Information Security: Procedures, Standards and Management

Information Security: Procedures, Standards and Management

Edited by Fiona Hobbs

Clanrye International
www.clanryeinternational.com

Clanrye International,
750 Third Avenue, 9th Floor,
New York, NY 10017, USA

ISBN: 978-1-63240-583-8

Cataloging-in-publication Data

Information security : procedures, standards and management / edited by Fiona Hobbs.
p. cm.
Includes bibliographical references and index.
ISBN 978-1-63240-583-8
1. Information storage and retrieval systems--Security measures. 2. Data protection. 3. Computer networks--Security measures 4. Computer security. 5. Information technology. 6. Management information systems. 7. Information resources management. I. Hobbs, Fiona.

TK5105.59 .I54 2017
658.478--dc23

For information on all Clanrye International publications visit our website at www.clanryeinternational.com

CLANRYE INTERNATIONAL

Printed in the United States of America.

Contents

Preface

The practice of defending, information from unauthorized access, use and disclosure along with destruction of data is known as information security. This defense mechanism is also known as InfoSec. This technology is widely used across the globe by various industries like hospitals, military etc. From theories to research to practical applications, case studies related to all contemporary topics of relevance to this field have been included like its different procedures and techniques of management. This book also outlines the threats that are common to data and information like software attacks, Trojan horses, viruses, worms, etc. The extensive content of this book provides the readers with a thorough understanding of the subject. It is a vital tool for all researching and studying this field.

Various studies have approached the subject by analyzing it with a single perspective, but the present book provides diverse methodologies and techniques to address this field. This book contains theories and applications needed for understanding the subject from different perspectives. The aim is to keep the readers informed about the progress in the field; therefore, the contributions were carefully examined to compile novel researches by specialists from across the globe.

Indeed, the job of the editor is the most crucial and challenging in compiling all chapters into a single book. In the end, I would extend my sincere thanks to the chapter authors for their profound work. I am also thankful for the support provided by my family and colleagues during the compilation of this book.

Editor

Target maneuver discrimination using ISAR image in interception

S.-J. Fan[1*], H.-T. Xiao[1], H.-Q. Fan[1] and J.-P. Fan[2]

Abstract

Discrimination for target maneuver magnitude and direction switching during the endgame is significant for interception performance improvement. Inverse synthetic aperture radar (ISAR) images carry the information related to target motion parameters. It is feasible to use them to discriminate the maneuver. An imaging model in interception is first formulated. The principle of maneuver discrimination using the ISAR images is then fully explored. A novel and practical discriminator is developed with a rigorous analysis of the scenario characteristics. The discriminator parameter selection and some important factors affecting the discrimination performance are discussed comprehensively. Finally, a simulation environment with software tools capable of generating target-realistic ISAR images is developed. The simulation results confirm the rationality of the design procedure and demonstrate that the proposed discriminator performs better than the classical innovation-based maneuver discriminator.

Keywords: Maneuver target, Motion discrimination, Inverse synthetic aperture radar, Interception

1 Introduction

The interception of highly maneuver target is a representative optimal control problem, and target maneuver is one of the main error sources for the nonzero miss distance as the guidance theory points out [1]. Fast response to a maneuver onset and exact discrimination of the acceleration change are important for interception performance improvement. Since target maneuvers are independently controlled and target acceleration cannot be measured directly by existing sensors, acceleration can only be acquired by means of state estimation.

Conventional works commonly adopt the acceleration magnitude change from zero to nonzero as the maneuver indication [2, 3]. However, a large amount of simulation studies and flight tests have demonstrated that maneuvering in a fixed direction (constant acceleration, denoted as type I maneuver) does not, usually, pose a real challenge to the interceptor guidance system. Rather, the more difficult problem (handled by the target acceleration estimator) is to detect a single, randomly timed maneuver direction switch (MDS) during the endgame [4] (denoted as type II maneuver). It was also found that such a bang-bang type of evasion maneuvers is the optimal one for interception avoidance [1, 5]. Hence, we focus on the maneuver discrimination for a single MDS in interception in this paper.

According to the information employed in the maneuver discriminator, current techniques can be mainly classified into two categories: innovation-based and feature-based. The innovation-based [6] maneuver detector and state estimator depend on the innovation information of the Kalman filter or its variation. Whether a single-model or multiple-model method, it is difficult to achieve a short discrimination delay while maintaining high correct probabilities, due to the Q effect [2]. This inherent drawback becomes more serious when a mismatch occurs between target acceleration and predesigned models. By employing maneuver information embedded in the features from sensors, the feature-based technique [6] breaks through the above obstacle. In an air-to-air interception scenario, the bank angle measurement from the image is utilized in estimator when the fighter plane is taking a bank-to-turn (BTT) maneuver [4]. The detection delay is greatly reduced compared to the classical innovation-based estimator. Many similar researches exploit maneuver information from optical

* Correspondence: robert_fsj@sina.com
[1]ATR, National University of Defense Technology, Changsha 410072, People's Republic of China
Full list of author information is available at the end of the article

sensors by estimating target orientation directly [7] or extracting image fluctuant features indirectly [8]. However, the target range and velocity cannot be measured by optical sensors directly which are helpful for the state estimation and guidance. The radar echo also conveys maneuver information due to the modulation effects on electromagnetic scattering, and it can easily handle the problems of the optical sensors. Some narrowband radar features including glint, radar cross section (RCS), and high-resolution Doppler profile (HRDP) have been exploited successfully for type I maneuver detection [6, 9, 10]. But the MDS discrimination is not involved in the aforementioned researches. The validity of these approaches needs to be further verified.

According to the information employed in the maneuver discriminator, current techniques can be mainly classified into two categories: innovation-based and feature-based. The former methods depend on the innovation information of the Kalman filter or its variations [6]. Due to the Q effect [2], it is difficult for both of the single-model and multiple-model methods to achieve a short discrimination delay while maintaining high correct probabilities. This inherent drawback becomes more serious with mismatch between target acceleration and predesigned models. However, employing maneuver information embedded in the features from sensors, feature-based techniques [6] overcome the above obstacle. For instance, in an air-to-air interception scenario where a fighter plane is taking a BTT maneuver [4], an estimator using the bank angle measurement from images can greatly reduce the detection delay, compared to the classical innovation-based estimator. Many similar researches exploit maneuver information from optical sensors by directly estimating target orientation [7] or indirectly extracting image fluctuant features [8]. Unfortunately, optical sensors cannot directly measure target range and velocity which are helpful for the state estimation and guidance. Radar sensors can also capture maneuver information and easily obtain target range and velocity, because of the modulation effect on electromagnetic scattering. Narrowband radar features including glint, RCS, and HRDP have been exploited to detect type I maneuver [6, 9, 10]. But their validity needs to be further verified for the MDS discrimination, which is not involved in the aforementioned researches.

Generally, compared with low-resolution radar features, high-resolution features from high-range resolution (HRR) or inverse synthetic aperture radar (ISAR) images gain more advantages in maneuver information extraction. As stated in [11], the relative orientation of missile-to-target in interception can be approximated by a turntable model, which makes the maneuver discrimination using ISAR images possible. In fact, the estimation of motion parameters per se including translational motion velocity, rotation velocity, and direction is key to autofocus and cross-range scaling in ISAR imaging, and many signal-domain and image-domain methods have been proposed [12–15]. In essence, these methods are mostly offline data processing regardless of application backgrounds and need an iterative optimization "matching." Notice that they comprehensively do not analyze the relationship between maneuver parameters and ISAR images as well as the impact factors on estimation error, such as resolution and relative orientation of missile-to-target. Yang et al. [16] derive the relationship between target ISAR image slope and turn rate in the ground moving target indicator (GMTI) radar surveillance. In this paper, we extend the air-to-ground scenario to an air-to-air interception scenario and estimate the lateral acceleration instead of the maneuvering turn. Moreover, the estimation in a quasi-steady state is extended to the transient period with a determination of maneuver switch instant.

Considering the interception of a skid-to-turn (STT) cruise missile taking a horizontal, planar "S" maneuver (denoted as type II maneuver) in penetration [17, 18], the sideslip angle will change, and a novel and practical target maneuver discriminator using ISAR images is proposed with rigorous analysis. For simplicity, we assume the target translational motion is well compensated, and employ the image-domain features, in consideration of the effect of echoes' quality on the signal-domain parameter estimation. The paper makes an elaborate and systematic analysis of the maneuver discrimination principle in Section 2. Section 3 discusses some important factors affecting the discrimination performance and then proposes a maneuver discriminator using ISAR images. Simulation results are presented in Section 4, and conclusion is drawn in Section 5.

2 Maneuver discrimination principle

Taking the initial line-of-sight (LOS) coordinate system as the inertial coordinate system, the geometry of the two-dimensional interception scenario is shown in Fig. 1, where R is the distance between target and missile, q is the LOS angle, and γ_M, a_M, and V_M and γ_T, a_T, and V_T are missile and target path angles, accelerations (perpendicular to the respective velocities), and speeds, respectively. Assuming first-order dynamics for both target and missile and both velocities are nearly constant, the following dynamics equations are satisfied:

$$\begin{cases} \dot{a}_i = \left(a_i^c - a_i\right)/\tau_i \\ \dot{V}_i = 0 \\ \dot{\gamma}_i = a_i/V_i, \end{cases} \quad (1)$$

where $i = M,T$ refers to missile and target, a_i^c is the acceleration command, and τ_i is the time constant. The

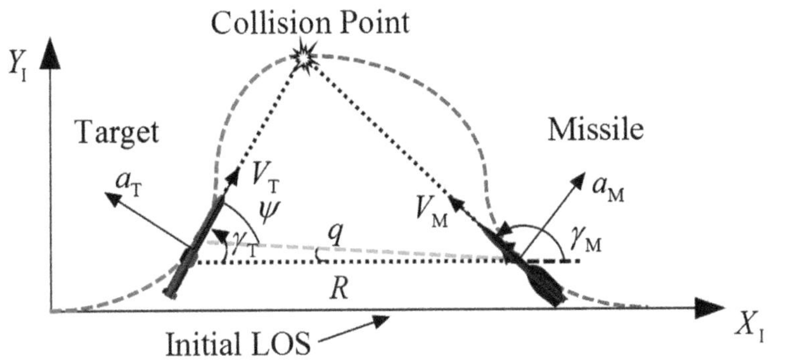

Fig. 1 Interception scenario geometry

relationship between motion parameters and relative orientation of missile-to-target in a three-dimensional interception scenario has been derived in [11]. A two-dimensional simplified analysis is presented to establish the ISAR imaging model as follows.

2.1 Imaging model

A right-handed coordinate system is attached to the target where the *x*-axis is pointing out of the nose, the *y*-axis to the left, and the *z*-axis to the top. Assuming the target velocity is along the *x*-axis, the pose angle ψ, relative to LOS, and its rates ω are formulated as

$$\begin{aligned}\psi &= \gamma_T - q \\ \omega &= \dot{\psi} = \dot{\gamma}_T - \dot{q}\end{aligned} \quad (2)$$

The positive pose angle is prescribed to the left and the positive turn is also to the left. The considerable disparities of ψ and ω in MDS are the basis of maneuver discrimination. In (2), $\dot{\gamma}_T$ and $\dot{q}$ represent the pose angle variety introduced by the target motion and relative motion of missile-to-target, respectively. It has been demonstrated in [11] that

$$|\dot{q}| \ll |\dot{\gamma}_T|. \quad (3)$$

This conclusion also can be explained by the expression of $\dot{q}$ in proportional navigation (PN) guidance law [19]:

$$\dot{q} = \frac{V_T \sin(\gamma_T - q) - V_M \sin(\gamma_M - q)}{R}. \quad (4)$$

In fact, the numerator of (4) is the "collision triangle" (the dotted triangle in Fig. 1) condition [19]. If the relative motion keeps the condition satisfied in the whole interception, i.e., $V_T \sin(\gamma_T - q) = V_M \sin(\gamma_M - q)$, $\dot{q} = 0$ is straightforward. In real interception scenario, $\dot{q}$ is influenced by many factors, including target maneuver, guidance law adopted, initial heading error, and estimation error. But the guidance law always keeps $\dot{q}$ within a small neighborhood of zero before the seeker head reaches its blind range. Hence, after translational motion compensation, the imaging model in two-dimensional interception can be approximated as a planar rotating object in Fig. 2, where rotation angular velocity is equal to the pose angle rate,

$$\omega = \dot{\psi} \approx \dot{\gamma}_T \quad (5)$$

Furthermore, assuming target centroid O as the origin, the scatterer on target of radial distance L is mapped on to the range-Doppler plane as follows under the far-field condition:

$$\begin{aligned}X &= L\cos\psi / \eta_r \\ Y &= \frac{-2v}{\lambda} / \eta_f = \frac{-2\omega L \sin\psi}{\lambda} / \eta_f,\end{aligned} \quad (6)$$

where v is the rotation linear velocity, λ is the wavelength, and η_r and η_f are the range and Doppler resolutions, respectively, defined by

$$\eta_r = c/(2B) \qquad \eta_f = 1/T_{img}. \quad (7)$$

In (7), c is the velocity of light, B is the signal bandwidth, and T_{img} is the imaging time. A typical target ISAR image is also illustrated in Fig. 2 which shows the scatterer distribution in the range-Doppler plane.

The above imaging model in interception differs significantly from that in surveillance of the ground-based radar (or other location-fixed radar) [6, 16]. In the latter situation, an ISAR image also can be obtained even if the target does not maneuver. However, from Fig. 2, we can see that only when the target takes the lateral maneuver (perpendicular to velocity), i.e., rotation, the imaging condition could be satisfied. This disparity provides the feasibility of maneuver discrimination using ISAR images in interception.

2.2 Relationship between maneuver parameters and images

The changes of target acceleration a_T and acceleration command a_T^c in type II maneuver are showed in Fig. 3.

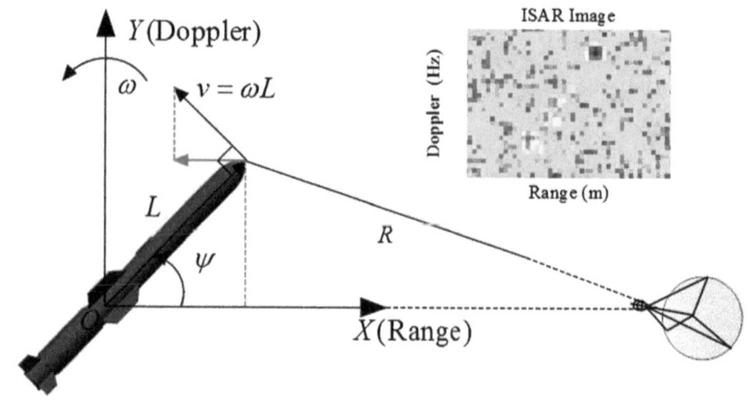

Fig. 2 Imaging model in two-dimensional interception

In maneuver discrimination, we focus on the acceleration command switch instant t_{sw} and the acceleration direction switch instant t_{dir}. t_{sw} is usually set to be the starting instant which is the reference to the discrimination delay evaluation. We follow this metric in our paper. By substituting (1) into (5), ω and its time derivative can thus be expressed as

$$\begin{aligned}\omega &= a_{\mathrm{T}}/V_{\mathrm{T}} \\ \dot{\omega} &= \left(a_{\mathrm{T}}^{\mathrm{c}} - a_{\mathrm{T}}\right)/V_{\mathrm{T}}\tau_{\mathrm{T}}.\end{aligned} \tag{8}$$

From (8), ω and $\dot{\omega}$ encapsulate the full information of target maneuver. On the other hand, from (6), ω can be derived by the scatterer position in the range-Doppler plane. Consequently, the maneuver information can be extracted theoretically by matching the target scatterers in ISAR images of different instants [13, 14]. For example [14], ω of airplane rotation is estimated by comparing the geometrical relationship differences of relative scatterers in two adjacent images. Actually, the equivalent scatterer number of missile-class target is significantly fewer than ship or airplane due to its smaller size. So the matching process needs the high-resolution images, and the scatterer association in different images must be well-handled. Fortunately, a "shaft-like" shape is available for extracting the line features from target ISAR images.

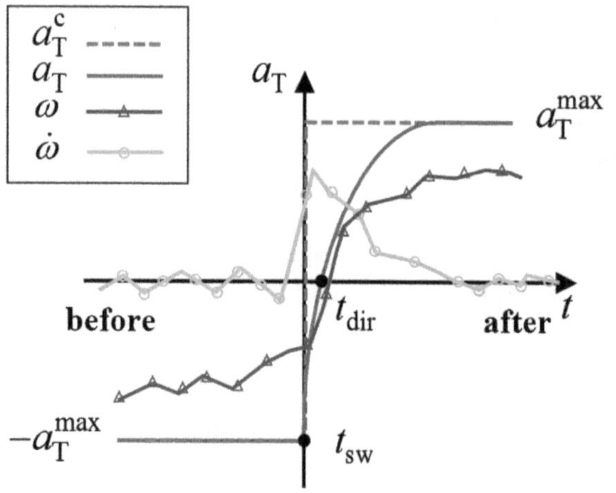

Fig. 3 The changes of a_T and a_T^c in type II maneuver

From (6), the slope of the target ISAR image can be expressed as

$$s = \frac{X}{Y} = -\frac{f_s}{T_{\mathrm{img}} f_0 \omega \tan\psi} = \frac{K}{\omega \tan\psi}, \tag{9}$$

where f_0 is the center frequency and $K = -f_s/T_{\mathrm{img}} f_0$ is a known constant. By substituting (8) into the time derivative of s, we obtain

$$\dot{s} = \frac{-K}{\sin\psi}\left(\frac{\dot{\omega}}{\omega^2}\cos\psi + \frac{1}{\sin\psi}\right). \tag{10}$$

Thus, the relationship between s and ω, also their time derivatives, is established. It is noted that these relationships are also related to the pose angle ψ. We firstly assume $\psi > 0$ in the following analysis and other situations are discussed later.

For the sake of clarity, type II maneuver is further divided into two types considering the different switch directions, i.e., type P and type N. According to Fig. 3, a detailed summary of maneuver parameters and slope features in type II maneuver is listed in Table 1.

$$\sin 2\psi > \frac{-2a_{\mathrm{T}}^2 \tau_{\mathrm{T}}}{\left(-a_{\mathrm{T}}^{\max} - a_{\mathrm{T}}\right) V_{\mathrm{T}}}, \quad \psi > 0 \tag{11}$$

According to the results summarized in Table 1, we can see that the value of $\dot{s}$ and the sign of s will change after the time instants t_{sw} and t_{dir}, respectively. Especially, if ψ satisfies (11) in the type P

Table 1 The summary of maneuver parameters and slope features in type II maneuver ($\psi > 0$)

		t_{sw}			t_{dir}		
		a^c	$\dot{\omega}$	$\dot{s}$	a	ω	s
Type P	Before	$+a_T^{max}$	0	$\frac{-K}{\sin^2\psi} > 0$	>0	>0	<0
	After	$-a_T^{max}$	−max	$< \frac{-K}{\sin^2\psi}$; if (11) is satisfied, < 0	<0	<0	>0
Type N	Before	$-a_T^{max}$	0	$\frac{-K}{\sin^2\psi} > 0$	<0	<0	>0
	After	$+a_T^{max}$	+max	$> \frac{-K}{\sin^2\psi}$	>0	>0	<0

maneuver, the MDS can be easily discriminated only by the sign of $\dot{s}$.

Notice that the above derivation entails the assumption that the rotation center of the target is known which is very difficult to fulfill in reality. As a matter of fact, the slope estimation can be realized by any two scatterers along the target radial axis or by some elaborate line-extraction algorithms in image processing. Both of them are independent of the position of rotation center. More detailed scheme will be given in the next section.

2.3 Discussion

We discuss the influence of ψ on the maneuver discrimination performance herein. As we know, most of the missile targets are of axial symmetry. The ISAR image acquired when $\psi < 0$ and $\omega < 0$ is the same as that when $\psi > 0$ and $\omega > 0$ according to Fig. 2. In other words, we only have the information of $|\psi|$ and $|\omega|$ from the ISAR images. Thereupon, some further remarks are made as follows (the sign of variable is denoted as sgn[·] for simplicity):

First of all, conclusions in Table 1 are contrary when $\psi < 0$ according to (9) and (10). It does not affect the detection of t_{sw} but misleads the MDS discrimination. Actually, sgn[s] only indicates whether the target is turning toward or away from the LOS without the knowledge of sgn[ψ].

Secondly, if ψ traverses zero in interception, either $+ \to 0 \to -$ or $- \to 0 \to +$, a "ghost phenomenon" is produced which means ω changing from $\omega < 0$ to $\omega > 0$. As a result, both sgn[s] and the value of $\dot{s}$ vary even though no MDS occurs. In this instance, the discrimination of type N maneuver suffers from the invalidation or ambiguity.

Thirdly, from the expression of $\dot{s}$ before the MDS occurs, i.e., $\dot{s} = \frac{-K}{\sin^2\psi}$, we know that the value of $\dot{s}$ varies along with ψ even there is no MDS. If the value of $\dot{s}$ is used as the test statistic, a float threshold is needed which is generated by a large amount of statistics at different ψ. But it is very hard to be realized in reality.

Finally, the performance of line extracting from the images strongly depends on the value of ψ. For example, within a small neighborhood of $\psi = 0$, the target image approximately remains perpendicular to the Doppler axis even if there is a rotation. The reason is that Doppler frequencies developed in both sides of a target from the front to the rear have the same small values with different signs. At the same time, the ISAR image spreads in several Doppler resolution bins due to the target width. Therefore, both sgn[s] and the value of $\dot{s}$ variations are unpredictable results from the line extracting errors.

In summary, the estimation of sgn[ψ] and a de-ambiguity processing are necessary for the former two situations in maneuver discrimination. From the point of an implementation view, only sgn[$\dot{s}$] and sgn[s] are selected in our paper as the indications of MDS. Although (11) should be satisfied in type P maneuver, it holds in most cases during [t_{sw},t_{dir}]. This situation will be testified in Section 4 where the effect of ψ on discrimination performance is also explained more thoroughly.

3 Discriminator design

3.1 Image pre-processing

The ISAR image series can be obtained by the sliding windowing method. The window length, i.e., T_{img}, determines the accumulated rotating angle for each ISAR image, and thus determines its Doppler resolution (inversely proportional to T_{img} in (7)). But long T_{img} implies great delay in discrimination. Hence, a tradeoff between delay and resolution should be considered. On the other hand, the sliding step length (denoted as ΔT) determines the aspect angle difference between neighboring ISAR images with a given ω. In reality, ΔT should be less than the missile control period but not too small. If so, the estimation of $\dot{s}$ is not reliable due to the slight difference between neighboring aspect angles.

Then, a target image is segmented out from the scene that is indicating which pixels are on-target. This usually can be done using CFAR detection followed by a sequence of binary morphological operations [16]. For the air-to-air endgame application in our paper, the signal-to-noise ratio (SNR) is quite high due to the low clutter and the enough radiation power. The major noise sources are scatterer amplitude and position fluctuations. So the target is segmented simply by the following two level thresholds:

$$\begin{aligned} TH_1 &= \overline{I(x,y)} = \sum_{j=1}^{N_D}\sum_{i=1}^{N_R} I\left(x_i, y_j\right)/N_D N_R \\ TH_2 &= C\cdot\sum_{j=1}^{N_D}\sum_{i=1}^{N_R} I'\left(x_i, y_j\right), \end{aligned} \tag{12}$$

where $I(x_i,y_j)$ is the original image pixel value, N_D and N_R are the numbers of pixels in the Doppler and range directions, respectively, $I'(x_i, y_j)$ is the image pixel value filtrated by the first-level threshold TH_1, and $C < 1$ is a scaling factor.

3.2 Estimation of s and $\dot{s}$

Many methods in curve fitting, image processing, and ISAR cross-range scaling can be utilized to estimate s [12–15]. Least squares (LS) and total least squares (TLS) methods are easy to operate but would be invalided if some shadowing or obstructions appeared in the ISAR image [20]. Some algorithms such as Radon and Hough transforms [13] and polar mapping [15] can solve this problem by an iterative optimization implementation of exhaustive searching in a wide angle range. However, they afford heavy computational burden for real-time missile-borne application.

As analyzed earlier, only sgn[s] and sgn[$\dot{s}$] are needed in most cases. Herein, the major axis direction in the image-domain analysis is used as the estimation of s [21], namely

$$\hat{s} = \tan\alpha = \tan\left[\frac{1}{2}\tan^{-1}\left(\frac{2\mu_{11}}{\mu_{20}-\mu_{02}}\right)\right], \tag{13}$$

where α is the oblique angle, μ_{pq} is the $(p + q)$ - th central moment of image defined as

$$\begin{aligned} \mu_{pq} &= \sum_{j=1}^{N_D}\sum_{i=1}^{N_R}(x_i-\bar{x})^p\left(y_j-\bar{y}\right)^q I\left(x_i, y_j\right), \\ \bar{x} &= \frac{m_{10}}{m_{00}},\ \bar{y} = \frac{m_{01}}{m_{00}} \qquad p,q = 0,1,2... \end{aligned} \tag{14}$$

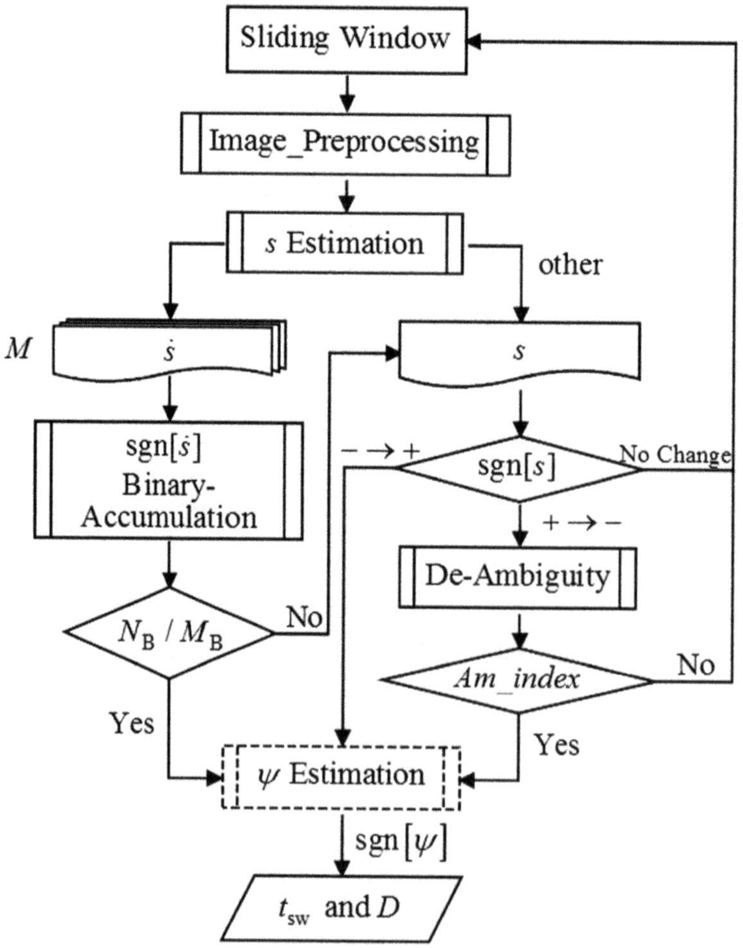

Fig. 4 Flow chart of the proposed maneuver discrimination scheme

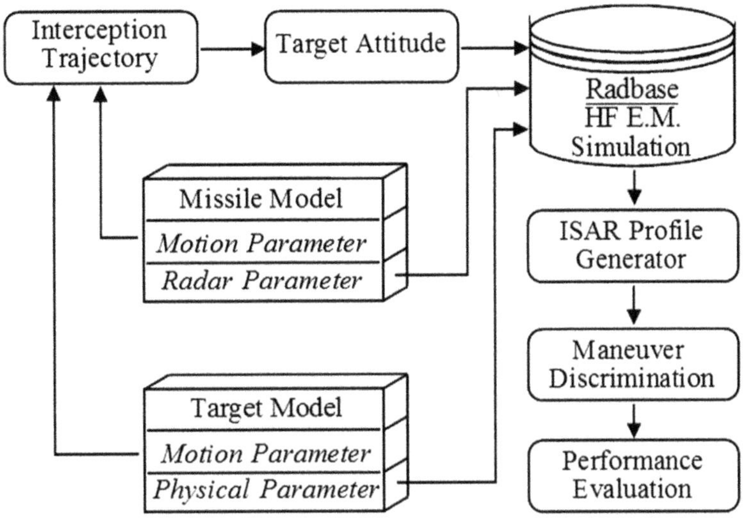

Fig. 5 Block diagram of simulation environment

and m_{pq} is the $(p+q)$ - th geometrical moment of image defined as

$$m_{pq} = \sum_{j=1}^{N_D}\sum_{i=1}^{N_R} x_i^p y_j^q I\left(x_i, y_j\right), \quad p, q = 0, 1, 2... \tag{15}$$

From (13) to (15), we see that the major axis direction can be obtained only by some multiplications and additions in one cycle. The estimation of $\dot{s}$, denoted as $\hat{\dot{s}}$ can be deduced by two neighboring frames of image sequence.

3.3 Estimation of ψ

With the knowledge of sgn[ψ], the real maneuver switch direction could be confirmed. An estimation method of ψ based on the target velocity vector $\boldsymbol{v}_{\mathrm{T}}$ and LOS vector $\boldsymbol{r}$ is proposed in [16], namely

$$\hat{\psi} = \cos^{-1}\left(\frac{\langle \hat{\boldsymbol{r}}, \hat{\boldsymbol{v}}_{\mathrm{T}}\rangle}{\hat{R}\hat{V}_{\mathrm{T}}}\right). \tag{16}$$

From (16), we know that the accurate estimation is not well because both the position and velocity of missile-to-target need to be estimated. As mentioned previously, the "collision triangle" condition holds approximately in the whole interception. $\hat{\psi}$ can also be obtained by this restriction

$$\hat{\psi} = \sin^{-1}\left(\frac{\hat{V}_{\mathrm{M}}\sin\hat{\gamma}_{\mathrm{M}}}{\hat{V}_{\mathrm{T}}}\right) \tag{17}$$

The target state estimation per se is quite accurate, so only the constant target speed needs to be estimated. Obviously, the estimation error of (17) is much smaller than that of (16).

3.4 De-ambiguity

In theory, the value of $\hat{\psi}$ can be used to solve the ambiguity caused by the ghost phenomenon as mentioned in type N maneuver. But the estimation delay still exists from (17) because it is essentially an innovation-based method. It is difficult to solve the ambiguity based on the value of $\hat{\psi}$. Although there is no MDS, it is noted that $|\omega|$ is maximal during ψ traversing zero, and thus $\hat{s}$ is quite accurate due to the high Doppler resolution. Therefore, if a change of sgn[$\hat{s}$] from positive to negative is detected, current frame or several frames before can be utilized to obtain an $\hat{s}$. The value of $\hat{s}$ depends on ψ

Table 2 Parameters of simulation environment

Parameter		Value
Target	Motion	$V_{\mathrm{T}} = 300\ \mathrm{m/s},\ a_{\mathrm{T}}^{\max} = 15\mathrm{g},\ \tau_{\mathrm{T}} = 0.2\ \mathrm{s}$
	Size	Length = 5 m, width = 1 m
Missile	Motion	$V_{\mathrm{M}} = 450\ \mathrm{m/s},\ a_{\mathrm{M}}^{\max} = 20\ \mathrm{g}\tau_{\mathrm{M}} = 0.2\ \mathrm{s}, T_c = 0.01\ s$
	Radar	$\lambda = 3\ \mathrm{cm}$, PRF = 32 kHz$N_p = 64, \Delta f = 10\ \mathrm{MHz}, B = 640\ \mathrm{MHz}$
Scenario		$R_0 = 2.25\ \mathrm{km}, \gamma_{\mathrm{T}}(0) \sim U(-15^{\circ}, 15^{\circ})$
Error		$\sigma_r = 1\ \mathrm{m}, \sigma_{v\mathrm{T}} = 10\ \mathrm{m/s}, \sigma_{a\mathrm{T}} = 1\ \mathrm{g}\sigma_{\mathrm{ang}} = 0.1\ \mathrm{mrad}, \Delta_{\mathrm{est}} = 0.2\ \mathrm{s}, \sigma_{a\mathrm{M}} = 0.1\ \mathrm{g}$

when MDS occurs, but it is almost constant when ψ is traversing zero. This disparity provides a feasible way to solve the ambiguity.

Finally, the flow chart of the proposed maneuver discrimination scheme is provided in Fig. 4.

Figure 4 shows that a two-stage detection is implemented employing $\mathrm{sgn}[\hat{\dot{s}}]$ and $\mathrm{sgn}[\hat{s}]$ at different instants t_{sw} and t_{dir}, respectively. Meanwhile, in order to increase the reliability of $\hat{\dot{s}}$, a "binary integration detection" or "N_B/M_B detection" scheme is adopted [22]. The detection of $\mathrm{sgn}[\hat{\dot{s}}]$ and $\mathrm{sgn}[\hat{s}]$ can be directly used as the indication of t_{sw}, whether the target is turning toward or away from the LOS. After $\hat{\psi}$ is integrated, the real maneuver switch direction (denoted as D in Fig. 4) is taken.

4 Simulation results

4.1 Simulation environment

The block diagram of simulation environment is shown in Fig. 5. A trajectory is generated in a missile-target interception scenario, and the target pose angle is calculated. The scatterer phase center data, that is, the position and complex RCS of each of the scatterers composing the target in different pose angles and frequencies, are obtained through the high-frequency electromagnetic simulation software RadBase [6]. Based on it, the ISAR images are generated considering the noise and clutter data. Finally, the performance of the maneuver discrimination is evaluated.

The simulation parameters are listed in Table 2, and the final time of the interception is about 3 s. The initial target heading angle uniformly distributed between ±15°, that means the missile is located in the head-on zone of the target. The differential game guidance laws (DGL1) and the step-frequency wideband waveform [23] are adopted by the missile. Regardless of the specific performance of estimator used, only the target acceleration estimation delay is considered, namely, $\Delta_{\mathrm{est}} = 0.2$ s. Estimation errors of other target states are assumed as the white Gaussian noises whose standard deviation is also listed in Table 2. Besides, the window sliding step length is set equal to the missile control period, namely, $\Delta T = T_c = 0.01$ s.

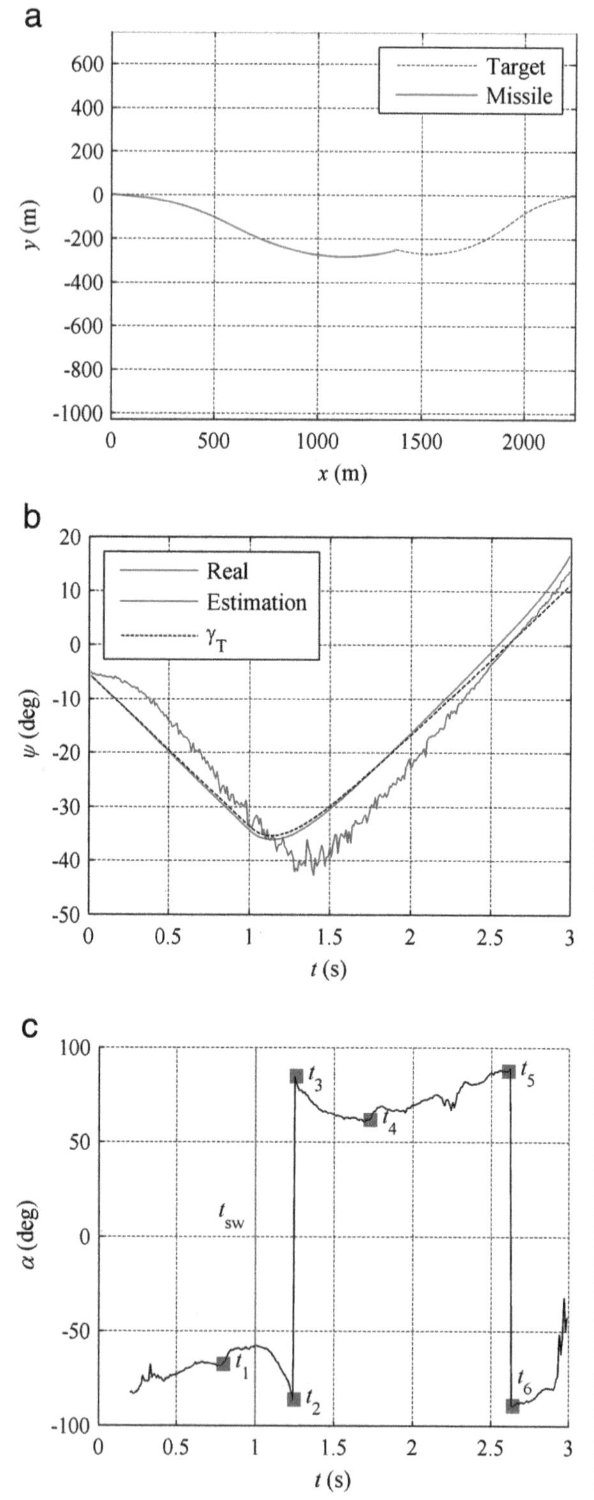

Fig. 6 A single run simulation result. **a** Trajectory. **b** Pose angle and target path angle. **c** Oblique angle

4.2 Simulation results

4.2.1 A single run trial

A single simulation run of missile-target interception trajectory is depicted in Fig. 6a, where the target performs a single MDS from −15 to 15 g at $t_{\mathrm{sw}} = 1$ s. Figure 6b illustrates the pose angle ψ and the target path angle γ_T during the whole interception. Note that $\psi \approx \gamma_T$ is almost satisfied except at the last phase when the LOS angle q variations are considerable. So the planar rotation imaging model is reasonable in interception. The estimation result of ψ from (17) is also added in Fig. 6b. It can be seen that the estimation delay is evident, but the sign estimation is quite accurate.

On the other hand, the oblique angle α in (13) instead of $\hat{s}$ is shown in Fig. 6c for clarity, where six sample time instants are marked in turn. The ISAR images and $\hat{s}$ corresponding to these time instants are illustrated, respectively, in Fig. 7. The imaging time $T_{img} = 0.2$ s and SNR = 10 dB [24] are prescribed in ISAR imaging. Combined with the variation of ψ in Fig. 6b, some cases are outlined below: in these images, most of target scatterers are visible due to the fast rotation rate ($|\omega| \approx 28^{\circ}$/s at Fig. 7a, d), so the target is turning about 5.6° in each imaging time interval. It makes easier to estimate the slope of the target. In the neighborhood of t_{dir} (Fig. 7b, c), the Doppler resolution degradation may adversely affect the accuracy of $\hat{s}$, but sgn[$\hat{s}$] reverses rapidly yet; sgn[$\hat{s}$] also reverses from positive to negative when $\psi$is traversing zero (Fig. 7e, f), but the Doppler resolution is distinctly higher than that in Fig. 7b, c. Another remarkable and important thing is the persistent decrement of $\hat{s}$ during $[t_{sw}, t_2]$ in Fig. 6c. That is to say, sgn[$\hat{s}$] reverses after MDS occurs. All of these cases are consistent with the analysis and discussion in the above sections.

4.2.2 Discriminator parameter design

As analyzed earlier, the discriminator parameter design strongly depends on ψ. So the influence of various discriminator parameters on discrimination performance is testified through a large amount of Monte Carlo simulations at different ψ. Note that type P maneuver in $\psi > 0$

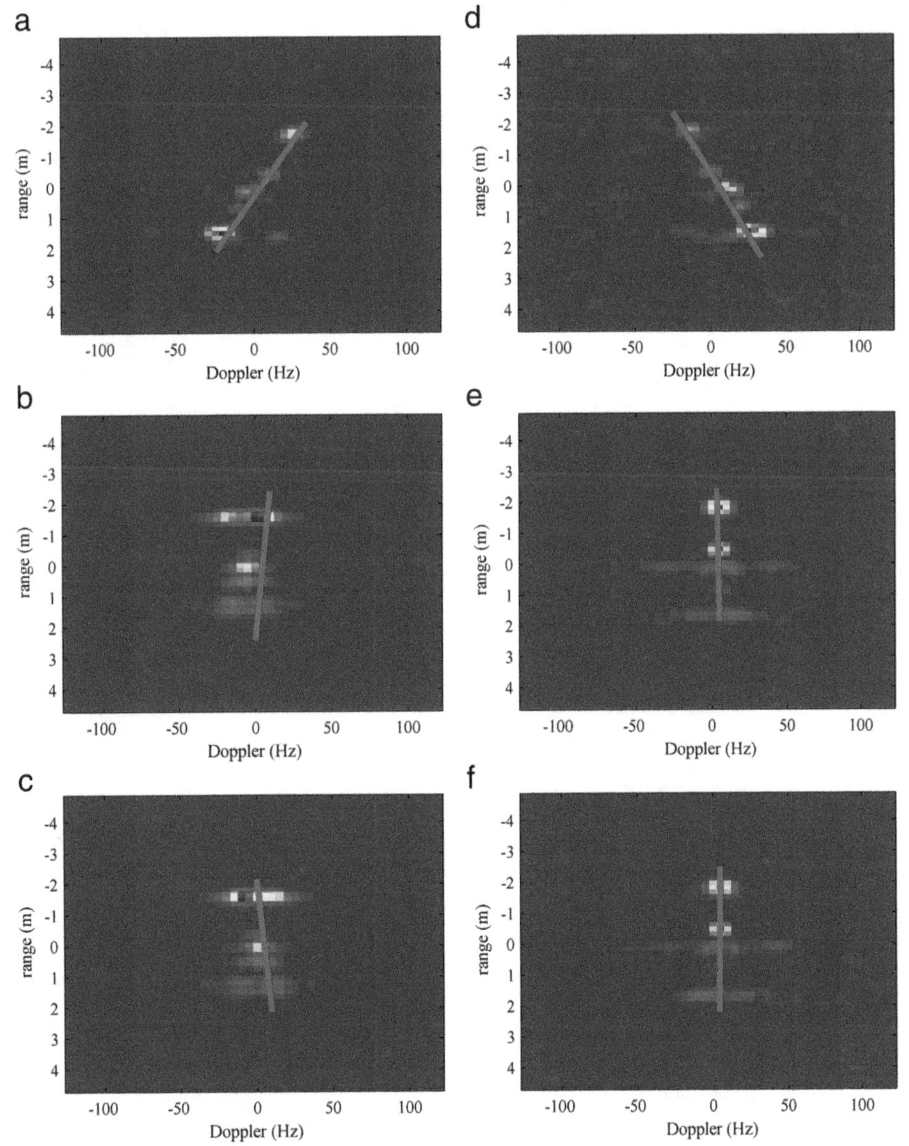

Fig. 7 ISAR images at different time instants. **a** $t_1 = 0.8$ s. **b** $t_2 = 1.24$ s. **c** $t_3 = 1.25$ s. **d** $t_4 = 1.7$ s. **e** $t_5 = 2.62$ s. **f** $t_6 = 2.63$ s

is equivalent to type N maneuver in $\psi < 0$ and vice versa. Hence, only the target takes a single MDS from 15 to −15 g is considered. In simulation, the angle interval is 5° and 1000 runs at each interval are picked out by changing t_{sw} and $\gamma_T(0)$. From the point of implementation view, γ_M should be smaller than the seeker gimbals angle [25] (35° in this paper) to make sure that the target will not fly off the field of view. Herein, ψ is limited to 60° according to the "collision triangle" condition.

Figure 8 shows the detection probability P_d and the false alarm probability P_{fa} of t_{sw} for N_B/M_B detection of $\hat{\dot{s}}$ when $T_{img} = 0.2$ s. The detection performance degrades when $\psi < 15°$ because the estimation errors of s increases and (11) is hardly to be satisfied. Both the detection and false alarm performance are good after $\psi >$ 30°. Since the detection of $\hat{\dot{s}}$ is just the first stage of MDS discrimination, the minimal P_{fa} is the top priority for the N_B/M_B selection. On the other hand, considering the delay increases as N_B and M_B increase, the N_B/M_B selection is a tradeoff between the delay and P_{fa}.

Similarly, the performance of de-ambiguity is shown in Fig. 9. As mentioned in Section 3.4, the mean value of α of ten frames before sgn[$\hat{\dot{s}}$] changes from positive to negative is chosen as a threshold (denoted as *AM_index*). In Fig. 9a, a cluster of the detection probability of type N maneuver (type P maneuver when $\psi < 0$) at different thresholds is exhibited. In contrast, the curves of false alarm probability in type P maneuver when $\psi > 0$ are illustrated in Fig. 9b. Different from the N_B/M_B selection, the *AM_index* selection should pursue a total maximum sum of $P_d - P_{fa}$.

At last, the detection probability of different window lengths is shown in Fig. 10. The imaging time T_{img} is normalized by the window sliding step length ΔT, for simplicity, namely, WL = $T_{img}/\Delta T$. The N_B/M_B is all "7/7" and the *AM_index* values are 65.88°, 87.2°, and 87.5°, respectively, in three cases. The detection probability of WL = 10 ($T_{img} = 0.1$ s) is low due to the low Doppler resolution. The detection probability of WL = 15 and WL = 20 are closer, but WL = 15 is a better choice due to a smaller

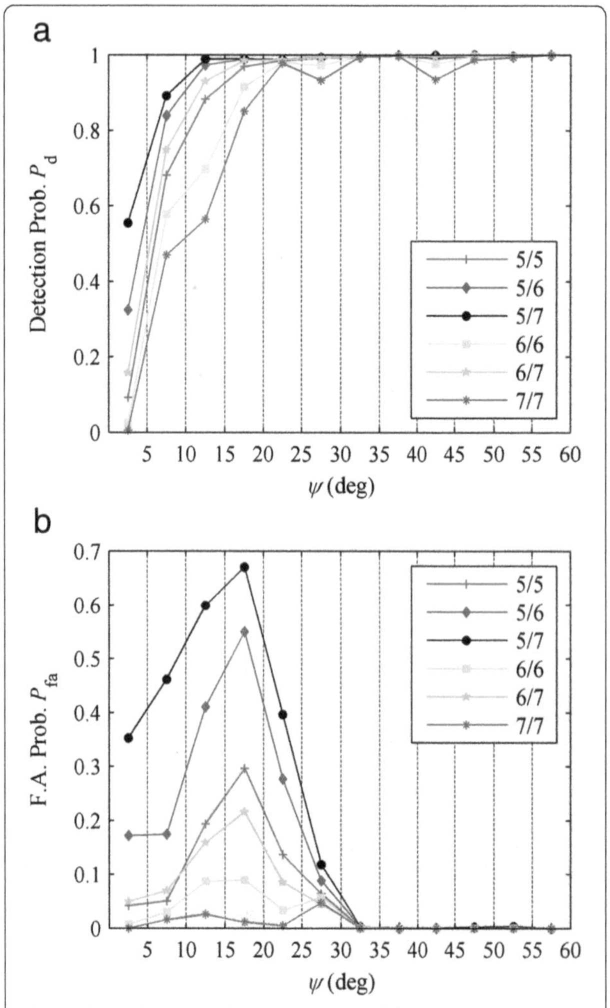

Fig. 8 The performance of N_B/M_B detection of $\hat{\dot{s}}$ ($T_{img} = 0.2$ s). **a** P_d. **b** P_{fa}

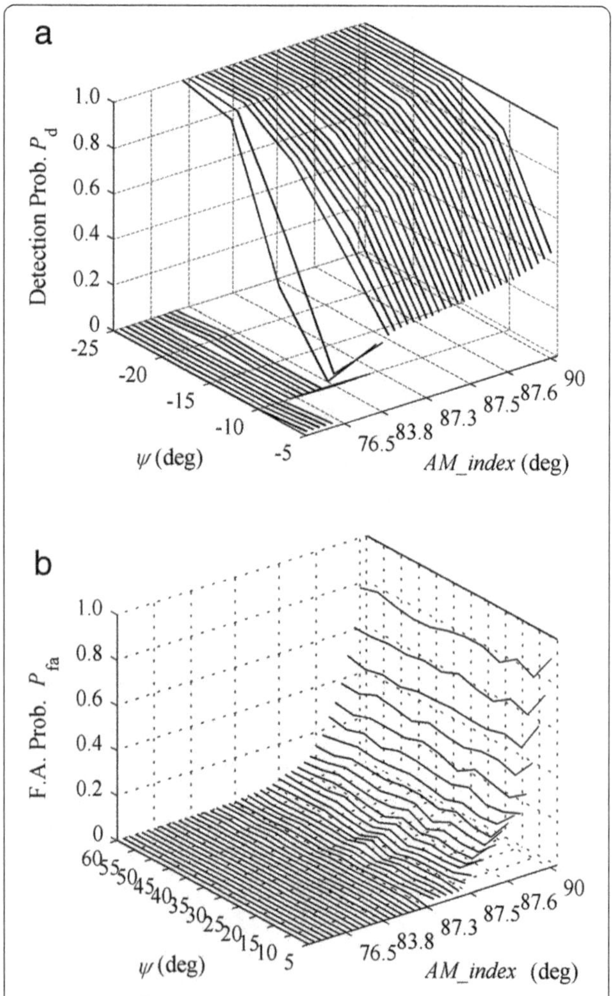

Fig. 9 The performance of de-ambiguity ($T_{img} = 0.2$ s). **a** P_d. **b** P_{fa}

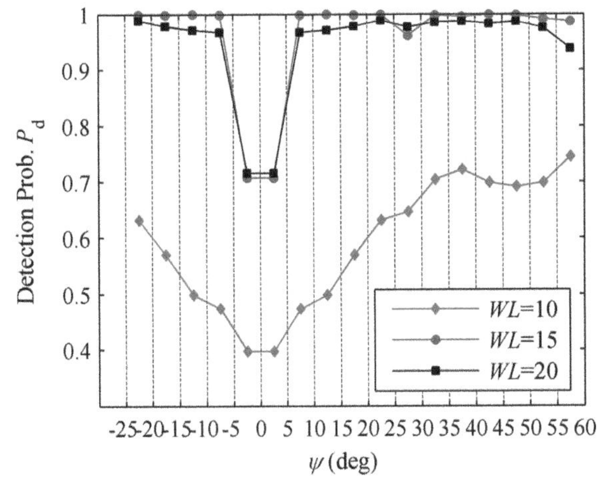

Fig. 10 The detection probability vs. different window lengths

delay. It is also apparent that the discrimination performance is extremely poor in the neighborhood of $\psi = 0$ ($[-5^{\circ}, 5^{\circ}]$) that justifies the conclusion in the former section.

4.2.3 Discrimination statistics

The total discrimination performance at $t_{sw} \in [0.2, 2.8]$ s in interception is shown in Fig. 11, and sets of 1000 Monte Carlo runs with random noise, random initial positions at each time interval are used. The window length WL = 15 and other discriminator parameters are the same as given in Fig. 10. The detection probability P_d, false alarm probability P_{fa}, miss probability P_m, and correct direction discrimination probability P_c (integrated $\text{sgn}[\hat{\psi}]$) are illustrated in Fig. 11a. It can be seen that the total successful discrimination probability in interception is quite good with the exception of $t_{sw} = 2.8$ s. Since the sufficient information cannot be collected to deliver a statistically significant decision at this time instant when WL = 15, P_m increases rapidly. Besides, the performance degrades slightly, especially $P_c < P_d$, when $t_{sw} < 1$ s, because the pose angle ψ is often in the neighborhood of zero when MDS occurs.

From Fig. 11b, the minimum discrimination delay is 0.07 s which is acquired by the "7/7" detection of $\hat{s}$ and the maximum delay does not exceed 0.26 s. The mean delay keeps about 0.15 s at all switch instants. Compared with the classical innovation-based maneuver detector, such as adaptive-H0 and the standard GLR detectors in [26], the mean delay in the same detection probability is an almost linear function of t_{sw} monotonically decreasing from 0.35 (at $t_{sw} = 0.2$ s) to 0.16 s (at $t_{sw} = 0.8$ s). The reason can be attributed to the constant angular noise, and the displacement noise is proportional to the range. The results are not shown here for conciseness.

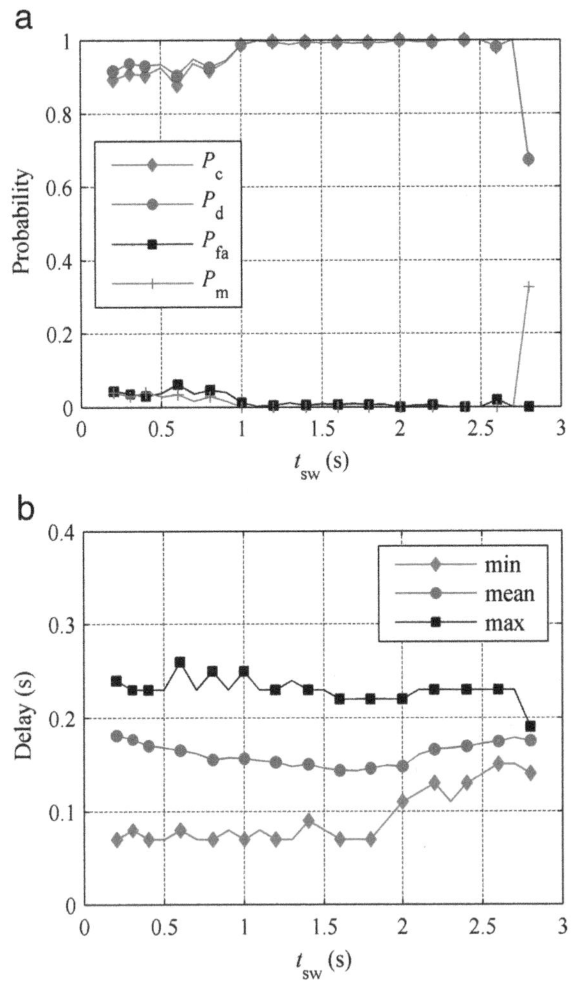

Fig. 11 The discrimination performance vs. switch time instant t_{sw}. **a** Probabilities. **b** Delay

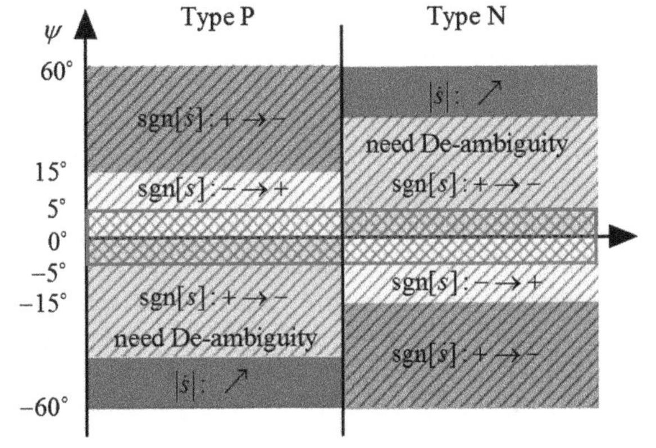

Fig. 12 The applicability summary of proposed discriminator

4.2.4 Applicability summary

According to the pose angle ψ and maneuver type, an applicability summary of the proposed discriminator based on the analysis and simulation results is illustrated as follows:

From Fig. 12, the feature or the test statistics used in the discriminator are the same in the same color zone and the deeper color means the shorter delay. In reality, MDS often occurs in the hatch zone due to the initial head-on geometry of missile-to-target and the short fly time in endgame, so sgn[s] and sgn[$\dot{s}$] are sufficient for discrimination. The upper bound is determined by the gimbal angle of missile under the "collision triangle" condition, and the lower bound depends on the estimation error of s (the red mesh boundary). Of course, real switch direction discrimination and de-ambiguity are necessary with the help of other information. Note that the applicability analysis in Fig. 12 is based on the particular scenario in this paper. Generally, the feature selection and the discriminator parameter design should be closely associated with the application characteristics.

5 Conclusions

Discriminating target maneuver using ISAR images is feasible because of the embedded information related to target motion parameters. This paper firstly sets up the imaging model in interception and mathematically derives the relationship between the bang-bang type maneuver parameters and ISAR image slope. Then, the principle of maneuver discrimination using the ISAR images is explored, and some important factors affecting the discrimination performance are discussed. A novel and practical discriminator is developed afterwards whose parameter is designed elaborately based on the endgame scenario characteristics. Finally, the simulation results give some operational guidelines to designer for choosing discriminator parameters in practice and demonstrate that the proposed discriminator performs better than the classical innovation-based maneuver discriminator.

Compared with the conventional maneuver detector, the proposed discriminator further provides the maneuver direction switch information which has been successfully used in both estimator [4] and guidance law [27]. In fact, as analyzed in this paper, we know that ω can be estimated directly from ISAR images or integrated in the conventional innovation-based estimator. It will certainly enhance the estimation performance. Moreover, although the analysis in this paper is based on STT maneuvering target, it is also feasible to extract the maneuver parameters for a BTT target. For example, the wings' rotation when the plane is taking a BTT maneuver is similar to the missile body's rotation. In this situation, maneuver discrimination based on the ISAR images is a very attractive research direction.

Competing interests
The authors declare that they have no competing interests.

Acknowledgements
This work was supported in part by the China National Science Foundation under Grant 61101186 and the Specialized Research Fund for the Doctoral Program of China Higher Education under Grant 20134307110012. The authors thank Dr. Zhou J. X. for her valuable suggestions. The authors would also like to thank the anonymous reviewers for their valuable suggestions on improving this paper.

Author details
[1]ATR, National University of Defense Technology, Changsha 410072, People's Republic of China. [2]College of Electronic Science and Engineering, National University of Defense Technology, Changsha 410072, People's Republic of China.

References

1. J Shinar, T Vladimir, What happens when certainty equivalence is not valid? Is there an optimal estimator for terminal guidance? Annu. Rev. Control. **27**, 119–130 (2003). doi:10.1016/j.arcontrol.2003.10.001
2. HQ Fan, S Wang, Q Fu, Survey of algorithms of target maneuver detection. Syst. Eng. Electron. **31**(5), 1064–1070 (2009)
3. JF Ru, VP Jikov, XR Li, A Bashi, Detection of target maneuver onset. IEEE Trans. Aerosp. Electron. Syst. **45**(2), 536–554 (2009)
4. Y Oshman, D Arad, Enhanced air-to-air missile tracking using target orientation observations. AIAA J Guid. Control. Dyn. **27**(4), 595–606 (2004). doi:10.2514/1.11155
5. J. Shinar, T. Shima, Robust missile guidance law against highly maneuvering targets. Paper presented at the 7th Mediterranean conference on control and automation, Haifa, Israel, 28–30 June 1999
6. YL Zhu, HQ Fan, JP Fan, ZQ Lu, Q Fu, Target turning maneuver detection using high resolution Doppler profile. IEEE Trans. Aerosp. Electron. Syst. **48**(1), 762–779 (2012). doi:10.1109/TAES.2012.6129669
7. DD Sworder, RG Hutchins, Maneuver estimation using measurements of orientation. IEEE Trans. Aerosp. Electron. Syst. **26**(4), 625–638 (1990)
8. S Shetty, AT Alouani, A multisensor tracking system with an image-based maneuver detector. IEEE Trans. Aerosp. Electron. Syst. **32**(1), 167–181 (1996)
9. EJ Hughes, M Leyland, Target manoeuvre detection using radar glint. Electron. Lett. **34**(17), 1695–1696 (1998)
10. H.Q. Fan, Dissertation, National University of Defense Technology, 2008
11. SJ Fan, HQ Fan, HT Xiao, JP Fan, Q Fu, Three-dimensional analysis of relationship between relative orientation and motion modes. Chin. J. Aeronaut. **27**(6), 1495–1504 (2014). doi:10.1016/j.cja.2014.10.016
12. ZW Xu, L Zhang, MD Xing, Precise cross-range scaling for ISAR images using feature registration. IEEE Trans. Geosci. Remote Sens. Lett. **11**(10), 1792–1796 (2014). doi:10.1109/LGRS.2014.2309604
13. CM Yeh, J Xu, YN Peng, XT Wang, J Yang, XG Xia, Cross-range scaling for ISAR via optical flow analysis. IEEE Aerosp. Electron. Syst. Mag. **27**(2), 14–22 (2012). doi:10.1109/MAES.2012.6163609
14. CM Yeh, J Xu, YN Peng, XM Shan, Rotational motion estimation for ISAR via triangle pose difference on two range-Doppler images. IET Radar. Sonar. Navig. **4**(4), 528–536 (2010). doi:10.1049/iet-rsn.2009.0042
15. SH Park, HT Kim, KT Kim, Cross-range scaling algorithm for ISAR images using 2-D Fourier transform and polar mapping. IEEE Trans. Geosci. Remote Sens. **49**(2), 868–877 (2011). doi:10.1109/TGRS.2010.2060731
16. C. Yang, W. Garber, R. Mitchell, E. Blasch, A simple maneuver indicator from target range-Doppler image. Paper presented at the 10th international conference information fusion, Quebec, Canada, 9–16 July 2007
17. B Etkin, LD Reid, *Dynamics of Flight: Stability and Control* (Wiley, New York, 1996)
18. J.R. Cloutier, T.S. Donald, Nonlinear hybrid bank-to-turn/ skid-to-turn missile autopilot design. Paper presented at the AIAA guidance, navigation, and control conference and exhibit, Montreal, Canada, 6–9 August 2001, 705–715
19. NF Palumbo, RA Blauwkamp, JM Lloyd, Modern homing missile guidance theory and techniques. J. Hopkins APL Tech. Dig. **29**(1), 42–59 (2010)
20. TK Moon, WC Stirling, *Mathematical Methods and Algorithms for Signal Processing* (Prentice Hall Press, Upper Saddle River, 2000)
21. JX Sun, *Image Analysis* (Chinese Science Press, Beijing, 2004), pp. 123–126

22. JV Harrington, An analysis of the detection of repeated signals in noise by binary integration. IEEE Trans. IT. **4**(1), 1–9 (1955).
23. Z Bao, MD Xing, T Wang, *Technology on Radar Imaging* (Publishing House of Electronics Industry Press, Beijing, 2005)
24. JX Zhou, ZG Shi, X Cheng, Q Fu, Automatic target recognition of SAR images based on global scattering center model. IEEE Trans. Geosci. Remote Sens. **49**(10), 3713–3729 (2011). doi:10.1109/TGRS.2011.2162526
25. MIL-HDBK-1211(MI). *'Missile flight simulation, part one: surface-to-air missiles'.* (US Department of Defense, Falls Church, VA, 1995)
26. D Dionne, H Michalska, Y Oshman, J Shinar, Novel adaptive generalized likelihood ratio detector with application to maneuvering target tracking. AIAA J. Guid. Control. Dyn. **29**(2), 465–474 (2006). doi:10.2514/1.13447
27. Y Oshman, D Arad, Differential-game-based guidance law using target orientation observations. IEEE Trans. Aerosp. Electron. Syst. **42**(1), 316–326 (2006). doi:10.1109/TAES.2006.1603425

2

Automatic and online setting of similarity thresholds in content-based visual information retrieval problems

Izaquiel L. Bessas[1], Flávio L. C. Pádua[1], Guilherme T. de Assis[2], Rodrigo T. N. Cardoso[3] and Anisio Lacerda[1*]

Abstract

Several information recovery systems use functions to determine similarity among objects in a collection. Such functions require a similarity threshold, from which it becomes possible to decide on the similarity between two given objects. Thus, depending on its value, the results returned by systems in a search may be satisfactory or not. However, the definition of similarity thresholds is difficult because it depends on several factors. Typically, specialists fix a threshold value for a given system, which is used in all searches. However, an expert-defined value is quite costly and not always possible. Therefore, this study proposes an approach for automatic and online estimation of the similarity threshold value, to be specifically used by content-based visual information retrieval system (image and video) search engines. The experimental results obtained with the proposed approach prove rather promising. For example, for one of the case studies, the performance of the proposed approach achieved 99.5 % efficiency in comparison with that obtained by a specialist using an empirical similarity threshold. Moreover, such automated approach becomes more scalable and less costly.

Keywords: Information retrieval, Content-based retrieval systems, Similarity thresholds

1 Introduction

Nowadays, multimedia databases are applied in various fields, storing large amounts of data. Thereby, the development of image and video content-based retrieval systems (capable of efficiently managing such data) has increased as well the academic interest in the area [1, 2]. For the development of such systems, some inherent problems must be solved: the selection of appropriate descriptors to represent images [1, 3]; the selection of appropriate similarity function to measure the similarity of the images being compared [1, 4]; and the definition of a suitable similarity threshold to be used by the systems [5–9].

The scope of possible techniques to solve the problems involved in the retrieval of content-based visual information makes necessary to use metrics that can assess the quality of the results obtained by different techniques. Such systems recover not only equal but also images similar to the searched image, making it necessary to evaluate responses returned to users. In this regard, some evaluation metrics are commonly used to describe the results obtained on an information retrieval system, namely precision, recall and F1 [10], which are classical metrics commonly used in information retrieval tasks.

After pre-processing input images (consultation), information retrieval systems compare them to the collection system and categorize them as either similar or dissimilar. Such verification is done through a similarity function *f*, which measures similarity between images. After image comparison, the result of the similarity function is tested against a δ similarity threshold to determine image similarity (the similarity threshold's minimum acceptable score [6–9]). Images compared with the input image whose similarity values are greater or equal to δ are considered similar, and the remaining are considered dissimilar. Typically, the values calculated by the similarity function *f* and defined for the value of δ similarity threshold are in a [0,1] range [5]; therefore, the closer the value returned by *f* is to 1, the more similar such images are.

*Correspondence: anisio@decom.cefetmg.br
[1] Computer Science Department, Centro Federal de Educação Tecnológica de Minas Gerais, Av. Amazonas, 7675 Belo Horizonte, Brazil
Full list of author information is available at the end of the article

Often, the solutions used to define δ are based on specialist-developed templates for specific searches, aimed at representing the entire collection. For each search, templates compute precision, recall and F1 values, considering different δ values. In this case, δ values maximizing F1 measurements for the highest number of searches are selected and fed to the information retrieval system. Setting the δ value in this fashion is laborious, making it unfeasible in most cases (mainly because of the need to know the entire collection).

Considering, for example, Fig. 1a, b, c, d displays the results of analysis of four separate (content-based retrieval) searches per image with the SAPTE system (a content-based multimedia information retrieval system [11, 12] (FLA Conceição, FLC Pádua, ACM Pereira, GT Assis, GD Silva, AAB Andrade: Semiodiscursive Analysis of TV Newscasts based on Data Mining and Image Pre-processing, to appear). For each image analysis result (Fig. 1a, b, c, d), corresponding F1 values are determined for different similarity threshold values. Here, the searched images are part of templates specifically designed to evaluate the system's performance; such images consist of key frames extracted from Rede Minas TV videos, present in SAPTE.

Figure 1a, b, c, d shows that to obtain the largest F1 value for a given search, a distinct δ value should also be considered for producing the best results. Therefore, automatic online setting of a δ value increases search effectiveness.

To automatically estimate δ in online applications, this study advocates the use of a metric based on internal criteria, possible to calculate without human intervention, as opposed to F1 calculation tied to external criteria and thus impossible to automate. Such metric is the silhouette coefficient [13] used to evaluate image clusters returning values within a $[-1\ldots1]$ interval (better clusters presenting values closer to 1).

Our approach with automatic and online estimation of the objective similarity threshold through a dynamic similarity threshold value associated to individual searches enhances the efficiency of content-based visual information retrieval. More efficient automatic information retrieval (without human intervention) contributes to generate specific web page repositories, along with improved information retrieval system feedback to users.

An example of improved search feedback to users is provided by SAPTE systems, as shown in Fig. 2a, b. These respectively represent the response of SAPTE to a given search using $\delta = 0.83$ (expert defined) and $\delta = 0.86$ (estimated by this study's approach). In Fig. 2a, the definition of a fixed threshold reached 0.53 in terms of F1 for a specific search, whereas this study's proposal F1 reached a more efficient 0.89 (Fig. 2b).

The main contribution of the present work consists in to present and validate a new effective and efficient

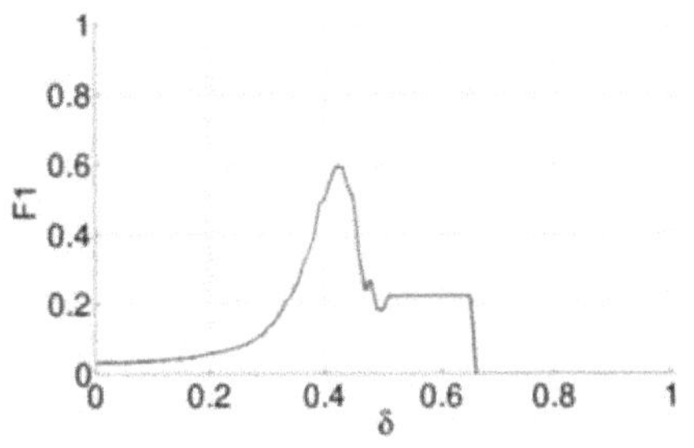

(a) Template 6 from CAPTE.

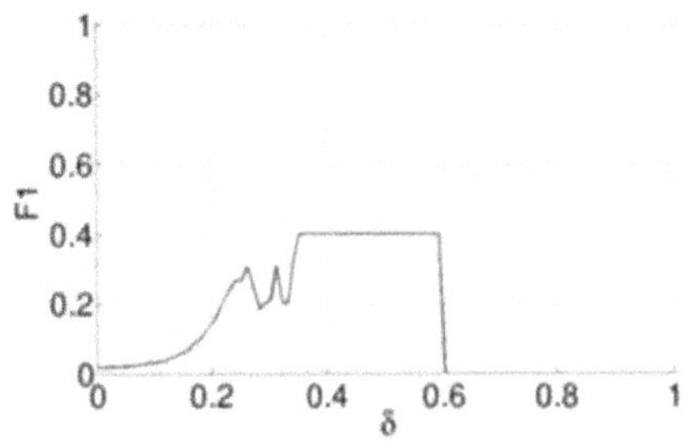

(b) Template 8 from CAPTE.

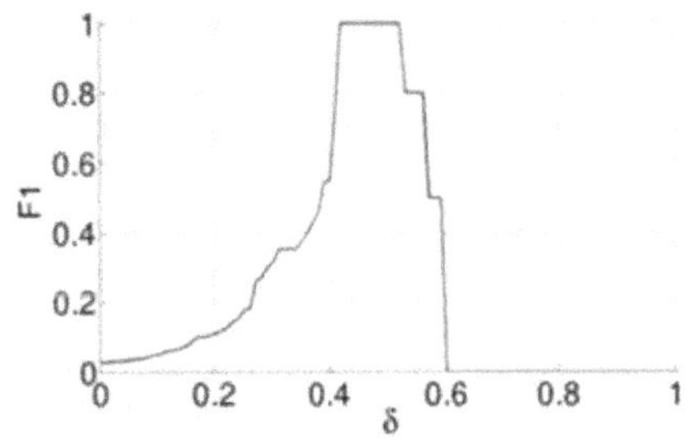

(c) Template 55 from CAPTE.

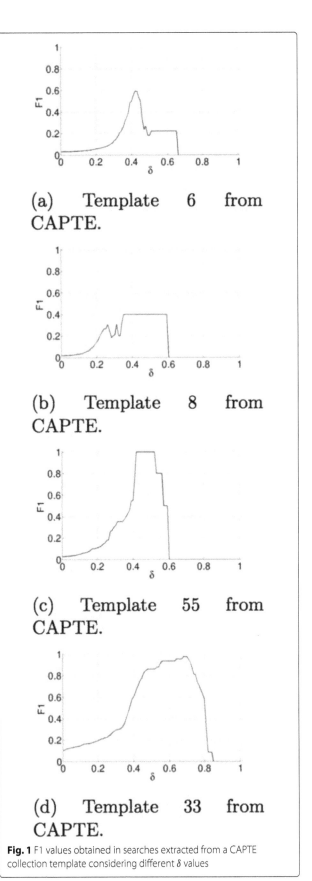

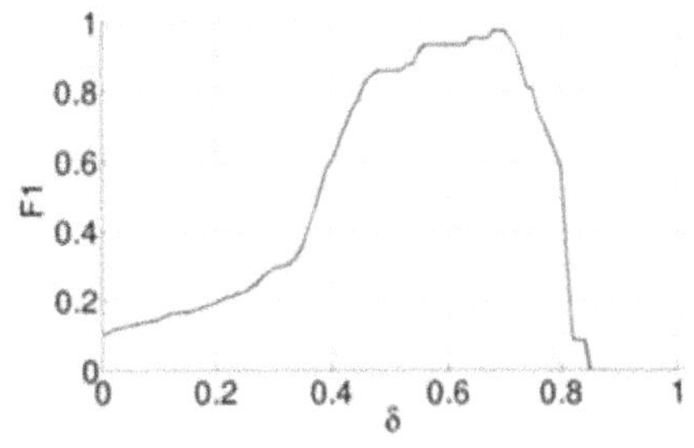

(d) Template 33 from CAPTE.

Fig. 1 F1 values obtained in searches extracted from a CAPTE collection template considering different δ values

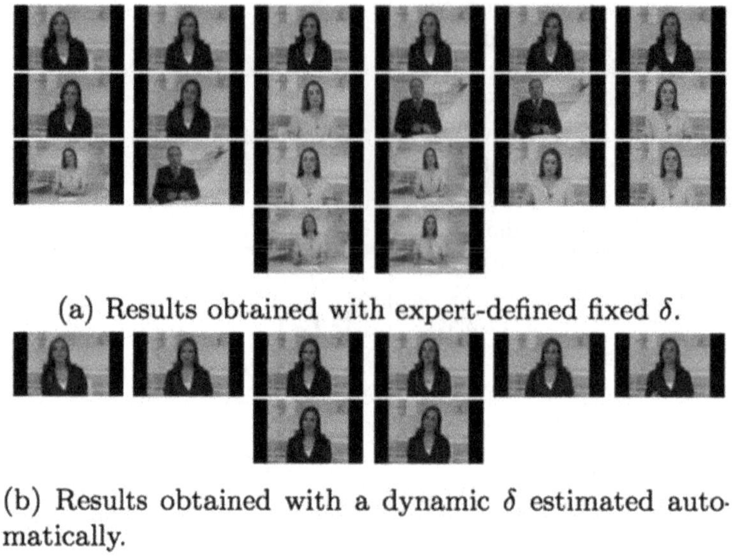
(a) Results obtained with expert-defined fixed δ.
(b) Results obtained with a dynamic δ estimated automatically.

Fig. 2 Results returned by a search held with a fixed δ (expert-defined) and a dynamic δ (estimated automatically)

approach, named automatic setting similarity threshold (ASTS), to automatically estimate similarity thresholds in content-based visual information retrieval (CBVIR) problems. As far as we know, this is the first work in the literature to propose a simple and successful solution for such a problem, which is specially challenging in online applications. We claim that ASTS represents a promising alternative to the current solutions, which are commonly based on specialist-developed templates. Unfortunately, the threshold setting processes of those solutions are prone to human error and demand on significant time and financial costs. Moreover, even though the aforementioned templates are computed by considering only subsets of specific searches, their application is extended to searches involving the entire dataset, what frequently produces unsatisfactory results to end-users. Unlike those solutions, ASTS is capable to automatically and online estimate similarity thresholds associated to individual searches, enhancing the effectiveness and the efficiency of CBVIR processes.

This paper is organized as follows: Section 2 presents related work. Section 3 presents and discusses our proposed approach. Section 4 presents experimental results. Section 5 shows final considerations and future work.

2 Related work

Among studies aimed at improving content-based visual information retrieval systems, this one particularly addresses effectiveness improvement (i.e. system's quality improvements through search, setting the automatic and online similarity threshold to be adopted).

Previous works outlined (aimed at improving such systems) address the development of techniques solving several related problems, namely the description mode of images contained in the system [2, 14–16], selection of the best similarity function [4, 17–19], creation of user profiles [20], machine learning, task clustering and indexing, stochastic algorithms [3, 20–26] and similarity threshold estimation [5–7, 9, 27, 28], the latter being the problem addressed in this paper.

For instance, in [3], the authors present a method that combines a k-means clustering algorithm with a B + tree structure to improve system results obtained through search, returning only images of the closest clusters. Another study [22] aims at improved search results. Here, we combine an evolutionary stochastic algorithm (particle swarm optimization) with feedback relevance to understand, by iterative learning, the most relevant features to users and then properly consider the image feature descriptors according to what was learned during the interaction with the user. In a previous study [21], a two-stepped recovery of multimedia information was developed, with content-based visual information retrieval being performed only in the second stage. The first step consists of searching the collection for a top-K cluster, and only after this, the cluster formation was compared by content-based visual information retrieval. Content-based visual information retrieval occurs on a reduced cluster of the collection, thus enhancing recovery efficiency.

Based on collection samples, a semi-automatic approach for the estimation of recall and precision values for various similarity thresholds minimizes efforts involved by static similarity threshold definitions [28, 29]. It requires expert input only where the number of distinct objects contained in each sample is concerned and uses two techniques to reduce human interaction, namely (i) sample use and (ii) similarity cluster process. Hence, the formed groups are used for automatic calculation of recall and precision then that resultant groups contain only objects that represent singular real objects. These clusters identify relevant objects so that when a particular object cluster is used for search, all its remaining objects are labeled relevant. Consequently, this approach generates a table of estimated recall and precision values from which it becomes possible to determine the appropriate similarity threshold for the application. Despite significantly reducing heavy expert reliance (usual in classical approaches), the proposed approach depends on specialist intervention to indicate the number of distinct objects contained in each sample. This limits the size of generated samples and reduces the number of distinct objects, making it possible for specialists to quantify them.

A new approach [5] combines two strategies to eliminate human intervention [28, 29], during the recall and precision values estimation process. They are (i) use of agglomerative hierarchical clustering algorithms and (ii) use of the silhouette coefficient for cluster evaluation. The first form clusters from different similarity thresholds without notifying the number of groups to be generated. Those are evaluated by the silhouette coefficient selecting the cluster with the highest silhouette coefficient value. Expert dependency is thus eliminated from the estimation process of the best similarity threshold and similarity function. This process is based on the premise that selected clusters (according to the validation of the clustering process) properly partition examined objects, meaning that each group represents only one real object. This premise, for example, was very important for the high linear correlation between the silhouette coefficient and F1 formally recorded in [5]. In expert-prepared templates used for recall and precision calculation, subjective external criteria may come into play. The absence of such information during the silhouette coefficient calculation potentially affects the linear correlation between this and F1 values.

In another study [5], the authors obtained relevant results by eliminating human intervention during the estimation of static similarity thresholds used by the system. However, the resultant information was used only as metadata for future similar applications, given the high computational cost of calculating silhouette coefficients, various different clusters and similarity functions for the entire collection (which excludes it from the dynamic definition of similarity thresholds). Despite being defined automatically, similarity threshold values remain used as a static similarity threshold, set and fixed for a given application. However, given that different searches may require different similarity threshold values, the definition of a single value for the latter ultimately compromises the efficiency of searches. Another relevant question regarding the use of a single similarity threshold value is that it may lose quality with the addition of new objects to the collection.

Unlike the previous methods, this work proposes an automatic and online approach, named automatic setting similarity threshold (ASTS), capable of estimating the most suitable similarity threshold value in accordance with the silhouette coefficient for individual searches, without any previous knowledge of the collection. The silhouette coefficient, originally proposed in [13] for interpretation and validation of consistency within general clusters of data, is used as a simple quality measure of the clustering step of ASTS, allowing the automatic estimation of similarity thresholds associated to individual searches. Note that the silhouette coefficient is an internal evaluation measure [30], which does not require an evaluated dataset, i.e. it does not require matching data instances to be known. As a result, our approach does not require human intervention.

3 Proposed approach

When using information retrieval systems, users expect to obtain a set of images somewhat connected with the searched object. Thus, provided answers should match the best image cluster present in the collection (collection images similar to the query). A previous study [13] indicates that a silhouette coefficient is a good cluster quality indicator, suggesting that this metric leads to a good F1 value if a good answer is obtained for any given search.

Figure 3 shows the proposed approach for automatic online setting of similarity thresholds. It can be described as follows: during searches, an input image supplied to the search system goes through a preprocessing (module 1) responsible for extracting the image's signature. A search and comparison (module 2) then analyzes the image signatures stored in the repository (database) and compares them with the desired image using a similarity function.

Importantly, the visual signatures of images are based on color, shape and texture information and are estimated by using the method proposed in [12]. In that work, the authors address the development of a unified approach to content-based indexing and retrieval of digital videos from television archives and estimate visual signatures to represent key frames of video recordings. More specifically, by using the method described in [12], we compute a visual signature for each image involved in our problem, containing 79 components (54 refer to color, 18 refer to texture and 7 refer to shape positions).

To ensure good recall, a low similarity threshold value ($\delta \approx 0$) is initially considered. When obtaining the result of the search and comparison module (possibly with high recall), the cluster of returned images is refined to increase the response's accuracy. Such refinement regroups the

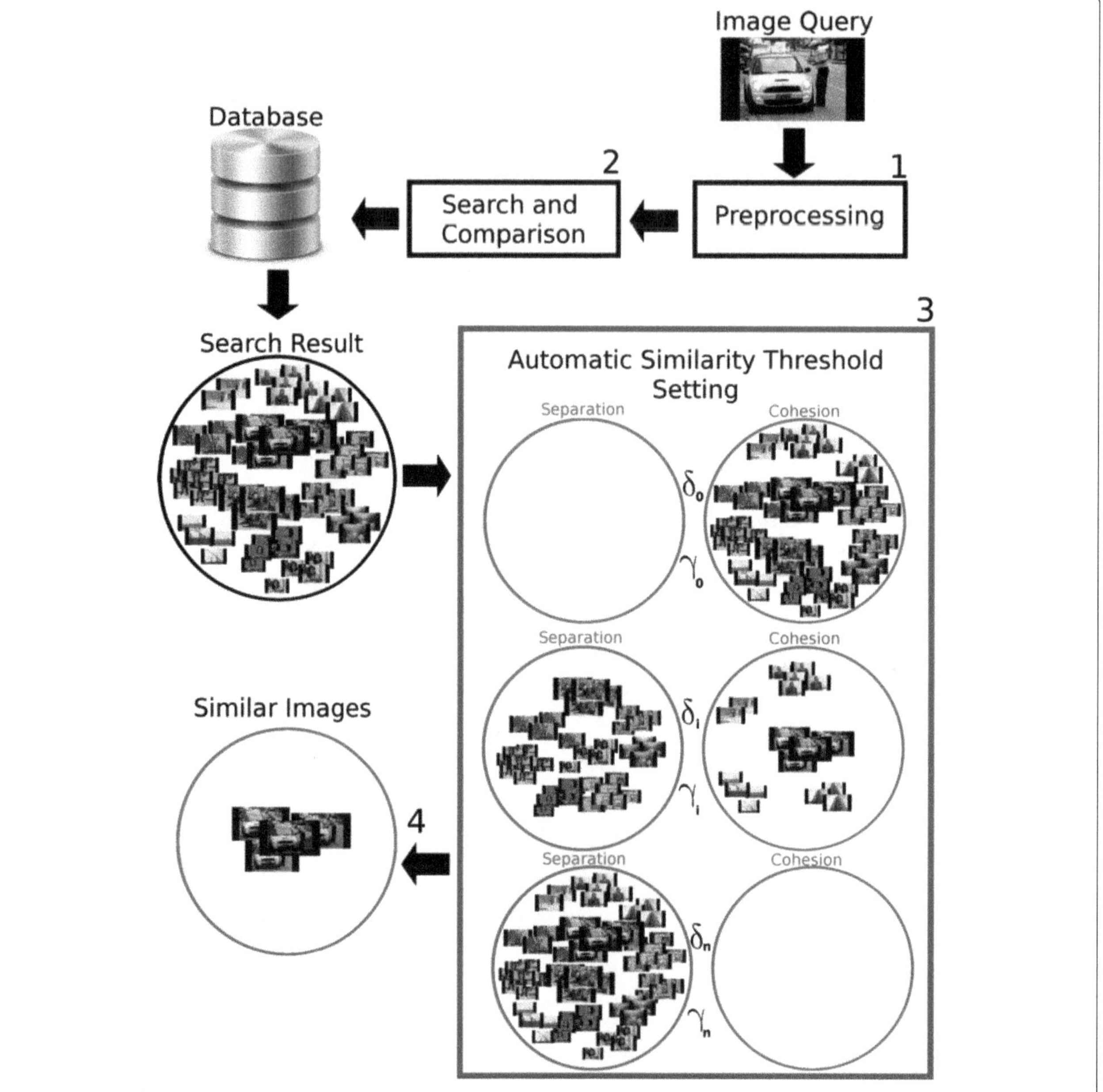

Fig. 3 Overview of the proposed approach

cluster of images initially returned by the search and comparison module into two clusters: (i) similar and (ii) dissimilar images to the query image. This step is executed by the similarity threshold automatic setting (module 3). The grouping is based on different similarity threshold values $(\delta_0, \ldots, \delta_{i-1}, \delta_i, \delta_{i+1}, \ldots, \delta_n)$, where the group of similar images contains objects with a degree of similarity greater than the δ_i similarity threshold value and the dissimilar images contain the remaining ones. Each δ_i is thus associated with a cluster evaluated by a silhouette coefficient (γ). The latter is associated with its corresponding δ_i. Each δ_i associated with a cluster is hereby also associated with a γ_i $(\gamma_0, \ldots, \gamma_{i-1}, \gamma_i, \gamma_{i+1}, \ldots, \gamma_n)$. Finally, users receive a group of similar images (module 4) tied to the largest γ_i value and to a more appropriate similarity threshold. In other words, it is a cluster of similar images matching the group that obtained the best silhouette coefficient evaluation.

Algorithm 1 generically describes the proposed approach steps to such an extent that it encompasses implementations ranging from deterministic algorithms such as ASTS proposed in this study and presented in Section 3.2. The proposed approach does not previously establish a stop condition, in a way that such a condition is set according to the implementation and what is expected of the application being used.

Algorithm 1: Proposed approach

Input: query image i_q, silimilarity threshold $\delta \approx 0$
Output: Sub-cluster of similar images (C_m) associated with the best δ

Search of i_q with a δ collection similarity threshold;
Response set I from the system;
repeat
    Generate new δ value;
    Regroup I according to δ in a sub-cluster of similar images (C_m) and dissimilar images sub-cluster (C_t);
    Evaluate C_m and C_t generated from δ, to obtain the γ related to this evaluation;
until *a stop criterion is achieved*;
Return a sub-cluster of similar images (C_m) associated with the hightest γ value;

This section is arranged as follows. In Section 3.1, we present the complexity analysis of the proposed approach. In Section 3.2, we present the ASTS algorithm, which is used to define the similarity threshold.

3.1 Complexity analysis

Once the silhouette coefficient is calculated for different pairs (δ, $[C_m, C_t]$), its computational cost is determined considering that the proposal tries to solve the problem online. The computational cost of the similarity threshold setting strategy uses a silhouette coefficient function to select the best answer. Algorithm 1 acts as the basis for this strategy cost calculation since it presents the proposed approach.

The operations related to distance calculation between vectors are used here as a metric to determine the computational cost of silhouette coefficients, adopting the formula used to calculate computational costs, as defined in [13]. The cohesion's computational cost is given by $O(n_m - 1)$, where n_m is the amount of images in a C_m cluster, and the computational cost of separation is $O\left(\sum_{j=1}^{K} n_t^j\right)$, where K is the number of groups of dissimilar images (C_t) and n_t is the number of images in each group C_t^j. The amount of clusters for the proposed approach is always two (one of similar images and other of dissimilar images to the query image). The result ($K = 1$) thus reduces the separation computational cost to $O(n_t)$. The silhouette coefficient calculation cost for a single object is $O(n_m - 1 + n_t)$; the silhouette coefficient calculation cost for cluster equals $O\left(n_m^2 - n_m + n_t\right)$. The total computational cost is $O\left(n_m^2\right)$ for each cluster silhouette coefficient calculation. The computational silhouette coefficient is therefore dictated by the quantity of images in C_m: the more images in a group, the higher is the computational cost of its silhouette coefficient calculation.

The computational cost of the proposed approach is defined by the number of times the silhouette coefficient calculation is performed. If N equals the number of times a silhouette coefficient is calculated to define the similarity threshold, the proposed approach cost is $O\left(N \times n_m^2\right)$. Thus, our proposed algorithm presents constant running time (apart from silhouette coefficient computation, which presents squared complexity).

Once the computational cost of the silhouette coefficient and the used similarity threshold setting strategy is known, adjustments can be made to achieve a better balance between runtime and effectiveness.

3.2 ASTS algorithm

The ASTS algorithm is a deterministic algorithm designed for automatic setting of similarity thresholds on the basis of a greedy paradigm. It consists of the heuristic used to estimate the best similarity threshold used in image searches (module 3 in Fig. 3). The ASTS is based on two steps: first, different similarity thresholds are explored to evaluate the quality of each one; second, the thresholds close to the best similarity threshold found by step 1 are exploited.

ASTS implementation requires establishing the following variables: l' and l'' – are the lower and upper limits for δ, respectively; α is the increment value of l' to l'', which generates δ values having the initial exploration function $(\delta_1, \ldots, \delta_{i-1}, \delta_i, \delta_{i+1}, \ldots, \delta_n)$, and $\alpha < (l'' - l')$; β evaluates the answers closer to the best solution found until then (with $\beta < \alpha$). The operation performed with the aid of β values is made through increases and decreases of the δ value associated with the best solution. Algorithm 2 details the ASTS operation.

According to Algorithm 2, once input variables (l', l'', α, β) are defined and a set of answers (I) is obtained via an information retrieval system, Eq. 1 generates δ values contained within an l' to l'' range (line 1). A cluster is made from each δ value $(\delta_1, \ldots, \delta_{i-1}, \delta_i, \delta_{i+1}, \ldots, \delta_n)$ generated by Eq. 1 so that for each δ_i, there is a cluster $(C_m^{\delta_i}, C_t^{\delta_i})$ (line 3). For each cluster $(C_m^{\delta_i}, C_t^{\delta_i})$ generated by δ_i, a silhouette coefficient (γ_{δ_i}) associated with the cluster is calculated reflecting its quality (line 4). This cluster generator method and respective silhouette coefficient evaluation is repeated for all δ values generated in Eq. 1 (line 2).

Once all solutions generated for the initial operation are evaluated, the solution with the highest γ_{δ_i} value is selected to ensure that it is the best one. The solution is then stored in two clusters with two variables $\left(\left(\delta_{\text{better}}^{+}, \gamma_{\text{better}}^{+}\right), \left(\delta_{\text{better}}^{-}, \gamma_{\text{better}}^{-}\right)\right)$ upon which improvement is refined by increases and decreases (line 5). Thus, the refining process of $\left(\delta_{\text{better}}^{+}, \gamma_{\text{better}}^{+}\right)$ is accomplished by increases and decreases in β values to the same β value in $\left(\delta_{\text{better}}^{-}, \gamma_{\text{better}}^{-}\right)$.

Algorithm 2: ASTS

Input: $I, l', l'', \alpha, \beta$

Output: R

1 generation of the initial δ values for exploration of the search space:

$$\delta_i = \begin{cases} l' & \text{se } i = 1, \\ \delta_{i-1} + \alpha & \text{se } 1 < i < n,\ n = \dfrac{l'' - l'}{\alpha} + 1 \\ l'' & \text{se } i = n \end{cases} \quad (1)$$

/* Creation of clusters for each threshold generated by Eq. 1, being evaluated by the silhouette coefficient */

2 **for** *todo* δ_i **do**

3 reassembles the answer set I, acording to δ_i, into two subgroups $C_m^{\delta_i}$ and $C_t^{\delta_i}$;

4 compute the silhouette coefficient γ_{δ_i} to get $C_m^{\delta_i}$ e $C_t^{\delta_i}$;

end

5 selects δ_i associated with the highest γ_{δ_i}, assigning it to δ^+_{better} and γ^+_{better}; the same values are assigned to δ^-_{better} and γ^-_{better};

/* Refinement of the best similarity threshold found earlier and defined in δ^+_{better} and γ^+_{better}through β increases */

6 **repeat**

7 $\delta_x = \delta^+_{melhor} + \beta$;

8 reassembles the answer set I according to δ_x into two subgroups $C_m^{\delta_x}$ and $C_t^{\delta_x}$;

9 compute silhouette coefficient γ_{δ_x} to obtain $C_m^{\delta_x}$ and $C_t^{\delta_x}$;

10 the γ^+_{better} value is replaced by γ_{δ_x} if $\gamma_{\delta_x} > \gamma^+_{better}$;

until *($\gamma^+_{better} \leq \gamma_{\delta_x}$) or ($\delta^+_{better} - \alpha \leq \delta_x \leq \delta^+_{better} + \alpha$) or ($l' \leq \delta_x \leq l''$);*

/* Refinement of the previous best similarity threshold and defined by δ^-_{better} and γ^-_{better} by β decreases */

11 **repeat**

12 $\delta_x = \delta^-_{better} - \beta$;

13 reassembles the answer set I according to δ_x into two subgroups $C_m^{\delta_x}$ and $C_t^{\delta_x}$;

14 compute silhouette coefficient γ_{δ_x} for $C_m^{\delta_x}$ and $C_t^{\delta_x}$;

15 γ^-_{better} is replaced by γ_{δ_x} if $\gamma_{\delta_x} > \gamma^-_{better}$;

until *($\gamma^-_{better} \leq \gamma_{\delta_x}$) or ($\delta^-_{better} - \alpha \leq \delta_x \leq \delta^-_{better} + \alpha$) or ($l' \leq \delta_x \leq l''$);*

16 Assigns R to the C_m cluster associated with the greatest value between γ^+_{better} and γ^-_{better};

With the best current solution selected, δ values are increased and decreased through β. These produce new δ_x similarity thresholds, which in turn generate new clusters that are evaluated and related to γ_{δ_x} values (lines 7, 8, 9, 12, 13, and 14). This procedure is repeated until a certain δ_x similarity threshold produces a γ_{δ_x} worse than that of the current best solution, i.e. $\gamma^+_{\text{better}} > \gamma_x$ e $\gamma^-_{\text{better}} > \gamma_x$ or until a limit value is reached: $(\delta^+_{\text{better}} - \alpha \leq \delta_x \leq \delta^+_{\text{better}} + \alpha)$ e $(\delta^-_{\text{better}} - \alpha \leq \delta_x \leq \delta^-_{\text{better}} + \alpha)$ or $(l' \leq \delta_x \leq l'')$ (lines 6 and 11). When a better solution is found, it replaces the current best (rows 10 and 15). Identical in their logic, both second and third operations repeat Algorithm 2 blocks (lines 6 and 11, respectively); while the first explores solutions close to the best current solution by similarity threshold increases, the second does so with decreases in the same value.

After finishing exploring solutions close to the initially selected better similarity threshold, Algorithm 2 returns to users a cluster of similar images associated with the highest value of γ – in range γ^+_{better} and γ^-_{better}.

4 Experimental results

To better present experimental results, this section is divided into four subsections. Section 4.1 describes experimental planning. Section 4.3 details the baselines used for performance comparison. Section 4.4 analyzes the linear correlation between F1 and silhouette coefficient metrics. Finally, Section 4.5 presents experimental results obtained by the proposed approach, comparing them against those of the defined baseline.

4.1 Experiment planning

The first experimental step was to select and organize the templates of three collections: "CAPTE" [11, 12], "Corel" [31] and "The INRIA Holidays dataset" [32].

The "CAPTE" collection consists of a set of 575 key frames extracted from 90 video blocks found on 11 TV shows aired on Rede Minas television channel [12]. The CAPTE collection is mainly composed of face images from the mentioned TV shows. The "Corel" collection consists of approximately 10,000 general purpose images, which are then reduced to 202 and distributed among 32 similar images classes manually labeled by researchers [31] (the template that was used in this study). "The INRIA Holidays dataset" collection [32] consists of 1491 general images separated into 316 semantically similar image classes.

With the collections and respective templates defined and ready to be used, its images were processed, generating a database of image signatures for each one of them. A previously described method [12] was used to estimate images signatures (module 3 in Fig. 3).

To calculate image similarity, five functions were analyzed to assess the similarity function with best F1 results, namely cosine of the θ angle, Manhattan distance, Euclidean distance, Pearson correlation coefficient and histogram intersection. These similarity functions were chosen because for their low computational cost and workability of the image signatures used.

4.2 Evaluation metric

We use a standard evaluation metric in information retrieval literature: f-measure (F1). This metric is defined in terms of precision (P) and recall (R). Precision is the ratio of the number of correctly returned images to the total number of returned images. Recall is the ratio of the number of correctly returned images to the total number of images that should be returned according to ground truth information. Finally, F1 measure is defined as the harmonic mean of precision and recall, as given by

$$F1 = \frac{2 \times P \times R}{P + R}$$

4.3 Baselines

Following, we detail each baseline used for performance comparison.

4.3.1 *Threshold impact on performance*

With the collections, the image description and the similarity functions established for each pair [template of a collection/similarity function], we calculated the F1 values associated with different values of similarity threshold. This threshold was expanded from zero to one, by 0.01 increments.

Hence, it was possible to determine which similarity threshold leads to higher F1 (optimal δ_{best}) for a given search using a specific similarity function. The optimal δ can thus be formally defined in Eq. 2:

$$\delta_{\text{best}} = \operatorname{argmax}\left(F1_{\delta_i}^{g_k,f}\right), \tag{2}$$

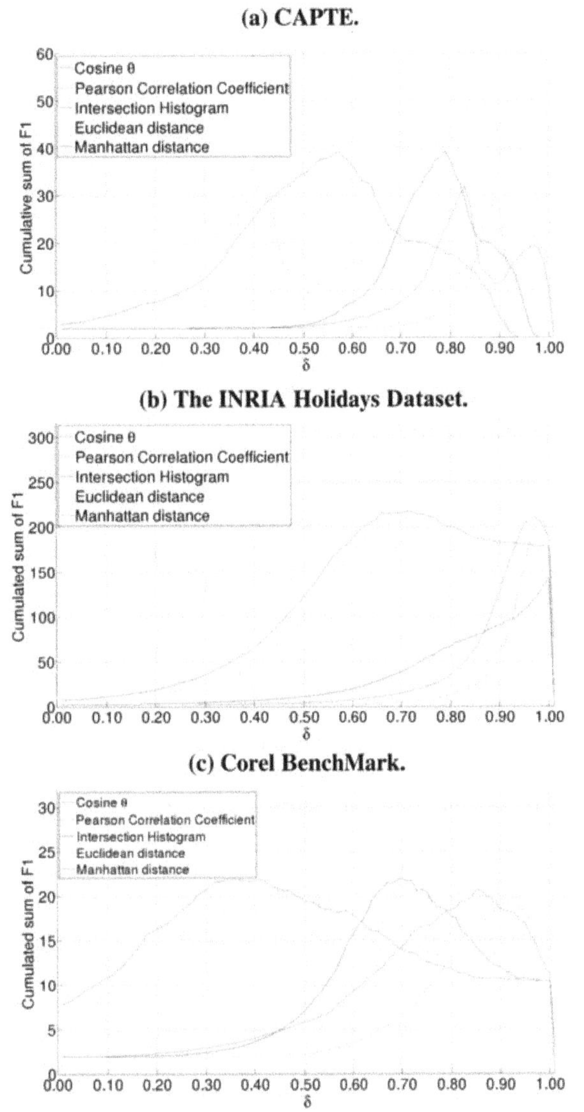

Fig. 4 Curve of the cumulative F1 sum for each pair [f, δ]: similarity function f; similarity threshold considered δ

where g_k represents the template related to a particular collection search k, f is the similarity function used and δ_i, for $i = 1, \ldots, n$ represents the similarity threshold considered. The optimal delta represents the value of similarity threshold associated with the highest F1 in a given search k for a specific collection when using similarity functions f. It is expected that optimal δ values close to the automatically set similarity threshold proposed (δ_γ) produce more effective results.

Figure 4a, b, c presents the cumulative F1 sum reached by each pair [collection/similarity function] for all tested δ values, representing "CAPTE", "The INRIA Holidays dataset" and "Corel" collections, respectively.

Figure 4a, b, c also shows that a unique similarity threshold value does not guarantee optimum performance in a content-based visual information retrieval system. However, it can produce satisfactory results if well defined. Through these figures, it is possible to determine similarity thresholds for each similarity function, leading to the system's greatest cumulative F1 sum. These similarity thresholds (fixed δ) form the baseline, as presented in Table 1. Cumulative F1 sum values for each fixed δ are used to compare and validate the results achieved with the approach proposed hereby (Table 2).

From Table 2, we observe that the best F1 values for all collections is given by the similarity function based on the Manhattan's distance, excepting "Corel benchmark" collection.

Table 1 Fixed δ values defined for each pair [collection/similarity function]

f	CAPTE	INRIA	Corel
Cosine of the θ angle	0.82	0.96	0.85
Pearson correlation coefficient	0.88	0.97	0.91
Histogram intersection	0.78	0.98	0.69
Euclidean distance	0.40	0.72	0.45
Manhattan distance	0.56	0.70	0.40

4.3.2 *k*-means analysis

Given that our proposed approach is based on clustering similar images, we investigate the performance of k-means algorithm [33] retrieving relevant images. The k-means algorithm is a classical method for clustering. Here, we represent images by their descriptors and vary the number of clusters (i.e. the k parameter) to evaluate the performance of k-means when compared to our proposed approach.

Specifically, we start by finding an initial set of images by conducting a query over the whole dataset. Hence, this set is used as input to k-means and a given number of expected clusters (i.e. k parameter). Finally, given the returned clusters found by k-means, we return to the user the cluster of images that have the highest average similarity value among the images within the cluster and the input image (i.e. the one used as query).

In Table 3, we present the results of cumulative F1 measure with distinct k values. The best results obtained by k-means refer to "Corel" datasets, which is also the best results for our approach (i.e. ASTS) when considering k equals to 4 and 8. For all tested k values, the proposed approach presents better results than the strong baseline, i.e. the k-means algorithm.

Moreover, the experiments show that as we increase the values of k, the performance of the k-means algorithm also increases. We believe that this happens because as we increase the number of clusters, the precision also increases. Another possibility is that precision increases but recall decreases, which is a well known trade-off in information retrieval literature. We avoid this by limiting the number of generated clusters to avoid empty empty groups of images.

Table 2 Cumulative F1 sum for each pair [collection/similarity function] for fixed δ values set (Table 1)

f	CAPTE	INRIA	Corel
Cosine of the θ angle	*31.73*	*211.96*	*20.68*
Pearson correlation coefficient	29.55	*207.22*	19.65
Histogram intersection	39.18	134.87	21.97
Euclidean distance	*31.73*	*211.10*	*20.57*
Manhattan distance	39.18	216.90	21.92

Table 3 Cumulative F1 sum for k-means algorithm with distinct k values

k	CAPTE	INRIA	Corel
$k = 2$	3.9492	6.0073	9.2071
$k = 4$	5.6523	9.6352	14.1657
$k = 8$	-	13.6408	18.3246

We also compare the performance of k-means algorithm and our proposed approach. For this comparison, we used the cumulative F1 measure and the Euclidean distance as similarity metric. The results are summarized in Table 4. We vary the k values for each query for all datasets and present the mean, standard deviation, absolute F1 values and the relative gains of our approach over the k-means algorithm.

The results presented in Table 4 show that the performance of our ASTS algorithm is mostly higher than the performance of the k-means baseline. A different behavior is observed for the "Corel" dataset when considering $k = 4$ and $k = 8$. Note that the performance of the k-means algorithm is worst than the performance of our approach when using fixed δ. We observe that our approach presents a better performance than the tested baseline. Besides the lower performance of k-means, it has a disadvantage that the number of clusters needs to be specified beforehand. This can be difficult for large datasets and, as shown in experiments, has considerable impact on the method's performance. Contrarily, the proposed ASTS algorithm avoids this problem, which represents an advantage for researchers and practitioners. Finally, we observe that even when keeping fixed values for δ the proposed ASTS algorithm has a higher performance than k-means algorithm for datasets "CAPTE" and "The INRIA Holidays dataset".

4.4 Linear correlation

A high linear correlation between F1 and silhouette coefficients ensures quality in this approach's estimations. Therefore, for each collection searched, linear correlation between these metrics was calculated. For all collections, observations revealed both high and low/almost nonlinear correlation between the metrics. Only the "Corel" collection obtained results where the linear correlation was less than zero.

However, a good linear correlation between these metrics is not always guaranteed because F1 calculations consider external criteria absent during the silhouette coefficient calculation (which works with internal criteria). To calculate F1, specialists may include subjective criteria for deciding on similarity or dissimilarity of search-returned images: criteria missing on the characteristics described by the images signatures that directly

Table 4 Cumulative F1 sum reached by ASTS and k-means for each k value

		CAPTE		
k value	F1 mean	Standard deviation	Cumulative F1 sum by k-means	Cumulative F1 sum k-means relative to δ_γ
2	0.0658	0.0669	3.9492	13.18 %
4	0.0942	0.1014	5.6523	18.86 %
		The INRIA Holidays dataset		
k value	F1 mean	Standard deviation	Cumulative F1 sum by k-means	Cumulative F1 sum k-means relative to δ_γ
2	0.0190	0.0429	6.0073	3.3 %
4	0.0304	0.0728	9.6352	5.3 %
8	0.0431	0.1125	13.5408	7.5 %
		Corel benchmark		
k value	F1 mean	Standard deviation	Cumulative F1 sum by k-means	Cumulative F1 sum k-means relative to δ_γ
2	0.2877	0.2474	9.2071	86.92 %
4	0.4426	0.3378	14.1657	133.73 %
8	0.5726	0.3562	18.3246	172.99 %

affect cluster evaluation through silhouette coefficient calculation. Therefore, a higher or lower linear correlation between F1 and silhouette coefficient may be obtained for different templates of the same collection.

Figure 5a, b, c[1] maps the linear correlation between such metrics for each search of the "CAPTE", "Corel" and "The INRIA Holidays dataset" collections. The "CAPTE" collection template reveals that 63 % of the searches achieved a linear correlation above 70 %, with an average linear correlation of 54 %. In total, 80 % of the "The INRIA Holidays dataset" templates queries reached a linear correlation above 70 %, with an average linear correlation of 78 %. The "Corel" template results were not as good as the first two: only 12 % of the searches attained linear correlation results above 70 %, with an average linear correlation of only 5 %.

As previously stated, a satisfactory linear correlation between F1 and silhouette coefficients is not always possible. However, the linear correlation between these metrics may improve: the closer the decision criteria on the similarity between images is to that used by experts and by the system, the better the linear correlation between F1 and the silhouette coefficient is. Thus, according to the results obtained in this subsection, a lower efficacy is expected for the "Corel" collection when using the proposed approach.

4.5 Proposed approach evaluation

To evaluate the proposed approach, the ASTS algorithm was implemented and executed for the three collections and for five defined similarity functions. The evaluation of the retrieval process is the same for all datasets. The input query image is randomly chosen from a given cluster and the ground truth data are the other images that compose the given cluster. The aim is having as high as possible values for precision and recall, which leads to high F1 values.

In [5], the authors conducted a set of experiments to evaluate the correlation between F1 and silhouette coefficient metrics, using four similarity functions on six datasets. These experiments demonstrated that, when the silhouette coefficient is highly correlated with the F1, the similarity threshold value that maximizes the F1, on a pair dataset/similarity function, also maximizes the silhouette coefficient. Based on this result, we can say that a high linear correlation between F1 and silhouette coefficient metrics ensures efficiency in our proposed approach. Therefore, for each collection searched, linear correlation between these metrics was calculated. For all collections, observations revealed both high and low/almost non-linear correlation between the metrics. Only the "Corel" collection obtained results where the linear correlation was less than zero.

ASTS automatically estimated similarity thresholds for each search with a different similarity threshold (δ_γ) set for each of those. Figure 6a, b, c shows this value and an optimal δ. We therefore used the Manhattan distance similarity function f, which performed better with fixed δ (Table 2).

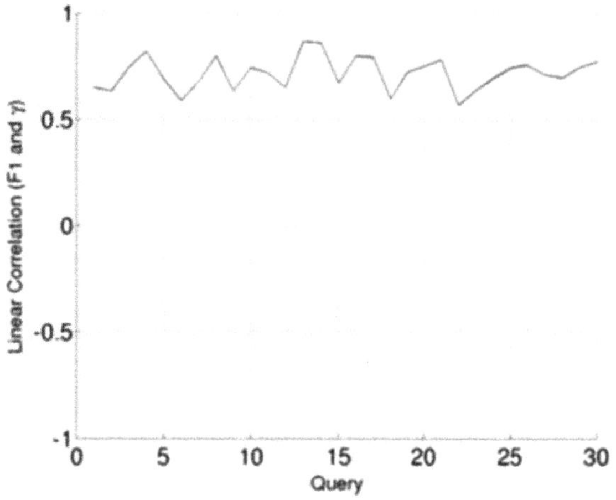

(a) CAPTE.

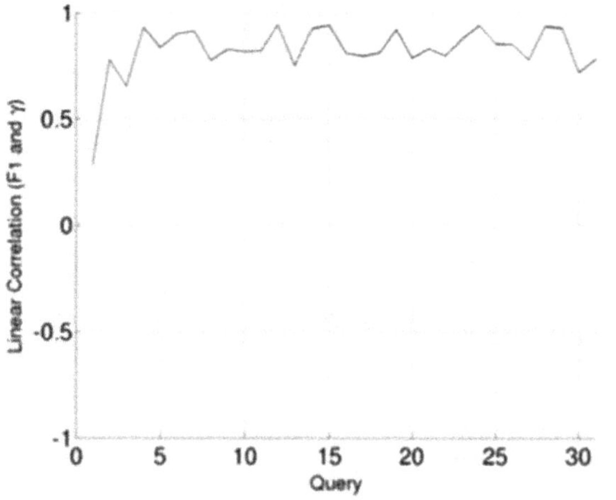

(b) The INRIA Holidays Dataset.

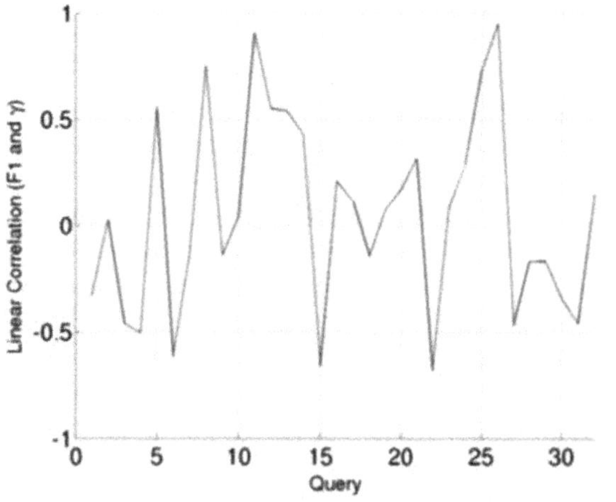

(c) Corel Bench Mark.

Fig. 5 Linear correlation between F1 and the silhouette coefficient for each template

Figure 6a, b shows that ASTS could estimate similarity thresholds (δ_γ) close to δ optimal values. Such behavior often leads to high F1 values. Figure 6c shows that most of ASTS searches estimated δ_γ values distant from optimal δ (given the linear correlation observed in this collection; see Section 4.4).

To assess result quality of the proposed approach, we compared our cumulative F1 sums with those attained by expert-set fixed similarity thresholds (baseline). Table 5 shows the cumulative F1 sum reached by ASTS, by similarity function used, considering all searches of the same collection. Table 2 presents the ASTS performance achieved by the baseline, in which we present F1 mean, F1 standard deviation, cumulative F1 for k-means and cumulative F1 for k-means relative to a fixed delta.

Table 5 shows the collections where ASTS achieved the best results ("CAPTE" and "The INRIA Holidays" dataset). In the "CAPTE" collection, all ASTS-evaluated similarity functions achieved performances greater than 70 % when compared with a cumulative F1 sum for a fixed similarity threshold. In addition, in two other cases, the sums resemble those obtained with a fixed similarity threshold (99.5 and 94.4 %). "The INRIA Holidays dataset" collection also obtained good results, except for the similarity histogram intersection function, which achieved only 55.2 % of what was achieved with this same function when using a fixed similarity threshold. However, the remaining collection reveals performances superior to 60 %: two cases stood out with 86.0 % (for Euclidean distance) and 83.3 % (for Manhattan distance). Only one case of the "Corel" collection achieved a performance superior to 70 %.

The greatest contribution of this study is the achievement of automatic results, without specialist input, matching the best results attained by expert-defined similarity thresholds (baseline), for a given collection. Other advantages of the proposed approach are as follows: (i) scalability, (ii) resistance to changes in image content, (iii) change in the similarity function, (iv) insertion and removal of new images in the collection, and (v) no previous knowledge of the collection. Furthermore, the approach proposed hereby has the potential to achieve results superior to those obtained via fixed similarity thresholds (because the dynamic setting of a suitable value for this threshold increases result effectiveness). Improvement of the linear correlation between F1 and silhouette coefficients is required though. As described above, expert F1 calculation presupposes a template of desired queries, separating similar from dissimilar images. The criteria considered when determining image similarity or dissimilarity depends on experts. Silhouette coefficient calculation groups images according to certain thresholds and similarity functions with the similarity calculation performed on the image

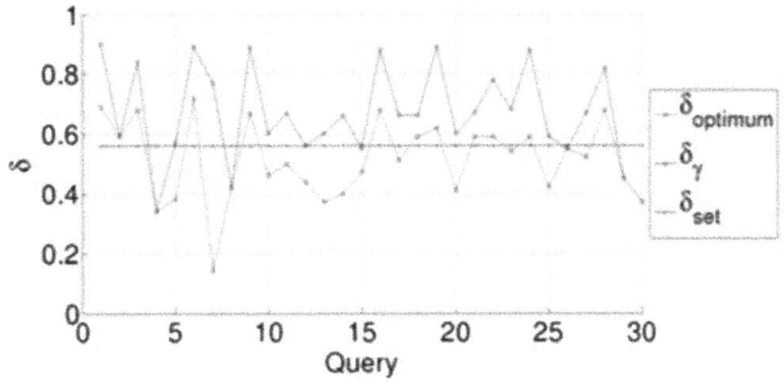

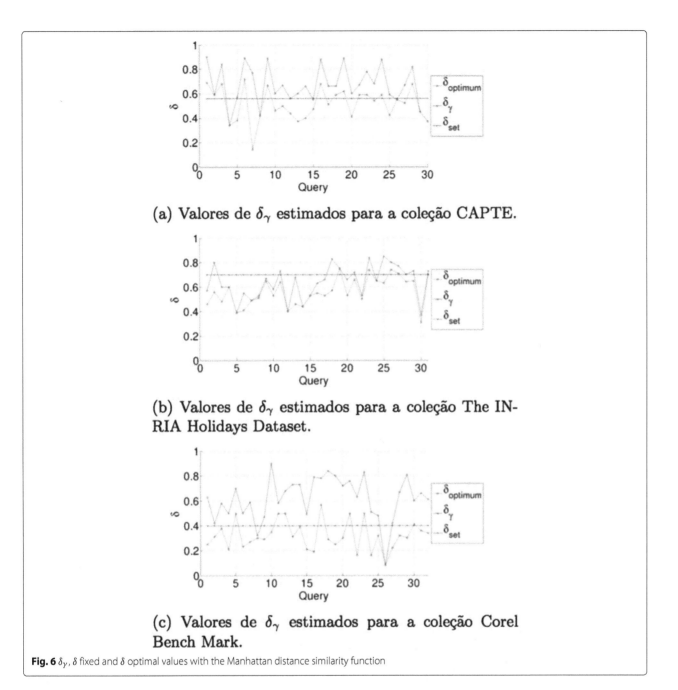

(a) Valores de δ_γ estimados para a coleção CAPTE.

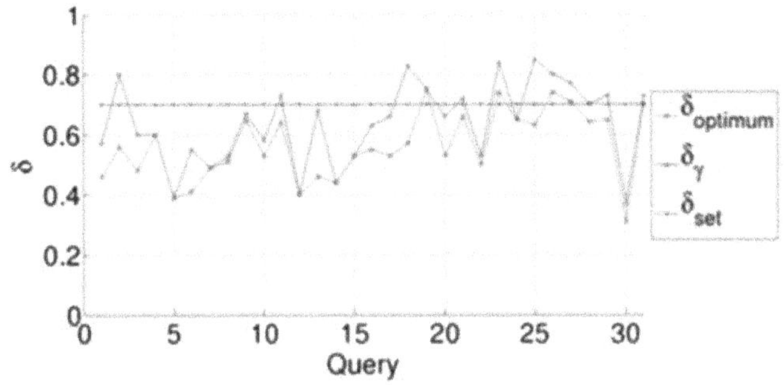

(b) Valores de δ_γ estimados para a coleção The INRIA Holidays Dataset.

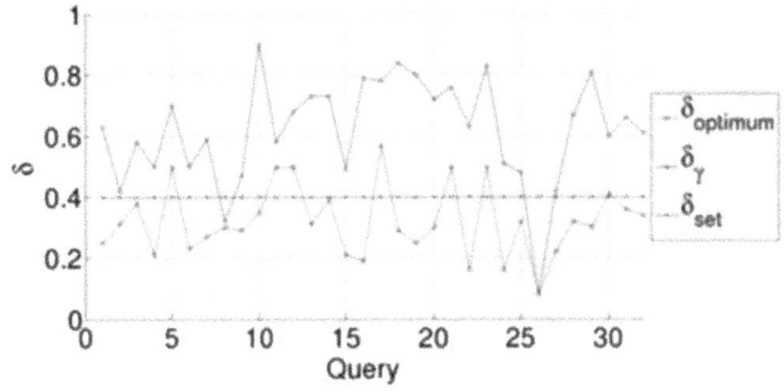

(c) Valores de δ_γ estimados para a coleção Corel Bench Mark.

Fig. 6 δ_γ, δ fixed and δ optimal values with the Manhattan distance similarity function

signature. Therefore, the closer the criterion used by specialists is to that used for similarity calculation by similarity functions f, the greater is the linear correlation between these measures and the better results become.

We also investigate the computational costs per query. The experiments were implemented in MATLAB and run on a Intel Core i7 2.1 GHz with 32 GB of memory. In Fig. 7, we show the running time for each query as well as the average for the CAPTE dataset[2]. As we can see, there is variation on running time for each query.

4.6 Parameter sensitivity

In this section, we investigate the impacts of different parameter settings on the overall performance of our method. First, we discuss the sensitivity of the α parameter, which refers to the number of initial solutions to be searched in the first step of our algorithm. Hence, we discuss the sensitivity of the β parameter, which refers to the number of answers closer to the best solution found at a given interaction.

Effect of α with fixed β. In Fig. 8, we present the resulting performance costs of our ASTS algorithm when varying α

Table 5 Cumulative F1 sum reached by ASTS for each similarity function

		CAPTE		
f	Mean	Standard deviation	Cumulative F1 sum	δ_γ compared to δ_{fixo}
Cosine of the θ angle	0.5263	0.3578	31.58	99.5 %
Pearson correlation coefficient	0.3591	0.3840	21.55	72.9 %
Histogram intersection	0.5244	0.3196	31.47	80.3 %
Euclidean distance	0.4995	0.3319	29.97	94.4 %
Manhattan distance	0.4913	0.3047	29.48	75.2 %
		The INRIA Holidays dataset		
f	Mean	Standard deviation	Cumulative F1 sum	δ_γ compared to δ_{fixo}
Cosine of the θ angle	0.5218	0.2330	164.90	77.8 %
Pearson correlation coefficient	0.4134	0.2923	130.64	63.0 %
Histogram intersection	0.2358	0.2262	74.54	55.2 %
Euclidean distance	0.5742	0.1498	181.47	86.0 %
Manhattan distance	0.5718	0.1467	180.70	83.3 %
		Corel benchmark		
f	Mean	Standard deviation	Cumulative F1 sum	δ_γ compared to δ_{fixo}
Cosine of the θ angle	0.3751	0.2078	12.00	58.0 %
Pearson correlation coeficcient	0.4520	0.2293	14.46	73.6 %
Histogram intersection	0.3318	0.1423	10.62	48.3 %
Euclidean distance	0.3310	0.1406	10.59	51.5 %
Manhattan distance	0.3310	0.1406	10.59	48.3 %

parameter. As we increase the α values from 0.1, the computational costs also increase, because we are considering more candidate solutions.

Effect of α and β combinations. In Fig. 9, we investigate how different combinations of α and β parameters affect computational performance of our ASTS algorithm. When decreasing values of β leads to more computational costs because we are considering a larger solution space. The opposite is also valid, i.e. increasing β values leads to less computational costs because we are considering more restricted regions in solution space.

5 Conclusions

The main challenge of this study is the dynamic and automatic setting of an appropriate similarity threshold value to be used in searches of content-based visual information retrieval systems. To accomplish this, we proposed an approach using a metric silhouette coefficient in which basic principles were implemented through an ASTS algorithm (also adopted here).

Performed tests revealed promising ASTS results. For example, the "CAPTE" and "The INRIA Holidays dataset" collections (with the greatest number of images) showed performance close to 100 %, obtained automatically (with cumulative F1 sums of the proposed approach compared with the baseline cumulative F1 sum). Notably, however, the templates of each collection contained semantically similar images (simple image signature techniques combined with similarity functions appropriate to this type of signature), thus producing good results. The techniques used on the "Corel" collection were not sufficient for the image descriptors to properly represent the characteristics that determine image resemblance, thus being irrelevant to the proposed approach.

In general, our approach achieved good results, often reaching high performances very close to those achieved by fixed specialist set similarity thresholds. Such results encourage the continuation of this work, to solve a question that significantly enhances the quality of content-based visual information retrieval systems.

We believe that pairing more robust image signatures with appropriate similarity functions to compare the first will lead to better results and a more efficient approach. The computational cost of signature calculation and comparison must be accounted for in proposals seeking to automatically determine similarity thresholds

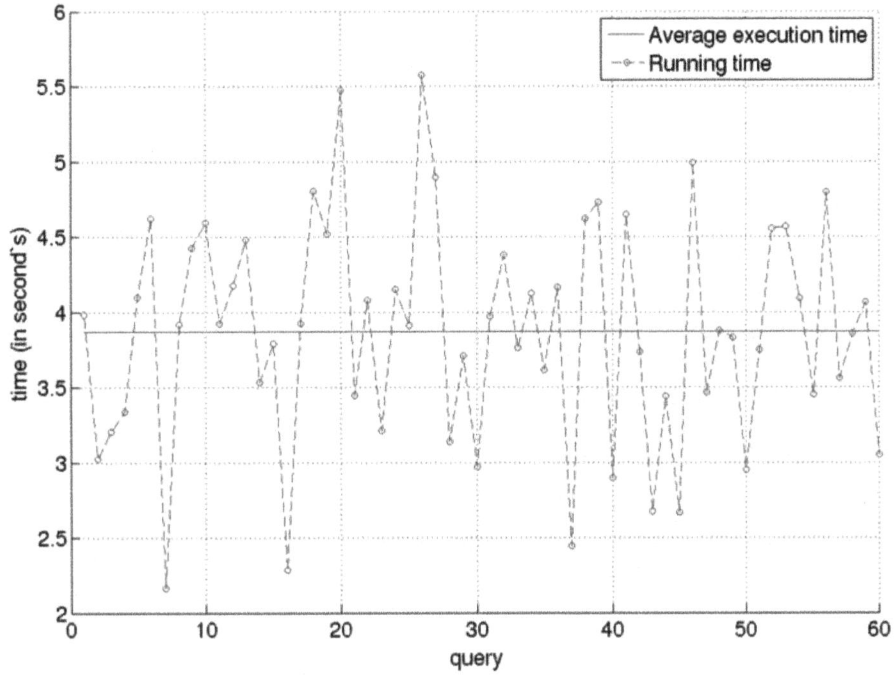

Fig. 7 Computational costs per query for CAPTE dataset

online. Image signatures used hereby are classic models. They work with global characteristic descriptors, describing images with a single vector (with low computational cost for both signature calculation and for its comparison through similarity functions). However, such signatures may not be so effective to describe image signatures working with local features. On the other hand, signature calculation on the basis of local characteristics and the calculation of its similarity (comparison of a set of vectors rather than a single vector) have high computational

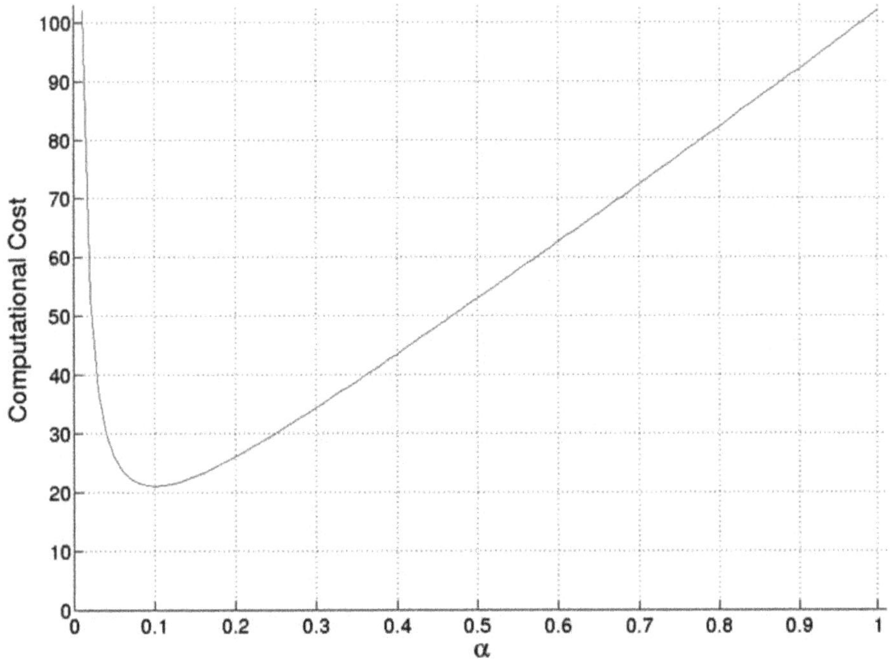

Fig. 8 Computational costs of ASTS algorithm varying α parameter with β parameter equals to 0.01

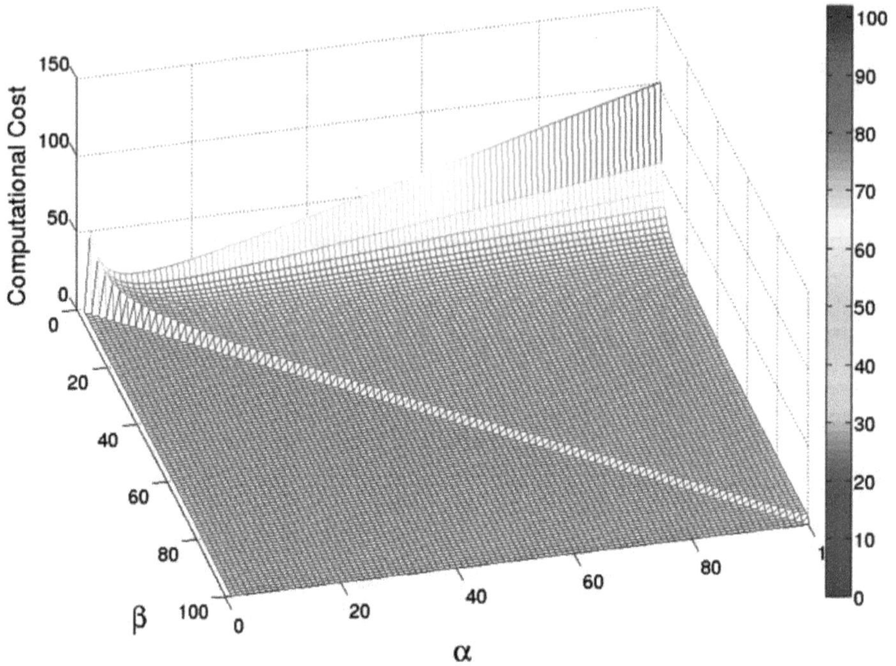

Fig. 9 Computational costs of ASTS algorithm varying α and β parameters

cost, particularly when compared to techniques working with global characteristics. It is therefore necessary to prevent silhouette coefficient computational cost increases, rendering the proposed approach unfeasible.

As future work, we plan to investigate better image representation as well as appropriate similarity functions to compare their signatures. Such way of representation and comparison directly impacts this proposal's effectiveness and efficiency. A balance between these two characteristics (or the predominance of one over the other) depends on what is expected of the system to which the proposed approach is applied. The improvement of such techniques aims to produce high linear correlation between silhouette coefficients and F1s, which will help to generate good results in the information retrieval process.

Endnotes

[1]Figures concerning the linear correlation for "CAPTE" and "The INRIA Holidays dataset" collection searches present only a data sample.

[2]Since results for Corel and INRIA datasets are similar, we omit these results.

Competing interests
The authors declare that they have no competing interests.

Acknowledgements
The authors gratefully acknowledge the financial support of FAPEMIG-Brazil under Procs. APQ-01180-10 and APQ-02269-11; CEFET-MG under Procs. PROPESQ-088/12, PROPESQ-076/09 and PROPESQ-10314/14; CAPES-Brazil and CNPq-Brazil.

Author details
[1]Computer Science Department, Centro Federal de Educação Tecnológica de Minas Gerais, Av. Amazonas, 7675 Belo Horizonte, Brazil. [2]Computer Science Department, Universidade Federal de Ouro Preto, Morro do Cruzeiro, Ouro Preto, Brazil. [3]Departamento de Física e Matemática, Centro Federal de Educação Tecnológica de Minas Gerais, Av. Amazonas, 7675 Belo Horizonte, Brazil.

References
1. R Datta, D Joshi, J Li, JZ Wang, Image retrieval: ideas, influences, and trends of the New Age. ACM Comput. Surv. **40**(2), 5–1560 (2008). doi:10.1145/1348246.1348248
2. MTF Tannús, Comparação de técnicas para a determinação de semelhança entre imagens digitais Master's thesis, Universidade Federal de Uberlândia (2008)
3. E Yildizer, AM Balci, TN Jarada, R Alhajj, Integrating wavelets with clustering and indexing for effective content-based image retrieval. Knowledge-Based Syst. **31**, 55–66 (2012)
4. G Chechik, V Sharma, U Shalit, S Bengio, Large scale online learning of image similarity through ranking. J. Mach. Learn. Res. **11**, 1109–1135 (2010)
5. JB dos Santos, CA Heuser, VP Moreira, LK Wives, Automatic threshold estimation for data matching applications. Inf. Sci. **181**(13), 2685–2699 (2011). doi:10.1016/j.ins.2010.05.029
6. E Schallehn, K-U Sattler, G Saake, Efficient similarity-based operations for data integration. Data & Knowledge Eng. **48**(3), 361–387 (2004)
7. M Ortega-Binderberger, Integrating similarity based retrieval and query refinement in databases. PhD thesis, University of Illinois at Urbana-Champaign (2002)
8. M Ortega-Binderberger, Integrating similarity based retrieval and query refinement in databases. Technical report, University of Illinois at Urbana-Champaign, Champaign, IL, USA (2002)
9. A Motro, VAGUE: A user interface to relational databases that permits vague queries. ACM Trans. Inf. Syst. (TOIS). **6**(3), 187–214 (1988)

10. RA Baeza-Yates, B Ribeiro-Neto, *Modern information retrieval.* (Addison-Wesley Longman Publishing Co., Inc, Boston, MA, USA, 1999)
11. MHR Pereira, CL de Souza, FLC Pádua, G Silva, GT de Assis, ACM Pereira, SAPTE: A multimedia information system to support the discourse analysis and information retrieval of television programs. Multimed Tools and Appl. **74**, 10923–10963 (2015)
12. CL de Souza, FLC Pádua, GT de Assis, GD Silva, CFG Nunes, A unified approach to content-based indexing and retrieval of digital videos from television archives. Artif. Intell. Res. **3**, 49–61 (2014)
13. P Rousseeuw, Silhouettes: A graphical aid to the interpretation and validation of cluster analysis. J. Comput. Appl. Math. **20**(1), 53–65 (1987)
14. RdS Torres, AX Falcão, Contour salience descriptors for effective image retrieval and analysis. Image and Vision Comput. **25**, 3–13 (2007)
15. A Vadivel, AK Majumdar, S Sural, in *Proceedings of International Conference on Intelligent Sensing and Information Processing, 2004*. Characteristics of weighted feature vector in content-based image retrieval applications, (2004), pp. 127–132. doi:10.1109/ICISIP.2004.1287638
16. T Gevers, AWM Smeulders, PicToSeek: combining color and shape invariant features for image retrieval. IEEE Trans. Image Process. **9**(1), 102–119 (2000)
17. AD Doulamis, ND Doulamis, Generalized nonlinear relevance feedback for interactive content-based retrieval and organization. Circuits and Syst. Video Technology, IEEE Trans. **14**(5), 656–671 (2004)
18. S Aksoy, RM Haralick, Feature normalization and likelihood-based similarity measures for image retrieval. Pattern Recogn. Lett. **22**(5), 563–582 (2001)
19. G-D Guo, AK Jain, W-Y Ma, H-J Zhang, Learning similarity measure for natural image retrieval with relevance feedback. Neural Networks, IEEE Trans. **13**(4), 811–820 (2002)
20. M Montebello, in *Proceedings of the 21st Annual International ACM SIGIR Conference on Research and Development in Information Retrieval.* Optimizing Recall/Precision Scores in IR over the WWW (ACM, New York, NY, USA, 1998), pp. 361–362. isbn: 1-58113-015-5
21. A Arampatzis, K Zagoris, SA Chatzichristofis, Dynamic two-stage image retrieval from large multimedia databases. Inf. Process. Manag. **49**(1), 274–285 (2013). doi:10.1016/j.ipm.2012.03.005
22. M Broilo, De Natale, FGB, A stochastic approach to image retrieval using relevance feedback and particle swarm optimization. Multimed. IEEE Trans. **12**(4), 267–277 (2010). doi:10.1109/TMM.2010.2046269
23. M Cord, PH Gosselin, S Philipp-Foliguet, Stochastic exploration and active learning for image retrieval. Image and Vision Comput. **25**(1), 14–23 (2007)
24. N Doulamis, A Doulamis, Evaluation of relevance feedback schemes in content-based in retrieval systems. Signal Process. Image Commun. **21**(4), 334–357 (2006)
25. S Tong, E Chang, in *Proceedings of the ninth ACM international conference on Multimedia*. Support vector machine active learning for image retrieval (ACM, New York, NY, USA, 2001), pp. 107–118
26. J-T Horng, C-C Yeh, Applying genetic algorithms to query optimization in document retrieval. Inf. Process. Manag. **36**, 737–759 (2000)
27. R da Silva, RK Stasiu, VM Orengo, CA Heuser, Measuring quality of similarity functions in approximate data matching. J. Informetrics. **1**(1), 35–46 (2007)
28. RK Stasiu, CA Heuser, R da Silva, in *Proceedings of the 17th International Conference on Advanced Information Systems Engineering*. Estimating Recall and Precision for Vague Queries in Databases (Springer-Verlag, Berlin, Heidelberg, 2005), pp. 187–200. isbn: 3-540-26095-1, 978-3-540-26095-0
29. RK Stasiu, CA Heuser, Quality evaluation of similarity functions for range queries. PhD thesis, Universidade Federal do Rio Grande do Sul (2007)
30. CD Manning, P Raghavan, H Schütze, et. al., *Introduction to information retrieval*, vol. 1. (Cambridge University Press, Cambridge, 2008), p. 496
31. Q Lv, W Josephson, Z Wang, M Charikar, K Li, Ferret: a toolkit for content-based similarity search of feature-rich data. ACM SIGOPS Oper. Syst. Rev. Proc. 2006 EuroSys Conf. **40**(4), 317–330 (2006)
32. H Jégou, M Douze, C Schmid, Improving bag-of-features for large scale image search. Int. J. Comput. Vision. **87**(3), 316–336 (2010)
33. CM Bishop, *Pattern recognition and machine learning*, 1st edn., vol. 1. (Springer, New York, 2006)

3

Unified LMI-based design of $\Delta\Sigma$ modulators

M. Rizwan Tariq* and Shuichi Ohno

Abstract

Optimal finite impulse response (FIR) error feedback filters for noise shaping in $\Delta\Sigma$ modulators are designed by using weighting functions based on the system norms. We minimize the weighted norms of the quantization error in the output of a $\Delta\Sigma$ modulator, which corresponds to the minimization of the system norm. Three norms, the H_2 system norm, the H_∞ system norm, and the l_1 norm of the impulse response of the system, are adopted. The optimization problem for three types of FIR filters are evaluated by using linear matrix inequalities (LMIs) and then solved numerically via semi-definite programming. Design examples are provided to demonstrate the effectiveness of our proposed methods.

Keywords: Delta-sigma modulation, Noise shaping, Quantization, Semi-definite programming

1 Introduction

Analog-to-digital (A/D) and digital-to-analog (D/A) data converters are some of the most important parts of the electronic systems which act as the interface between the digital signal world and the real analog world. In A/D converters, the continuous-valued signals are discretized and quantized for transmission in wireline or wireless systems [1]. The process of quantization maps the continuous-valued signal to the discrete-valued signal. This usually introduces an undesirable effect, which is known as quantization noise. The important aspect of these converters is their ability to determine whether and how much the conversion can correctly keep the important information of signals, while suppressing undesirable noises.

Currently, the delta-sigma ($\Delta\Sigma$) modulation is a popular technique for making high-resolution A/D and D/A converters [2, 3]. Modern $\Delta\Sigma$ converters offer several benefits including high resolution, low power consumption, and low cost, making them a reasonable choice for the A/D converter for many signal processing applications such as audio devices [4, 5]. These $\Delta\Sigma$ A/D converters are effective for converting analog signals over a wide range of frequencies, from DC to several megahertz.

*Correspondence: rizwan-tariq@hiroshima-u.ac.jp
Department of System Cybernetics, Hiroshima University, Saijo, Higashi-Hiroshima, Japan

The $\Delta\Sigma$ modulator mainly consists of a static uniform quantizer and an error feedback filter to shape quantization noise [6], which is called noise shaping filter. The input to the modulator is an oversampled signal which is to be digitized. In oversampling, the signal is sampled at a frequency much higher than the Nyquist frequency (two times the input bandwidth) which reduces the effect of the quantization noise in the frequency band carrying the information signal, while the total noise remains the same.

The high-rate digital output of the modulator has two components, one is the signal which is located in the low-frequency region and the other is the noise which has to be reduced.

In the design of a $\Delta\Sigma$ modulator, the objective is to minimize the in-band quantization noise which as a result improves the signal-to-quantization-noise ratio (SQNR) of a $\Delta\Sigma$ modulator. It has been observed that the technique of oversampling alone may not be enough to improve the SQNR in the band of interest, and we need to exploit the noise shaping properties of the $\Delta\Sigma$ modulator to further reduce the in-band quantization noise. This can be achieved by using a feedback filter which employs the noise shaping to obtain a high SQNR while keeping the oversampling ratio (OSR) not too high. Although the overall quantization noise may not be changed by the noise shaping, the SQNR is increased in the information signal frequency band of the frequency spectrum. Our objective is to design the finite impulse response (FIR) noise shaping filter of the $\Delta\Sigma$ modulator so that we can minimize the noise in the frequency region which constitutes our signal bandwidth.

Several designs for feedback filters have been proposed which also use the noise spectrum shaping technique [7, 8]. The FIR error spectrum shaping filters have been proposed for recursive digital filters composed of cascaded second order section in [9]. In [10], the noise transfer function (NTF) is assumed to have an infinite impulse response which is converted to a minimization problem by virtue of generalized Kalman-Yakubovich-Popov (GKYP) lemma. Then, an iterative algorithm is developed to solve this minimization problem subject to quadratic matrix inequalities. The method in [11] is a min-max design to optimize the NTF via GKYP lemma. This approach minimizes the worst case gain of the NTF over the signal frequency band and is shown to be able to improve the overall SNR of $\Delta\Sigma$ modulators as well. However, the method in [11] cannot incorporate the system connected to the quantizer into its design, while we consider a non-ideal output filter to minimize the quantization noise. In [12, 13], the optimization problem based on H_2 norm is formulated as a convex quadratic optimization problem where the weighting function (output filter) impulse response in truncated to finite number of samples.

In this paper, to keep $\Delta\Sigma$ modulators versatile, we utilize the weighting function to design $\Delta\Sigma$ modulators. We minimize the weighted quantization noise in the output of the $\Delta\Sigma$ modulator. Three norms are adopted to measure the quantity of the weighted quantization noise. One is the variance of the weighted quantization noise when the quantization errors at different time are assumed to be independent of each other. The others are the l_2 and the l_∞ norms of the weighted quantization noise. They correspond to the minimization of the H_2 system norm, the H_∞ system norm, and the l_1 norm of the impulse response of a system, respectively, and can be formulated as convex optimization problems with linear matrix inequalities (LMIs), which can be solved efficiently. The three norms considered in this paper are the most commonly used norms for quantifying signals. Our proposed method based on LMIs is termed unified for these three most commonly used norms only. If one imposes a constraint on the filter, then there are nine combinations for the design, three types of objectives, and three types of constraints, which can be handled by LMIs. One of these nine combinations, H_2 norm subjected to the Lee criterion, is similar to the design criteria of the method in [12, 13]. However, for our proposed H_2 norm design, we provide an alternate approach based on expressing the H_2 norm by using LMIs. The similarity lies in the fact that our proposed design and the method in [12, 13] use the idea of incorporating the non-ideal output filter for the minimization of the quantization noise.

The stability condition of $\Delta\Sigma$ modulators is also described by an LMI, which is incorporated into our design. Simulations with our designed noise shaping filters are performed, and comparisons with existing methods are made to demonstrate the effectiveness of our proposed design.

This paper is organized as follows: Section 2 gives the input/output relation of a linearized $\Delta\Sigma$ modulator with a weighting function. Then, we formulate our design problem which minimizes the weighted quantization noise under the stability condition. Section 3 is the main section of this paper, and we propose the design of the FIR feedback filter using LMIs for H_2, H_∞, and l_1 system norms. Section 4 gives design examples to show advantages of our method using simulation results. Section 5 provides us with the conclusion of our study.

Notation: Throughout this paper, $\mathbb{R}$ and $\mathbb{Z}$ denote a set of real numbers and a set of integer respectively. S denotes the set of all stable, proper, and rational transfer functions with real coefficients. The subscript $(\cdot)_+$ is used to indicate a subset restricted to non-negative numbers.

2 $\Delta\Sigma$ modulator and output weighting filter

Let us consider a general linearized model of a $\Delta\Sigma$ modulator for analyzing the noise shaping characteristics and designing the optimal noise shaping filter. We only consider the discretized single-input/single-output system with discrete-time signals. Let us denote the z transform of a sequence $f = \{f_k\}_{k=0}^{\infty}$ as $F[z] = \sum_{k=0}^{\infty} f_k z^{\ \ k}$ and express the output (sequence) b of the linear time invariant (LTI) system $F[z]$ to the input $a = \{a_k\}_{k=0}^{\infty}$ as $b = F[z]\, a$.

Figure 1 shows the error feedback configuration of a $\Delta\Sigma$ modulator. The input to the modulator is y, while the output is u. The filter $P[z]$ acts as a pre-filter to shape the frequency response of the input signal, and $Q(\cdot)$ is our static quantizer. The quantization error w is filtered by $R[z] \quad 1$ and is fed back to y. We assume that $\lim_{z \quad \infty} R[z] = 1$, i.e., the zeroth coefficient of the impulse response of $R[z]$ is 1, which implies $R[z] \quad 1$ is strictly proper. We also assume that

$$P[z]\,, R[z] \quad S. \tag{1}$$

The static uniform quantizer can be described by two parameters, the quantization interval $d \quad \mathbb{R}_+$ and the saturation level $L \quad \mathbb{Z}_+$. For the continuous-valued input ξ, let the output of the static uniform quantizer be

$$Q(\xi) = \begin{cases} id, \ \xi \quad \left(\left(i \quad \tfrac{1}{2}\right)d, \left(i+\tfrac{1}{2}\right)d\right) \text{ and } |\xi| \quad L \\ L, \qquad\qquad \xi > L \\ \ \ L, \qquad\qquad \xi < \ \ L \end{cases}, \tag{2}$$

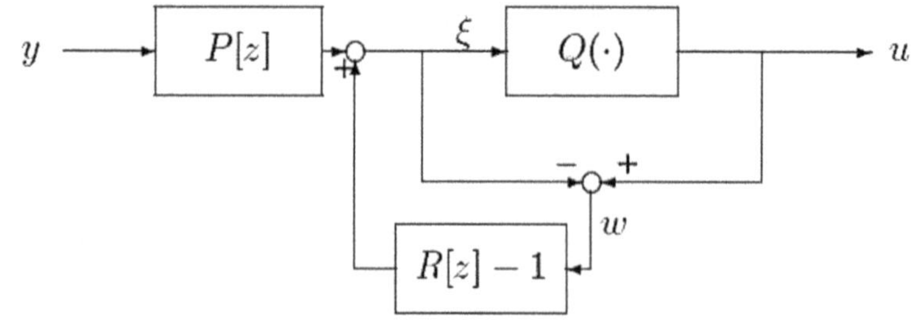

Fig. 1 Error feedback structure of linearized $\Delta\Sigma$ modulator

where d is the quantization interval and i is an integer. We assume that the saturation level is sufficiently large to avoid the saturation.

The difference between the input and the output of the static quantizer Q is known as a quantization error, which is denoted at time k as

$$w_k = u_k \quad \xi_k. \tag{3}$$

The quantization error is filtered by the noise shaping filter and added to the input to the static quantizer. Then, the input to the static quantizer is expressed as

$$\xi = P[\mathrm{z}]\, y + (R[\mathrm{z}] \quad 1)w. \tag{4}$$

Then, we have

$$u = w + \xi = P[\mathrm{z}]\, y + R[\mathrm{z}]\, w. \tag{5}$$

The gain from the input y to the output of the modulator u is known as as signal transfer function (STF), while the gain between the quantization error w and the modulator output u is commonly known as noise transfer function (NTF). In our setting, the STF and NTF for the $\Delta\Sigma$ modulator are $P[\mathrm{z}]$ and $R[\mathrm{z}]$, respectively.

The feedback loop acts in such a way that the quantization noise is shifted away from a certain frequency band. If the input to the modulator lies within this certain frequency band, then most of the noise due to quantization lies outside the frequency band of interest.

To design the noise shaping filter, we utilize a weighting function $H_W[\mathrm{z}]$. More specifically, we consider the weighted quantization noise ϵ defined as

$$\epsilon = H_W[\mathrm{z}]\, R[\mathrm{z}]\, w, \tag{6}$$

where $H_W[\mathrm{z}] \quad S$. Without loss of generality, we normalize the maximum magnitude of $H_W[\mathrm{z}]$ to be in unity. The weighting function is selected to reduce the effect of the quantization noise in the passband of the y. For example, when the passband of y is $[\quad \omega_p, \omega_p]$, we will use the weighting filter that meets $H_W\left[e^{j\omega}\right] \quad 1$ for $\omega \quad [\quad \omega_p, \omega_p]$ and $|H_W\left[e^{j\omega}\right]|$ is small enough outside the passband to let most of the noise be outside the passband.

Suppose that the output of our $\Delta\Sigma$ modulator u is connected to a system $H_S[\mathrm{z}]$ whose output is denoted by v. Then, we have

$$v = H_S[\mathrm{z}]\, u. \tag{7}$$

Substituting (5) into (7), we get

$$v = H_S[\mathrm{z}]\, P[\mathrm{z}]\, y + H_S[\mathrm{z}]\, R[\mathrm{z}]\, w. \tag{8}$$

In [12], the noise $H_S[\mathrm{z}]\, R[\mathrm{z}]\, w$ is minimized based on the H_2 system norm to reduce the in-band quantization noise. When $H_W[\mathrm{z}] = H_S[\mathrm{z}]$, our minimization based on the H_2 system norm is equivalent to the minimization of [12]. Then, the difference between the proposed method and [12] lies in the usage of different optimization procedures for solving the H_2 norm objective function. As pointed out in [12], if one knows the system $H_S[\mathrm{z}]$ connected to the $\Delta\Sigma$ modulator, one should set $H_W[\mathrm{z}] = H_S[\mathrm{z}]$. If not, we could design more general $\Delta\Sigma$ modulators using weighting functions. Thus, our objective is to obtain the optimal filter $R[\mathrm{z}]$ in (8) for a given $H_W[\mathrm{z}]$ that minimizes $\epsilon = H_W[\mathrm{z}]\, R[\mathrm{z}]\, w$ in a sense.

The signal w which is the difference between the input and the output of the static uniform quantizer satisfies

$$|w_k| \quad \frac{d}{2}. \tag{9}$$

Since the transfer function from w to ϵ is linear, we can put $d = 2$ without the loss of generality so that $|w_k| \quad 1$ and hence $|w_k|^2 \quad 1$.

Let us define the H_2 norm of a system $H[z] = \sum_{k=0}^{\infty} h_k z^{-k}$ as

$$||H[z]||_2 = \left[\sum_{k=0}^{\infty} |h_k|^2 \right]^{\frac{1}{2}}. \tag{10}$$

The quantization error may be modeled as a uniform random variable with zero mean and variance σ_w^2 [2]. If the errors at different times are independent of each other, then the variance of the weighted quantization noise ϵ_k is given by

$$\sigma_\epsilon^2 = ||H_W[z] R[z]||_2^2 \sigma_w^2. \tag{11}$$

As a deterministic sequence, the weighted quantization noise signal ϵ may be measured with its l_p norm defined as

$$||\epsilon||_p = \left[\sum_{k=0}^{\infty} |\epsilon_k|^p \right]^{\frac{1}{p}}. \tag{12}$$

Among l_p, the l_2 and the l_∞ norm are often utilized. The l_∞ norm of a discrete signal $\{\epsilon_k\}_{k=0}^{\infty}$ is defined as

$$||\epsilon||_\infty = \sup_k |\epsilon_k|. \tag{13}$$

The value of $||\epsilon||_\infty$ is the largest absolute value of the error signal and hence can be used to consider the worst case errors. On the other hand, the l_2 norm is defined as

$$||\epsilon||_2 = \left[\sum_{k=0}^{\infty} |\epsilon_k|^2 \right]^{\frac{1}{2}}. \tag{14}$$

The stability of $\Delta\Sigma$ modulators should also be considered. Here we consider the l_p bounded stability. Suppose that y is bounded such that $||y||_p < \gamma_y$ for a finite γ_y. Then, it is easy to see that if $||R[z]\, w||_p$ is bounded, then the input ξ to the static quantizer, which is the internal variable of the $\Delta\Sigma$ modulator, is bounded. Thus, to guarantee the l_p stability of the $\Delta\Sigma$ modulator, it is sufficient to assure

$$||R[z]\, w||_p < \gamma, \tag{15}$$

for a finite γ.

If one takes the $p = 2$ norm, then

$$\sup_w ||R[z]\, w||_2 \leq ||R[z]||_\infty ||w||_2, \tag{16}$$

where $||R[z]||_\infty$ is the H_∞ system norm defined as

$$||R[z]||_\infty = \max_\omega |R\left[e^{j\omega}\right]|. \tag{17}$$

The constraint on the H_∞ norm of the NTF is known as Lee criterion [6, 14]. The peak value of the NTF magnitude response must be bounded to some constant value γ, where the value of γ depends on the number of saturation levels. For the case of binary quantizers, the value of γ is usually set as 1.5.

In summary, we would like to minimize σ_ϵ^2, $||\epsilon||_2$, or $||\epsilon||_\infty$ under the stability condition (15), assuming that the variance of w_k, $||w||_2$ or $||w||_\infty$ is finite. It should be noted that without the weighting function, we only have the trivial solution such that $R[z] = 1$, that is, the error feedback is not necessary.

3 Design of FIR noise shaping filters using linear matrix inequalities

Since FIR filters are often preferred, we confine our attention to design of FIR filters of order n, denoting

$$R[z] = \sum_{k=0}^{n} r_k z^{-k}, \quad r_0 = 1. \tag{18}$$

The coefficient r_0 of the impulse response of the FIR filter $R[z]$ is unitary to ensure $R[z] \in S$, which makes the noise shaping filter strictly proper.

Let us denote the matrices of a state-space realization of $R[z]$ by $(A_R, B_R, C_R, 1)$, where

$$A_R = \begin{bmatrix} 0 & 1 & & 0 \\ \vdots & \ddots & \ddots & \\ \vdots & & \ddots & 1 \\ 0 & \cdots & \cdots & 0 \end{bmatrix}, \quad B_R = \begin{bmatrix} 0 \\ \vdots \\ 0 \\ 1 \end{bmatrix} \tag{19}$$

$$C_R(r) = \left[\, r_n, \; r_{n-1}, \; \cdots \; r_1 \,\right]. \tag{20}$$

It is noted that A_R and B_R are constant. Our design parameter is

$$r = [r_1, \ldots, r_n] \tag{21}$$

which defines $C_R(r)$ above.

The weighted quantization noise ϵ in (6) to be minimized is characterized by the the composite system $H_W[z]\, R[z]$, which has to be internally stable.

Let $H_W[z]$ be a proper function, whose (A, B, C, D) matrices of a state-space realization is (A_H, B_H, C_H, D_H). Let the order of $R[z]$ be n and let $(A_R, B_R, C_R, 1)$ be (A, B, C, D) matrices of a state-space realization of $R[z]$. Then, one can express the state-space realization of $H_W[z]\, R[z]$ as

$$x_{k+1} = A x_k + B w_k \tag{22}$$

$$\epsilon_k = C x_k + D w_k \tag{23}$$

where

$$A = \begin{bmatrix} A_R & B_R C_H \\ \mathbf{0} & A_H \end{bmatrix}, \quad B = \begin{bmatrix} B_R D_H \\ B_H \end{bmatrix},$$

$$C = \left[\, C_R \;\; C_H \,\right], \quad D = D_H. \tag{24}$$

First of all, let us consider the minimization of the variance σ_ϵ^2 of the weighted quantization error under the white noise assumption. It is sufficient to minimize the H_2 norm of $H_W[z]\, R[z]$ to minimize σ_ϵ^2 given by (11).

For FIR $R[z]$, $||H_W[z]\, R[z]||_2^2$ can be expressed as a quadratic function of $r = [r_1, \ldots, r_n]$ by using inverse Fourier transform of $|H_W\left[e^{j\omega}\right]|^2$ [8], which requires numerical integrations. On the other hand, a truncated impulse response of $H_W[z]\,R[z]$ is utilized in [12], where the order of some parameters is scaled by the length of the truncated impulse response. Here, we adopt LMIs to numerically evaluate the H_2 norm based on the next lemma.

Lemma 1. *([15]) Let $G[z]$ be a proper stable rational function, whose state-space realization is (A, B, C, D). Then, A is Schur and*

$$||G[z]\,||_2^2 < \mu_2 \tag{25}$$

if and only if there exist positive definite matrices P and Z which satisfy

$$APA^T \quad P + BB^T \quad 0 \tag{26}$$

$$Z \quad DD^T \quad CPC^T \quad 0 \tag{27}$$

$$\mathrm{trace}(Z) < \mu_2. \tag{28}$$

Using the Schur complement, one can show that (26) holds true if and only if

$$\begin{bmatrix} P & PA & PB \\ A^T P & P & 0 \\ B^T P & \mathbf{0} & 1 \end{bmatrix} \quad 0. \tag{29}$$

Similarly, since our system has a single input and a single output, Eq. (27) for (A, B, C, D) can be expressed as

$$\begin{bmatrix} \mu_2 & C & D \\ C^T & P & \mathbf{0} \\ D^T & \mathbf{0} & 1 \end{bmatrix} \quad 0. \tag{30}$$

On the other hand, the l_2 norm of the weighted quantization noise is bounded as

$$||\epsilon||_2 = ||H_W[z]\,R[z]\,w||_2 \quad ||H_W[z]\,R[z]\,||_\infty ||w||_2. \tag{31}$$

We can utilize the bounded real lemma that provides us an LMI to evaluate the gain.

Lemma 2. *([16]) Let $G[z]$ be a proper stable rational function, whose state-space realization is (A, B, C, D). Then, A is Schur and*

$$||G[z]\,||_\infty^2 < \mu_\infty \tag{32}$$

if and only if there exists a positive definite matrix P which satisfies

$$\begin{bmatrix} A^T PA \quad P + C^T C & A^T PB + C^T D \\ B^T PA + D^T C & B^T PB + D^T D \quad \mu_\infty I \end{bmatrix} \quad 0. \tag{33}$$

By using the Schur complement, (33) can be converted into an LMI given by

$$\begin{bmatrix} P & PA & PB & \mathbf{0} \\ A^T P & P & \mathbf{0} & C^T \\ B^T P & 0 & \mu_\infty & D^T \\ \mathbf{0} & C & D & 1 \end{bmatrix} \quad 0. \tag{34}$$

Let us define the l_∞ norm of the impulse response of a system $H[z] = \sum_{k=0}^{\infty} h_k z^{\ \ k}$ as

$$||H[z]\,||_{\mathrm{imp}} = \sum_{k=0}^{\infty} |h_k|. \tag{35}$$

We call $||H[z]\,||_{\mathrm{imp}}$ as H_{imp} norm for convenience. Then, the l_∞ norm $||\epsilon_k||_\infty$ is bounded as

$$||\epsilon||_\infty = ||H_W[z]\,R[z]\,w||_\infty \quad ||H_W[z]\,R[z]\,||_{\mathrm{imp}} ||w||_\infty$$

$$= ||H_W[z]\,R[z]\,||_{\mathrm{imp}}. \tag{36}$$

We can reduce $||\epsilon||_\infty$ by minimizing $||H_W[z]\,R[z]\,||_{\mathrm{imp}}$.

Unlike the H_2 norm and the H_∞ norm, only upper bounds of the H_{imp} norm are available. In [17, 18], an upper bound based on the invariant set of a discrete-time system has been utilized to design infinite impulse response (IIR) error feedback filters for dynamic quantizers. The invariant set of a discrete-time system is defined as follows [19]:

Definition 1. Let $x_k \quad \mathbb{R}^n$ be the state vector of the LTI system given by

$$x_{k+1} = Ax_k + Bw_k \tag{37}$$

where $A \quad \mathbb{R}^{n \times n}$, $B \quad \mathbb{R}^{n \times m}$ and $w_k \quad \mathbb{R}^m$. A set $\mathcal{X}$ that satisfies $x_{k+1} \quad \mathcal{X}$ if $x_k \quad \mathcal{X}$ and $w_k^T w_k \quad 1$ is called an invariant set of the system given by (37).

The following lemma describes how to obtain an ellipsoid which is an invariant set of the system (37).

Lemma 3. *([19]) Let $\mathcal{E}(P)$ be the ellipsoid defined by an $n \times n$ real symmetric matrix $P \quad 0$ as $\mathcal{E}(P) = \{x \quad \mathbb{R}^n : x^T Px \quad 1\}$.*

The ellipsoid $\mathcal{E}(P)$ is an invariant set of the system (37) if and only if there exists a scalar $\alpha \quad [0, 1 \quad \rho^2(A)]$ which satisfies

$$\begin{bmatrix} A^T PA \quad (1 \quad \alpha)P & A^T PB \\ B^T PA & B^T PB \quad \alpha I \end{bmatrix} \quad 0 \tag{38}$$

where $\rho(A)$ is the spectrum radius of A.

It should be noted that unlike H_2 and H_∞, H_{imp} depends on parameter α.

If $x_k \quad \mathcal{E}(P)$, then

$$\sup_{x_k \ \mathcal{E}(P)} |Cx_k|^2 = CP^{\ \ 1} C^T. \tag{39}$$

It follows from $|\epsilon_k| = |Cx_k + Dw_k| \quad |Cx_k| + |Dw_k|$ that

$$||H_W[z]\,R[z]\,||_{\mathrm{imp}} \quad |CP^{\ \ 1} C^T|^{\frac{1}{2}} + |D|. \tag{40}$$

Thus, we can conclude that $|CP^{\ \ 1} C^T|^{\frac{1}{2}} + |D|$ is an upper bound of the norm.

Since D is constant, we minimize $CP^{\ \ 1} C^T$ with respect to α and $C_R(r)$. It should be also remarked that we can

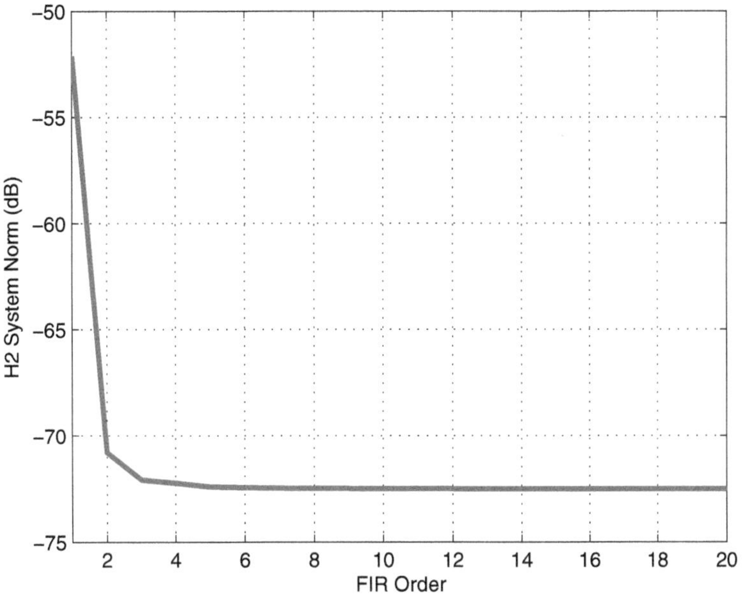

Fig. 2 The H_2 norm of $H_W[z]\,R[z]$ as a function of order of $R[z]$ for the first-order lowpass weighting function, where $R[z]$ is designed based on the H_2 norm

assume that $\alpha = 0$ since our B matrix is not zero. Similarly, we can express (38) with (A, B, C, D) as

$$\begin{bmatrix} (1 \quad \alpha)P & 0 & A^TP \\ \mathbf{0} & \alpha & B^TP \\ PA & PB & P \end{bmatrix} \quad 0. \tag{41}$$

Moreover, using the Schur complement, we can express $CP\ ^{1}C^T \quad \mu$ as an LMI given by

$$\begin{bmatrix} P & C^T \\ C & \mu \end{bmatrix} \quad 0. \tag{42}$$

For a fixed α, the minimization of μ is a semidefinite program, which can be numerically solved by existing optimization packages, e.g., CVX [20]. Then, all we have to do is to find α which gives the minimum. Since A is our

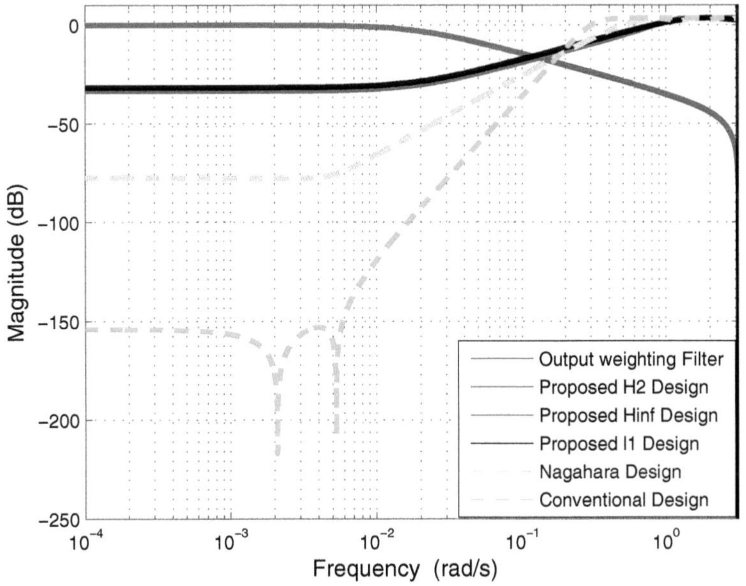

Fig. 3 Frequency responses of filters designed by the proposed method and the referenced methods. The weighting function is of order unity

design parameter, a line search for α (0, 1) is required to obtain the minimum. The optimal (A, B, C, D) is given by the arguments corresponding to the optimal α.

Not only the objective function but also the condition (15) on the stability can be described by LMIs. For example, as shown in [11], it follows from Lemma 2 that the Lee criterion

$$||R[z]||_{\infty} < \gamma \tag{43}$$

is satisfied if and only if there exists a positive definite matrix P_R which meets

$$\begin{bmatrix} P_R & P_R A_R & P_R B_R & \mathbf{0} \\ A_R^T P_R & P_R & \mathbf{0} & C_R^T \\ B_R^T P_R & 0 & \gamma^2 & 1 \\ \mathbf{0} & C_R & 1 & 1 \end{bmatrix} \quad 0. \tag{44}$$

Thus, if one would like to design the FIR noise shaping filter that minimizes σ_ϵ^2 under the Lee criterion, it suffices to solve the following convex optimization problem

$$\min_{r_1,\ldots,r_n} \mu_2 \tag{45}$$

subject to (29), (30), and (44).

The LMIs for other stability conditions $||R[z]||_2 < \gamma$ and $||R[z]||_{\text{imp}} < \gamma$ can be obtained similarly, which are omitted to avoid the duplication.

In summary, our unified approach enables the design of the FIR noise shaping filter to minimize the H_2, the H_∞, or the l_1 system norm under the H_2, the H_∞, or the l_1 norm constraint. Moreover, since norms are described by LMIs, different types of problems can be solved numerically. For example, some signal processing applications may require us to design an error feedback filter for a $\Delta\Sigma$ modulator by adding a constraint that limits the magnitude of the weighted quantization noise to a certain value. Then, our design objective is to design the noise shaping filter that attains the optimal value of the stability threshold γ under the maximum weighted quantization noise constraint. If we adopt the Lee criterion, we can obtain the most stable error feedback filter by minimizing (43) subject to $||\epsilon||_\infty$ c, where c is the maximum bound on the weighted quantization noise ϵ, by using LMIs in (41), (42), and (44).

4 Design examples

In this section, simulations for lowpass and bandpass $\Delta\Sigma$ modulators have been shown using the proposed design method based on H_2, H_∞, and l_1 system norms. For the design of a conventional $\Delta\Sigma$ modulator by NTF zero optimization method [6], the DELSIG toolbox [21] is utilized to obtain the frequency response of an IIR noise shaping filter with *synthesizeNTF* MATLAB function. The frequency response and the noise shaping characteristics of the FIR feedback filter proposed in [11] are also compared with our designed filters. As our proposed H_2 norm minimization is mathematically equivalent to the method proposed in [12], the numerical results which we have performed also show that there is no significant difference between our proposed H_2 norm method and [12]. To avoid redundancy in our simulations, we omit the comparison with [12].

All simulation results are obtained by using MATLAB programming, while semi-definite programming (SDP)

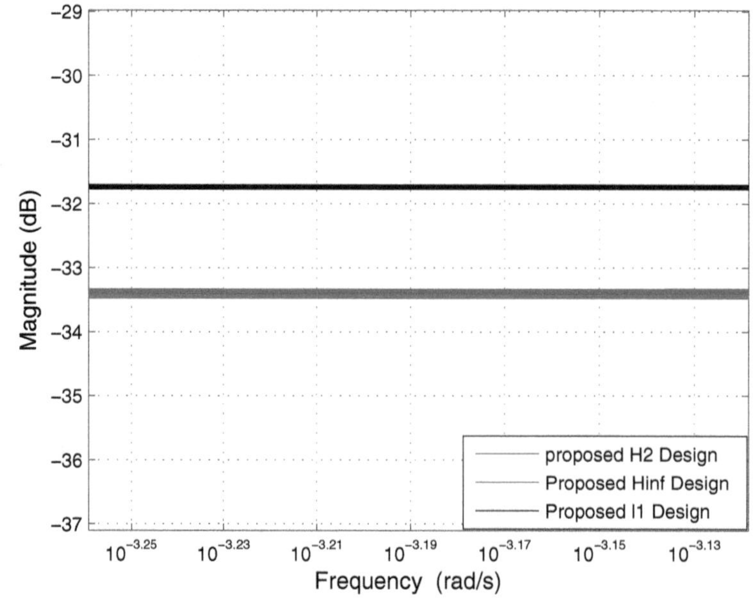

Fig. 4 Enlarged frequency response of our proposed filters in Fig. 3

problems are solved by using CVX tool [20], which is an effective solver for convex optimization problems.

4.1 Lowpass ΔΣ modulator with the first-order weighting function

Now, let us design a lowpass ΔΣ modulator by using a first-order lowpass Butterworth filter as our weighting function $H_W[z]$. The first-order Butterworth filter provides us the maximum flat response in the passband at the expense of a wide transition band as the filter changes from the passband to the stopband. The input signal y to the lowpass ΔΣ modulator is assumed to be oversampled with an oversampling ratio (OSR) of 512. Then, the cut-off frequency of the first-order Butterworth filter is set at $\pi/\text{OSR} \quad 0.0061$ in the normalized angular frequency interval $[0, \pi]$.

For the stability of the ΔΣ modulator, we assume the value of the Lee coefficient γ to be 1.5 which is equivalent to 3.52 in decibels ; however, the value of γ can be increased further as long as the ΔΣ modulator remains stable.

The order of the FIR feedback filter $R[z]$ is chosen based on the convergence behavior of the objective function. Figure 2 shows that the H_2 norm of $H_W[z]\,R[z]$ reaches a value as we keep on increasing the order of FIR filter.

Table 1 $||H_W[z]\,R[z]\,||_2$, $||H_W[z]\,R[z]\,||_\infty$, and l_1 norms of the impulse response of $H_W[z]\,R[z]$ for the first-order lowpass weighting function

	H_2 norm	H_∞ norm	l_1 norm
H_2 norm design	1.54×10^{2}	2.19×10^{2}	2.62×10^{2}
H_∞ norm design	1.54×10^{2}	2.16×10^{2}	2.59×10^{2}
l_1 norm design	1.63×10^{2}	2.59×10^{2}	2.59×10^{2}
Nagahara design [11]	1.92×10^{2}	3.82×10^{2}	4.89×10^{2}
Conventional design [6]	2.61×10^{2}	6.92×10^{2}	11×10^{2}

Above the FIR order 8, the norm of the weighted quantization noise remains almost constant in terms of the H_2 norm, resulting in a high convergence rate. In this example, the FIR feedback filter $R[z]$ for noise shaping is set to be 8.

Figure 3 depicts the frequency responses of H_2, H_∞, and l_1 norm-based filters compared with the referenced methods in [6] and [11]. The order of FIR feedback filter in [11] is also chosen to be 8, while the order of IIR feedback filter for the conventional design [6] is set to be 4. Our designed FIR filters have almost the same frequency response. It can be observed that the frequency responses of our designed FIR filters have

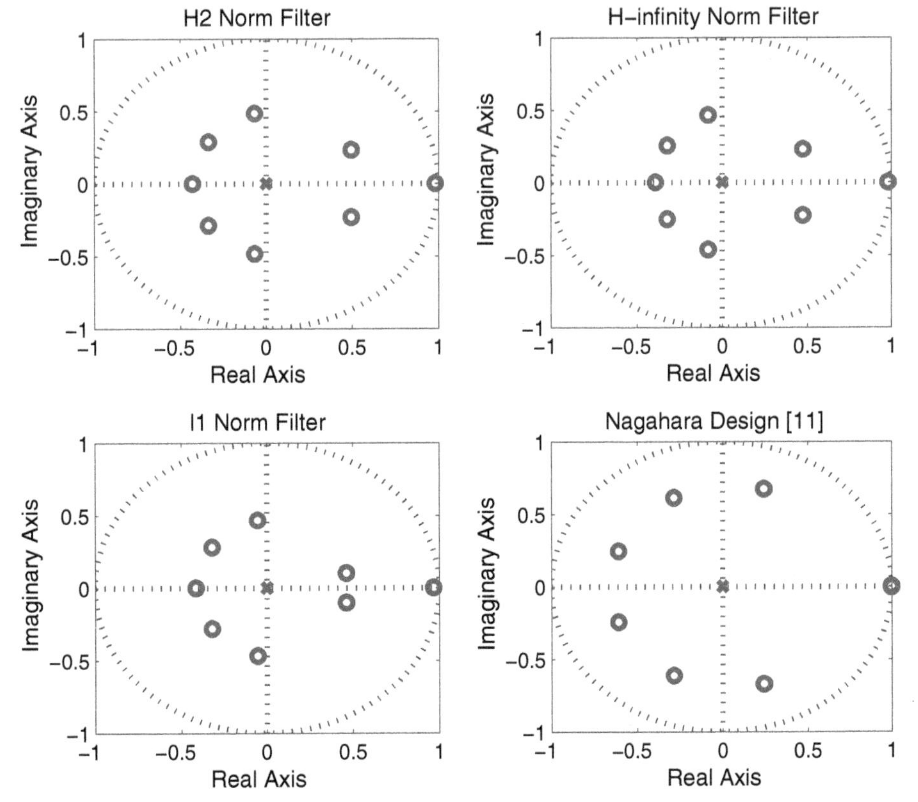

Fig. 5 Pole-zero placements of proposed designs and Nagahara design [11]

uniform attenuation in the low-frequency region of the frequency spectrum, while the conventional design shows a peak in the magnitude response near the cut-off frequency.

To precisely see the difference between the magnitude responses of our designed filters in low-frequency region, the enlarged view of Fig. 3 is shown in Fig. 4.

The method in [11] designs the FIR noise shaping filter based on the weighted H_∞ norm of $R[z]$. Near the cut-off frequency, the magnitude response of the FIR filter in [11] increases rapidly showing the high steepness in the transition band, while all of our proposed filters exhibit good performance, matching the steepness of the weighting function. Note that the maximum magnitude value of all filters are bounded to 3.52 dB approximately due to stability constraint which utilizes the Lee coefficient $\gamma = 1.5$.

Table 1 lists the H_2 norm $||H_W[z]\,R[z]\,||_2$, the H_∞ norm $||H_W[z]\,R[z]\,||_\infty$, and the l_1 norm of the impulse response of $H_W[z]\,R[z]$ for our designed FIR filters compared with the referenced designs in [6] and [11]. All three designed filters have less H_2, H_∞, and l_1 norms as compared with optimal feedback filters in [6] and [11]. Although the referenced designs have lower gains in the passband as observed in Fig. 3, our designed filters have better performance in the weighted norms. This is because the referenced designs only take into account the passband, while our design does the whole band by incorporating a lowpass output filter which is assumed to be non-ideal in practice. Indeed, if an ideal lowpass filter can be used as our weighting function, our H_∞ norm-based filter is equivalent to the weighted H_∞ norm-based filter in [11]. Since any ideal lowpass filter is not available in practice, it is important to consider the noise in the stopband. Our method can trade off the properties of the noise shaping filter in the passband and the stopband using an appropriate weighting function.

The H_∞ and l_1 norm designs exhibit an equivalent l_1 norm, while the H_2 and H_∞ norm designs have an equivalent H_2 norm. This may be partially due to the implementation and the numerical errors in our numerical optimization. It should be noted that we minimize the upper bounds, which implies that we cannot guarantee that the quantizer designed based on a norm is optimal in the sense of the norm.

Figure 5 shows the pole-zero placement for the lowpass $\Delta\Sigma$ modulator with proposed error feedback filters compared with the FIR filter in [11].

4.2 Lowpass $\Delta\Sigma$ modulator with the fourth-order weighting function

Now let us introduce a higher order lowpass Butterworth filter of order 4 as our weighting function, where the OSR is 32. The maximum magnitude of NTF is limited to 3.52 dB by using the Lee coefficient $\gamma = 1.5$. The fourth-order Butterworth filter with a cut-off frequency of π/OSR 0.0098 has a better stopband attenuation than the first-order Butterworth filter by increasing the steepness of the passband to the stopband transition at the cost of reduced passband flatness.

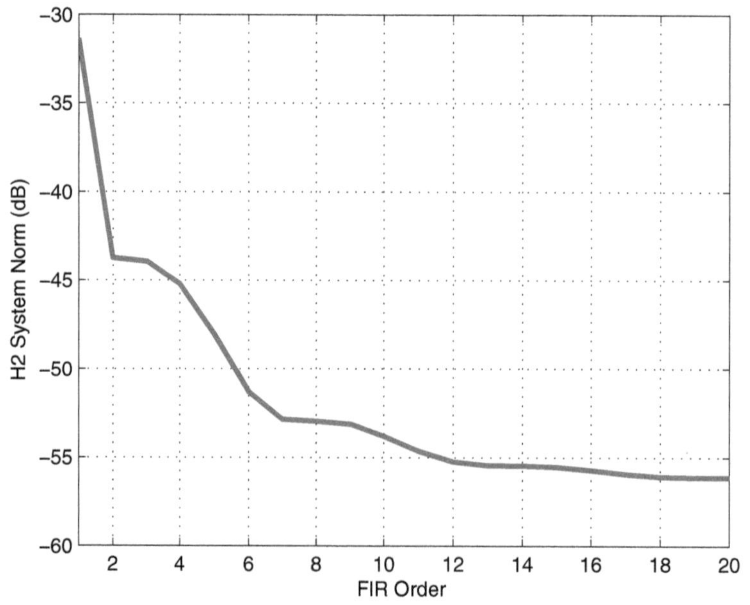

Fig. 6 The H_2 norm of $H_W[z]\,R[z]$ as a function of order of $R[z]$ for the fourth-order lowpass weighting function, where $R[z]$ is designed based on the H_2 norm

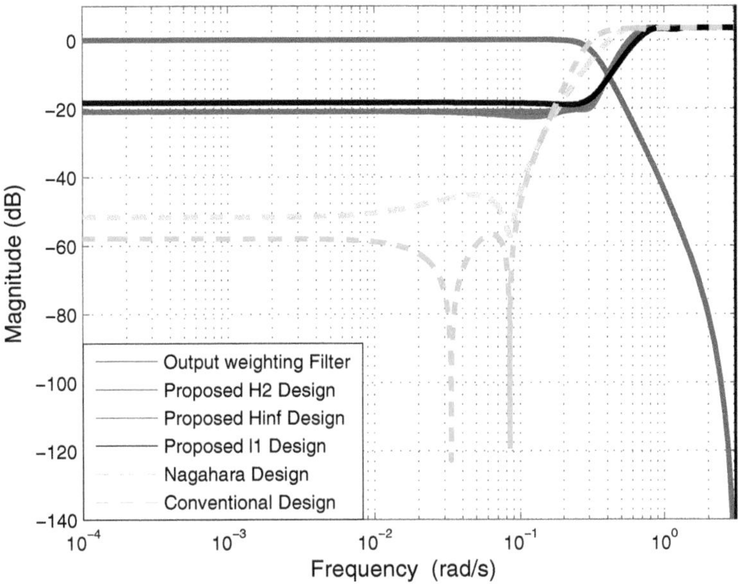

Fig. 7 Frequency responses of the filters designed by the proposed method and the referenced methods. The weighting function is of order 4

For this lowpass $\Delta\Sigma$ modulator, Fig. 6 shows the convergence behavior of the H_2 norm of $H_W[z]R[z]$ for the H_2 norm-based design. From this, the FIR feedback filter of order 20 is chosen for th epro-posed designs and referenced design in [11], while the IIR feedback filter for conventional design [6] is of order 4.

In Fig. 7, we give the frequency responses of proposed H_2, H_∞, and l_1 norm-based filters compared with the referenced methods. Our proposed designs show better performance by providing uniform attenuation in the low-frequency region and exhibiting better magnitude responses near the cut-off frequency as compared to the referenced methods in [11] and [6], for the three designed noise shaping filters.

Table 2 shows the H_2 norm, the H_∞ norm, and the l_1 norm of the impulse response of $H_W[z]R[z]$ for our designed FIR filters compared with the referenced designs in [6] and [11]. It can be observed that all three designed filters have less H_2, H_∞ and, l_1 norms than the optimal feedback filters in [6] and [11]. The H_2, H_∞, and l_1 norm designs have the least H_2, H_∞, and l_1 norms, respectively.

Table 2 $||H_W[z]\,R[z]\,||_2$, $||H_W[z]\,R[z]\,||_\infty$, and l_1 norms of the impulse response of $H_W[z]\,R[z]$ for the fourth-order lowpass weighting function

	H_2 norm	H_∞ norm	l_1 norm
H_2 norm design	3.95×10^{2}	9.71×10^{2}	1.40×10^{1}
H_∞ norm design	4.07×10^{2}	9.09×10^{2}	1.24×10^{1}
l_1 norm design	4.43×10^{2}	1.22×10^{1}	1.23×10^{1}
Nagahara design [11]	9.18×10^{2}	3.53×10^{1}	4.74×10^{1}
Conventional design [6]	1.49×10^{1}	6.69×10^{1}	9.01×10^{1}

To assess the performance of the lowpass $\Delta\Sigma$ modulator with an error feedback filter obtained by our proposed H_2 norm-based design, the MATLAB function *simulateDSM* in DELSIG toolbox [21] is used to simulate the $\Delta\Sigma$ modulator for obtaining the digital output. The input to the $\Delta\Sigma$ modulator is a sinusoidal wave with a frequency of 100 Hz and and amplitude of 0.5. We assume a uniform quantizer with saturation levels $L = 2$ and quantization interval $d = 2$.

The output of this uniform quantizer is a digital signal which is represented by using $+1$ and 1 volts for binary 0 and 1, respectively, which is shown in the upper part of Fig. 8. The lower part of Fig. 8 is the frequency spectrum of the digital output, which gives the performance of our lowpass $\Delta\Sigma$ modulator. Our lowpass $\Delta\Sigma$ modulator attenuates the quantization noise in the frequency region which contains the information signal. The frequency notch for the input signal appears at 100 Hz, which is the same with the sinusoidal wave, and the magnitude of quantization noise is low in the passband. Our proposed H_2 filter efficiently shifts the quantization noise towards the high-frequency region which does not carry much information. Similar results can be found for H_∞ and l_1 norm-based designs, which are omitted.

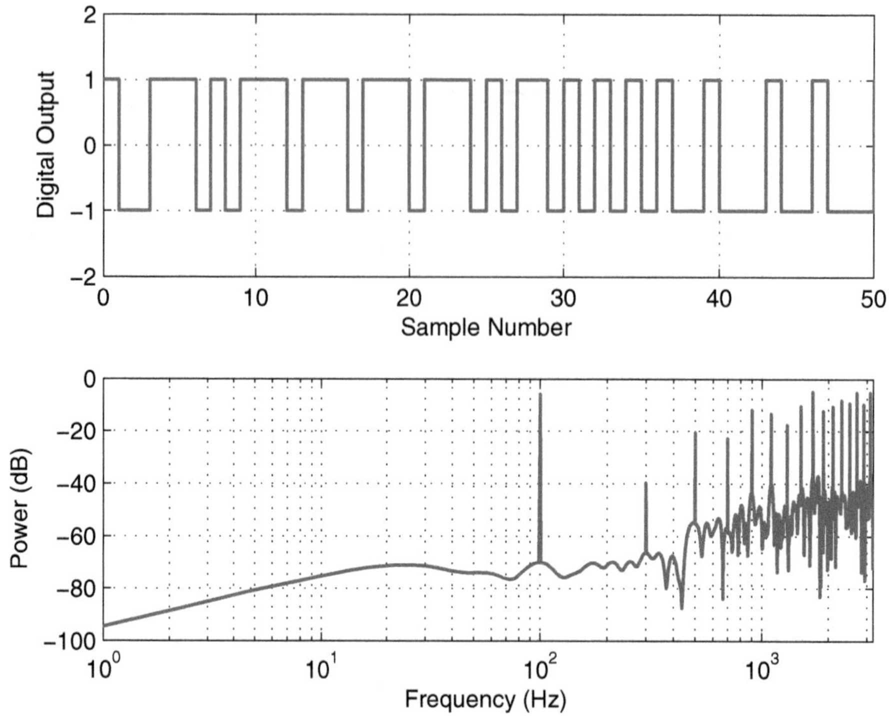

Fig. 8 Output and frequency spectrum plot of the lowpass $\Delta\Sigma$ modulator obtained by the proposed H_2 norm-based design

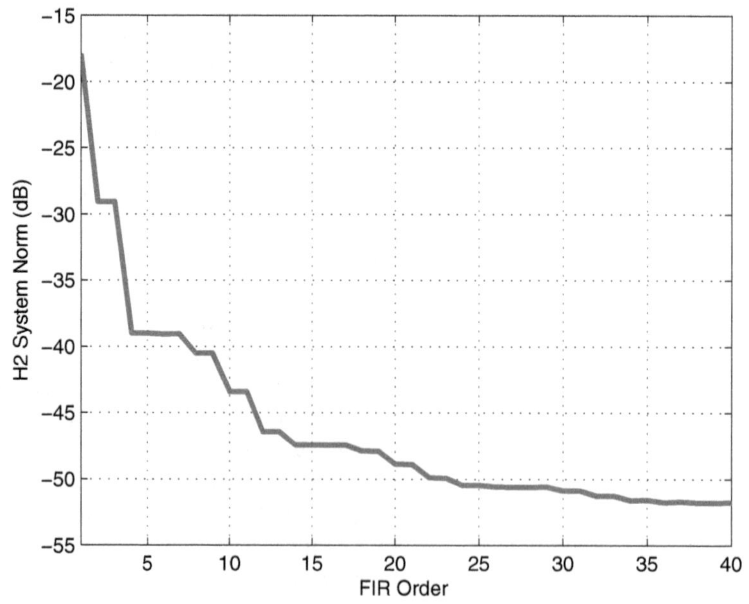

Fig. 9 The H_2 norm of $H_W[z]\,R[z]$ as a function of order of $R[z]$ for the sixth-order bandpass weighting function, where $R[z]$ is designed based on the H_2 norm

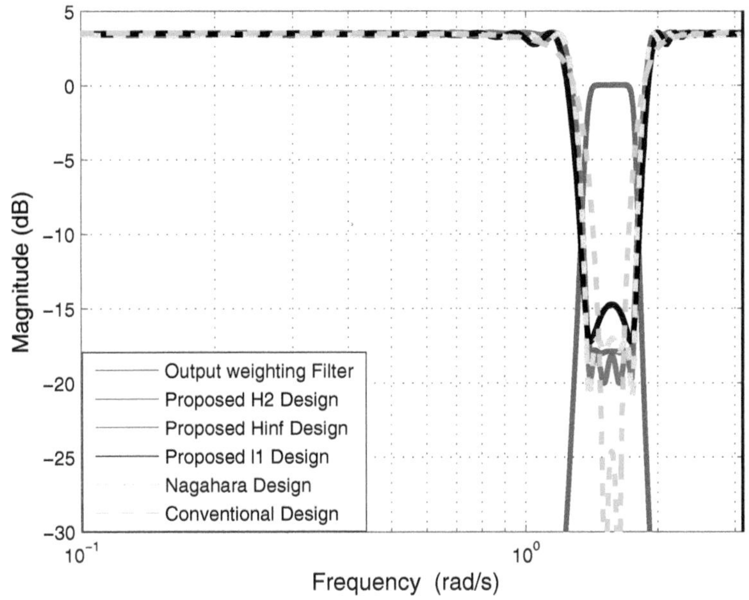

Fig. 10 Frequency responses of filters designed by the proposed method and the conventional method. The weighting function is of order 6

4.3 Bandpass ΔΣ modulator with the sixth order weighting function

Finally, we adopt a sixth-order bandpass Butterworth filter as our weighting function, whose frequency response is found in Fig. 10.

The input to the modulator is assumed to have the center frequency $\omega \;= \pi/2$ and bandwidth parameter $\Omega = \pi/16$. For the passband $\omega \quad [\pi/2 \quad \pi/16, \pi/2+\pi/16]$, we use the bandpass Butterworth filter that meets $H_W[e^{j\omega}]$ 1 for $\omega \quad [\omega \quad \Omega, \omega + \Omega]$, and $|H_W[e^{j\omega}]|$ is small enough outside the passband to let most of the noise be outside the passband. For the conventional design [6], OSR is set to be 16.

As illustrated in Fig. 9 the H_2 norm of $H_W[z]\,R[z]$ for H_2 norm-based design converges slowly compared to the previous examples. A longer order is required to adjust to the sixth-order bandpass Butterworth filter. Thus, the order of proposed FIR feedback filters $R[z]$ is chosen to be 40. The order of FIR feedback filter in [11] is also set to be 40. For the conventional bandpass ΔΣ modulator [6],

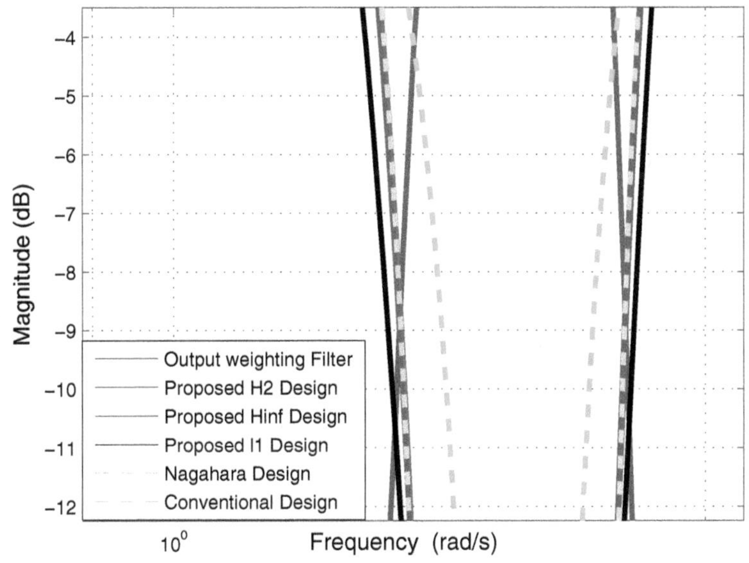

Fig. 11 Enlarged frequency response of our proposed filters in Fig. 10

Table 3 $||H_W[z]\,R[z]\,||_2$, $||H_W[z]\,R[z]\,||_\infty$, and l_1 norms of the impulse response of $H_W[z]\,R[z]$ for the sixth-order bandpass weighting function

	H_2 norm	H_∞ norm	l_1 norm
H_2 norm design	$5.08 \times 10^{\ 2}$	$1.385 \times 10^{\ 1}$	$2.094 \times 10^{\ 1}$
H_∞ norm design	$5.38 \times 10^{\ 2}$	$1.277 \times 10^{\ 1}$	$1.916 \times 10^{\ 1}$
l_1 norm design	$6.08 \times 10^{\ 2}$	$1.833 \times 10^{\ 1}$	$1.858 \times 10^{\ 1}$
Nagahara design [11]	$5.45 \times 10^{\ 2}$	$1.408 \times 10^{\ 1}$	$2.222 \times 10^{\ 1}$
Conventional design [6]	$10.19 \times 10^{\ 2}$	$4.253 \times 10^{\ 1}$	$5.461 \times 10^{\ 1}$

the order of the IIR feedback filter is 4, whereas the center frequency is $f\ = 1/4$.

We compare the frequency responses of our proposed FIR feedback filters for the bandpass $\Delta\Sigma$ modulator with the referenced designs in [6] and [11]. Figure 10 shows that the magnitude responses of proposed H_2 and H_∞ design FIR filters have higher attenuation levels as compared to the method proposed in [11]. Again, the magnitude responses of our proposed design filters are uniformly attenuated over the passband, while the conventional design shows a peak near the edges of the band which can be observed in Fig. 11.

Table 3 gives the H_2 norm, the H_∞ norm, and the l_1 norm of the impulse response of $H_W[z]\,R[z]$ for our designed FIR filters compared with the referenced designs in [6] and [11]. Again, our proposed H_2, H_∞, and l_1 norm designs have the least H_2, H_∞, and l_1 norms, respectively.

4.4 Stability under the l_∞ norm constraint on the weighted quantization noise

Here, to obtain the most stable error feedback filter for a lowpass $\Delta\Sigma$ modulator, we minimize (43) under the l_∞ norm constraint on the weighted quantization noise such that $||\epsilon||_\infty\ = 1.96 \times 10^{\ 2}$. We use the same first-order Butterworth filter in Section 4.1.

The minimum magnitude value of the in-band quantization noise is 34.2 dB. The obtained upper bound of the Lee criterion is $\gamma\ = 1.92$, which is equivalent to 5.7dB. It is larger than 1.5 used in the l_1 norm design in Table 1, since we impose a slight tighter constraint on the $||\epsilon||_\infty =$ $1.96 \times 10^{\ 2}$ than $2.59 \times 10^{\ 2}$ in Table 1. The frequency response of the designed feedback filter is illustrated in Fig. 12.

5 Conclusions

We have proposed a design method of the FIR noise shaping filters of $\Delta\Sigma$ modulators based on H_2, H_∞, and l_1 norms. The minimization of the norm of the weighted quantization error is cast into a convex optimization problem by using LMIs, which can be efficiently and numerically solved. To ensure the stability of a $\Delta\Sigma$ modulator, we have also included LMI constraints which subsumes the Lee criterion. Our results show that the frequency response of our filters exhibits good performance throughout the low-frequency region providing uniform attenuation and matching the weighting function. Also, our proposed H_2, H_∞, and l_1 norm designed error feedback filters are shown to provide us with minimum H_2,

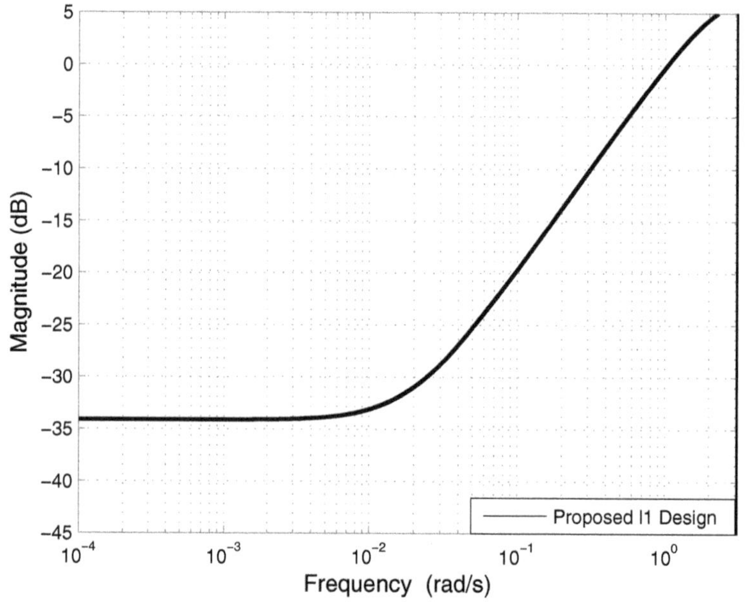

Fig. 12 Frequency response of the error feedback filter designed by minimizing the upper bound of the Lee coefficient under the constraint on the l_∞ norm of the weighted quantization noise

H_∞, and l_1 norms of the weighted quantization error, respectively, which shows the effectiveness of our proposed design method.

Competing interests

The authors declare that they have no competing interests.

References

1. J Proakis, *Digital Communications*, 4th. (McGraw-Hill, New York, 2001)
2. JC Candy, GC Temes, *Oversampling Delta-Sigma Data Converters*. (IEEE Press, New York, 1991)
3. KCH Chao, S Nadeem, WL Lee, CG Sodini, A higher order topology for interpolative modulator for oversampling A/D conversion. IEEE Trans. Circuits Syst. **37**, 309–318 (1990)
4. E Janssen, D Reefman, Super-audio CD: an introduction. IEEE Signal Process. Mag. **20**(4), 83–90 (2003)
5. U Zoler, *Digital Audio Signal Processing*, 2nd. (Wiley, New York, 2008)
6. R Schreier, GC Temes, *Understanding Delta-Sigma Data Converters*, 1st. (Wiley-IEEE Press, US, 2004)
7. Tran-Thong, B Liu, Error spectrum shaping in narrow-band recursive filters. IEEE Trans. Acoustics, Speech Signal Process. **25**(2), 200–203 (1977)
8. T Laakso, I Hartimo, Noise reduction in recursive digital filters using high-order error feedback. IEEE Trans. Signal Process. **40**(5), 1096–1107 (1992)
9. W Higgins, DC J Munson, Noise reduction strategies for digital filters: error spectrum shaping versus the optimal linear state-space formulation. IEEE Trans. Acoustics Speech Signal Process. **30**(6), 963–973 (1982)
10. X Li, C Yu, H Gao, Design of delta-sigma modulators via generalized Kalman-Yakubovich-Popov lemma. Automatica. **50**, 2700–2708 (2014)
11. M Nagahara, Y Yamamoto, Frequency domain min-max optimization of noise-shaping delta-sigma modulators. IEEE Trans. Signal Process. **60**(6), 2828–2839 (2012)
12. S Callegari, F Bizzarri, Output filter aware optimization of the noise shaping properties of delta-sigma modulators via semi-definite programming. IEEE Trans. Circuits Syst. I. **60**(9), 2352–2365 (2013)
13. S Callegari, F Bizzarri, Noise weighting in the design of delta-sigma modulators (with a psychoacoustic coder as an example). IEEE Trans. Circuits Syst. II: Express Briefs. **60**(11), 756–760 (2013)
14. KCH Chao, WLL S. Nadeem, CG Sodini, A higher order topology for interpolative modulators for oversampling a/d converters. IEEE Trans. Circuits Syst. **37**(3), 309–318 (1997)
15. S Boyd, LE Ghaoul, E Feron, *Linear Matrix Inequalities in System and Control Theory*. (Society for Industrial and Applied Mathematics, USA, 1997)
16. P Gahinet, P Apkarian, A linear matrix inequality approach to h_∞ control. Int. J. Robust Nonlinear Control. **4**, 421–448 (1994)
17. K Sawada, S Shin, Synthesis of dynamic quantizers for quantized feedback systems within invariant set analysis framework. Am. Control Conf. (ACC), 1662–1667 (2011)
18. S Ohno, Y Wakasa, M Nagata, Optimal error feedback filters for uniform quantizers at remote sensors. IEEE Int. Conf. Acoustics, Speech Signal Process, 3866–3870 (2015)
19. H Shingin, Y Ohta, in *10th IFAC/IFORS/IMACS/IFIP Symposium on Large Scale systems: Theory and Applications (LSS)*. Optimal invariant sets for discrete-time systems: approximation of reachable sets for bounded inputs, (2004), pp. 401–406
20. M Grant, S Boyd, Cvx: Matlab software for disciplined convex programming, version 2.0 beta (2012). http://cvxr.com/cvx/. Accessed date Feb 2015
21. R Schreier, Delta sigma toolbox [online]. http://jp.mathworks.com/matlabcentral/fileexchange/19-delta-sigma-toolbox. Accessed date Feb 2015

4

Distributed Gram-Schmidt orthogonalization with simultaneous elements refinement

Ondrej Slučiak[1], Hana Straková[2], Markus Rupp[1*] and Wilfried Gansterer[2]

Abstract

We present a novel distributed QR factorization algorithm for orthogonalizing a set of vectors in a decentralized wireless sensor network. The algorithm is based on the classical Gram-Schmidt orthogonalization with all projections and inner products reformulated in a recursive manner. In contrast to existing distributed orthogonalization algorithms, all elements of the resulting matrices **Q** and **R** are computed simultaneously and refined iteratively after each transmission. Thus, the algorithm allows a trade-off between run time and accuracy. Moreover, the number of transmitted messages is considerably smaller in comparison to state-of-the-art algorithms. We thoroughly study its numerical properties and performance from various aspects. We also investigate the algorithm's robustness to link failures and provide a comparison with existing distributed QR factorization algorithms in terms of communication cost and memory requirements.

Keywords: Distributed processing, Gram-Schmidt orthogonalization, QR factorization

1 Introduction

Orthogonalizing a set of vectors is a well-known problem in linear algebra. Representing the set of vectors by a matrix $\mathbf{A} \in \mathbb{R}^{n\times m}$, with $n \geq m$, several orthogonalization methods are possible. One example is the so-called *reduced QR factorization* (matrix decomposition), $\mathbf{A} = \mathbf{QR}$, with a matrix $\mathbf{Q} \in \mathbb{R}^{n\times m}$ having orthonormal columns, and an upper triangular matrix $\mathbf{R} \in \mathbb{R}^{m\times m}$ containing the coefficients of the basis transformation [1]. In the signal processing area, QR factorization is used widely in many applications, e. g., when solving linear least squares problems or decorrelation [2–4]. In adaptive filtering, a decorrelation method is typically used as a pre-step for increasing the learning rate of the adaptive algorithm [5], ([6], p. 351), ([7], p. 700).

From an algorithmic point of view, there are many methods for computing QR factorization with different numerical properties. A standard approach is the *Gram-Schmidt orthogonalization algorithm*, which computes a set of orthonormal vectors spanning the same space as the given set of vectors. Other methods include Householder reflections or Givens rotations, which are not considered in this paper.

Optimization of QR factorization algorithms for a specific target hardware has been addressed in the literature several times (e.g., [8, 9]). Parallel algorithms for computing QR factorization, which are applicable for reliable systems with fixed, regular, and globally known topology, have been investigated extensively (e.g., [10–13]).

Besides parallel algorithms, there are two other potential approaches for computation across a distributed network. In the standard—centralized—approach, the data are collected from all nodes and the computation is performed at a fusion center. Another approach is to consider distributed algorithms for fully *decentralized* networks without any fusion center where all nodes have the same functionality and each of them communicates only with its neighbors. Such an approach is typical for sensor-actuator networks or autonomous swarms of robotic networks [14]. Nevertheless, the investigation of *distributed* QR factorization algorithms designed for loosely coupled distributed systems with independently operating distributed memory nodes and with possibly unreliable communication links has only started recently [3, 15, 16].

*Correspondence: mrupp@nt.tuwien.ac.at
[1] TU Wien, Institute of Telecommunications, Gusshausstrasse 25/E389, 1040 Vienna, Austria
Full list of author information is available at the end of the article

In the following, we focus on algorithms for such decentralized networks.

1.1 Motivation

The main goal of this paper is to present a novel distributed QR factorization algorithm—DS-CGS—which is based on the classical Gram-Schmidt orthogonalization. The algorithm does not require any fusion center and assumes only local communication between neighboring nodes without any global knowledge about the topology. In contrast to existing distributed approaches, the DS-CGS algorithm computes the approximations of all elements of the new orthonormal basis *simultaneously* and as the algorithm proceeds, the values at *all* nodes are refined iteratively, approximating the exact values of **Q** and **R**. Therefore, it can deliver an estimate of the full matrix result *at any moment* of the computation. As we will show, this approach is, among others, superior to existing methods in terms of the number of transmitted messages in the network.

In Section 2, we briefly recall the concept of a consensus algorithm which we use later in the distributed orthogonalization algorithm. In Section 3, we review the basics of the QR decomposition and existing distributed methods. In Section 4, we describe the proposed distributed Gram-Schmidt orthogonalization algorithm with simultaneous refinements of all elements (DS-CGS). We experimentally compare DS-CGS with other distributed approaches in Section 5 where we also investigate the properties of DS-CGS from many different viewpoints. Section 6 concludes the paper.

1.2 Notation and terminology

In what follows, we use k as the node index, $\mathcal{N}_k$ denotes the set of neighbors of node k, N denotes the (known) number of nodes in the network, $\mathcal{E}$ the set of edges (links) of the network, d_k the kth node degree ($d_k = |\mathcal{N}_k|$), $\bar{d}$ the average node degree of the network, and t a discrete time (iteration) index.

We will describe the behavior of the distributed algorithm from a network (global) point of view with the corresponding vector/matrix notation. For example, the (column) vector of all ones denoted by **1**, corresponds to all nodes having value 1. In general, we denote the number of rows of a matrix by n and the number of columns by m. Element-wise division of two vectors is denoted as $\mathbf{z} = \frac{\mathbf{x}}{\mathbf{y}} \equiv \frac{x_i}{y_i}, \forall i$, element-wise multiplication of two vectors as $\mathbf{z} = \mathbf{x} \circ \mathbf{y} \equiv x_i y_i, \forall i$ and of two matrices as $\mathbf{Z} = \mathbf{X} \circ \mathbf{Y}$. The operation $\mathbf{X} \circledast \mathbf{Y}$ is defined as follows: Having two matrices $\mathbf{X} = (\mathbf{x}_1, \mathbf{x}_2, \ldots, \mathbf{x}_m)$ and $\mathbf{Y} = (\mathbf{y}_1, \mathbf{y}_2, \ldots, \mathbf{y}_m)$, the resulting matrix $\mathbf{Z} = \mathbf{X} \circledast \mathbf{Y}$ is a stacked matrix of all matrices $\mathbf{Z}_i$ such that $\mathbf{Z}_i = (\mathbf{x}_1, \mathbf{x}_2, \ldots, \mathbf{x}_i) \circ ((\underbrace{1, 1, \ldots, 1}_{i}) \otimes \mathbf{y}_{i+1})$ ($\otimes$ denotes the Kronecker product; $i = 1, 2, \ldots, m-1$), i.e., $\mathbf{Z} = (\underbrace{\mathbf{x}_1 \circ \mathbf{y}_2}_{\mathbf{Z}_1}, \underbrace{\mathbf{x}_1 \circ \mathbf{y}_3, \mathbf{x}_2 \circ \mathbf{y}_3}_{\mathbf{Z}_2}, \ldots, \underbrace{\mathbf{x}_{m-2} \circ \mathbf{y}_m, \mathbf{x}_{m-1} \circ \mathbf{y}_m}_{\mathbf{Z}_{m-1}})$, thus creating a big matrix containing combinations of column vectors: $\mathbf{Z} \in \mathbb{R}^{n \times \frac{m^2-m}{2}}$. This later corresponds in our algorithm to the off-diagonal elements of the matrix **R**. Also note that all variables with the "hat" symbol, e.g., $\hat{\mathbf{u}}(t)$ represent variables that are computed locally at nodes, while variables with the "tilde" symbol, e.g., $\tilde{\mathbf{u}}(t)$, are updated based on the information from neighbors.

2 Average consensus algorithm

We model a wireless sensor network (WSN) by synchronously working nodes which broadcast their data into their neighborhood within a radius ρ (so-called geometric topology). The WSN is considered to be static, connected, and with error-free transmissions (except for Section 5.4 ahead). Although the practicality of synchronicity can be argued [17, 18], we note that it is not an unrealizable assumption [19].

In the following, we briefly review the classical consensus algorithm for computing the *average* of values distributed in a network. Note that the algorithm can be easily adapted to computing a *sum* by multiplying the final average value (arithmetic mean) by the total number of nodes N.

The distributed average consensus algorithm computes an estimate of the global *average* of distributed initial data $\mathbf{x}(0)$ at each node k of a WSN. In every iteration t, each node updates its estimate using the weighted data received from its neighbors, i.e.,

$$x_k(t) = [\mathbf{W}]_{kk}\, x_k(t-1) + \sum_{k' \in \mathcal{N}_k} [\mathbf{W}]_{kk'}\, x_{k'}(t-1)$$

or from a global (network) point of view

$$\mathbf{x}(t) = \mathbf{W}\mathbf{x}(t-1). \tag{1}$$

The selection of the *weight matrix* **W**, representing the connections in a strongly connected network, crucially influences the convergence of the average consensus algorithm [20–22]. The main condition for the algorithm to converge is that the largest eigenvalue of **W** is equal to 1, i.e., $\lambda_{\max} = 1$, with multiplicity one, and that each row of **W** sums up to 1. It can then be directly shown [20] that the value $x_k(t)$ at each node converges to a common global value, e.g., average of the initial values.

If not stated otherwise, we use the so-called Metropolis weights [22] for matrix **W**, i.e.,

$$[\mathbf{W}]_{ij} = \begin{cases} \frac{1}{1+\max\{d_i, d_j\}} & \text{if } (i,j) \in \mathcal{E}, \\ 1 - \sum_{i' \in \mathcal{N}_i} [\mathbf{W}]_{ii'} & \text{if } i = j, \\ 0 & \text{otherwise.} \end{cases} \tag{2}$$

These weights guarantee that the consensus algorithm converges to the average of the initial values.

3 QR factorization

As mentioned in Section 1, there exist many algorithms for computing the QR factorization with different properties [1, 23]. In this paper we utilize the QR decomposition based on the *classical* Gram-Schmidt orthogonalization method (in ℓ^2 space).

3.1 Centralized classical Gram-Schmidt orthogonalization

Given matrix $\mathbf{A} = (\mathbf{a}_1, \mathbf{a}_2, \ldots, \mathbf{a}_m) \in \mathbb{R}^{n \times m}$, $n \geq m$, classical Gram-Schmidt orthogonalization (CGS) computes a matrix $\mathbf{Q} \in \mathbb{R}^{n \times m}$ with orthonormal columns and an upper-triangular matrix $\mathbf{R} \in \mathbb{R}^{m \times m}$, such that $\mathbf{A} = \mathbf{QR}$. Denoting

$$\mathbf{Q} = (\mathbf{q}_1 \quad \mathbf{q}_2 \quad \cdots \quad \mathbf{q}_m)$$

$$\mathbf{R} = \begin{pmatrix} \langle \mathbf{q}_1, \mathbf{a}_1 \rangle & \langle \mathbf{q}_1, \mathbf{a}_2 \rangle & \ldots & \langle \mathbf{q}_1, \mathbf{a}_m \rangle \\ 0 & \langle \mathbf{q}_2, \mathbf{a}_2 \rangle & \langle \mathbf{q}_2, \mathbf{a}_3 \rangle & \ldots \\ \vdots & & \ddots & \ldots \\ 0 & \ldots & 0 & \langle \mathbf{q}_m, \mathbf{a}_m \rangle \end{pmatrix}, \tag{3}$$

we have

$$\mathbf{q}_i = \frac{\mathbf{u}_i}{\|\mathbf{u}_i\|_2}, i = 1, 2, \ldots, m, \tag{4}$$

and

$$\mathbf{u}_i = \mathbf{a}_i - \sum_{j=1}^{i-1} \frac{\langle \mathbf{q}_j, \mathbf{a}_i \rangle}{\langle \mathbf{q}_j, \mathbf{q}_j \rangle} \mathbf{q}_j, \quad i = 1, 2, \ldots, m, \tag{5}$$

where $\|\mathbf{u}\|_2 = \sqrt{\sum_{i=1}^{n} u_i^2}$ and $\langle \mathbf{q}, \mathbf{a} \rangle = \sum_{i=1}^{n} q_i a_i$.

It is known that the algorithm is numerically sensitive depending on the singular values (condition number) of matrix $\mathbf{A}$ as well as it can produce vectors $\mathbf{q}_i$ far from orthogonal when the matrix $\mathbf{A}$ is close to being rank deficient even in a floating-point precision [23]. Numerical stability can be improved by other methods, e.g., modified Gram-Schmidt method, Householder transformations, or Givens rotations [1, 23].

3.2 Existing distributed methods

Assuming that each node k stores its local values u_k^2 and $q_k a_k$, it is then straightforward to redefine the CGS in a distributed way, suitable for a WSN, by following the definition of the ℓ^2 norm, i.e., $\|\mathbf{u}\|_2^2 = u_1^2 + u_2^2 + \cdots + u_n^2$ (cf. (4)), and inner products, $\langle \mathbf{q}, \mathbf{a} \rangle = q_1 a_1 + q_2 a_2 + \cdots + q_n a_n$ (cf. (5)). The summations can then be computed using any distributed aggregation algorithm, e.g., average consensus [20][1] (see Section 2), and asynchronous gossiping algorithms [24], using only communication with the neighbors.

Nevertheless, to our knowledge, all existing distributed algorithms for orthogonalizing a set of vectors are based on the gossip-based *push-sum algorithm* [16, 24]. Specifically in [3], authors used a distributed CGS based on gossiping for solving a distributed least squares problem and in [15], a gossip-based distributed algorithm for *modified* Gram-Schmidt orthogonalization (MGS) was designed and analyzed. The authors also provided a quantitative comparison to existing parallel algorithms for QR factorization. A slight modification of the latter algorithm was introduced in [25], which we use for comparison in this paper. We denote the two Gossip-based distributed Gram-Schmidt orthogonalization algorithms as G-CGS [3] and G-MGS [25], respectively.

Since the classical Gram-Schmidt orthogonalization computes each column of the matrix $\mathbf{Q}$ from the previous column recursively, i.e., to know vector $\mathbf{q}_2$, we need to compute the norm of $\mathbf{u}_2$ which depends on vector $\mathbf{q}_1$, the existing distributed algorithms always need to wait for convergence of one column before proceeding with the next column. This may be a big disadvantage in WSNs as it requires a lot of transmissions. Also, if the algorithm fails at some moment, e.g., due to transmission errors, the matrices $\mathbf{Q}$ and $\mathbf{R}$ are incomplete and unusable for further application.

In contrast, the distributed algorithm proposed in this paper overcomes these disadvantages and computes approximations of all elements of the matrices $\mathbf{Q}$ and $\mathbf{R}$ simultaneously. All the norms and inner products are refined iteratively which leads to a significant decrease of transmitted messages, and also the algorithm brings an intermediate approximation of the whole matrices $\mathbf{Q}$ and $\mathbf{R}$ at any time instance.

4 Distributed classical Gram-Schmidt with simultaneous elements refinement

As mentioned in Section 3.2, the Gram-Schmidt orthogonalization method can be computed in a distributed way using any distributed aggregation algorithm. We refer to CGS based on the average consensus (see Section 2) as AC-CGS. AC-CGS as well as G-CGS [3] and G-MGS [25] have the following substantial drawback.

In all Gram-Schmidt orthogonalization methods, the computation of the norms $\|\mathbf{u}_i\|$ and the inner products $\langle \mathbf{q}_j, \mathbf{a}_i \rangle$, $\langle \mathbf{q}_j, \mathbf{q}_j \rangle$, occurring in the matrices $\mathbf{Q}$ and $\mathbf{R}$, depends on the norms and inner products computed from the previous columns of the input matrix $\mathbf{A}$. Therefore, each node k must *wait* until the estimates of the previous norms $\|\mathbf{u}_j\|$ $(j < i)$ have achieved an acceptable accuracy before processing the next norm $\|\mathbf{u}_i\|$ (a "cascading" approach; see [15]). The same holds also for computing the inner products. We here present a novel approach overcoming this drawback.

Rewriting Eqs. (4) and (5) by a recursion, we obtain

$$\hat{\mathbf{q}}_i(t) = \frac{\hat{\mathbf{u}}_i(t)}{\sqrt{N \tilde{\mathbf{u}}_i(t-1)}}, \qquad i = 1, 2, \ldots, m, \tag{6}$$

$$\hat{\mathbf{u}}_i(t) = \mathbf{a}_i - \mathbf{p}_i(t), \qquad i = 1, 2, \ldots, m, \tag{7}$$

where $\tilde{\mathbf{u}}_i(t)$ is the approximation of $1/N\,\|\mathbf{u}_i\|_2^2\,\mathbf{1}$ at time t and

$$\mathbf{p}_i(t) = \sum_{j=1}^{i-1} \frac{\tilde{\mathbf{p}}^{(2)}_{j+(i-1)(i-2)/2}(t-1) \circ \hat{\mathbf{q}}_j(t-1)}{\tilde{\mathbf{q}}_j(t-1)},$$

with $\tilde{\mathbf{p}}^{(2)}_{j+(i-1)(i-2)/2}(t)$ being an approximation of the off-diagonal inner products $1/N\langle \mathbf{q}_j, \mathbf{a}_i\rangle \mathbf{1}$ ($\forall j < i$) of matrix $\mathbf{R}$ (cf. (3)) and $\tilde{\mathbf{q}}_j(t)$ an approximation of $1/N\langle \mathbf{q}_j, \mathbf{q}_j\rangle \mathbf{1}$ at time t. Similarly, we define $\tilde{\mathbf{p}}^{(1)}_i(t)$ to be an approximation of $1/N\langle \mathbf{q}_i, \mathbf{a}_i\rangle \mathbf{1}$. As we show later, $\tilde{\mathbf{u}}_i(t)$, $\tilde{\mathbf{q}}_j(t)$, $\tilde{\mathbf{p}}^{(1)}_i(t)$, and $\tilde{\mathbf{p}}^{(2)}_{j+(i-1)(i-2)/2}(t)$ converge to $1/N\,\|\mathbf{u}_i\|_2^2\,\mathbf{1}$, $1/N\langle \mathbf{q}_j, \mathbf{q}_j\rangle \mathbf{1}$, $1/N\langle \mathbf{q}_i, \mathbf{a}_i\rangle \mathbf{1}$, and $1/N\langle \mathbf{q}_j, \mathbf{a}_i\rangle \mathbf{1}$, respectively.

Similarly to the state-of-the-art methods (see Section 3.2), we further assume that the matrices $\mathbf{A} \in \mathbb{R}^{n\times m}$ and $\mathbf{Q} \in \mathbb{R}^{n\times m}$ are distributed over the network row-wise, meaning that each node stores at least one row of the matrix $\mathbf{A}$ and corresponding rows of the matrix $\mathbf{Q}$ and each node stores the whole matrix $\mathbf{R}$. In case $n > N$, more rows must be stored at the node and each node must sum the data locally before broadcasting to neighbors. Obviously, the data distribution over the network influences the speed of convergence of the algorithm, as can be seen also in the simulations ahead (see Section 5).

Notation $\mathbf{A}_k, \mathbf{Q}_k(t)$ here represent the rows of the matrices $\mathbf{A}$ and $\mathbf{Q}$ at a given node k at time t. If more rows are stored in one node, $\mathbf{A}_k$ and $\mathbf{Q}_k(t)$ are matrices, otherwise they are row vectors. Matrix $\mathbf{R}^{(k)}(t)$ represents the whole matrix $\mathbf{R}$ at node k at time t.

From a *global* (network) point of view, the algorithm is defined in Algorithm 1.

Proof of convergence of DS-CGS. For the first column, vector $i = 1$, $\hat{\mathbf{u}}_1(t) = \mathbf{a}_1$, and thus the convergence results of the average consensus, see Section 2, apply, i.e., as $t \to \infty$, the nodes will monotonically reach the common values, i.e., $\tilde{\mathbf{u}}_1(t) = 1/N\|\mathbf{a}_1\|_2^2\mathbf{1}$ and thus also, $\hat{\mathbf{q}}_1(t) = \frac{\mathbf{a}_1}{\|\mathbf{a}_1\|_2^2}$, $\tilde{\mathbf{q}}_1(t) = 1/N\mathbf{1}$, $\tilde{\mathbf{p}}^{(1)}_1(t) = 1/N\|\mathbf{a}_1\|_2^2\mathbf{1}$, and $\tilde{\mathbf{p}}^{(2)}_1(t) = 1/N\langle \mathbf{a}_1, \mathbf{a}_2\rangle \mathbf{1}$.

Furthermore, for all columns $i > 1$, all the elements depend only on the first column ($i = 1$), e.g., Eq. (7), $\hat{\mathbf{u}}_2(t) = \mathbf{a}_2 - \frac{\tilde{\mathbf{p}}^{(2)}_1(t-1)\circ\hat{\mathbf{q}}_1(t-1)}{\tilde{\mathbf{q}}_1(t-1)}$ $\left(\text{from Eq. (6) } \hat{\mathbf{q}}_1(t) = \frac{\hat{\mathbf{u}}_1(t)}{\sqrt{N\tilde{\mathbf{u}}_1(t-1)}}\right)$. Thus, eventually, $\hat{\mathbf{u}}_2(t)$ will converge to $\mathbf{u}_2$ (Eq. (5)) and similarly will do all norms and inner products (Eqs. (4) and (5)) of matrix $\mathbf{Q}$ and $\mathbf{R}$. □

Intuitively, we can see that as $\tilde{\mathbf{u}}_1(t)$ converges to its steady state, all other variables converge, with some "delay," to their steady states as well. We may say that as the first column converges, it "drags" other elements to their steady states. In the worst case, the consequent (following) column starts to converge only when the previous column is fully converged. This behavior differs from the known methods where we have to wait for $\tilde{\mathbf{u}}_1(t)$ to be converged before computing other terms.

Algorithm 1: DISTRIBUTED GRAM-SCHMIDT ORTHOGONALIZATION WITH SIMULTANEOUS REFINEMENT (DS–CGS)

- Input matrix $\mathbf{A} = (\mathbf{a}_1, \mathbf{a}_2, \ldots, \mathbf{a}_m) \in \mathbb{R}^{n\times m}$ with $n \geq m$ is distributed row-wise across N nodes. If $n > N$, some nodes store more than one row. Each node computes the rows of $\mathbf{Q}$ corresponding to the stored rows of $\mathbf{A}$ and an estimate of the whole matrix $\mathbf{R}$. indices: $k = 1, 2, \ldots, N$ (nodes); $i = 1, 2, \ldots, m$ (columns).

1. Initialization ($t = 0$):

$$\tilde{\mathbf{U}}(0) = \mathbf{A}\circ\mathbf{A}, \quad \hat{\mathbf{U}}(0) = \mathbf{A},$$
$$\tilde{\mathbf{Q}}(0) = \mathbf{A}\circ\mathbf{A}, \quad \hat{\mathbf{Q}}(0) = \mathbf{A},$$
$$\tilde{\mathbf{P}}^{(1)}(0) = \mathbf{A}\circ\mathbf{A}, \ \tilde{\mathbf{P}}^{(2)}(0) = \mathbf{A}\circledast\mathbf{A}$$

2. Repeat for $t = 1, 2, \ldots$

   (a) Compute locally at each node k

$$\mathbf{p}_i(t) = \sum_{j=1}^{i-1} \frac{\tilde{\mathbf{p}}^{(2)}_{j+(i-1)(i-2)/2}(t-1)\circ\hat{\mathbf{q}}_j(t-1)}{\tilde{\mathbf{q}}_j(t-1)}$$
$$\hat{\mathbf{u}}_i(t) = \mathbf{a}_i - \mathbf{p}_i(t)$$
$$\hat{\mathbf{q}}_i(t) = \frac{\hat{\mathbf{u}}_i(t)}{\sqrt{N\tilde{\mathbf{u}}_i(t-1)}}$$

   (b) At each node k store

$$\mathbf{Q}_k(t) = (\hat{q}_{k,1}(t), \hat{q}_{k,2}(t), \ldots, \hat{q}_{k,m}(t)), \quad \text{and}$$

$$\mathbf{R}^{(k)}(t) = N\begin{pmatrix} \tilde{p}^{(1)}_{k,1}(t)\ \tilde{p}^{(2)}_{k,1}(t) & \cdots & \tilde{p}^{(2)}_{k,(m^2-3m+4)/2}(t) \\ 0 \quad \tilde{p}^{(1)}_{k,2}(t)\ \tilde{p}^{(2)}_{k,3}(t) & & \cdots \\ \vdots & \ddots & \cdots \\ 0 \quad \cdots \quad 0 & & \tilde{p}^{(1)}_{k,m}(t) \end{pmatrix}$$

   (c) Aggregate data

$$\begin{aligned}
\Psi^{(1)} &= \tilde{\mathbf{U}}(t-1) &&+ \hat{\mathbf{U}}(t)\circ\hat{\mathbf{U}}(t) - \hat{\mathbf{U}}(t-1)\circ\hat{\mathbf{U}}(t-1)\\
\Psi^{(2)} &= \tilde{\mathbf{Q}}(t-1) &&+ \hat{\mathbf{Q}}(t)\circ\hat{\mathbf{Q}}(t) - \hat{\mathbf{Q}}(t-1)\circ\hat{\mathbf{Q}}(t-1)\\
\Psi^{(3)} &= \tilde{\mathbf{P}}^{(1)}(t-1) &&+ \hat{\mathbf{Q}}(t)\circ\mathbf{A} - \hat{\mathbf{Q}}(t-1)\circ\mathbf{A}\\
\Psi^{(4)} &= \underbrace{\tilde{\mathbf{P}}^{(2)}(t-1)}_{} &&+ \underbrace{\hat{\mathbf{Q}}(t)\circledast\mathbf{A} - \hat{\mathbf{Q}}(t-1)\circledast\mathbf{A}}_{}
\end{aligned}$$

$$\boldsymbol{\Psi}(t) = \mathbf{X}(t-1) \quad + \quad \Delta\mathbf{S}(t)$$

   (d) If $n > N$, sum $\boldsymbol{\Psi}(t)$ locally at the nodes and broadcast $\boldsymbol{\Psi}(t) = \left(\Psi^{(1)}, \Psi^{(2)}, \Psi^{(3)}, \Psi^{(4)}\right)$, ($\boldsymbol{\Psi}(t) \in \mathbb{R}^{N\times \frac{m^2+5m}{2}}$) to the neighbors, i.e.,

$$\underbrace{\left(\tilde{\mathbf{U}}(t), \tilde{\mathbf{Q}}(t), \tilde{\mathbf{P}}^{(1)}(t), \tilde{\mathbf{P}}^{(2)}(t)\right)}_{\mathbf{X}(t)} = \mathbf{W}\boldsymbol{\Psi}(t).$$

Note that instead of knowing the number of nodes N and using it as a normalization constant, we could transmit an additional weight vector $\boldsymbol{\omega}(t) \in \mathbb{R}^{N\times 1}$, i.e., $\Psi^{(0)}(t) = \boldsymbol{\omega}(t)$ and $\boldsymbol{\Psi}(t) = (\Psi^{(0)}(t), \Psi^{(1)}(t), \Psi^{(2)}(t), \Psi^{(3)}(t), \Psi^{(4)}(t))$, such that $\boldsymbol{\omega}(0) = (1, 0, \ldots, 0)^\top$ and Eq. (6) would change only slightly[2], i.e.,

$$\hat{\mathbf{q}}_i(t) = \frac{\hat{\mathbf{u}}_i(t)}{\sqrt{\frac{1}{\boldsymbol{\omega}(t)} \circ \tilde{\mathbf{u}}_i(t-1)}}.$$

We note that the normalization constant N (or $\boldsymbol{\omega}(t)$, respectively) affects only[3] the *orthonormality* (columns remain orthogonal but not normalized) of the columns of the matrix $\mathbf{Q}(t)$, and in case only orthogonality is sufficient, as in [26], we can omit this constant. We can, thus, overcome the necessity of knowing the number of the nodes or reduce the number of transmitted data in the network, respectively.

4.1 Relation to dynamic consensus algorithm

The dynamic consensus algorithm is a distributed algorithm which is able to track the average of a time-varying input signal. There exist many variations of the algorithm, e.g., [27–33]. Comparing the proposed DS-CGS algorithm with a dynamic consensus algorithm from [30, 32], we observe an interesting resemblance.

Formulating DS-CGS from a global point of view, i.e.,

$$\mathbf{X}(t) = \mathbf{W}\left[\mathbf{X}(t-1) + \triangle\mathbf{S}(t)\right],$$

we observe that it is a variant of the dynamic consensus algorithm with an "input signal" $\mathbf{S}(t)$. However, the "input signal" $\mathbf{S}(t)$ in our case is very complicated as it depends on $\mathbf{X}(t-1)$ and $\mathbf{S}(t-1)$ and cannot be considered as an independent signal as it is usually considered in dynamic consensus algorithms. Therefore, it is difficult to analyze the properties of this input signal and convergence conditions of DS-CGS based on the dynamic consensus algorithm. It is also beyond the scope and focus of this paper to analyze this algorithm in general. Nevertheless, some analysis of this type of dynamic consensus algorithm, for a general input signal, together with the bounds on convergence speed, has been conducted in [34].

5 Performance of DS-CGS

In our simulations, we consider a connected WSN with $N = 30$ nodes. We explore the behavior of DS-CGS for various topologies: *fully connected* (each node is connected to every other node), *regular* (each node has the same degree d), and *geometric* (each (randomly deployed) node is connected to all nodes within some radius ρ—a WSN model). If not stated otherwise, the randomly generated input matrix $\mathbf{A} \in \mathbb{R}^{300\times 100}$ has uniformly distributed elements from the interval $[0, 1]$ and a low condition number $\kappa(\mathbf{A}) = 35.7$. In Section 5.3.2, we, however, investigate the influence of various input matrices with different condition numbers on the algorithm's performance.

Also, except for the Sections 5.3.1 and 5.4, for the consensus weight matrix we use the metropolis weights (Eq. (2)).

The confidence intervals were computed from the several instantiations using a bootstrap method [35].

5.1 Orthogonality and factorization error

As performance metrics in the simulations, we use the following:

- *Relative factorization error*— $\frac{\left\|\mathbf{A}-\mathbf{Q}(t)\mathbf{R}^{(k)}(t)\right\|_2}{\|\mathbf{A}\|_2}$ —which measures the accuracy of the QR factorization at node k,
- *Orthogonality error*— $\left\|\mathbf{I} - \mathbf{Q}(t)^\top\mathbf{Q}(t)\right\|_2$ —which measures the orthogonality of the matrix $\mathbf{Q}(t)$ (see step 2 of the algorithm).

Note that both errors are calculated from the network (global) perspective and as depicted, they are not known locally at the nodes, since only $\mathbf{R}^{(k)}(t)$ is local at each node, whereas $\mathbf{Q}(t)$ is distributed row-wise across the nodes ($\mathbf{Q}_k(t)$). From now on, we simplify the notation by dropping the index t in $\mathbf{Q}(t)$ and $\mathbf{R}^{(k)}(t)$. The simulation results for a geometric topology with an average node degree $\bar{d} = 8.533$ are depicted in Fig. 1. Since both errors behave almost identically (compare Fig. 1a, b) and since each node k can compute a *local factorization error* $\left\|\mathbf{A}_k - \mathbf{Q}_k\mathbf{R}^{(k)}\right\|_2 / \|\mathbf{A}_k\|_2$ from its local data, we conjecture that such local error evaluation can be used also as a local stopping criterion in practice. Note that this fact was used in [26] for estimating a network size.

Note that the error at the beginning stage in Fig. 1 is caused by the disagreement and not converged norms and inner products across the nodes, i.e., the values of $\tilde{\mathbf{U}}(t)$, $\tilde{\mathbf{Q}}(t)$, $\tilde{\mathbf{P}}^{(1)}(t)$, and $\tilde{\mathbf{P}}^{(2)}(t)$. We also observe that the error floor[4] is highly influenced by the network topology, weights of matrix $\mathbf{W}$, and condition number of input matrix $\mathbf{A}$. We investigate these properties in Section 5.3.

5.2 Initial data distribution

If $n > N$, some nodes store more than one row of $\mathbf{A}$. Thus, before doing distributed summation (broadcasting to neighbors), every node has to locally sum the values of its local rows.

Simulations show that the convergence behavior of DS-CGS strongly depends on the distribution of the rows across the network (see Fig. 2). We investigate the following cases: (1) each node stores ten rows of $\mathbf{A}$ ("uniform"); (2) 271 rows are stored in the node with the lowest degree, the other 29 rows in the remaining 29 nodes; and (3) 271

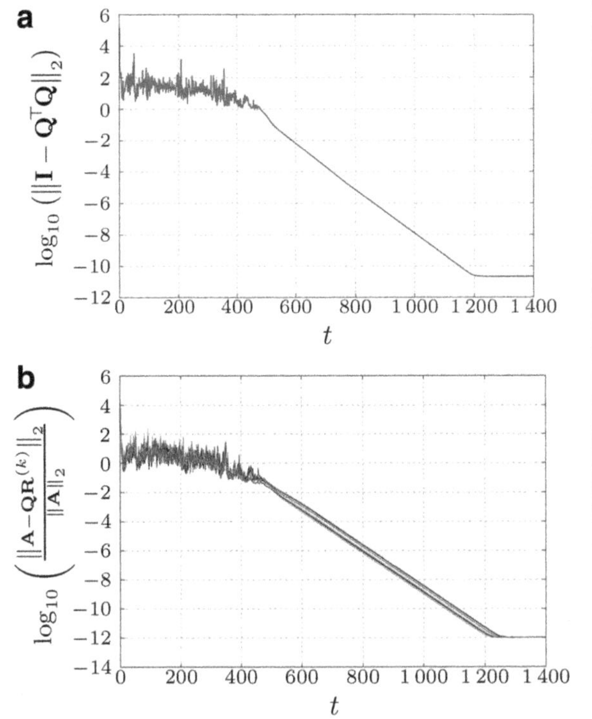

Fig. 1 Example of orthogonality (**a**) and factorization error (**b**) for each node k for a geometric topology with $d = 8.533$. $N = 30, k = 1, 2, \ldots, 30$

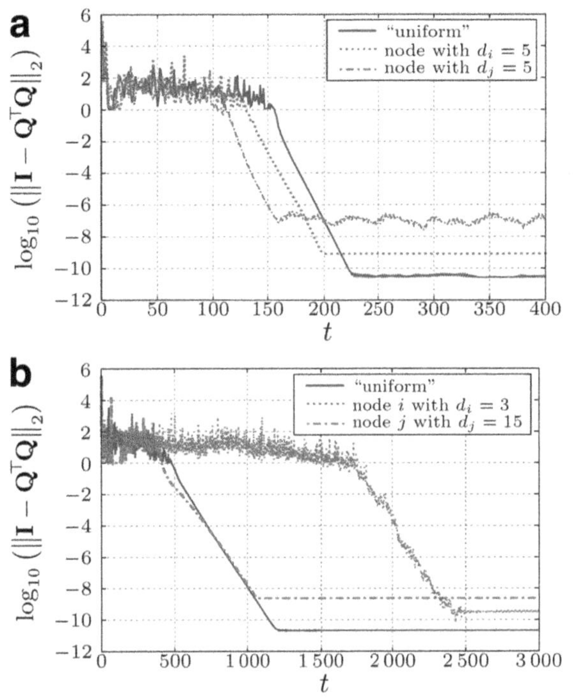

Fig. 2 Convergence for networks with different topology and initial data distribution: either all nodes store the same amount of data ("uniform") or most of the data is stored in one node (with minimum or maximum degree) (**a** - Regular topology with $\overline{d} = 5$; **b** - Geometric topology with $\overline{d} = 5$). In case of the regular topology (**a**), the nodes *i,j* are picked randomly

rows are stored in the node with the highest degree, the rest in the remaining 29 nodes.

We observe that not only the initial distribution of the data influences the convergence behavior but also the topology of the underlying network. In the case of a regular topology (Fig. 2a), the influence of the distribution is small and relatively weak in terms of convergence time but stronger in terms of the final accuracy achieved. We recognize that the difference between the nodes comes only from the variance of the values in input matrix **A**. On the other hand, in case of a highly irregular geometric topology (see Fig. 2b), where the node with most neighbors stores most of the data, the algorithm converges much faster than in the case when most of the data are stored in a node with only few neighbors.

We further observe that in the "uniform" case, the algorithm behaves slightly differently for different distributions of the rows (although still having ten rows in each node). In Fig. 3, we show results for six different placements of the data across the nodes for three different topologies, where we depict the mean value and the corresponding confidence intervals of the simulated orthogonality error. As we can observe, in case of the fully connected topology, the data distribution is of no importance, since all the nodes exchange data in every step with all other nodes. In case of the geometric topology, however, the convergence of the algorithm is influenced by the distribution of data, even if every node contains the same number of rows (ten rows in each node). This can be recognized by bigger confidence intervals of the orthogonality error. Nevertheless, the speed of convergence for all cases is bigger than the case when most data is stored in the "sparsest" node (cf. Fig. 2b). In case of the regular topology, the difference is small only due to numerical accuracy of the mixing parameters.

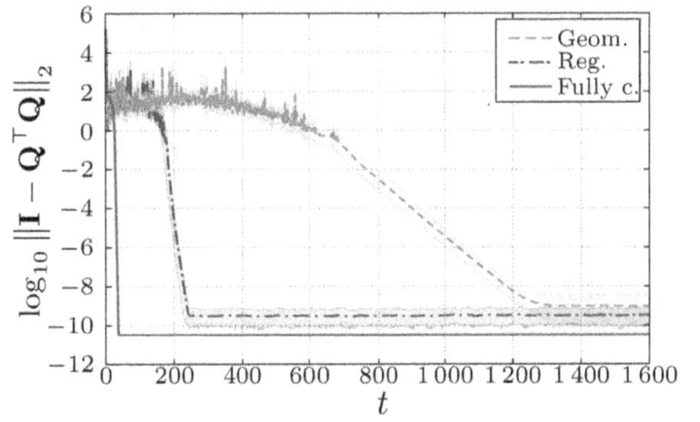

Fig. 3 "Uniform" distribution for different topologies. (*Boldface line* is the mean value across six different uniform data distributions. *Shaded areas* are 95 % confidence intervals)

5.3 Numerical sensitivity

As mentioned in Section 3.1, the classical Gram-Schmidt orthogonalization possesses some undesirable numerical properties [1, 23]. In comparison to *centralized* algorithms, numerical stability of DS-CGS is furthermore influenced by the precision of the mixing weight matrix $\mathbf{W}$, the network topology, and properties of input matrix $\mathbf{A}$, i.e., its condition number (see Fig. 5 ahead) and the distribution of the numbers in the rows of the matrix (see Figs. 2 and 3). In this section, we provide simulation results showing these dependencies.

5.3.1 Weights

As mentioned in Section 2, matrix $\mathbf{W}$ can be selected in many ways. Mainly, the selection of the weights influences the speed of convergence. Unlike previous simulations, where we used the metropolis weights (see Eq. (2)), here we selected constant weights for matrix $\mathbf{W}$ [20], i.e.,

$$[\mathbf{W}]_{ij} = \begin{cases} \frac{c}{N} & \text{if } (i,j) \in \mathcal{E}, \\ 1 - \frac{c}{N} d_i & \text{if } i = j, \\ 0 & \text{otherwise,} \end{cases} \tag{8}$$

where $c \in (0, 1]$. Such weights, in general, lead to slower convergence. However, we can also see in Fig. 4 that the weights influence not only the speed of convergence but also the numerical accuracy of the algorithm (different error floors).

5.3.2 Condition numbers

It is well known that the classical Gram-Schmidt orthogonalization is numerically unstable [23]. In cases when input matrix $\mathbf{A}$ is ill-conditioned (high condition number) or rank-deficient (matrix contains linear dependent columns), the computed vectors $\mathbf{Q}$ can be far from orthogonal even when computed with high precision.

In this section, we study the influence of the condition number of input matrix $\mathbf{A}$ on the accuracy of the orthogonality. The condition number is defined with respect to inversion as the ratio of the largest and smallest singular value. In comparison to classical (centralized) Gram-Schmidt orthogonalization, we observe (Fig. 5a) that the DS-CGS algorithm behaves similarly, although it reaches neither the accuracy of AC-CGS nor of the centralized algorithm (even in the fully connected network). We observe in all of the simulations that the orthogonality error in the first phase can reach very high values (due to divisions by numbers close to zero), which may influence the numerical accuracy in the final phase.

We further observe that the algorithm requires matrix $\mathbf{A}$ to be very well-conditioned even for the fully connected network. Unlike other methods, the factorization error in case of DS-CGS has the same characteristics as the orthogonality error and is also influenced by the condition number of the input matrix, see Fig. 5b. Although, as we noted in Section 5.1, orthogonality and factorization error of DS-CGS behave almost identically, the dependence of condition number $\kappa(\mathbf{A})$ on the factorization error would need a further investigation.

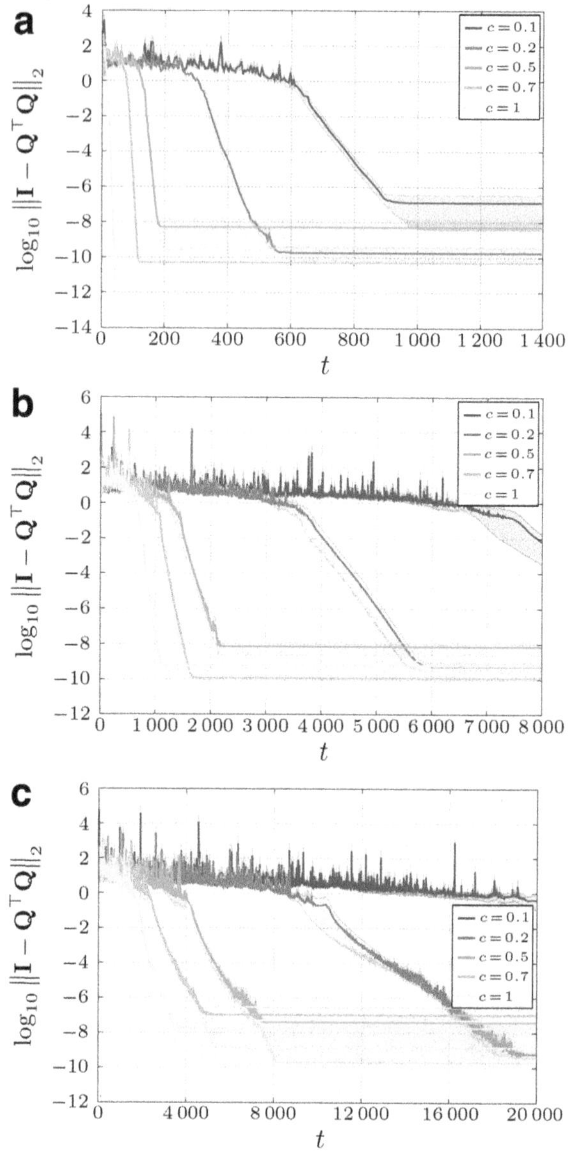

Fig. 4 Influence of different constant weights c (Eq. (8)) on the algorithm's accuracy and convergence speed for three different topologies (**a** - Fully connected topology; **b** - Regular topology; **c** - Geometric topology) averaged over ten different input matrices (**a–c**). (*Shaded areas* are 95 % confidence intervals)

Figure 5 also shows that G-MGS is the most robust method in comparison to the others. This is caused by the usage of the *modified* Gram-Schmidt orthogonalization instead of the classical one.

5.3.3 Mixing precision

Another factor influencing the algorithm's performance is the numerical precision of the mixing weights $\mathbf{W}$. Here,

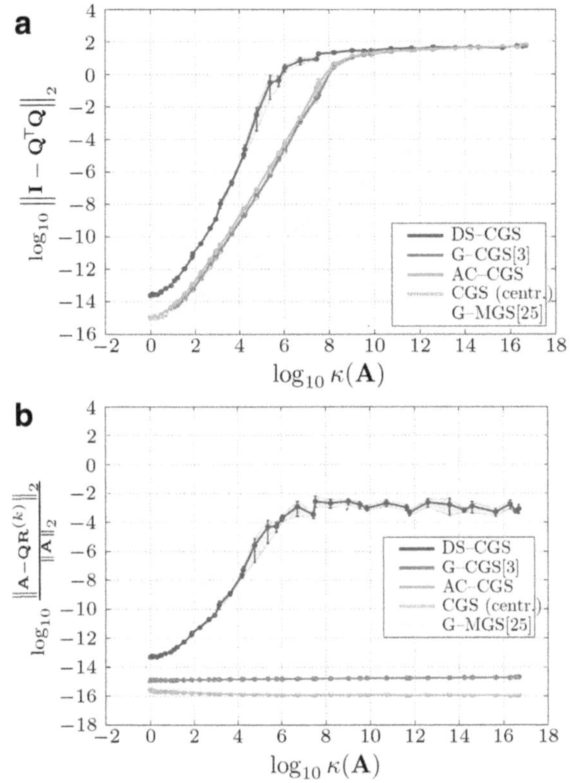

Fig. 5 Impact of the condition number $\kappa(\mathbf{A})$ of matrix $\mathbf{A}$ on the orthogonality (**a**) and factorization error (**b**). Averaged over ten matrices for each condition number. Fully connected network. (*Both axes* are in logarithmic scale. *Shaded areas* are 95 % confidence intervals)

we simulate the case of a geometric topology with the Metropolis weights model, where the weights are of given precision—characterized by the number of variable decimal digits (4, 8, 16, 32, "Infinite").[5]

If we compare Fig. 6 with Fig. 7, we find that the numerical precision of the mixing weights have bigger influence in cases when the input matrix is worse conditioned. In Figs. 8 and 9, we can see the difference between

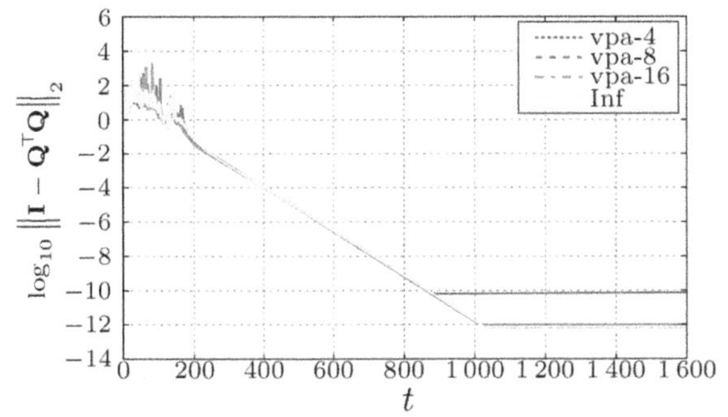

Fig. 6 Influence of the numerical precision of the mixing weights on the orthogonality error of DS-CGS. Geometric topology, matrix $\mathbf{A}$ with low condition number ($\kappa(\mathbf{A}) = 1.04$)

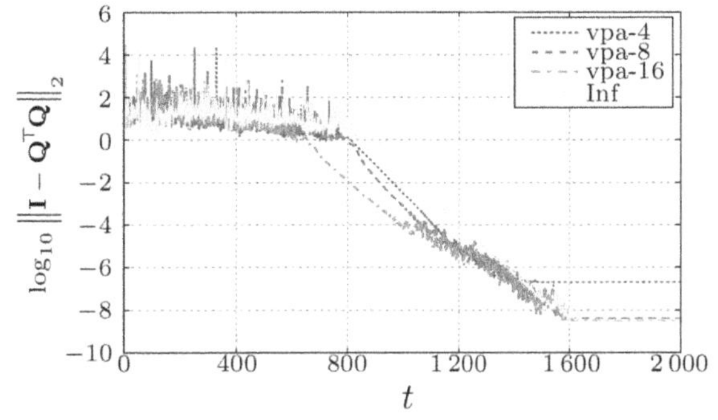

Fig. 7 Influence of the numerical precision of the mixing weights on the orthogonality error of DS-CGS. Geometric topology, matrix $\mathbf{A}$ with higher condition number ($\kappa(\mathbf{A}) = 76.33$)

orthogonality errors for various precisions. We observe that for the matrix $\mathbf{A}$ with higher condition number, the higher mixing precision has bigger impact on the result.

As we find in Fig. 6, the error floor moves with the mixing precision. However, we must note that even for the "infinite" mixing precision the orthogonality error stalls at an accuracy ($\sim 10^{-12}$) lower than the used machine precision—taking into account also the conversion to double precision. From the simulations, we conclude that this is caused by high numerical dynamic range in the first phases of the algorithm as well as by the errors created by the misagreement among the nodes during the transient phase of the algorithm.

5.4 Robustness to link failures

In case of distributed algorithms, it is of big importance that the algorithm is robust against network failures. Typical failures in WSN are message losses or link failures, which occur due to many reasons, e.g., channel fading, congestions, message collisions, moving nodes, or dynamic topology.

We model link failures as a temporary drop-out of a bidirectional connection between two nodes, meaning

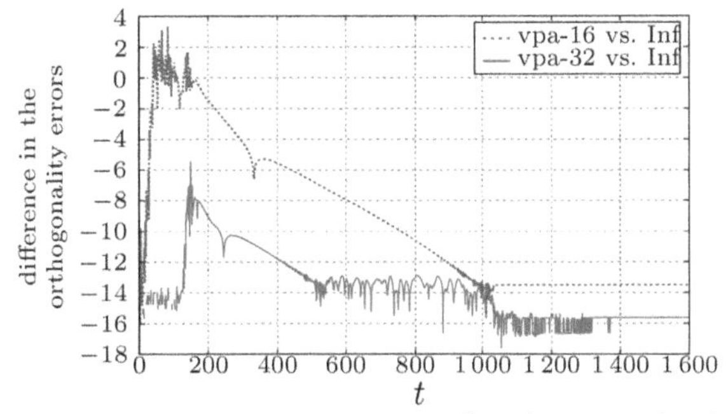

Fig. 8 Difference in the orthogonality error $\left(\log_{10}\left|\|\mathbf{I}-\mathbf{Q}^T\mathbf{Q}\|_2^{(\text{vpa}-i)} - \|\mathbf{I}-\mathbf{Q}^T\mathbf{Q}\|_2^{(\text{Inf})}\right|\right)$ for the case of 16 and 32 decimal digits versus "infinite" precision (converted to double)

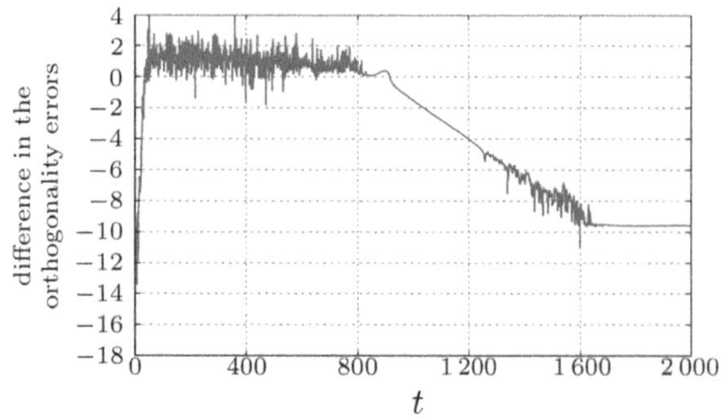

Fig. 9 Difference in the orthogonality error $\left(\log_{10}\left|\|\mathbf{I}-\mathbf{Q}^{\mathsf{T}}\mathbf{Q}\|_2^{(\text{vpa}-16)} - \|\mathbf{I}-\mathbf{Q}^{\mathsf{T}}\mathbf{Q}\|_2^{(\text{inf})}\right|\right)$ for the case of 16 decimal digits versus "infinite" precision (converted to double). Note that in comparison to Fig. 8, the difference between "infinite" and more than 16 digits is below the machine precision (exact same results)

that no message can be transmitted between the nodes. In every time step, we randomly remove some percentage of links in the network. As a weight model, we picked the constant weights model, Eq. (8), due to its property that every node can compute at each time step the weights *locally* based only on the number of received messages (d_i). Thus, no global knowledge is required. However, the nodes must still work synchronously.[6]

From Fig. 10, we conclude that the algorithm is very robust and even if we drop in every time step, a big percentage (up to 60 %) of the links, the algorithm still achieves some accuracy (at least 10^{-2}; Fig. 10c).

It is worth noting that moving nodes and dynamic network topology can be modeled in the same way. We therefore argue that the algorithm is robust also to such scenarios (assuming that synchronicity is guaranteed).

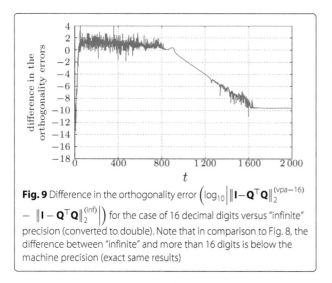

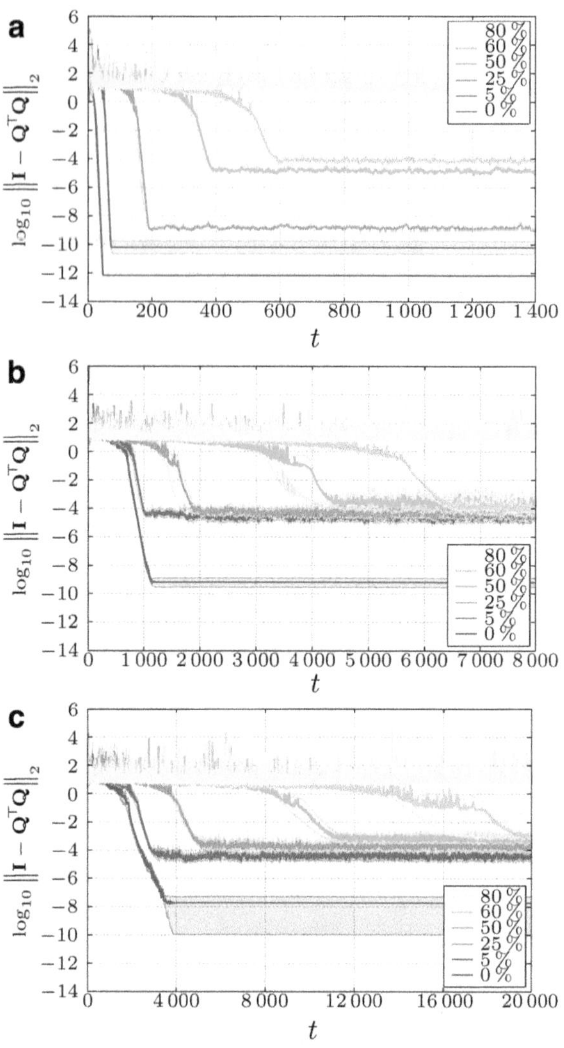

Fig. 10 Robustness to link failures for different percentages of failed links at every time step (**a** - Fully connected; **b** - Regular topology; **c** - Geometric topology). Constant weight model with $c = 1$, i.e., the fastest option (see Fig. 4). (*Shaded areas* are 95 % confidence intervals)

5.5 Performance comparison with existing algorithms

We compare our new DS-CGS algorithm with AC-CGS, G-CGS, and G-MGS introduced in Section 3.2. Although all approaches have iterative aspects, the cost per iteration strongly differs for each algorithm. Thus, instead of providing a comparison in terms of number of iterations to converge, we compare the communication cost needed for achieving a certain accuracy of the result. We investigate the total number of messages sent as well as the total amount of data (real numbers) exchanged.

Simulation results for various topologies are shown in Figs. 11 and 12. The gossip-based approaches exchange, in general, less data (Fig. 12), but since their message size is much smaller than in DS-CGS, the total number of messages sent is higher (Fig. 11).

Because the message size of AC-CGS is even smaller than in the gossip-based approaches, it sends the highest number of messages. Since the energy consumption in a WSN is mostly influenced by the number of transmissions [36, 37], it is better to transmit as few messages as possible (with any payload size); therefore, DS-CGS is the most suitable method for a WSN scenario. However, we notice that in many cases, DS-CGS does not achieve the same final accuracy of the result as the other methods.

Note that in fully connected networks, AC-CGS delivers a highly accurate result from the beginning, because within the first iterations, all nodes exchange the required information with all other nodes.

In Table 1, we summarize the total communication cost and local memory requirements of the algorithms. However, due to different parameters, it is difficult to rank the approaches in a general case. The requirements depend especially on the topology of the underlying network, the

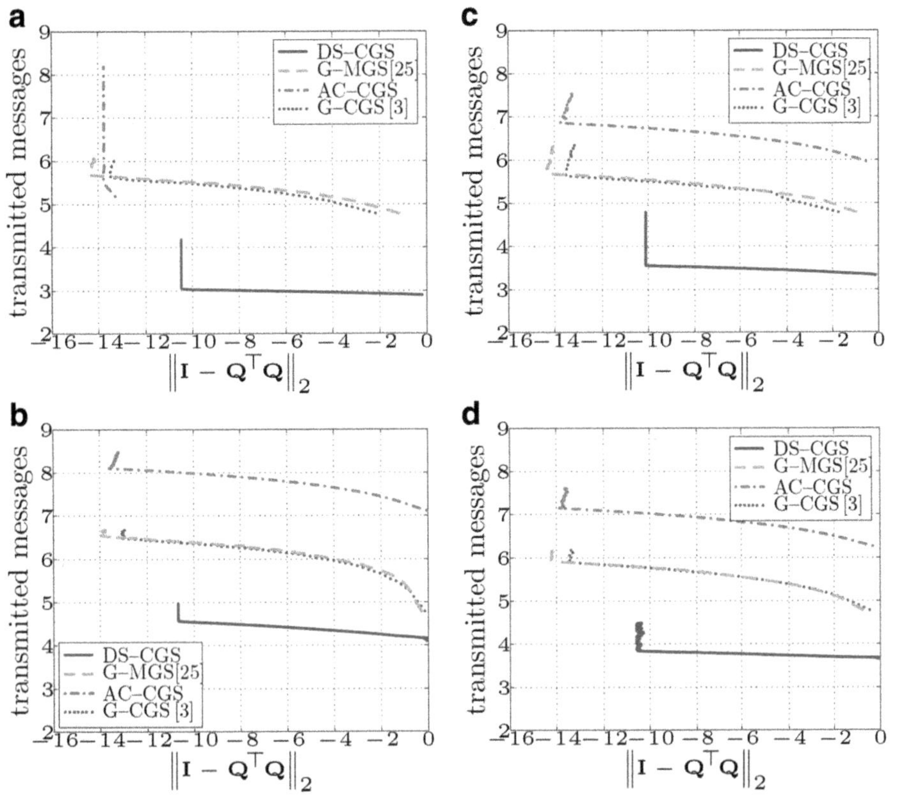

Fig. 11 Total number of transmitted messages in the network vs. orthogonality error (*both axes* are in *logarithmic* scale $\log_{10}$) (**a** - Fully connected topology; **b** - Geometric topology with $\bar{d} = 8.53$; **c** - Geometric topology with $\bar{d} = 24.46$; **d** - Regular topology with $\bar{d} = 5$)

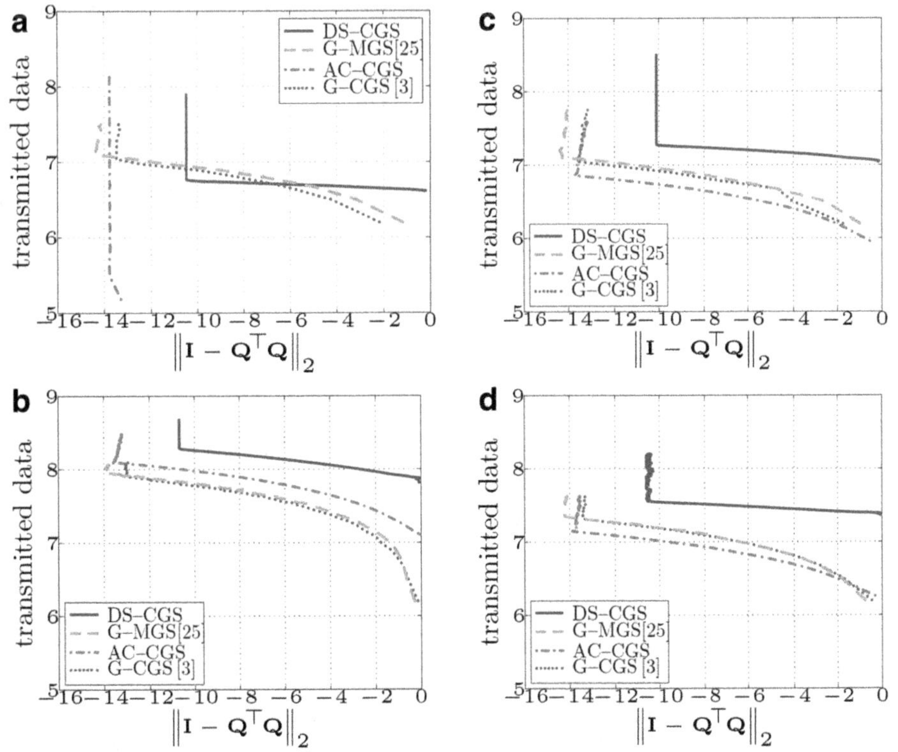

Fig. 12 Total number of transmitted real numbers (data) in the network vs. orthogonality error (*both axes* are in *logarithmic* scale $\log_{10}$) (**a** - Fully connected topology; **b** - Geometric topology with $\bar{d} = 8.53$; **c** - Geometric topology with $\bar{d} = 24.46$; **d** - Regular topology with $\bar{d} = 5$)

Table 1 Comparison of various distributed QR factorization algorithms

	Total number of sent messages	Total amount of data (real numbers)	Local memory requirements per node
DS-CGS	$N \cdot I^{(d)}$	$N \cdot I^{(d)} \cdot \frac{m^2+5m}{2}$	$O(mn/N+m^2)$
AC-CGS	$N \cdot I^{(s)} \cdot \frac{(m+1)m}{2}$	$N \cdot I^{(s)} \cdot \frac{(m+1)m}{2}$	$O(mn/N+m^2)$
G-CGS	$N \cdot R \cdot (2m-1)$	$N \cdot R \cdot \frac{m^2+5m-2}{2}$	$O(nm/N)$
G-MGS	$N \cdot R \cdot (2m-1)$	$N \cdot R \cdot \frac{m^2+5m-2}{2}$	$O(nm/N)$

$I^{(d)}$ denotes the number of iterations of "dynamic" consensus, $I^{(s)}$ the number of iterations of "static" consensus, R the number of rounds per push-sum, N the number of nodes, m the number of columns of the input matrix

number of iterations $I^{(s)}$ and $I^{(d)}$ required for convergence in "static" and "dynamic" consensus-based algorithms or the number of rounds R needed for convergence of push-sum in the gossip-based approaches. For example, in a *fully connected* network $R = O(\log N)$ [24], $I^{(s)} = 1$. Thus, AC-CGS requires $O(m^2N)$ messages sent as well as data exchanged, whereas gossip-based approaches need $O(mN \log N)$ messages and $O(m^2N \log N)$ data. Note that G-CGS and G-MGS have theoretically identical communication cost; however, G-MGS is numerically more stable (see Fig. 5) and achieves a higher final accuracy (see Figs. 11 and 12). In case of DS-CGS and a fully connected network, we can interpret DS-CGS in the worst case as m consequent static consensus algorithms (one for each column); thus, $I^{(d)} = O(m)$, and the number of transmitted messages is $O(mN)$ and data $O(m^3N)$. Nevertheless, theoretical convergence bounds of DS-CGS (on $I^{(d)}$) remain an open research question.

6 Conclusions

We presented a novel distributed algorithm for computing QR decomposition and provided an analysis of its properties. In contrast to existing methods, which compute the columns of the resulting matrix $\mathbf{Q}$ consecutively, our method iteratively refines all elements at once. Thus, in any moment, the algorithm can deliver an estimate of both matrices $\mathbf{Q}$ and $\mathbf{R}$. The algorithm dramatically outperforms known distributed orthogonalization algorithms in terms of transmitted messages, which makes it suitable for energy-constrained WSNs. Based on our empirical observation, we argue that the evaluation of the local factorization error at each node might lead to a suitable stopping criterion for the algorithm. We also provided a thorough study of its numerical properties, analyzing the influence of the precision of the mixing weights and condition numbers of the input matrix. We furthermore analyzed the robustness of the algorithm to link failures and showed that the algorithm is capable to reach a certain accuracy even for a high percentage of link failures.

The biggest drawback of the algorithm is the necessity to have synchronously working nodes. This leads to poor robustness when the messages are sent (or lost) asynchronously. As we showed, since the algorithm originates from the classical Gram-Schmidt orthogonalization, also the numerical sensitivity of the algorithm is a big issue and needs to be addressed in the future. The optimization of the weights and design of algorithm in such way that it avoids a big dynamic numerical range, especially in the first phases, is also of interest.

An alternative approach, not considered here, which could be worth of future research, would be to find a distributed algorithm as an optimization problem, e.g., $\min_{\text{s.t. } \mathbf{Q}^\top\mathbf{Q}=\mathbf{I}} \|\mathbf{A} - \mathbf{QR}\|$. In literature, there exist many distributed optimization methods, e.g., [38, 39], which could lead to even superior algorithms, with even faster convergence and smaller error floors.

Last but not least, theoretical bounds of DS-CGS for the convergence time and rate remain an open issue. A first application of the algorithm has already been proposed in [26]. Also, since the proposed algorithm is not restricted to the usage in wireless sensor networks only, a transfer of the proposed algorithm onto so-called network-on-chip platforms [40] could possibly lead to further new interesting and practical applications as well.

Endnotes

[1]Knowing n, $\|\mathbf{u}\|_2^2 = n \lim_{t\to\infty} \mathbf{W}^t(\mathbf{u} \circ \mathbf{u}) = \sum_{i=1}^n u_i^2$.

[2]$\lim_{t\to\infty} \boldsymbol{\omega}(t) = 1/N\mathbf{1}$.

[3]Not considering numerical properties.

[4]Error level at which the algorithm stalls at given computational precision.

[5]The simulations were performed in Matlab R2011b 64-bit using the Symbolic Math Toolbox with variable precision arithmetic. "Infinite" precision denotes weights represented as an exact ratio of two numbers. The depicted result after "infinite" precision multiplication was converted to double precision.

[6]If there is a link, nodes see each other and immediately exchange messages. From a mathematical point of view, this implies that weight matrix $\mathbf{W}$ will be doubly stochastic [1] in every time step.

Appendix: local algorithm

For a better clarity, we here reformulate DS-CGS algorithm from the point of view of an individual node i (local point of view). Note that input matrix $\mathbf{A}$ is stored row-wise in the nodes, and for simplicity, we show here the case when the number of rows of matrix $\mathbf{A} \in \mathbb{R}^{N\times m}$ is equal to the number of nodes in the network. For a formulation from the network (global) point of view and arbitrary size of matrix $\mathbf{A}$, see Section 4.

1. Initialization ($t = 0$). Node i stores the following vectors.

$$\hat{\mathbf{u}}_i(0) = (a_{i,1},\ a_{i,2},\ \ldots\ a_{i,m})$$
$$\hat{\mathbf{q}}_i(0) = (a_{i,1},\ a_{i,2},\ \ldots\ a_{i,m})$$
$$\tilde{\mathbf{u}}_i(0) = (a_{i,1}^2,\ a_{i,2}^2,\ \ldots\ a_{i,m}^2)$$
$$\tilde{\mathbf{q}}_i(0) = (a_{i,1}^2,\ a_{i,2}^2,\ \ldots\ a_{i,m}^2)$$
$$\tilde{\mathbf{p}}_i^{(1)}(0) = (a_{i,1}^2,\ a_{i,2}^2,\ \ldots\ a_{i,m}^2)$$
$$\tilde{\mathbf{p}}_i^{(2)}(0) = (a_{i,1}a_{i,2},\ a_{i,1}a_{i,3},\ a_{i,2}a_{i,3},\ \ldots\ a_{i,m-1}a_{i,m})$$

2. Repeat for $t = 1, 2, \ldots$

(a) Compute vectors locally.

$$\mathbf{p}_i(t) = \Big(0,\ \tilde{p}_{i1}^{(2)}(t-1)\frac{\hat{q}_{i,1}(t-1)}{\tilde{q}_{i,1}(t-1)},\ \tilde{p}_{i,2}^{(2)}(t-1)\frac{\hat{q}_{i,1}(t-1)}{\tilde{q}_{i,1}(t-1)} + \tilde{p}_{i,3}^{(2)}(t-1)\frac{\hat{q}_{i,2}(t-1)}{\tilde{q}_{i,2}(t-1)},\ \ldots,\ \sum_{j=1}^{m-1}\tilde{p}_{i,j+(m-1)(m-2)/2}^{(2)}(t-1)\frac{\hat{q}_{i,j}(t-1)}{\tilde{q}_{i,j}(t-1)}\Big)$$

$$\hat{\mathbf{u}}_i(t) = \big(a_{i,1} - p_{i,1}(t),\ a_{i,2} - p_{i,2}(t),\ \ldots,\ a_{i,m} - p_{i,m}(t)\big)$$

$$\hat{\mathbf{q}}_i(t) = \left(\frac{\hat{u}_{i,1}(t)}{\sqrt{N\tilde{u}_{i,1}(t-1)}},\ \frac{\hat{u}_{i,2}(t)}{\sqrt{N\tilde{u}_{i,2}(t-1)}},\ \ldots,\ \frac{\hat{u}_{i,m}(t)}{\sqrt{N\tilde{u}_{i,m}(t-1)}}\right)$$

(b) Store the local part of the resulting matrix $\mathbf{Q}$ and the whole matrix $\mathbf{R}$, i.e.,

$$\hat{\mathbf{q}}_i(t) = \left(\frac{\hat{u}_{i,1}(t)}{\sqrt{N\tilde{u}_{i,1}(t-1)}},\ \frac{\hat{u}_{i,2}(t)}{\sqrt{N\tilde{u}_{i,2}(t-1)}},\ \ldots,\ \frac{\hat{u}_{i,m}(t)}{\sqrt{N\tilde{u}_{i,m}(t-1)}}\right)$$

$$\mathbf{R}^{(i)}(t) = N\begin{pmatrix} \tilde{p}_{i,1}^{(1)}(t) & \tilde{p}_{i,1}^{(2)}(t) & \cdots & \tilde{p}_{i,(m^2-3m+4)/2}^{(2)}(t) \\ 0 & \tilde{p}_{i,2}^{(1)}(t) & \tilde{p}_{i,3}^{(2)}(t) & \cdots \\ \vdots & & \ddots & \cdots \\ 0 & \cdots & 0 & \tilde{p}_{i,m}^{(1)}(t) \end{pmatrix}$$

(c) Aggregate the following data into one message:

$$\boldsymbol{\psi}_i^{(1)} = \big(\tilde{u}_{i,1}(t-1) + \hat{u}_{i,1}^2(t) - \hat{u}_{i,1}^2(t-1),\ \ldots,\ \tilde{u}_{i,m}(t-1) + \hat{u}_{i,m}^2(t) - \hat{u}_{i,m}^2(t-1)\big)$$

$$\boldsymbol{\psi}_i^{(2)} = \big(\tilde{q}_{i,1}(t-1) + \hat{q}_{i,1}^2(t) - \hat{q}_{i,1}^2(t-1),\ \ldots,\ \tilde{q}_{i,m}(t-1) + \hat{q}_{i,m}^2(t) - \hat{q}_{i,m}^2(t-1)\big)$$

$$\boldsymbol{\psi}_i^{(3)} = \Big(\tilde{p}_{i,1}^{(1)}(t-1) + a_{i,1}\hat{q}_{i,1}(t) - a_{i,1}\hat{q}_{i,1}(t-1),\ \ldots,\ \tilde{p}_{i,m}^{(1)}(t-1) + a_{i,m}\hat{q}_{i,m}(t) - a_{i,m}\hat{q}_{i,m}(t-1)\Big)$$

$$\boldsymbol{\psi}_i^{(4)} = \Big(\tilde{p}_{i,1}^{(2)}(t-1) + \hat{q}_{i,1}(t)a_{i,2} - \hat{q}_{i,1}(t-1)a_{i,2},\ \tilde{p}_{i,2}^{(2)}(t-1) + \hat{q}_{i,1}(t)a_{i,3} - \hat{q}_{i,1}(t-1)a_{i,3},\ \ldots,\ \tilde{p}_{i,(m^2-m)/2}^{(2)}(t-1) + \hat{q}_{i,m-1}(t)a_{i,m} - \hat{q}_{i,m-1}(t-1)a_{i,m}\Big)$$

(d) Broadcast the message containing the vectors $\left\{\boldsymbol{\psi}_i^{(1)}, \boldsymbol{\psi}_i^{(2)}, \boldsymbol{\psi}_i^{(3)}, \boldsymbol{\psi}_i^{(4)}\right\}$ to the neighbors and update the own local data $\left\{\tilde{\mathbf{u}}_i(t), \tilde{\mathbf{q}}_i(t), \tilde{\mathbf{p}}_i^{(1)}(t), \tilde{\mathbf{p}}_i^{(2)}(t)\right\}$ from received data.

Competing interests

The authors declare that they have no competing interests.

Acknowledgements

This work was supported by the Austrian Science Fund (FWF) under project grants S10608-N13 and S10611-N13 within the National Research Network SISE. Preliminary parts of this work were previously published at the 46th Asilomar Conf. Sig., Syst., Comp., Pacific Grove, CA, USA, Nov. 2012 [32].

Author details

[1] TU Wien, Institute of Telecommunications, Gusshausstrasse 25/E389, 1040 Vienna, Austria. [2] University of Vienna, Faculty of Computer Science, Theory and Applications of Algorithms, Währingerstrasse 29, 1090 Vienna, Austria.

References

1. GH Golub, CF Van Loan, *Matrix Computations*, 3rd Ed. (Johns Hopkins Univ. Press, Baltimore, USA, 1996)
2. JM Lees, RS Crosson, in *Spatial Statistics and Imaging*, ed. by A Possolo. Bayesian ART versus conjugate gradient methods in tomographic seismic imaging: an application at Mount St. Helens, Washington, vol. 20 (IMS Lecture Noted-Monograph Series, Hayward, CA, 1991), pp. 186–208
3. C Dumard, E Riegler, in *Int. Conf. on Telecom. ICT '09*. Distributed sphere decoding (IEEE, Marrakech, 2009), pp. 172–177
4. G Tauböck, M Hampejs, P Svac, G Matz, F Hlawatsch, K Gröchenig, Low-complexity ICI/ISI equalization in doubly dispersive multicarrier systems using a decision-feedback LSQR algorithm. IEEE Trans. Signal Process. **59**(5), 2432–2436 (2011)
5. E Hänsler, G Schmidt, *Acoustic Echo and Noise Control*. (Wiley, Chichester, New York, Brisabne, Toronto, Singapore, 2004)
6. PSR Diniz, *Adaptive Filtering—Algorithms and Practical Implementation*. (Springer, US, 2008)
7. AH Sayed, *Adaptation, Learning, and Optimization over Networks*, vol. 7. (Foundations and Trends in Machine Learning, Boston-Delft, 2014)
8. K-J Cho, Y-N Xu, J-G Chung, in *IEEE Workshop on Signal Processing Systems*. Hardware efficient QR decomposition for GDFE (IEEE, Shanghai, China, 2007), pp. 412–417
9. X Wang, M Leeser, A truly two-dimensional systolic array FPGA implementation of QR decomposition. ACM Trans. Embed. Comput. Syst. **9**(1), 3–1317 (2009)
10. A Buttari, J Langou, J Kurzak, J Dongarra, in *Proc. of the 7th International Conference on Parallel Processing and Applied Mathematics*. Parallel tiled QR factorization for multicore architectures (Springer, Berlin, Heidelberg, 2008), pp. 639–648
11. J Demmel, L Grigori, MF Hoemmen, J Langou, Communication-optimal parallel and sequential QR and LU factorizations (2008). Technical report, no. UCB/EECS-2008-89, EECS Department, University of California, Berkeley
12. F Song, H Ltaief, B Hadri, J Dongarra, in *International Conference for High Performance Computing, Networking, Storage and Analysis*. Scalable tile communication-avoiding QR factorization on multicore cluster systems (IEEE Computer Society, Washington, DC, USA, 2010), pp. 1–11
13. M Shabany, D Patel, PG Gulak, A low-latency low-power QR-decomposition ASIC implementation in 0.13μm CMOS. IEEE Trans. Circ. Syst. I. **60**(2), 327–340 (2013)
14. A Nayak, I Stojmenović, *Wireless Sensor and Actuator Networks: Algorithms and Protocols for Scalable Coordination and Data Communication*. (Wiley, Hoboken, NJ, 2010)
15. H Straková, WN Gansterer, T Zemen, in *Proc. of the 9th International Conference on Parallel Processing and Applied Mathematics, Part I. Lecture Notes in Computer Science*. Distributed QR factorization based on randomized algorithms, vol. 7203 (Springer Berlin Heidelberg, Berlin, Heidelberg, 2012), pp. 235–244
16. H Straková, Truly distributed approaches to orthogonalization and orthogonal iteration on the basis of gossip algorithms (2013). PhD thesis, University of Vienna

17. O Slučiak, M Rupp, in *Proc. of the 36th IEEE International Conference on Acoustics, Speech and Signal Processing (ICASSP)*. Reaching consensus in asynchronous WSNs: algebraic approach, (Prague, 2011), pp. 3300–3303. Chap. Acoustics, Speech and Signal Processing (ICASSP), 2011
18. O Slučiak, M Rupp, in *Proc. of Statistical Sig. Proc. Workshop (SSP)*. Almost sure convergence of consensus algorithms by relaxed projection mappings (IEEE, Ann Arbor, MI, USA, 2012), pp. 632–635
19. F Sivrikaya, B Yener, Time synchronization in sensor networks: a survey. IEEE Netw. Mag. Special Issues Ad Hoc Netw. Data Commun. Topol. Control. **18**(4), 45–50 (2004)
20. R Olfati-Saber, JA Fax, RM Murray, Consensus and cooperation in networked multi-agent systems. Proc. IEEE. **95**(1), 215–233 (2007)
21. L Xiao, S Boyd, Fast linear iterations for distributed averaging. Syst. Control Lett. **53**, 65–78 (2004)
22. L Xiao, S Boyd, S Lall, in *Proc. ACM/IEEE IPSN–05*. A scheme for robust distributed sensor fusion based on average consensus (IEEE, Los Angeles, USA, 2005), pp. 63–70
23. LN Trefethen, D Bau III, *Numerical Linear Algebra*. (SIAM: Society for Industrial and Applied Mathematics, Philadelphia, 1997), p. 373
24. D Kempe, A Dobra, J Gehrke, in *Foundations of Computer Science, 2003. Proceedings. 44th Annual IEEE Symposium on*. Gossip-based computation of aggregate information, (2003), pp. 482–491. ISSN:0272-5428, doi:10.1109/SFCS.2003.1238221
25. H Straková, WN Gansterer, in *21st Euromicro Int. Conf. on Parallel, Distributed, and Network-Based Processing (PDP)*. A distributed eigensolver for loosely coupled networks (IEEE, Belfast, UK, 2013), pp. 51–57
26. O Slučiak, M Rupp, Network size estimation using distributed orthogonalization. IEEE Sig. Proc. Lett. **20**(4), 347–350 (2013)
27. P Braca, S Marano, V Matta, in *Proc. Int. Conf. Inf. Fusion (FUSION 2008)*. Running consensus in wireless sensor networks (IEEE, Cologne, Germany, 2008), pp. 152–157
28. W Ren, in *Proc. of the 2007 American Control Conference*. Consensus seeking in multi-vehicle systems with a time-varying reference state (IEEE, New York, NY, 2007), pp. 717–722
29. V Schwarz, C Novak, G Matz, in *Proc. 43rd Asilomar Conf. on Sig., Syst., Comp*. Broadcast-based dynamic consensus propagation in wireless sensor networks (IEEE, Pacific Grove, CA, 2009), pp. 255–259
30. M Zhu, S Martínez, Discrete-time dynamic average consensus. Automatica. **46**(2), 322–329 (2010)
31. O Slučiak, O Hlinka, M Rupp, F Hlawatsch, PM Djurić, in *Rec. of the 45th Asilomar Conf. on Signals, Systems, and Computers*. Sequential likelihood consensus and its application to distributed particle filtering with reduced communications and latency (IEEE, Pacific Grove, CA, 2011), pp. 1766–1770
32. O Slučiak, H Straková, M Rupp, WN Gansterer, in *Rec. of the 46th Asilomar Conf. on Signals, Systems, and Computers*. Distributed Gram-Schmidt orthogonalization based on dynamic consensus (IEEE, Pacific Grove, CA, 2012), pp. 1207–1211
33. P Braca, S Marano, V Matta, AH Sayed, in *Proc. of the 39th IEEE International Conference on Acoustics, Speech and Signal Processing (ICASSP)*. Large deviations analysis of adaptive distributed detection (IEEE, Florence, Italy, 2014), pp. 6153–6157
34. O Slučiak, Convergence analysis of distributed consensus algorithms (2013). PhD thesis, TU Vienna
35. B Efron, RJ Tibshirani, *An Introduction to the Bootstrap*. (Chapman & Hall/CRC Monographs on Statistics & Applied Probability 57, London, UK, 1994)
36. P Rost, G Fettweis, in *GLOBECOM Workshops, 2010 IEEE*. On the transmission-computation-energy tradeoff in wireless and fixed networks (IEEE, Miami, FL, 2010), pp. 1394–1399
37. R Shorey, A Ananda, MC Chan, WT Ooi, *Mobile, Wireless, and Sensor Networks: Technology, Applications, and Future Directions*. (Wiley, Hoboken, NJ, 2006)
38. B Johansson, On distributed optimization in networked systems (2008). PhD thesis, KTH, Stockholm
39. I Matei, JS Baras, Performance evaluation of the consensus-based distributed subgradient method under random communication topologies. IEEE J. Sel. Top. Signal Process. **5**(4), 754–771 (2011)
40. L Benini, GD Micheli, Networks on chips: a new SoC paradigm. IEEE Comput. **35**(1), 70–78 (2002)

5

Signal processing techniques for seat belt microphone arrays

Vasudev Kandade Rajan[1*], Mohamed Krini[2†], Klaus Rodemer[2] and Gerhard Schmidt[1†]

Abstract

Microphones integrated on a seat belt are an interesting alternative to conventional sensor positions used for hands-free telephony or speech dialog systems in automobile environments. In the setup presented in this contribution, the seat belt consists of three microphones which usually lay around the shoulder and chest of a sitting passenger. The main benefit of belt microphones is the small distance from the talker's mouth to the sensor. As a consequence, an improved signal quality in terms of a better signal-to-noise ratio (SNR) compared to other sensor positions, e.g., at the rear view mirror, the steering wheel, or the center console, can be achieved. However, the belt microphone arrangement varies considerably due to movements of the passenger and depends on the size of the passenger. Furthermore, additional noise sources arise for seat belt microphones: they can easily be touched, e.g., by clothes, or might be in the path of an air-stream from the automotive ventilation system. This contribution presents several robust signal enhancement algorithms designed for belt microphones in multi-seat scenarios. The belt microphone with the highest SNR (usually closest to the speaker's mouth) is selected for speech signal enhancement. Further improvements can be achieved if all belt microphone signals are combined to a single output signal. The proposed signal enhancement system for belt microphones includes a robust echo cancelation scheme, three different microphone combining approaches, a sophisticated noise estimation scheme to track stationary as well as non-stationary noise, and a speech mixer to combine the signals from each seat belt to a single channel output in a multi-seat scenario.

Keywords: Seat belt microphones, Microphone arrays, Speech enhancement, Moving microphones

1 Introduction

If speech-based services such as hands-free telephony [1, 2], in-car communication [3, 4], or voice control [5] should be used in cars, microphones that convert the acoustic signals into electric counterparts are required. In order to capture the speech signals of the passengers in an optimal way, the question on the placement of the microphones is natural. Here, several competing interests arise. Engineers who are responsible for optimizing the performance of voice control systems might favor a small distance between the microphone and the mouth of the speaker. This might lead to solutions that are not preferred by designers and final customers (being the second and third group in that process).

*Correspondence: vakr@tf.uni-kiel.de
†Equal contributors
[1] Digital Signal Processing and System Theory, University of Kiel, Kaiserstrasse 2, Kiel, Germany
Full list of author information is available at the end of the article

Currently, several positions have been found as a compromise among the three groups: automotive microphones are placed in the roof of the car (e.g., BMW), in the rear-view mirror (e.g., Daimler), in the overhead console (e.g., Audi), or on the steering wheel (e.g., Porsche) to mention just a few positions. When selecting those places, usually the expected average noise and speech levels are taken into account.

While the speech level is mainly a function of the distance between the talker's mouths and the microphones, the noise level depends on a lot of factors such as the noise distribution in the passenger compartment. In addition, it is evaluated if the position allows for simple wiring and if the microphone can be used for more than one passenger. Some systems also like to exploit spatial filtering such as beamforming [6] or diversity-based approaches [7]. Then, it must be ensured that more than one microphone can be mounted.

Recently, a new interesting microphone position and type is available (see Fig. 1): microphones that are

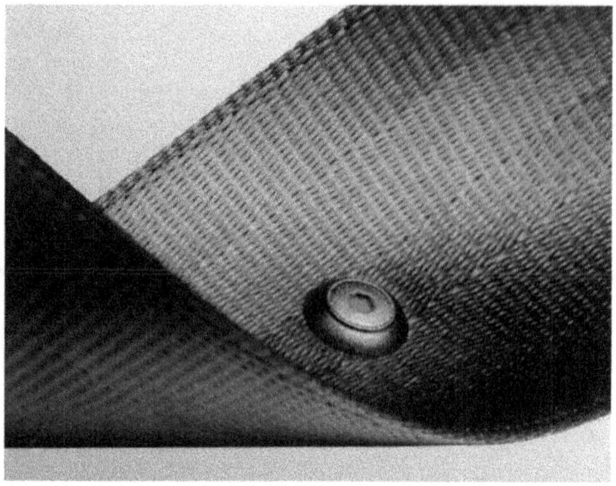

Fig. 1 Belt microphone (with permission from [8])

integrated into the seat belt [8]. From here on, such microphones will shortly be called as *belt microphones*. Details about belt microphones will be presented in the next chapter.

2 Belt microphones

In the following, we will view the belt microphones as an array consisting of three sensors. All of them are omnidirectional microphones, spaced 160 mm apart, fixed on one seat belt. Each microphone is approximately 10 mm in diameter, and all wiring needed for voltage supply and signal transport is weaved into the seat belts so that it appears invisible. The microphones are able to receive signals between 100 and 8500 Hz at a maximum sound pressure level of 115 dB. Figure 2 shows an example of a seat belt microphone system installed in a vehicle.

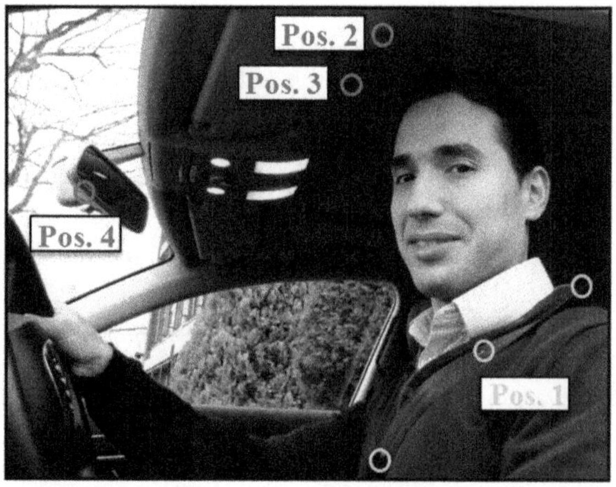

Fig. 2 Belt microphones (*Pos. 1*) and microphones positioned at the roof and at the mirror (*Pos. 2–4*)

The region of placement of these microphones is roughly between the shoulder and the center of the upper body of a sitting passenger. The exact position can vary considerably depending on the size of the passenger and also the seat position. However, due to the arrangement of the three microphones, at least one is usually close to the speaker's mouth. It is important to note that the entire geometry is likely to change due to movements of the passenger. The array can be of linear type with all microphones in one line, but could also be spread on a convex curve.

In Fig. 3, a belt microphone system is compared with three hands-free microphones placed at different positions (see Fig. 2) in terms of the average signal-to-noise ratio (SNR) for driving speeds between 120 and 160 km/h.

The distances from different microphone positions to the mouth are 20–27 cm (Pos. 1), 28 cm (Pos. 2/3), and 58 cm (Pos. 4). All microphones are calibrated to have the same speech power at standstill. This comparison shows that at higher frequencies, the behavior of all microphones is almost similar, whereas at low and medium frequencies, the belt microphone outperforms conventional hands-free microphones. An improvement of up to 6–10 dB in SNR can be achieved.

Even if belt microphones have a strong potential to improve the speech acquisition in automotive environments, we face several challenges with this microphone type. We will highlight the three major ones in the following paragraphs:

- **Continuously changing echo paths**
  An undesired characteristic of belt microphones is their changing position. Every time the driver or passenger moves his/her body, the positions of the microphones are changed. This is a recurring phenomenon during the course of normal driving. It is not an easy task for adaptive signal processing schemes such as echo cancelation filters to cope up with this movement. Every time the position is changed, the "true" frequency response is different from the estimated one which results in echo bursts. The sudden appearance of echoes can be quite unpleasant for the remote communication partner and can occur several times during a conversation. This serious restriction must be handled with robust and reliable detection and suppression schemes. It motivates the (re-) investigation of so-called room change detectors and shadow filters approaches.
- **Array processing**
  Another challenge resulting from the varying microphone positions is to process them as an array. One promising algorithm to this problem is the so-called adaptive microphone selection [9]. The

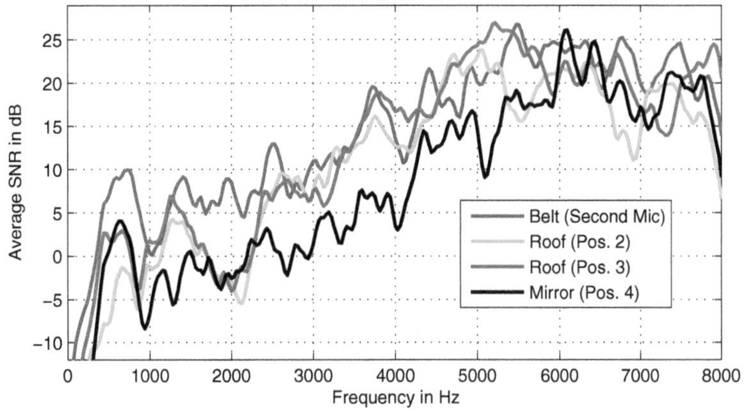

Fig. 3 SNR measured at different microphone positions

algorithm applies a sensor switching based on the corresponding SNR.
However, for optimal usage of the array structure, all microphone signals should be processed and utilized simultaneously. This motivates the investigation of robust adaptive beamforming schemes.

- **Additional noise sources**

  An additional noise source arises for seat belt microphones because they are placed directly at the passenger's body. They might be touched accidentally by hand or rubbed by clothes such as ties, zippers of a jacket. Ventilation systems can severely degrade the signal quality when the air-stream is directed towards the passenger. Therefore, more sophisticated noise estimation schemes that are also able to track non-stationary noise sources are of great interest.

3 Structure of the contribution and notation

The authors have organized this article around the signal enhancement scheme designed for belt microphones in a multi-seat scenario as shown in Fig 4. All signal processing solutions involving various tasks like echo cancelation, speaker localization, signal equalization and delay alignment, microphone combination, noise estimation, residual echo and noise suppression, and speech mixer will be described in the following sections. Section 4.1 introduces a robust echo cancelation scheme to solve the major challenge of continuously changing echo paths with belt microphones. A reliable and robust localization of the moving signal source (passenger) will be presented in Section 4.2. The equalization and alignment methods for effectively combining the belt microphone signals for each seat will be illustrated in Section 4.3. Three different methods for combining belt microphones on each seat will be presented and their performance will be compared to each other in Section 4.4. A sophisticated low computational complexity noise estimation method which is able to track stationary as well as non-stationary noise will be discussed in Section 4.5. This is followed by Section 4.6, in which the residual echo and noise suppression scheme for attenuating different kinds of interferences at the output of the combiner will be considered. Details of a speech mixer that combines the different belt microphones from various seats to a single output will be illustrated in Section 4.7. Finally, the contribution concludes with a summary and an outlook in Sections 5 and 6, respectively.

All presented algorithms designed for belt microphones operate in the short-term frequency domain [10]. Thus, the entire structure is embedded into *analysis* and *synthesis filter banks*. For some applications, e.g., in-car communication (ICC) systems, special restrictions such as a low delay have to be fulfilled by the filter banks [11, 12].

In the following, we will use a sample rate $f_s = 16$ kHz, a frame shift of $r = 128$ samples, and a fast Fourier transform (FFT) order of $N_{FFT} = 512$ where the samples are weighted with a Hann window. As an example, the output of the analysis filter bank of the belt microphone signal contains the corresponding short-term spectra of the $M = 3$ microphone signals $Y_l^{(p)}(\mu, k)$, where the index $l \in \{0, \ldots, M-1\}$ is the microphone index, $(p) \in \{0, \ldots, P-1\}$ indicates the seat index, $\mu \in \{0, 1, \ldots, N_{FFT}-1\}$ is the subband, and k is the frame index. Since the input signals are assumed to be real, it is sufficient to store and process only the first $N_{Sbb} = N_{FFT}/2 + 1$ frequency supporting points. For better readability, the seat index (p) and the microphone index l are dropped in most of the following sections. However, when we discuss beamforming and how the

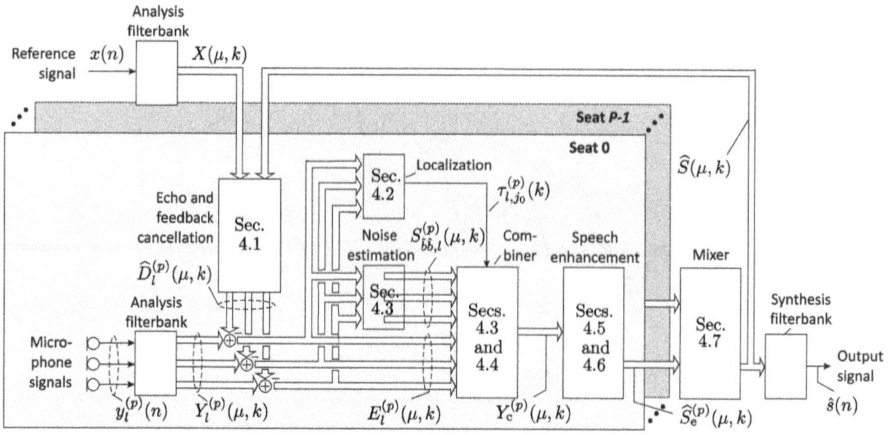

Fig. 4 Overview of the proposed signal enhancement system for processing belt microphones. The numbers in the frames refer to the related sections of this article

enhanced spectra of the individual seats can be combined, the indices will reappear.

4 Signal processing techniques for belt microphones

In the following subsections, the signal enhancement scheme designed for belt microphones in a multi-seat scenario will be described in detail.

4.1 Belt microphones used in echo path estimation

Belt microphones, like other automotive microphones, are often used for communication with a remote person. The setup is such that the remote person's voice is played back locally inside the automobile cabin which results in the well-understood problem of acoustic echoes [13]. The signals recorded by the belt microphones consist of these undesired echo components (besides the desired speech signals). As described in the previous section, the major challenge in using belt microphones for such a scenario is the continuously changing echo path. Along with the need for a robustly controlled adaptive filter, a method to handle the sudden changes in echo path is necessary. The task of the echo canceler is to produce a signal which is an estimate of the true echo signal.

4.1.1 Design of the echo canceler

The echo canceler is designed to operate in the subband domain as shown in Fig. 4. This subband domain operation offers an advantage of keeping the computational load low. In a multi-channel scenario such as here with at least three microphones per seat belt along with multiple seats, the total number of cancelation filters required are dependent on the number of loudspeakers present in the cabin as well. The number of cancelation filters required is given by number of loudspeakers × $(P \times M)$, where the loudspeakers are referred to as the reference channels and $(P \times M)$ is the total number of microphones for all seats. The echo path from each loudspeaker to a microphone is modeled as a finite impulse response (FIR) filter. The principle behind echo cancelation is first to estimate the total echoes at the microphone which is then subtracted from the microphone signal. For the sake of simplicity, a single channel setup is considered here although the method of cancelation remains the same for each filter. The belt microphone signal and its spectrum is represented by $y(n)$ and $Y(\mu, k)$, respectively. $Y(\mu, k)$ consists of the echo $D(\mu, k)$, the local speech component $S(\mu, k)$, and the background noise $B(\mu, k)$, respectively. Thus, the short-term spectrum of each belt microphone is given by

$$Y(\mu, k) = D(\mu, k) + S(\mu, k) + B(\mu, k). \quad (1)$$

The estimated echo spectrum by the echo canceler is represented by $\widehat{D}(\mu, k)$. This estimated spectrum is subtracted from the belt microphone spectrum to get the error spectrum given by

$$E(\mu, k) = Y(\mu, k) - \widehat{D}(\mu, k), \quad (2)$$

where the estimated echo is obtained by the convolution of the reference spectrum with the estimated multi-path transmission from the loudspeaker to the microphone

$$\widehat{D}(\mu, k) = \widehat{\boldsymbol{H}}^{\mathrm{H}}(\mu, k)\, \boldsymbol{X}(\mu, k), \quad (3)$$

with

$$\widehat{\boldsymbol{H}}(\mu, k) = \left[\widehat{H}(\mu, k, 0), \ldots, \widehat{H}(\mu, k, L-1)\right]^{\mathrm{T}}, \quad (4)$$

$$\boldsymbol{X}(\mu, k) = \left[X(\mu, k), \ldots X(\mu, k-L+1)\right]^{\mathrm{T}}, \quad (5)$$

where L is the length of the FIR filter. The echo path is estimated in terms of its frequency response between the loudspeaker and the seat belt microphones represented by $\widehat{\boldsymbol{H}}(\mu, k)$. The coefficients of the FIR filters are updated using the normalized least-mean square (NLMS) update rule [14]

$$\widehat{\boldsymbol{H}}(\mu,k+1)=\widehat{\boldsymbol{H}}(\mu,k)+\nu(\mu,k)\frac{\boldsymbol{X}(\mu,k)\,E^{*}(\mu,k)}{\|\boldsymbol{X}(\mu,k)\|^{2}}, \quad (6)$$

where $\nu(\mu,k)$ is the adaptive step-size control parameter. The step-size parameter in the NLMS equation controls the filter update and ranges between 0 and 1 [14]. This parameter is a critical aspect of modern day echo cancelers. It enables the system to

- Update the filters based on the reference spectral power distribution
- Inherit double-talk detection capabilities
- Protect the filters in high noise scenarios

A pseudo-optimal step-size control for the NLMS algorithm is derived in [15]. The result is given by

$$\nu_{\text{opt}}(\mu,k)=\frac{\mathrm{E}\left\{|E_{\text{u}}(\mu,k)|^{2}\right\}}{\mathrm{E}\left\{|E(\mu,k)|^{2}\right\}}, \quad (7)$$

where $E_{\text{u}}(\mu,k)$ is the undisturbed error spectrum

$$E_{\text{u}}(\mu,k)=E(\mu,k)-S(\mu,k)-B(\mu,k) \quad (8)$$

and E{...} is the expectation operator. For the application of belt microphone, the pseudo-optimal step-size is approximated by

$$\nu(\mu,k)=\frac{\overline{X}^{2}(\mu,k)\,\beta_{\text{coupl}}^{2}(\mu,k)}{\overline{E}^{2}(\mu,k)}, \quad (9)$$

where $\beta_{\text{coupl}}(\mu,k)$ is referred to as the coupling between the reference spectrum and the error spectrum. The magnitude spectra of the reference signal $X(\mu,k)$ and the error signal $E(\mu,k)$ are smoothed by first-order infinite impulse response (IIR) filtering:

$$\overline{E}(\mu,k) = \beta_0\,|E(\mu,k)|+(1-\beta_0)\overline{E}(\mu,k-1), \quad (10)$$

$$\overline{X}(\mu,k) = \beta_0\left|X\left(\mu,k-\delta_{\text{delay}}(k)\right)\right| +(1-\beta_0)\,\overline{X}(\mu,k-1). \quad (11)$$

In Eq. (11), the variable $\delta_{\text{delay}}(k)$ captures the delay of the impulse response between the loudspeaker and the belt microphone. This variable helps in choosing the value of the input along time that has the largest contribution to the echo. This delay is computed by averaging the largest value per subband in the estimated frequency response matrix. The coupling factors have two roles to play:

- To ensure the tracking of the ratio of the squared magnitudes of the reference and the error signal
- To indicate the instantaneous coupling between the two quantities

It is desired that the filters converge to the true frequency response as fast as possible. Given this, the coupling factors are computed and adjusted based on multiplicative constants. These time constants are responsible for the speed and accuracy trade-off of the tracking according to

$$\beta_{\text{coupl}}(\mu,k)=\begin{cases}\tilde{\beta}_{\text{coupl}}(\mu,k-1)\,\Delta_{\beta,\text{inc}}, \\ \text{if}\ \overline{X}(\mu,k)\,\beta_{\text{coupl}}(\mu,k-1)<\overline{E}(\mu,k), \\ \tilde{\beta}_{\text{coupl}}(\mu,k-1)\,\Delta_{\beta,\text{dec}}, \\ \text{else,}\end{cases} \quad (12)$$

where $\Delta_{\beta,\text{inc}}$ and $\Delta_{\beta,\text{dec}}$ are the increment and decrement time constants. The definition of $\tilde{\beta}_{\text{coupl}}(\mu,k)$ will be given in the next section. After sufficient excitation time, the filters converge to the desired frequency response.

4.1.2 *Accommodating the altering position of belt microphones*

The constantly altering position of the belt microphones results in an incorrectly estimated frequency response $\widehat{\boldsymbol{H}}(\mu,k)$ as compared to the true frequency response. The coupling factors absorb the change to a certain extent. For example the minor movement of the microphone caused due to breathing, slight movement of body, etc. is accounted by the multiplicative constants. Nevertheless, depending on the chosen time constants ($\Delta_{\beta\ \text{inc}}$, $\Delta_{\beta\ \text{dec}}$ in Eq. (12)), echo leakage can occur during the time of re-adaptation. In cases where the shift is more significant, it can freeze the system. This particular problem has been addressed by several authors earlier [16–18]. The problem of changes in the true echo paths causes the estimated echo path to be different from the current echo path. The altering position of the belt microphones is modeled here as a change in the echo path. A change in the system distance can be caused by other factors like a adjusting the volume of the playback of the reference signal, or delay change of the entire system could also lead to an increase in the system distance. Such behaviors are called "echo path change" or "room change" in the literature [19, 20]. Several algorithms are suggested for detecting echo path changes mostly in combination with double-talk detection methods [21, 22]. The approach proposed in [22] is based on correlation techniques in the time-domain, whereas in [21], a subband-based solution with two filters is presented. One filter is responsible for the single-talk echo cancelation and the second for the double-talk and echo path change detection.

4.1.3 *Coupling trigger to handle room changes*

After room changes, the re-adaptation of the estimated filter coefficients seems to be an appropriate action to converge to the new frequency response. The solution presented here is integrated into the adaptive step-size control approach presented in the previous section. The coupling factors, which adjust the filter update according to Eq. (9), are triggered. The factors responsible for the computation of the step-size are:

- The short-term spectrum of undisturbed error
- The short-term spectrum of the (measurable) disturbed error

The average short-term magnitude of the undisturbed error spectrum $E_{\mathrm{u}}(\mu, k)$ is computed by multiplying the smoothed magnitude of the reference spectrum with the coupling factors. This can be seen as the estimated ratio of the squared magnitudes of the reference signal and the error signal.

When the filters reach a certain convergence, the resulting step-size will be small due to converged values of the coupling factor and the error signal. At this stage, a change in the computed step-size can only be achieved by a change in the coupling factors. This will cause the computed step-size to be large (close to one) since the high value of the coupling factor will ensure that the numerator is greater than the denominator (see Eq. (9). The consistently large step-size will ensure that the filters converge to the new frequency response. The coupling factors need a certain time to reach the new convergence levels. During this time, as during normal operation of the system, the residual echo power is computed according to

$$\mathrm{E}\left\{|E_{\mathrm{u}}(\mu,k)|^2\right\} \approx \overline{X}^2(\mu,k)\,\beta^2_{\mathrm{coupl}}(\mu,k). \qquad (13)$$

The computed residual echo power is suppressed by the postfilter as described in Section 4.6. By triggering the coupling factors, echo artifacts caused, e.g., by movements of the belts, can be handled now. It is now clear that a forced change in the coupling factor can handle the room change which gives the filters and the NLMS algorithm time to adapt to the new frequency response without *freezing* the system. The question now is to detect such events. During remote-side single talk, the short-term power of the error spectrum $E(\mu, k)$ will suddenly increase when the belt microphones alter their positions. This occurs as the estimated filter coefficients are incorrect and the convolution with the reference signal does not lead to the amount of echo that is actually present in the belt microphone signal.

An ideal solution for the recovering from the room change is to have a parallel set of filters that contain the coefficients of the new frequency response. Since this is hard to achieve, filters that indicate in this direction are useful. Such schemes can be realized with a second set of filters, in parallel to the main filters, referred to as *shadow filters* [23, 24]. The shadow filters are updated with the same NLMS update rule as for the main filters, but the step-size parameter is always set to 1 whenever there is activity in the reference signal. This ensures that the shadow filters converge very quickly to the true frequency response but with the problem of very quick divergence.

To reduce the overall computational load of the system, shadow filters are not placed in parallel to every subband but only a few chosen subbands. The index μ_{sh} refers to the shadow filter subbands which is $\mu_{\mathrm{sh}} \subset \mu$. Since the shadow filters are always updated with step-size 1, they adapt much faster than the main filters. During the time of change in the position of the belt microphones, the power of the error signal produced by the shadow filters is much lower than the power of the error of the main filters. It is exactly with this error power difference that a room change can be detected:

$$\tilde{\beta}_{\mathrm{coupl}}(\mu,k) = \begin{cases} \frac{\overline{E}(\mu,k)}{\overline{X}(\mu,k)}, \\ \quad \text{if } \overline{E}_{\mathrm{main}}(k) > T_{\mathrm{change}}\,\overline{E}_{\mathrm{sh}}(k), \\ \beta_{\mathrm{coupl}}(\mu,k), \\ \quad \text{else,} \end{cases} \qquad (14)$$

with

$$\overline{E}_{\mathrm{sh}}(k) = \sum_{\mu_{\mathrm{sh}}=0}^{N_{\mathrm{Sbb,sh}}-1} |E_{\mathrm{sh}}(\mu_{\mathrm{sh}},k)|^2, \qquad (15)$$

$$\overline{E}_{\mathrm{main}}(k) = \sum_{\mu_{\mathrm{sh}}=0}^{N_{\mathrm{Sbb,sh}}-1} |E(\mu_{\mathrm{sh}},k)|^2. \qquad (16)$$

$N_{\mathrm{Sbb,sh}}$ is the total number of subbands for which shadow filters have been placed. $E_{\mathrm{sh}}(\mu_{\mathrm{sh}}, k)$ is the error signal obtained from the shadow filters similar to the main filters. During normal updates, the shadow filters will diverge because of a lack of optimum control. During this time, the error power of the main filters is lower than the error power of the shadow filters and is detected according to

$$\overline{E}_{\mathrm{sh}}(k) > T_{\mathrm{div}}\,\overline{E}_{\mathrm{main}}(k), \qquad (17)$$

where T_{div} is the threshold at which the divergence of the shadow filters is detected. When this occurs, the coefficients from the main filter are copied to the shadow filters.

4.1.4 Results

The echo canceler presented before has been tested in various scenarios. The test setup consisted of one reference signal originating from the phone which is played back via the loudspeakers in the car with engines turned on. This signal is picked up as an echo by the belt microphones. The echo canceler filter length was set to about 100 ms. The entire echo canceler was tuned for performance in terms of smoothing constants, multiplicative constants of the coupling factors, etc.

The first scenario for testing the echo canceler is a regular speech activity from both the remote side and the local side in the following order: a remote-side single talk, a local-side single-talk, and a double-talk. The test determines the amount of echo suppression by the echo canceler alone without the postfilter applied to suppress the residual echo. The plots in Fig. 5 compare the microphone signal spectrogram of the first belt microphone versus the corresponding error signal. The time spans of each activity situation are shown encircled along with the echo canceled regions. A cancelation of between −20 and −30 dB is achieved during the remote-side single-talk situation. During the local-side-only speech-activity, the speech is completely retained as seen clearly in the spectrograms. During the double-talk situation, one of the important factors is that the echo cancelation filters do not diverge. Also, when postfilter is applied, the conversation must be as transparent as possible. Transparent conversation here means the retention of the local speech components against the suppression of the echo components. An overview of the results of some important tests performed under the ITU tests [25] is shown through a quality pie in Fig. 6. All tests except the distortion RCV and distortion SND belong to the echo canceler. The green color indicates that the ITU tests have passed, while the yellow area indicates that the test has failed. The red area indicates the area to be covered in order to pass the test. The most important tests are the double talk-tests (preceding with DT-) which have all passed with the highest class of class 1. More details about the test can be found in the ITU recommendation document [25].

The second test scenario focuses on the room-change detection. For this test, the microphone signal was simulated in such a way that after about 9.5 s time, the impulse response is changed to another impulse response, both belonging to typical belt microphone positions. Figure 7 shows the microphone signal and the point at which the room change was applied. The second plot shows the error signal in which the echo reappears after the room change. The third plot is the trigger signal which indicates that the room change condition is met according to Eq. (14). Finally, the reaction of the coupling factor $\beta_{\text{coupl}}(\mu, k)$ is seen which is reset to about 0 dB after each trigger. The coupling factor is plotted for subband $\mu = 29$, but the trigger is applied to all subbands. The tunable threshold parameter T_{change} for this scenario was set at 25 dB. This parameter will determine the reaction time of the trigger to the room change. During the time after the room change and before the coupling trigger, there will be echo blips which would be suppressed by the postfilter through the residual echo. The power of the echo blips is dependent mainly on the distance between the adapted frequency response and the changed frequency response. During subjective tests, it has been seen that these blips mostly go unnoticed by the remote listener. During initial adaptation and re-adaptation after a room change, there will be many re-triggers because the filters are still converging to the changed frequency response. This is also seen in the third and the fourth plots where after the first trigger, there are four follow-up triggers which again reset the coupling factors. This results in a slightly higher residual echo power. This can be improved by averaging the trigger indicator over time, holding the room-change detection for a while after the first trigger.

4.2 Localization

Based on the array geometry of the three microphones on each seat belt, the microphone signals can be combined with a beamformer as described in Section 4.4. Because

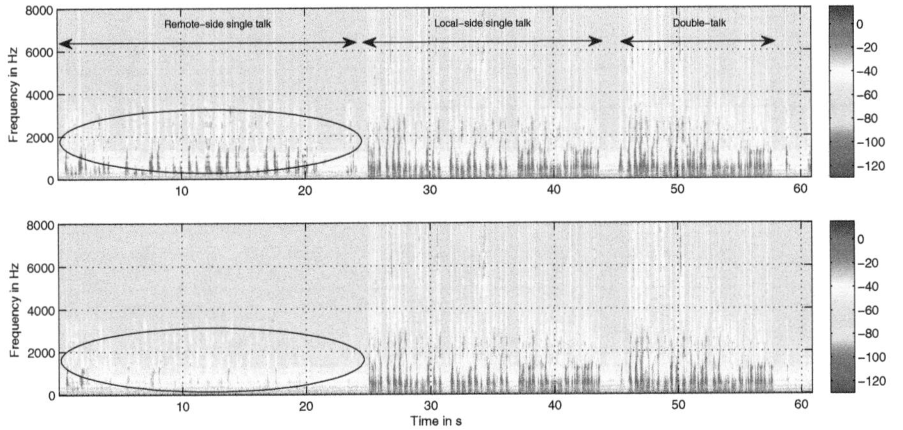

Fig. 5 Spectrogram comparison of the first microphone of the belt (*top*) with the echo canceled error signal (*bottom*)

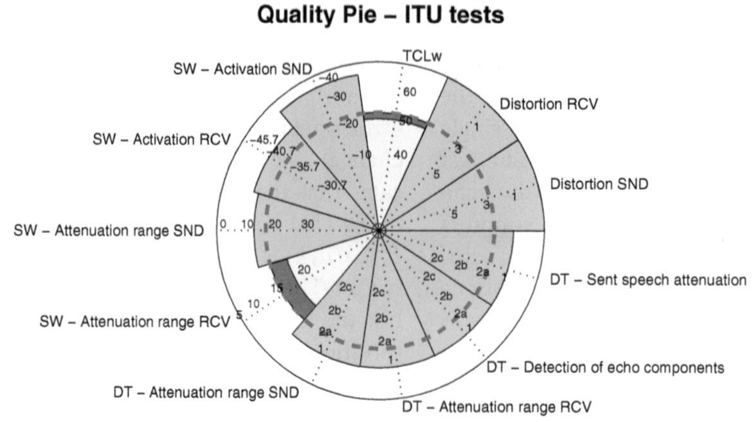

Fig. 6 Results overview for ITU tests

of the highly varying geometry of the array and changing position of the signal source, it is nearly impossible to generate any a priori knowledge about the direction of the beamformer. Therefore, a reliable and robust localization of the signal source has to be applied. To estimate the delays $\tau_{l,j}(k)$ in samples between the microphones and thereby the direction of the beamformer, a *generalized cross correlation* (GCC) function is utilized as presented in [26]. Here, a pairwise instantaneous *cross power spectral density* (CPSD) $\tilde{S}_{e_l,e_j}(\mu,k) = E_l(\mu,k)\,E_j^*(\mu,k)$ between the error spectra is determined for $l \neq j$. The CPSD is smoothed to avoid the jumps and variations seen on the instantaneous spectra through a first-order IIR filter given by[1]

$$\overline{S}_{e_l,e_j}(\mu,k) = \alpha_{\mathrm{E}}\,\tilde{S}_{e_l,e_j}(\mu,k) + (1-\alpha_{\mathrm{E}})\,\overline{S}_{e_l,e_j}(\mu,k-1), \tag{18}$$

where the smoothing constant α_{E} is chosen to be around 0.8 (240 dB/s). The delay is computed by the argument that maximizes the inverse Fourier transform of that quantity. Before transforming it, a weighting can be applied. We utilized here the so-called phase transformation (PHAT) [27] leading to the following normalized cross correlation:

$$s_{e_l,e_j}(\kappa,k) = \frac{1}{N_{\mathrm{FFT}}}\sum_{\mu=0}^{N_{\mathrm{FFT}}-1}\frac{\overline{S}_{e_l,e_j}(\mu,k)}{\left|\overline{S}_{e_l,e_j}(\mu,k)\right|}\,e^{j\frac{2\pi\mu}{N_{\mathrm{FFT}}}\kappa}. \tag{19}$$

The time-domain transformed samples are indexed by κ. Optionally, a lower FFT size can be used to reduce the computational complexity by dropping bins above, e.g., 3500 Hz. The robustness can be improved by setting the lowest bins to zero before applying the transform. The maximum distance between the belt microphones is 320 mm, and hence, the delay is limited to this distance given by $\tau_{\max}$. From the time-domain transformed frame,

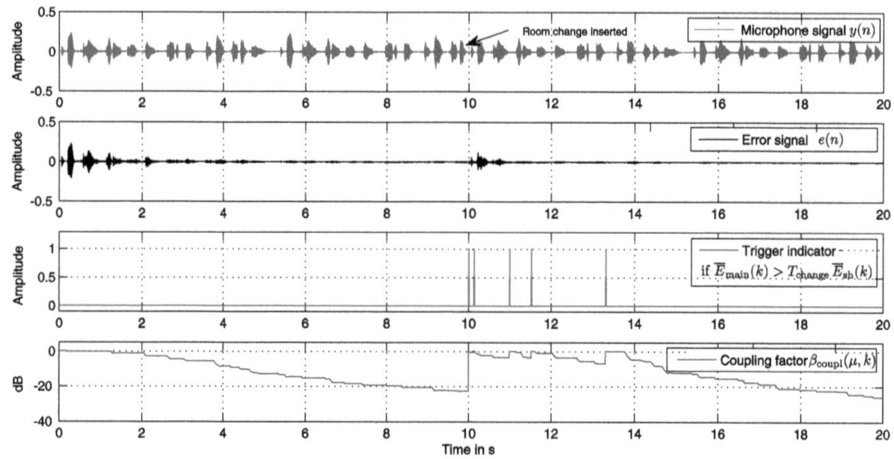

Fig. 7 Plots showing triggering of the coupling factor (shown for subband around 1 kHz) due to a room change detected by the trigger indicator. The room change was inserted after about 9.5 s as shown in the microphone signal

the delay $\tau_{l,j}(k)$ is computed by finding the argument κ that maximizes the cross correlation function $s_{e_l,e_j}(\kappa,k)$:

$$\tau_{l,j}(k) = \underset{-\tau_{\max}<\kappa<\tau_{\max}}{\operatorname{argmax}} \left\{ s_{e_l,e_j}(\kappa,k) \right\}. \quad (20)$$

4.3 Signal equalization and delay alignment

The nature of the belt microphones is such that they usually pickup slightly varied ambient noise even if they are in the same environment. To achieve good combination performance, it is important to correct this by equalizing the noise for all the microphones. This is achieved by using a simple multiplicative constant based on the noise PSD estimation for each microphone given by

$$\widehat{B}_l(\mu,k) = \begin{cases} \delta_{\text{inc}}\,\widehat{B}_l(\mu,k-1), & \text{if } \overline{E}_l(\mu,k) > \widehat{B}_l(\mu,k-1), \\ \delta_{\text{dec}}\,\widehat{B}_l(\mu,k-1), & \text{else}, \end{cases} \quad (21)$$

where $\widehat{B}_l(\mu,k)$ is the estimated magnitude spectrum of background noise for each microphone, δ_{inc} is the incremental constant, and δ_{dec} is the decremental constant, with $0 \ll \delta_{\text{dec}} < 1 < \delta_{\text{inc}}$. $\overline{E}_l(\mu,k)$ is a smoothed version of the magnitude of the spectrum $E_l(\mu,k)$ as opposed to a complex smoothed spectra obtained similarly as shown in Eq. (18). A slowly varying equalization factor $K_l(\mu,k)$ per microphone is computed and tracked based on the average background noise $\widehat{B}_{\text{avg}}(\mu,k) = 1/M \sum_{l=0}^{M-1} \widehat{B}_l(\mu,k)$ of all the three microphones given by

$$K_l(\mu,k) = \begin{cases} \delta_{\text{gain-inc}}\,K_l(\mu,k-1), & \text{if } \widehat{B}_{\text{avg}}(\mu,k) > \widehat{B}_l(\mu,k), \\ \delta_{\text{gain-dec}}\,K_l(\mu,k-1), & \text{else}. \end{cases} \quad (22)$$

The equalization factor, which is bounded by a maximum and a minimum value for safety reasons, is applied to the error spectra along with the estimated delay to obtain the pre-processed spectra on which the beamforming technique is applied. This is performed by

$$\widetilde{E}_l(\mu,k) = K_l(\mu,k)\,E_l(\mu,k)\,e^{-j\frac{2\pi\mu}{N_{\text{FFT}}}\tau_{l,j_0}(k)}. \quad (23)$$

Usually, the center microphone is used as a (delay) reference, meaning that we use $j_0 = 1$ in Eq. (23).

4.4 Combining belt microphones

The microphone combination computes one signal for each passenger from a subset of all microphones. From the arrangement of $M = 3$ microphones positioned on a seat belt, that microphone can be selected which has the best overall signal quality in terms of high SNR. Further improvements can be achieved if all microphone signals are combined to a single output signal. In the following subsections, three different combining methods are presented and compared to each other in terms of SNR and signal-to-interference ratio (SIR).

4.4.1 *Max-SNR approach*

A straightforward and robust method is to use only the microphone with the best signal quality that is measured based on instantaneous SNR:

$$\Gamma_l(\mu,k) = \frac{|E_l(\mu,k)|^2}{\left|\widehat{B}_l(\mu,k)\right|^2}. \quad (24)$$

This measure is smoothed over time and also decreased if the microphone signal suffers frequently from degradations by instationary distortions. The smoothed SNR $\overline{\Gamma}_l(\mu,k)$ is only updated during local speech activity of pth passenger and while no activity on the reference channel and from the neighboring speaker's is detected. The signal combination is done in two stages:

1. Select the microphone $i \in \{0,\ldots,M-1\}$ with the best quality measure:

   $$\overline{\Gamma}_i(k) = \frac{1}{N_{\text{FFT}}} \sum_{\mu=0}^{N_{\text{FFT}}-1} \overline{\Gamma}_i(\mu,k). \quad (25)$$

   In order to avoid frequent switching in case the measures are close together, a hysteresis is introduced.
2. If instationary distortions have been detected in the microphone that is currently selected, the disturbed frequency bins are replaced by those of signal with the next best quality. In case that all signals are distorted, comfort noise is injected.

The estimates of the time delays between microphones can also be exploited and combined with the smoothed SNR for enhanced microphone selection. Details can be found, e.g., in [28].

4.4.2 *SNR-based weighting*

For combining the microphone signals to one output signal, a modified filter and sum beamformer is used with an SNR-based signal weighting. In the literature, e.g., in [7, 29], SNR-based beamforming is widely presented. The SNR-based weighting beamformer is a modified filter-and-sum beamformer which means that each input to the beamformer will be filtered and the sum of all the filtered inputs forms the output of the beamformer. In the context of this paper, the inputs to the beamformer are the three equalized and delay-aligned belt microphone spectra. This is shown in Eq. (26)

$$Y_{\text{fb}}(\mu,k) = \sum_{l=0}^{M-1} G_l(\mu,k)\,\widetilde{E}_l(\mu,k). \quad (26)$$

The filter weights $G_l(\mu,k)$ are a function of the normalized SNR computed per subband for the respective microphone. The SNR per subband $\Gamma_l(\mu,k)$ is computed according to Eq. (24). The normalized SNR is computed by dividing the subband SNR by the sum of all the subband SNRs of three microphones given by

$$\widetilde{\Gamma}_l(\mu,k) = \frac{\Gamma_l(\mu,k)}{\sum\limits_{j=0}^{M-1} \Gamma_j(\mu,k)}. \tag{27}$$

Since the short-term SNR of the individual microphone signals is highly varying, the filter function is computed as a smoothed version of the normalized SNRs. In addition, the filter function should be updated only during speech activity. The smoothing is again performed by an IIR filter with the smoothing constant that is switched between a constant and 0 to ensure that the previous values are kept during non-speech frames. This is captured in Eqs. (28) and (29):

$$G_l(\mu,k) = [1-\alpha_l(k)]\, G_l(\mu,k-1) + \alpha_l(k)\, \widetilde{\Gamma}_l(\mu,k), \tag{28}$$

where

$$\alpha_l(k) = \begin{cases} \alpha_{\mathrm{SNR}}, & \text{if } \frac{1}{N_{\mathrm{FFT}}} \sum\limits_{\mu=0}^{N_{\mathrm{FFT}}-1} \overline{\Gamma}_l(\mu,k) > T_{\mathrm{SNR}}, \\ 0, & \text{else,} \end{cases} \tag{29}$$

where α_{SNR} is the smoothing constant and T_{SNR} is the SNR threshold parameter for voice activity detection.

4.4.3 Adaptive beamformer

In the following, we will describe details about all components that are necessary to perform a robust beamforming approach with belt microphones. Before proceeding with combining the three microphone spectra using an adaptive beamformer based on the *generalized sidelobe canceler* [30], they are pre-processed with two blocks, namely the *delay alignment* and *equalization*. In addition, a *localization* as shown in Fig. 8 is computed. The delay alignment is performed in order to compensate the elapsed time between the mouth of the talking passenger and the individual microphones. Localization and equalization are realized as described in Sections 4.2 and 4.3.

The SNR-weighted beamformer presented in the previous section referred to as the *first beamformer* (see Fig. 8) is used as a precursor to the adaptive blocking matrix and the interference canceler presented in the following section.

Adaptive blocking matrix: The adaptive blocking matrix (ABM) generates a noise reference for the interference canceler (IC) as shown in Fig. 8. A fixed blocking matrix [31], which subtracts adjacent equalized and time-aligned microphone subband signals, is not suitable for belt microphones due to the strong microphone SNR variations. The ABM subtracts adaptively filtered versions of the first beamformer output $Y_{\mathrm{fb}}(\mu,k)$ from each channel input $\widetilde{E}_l(\mu,k)$ and provides the noise reference signals $U_l(\mu,k)$ for the IC with $l \in \{0,\ldots,M-1\}$. The SNR differences between belt microphones and the mismatch of the steering direction can be compensated. Filters of the blocking matrix are adapted using the NLMS algorithm:

$$\boldsymbol{V}_l(\mu,k+1) = \boldsymbol{V}_l(\mu,k) + \beta_{\mathrm{bm}}(\mu,k)\, \frac{\boldsymbol{Y}_{\mathrm{fb}}(\mu,k)\, U_l^*(\mu,k)}{\|\boldsymbol{Y}_{\mathrm{fb}}(\mu,k)\|^2}, \tag{30}$$

where

$$\boldsymbol{V}_l(\mu,k) = [V_l(\mu,k,0),\ldots,V_l(\mu,k,N_{\mathrm{bm}}-1)]^{\mathrm{T}} \tag{31}$$

denote the subband filter coefficients and N_{bm} is the filter length. The vector

$$\boldsymbol{Y}_{\mathrm{fb}}(\mu,k) = [Y_{\mathrm{fb}}(\mu,k),\ldots,Y_{\mathrm{fb}}(\mu,k-N_{\mathrm{bm}}+1)]^{\mathrm{T}} \tag{32}$$

comprises the current and the last $N_{\mathrm{bm}} - 1$ subband outputs of the first beamformer. The filters of the blocking matrix are adapted only if speech is picked up from the steering direction. For improved robustness, the filter coefficients can be limited (in terms of their magnitudes) by an upper and lower threshold [32, 33]. The step-size $\beta_{\mathrm{bm}}(\mu,k)$ is used to control the speed of the adaptation in every subband.

Interference canceler: The subband signals $U_l(\mu,k)$ are passed to the IC which adaptively removes the signal components that are correlated to the interference input signals from the beamformer output $Y_{\mathrm{fb}}(\mu,k)$. The adaptive filters

$$\boldsymbol{W}_l(\mu,k) = [W_l(\mu,k,0),\ldots,W_l(\mu,k,N_{\mathrm{ic}}-1)]^{\mathrm{T}} \tag{33}$$

of the IC are not adapted if speech is coming from the steering direction to avoid signal cancelation. N_{ic} denotes the filter length. For filter adaptation, again the NLMS algorithm is used:

$$\boldsymbol{W}_l(\mu,k+1) = \boldsymbol{W}_l(\mu,k) + \beta_{\mathrm{ic}}(\mu,k)\, \frac{\boldsymbol{U}_l(\mu,k)\, Y_{\mathrm{c}}^*(\mu,k)}{\sum\limits_{l=0}^{M-1} \|\boldsymbol{U}_l(\mu,k)\|^2}. \tag{34}$$

The vector $U_l(\mu,k) = [U_l(\mu,k),\ldots,U_l(\mu,k-N_{\mathrm{ic}}+1)]^{\mathrm{T}}$ comprises the last $N_{\mathrm{ic}} - 1$ output signals of the ABM. The adaptive beamformer output is determined by

$$Y_{\mathrm{c}}(\mu,k) = Y_{\mathrm{fb}}(\mu,k) - \sum_{l=0}^{M-1} \boldsymbol{U}_l^{\mathrm{H}}(\mu,k)\, \boldsymbol{W}_l(\mu,k). \tag{35}$$

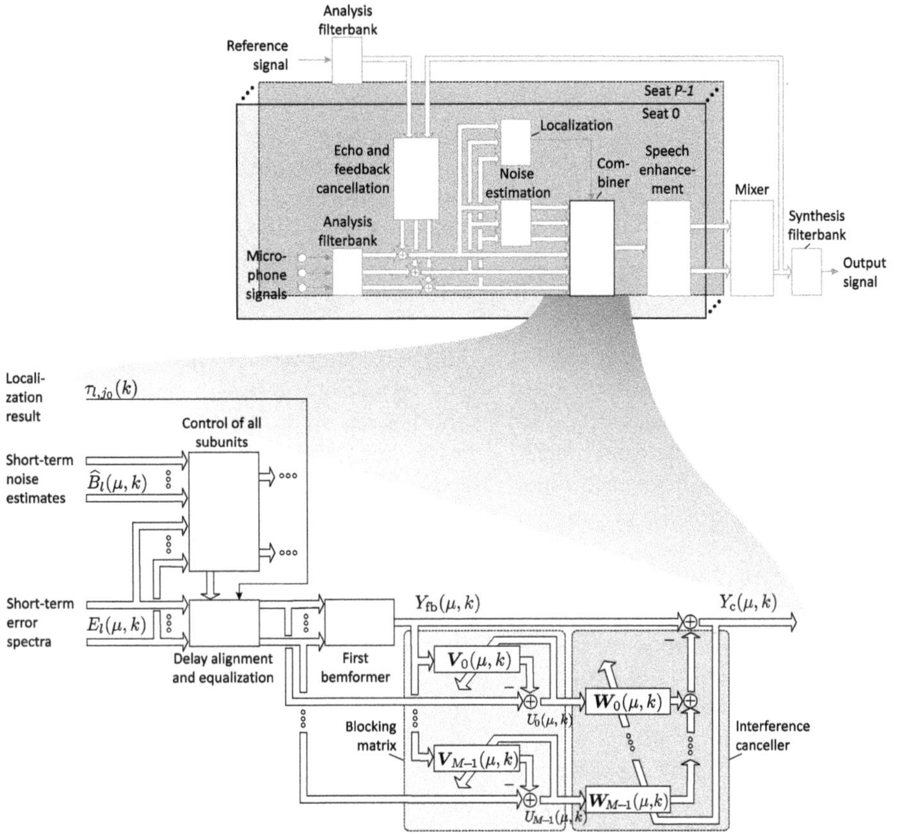

Fig. 8 Overview of the proposed adaptive beamformer for belt microphones and its integration in the entire processing structure

In order to increase the robustness of the beamformer, the norm of the adaptive filter coefficients can be limited [32, 33]. The control of the step-size $\beta_{\mathrm{ic}}(\mu, k)$ is described in the following section.

Adaptation control: The step-sizes for the ABM and the IC are controlled based on the speech activity estimation from the steering direction. As a measure for the speech activity, a ratio of the smoothed short-term powers $S_{y_{\mathrm{fb}}y_{\mathrm{fb}}}(\mu, k)$ and $S_{uu}(\mu, k)$ of the first beamformer and of the ABM output, respectively, averaged over a certain frequency range, is used:

$$r_{\mathrm{SD}}(k) = \frac{\sum_{\mu=N_{\mathrm{u}}}^{N_{\mathrm{o}}} S_{y_{\mathrm{fb}}y_{\mathrm{fb}}}(\mu, k)}{\sum_{\mu=N_{\mathrm{u}}}^{N_{\mathrm{o}}} S_{uu}(\mu, k)}. \tag{36}$$

The short-term powers are smoothed through a first-order IIR filter according to:

$$S_{y_{\mathrm{fb}}y_{\mathrm{fb}}}(\mu, k) = (1-\alpha)\, S_{y_{\mathrm{fb}}y_{\mathrm{fb}}}(\mu, k-1) + \alpha\, |Y_{\mathrm{fb}}(\mu, k)|^2 \tag{37}$$

and

$$S_{uu}(\mu, k) = (1-\alpha)\, S_{uu}(\mu, k-1) + \alpha\, \beta(\mu, k) \sum_{l=0}^{M-1} |U_l(\mu, k)|^2 . \tag{38}$$

The smoothing constant is chosen around α = 750 dB/s, and the lower and upper frequencies used in Eq. (36) were set by $\Omega_{N_{\mathrm{u}}} = 1$ kHz and $\Omega_{N_{\mathrm{o}}} = 6$ kHz. $\beta(\mu, k)$ is controlled such that in periods of stationary background noise, the ratio $r_{\mathrm{SD}}(k)$ becomes one. Only high values of $r_{\mathrm{SD}}(k)$ indicate signal energy from the steering direction. Thus, the filters of the ABM are adjusted only when $r_{\mathrm{SD}}(k)$ exceeds a predetermined threshold $t_{\mathrm{bm}} = 0.3$ using:

$$\beta_{\mathrm{bm}}(\mu, k) = \begin{cases} \beta_{\mathrm{bm}}^{(\max)}, \text{ if } S_{b_{\mathrm{fb}}b_{\mathrm{fb}}}(\mu, k)\, K < \left|Y_{\mathrm{fb}}(\mu, k)\right|^2 \\ \qquad \wedge\, r_{\mathrm{sd}}(k) \geq t_{\mathrm{bm}}\,, \\ 0, \qquad \text{else}\,, \end{cases} \tag{39}$$

where $S_{b_{\mathrm{fb}}b_{\mathrm{fb}}}(\mu, k)$ denotes the estimated PSD of the noise at the first beamformer output and K is set to 6 dB. The adaptive filters of the IC are controlled using:

$$\beta_{\text{ic}}(k) = \begin{cases} \beta_{\text{ic}}^{(\max)}, & \text{if } r_{\text{sd}}(k) < t_{\text{ic}}, \\ 0, & \text{else}, \end{cases} \tag{40}$$

with $t_{\text{ic}} = 0.2$. The maximum step-sizes can be set to $\beta_{\text{ic}}^{(\max)} = 0.1$ and $\beta_{\text{bm}}^{(\max)} = 0.2$.

4.4.4 Results

For evaluating the performance of the adaptive beamformer, real-world recordings have been made at a speed of 120 km/h using the microphones on the driver's seat belt. The belt position was set to a worst-case position for the beamformer. Thus, the distance of the three microphones of the belt was highly different from each other, and therefore, the single microphone SNRs are varying significantly.

A frequency-selective SNR and SIR analysis has been made to compare the non-adaptive and the adaptive beamformers with the best single microphone. For the analysis, the speech signal with a duration of about 120 s recorded in a car at 120 km/h has been used. No remote speech was considered for this test scenario. During the first 60 s, the passenger sitting beside the drive was speaking (interference speech). Afterward, the driver was active also for about 60 s (desired speech). The number of filter taps for the interference canceler and for the adaptive blocking matrix were chosen as $N_{\text{ic}} = 3$ and $N_{\text{bm}} = 3$. The maximum step-sizes for the adaptive filters were set as indicated in the last paragraph. For a simple analysis, two belt microphones with high SNRs have been used to reduce computational complexity. The results in terms of SNR can be seen in Fig. 9. The SNR performance of the first beamformer is slightly better than that of the single best microphones (on average about 2 dB). The overall SNR performance can be further increased by about 5 dB when using the proposed adaptive beamformer compared to the best belt microphone. The SIR analysis as shown in Fig. 10 indicates that on average, about 2 dB SIR improvement with the first beamformer and 6 dB with the adaptive beamformer can be achieved. The proposed adaptive beamformer is suitable for highly suboptimal array geometries and shows robust performance when the signal source position is changing fast. The SIR can be further enhanced if a spatial postfilter is applied as postprocessor for adaptive beamforming.

4.5 Belt microphones in speech enhancement: low complexity noise estimation

Another common problem faced in the automobile environment is the presence of highly varying background noise. With increasing number of microphones like in the case of belt microphones, a reliable and robust noise estimation scheme that requires a low computational complexity is essential. A straightforward solution to estimate the noise accurately is to track the segments of the beamformer output spectrum that do not contain speech. Naturally, the behavior of this spectrum is dependent on the nature of noise present in the given environment which can be classified as non-stationarity in many cases in automobiles. Generally for such environments, the noise spectrum can be described as non-flat with a low-pass characteristic dominated below 500 Hz. Apart from this low-pass characteristic, changes in speed, opening and closing of windows, passing cars, etc. cause the noise floor to vary with time. A close look at one frequency bin of the noise spectrum reveals the following properties:

1. Instantaneous power can vary a large extent from the mean power even during steady conditions.
2. A steady increase or a steady decrease of power is observed during certain situations (e.g., during acceleration).

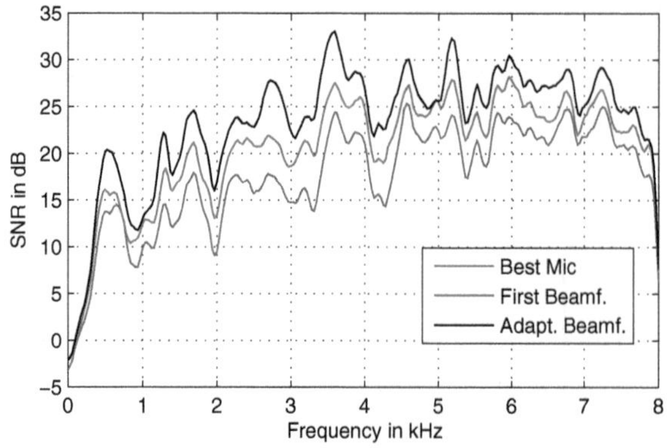

Fig. 9 SNR comparison between the best belt microphone and the beamformer outputs

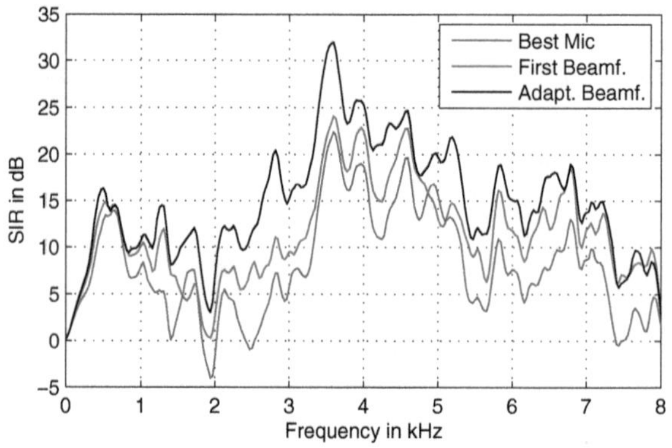

Fig. 10 SIR comparison between the best belt microphone and the beamformer outputs

The signal model considered here is an additive noise which is described by

$$Y_c(\mu,k) = S(\mu,k) + B_c(\mu,k), \tag{41}$$

where $S(\mu,k)$ is the local speech in the echo canceled and beamformed spectrum and $B_c(\mu,k)$ is the local background noise. Consider a simple estimator used to track the change in magnitude per subband

$$\widehat{B}_c(\mu,k) = \begin{cases} \widehat{B}_c(\mu,k-1)\,\Delta_{\text{inc}}, & \text{if } \overline{Y_c}(\mu,k) > \widehat{B}_c(\mu,k-1), \\ \widehat{B}_c(\mu,k-1)\,\Delta_{\text{dec}}, & \text{else,} \end{cases} \tag{42}$$

where $\widehat{B}_c(\mu,k)$ is the estimated background noise magnitude spectrum. This estimator follows a smoothed input $\overline{Y_c}(\mu,k)$ based on the previous noise estimate. The speed at which it tracks the noise floor is controlled by the increment constant Δ_{inc} and the decrement constant Δ_{dec}. The advantage of this algorithm is its low computational complexity. With careful tuning of increment and decrement constants combined with a highly smoothed input, an estimate of the background noise can be obtained. However, this estimator would fail for the following reasons

- Low time-constants will lag in tracking the noise power
- High time-constants will estimate speech as noise

4.5.1 *Idea of the proposed noise estimator*

Using the simple estimator in Eq. (42) as the basis, an improved noise estimation algorithm is proposed that tries to find a balance by keeping the computational complexity low and offering fast and accurate tracking. By recursive averaging of the estimated background noise in combination with the smoothed input spectrum, the noise estimate is obtained by

$$\begin{aligned} \widehat{B}_f(\mu,k) &= W_{\widehat{B}}(\mu,k)\,\overline{Y_c}(\mu,k) \\ &\quad + \big(1 - W_{\widehat{B}}(\mu,k)\big)\,\widehat{B}_{\text{pre}}(\mu,k), \end{aligned} \tag{43}$$

where the time-varying parameters $W_{\widehat{B}}(\mu,k)$ along with $\Delta_{\text{final}}(\mu,k)$ (applied to estimate $\widehat{B}_{\text{pre}}(\mu,k)$) control the estimation. $\widehat{B}_{\text{pre}}(\mu,k)$ is a slow varying noise estimation used similar to the basic noise estimation signal. The principle behind the new estimator is to choose the most suitable multiplicative constant in a given specific situation through the $\Delta_{\text{final}}(\mu,k)$ parameter. Common situations are the presence of speech, a consistent background noise, increasing background noise, decreasing background noise, etc. A measure called *trend* is computed which indicates if the long-term direction of the input signal is going up or down. Details are described in the following paragraphs. The incremental and decremental time-constants along with the trend are finally applied together in Eq. (51).

4.5.2 *Smoothing the input spectrum*

The tracking of the noise estimator is dependent on the smoothed input signal $\overline{Y_c}(\mu,k)$. The input spectrum is smoothed using a first-order IIR filter

$$\overline{Y_c}(\mu,k) = \gamma_{\text{smth}}\,|Y_c(\mu,k)| + (1-\gamma_{\text{smth}})\,\overline{Y_c}(\mu,k-1), \tag{44}$$

where γ_{smth} is the smoothing constant. The smoothing constant must be chosen in such a way that it retains fine variations of the input spectrum as well as eliminate the high variation of the instantaneous spectrum. A value of 300 dB/s is chosen here.[2] Optionally, additional frequency-domain smoothing can be applied.

4.5.3 *Trend: long-term activity measurement*

One of the difficulties for noise estimators in non-stationary environments is differentiating between a speech part and an actual change in the noise level. This problem can be partially overcome by measuring the duration for a power increase, i.e., the difference between the estimated background noise level and the instantaneous power. If the increase is due to a speech source, then the power difference will drop down after the utterance of a syllable, whereas the power difference continues to stay high for a longer duration. This can be utilized as an indication of an increased background noise. By using these power differences, a trend measure is computed by the proposed noise estimation algorithm. By observing the direction of the trend, the noise floor changes can be tracked by avoiding track speech-like parts of the spectrum. The decision about the current state of the frame is made by comparing if the estimated noise of the previous frame is smaller than the smoothed input spectrum of the current frame, and a set of values are obtained. A positive value indicates that the direction is going up, and a negative value indicates that the direction is going down

$$A_{\text{curr}}(\mu,k) = \begin{cases} A_{\text{up}}, & \text{if } \overline{Y_c}(\mu,k) > \widehat{B}_c(\mu,k-1), \\ A_{\text{down}}, & \text{else,} \end{cases} \tag{45}$$

where $\widehat{B}_c(\mu,k-1)$ is the estimated noise of the previous frame. The values $A_{\text{up}} = 1$ and $A_{\text{down}} = -4$ are chosen empirically. The trend is smoothed along both the time and the frequency axis. A zero-phase forward-backward filter is used for smoothing along the frequency axis. Smoothing along the frequency ensures that isolated peaks caused by non-speech-like activities are suppressed.

Smoothing is applied by using

$$\overline{A_{tr}}(\mu,k) = \gamma_{tr\text{-}fq}\, A_{curr}(\mu,k) + (1-\gamma_{tr\text{-}fq})\overline{A_{tr}}(\mu-1,k), \quad (46)$$

for $\mu = 1, \ldots, N_{Sbb}$ and similarly backward smoothing is applied. Both frequency smoothing constants $\gamma_{tr\text{-}fq}$ are chosen to be at about 35 dB/Hz. This is temporally smoothed to obtain the time-smoothed trend factor $\overline{\overline{A_{tr}}}(\mu,k)$ by an IIR filter

$$\overline{\overline{A_{tr}}}(\mu,k) = \gamma_{tr\text{-}tm}\, \overline{A_{tr}}(\mu,k) + (1-\gamma_{tr\text{-}tm})\, \overline{\overline{A_{tr}}}(\mu,k-1), \quad (47)$$

where $\gamma_{tr\text{-}tm}$ is the smoothing constant chosen to be at about 15 dB/s. The behavior of the double-smoothed trend factor $\overline{\overline{A_{tr}}}(\mu,k)$ can be summarized as follows. The trend factor is a long-term indicator of the power level of the input spectrum. During speech parts, the trend factor temporarily goes up but comes down quickly. When the true background noise increases, then the trend goes up and stays there until the noise estimate catches up. A similar behavior is seen for a decreasing background noise power. This trend measure is used to further *push* the noise estimate in the desired direction. The trend is compared to an upward threshold and a downward threshold. When either of these thresholds are reached, then the respective time-constant to be used later is chosen by

$$\Delta_{tr}(\mu,k) = \begin{cases} \Delta_{tr\text{-}up}, & \text{if } \overline{\overline{A_{tr}}}(\mu,k) > T_{tr\text{-}up}, \\ \Delta_{tr\text{-}down}, & \text{else if } \overline{\overline{A_{tr}}}(\mu,k) < T_{tr\text{-}down}, \\ 1, & \text{else.} \end{cases} \quad (48)$$

The values of $\Delta_{tr\text{-}up}$ and $\Delta_{tr\text{-}down}$ are chosen to be at 20 and −20 dB/s. The trend multiplicative $\Delta_{tr}(\mu,k)$ is used later in Eq. (50) to obtain the final multiplicative constant.

4.5.4 Tracking constants based on activity detection

The tracking of the noise estimation has to be performed for two cases:

- When the smoothed input is greater than the estimated noise
- When the smoothed input is smaller than the estimated noise

Incrementing the noise estimate The short-term input spectrum can be greater than the estimated noise due to three reasons:

- When there is speech activity
- When the previous noise estimate has dipped too low and has to rise up
- When there is a continuous increase in the true background noise

The first case is handled by checking if the level of $\overline{Y_c}(\mu,k)$ is greater than a certain SNR threshold T_{snr}, in which case the chosen incremental constant Δ_{speech} has to be very slow because speech should not be tracked. For the second case, the incremental constant is set to Δ_{noise} which means that this is a case of normal rise and fall during tracking. For the case of a continuous increase in the true background noise, the estimate must catch up with it as fast as possible. For this, a counter $k_{cnt}(\mu,k)$ is utilized. The variable counts the duration for which the input spectrum has stayed above the estimated noise. If this counter reaches a threshold $K_{inc\text{-}max}$, then the $\Delta_{inc\text{-}fast}$ is chosen. The counter is incremented by 1 every time $\overline{Y_c}(\mu,k)$ is greater than $\widehat{B}_c(\mu,k-1)$ and reset to 0 otherwise. Equation (49) captures these conditions

$$\Delta_{inc}(\mu,k) = \begin{cases} \Delta_{inc\text{-}fast}, & \text{if } k_{cnt}(\mu,k) > K_{inc\text{-}max}, \\ \Delta_{speech}, & \text{else if } \overline{Y_c}(\mu,k) > \widehat{B}_c(\mu,k-1)\, T_{snr}, \\ \Delta_{noise}, & \text{else.} \end{cases} \quad (49)$$

The value for the fast increment $\Delta_{inc\text{-}fast}$ is chosen to be at about 40 dB/s. For the speech case, Δ_{speech} has to very slow and is chosen to be at about 0.5 dB/s (where T_{snr} is the SNR threshold for speech presence), and finally, the Δ_{noise} is chosen to be at about 6 dB/s.

Decrementing the noise estimate The choice of a decrementing constant does not have to be as explicit as the incrementing case. This is because of lesser ambiguity when $\overline{Y_c}(\mu,k)$ is smaller than $\widehat{B}_c(\mu,k-1)$ as a decrease in power usually settles down to the background noise power level. Here, the noise estimator chooses a decremental constant Δ_{dec} by default. The value for falling edge is chosen to be at about −20 dB/s. For a subband μ, only one of the above two stated conditions is chosen. From either of the two conditions, a final multiplicative constant is determined

$$\Delta_{final}(\mu,k) = \begin{cases} \Delta_{inc}(\mu,k), & \text{if } \overline{Y_c}(\mu,k) > \widehat{B}_c(\mu,k-1), \\ \Delta_{dec}, & \text{else.} \end{cases} \quad (50)$$

4.5.5 Combining all detection schemes

The input spectrum consists of only background noise when no speech-like activity is present. During this time, the best estimate is to set the noise estimate equal to the input spectrum. When the estimated noise is lower than the input spectrum, the noise estimate and the input spectrum are combined with a certain weight. The weights are computed according to Eq. (52). A pre-estimate $\widehat{B}_{\text{pre}}(\mu,k)$ is obtained for computing the weights. The pre-estimate is used in combination with the input spectrum. It is obtained by multiplying the estimate from the previous frame with the multiplicative constant $\Delta_{\text{final}}(\mu,k)$ and the trend constant $\Delta_{\text{tr}}(\mu,k)$

$$\widehat{B}_{\text{pre}}(\mu,k) = \Delta_{\text{final}}(\mu,k)\ \Delta_{\text{tr}}(\mu,k)\ \widehat{B}_{\text{pre}}(\mu,k-1). \quad (51)$$

The weighting factor for combining the input spectrum and the pre-estimate is given by

$$W_{\widehat{B}}(\mu,k) = \min\left\{1, \left(\frac{\widehat{B}_{\text{pre}}(\mu,k)}{\overline{Y_{\text{c}}}(\mu,k)}\right)^2\right\}. \quad (52)$$

The final noise estimate is computed by applying this weighting factor as shown in Eq. (43). During the first few frames of the noise estimation algorithm, the input spectrum itself is directly chosen as the noise estimate for faster convergence. The plot in Fig. 11 shows the result of the noise estimation algorithm for subband $\mu = 34$.

4.5.6 *Results*

The proposed algorithm was evaluated under different automobile noise conditions to test the performance in realistic situations encountered while driving. Noise recordings were performed under different speeds, with the air-condition system turned on and off, opening/closing of a window, accelerating to a high speed, breaking to a low speed, etc. The so-called Harvard sentences [34] were used for mixing speech for different SNRs. Noise recordings from one of the belt microphones were used for the evaluation. Two sentences of male and female speakers in a total length of 20 s were used for the evaluation. Figure 12 shows the log-error distance plot of the proposed noise estimation algorithm as compared to the speech presence probability (SPP) scheme [35] and the minimum statistics method [36] as these were the best among the five estimation schemes that were evaluated in our tests for different SNRs [37–39]. These schemes were evaluated as a noise estimation scheme applied to the belt microphone system. The log-error measure is a way to compute the distance between the true noise $\widehat{B}(\mu,k)$ and the estimated noise $\widehat{B}_{\text{f}}(\mu,k)$ given by [40]

$$\Delta_B(\mu,k) = 20\,\log_{10}|B(\mu,k)| - 20\,\log_{10}\left|\widehat{B}_f(\mu,k)\right|,$$

$$Log_{\text{err}} = \frac{1}{L_{\text{seg}}\,N_{\text{Sbb}}}\sum_{k=0}^{L_{\text{seg}}-1}\sum_{\mu=0}^{N_{\text{Sbb}}-1}|\Delta_B(\mu,k)|, \quad (53)$$

where L_{seg} is the number of frames of the noisy signal. The errors for the proposed scheme occur mainly when a rising noise has to be followed. The SPP-based estimate follows the noise well but also follows some speech segments, thereby distorting parts of speech. The minimum-statistics-based estimation was not able to follow the rising spectrum parts fast enough. The proposed algorithm performed better in terms of segmental SNR and overall SNR improvement. The estimated noise PSD is used by the postfilter to suppress the noise and residual echoes by using a suppression filter that is presented in the next section.

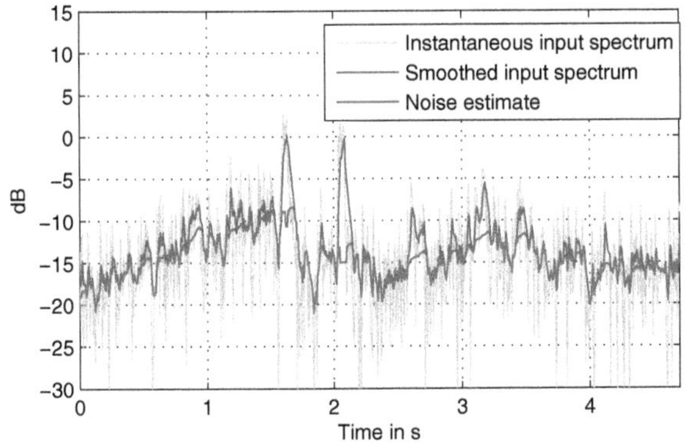

Fig. 11 Plot showing the noise estimate at subband $\mu = 34$

4.6 Residual echo and noise suppression

The output of the adaptive beamformer contains two unwanted components:

- The residual echo from the echo canceler which is caused due to imperfect cancelation
- The background noise of the automobile

Although an estimate of the residual echo $E_u(\mu,k)$ is already available from the echo canceler as per Eq. (13), the application of the adaptive beamformer on the error spectra modifies the estimated residual echo. The residual echo now needs to be re-estimated. Adaptive beamforming can be viewed as spatial filtering applied on the belt microphones. Hence, the filter applied on the error spectra cannot be directly applied on residual echo magnitude estimates. Given this, a good approximate of the residual echo can be obtained from the already available estimate for each microphone on the belt microphone array by applying a maximum over the entire array to get $\widehat{E}_u^2(\mu,k)$. Even if the gain by the beamformer is not included here, it turned out that this approach leads to satisfying results in terms of the echo and so-called double-talk performance of the overall system:

$$\widehat{E}_u(\mu,k) = \max_{l=0\ldots M-1}\left\{\overline{X}_l(\mu,k)\,\beta_{\text{coupl},l}(\mu,k)\right\}. \quad (54)$$

The residual echo estimate along with the background noise estimate $\widehat{B}_{\text{f}}(\mu,k)$ is suppressed by a modified

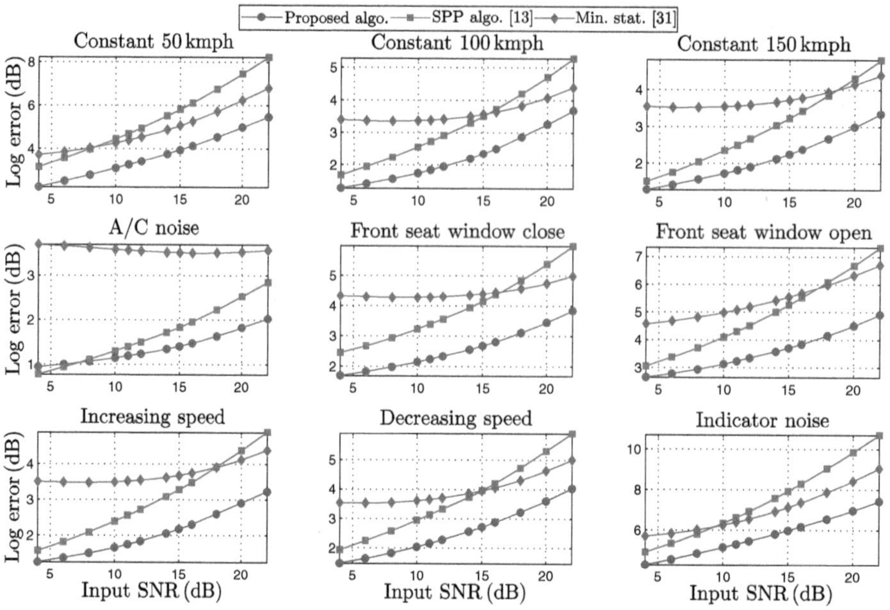

Fig. 12 Log-error plot of the proposed algorithm as compared to SPP [35] and MS [36] under various automobile noise conditions

Wiener filter [41] in the subband domain given by

$$\tilde{\zeta}_{\mathrm{i}}(\mu,k) = 1 - \frac{\Lambda_{\mathrm{res}}\,\widehat{E}_{\mathrm{u}}^2(\mu,k) + \Lambda_{\mathrm{ns}}\,\widehat{B}_{\mathrm{f}}^2(\mu,k)}{|Y_{\mathrm{c}}(\mu,k)|^2}, \tag{55}$$

where $\tilde{\zeta}(\mu,k)$ is the instantaneous Wiener filter. The filter is usually limited by a floor value (usually about -8 to -15 dB) to control the maximum attenuation applied by the filter:

$$\zeta(\mu,k) = \max\left\{\tilde{\zeta}(\mu,k),\ \zeta_{\mathrm{floor}}\right\}. \tag{56}$$

Equation (55) also contains two parameters Λ_{res} and the Λ_{ns} which are overestimation factors applied for the residual echo and the background noise estimate, respectively. This ensures that estimated values are compensated for incorrect estimates especially when the filter does not attenuate sufficiently. The output of the noise suppression filter is the estimated clean speech for each belt. It is obtained by

$$\widehat{S}_{\mathrm{e}}(\mu,k) = \tilde{\zeta}(\mu,k)\,Y_{\mathrm{c}}(\mu,k). \tag{57}$$

Whenever the estimated residual echo is larger than the background noise level reduced by the spectral floor, the output signal is replaced by so-called comfort noise at an appropriate level. Therefore, the following condition is checked:

$$\widehat{E}_{\mathrm{u}}(\mu,k) > \widehat{B}_{\mathrm{f}}(\mu,k)\,\zeta_{\mathrm{floor}}. \tag{58}$$

4.7 Belt microphones in multi-seat scenarios: speech mixer

In a setup which involves multiple seat belts fitted with belt microphones, all channels have to be mixed before they can be sent out via the single channel phone uplink. A first solution for mixing the channels is to simply add all of them. This would lead to a simple mixing scheme, but the overall broadband noise would increase. The solution presented here performs what is called *noise equalization* among the various seats before mixing them with individual time-varying weights. The weights are determined mainly on whether the channels (after beamforming and posfiltering) are active, meaning that the passenger on the specific seat is speaking. Before the channels are added, the noise in every channel should be the same. This is done by means of noise equalization, which is described at the end of this section. In general, the output of the speech mixer signal is computed by

$$\widehat{S}(\mu,k) = \sum_{p=0}^{P-1} \widehat{S}^{(p)}_{\mathrm{e,noise\text{-}eq}}(\mu,k)\,w^{(p)}(k), \tag{59}$$

where $\widehat{S}(\mu,k)$ is the output signal and $\widehat{S}^{(p)}_{\mathrm{e,noise\text{-}eq}}(\mu,k)$ are the noise equalized input channels to be mixed. Since we will combine now the outputs of the individual seats, the index (p) is no longer omitted. The time-varying weights $w^{(p)}(k)$ are combinations of two factors

$$w^{(p)}(k) = a^{(p)}(k)\,b(k). \tag{60}$$

The activity weight $a^{(p)}(k)$ is based on whether the channel has been detected to have activity and the background noise weight $b(k)$ *normalizes* the background noise to stay constant assuming all noise components from the individual seat being mutually orthogonal. Figure 13 shows the signal flow diagram of the speech mixer with the activity and the background noise weights.

The activity weight $a^{(p)}(k)$ controls the opening and closing of a given channel, and hence, the value of this weight lies between 0 dB and A_{att}. The background noise weight $b(k)$ is computed based on these activity weights:

$$b(k) = \frac{1}{\sqrt{\sum_{p=0}^{P-1} \left(a^{(p)}(k)\right)^2}}. \tag{61}$$

The background noise weight is derived by assuming the remaining noise output in terms of its power spectral density should be the same as the noise level of all inputs after equalization:

$$\mathrm{E}\left\{\left|\widehat{S}(\mu,k)\right|^2\right\}\Big|_{\text{during speech pauses}} \overset{!}{=} \mathrm{E}\left\{\left|\widehat{S}^{(p)}_{\text{e,noise-eq}}(\mu,k)\right|^2\right\}\Big|_{\text{during speech pauses}} \quad \forall p, \tag{62}$$

where $\overset{!}{=}$ indicates "should be equal to." Starting from that condition, using mutual orthogonality among all seat outputs, and restricting the weight $b(k)$ to be positive, leads to the solution given in Eq. (61).

4.7.1 *Activity detection*

The acoustic arrangement of the belt microphones in a car is such that when only one talker is active, his/her voice is also captured by belt microphones of other passenger seats which could result in incorrect detection for the non-speaking passengers. If there is no mechanism to differentiate this, then the result will be an addition of all the channels. The problem here is to identify the "true" passenger microphone where the talker is active. The approach adopted here is to find the loudest channel among the available channels. The activity decision for the loudest channel is set to 1, and the other channels are decayed with a falling constant up to A_{att}. Before a loudest channel search is performed, a simple VAD is performed as a pre-detection. The pre-detection ensures that channels where the signal is not loud enough is omitted from the loudness search. For example, the belt microphone immediately behind the driver's seat can be omitted from the loudness search when only the driver is active. The loudest channel search is performed over the subbands with a minimum SNR T_{loud} as compared to the background noise $\widehat{B}_{\text{f}}(\mu,k)$

$$\tilde{\chi}^{(p)}(\mu,k) = \begin{cases} 1, \text{ if } \left|\widehat{S}^{(p)}_{\text{e}}(\mu,k)\right| > T_{\text{loud}}\,\widehat{B}^{(p)}_{\text{f}}(\mu,k), \\ 0, \text{ else,} \end{cases} \tag{63}$$

where the computation of the noise level $\widehat{B}^{(p)}_{\text{f}}(\mu,k)$ was presented in Eq. (43). The individual subbands are summed to obtain a value per passenger

$$\chi^{(p)}(k) = \sum_{\mu=0}^{N_{\text{FFT}}-1} \tilde{\chi}^{(p)}(\mu,k). \tag{64}$$

A maximum search is performed over the $\chi^{(p)}(k)$ value to obtain the loudest passenger index $p_{\max}(k)$ given by

$$p_{\max}(k) = \begin{cases} p_{\max}(k-1), \\ \qquad \text{if } \max\limits_{p}\left\{\chi^{(p)}(k)\right\} < \chi_{\min}, \\ \operatorname*{argmax}\limits_{p}\left\{\chi^{(p)}(k)\right\}, \\ \qquad \text{else.} \end{cases} \tag{65}$$

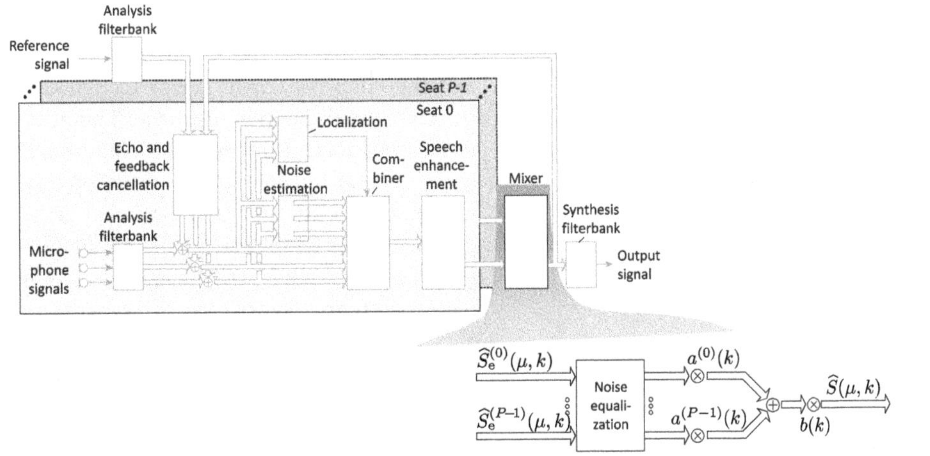

Fig. 13 Input-output signal flow of the mixer (depicting the two types of weights) and its position in the entire processing structure

However, the index of the loudest passenger is only updated if a sufficient amount of subbands show a large SNR. The weights resulting for the activity decision are changing on the bases of multiplicative time-constants. This ensures a smooth transition when the estimated talker's activity is switching from one passenger to another. To compute the activity weights $a^{(p)}(k)$, first, a default time-constant $\Delta_{\text{act-def}}$ is applied to the activity weights. This is then followed by a faster incremental time constant if the current channel is found to be the loudest; else, it is decremented with a slow time constant. The activity decisions are then set according to

$$a_{def}^{(p)}(k) = \min\left\{a^{(p)}(k-1)\,\Delta_{\text{act-def}}, A_{\text{att}}\right\}, \tag{66}$$

with

$$a^{(p)}(k) = \begin{cases} \min\left\{a_{\text{def}}^{(p)}(k)\,\Delta_{\text{act-inc}}, 1\right\}, \\ \quad \text{if } p = p_{\max}(k), \\ \max\left\{a_{\text{def}}^{(p)}(k)\,\Delta_{\text{act-dec}}, A_{\text{att}}\right\}, \\ \quad \text{else.} \end{cases} \tag{67}$$

4.7.2 *Noise equalization*

Before the channels can be added, the noise for every channel has to be the same. This is achieved by a slowly changing average-noise-gain tracker $G^{(p)}(\mu, k)$ multiplied with every channel. The noise gains are aimed to bring all channels to an average noise level. This is performed by a two-stage procedure. First, the gains of the last frame are updated in a preliminary fashion ($G^{(p)}(\mu, k-1) \rightarrow \widetilde{G}^{(p)}(\mu, k)$). Afterwards, the preliminary gains are limited, resulting in the final gains for the current frame ($\widetilde{G}^{(p)}(\mu, k) \rightarrow G^{(p)}(\mu, k)$). An average noise $\widehat{B}_{\text{f,avg}}(\mu, k)$ of all channels is computed by

$$\widehat{B}_{\text{f,avg}}(\mu, k) = \frac{1}{P}\sum_{p=0}^{P-1}\widehat{B}_{\text{f}}^{(p)}(\mu, k). \tag{68}$$

The background noise estimates are the ones that were used in the postfilter section (see Eq. (43)). The noise gains per channel are tracked with the help of slow time constants:

$$\widetilde{G}^{(p)}(\mu, k) = \begin{cases} G^{(p)}(\mu, k-1)\,\Delta_{gain-inc}, \\ \text{if } \widehat{B}_{\text{f}}^{(p)}(\mu, k)\, G^{(p)}(\mu, k-1) \\ \qquad < \widehat{B}_{f,avg}(\mu, k), \\ G^{(p)}(\mu, k-1)\,\Delta_{\text{gain-dec}}, \text{else.} \end{cases} \tag{69}$$

The gains $G^{(p)}(\mu, k)$ are finally limited by G_{max} and $G_{\min}$:

$$G^{(p)}(\mu, k) = \max\left\{G_{\min}, \min\left\{G_{\max}, \widetilde{G}^{(p)}(\mu, k)\right\}\right\}. \tag{70}$$

These noise gains are applied to the respective input channels resulting in

$$\widehat{S}_{\text{e,noise-eq}}^{(p)}(\mu, k) = \widehat{S}_{\text{e}}^{(p)}(\mu, k)\, G^{(p)}(\mu, k). \tag{71}$$

Although the usefulness of the speech mixer for a multi-seat conference is easy to see, there are no readily available evaluation methods for the mixer. One way to evaluate the mixer is to measure how fast the activity detection switches for continuously changing speakers in different seat positions. The noise equalizer can be evaluated by creating different noise situations at each seat position. Due to time and space constraints, the speech mixer presented here was subjectively evaluated by a remote speaker for scenarios involving conversation with passengers seated in different seat positions in real driving conditions. During the first part of the conversation, the mixer was turned off, and for second part of the conversation, the mixer was turned on. The remote speakers always positively acknowledged the improved speech situation from the car when the mixer was turned on.

5 Summary

The paper highlighted various positions in which microphones can be placed inside an automobile for capturing speech and compared conventional sensors to belt microphones. The natural SNR advantage of the belt microphones is hindered by various properties of the seat belt. For example, movement relative to the local speaker and the loudspeaker lead to acoustic echo path changes. The work presented in this paper has tried to solve these problems using appropriate signal processing schemes. First, the problem of continuously changing echo paths is managed by combining existing methods in step-size control with improvements through a delay estimate for faster adaptation. To tackle a large change in the echo path, a shadow-filter-based approach was presented. By using these additional filter, the coupling factors between the reference and error spectra are triggered to new values whenever a room change was detected. The results showed that the detection of the room change and the coupling trigger helps in quickly re-adapting to the changed frequency response. The next stage of signal processing were three different approaches for acquiring the local speech in the form of choosing a single microphone with the best SNR, an SNR-based microphone combination, and finally an adaptive beamformer where a first SNR-based beamformer is used in combination with an adaptive blocking matrix and an interference canceler. The adaptive blocking matrix is used to generate a reference for the interference canceler. Real measurement in cars showed that even with this highly time-varying setup, still some benefit could be achieved with beamforming techniques. For the estimation of the overall background noise of the vehicle, a simple but reliable and effective noise estimation method based on switching multiplicative constants was presented. The switching is based mainly on a long-term activity measure, the previous noise estimates, and the smoothed input spectrum. This results in an overall improved performance for the automobile noise situations compared to two other well-established noise estimation schemes. As a last step, a speech mixer was presented that combines the different belts from various seats to a single output. The mixer is designed in such a way that it differentiates between single-talker and multiple-talker situations by controlling the attenuation applied for every belt. The mixer also performs a simple noise equalization to maintain a constant background noise even if the individual belts might have different individual noise levels. The work shows that much of the problems presented initially for the belt microphones have been successfully handled through the various signal processing techniques developed. These techniques are supported with results using measures commonly applied by the research community.

6 Conclusions

This paper has shown that belt microphones can be used as an alternative to traditionally placed microphones. The algorithms presented in this paper are applied in real systems, and the results were rather promising. The expected problems, such as short echo bursts after movements of the passengers, can be avoided by appropriate control schemes. The presented methods have also taken into account multiple inputs, and an extension to multiple output is rather straightforward. The methods have also been tested against industry standards like the ITU [25] specifications.

The next steps towards improving the system can be made in several directions: since the echo cancelation schemes involve(s) several adaptive filters and control units, methods to reduce complexity by reducing processing bands, finding a correlation between the loudspeaker and the different microphone arrays can be explored. On the same line, the overall complexity of the adaptive beamformer could be reduced by further using the same attempts. In terms of noise estimation and suppression, other methods like a time-varying attenuation floor as presented in [42] can be examined. These methods also have the potential to be extended further to other systems like high-quality multichannel audio-video conferencing systems. Finally, the belt microphones itself can be used to measure the noise level as heard by the passengers since they are close to the ears. This information can be used to control the gain of the level control unit for the remote-side signals. The same holds for the adjustment of the playback level of music signals.

Endnotes

[1] Again, we dropped the superscript (p) for better readability here, since the same processing scheme is applied to all seats. The subscript l, however, is required now—in contrast to the previous sections.

[2] In order to be independent of the sample rate and frameshift, all time-constants are denoted in dB/s.

Competing interests

The authors declare that they have no competing interests.

Acknowledgements

The authors would like to thank all the colleagues at Digital Signal Processing and System Theory, University of Kiel, and paragon AG who helped in different ways while conducting various driving tests and different recordings, and special thanks for reviewing the manuscript and providing valuable inputs at various stages of development.

Author details

[1] Digital Signal Processing and System Theory, University of Kiel, Kaiserstrasse 2, Kiel, Germany. [2] Division Acoustics, paragon AG, Schwalbenweg 29, Delbrueck, Germany.

References

1. E Hänsler, The Hands-free telephone problem: an annotated bibliography. Signal Process. **27**(3), 259–271 (1992)
2. E Hänsler, The hands-free telephone problem: an annotated bibliography update. Ann. Telecommun. Annales des Télécommun. **79**(7-8), 360–367 (1994)
3. G Schmidt, T Haulick. Signal processing for in-car communication systems.Signal Process. **86**(6), 1307–1326 (2006)
4. J Withopf, C Lüke, H Özer, G Schmidt, in *5th Biennial Workshop on Digital Signal Processing for In-Vehicle Systems*. Signal Processing for In-car Communication Systems (Kiel, Germany, p. 2011. http://www.dss.tf.uni-kiel.de/en/events/workshops/dsp-in-vehicles-2011/the-5th-biennial-workshop-on-digital-signal-processing-for-in-vehicle-systems
5. H Höge, S Hohenner, B Kämmerer, N Kunstmann, S Schachtl, M Schönle, P Setiawan, in *Automatic Speech Recognition on Mobile Devices and Over Communication Networks Advances in Pattern Recognition*, ed. by Z Tan, B Lindberg. Automotive Speech Recognition, vol. 2008 Spinger, Berlin, Germany, 2008), pp. 347–373
6. M Brandstein, *D Ward, Microphone Arrays*. (Springer, Berlin, Germany, 2001)
7. J Freudenberger, Microphone diversity combining for in-car applications. EURASIP J. Adv. Signal Process. **2010** (2010). http://asp.eurasipjournals.springeropen.com/articles/10.1155/2010/509541
8. AG Paragon. http://www.paragon.ag. Accessed 25 Feb 2016
9. J Withopf, G Schmidt, in *Speech Communication; 10. ITG Symposium; Proceedings of*. Suppression of Instationary Distortions in Automotive Environments, (Germany, 2012). http://ieeexplore.ieee.org/xpl/articleDetails.jsp?arnumber=6309586&queryText=Suppression%20of%20Instationary%20Distortions%20in%20Automotive%20Environments&newsearch=true
10. JB Allen, Short-term spectral analysis, synthesis, and modification by discrete fourier transform. IEEE Trans. Acoust. Speech Signal Process. **25**(3), 235–238 (1977)
11. D Mauler, R Martin, in *Acoustics Speech and Signal Processing (ICASSP), 2010 IEEE International Conference on*. Optimization of switchable windows for low-delay spectral analysis-synthesis, (2010), pp. 4718–4721. doi:10.1109/ICASSP.2010.5495181, http://ieeexplore.ieee.org/xpl/articleDetails.jsp?arnumber=5495181&newsearch=true&queryText=Optimization%20of%20Switchable%20Windows%20for%20Low-Delay%20Spectral%20Analysis-Synthesis
12. J Withopf, L Jassoume, G Schmidt, A Theiss, in *DAGA 2012 Ű 38. Deutsche Jahrestagung für Akustik*. Modified Overlap-Add Filter Bank With Reduced Delay (Darmstadt, Germany, p. 2012. https://www.dega-akustik.de/publikationen/daga-tagungen/verzeichnisse.html

13. MM Sondhi, The history of echo cancellation. IEEE Signal Process. Mag. **23**(5), 95–102 (2006)
14. S Haykin, *Adaptive Filter Theory*, 3rd ed. Prentice-Hall, Inc., Upper Saddle River, NJ, USA, 1996)
15. C Breining, P Dreiseitel, E Hänsler, A Mader, B Nitsch, H Puder, T Schertler, G Schmidt, J Tilp. IEEE Signal Process. Mag. **16**(4), 42–69 (1999)
16. C Antweiler, J Grunwald, H Quack, in *IEEE International Conference on Acoustics, Speech, and Signal Processing*. Approximation of optimal step size control for acoustic echo cancellation, vol. 1, (1997), pp. 295–298. doi:10.1109/ICASSP.1997.599627, http://ieeexplore.ieee.org/xpl/articleDetails.jsp?arnumber=599627&newsearch=true&queryText=Approximation%20of%20optimal%20step%20size%20control%20for%20acoustic%20echo%20cancellation,%20acoustics,%20speech,%20and%20signal
17. MA Iqbal, SL Grant, in *Acoustics, Speech and Signal Processing, 2008. ICASSP 2008. IEEE International Conference on*. Novel variable step size NLMS algorithms for echo cancellation, (2008), pp. 241–244. doi:10.1109/ICASSP.2008.4517591, http://ieeexplore.ieee.org/xpl/articleDetails.jsp?arnumber=4517591&newsearch=true&queryText=Novel%20variable%20step%20size%20nlms%20algorithms%20for%20echo%20cancellation
18. C Paleologu, J Benesty, S Ciochina, A variable step-size affine projection algorithm designed for acoustic echo cancellation.Audio Speech Lang. Process. IEEE Trans. **16**(8), 1466–1478 (2008)
19. C Carlemalm, A Logothetis, in *Acoustics, Speech, and Signal Processing, 1997. ICASSP-97., 1997 IEEE International Conference on*. On detection of double talk and changes in the echo path using a Markov modulated channel model, vol. 5, (1997), pp. 3869–3872. doi:10.1109/ICASSP.1997.604743, http://ieeexplore.ieee.org/xpl/articleDetails.jsp?arnumber=604743&newsearch=true&queryText=On%20detection%20of%20double%20talk%20and%20changes%20in%20the%20echo%20path%20using%20a%20Markov%20modulated%20channel%20model
20. WC Lee, KH Jeong, DH Youn, in *Circuits and Systems, 1997. Proceedings of the 40th Midwest Symposium on*. A robust stereophonic subband adaptive acoustic echo canceller, vol. 2, (1997), pp. 1350–1353. doi:10.1109/MWSCAS.1997.662332, http://ieeexplore.ieee.org/xpl/articleDetails.jsp?arnumber=662332&newsearch=true&queryText=A%20robust%20stereophonic%20subband%20adaptive%20acoustic%20echo%20canceller
21. F Amano, HP Meana, A de Luca, G Duchen, A multirate acoustic echo canceler structure. IEEE Trans. Commun. **43**(7), 2172–2176 (1995)
22. MA Iqbal, SL Grant, in *Region 5 Technical Conference, 2007 IEEE*. A novel normalized cross-correlation based echo-path change detector, (2007), pp. 249–251. doi:10.1109/TPSD.2007.4380390, http://ieeexplore.ieee.org/xpl/articleDetails.jsp?arnumber=4380390&newsearch=true&queryText=A%20Novel%20Normalized%20Cross-Correlation%20Based%20Echo-Path%20Change%20Detector
23. W Armbrüster, in *Signal Processing*. Wideband Acoustic Echo Canceller with Two Filter Structure (Elsevier, Belgium, 1992), pp. 1611–1614. http://www.sciencedirect.com/science/article/pii/B9780444895875501055, https://s100.copyright.com/AppDispatchServlet?publisherName=ELS&contentID=B9780444895875501055&orderBeanReset=true
24. K Ochiai, T Araseki, T Ogihara, Echo canceller with tow echo path models. IEEE Trans. Commun. COM-25, 589–595 (1977)
25. ITU: ITU-T P.1110 – Wideband hands-free communication in motor vehicles (2015). http://www.itu.int/. Accessed 4 July 2015
26. C Knapp, G Carter, The generalized correlation method for estimation of time delay. IEEE Trans. Acoust. Speech Signal Process. **24**(4), 320–327 (1976)
27. GC Carter, AH Nuttall, P Cable, The smoothed coherence transform. IEEE Trans. Acoust. Speech Signal Process. **61**(10), 1497–1498 (1973)
28. M Krini, K Rodemer, *Seat Belt-Microphone Systems and their Application to Speech Signal Enhancement*. (Oldenburg, Germany, p. 2014
29. M Krini, VK Rajan, K Rodemer, G Schmidt, *Adaptive Beamforming for Microphone Arrays on Seat Belts*. Nuremberg, Germany, 2015). https://www.dega-akustik.de/publikationen/daga-tagungen/verzeichnisse.html
30. LJ Griffiths, CW Jim, An alternative approach to linearly constrained adaptive beamforming. IEEE Trans. Antennas Propag. **30**(1), 24–34 (1982)
31. DH Johnson, DE Dudgeon. 1st ed., in *Englewood Cliffs, NJ, USA*. Array Signal Processing: Concepts and Techniques (Prentice Hall, 1993)
32. H Cox, RM Zeskind, MM Owen, Robust adaptive beamforming. IEEE Trans. Acoust. Speech Signal Process. **35**(10), 1365–1375 (1987)
33. O Hoshuyama, A Sugiyama, A robust adaptive beamformer for microphone arrays with a blocking matrix using constrained adaptive filters. IEEE Trans. Signal Process. **61**(10), 1497–1498 (1973)
34. IEEE, Recommended practice for speech quality measurements. IEEE Trans. Audio Electroacoustics. **17**(3), 225–246 (1969)
35. T Gerkmann, RC Hendriks, Unbiased MMSE-based noise power estimation with low complexity and low tracking delay. IEEE Trans. Audio Speech Lang. Process. **20**(4), 1383–1393 (2012)
36. R Martin, Noise power spectral density estimation based on optimal smoothing and minimum statistics. IEEE Trans. Speech Audio Process. **9**(5), 504–512 (2001)
37. I Cohen, Noise spectrum estimation in adverse environments: improved minima controlled recursive averaging. IEEE Trans. Speech Audio Process. **11**(5), 466–475 (2003)
38. G Doblinger, Computationally efficient speech enhancement by spectral minima tracking in subbands. Proc. Eurospeech. **2**, 1513–1516 (1995)
39. HG Hirsch, C Ehrlicher, in *Acoustics, Speech, and Signal Processing, 1995. ICASSP-95., 1995 International Conference on*. Noise estimation techniques for robust speech recognition, vol. 1, (1995), pp. 153–156. doi:10.1109/ICASSP.1995.479387, http://ieeexplore.ieee.org/xpl/articleDetails.jsp?arnumber=479387&queryText=Noise%20estimation%20techniques%20for%20robust%20speech%20recognition&newsearch=true
40. PC Loizou, *Speech Enhancement: Theory and Practice. Signal Processing and Communications*, 1st ed. (CRC press, 2007). https://www.crcpress.com/Speech-Enhancement-Theory-and-Practice/Loizou/9780849350320
41. N Wiener, *Extrapolation, Interpolation and Smoothing of Stationary Time Series: With Engineering Applications*. (MIT Press, 1949). http://ieeexplore.ieee.org/xpl/articleDetails.jsp?arnumber=6284744, http://ieeexplore.ieee.org/xpl/bkabstractplus.jsp?bkn=6267356
42. VK Rajan, C Baasch, M Krini, G Schmidt, in *Speech Communication; 11. ITG Symposium; Proceedings of*. Improvement in Listener Comfort Through Noise Shaping Using a Modified Wiener Filter Approach (Nuremberg, Germany, 2014), pp. 1–4. http://ieeexplore.ieee.org/xpl/articleDetails.jsp?arnumber=6926063&newsearch=true&queryText=Improvement%20in%20Listener%20Comfort%20Through%20Noise%20Shaping%20Using%20a%20Modified%20Wiener%20Filter%20Approach

6

Generalization of interpolation DFT algorithms and frequency estimators with high image component interference rejection

Jiufei Luo[1*], Shuaicheng Hou[2], Xinyi Li[3], Qi Ouyang[2] and Yi Zhang[1]

Abstract

This paper focuses on the problem of frequency estimation of noise-contaminated sinusoidal. A basic tool to solve this problem is the interpolated discrete Fourier transform (DFT) algorithms, in which the influences of the spectral leakage from negative frequency are often neglected, resulting in significant errors in estimation when the signals contained small cycles. In this paper, analytic expressions of the interference due to the image component are derived and its influences on the traditional two-point interpolated DFT algorithms are analyzed. Based on the achieved expressions, the interpolated DFT algorithms are generalized and a novel frequency estimator with high image component interference rejection is proposed. Simulation results show that the frequency errors returned by the new algorithm are very small even though only one or two cycles are obtained. Comparative studies indicate that the new algorithm also has a good performance in the noise condition. With the advantages of high precision and strong robustness against additive noise, the proposed algorithm is a good choice for frequency estimation when the negative frequency interference is the dominant error source.

Keywords: Frequency estimation, Discrete Fourier transform, Spectral leakage, Image frequency interference

1 Introduction

Spectral analysis based on the discrete Fourier transform (DFT) and implemented by the fast Fourier transform (FFT) has been widely used in many fields for several decades. However, there are two drawbacks in the classic version: the spectral leakage effect (SLE) caused by the lack of periodicity and the picket fence effect (PFE) due to the frequency sampling [1]. These effects will lead to significant errors in spectral analysis such as parameter estimation [2, 3]. In order to obtain accurate estimates of signal parameters, a lot of solutions were proposed [4–14]. The interpolation discrete Fourier transform (IpDFT) algorithm is one of the most popular algorithms.

* Correspondence: jiufluo@gmail.com
[1]School of Advanced Manufacture Engineering, Chongqing University of Posts and Telecommunications, Chongqing 400065, People's Republic of China
Full list of author information is available at the end of the article

Early in 1970s, interpolation algorithms based on the moduli of two FFT spectral bins were presented by Rife et al. [4]. Various improved algorithms have been put forward in the following decades, such as the weighted interpolated DFT (WIDFT) proposed by Agrez [9] and the multi-point interpolated DFT approach (WMIpDFT) by Belega and Dallet [12]. Specifically, simple analytical solutions can be obtained when the maximum sidelobe decay windows (MSDW, also known as Rife–Vincent class I windows) are adopted [11]. However, the algorithms mentioned above are all established on a very important assumption that the leakage coming from the image component plays a minor role and could be ignored [11–13]. In fact, if signals contain a small number of cycles, the negative frequency component usually will exercise great influences on the estimators [15]. Although the multi-point IpDFT methods can reduce the sensitivity to some extent, frequency estimation errors due to the spectral interference from the image component still remain significant [15], especially for the signals with a few cycles. Furthermore, it should be emphasized that the reduction of systematic errors by the weighted interpolated DFT or multi-point IpDFT methods is at the expense of worse noise properties [9, 12]. In engineering practice, noise properties usually are more important than systematic errors. The accuracy could be improved with longer records as well, but the cost is increased response time [16]. As a result, we often have to make a tradeoff between the estimation accuracy and the overall system responsiveness. Consequently, it is of great significance to propose a new and simple algorithm by which accurate parameter estimates can be achieved with short intervals, especially for those fields where real-time response is required [16–18].

Recently, Belega et al. proposed an improved three-point IpDFT which exhibits a high rejection capability with respect to the interference from negative frequency [15]. In this paper, we proposed a novel frequency estimator by which the leakage coming from image component can be further reduced compared with the algorithm proposed by Belega et al. More importantly, it also keeps good noise properties due to a two-point-based mechanism. The remaining parts are organized as follows. In Section 2, we present a concise summary of the traditional interpolation algorithms. Symbols and basic equations used throughout the paper are defined in this section as well. In Section 3, the analytical expressions of the interference from the negative frequency are derived. With the properties of the derived expressions, we generalize the interpolation DFT algorithms. In Section 4, the frequency estimators with high interference rejection of image component are proposed. In Section 5, some computer simulations are carried out and the performance of the proposed algorithms are compared with some other state-of-the-art IpDFT methods. Finally, main conclusions are drawn in Section 6.

2 Theoretical background

In order to explain the basis of the frequency-estimating procedure, first, let $x_{\mathrm{raw}}(n)$ be the samples of a discrete cosine wave in the form

$$x_{\mathrm{raw}}(n) = A_0 \cos(2\pi f_0 n \Delta T + \varphi_0) \qquad n = 0, 1, 2, \ldots \tag{1}$$

where A_0, f_0, and φ_0 are the amplitude, frequency, and phase, respectively. ΔT denotes the sampling interval and n is the index of the samples. Sampling rate $f_s = 1/\Delta T$ is supposed to fulfill the Nyquist sampling theorem so that aliasing of spectrum does not occur. When N samples are acquired, f_0 is normalized by the frequency resolution $\Delta f = f_s/N$ and is expressed as

$$\lambda_0 = \frac{f_0}{\Delta f} = \frac{f_0}{f_s/N}, \tag{2}$$

where λ_0 is the normalized frequency expressed in bins [12]. Usually, samples are weighted by a window function $w_N(n)$ before DFT

$$x(n) = x_{\mathrm{raw}}(n) w_N(n) \tag{3}$$

The DFT of N weighted samples at the spectral line k is given by

$$X(k) = \frac{A_0}{2} e^{j\varphi_0} W_N(k - \lambda_0) + \frac{A_0}{2} e^{-j\varphi_0} W_N(k + \lambda_0), \tag{4}$$

where $W_N(\cdot)$ denotes the DTFT of the window $w_N(n)$. If the bin number with the largest magnitude is l, then the largest magnitude is given by

$$|X(l)| = \left| \frac{A_0}{2} e^{j\varphi_0} W_N(l - \lambda_0) + \frac{A_0}{2} e^{-j\varphi_0} W_N(l + \lambda_0) \right| \tag{5}$$

The second largest magnitude is given by

$$|X(l \pm 1)| = \left| \frac{A_0}{2} e^{j\varphi_0} W_N(l - \lambda_0 \pm 1) + \frac{A_0}{2} e^{-j\varphi_0} W_N(l + \lambda_0 \pm 1) \right|, \tag{6}$$

where it takes the negative if $l - \lambda_0 > 0$ and the positive if $l - \lambda_0 < 0$. The second terms on the right in (5) and (6) represent the image component in the spectrum. The interference is very small compared with the first term as long as l is far from zero frequency and Nyquist frequency. In this situation, $W_N(l + \lambda_0)$ can be ignored and (5) is reduced to

$$|X(l)| = \frac{A_0}{2} |W_N(l - \lambda_0)| \tag{7}$$

Similarly, (6) can be rewritten as

$$|X(l \pm 1)| \cong \frac{A_0}{2} |W_N(l - \lambda_0 \pm 1)| \tag{8}$$

For the two-point (2p) interpolation algorithm [6, 8, 11], we introduce α defined as the ratio of the two largest magnitudes

$$\alpha = \frac{|X(l \pm 1)|}{|X(l)|} \cong \frac{W_N(l - \lambda_0 \pm 1)}{W_N(l - \lambda_0)} \tag{9}$$

It can be clearly seen from Eq. (9) that the ratio α only depends on the normalized frequency λ_0 if the data window is already known. In particular, λ_0 can be determined by simple and explicit forms when the maximum sidelobe decay windows are used [11],

$$\lambda_0 = l \pm \frac{H\alpha - H + 1}{\alpha + 1} \tag{10}$$

In (10), H denotes the number of terms in the maximum sidelobe decay window. For other windows, λ_0 can be obtained by the polynomial approximation method [13].

Similarly, with proper combination of three or more spectral lines, a ratio α can be obtained which only depends on the selected window and λ_0 [9, 12]. Once the data window is chosen, λ_0 can be solely determined by α,

$$\lambda_0 = h(\alpha) \tag{11}$$

If the maximum sidelobe decay windows are selected, α can be obtained from (10). Once α is determined, the normalized frequency can be computed and the frequency can be worked out in Eq. (2).

As shown above, the second terms on the right in Eqs. (5) and (6) representing the interferences from the image component in the spectrum have been neglected. The approximation will be reasonable if $\lambda_0 > 5$ and $\lambda_0 < N/2 - 5$. However, if λ_0 were out of the specified ranges, significant errors would be generated [15]. Therefore, it is of great importance and necessary to deduce a simple algorithm that is applicable even when λ_0 is in the extreme ranges.

3 Generalization of interpolation DFT algorithms

In Section 2, it was already known that

$$X(l) = \frac{A_0}{2} e^{j\varphi_0} W_N(-\delta) + \frac{A_0}{2} e^{-j\varphi_0} W_N(2l + \delta), \tag{12}$$

where $W_N(\cdot)$ is the DTFT of the window $w_N(n)$ and

$$\delta = \lambda_0 - l \tag{13}$$

It should be pointed out that due to the actual processing requirements of causality, $w_N(n)$ is a time-shifting window, where $n = 0, 1 \cdots N - 1$. It can be obtained by

$$w_N(n) = w(n - N/2) \tag{14}$$

$w(n)$ is assumed to be a DFT-even window [2], which is symmetric with respect to the origin. According to the time-shifting property of DFT, we have

$$W_N(k) = W(k) e^{-jk\pi}, \tag{15}$$

where $W(k)$ is the DTFT of the window $w(n)$ and the complex exponential factor corresponds to the time shift. $W(k)$ is also symmetric and real because $w(n)$ is symmetric and real. Substituting Eq. (15) into Eq. (12), $X(l)$ can be rewritten as

$$X(l) = \frac{A_0}{2} e^{j(\delta\pi + \varphi_0)} W(-\delta) + \frac{A_0}{2} e^{-j(2l\pi + \delta\pi + \varphi_0)} W(2l + \delta) \tag{16a}$$

Because the period of the complex sinusoidal is 2π, Eq. (16a) can be further expressed as

$$X(l) = \frac{A_0}{2} e^{j(\delta\pi + \varphi_0)} W(-\delta) + \frac{A_0}{2} e^{-j(\delta\pi + \varphi_0)} W(2l + \delta) \tag{16b}$$

The real and imaginary parts are expressed as

$$X_R(l) = \frac{A_0}{2} \cos(\varphi_0 + \delta\pi)[W(-\delta) + W(2l + \delta)], \tag{17a}$$

and

$$X_I(l) = \frac{A_0}{2} \sin(\varphi_0 + \delta\pi)[W(-\delta) - W(2l + \delta)], \tag{17b}$$

respectively. Accordingly, we have

$$X_R(l \pm 1) = -\frac{A_0}{2} \cos(\varphi_0 + \delta\pi)[W(-\delta \pm 1) + W(2l + \delta \pm 1)], \tag{18a}$$

and

$$X_I(l + 1) = -\frac{A_0}{2} \sin(\varphi_0 + \delta\pi)[W(-\delta \pm 1) - W(2l + \delta \pm 1)] \tag{18b}$$

Now, we introduce two variables α_R, α_I defined as

$$\alpha_R = \left| \frac{X_R(l \pm 1)}{X_R(l)} \right| = \frac{W(-\delta \pm 1) + W(2l + \delta \pm 1)}{W(-\delta) + W(2l + \delta)}, \tag{19a}$$

and

$$\alpha_I = \left| \frac{X_I(l \pm 1)}{X_I(l)} \right| = \frac{W(-\delta \pm 1) - W(2l + \delta \pm 1)}{W(-\delta) - W(2l + \delta)} \tag{19b}$$

It is assumed, similar to that in Section 2, that λ_0 is far enough from the origin so that the leakage terms $W(2l + \delta)$ and $W(2l + \delta \pm 1)$ are very small compared to $W(-\delta)$ and $W(-\delta \pm 1)$ and could be ignored. With this assumption, we can get the following relationship

$$\alpha_R \cong \alpha_I \cong \alpha \cong \frac{W(-\delta \pm 1)}{W(-\delta)} \tag{20}$$

The relationship indicates that the ratio of the real or imaginary part can also be used for estimation if the interference from the image part can be neglected. Note that a very important phenomenon is implied from Eqs. (19a) and (19b) that the ratio is phase independent, i.e., the phase does not affect the result of frequency estimation.

In other words, the frequency estimate only depends on the frequency itself.

We proceed to analyze the traditional algorithm without making approximation. The moduli of $X(l)$ and $X(l \pm 1)$ can be obtained by the square roots of $J(l)$ and $J(l+1)$, respectively, according to the results in Eqs. (17a), (17b), (18a), and (18b).

$$J(l) = \frac{A_0^2}{4}\left[W^2(-\delta) + W^2(2l+\delta)\right] + \frac{A_0^2}{2}\cos(2\phi_0 + 2\delta\pi)W(-\delta)W(2l+\delta) \tag{21a}$$

$$J(l\pm 1) = \frac{A_0^2}{4}\left[W^2(-\delta\pm 1) + W^2(2l+\delta\pm 1)\right] + \frac{A_0^2}{2}\cos(2\phi_0 + 2\delta\pi)W(-\delta\pm 1)W(2l+\delta\pm 1) \tag{21b}$$

Without making approximation, Eq. (10) becomes

$$\bar{\alpha} = \frac{|X(l\pm 1)|}{|X(l)|} = \frac{\sqrt{J(l\pm 1)}}{\sqrt{J(l)}} \tag{22}$$

Obviously, $\bar{\alpha}$ is phase dependent. Also, for Hanning window, (namely two-term MSD window) it can be proved that (see Appendix 1)

$$\lambda_R \geq \bar{\lambda} \geq \lambda_I, \tag{23}$$

where λ_R, λ_I, and $\bar{\lambda}$ are corresponding estimation values by α_R, α_I and $\bar{\alpha}$. If $\delta \neq 0$, the first equality sign is only for $\phi_0 + \delta\pi = 0$ or π and the second equality sign is only for $\phi_0 + \delta\pi = \pm\pi/2$. Systematic error will be introduced no matter which of the three ratios is used in formula (11). The difference is that α_R is only affected by the real part of negative frequency and α_I is only affected by the imaginary part of the negative frequency component, while $\bar{\alpha}$ is affected by both the real and imaginary parts.

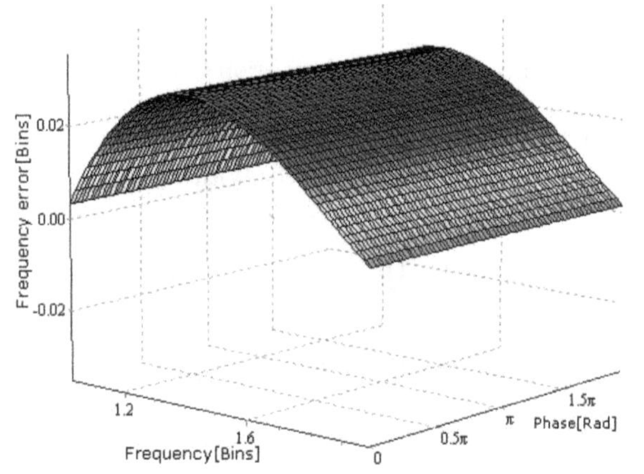

Fig. 1 Frequency estimation errors when Hanning window is used ($\alpha = \alpha_R$)

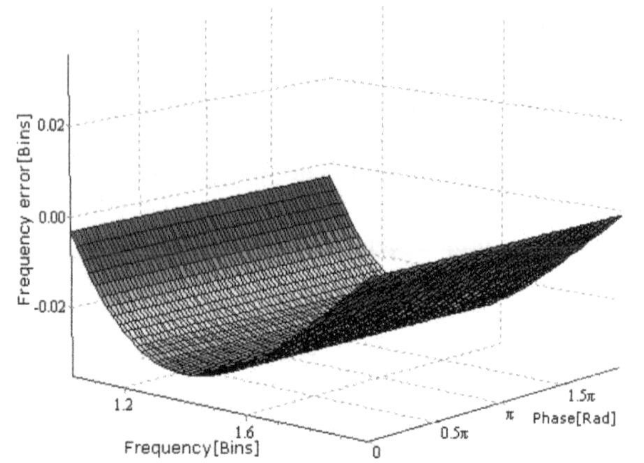

Fig. 2 Frequency estimation errors when Hanning window is used ($\alpha = \alpha_I$)

Inspired by modulus-based ratio, we can extend the ratio to a more general notation. With a proper combination of the real and imaginary parts of $X(l)$ and $X(l \pm 1)$, we can get various kinds of ratios. For example, $\hat{\alpha}$ can be defined as

$$\hat{\alpha} = \frac{|X_R(l\pm 1)| + |X_I(l\pm 1)|}{|X_R(l)| + |X_I(l)|} \tag{24}$$

Similar to $\bar{\alpha}$, we have

$$\hat{\alpha} \cong \frac{W(-\delta \pm 1)}{W_N(-\delta)}, \tag{25}$$

and for Hanning window, we can also obtain

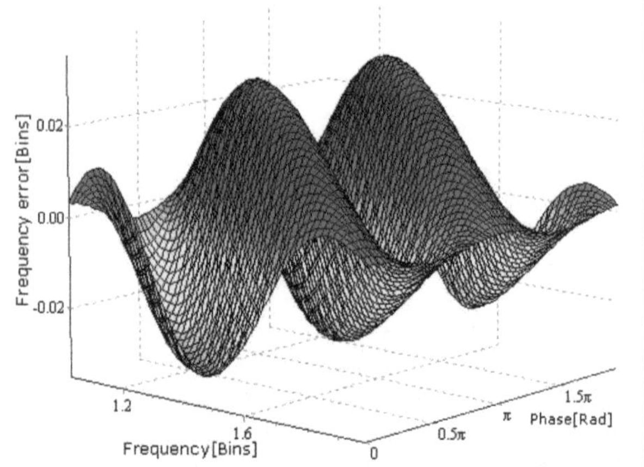

Fig. 3 Frequency estimation errors when Hanning window is used ($\alpha = \bar{\alpha}$)

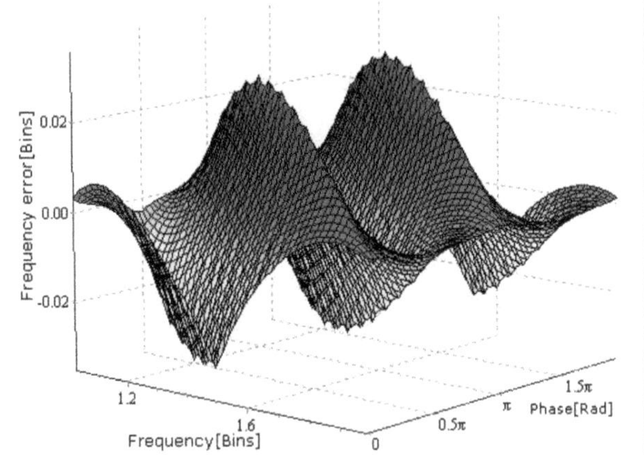

Fig. 4 Frequency estimation errors when Hanning window is used ($\alpha = \hat{\alpha}$)

$$\lambda_R \geq \hat{\lambda} \geq \lambda_I, \tag{26}$$

where $\hat{\lambda}$ is estimation value by $\hat{\alpha}$. It is indicated that a new estimator can be obtained if α in formula (11) is replaced by $\hat{\alpha}$. The proof of Eq. (26) is similar to that of Eq. (23). Frequency estimation errors of the four estimators when $1 < \lambda_0 < 2$ (samples are weighted by Hanning window) are shown in Figs. 1, 2, 3, and 4. In Figs. 1 and 2, it can be seen that for a certain frequency, the frequency error is constant in spite of the variable phase. It is confirmed that the frequency estimators, based on the α_R, α_I separately, are independent of the signal phase, while the estimators based on $\bar{\alpha}, \hat{\alpha}$ are the functions of both the frequency and the phase. Comparing the estimated errors in Figs. 1, 2, 3, and 4, we can also see that the simulation results coincide well with the theoretical analysis in Eqs. (23) and (26). The difference between the two estimators in Figs. 3 and 4 is that the developing trend of errors in Fig. 3 is smoother than that in Fig. 4. We now have to emphasize again that maximum absolute errors are obtained when the phase and the offset satisfy the relationship $\phi_0 + \delta\pi = 0$ or $\phi_0 + \delta\pi = \pi/2$. For a certain offset, the maximum error is equal to the error shown in Figs. 1 and 2. In addition, we can also construct other types of ratio to create new estimators by combining the real and imaginary parts of $X(l)$ and $X(l \pm 1)$ properly.

4 Algorithms with high image component interference rejection

As we can see in Figs. 1, 2, 3, and 4, the maximum error due to negative frequency can reach as high as 0.04 for all the estimators. Simulation results show that it can be even up to nearly 0.1 for the rectangle window and up to 0.2 for the three-term maximum decay window. As a result, it is of great significance to reduce the interference resulting from the negative frequency. A new interpolated algorithm which has strong resistance against interference from the negative frequency component is proposed in this section.

4.1 Simple algorithms with high image component interference rejection

Recalling Eqs. (19a) and (19b) and observing Figs. 1 and 2, we can infer that there is nearly a complementary relationship between the two estimators. A proper combination of the two estimators can probably result in an intrinsic rejection of negative frequency leakage. Hence, we introduce α_1 defined as the arithmetic mean value of α_R and α_I,

$$\begin{aligned}\alpha_1 &= (\alpha_R + \alpha_I)/2 \\ &= \frac{W(-\delta \pm 1) - W(2l + \delta \pm 1) W(2l + \delta)/W(-\delta)}{W(-\delta) - W^2(2l + \delta)/W(-\delta)}\end{aligned} \tag{27a}$$

Now, the interference terms are $W(2l + \delta \pm 1)W(2l + \delta)/W(-\delta)$ and $W^2(2l + \delta)/W(-\delta)$, much smaller than the original terms $W(2l + \delta \pm 1)$ and $W(2l + \delta)$. Most errors are eliminated by a simple arithmetic average operation. Similarly, we can also introduce α_2, α_3, and α_4 defined as the geometric mean value, the harmonic mean value, and the quadratic mean of α_R and α_I, respectively, as indicated in

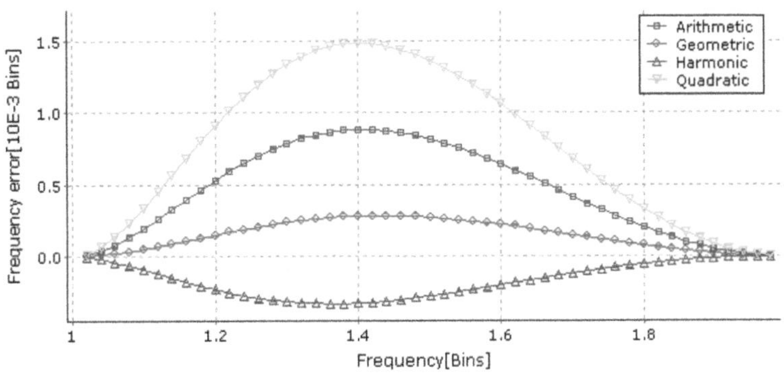

Fig. 5 Frequency estimation errors based on different means of α_R and α_I when Hanning window is used

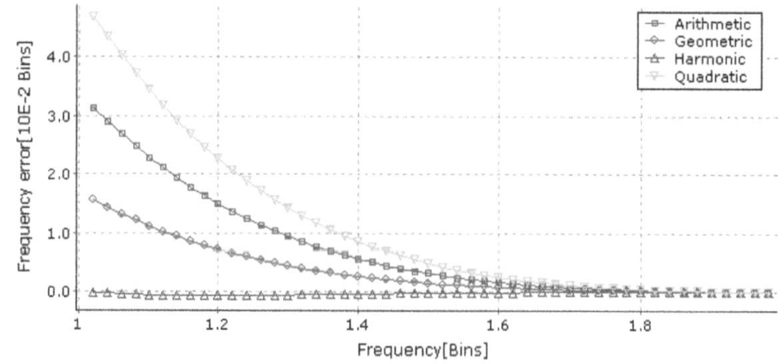

Fig. 6 Frequency estimation errors based on different means of α_R and α_I when three-term MSD window is used

$$\alpha_2 = \sqrt{\alpha_R \alpha_I} = \sqrt{\frac{W^2(-\delta \pm 1) - W^2(2l + \delta \pm 1)}{W^2(-\delta) - W^2(2l + \delta)}}, \tag{27b}$$

$$\alpha_3 = \frac{2}{1/\alpha_R + 1/\alpha_I} = \frac{\alpha_2^2}{\alpha_1}, \tag{27c}$$

and

$$\alpha_4 = \sqrt{(\alpha_R^2 + \alpha_I^2)/2} = \sqrt{2\alpha_1^2 - \alpha_2^2} \tag{27d}$$

Similar to α_1, the interference terms of α_2 become much smaller as well. α_3 and α_4 can be written as simple functions of α_1 and α_2, respectively. The values of the four means are approximately equal. To demonstrate the ability of negative frequency leakage rejection, the frequency errors of the four estimators are displayed when $1 < \lambda_0 < 2$. Note that the four estimators are also phase independent because no phase information is involved in the ratios shown in Eqs. (27a)–(27d). Consequently, the phase was just set to zero. Figures 5 and 6 show the estimation results as a function of the frequency. It can be seen that the frequency errors sharply decrease compared with the modulus-based algorithms. In particular, the remaining error for the one based on the harmonic mean value is less than 10^{-3}, which is small enough for the engineering practice.

4.2 Further improved interpolation algorithms with slide DFT

However, there is a serious defect in the above algorithms in which the weighed ratio is used. The algorithms may become quite vulnerable if $\cos(\phi_0 + \delta\pi) \approx 0$ or $\sin(\phi_0 + \delta\pi) \approx 0$. Under such two circumstances, the imaginary parts or the real parts would be so small that even a small disturbance would lead to a dramatic change in α_R or α_I, resulting of significant errors in the final frequency estimates. Theoretical cosine waves corrupted by low-level random noise were generated to confirm the defect, and the vulnerability of two frequency estimators based on α_R and α_I is shown in Figs. 7 and 8, respectively. It is clearly shown that radical changes appear when $\cos(\phi_0 + \delta\pi) \approx 0$ for α_R and $\sin(\phi_0 + \delta\pi) \approx 0$ for

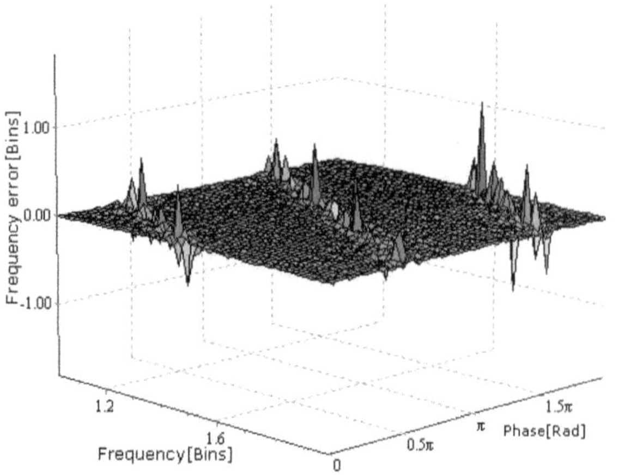

Fig. 7 The phenomenon of "Luo-arêtes" in the α_R-based estimator (Hanning window)

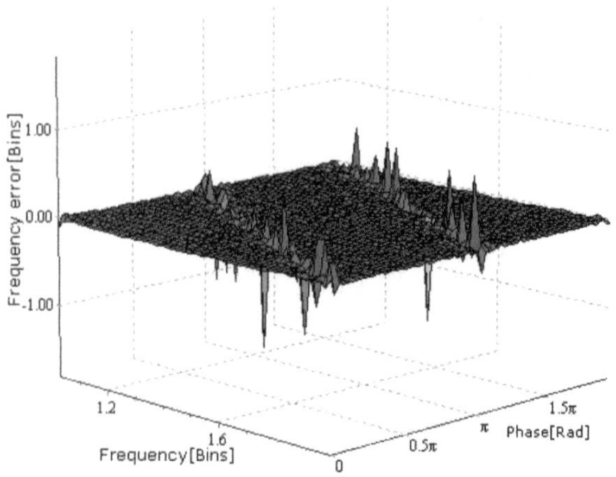

Fig. 8 The phenomenon of "Luo-arêtes" in the α_I-based estimator (Hanning window)

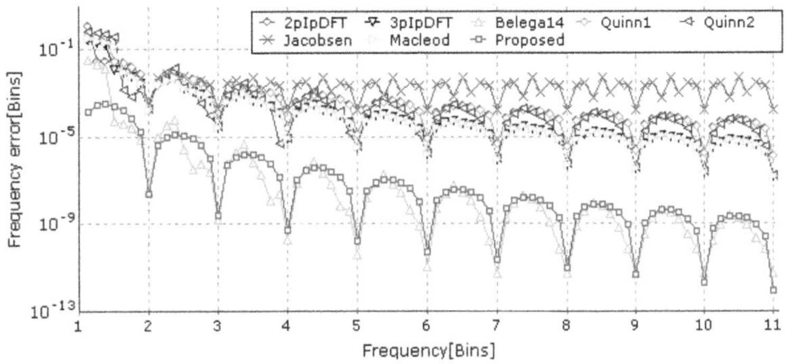

Fig. 9 Maximum estimation error as a function of λ_0 for different estimators without noise (Hanning window)

α_I. Sharp peaks along these lines are observed in the surface of the frequency errors. They look like knife-edge arêtes so we call them "Luo–arêtes." In contrast, for the frequencies that are not in the vicinity of these lines, errors are very small and remain stable.

To avoid the "Luo–arêtes," a further improved algorithm has been proposed. The fact that α_R and α_I (including various kinds of mean values of the two) are phase independent and the change of phase has no influences on frequency estimates help us get a robust ratio by time-shifting technique. Now, consider a discrete sequence with N samples $x(0), x(1)\cdots x(N-1)$ and assume that its observed phase is ϕ_1. After delaying for L samples, we get a time-shifted sequence $x(L), x(L+1)\cdots x(N+L-1)$ and its observed phase ϕ_2 can be expressed as

$$\phi_2 = \phi_1 + 2\pi f_0 L\Delta T = \phi_1 + 2\pi f_0 L/f_s = \phi_1 + 2\pi\lambda_0 L/N \quad (28)$$

In the above equation, ΔT is the sampling interval, f_0 is the theoretical frequency and λ_0 is the normalized frequency scaled by frequency resolution. As λ_0 is unknown, we can use its largest bin number l, instead.

$$L \approx N\frac{\phi_2-\phi_1}{2\pi l} \quad (29)$$

The actual observed phase of the time delay sequence is $\phi'_2 = \phi_1 + 2\pi l L/N$ and the phase error is

$$\phi_2' - \phi_2 = \Delta\phi_2 = 2\pi\delta L/N \quad (30)$$

Generally, we have $l > 1$ and $\phi_2 - \phi_1 < \pi/2$ so that $L/N < 1/4$. Considering $\delta \in [-0.5, 0.5)$, the absolute phase error is less than $\pi/4$. For α_R, if ϕ_2 was set to 0 or π, ϕ'_2 was limited in the range of $(-\pi/4, \pi/4)$ or $(3\pi/4, 5\pi/4)$. For α_I, if ϕ_2 was set to $\pi/2$ or $-\pi/2$, ϕ'_2 was limited in the range of $(\pi/4, 3\pi/4)$ or $(-3\pi/4, -\pi/4)$. It is indicated that we can adjust the observed phase by the time-shifting technique so that we can get a robust ratio to avoid the "Luo–arêtes." In addition, we can obtain the spectral lines l and $l \pm 1$ of the time-delayed sequence by means of the sliding discrete Fourier transform (SDFT) [19, 20]. It will be more efficient compared with another separate FFT or DFT.

5 Comparison with other state-of-the-art methods

In this section, some computer simulations were conducted to verify the effectiveness and the accuracy of the proposed algorithms. For conciseness, only the results of

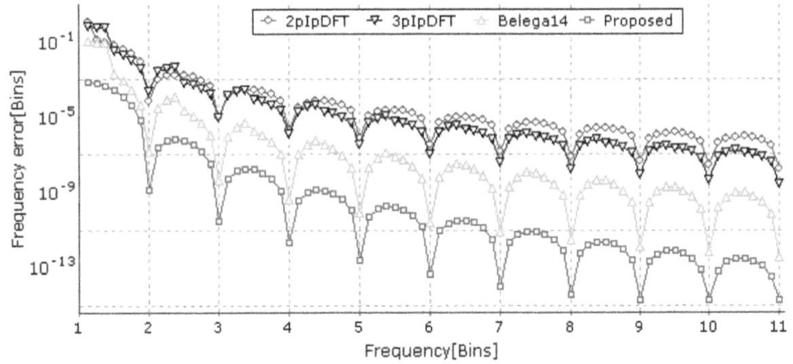

Fig. 10 Maximum estimation error as a function of λ_0 for different estimators without noise (three-term MSD window)

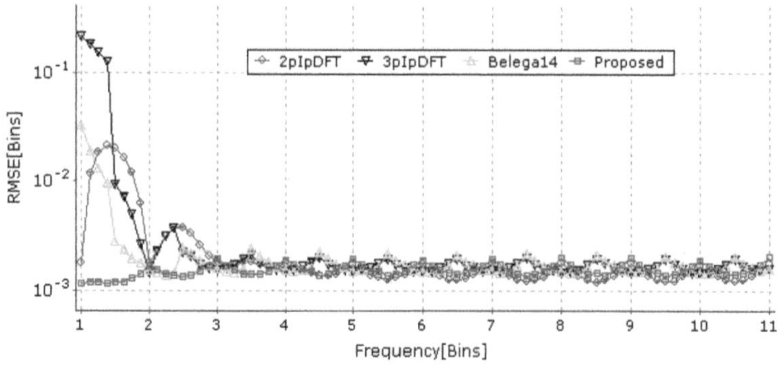

Fig. 11 RMSE for different algorithms (SNR = 30 dB, Hanning window)

the algorithm based on the harmonic mean of α_R and α_I were shown. All simulation results are returned by the algorithm proposed in Section 4.2. In addition, the results of the traditional IpDFT algorithm (2pIpDFT) [5, 8, 11], the classical three-point IpDFT algorithm (3pIpDFT) [9, 12], Quinn's two-point-based estimator (Quinn1, only applicable for Hanning window), and Quinn's three-point-based optimal estimator (Quinn2, only applicable for Hanning window) [21–23], the estimator proposed by Macleod in 1998 (Macleod, only applicable for Hanning window) [24], the three-point complex spectrum-based estimator (Jacobsen, only applicable for Hanning window) [25] referred by Jacobsen and Kootsookos in 2007, and the improved three-point IpDFT algorithm with high image frequency interference rejection capability recently proposed by Belega (Belega14) [15], were also displayed for comparison. In all the considered IpDFT-based algorithms, both the two-term and three-term MSD windows were adopted. For simplicity but without loss of generality, parameters used in all the simulation experiments were as follows, the amplitude of the cosine wave $A = 1$, the number of samples $N = 512$, and the sampling rate $f_s = 512$. The results shown in this section were scaled by frequency resolution and expressed in bins.

5.1 Theoretical cosine wave without noise

To demonstrate the excellent rejection capability against the interference from negative frequency, theoretical signals contain a small number of cycles. The normalized frequency λ_0 is varied in the range (1, 11) with a step of 1/8. For each frequency, the phase θ is varied in the range $[-\pi, \pi)$ with a step of $\pi/72$. The maximum absolute frequency errors $|\delta|_{max}$ are shown in Figs. 9 and 10 as a function of λ_0 for the two-term and three-term MSD windows, respectively. It is clearly revealed that the errors due to negative frequency interference are remarkably reduced. In general, both the proposed method and the improved three-point IpDFT method outperform other estimators throughout the entire range of considered λ_0. When the Hanning window is adopted, Jacobsen's estimator has the worst performance. The traditional IpDFT algorithm, Quinn's two-point-based estimator, and Quinn's three-point-based optimal estimator have similar trend. The classical three-point IpDFT algorithm and Macleod's estimator provide better results than the above three estimators. If $\lambda_0 < 4.5$ (especially $\lambda_0 < 1.5$) and $\delta > 0$, the new method provides better performance than the improved three-point IpDFT and the opposite holds if $\delta < 0$. When $\lambda_0 > 4.5$, the improved three-point IpDFT shows a

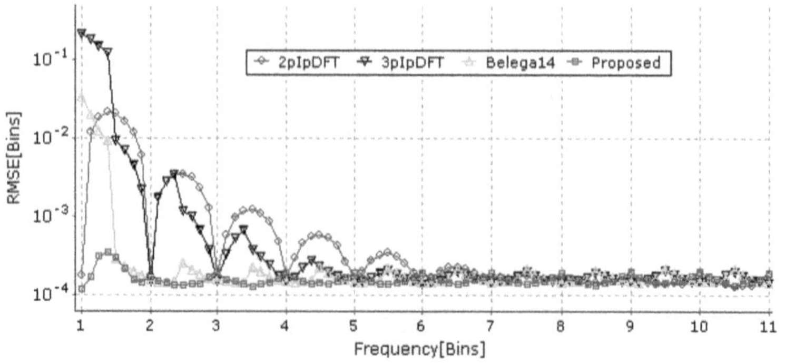

Fig. 12 RMSE for different algorithms (SNR = 50 dB, Hanning window)

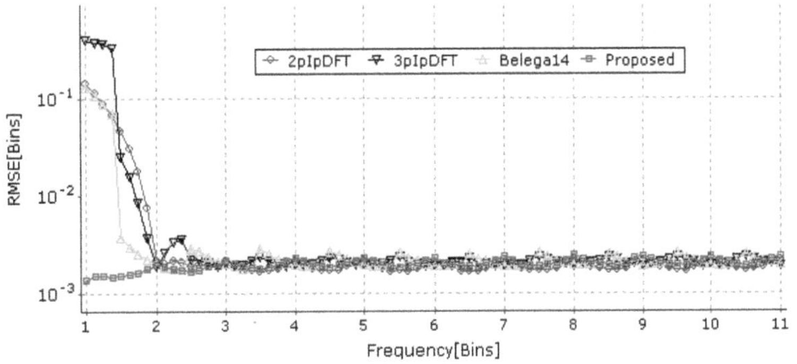

Fig. 13 RMSE for different algorithms (SNR = 30 dB, three-term MSD window)

small advantage than the proposed algorithm. When the three-term MSD window is adopted, the new estimator has overwhelming advantage over the rest. It should be pointed out that regardless of the adopted window type and the value of λ_0, the maximum frequency error of the new algorithm never goes above 10^{-3}, even though only one or two cycles are obtained.

5.2 Theoretical cosine wave corrupted by additive noise

In this subsection, we considered the ideal cosine wave contaminated with the additive Gaussian noise. Similar to [15], we investigated the RMSE of estimates returned by the considered estimators as a function of λ_0 for certain SNRs. For each frequency, 50,000 instances were generated with a random phase. For conciseness, four algorithms are considered, including the traditional IpDFT algorithm (2pIpDFT), the classical three-point IpDFT algorithm (3pIpDFT), the improved three-point IpDFT algorithm with high image frequency interference rejection capability (Belega14), and the proposed algorithm. Results with SNR = 30 dB and 50 dB for Hanning window and three-term MSD window were shown in Figs. 11, 12, 13, and 14, respectively. The results for Hanning window agree well with those in [15]. As shown in Figs. 11 and 12, the estimated RMSE of the proposed method is always in a low level with a small fluctuation and essentially the novel method has no competitor for $\lambda_0 < 3$. When λ_0 becomes larger, the estimated RMSE of four estimators tend to be in a similar level and it is interesting to find that the two-point-based algorithms show a better performance at the worst incoherent sampling condition ($\delta \approx 0.5$), while the three-point-based algorithms provide better results when λ_0 is close to integer values ($\delta \approx 0$).

When the three-term MSD window is adopted, the overall trend is similar to that of Hanning window. For $\lambda_0 < 2$, the performance of the traditional 2pIpDFT and 3pIpDFT is worse than Hanning window due to the wider mainlobe of the three-term MSD window. For $\lambda_0 > 2$, they have better performances because of the faster sidelobe decay rate. For the same SNR, the RMSE values of the two algorithms employing three-term MSD window decrease faster than that employing Hanning window before reaching the ultimate stable level. Meanwhile, the ultimate stable level is higher than that employing Hanning window because of the worse noise properties of the three-term MSD window. The performance of the proposed algorithm maintains its superiority to the other three algorithms for $\lambda_0 < 3$. To sum up, the traditional two-point- or three-point-based algorithms are very good choices because of their simplicity when random noise has a significant influence on the uncertainty of estimates.

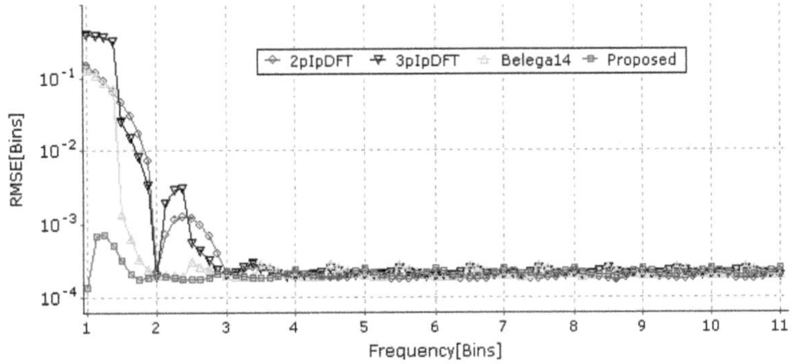

Fig. 14 RMSE for different algorithms (SNR = 50 dB, three-term MSD window)

The proposed algorithm is strongly recommended when the image frequency interference is the main error source especially when a small number of cycles are contained in samples.

6 Conclusions

Frequency estimation by the IpDFT method is studied in this paper. We have quantitatively analyzed the influences of the interference from the image component and generalized the interpolated DFT algorithms. Based on the analysis, novel frequency estimators are proposed, which have strong rejection against the high image component interference. Accuracy of the novel algorithm has been confirmed by simulations. Comparative studies reveal that the proposed algorithm has a better performance than the traditional algorithms when the spectral interference from negative frequency component is significant, especially for the cycles less than one and a half. This proposed algorithm is simple to understand, easy to implement, and very suitable for real-time analysis.

7 Appendices

7.1 Appendix 1

According to the conclusion in Eq. (10), we can get the frequency estimation by

$$\lambda = l \pm \frac{2\alpha - 1}{\alpha + 1}, \tag{A1}$$

when Hanning window is used.

Accordingly, we can obtain frequency estimations

$$\lambda_R = l \pm \frac{2\alpha_R - 1}{\alpha_R + 1} = l \pm \left(2 - \frac{3}{\alpha_R + 1}\right), \tag{A2a}$$

$$\lambda_I = l \pm \frac{2\alpha_I - 1}{\alpha_I + 1} = l \pm \left(2 - \frac{3}{\alpha_I + 1}\right), \tag{A2b}$$

and

$$\bar{\lambda} = l \pm \frac{2\bar{\alpha} - 1}{\bar{\alpha} + 1} = l \pm \left(2 - \frac{3}{\bar{\alpha} + 1}\right), \tag{A2c}$$

by three kinds of ratio α_R, α_I, and $\bar{\alpha}$, respectively.

Further, combining Eq. (A2a) with Eq. (A2c) and Eq. (A2b) with Eq. (A2c), we get the following two equations

$$\hat{\lambda}_R - \bar{\lambda} = \pm\left(\frac{3}{\bar{\alpha} + 1} - \frac{3}{\alpha_R + 1}\right) = \pm 3 \frac{\alpha_R - \bar{\alpha}}{(\bar{\alpha} + 1)(\alpha_R + 1)} \tag{A3a}$$

and

$$\hat{\lambda}_I - \bar{\lambda} = \pm\left(\frac{3}{\bar{\alpha} + 1} - \frac{3}{\alpha_I + 1}\right) = \pm 3 \frac{\alpha_I - \bar{\alpha}}{(\bar{\alpha} + 1)(\alpha_I + 1)} \tag{A3b}$$

The above equations indicate the following conclusions.

(1) For $\delta > 0$, since $\alpha_R > \bar{\alpha}$, $\alpha_I < \bar{\alpha}$ (Appendix 2) and it takes the positive in (A3a) and (A3b), we get $\hat{\lambda}_R > \bar{\lambda}$ and $\hat{\lambda}_I < \bar{\lambda}$.

(2) For $\delta < 0$, since $\alpha_R < \bar{\alpha}$, $\alpha_I > \bar{\alpha}$ (Appendix 2) and it takes the negative in (A3a) and (A3b),we get $\hat{\lambda}_R > \bar{\lambda}$ and $\hat{\lambda}_I < \bar{\lambda}$.

Finally, for both $\delta > 0$ and $\delta < 0$, we have $\hat{\lambda}_R > \bar{\lambda}$ and $\hat{\lambda}_I < \bar{\lambda}$. Furthermore, if $\delta \neq 0$, when $\varphi_0 + \delta\pi = 0$ or π, we have $\hat{\lambda}_R = \bar{\lambda}$; and when $\varphi_0 + \delta\pi = \pm\pi/2$, we have $\hat{\lambda}_I = \bar{\lambda}$.

7.2 Appendix 2

It is already known that $\alpha_R = \frac{W_1 + W_{2l+1}}{W_0 + W_{2l}}$, $\alpha_I = \frac{W_1 - W_{2l+1}}{W_0 - W_{2l}}$, $\bar{\alpha} = \sqrt{\frac{W_1^2 + W_{2l+1}^2 + 2uW_1W_{2l+1}}{W_0^2 + W_{2l}^2 + 2uW_0W_{2l}}}$ from Section 3, where $W_0 = W(-\delta)$, $W_1 = W(-\delta \pm 1)$, $W_{2l} = W(2l + \delta)$, $W_{2l+1} = W(2l + \delta \pm 1)$ and $u = \cos(2\varphi_0 + 2\delta\pi)$ according to Eqs. (19a), (19b), and (22). We define

$$E = \alpha_R^2 - \bar{\alpha}^2 = \frac{W_1^2 + W_{2l+1}^2 + 2W_1W_{2l+1}}{W_0^2 + W_{2l}^2 + 2W_0W_{2l}} - \frac{W_1^2 + W_{2l+1}^2 + 2uW_1W_{2l+1}}{W_0^2 + W_{2l}^2 + 2uW_0W_{2l}}, \tag{B1a}$$

and

$$F = \alpha_I^2 - \bar{\alpha}^2 = \frac{W_1^2 + W_{2l+1}^2 - 2W_1W_{2l+1}}{W_0^2 + W_{2l}^2 - 2W_0W_{2l}} - \frac{W_1^2 + W_{2l+1}^2 + 2uW_1W_{2l+1}}{W_0^2 + W_{2l}^2 + 2uW_0W_{2l}} \tag{B1b}$$

After some algebraic manipulation, we obtain

$$E = 2(1-u)\frac{G}{(W_0 + W_{2l})^2(W_0^2 + W_{2l}^2 + 2uW_0 W_{2l})}, \tag{B2a}$$

and

$$F = 2(1+u)\frac{-G}{(W_0 - W_{2l})^2(W_0^2 + W_{2l}^2 + 2uW_0 W_{2l})}, \tag{B2b}$$

where $G = (W_0\ W_1 - W_{2l}W_{2l+1})(W_0\ W_{2l+1} - W_1\ W_{2l})$. When Hanning window is used, we know that $W_0 > W_1 > 0$, $W_1 >> |W_{2l}|$, and $W_1 >> |W_{2l+1}|$.

(1) For $\delta > 0$, we have $W_{2l} < 0$ and $W_{2l+1} > 0$ for Hanning window, so $G > 0$. Then, we have $\alpha_R > \bar{\alpha}$ and $\alpha_I < \bar{\alpha}$.
(2) For $\delta < 0$, we have $W_{2l} > 0$ and $W_{2l+1} < 0$ for Hanning window, so $G < 0$. Then, we have $\alpha_R < \bar{\alpha}$ and $\alpha_I > \bar{\alpha}$.

It should be pointed that for $\delta \neq 0$, the requirement for $\alpha_R = \bar{\alpha}$ is that $\mu = 1$ and the requirement for $\alpha_I = \bar{\alpha}$ is that $\mu = -1$. That means that $\phi_0 + \delta\pi = 0$ or π for $\alpha_R = \bar{\alpha}$ and $\phi_0 + \delta\pi = \pm\pi/2$ for $\alpha_I = \bar{\alpha}$.

Competing interests
The authors declare that they have no competing interests.

Acknowledgements
The authors want to thank the anonymous reviewers for their helpful comments, which significantly improved the quality of the paper. This research was supported by the Science Foundation for Young Scientists (Grant No. E010A2015063) and Startup Fund for Doctors (Grant No. E010A2015037) of Chongqing University of Posts and Telecommunications, Chongqing Science and Technology Commission (Grant No. cstc2015jcyjB0241) and also was partly supported by the National Natural Science Foundation of China (Grant No. 51374264).

Author details
[1]School of Advanced Manufacture Engineering, Chongqing University of Posts and Telecommunications, Chongqing 400065, People's Republic of China. [2]School of Automation, Chongqing University, Chongqing 400044, People's Republic of China. [3]Department of Mechanical Engineering, Chongqing University, Chongqing 400044, People's Republic of China.

References
1. KF Chen, JT Jiang, S Crowsen, Against the long-range spectral leakage of the cosine window family. Comput Phys Commun **180**, 904–911 (2009)
2. FJ Harris, On the use of windows for harmonic analysis with the discrete Fourier transform. Proc IEEE **66**, 51–83 (1978)
3. J Luo, M Xie, Phase difference methods based on asymmetric windows. Mech Syst Signal Process **54**, 52–67 (2015)
4. DC Rife, G Vincent, Use of the discrete Fourier transform in the measurement of frequencies and levels of tones. Bell Syst Tech J **49**, 197–228 (1970)
5. VK Jain, WL Collins, DC Davis, High-accuracy analog measurements via interpolated FFT. Instrumentation and Measurement, IEEE Transactions on **28**, 113–122 (1979)
6. T Grandke, Interpolation algorithms for discrete Fourier transforms of weighted signals. Instrumentation and Measurement, IEEE Transactions on **32**, 350–355 (1983)
7. M Xie, K Ding, Corrections for frequency, amplitude and phase in a fast Fourier transform of a harmonic signal. Mech Syst Signal Process **10**, 211–221 (1996)
8. J Luo, Z Xie, M Xie, Frequency estimation of the weighted real tones or resolved multiple tones by iterative interpolation DFT algorithm. Digital signal processing **41**, 118–129 (2015)
9. D Agrez, Weighted multipoint interpolated DFT to improve amplitude estimation of multifrequency signal. Instrumentation and Measurement, IEEE Transactions on **51**, 287–292 (2002)
10. J Luo, Z Xie, M Xie, Interpolated DFT algorithms with zero padding for classic windows. Mech Syst Signal Process **70–71**, 118–129 (2016)
11. D Belega, D Dallet, Multifrequency signal analysis by Interpolated DFT method with maximum sidelobe decay windows. Measurement **42**, 420–426 (2009)
12. D Belega, D Dallet, D Petri, Accuracy of sine wave frequency estimation by multipoint interpolated DFT approach. Instrumentation and Measurement, IEEE Transactions on **59**, 2808–2815 (2010)
13. J-R Liao, C-M Chen, Phase correction of discrete Fourier transform coefficients to reduce frequency estimation bias of single tone complex sinusoid. Signal Process **94**, 108–117 (2014)
14. J-R Liao, S Lo, Analytical solutions for frequency estimators by interpolation of DFT coefficients. Signal Process **100**, 93–100 (2014)
15. D Belega, D Petri, D Dallet, Frequency estimation of a sinusoidal signal via a three-point interpolated DFT method with high image component interference rejection capability. Digital Signal Processing **24**, 162–169 (2014)
16. D Belega, D Petri, Accuracy analysis of the multicycle synchrophasor estimator provided by the interpolated DFT algorithm. IEEE Trans Instrum Meas **62**, 942–953 (2013)
17. P Castello, M Lixia, C Muscas, PA Pegoraro, Impact of the model on the accuracy of synchrophasor measurement. Instrumentation and Measurement, IEEE Transactions on **61**, 2179–2188 (2012)
18. Y Tu, H Zhang, Method for CMF signal processing based on the recursive DTFT algorithm with negative frequency contribution. Instrumentation and Measurement, IEEE Transactions on **57**, 2647–2654 (2008)
19. E Jacobsen, R Lyons, The sliding DFT. Signal Processing Magazine, IEEE **20**, 74–80 (2003)
20. K Duda, Accurate, guaranteed stable, sliding discrete Fourier transform [DSP tips & tricks]. Signal Processing Magazine, IEEE **27**, 124–127 (2010)
21. B.G. Quinn, Frequency estimation using tapered data, in *Proceedings of IEEE International Conference on Acoustics, Speech and Signal Processing, ICASSP 2006*, (IEEE, Piscataway, 2006), pp. 73–76.
22. B.G. Quinn, in *Handbook of Statistics: Time Series Analysis: Methods and Applications*, T.S. Rao, S.S. Rao, C.R. Rao (Eds.). The estimation of frequency, (Elsevier Press, North Holland,2012), pp. 585–621.
23. B.G. Quinn, E.J. Hannan, *The Estimation and Tracking of Frequency*, (Cambridge University Press, New York, 2001), pp. 180–206.
24. MD Macleod, Fast nearly ML estimation of the parameters of real or complex single tones or resolved multiple tones. IEEE Trans Signal Process **46**, 141–148 (1998)
25. E Jacobsen, P Kootsookos, Fast, accurate frequency estimators [DSP tips & tricks]. IEEE Signal Process Mag **24**, 123–125 (2007)

7

To the theory of adaptive signal processing in systems with centrally symmetric receive channels

David I. Lekhovytskiy

Abstract

This paper presents the analytical derivation of joint probability density functions (pdfs) of the maximum likelihood (ML) estimates of a real and complex persymmetric correlation matrices (PCM) of multivariate Gaussian processes. It is oriented at the modifications of the classical Wishart's–Goodman's pdfs adapted to the ML estimates of the data CMs in a wide class of signal processing (SP) problems in systems with centrally symmetric (CS) receive channels. The importance of the derived modified pdfs for such CS systems could be as great as that of the classical Wishart's–Goodman's pdfs for systems with arbitrary receive channels. Some properties of the new obtained joint pdfs are featured.

Keywords: Central symmetry, Correlation matrix, Maximum likelihood estimate, Persymmetry, Probability density function, Wishart–Goodman distribution

1 Introduction

The multivariate statistical analysis of random processes widely uses the Wishart distribution, which describes statistical properties of a maximum likelihood (ML) estimate of the real-valued positively definite correlation matrix (CM) of multivariate Gaussian processes/fields [1–5]. For the ML estimate of the complex-valued Hermitian positively definite general-type data CM, such distribution is derived by Goodman [6–10]. An importance of both these distributions is caused by the fact that the ML CM estimates are widely used in many signal processing contexts: for radar applications [9, 11–17], for "superresolving" direction of arrival (DOA) estimation [7, 12, 18, 19], for multichannel communication systems [10], feature enhanced radar imaging with synthetic aperture radar (SAR) sensors [20, 21], digital beamforming in adaptive array (AA) systems, and fractional SAR modalities [22–25].

The Wishart–Goodman distributions are true for a general type data CM (GCM) of Gaussian processes/fields. These distributions in their classical forms do not take into account CM structure practically possible specificity caused by the peculiarities of signal processing (SP) system. At the same time, prior knowledge about the CM structure specificity could considerably enhance the processing efficiency and analysis precision due to a considerable decrease in the dimensionality of the parameter vectors involved into the adaptation process [13, 26].

The well-known example of such specificity is a persymmetry, i.e., symmetry relative to the secondary diagonal, of symmetric (real-valued) and Hermitian (complex-valued) CMs. Persymmetric CM (PCM) coincides with a result of itself turn relative to the secondary diagonal and thus is completely determined by a set of parameters (CM elements) which quantity is approximately twice less than that for respective general-type CM.

In multichannel (in space or time) signal processing systems, the CM persymmetry could be caused, in particular, by central symmetry (CS) of pairwise-identical receive channels arrangement. Such CS is peculiar to numerous different-purpose space-time signal processing systems (see, for instance, references 1–7 in [27]).

The ML for Hermitian PCM was derived for the first time by Nitzberg in his paper [28]. From the moment of this paper publication, numerous works have been performed to investigate an efficiency of this estimate use

Correspondence: lekhovitskiy@rambler.ru
Kharkiv National University of Radio Electronics, 14 Lenin Avenue, 61166 Kharkiv, Ukraine

in CS systems of space-time adaptive signal processing [29–38]. Extensive supplementary list of relevant references is given in [16, 27].

In spite of a diversity of all these works, one common feature is inherent to all of them. Each such work sets an objective to determine statistical characteristics of one or another of function of ML estimate of relevant persymmetric correlation matrix (being usually the Hermitian one) since this function serves as a criterion of respective SP system efficiency. Thus, in [38], such function is "the persymmetric multiband generalized ratio algorithm (PGLR)" and the probability of false alarm and the probability of detection are obtained for this function. Works [28–35] investigate the relative losses, introduced in [9], in signal-to-(interference + noise) ratio (SINR) at the output of CS adaptive detector. These losses are taken relatively to those at the output of optimal detector, and probability density functions (pdfs), mean values, and variances are derived for them. Other criteria and their statistical characteristics under CM persymmetry are considered in [37].

The objectives been set are usually attained by the methods, which have specific distinctions from those been used for an analysis of efficiency of adaptive processing based on ML estimates of GCM. These distinctions are caused by the fact that, under generally concerned conditions, the PCM's initial ML estimate [28] as well as its variants [30, 36, 39] are the sum of two summands. Both these summands have the Wishart (or Wishart–Goodman) distribution with the same matrix of parameters which, however, are not independent [34]. This fact forbids to use directly the methodology, developed in [7, 9, 10], in order to find the statistical characteristics of functions of GCM ML estimates by using Wishart's–Goodman's probability density function (pdf).

For PCM, it is possible to proceed to this methodology after a number of preliminary mathematical transformations [35, 38], which overcome the abovementioned mutual dependence of summands in PCM ML estimate.

Having analyzed these transformations, the author noticed that they solve the problems formulated in [35, 38] as well as "suggest" a way to derive directly a pdf of PCM ML estimates. Such problem, which has not been set and solved in these works, seemed interesting from theoretical and practical considerations. This has stimulated such problem formulation and solution. It was expected that the importance of these distributions for CS systems with PCM of Gaussian inputs should be as great as that of the Wishart's–Goodman's distributions for systems with arbitrary characteristics of receive channels.

The goal of this paper is twofold: (i) to derive closed form analytical expressions for the pdfs of the ML estimates of persymmetric real and complex CMs of Gaussian processes/fields of various natures and (ii) to feature their usefulness in statistical data characterization and operational performance analysis in applications to SP systems that possess a space-time receive channel CS property.

The rest of the paper is organized as follows. Section 2 reviews the persymmetric CMs models. In Sections 3 and 4, we derive the distributions of ML estimates of real and complex persymmetric CMs, respectively, in a closed analytical form. Section 5 exemplifies the usage of the derived distributions in some characteristic applications related to multichannel adaptive SP problems. Conclusion in Section 6 resumes the study.

2 Overview of properties of persymmetric correlation matrices

A. The real $M \times M$ matrix $\mathbf{R} = [r_{i\ell}]_{i,\ell=1}^{M}$ is persymmetric if it coincides with the matrix obtained after rotation of $\mathbf{R}$ with respect to the secondary diagonal, i.e., when the property

$$\mathbf{R} = \mathbf{\Pi}_M \cdot \mathbf{R}^T \cdot \mathbf{\Pi}_M, \quad r_{i\ell} = r_{M+1-\ell,\, M+1-i}, \quad i, \ell \in 1, M, \tag{1}$$

for a real matrix (i.e., matrix composed of real-valued entries) holds.

If the correlation (symmetric) matrix plays a role of $\mathbf{R}$, then the additional equations are true

$$\mathbf{R} = \mathbf{\Pi}_M \cdot \mathbf{R}^T \cdot \mathbf{\Pi}_M = \mathbf{\Pi}_M \cdot \mathbf{R} \cdot \mathbf{\Pi}_M = \mathbf{R}^T,$$
$$r_{i\ell} = r_{M+1-\ell, M+1-i} = r_{M+1-i, M+1-\ell} = r_{\ell i}, \quad i, \ell \in 1, M. \tag{2}$$

Hereinafter, superscript "T" denotes a vector/matrix transposition;

$$\mathbf{\Pi}_\nu = \sum_{i=1}^{\nu} \mathbf{e}_i \cdot \mathbf{e}_{\nu+1-i}^T = \mathbf{\Pi}_\nu^T, \quad \mathbf{\Pi}_\nu \cdot \mathbf{\Pi}_\nu^T = \mathbf{I}_\nu, \quad \mathbf{\Pi}_\nu = \mathbf{\Pi}_\nu^T \tag{3}$$

is the $\nu \times \nu$ orthogonal symmetric permutation matrix with unit entries on its secondary diagonal, and $\mathbf{e}_i$ represents the $i-$ th $(i \in 1, \nu)$ column of the $\nu \times \nu$ unity matrix $\mathbf{I}_\nu$.

For even M $(M = 2 \cdot L)$, matrix (2) allows the following block representation

$$\mathbf{R} = \left[\begin{array}{c|c} \mathbf{R}_{11} & \mathbf{R}_{12} \\ \hline \mathbf{\Pi}_L \cdot \mathbf{R}_{12} \cdot \mathbf{\Pi}_L & \mathbf{\Pi}_L \cdot \mathbf{R}_{11} \cdot \mathbf{\Pi}_L \end{array}\right], \quad \begin{array}{l} \mathbf{R}_{11} = \mathbf{R}_{11}^T, \\ \mathbf{R}_{12} = \mathbf{\Pi}_L \cdot \mathbf{R}_{12}^T \cdot \mathbf{\Pi}_L, \end{array} \tag{4}$$

where $\mathbf{R}_{11}$ and $\mathbf{R}_{12}$ represent the corresponding $L \times L$ blocks in (4).

Let us introduce the $2 \cdot L \times 2 \cdot L = M \times M$ matrix

$$\mathbf{S}_M = [s_{i\ell}]_{i,\ell=1}^{2\cdot L} = \frac{1}{\sqrt{2}}(\mathbf{I}_M + \mathbf{J}_M \cdot \mathbf{\Pi}_M)$$
$$= \frac{1}{\sqrt{2}}\begin{bmatrix} \mathbf{I}_L & \mathbf{\Pi}_L \\ -\mathbf{\Pi}_L & \mathbf{I}_L \end{bmatrix}, \ \mathbf{J}_M = \begin{bmatrix} \mathbf{I}_L & 0 \\ 0 & -\mathbf{I}_L \end{bmatrix} \tag{5}$$

that possesses the following properties (easily verifiable via simple algebraic manipulations)

$$\mathbf{S}_M \cdot \mathbf{S}_M^T = \mathbf{I}_M, \quad \mathbf{S}_M \cdot \mathbf{\Pi}_M = \mathbf{J}_M \cdot \mathbf{S}_M, \quad \mathbf{J}_M \cdot \mathbf{\Pi}_M = -\mathbf{\Pi}_M \cdot \mathbf{J}_M. \tag{6}$$

Using (6), matrix $\mathbf{R}$ (4) can be transformed into the following block-diagonal form

$$\mathbf{R}_M = \mathbf{S}_M \cdot \mathbf{R} \cdot \mathbf{S}_M^T = \begin{bmatrix} \mathbf{R}_{\sum} & \mathbf{0} \\ \mathbf{0} & \mathbf{\Pi}_L \cdot \mathbf{R}_\Delta \cdot \mathbf{\Pi}_L \end{bmatrix}, \quad \begin{matrix} \mathbf{R}_{\sum} = \mathbf{R}_{11} + \mathbf{R}_{12} \cdot \mathbf{\Pi}_L, \\ \mathbf{R}_\Delta = \mathbf{R}_{11} - \mathbf{R}_{12} \cdot \mathbf{\Pi}_L, \end{matrix} \tag{7}$$

with the determinant

$$\det \mathbf{R}_M = |\mathbf{R}_M| = \left|\mathbf{R}_{\sum}\right| \cdot |\mathbf{\Pi}_L \cdot \mathbf{R}_\Delta \cdot \mathbf{\Pi}_L| = \left|\mathbf{R}_{\sum}\right| \cdot |\mathbf{R}_\Delta| = |\mathbf{R}| \tag{8}$$

that coincides with the determinant of the initial matrix

$$\mathbf{R} = \mathbf{S}_M^T \cdot \mathbf{R}_M \cdot \mathbf{S}_M \tag{9}$$

due to orthogonality (6) of matrix $\mathbf{S}_L$ defined in (5).

B. The complex $M \times M$ matrix $\mathbf{C} = [c_{i\ell}]_{i,\ell=1}^{M} = \mathbf{C}' + j \cdot \mathbf{C}''$ is persymmetric if the following equalities

$$\mathbf{C} = \mathbf{\Pi}_M \cdot \mathbf{C}^T \cdot \mathbf{\Pi}_M, \quad \mathbf{C}' = \mathbf{\Pi}_M \cdot \mathbf{C}'^T \cdot \mathbf{\Pi}_M, \quad \mathbf{C}'' = \mathbf{\Pi}_M \cdot \mathbf{C}''^T \cdot \mathbf{\Pi}_M \tag{10}$$

hold.

If matrix C is associated with a correlation (Hermitian) matrix, the following additional equalities are true

$$\begin{aligned} &\mathbf{C} = \mathbf{\Pi}_M \cdot \mathbf{C}^T \cdot \mathbf{\Pi}_M = \mathbf{\Pi}_M \cdot \mathbf{C}^\sim \cdot \mathbf{\Pi}_M = \mathbf{C}^*, \quad \mathbf{C}^T = \mathbf{C}^\sim, \\ &\mathbf{C}' = \mathbf{\Pi}_M \cdot \mathbf{C}'^T \cdot \mathbf{\Pi}_M = \mathbf{\Pi}_M \cdot \mathbf{C}' \cdot \mathbf{\Pi}_M = \mathbf{C}'^T, \\ &\mathbf{C}'' = \mathbf{\Pi}_M \cdot \mathbf{C}''^T \cdot \mathbf{\Pi}_M = -\mathbf{\Pi}_M \cdot \mathbf{C}'' \cdot \mathbf{\Pi}_M = -\mathbf{C}''^T. \end{aligned} \tag{11}$$

Here, superscripts ($\sim$) and (*) define complex conjugation and Hermitian conjugation (complex conjugation and transposition), respectively.

Let us introduce the unitary $M \times M$ matrix [31, 35, 38]

$$\mathbf{T} = [t_{i,\ell}]_{i,\ell=1}^{M} = \frac{1}{\sqrt{2}}(\mathbf{I}_M - j \cdot \mathbf{\Pi}_M) \tag{12}$$

that obviously satisfy the properties

$$\mathbf{T} = \mathbf{T}^T = \mathbf{\Pi}_M \cdot \mathbf{T} \cdot \mathbf{\Pi}_M = -j \cdot \mathbf{T}^\sim \cdot \mathbf{\Pi}_M = -j \cdot \mathbf{\Pi}_M \cdot \mathbf{T}^*, \mathbf{T} \cdot \mathbf{T}^* = \mathbf{I}_M. \tag{13}$$

Using (13), matrix (11) can be next transformed into the real symmetric $M \times M$ matrix

$$\mathbf{C}_r = \mathbf{T} \cdot \mathbf{C} \cdot \mathbf{T}^* = \mathbf{C}' + \mathbf{C}''^T \cdot \mathbf{\Pi}_M = \mathbf{C}_r^T = \mathbf{C}' + \mathbf{\Pi}_M \cdot \mathbf{C}'' \tag{14}$$

with the determinant

$$|\mathbf{C}_r| = \left|\mathbf{C}' + \mathbf{C}''^T \cdot \mathbf{\Pi}_M\right| = |\mathbf{C}' + \mathbf{\Pi}_M \cdot \mathbf{C}''| = |\mathbf{C}|, \tag{15}$$

which coincides with that of the initial matrix

$$\mathbf{C} = \mathbf{T}^* \cdot \mathbf{C}_r \cdot \mathbf{T} \tag{16}$$

due to the unitary model (13) of matrix $\mathbf{T}$ defined by (12).

3 pdf of ML estimate of real persymmetric CM

A. Let $M-$ variate random real (i.e., composed of real-valued entries) Gaussian (normal) vectors $\mathbf{y}_i = \left[y_\ell^{(i)}\right]_{\ell=1}^{M}$ of the $K-$ variate sample $\mathbf{Y} = [\mathbf{y}_i]_{i=1}^{K}$ be mutually independent and have zero means and identical non-negative definite $M \times M$ CMs $\mathbf{R}$, i.e.,

$$\begin{aligned} &\mathbf{Y} = [\mathbf{y}_i]_{i=1}^{K}, \quad \mathbf{y}_i = N(0, \mathbf{R}), \quad \overline{\mathbf{y}}_i = 0, \\ &\overline{\mathbf{y}_i \cdot \mathbf{y}_\ell^*} = \mathbf{R} \cdot \delta(i-\ell), \quad i, \ell \in 1, K, \end{aligned} \tag{17}$$

where $\delta(x)$ is the Kroneker symbol, and overbar defines the statistical averaging operator.

The joint pdf $p(\mathbf{Y})$ of elements of sample $\mathbf{Y}$ in this case is given by [3, 5, 12]

$$p(\mathbf{Y}) = (2\pi)^{-K \cdot M/2} \cdot |\mathbf{R}|^{-K/2} \cdot \exp\left\{-\frac{1}{2} \cdot tr\left(\mathbf{R}^{-1} \cdot \mathbf{A}_r\right)\right\}, \tag{18}$$

where $tr(\mathbf{\Phi})$ is the trace (sum of diagonal elements) of a matrix $\mathbf{\Phi}$, and

$$\mathbf{A}_r = \{a_{i\ell}\}_{i,\ell=1}^{M} = \mathbf{Y} \cdot \mathbf{Y}^T = \sum_{i=1}^{K} \mathbf{y}_i \cdot \mathbf{y}_i^T = \mathbf{A}_r^T = K \cdot \hat{\mathbf{R}}, \tag{19}$$

represents the $M \times M$ sample (random) CM.

Under conditions (17) and (18), matrix $\hat{\mathbf{R}} = K^{-1} \cdot \mathbf{A}_r$ represents an ML estimate of the real-valued general form CM $\mathbf{R}$ [3, 11–13], and matrix $\mathbf{A}_r$ has the Wishart distribution $W_M^{(\mathbf{R})}(\mathbf{A}_r, K, \mathbf{R})$ with $K - M$ degrees of freedom and parameter matrix $\mathbf{R}$ [2–5, 40]. Then,

$$p(\mathbf{A}_r) = W_M^{(\mathbf{R})}(\mathbf{A}_r, K, \mathbf{R}) = \frac{F_M^{(\mathbf{R})}(\mathbf{A}_r, K, \mathbf{R})}{f_M^{(\mathbf{R})}(K, \mathbf{R})}, \quad (20a)$$

where

$$F_M^{(\mathbf{R})}(\mathbf{A}_r, K, \mathbf{R}) = |\mathbf{A}_r|^{\frac{K-M-1}{2}} \cdot exp\left\{-\frac{1}{2} \cdot tr\left(\mathbf{R}^{-1} \cdot \mathbf{A}_r\right)\right\}, \quad (20b)$$

$$f_M^{(\mathbf{R})}(K, \mathbf{R}) = 2^{K \cdot M/2} \cdot \pi^{M \cdot (M-1)/4} \cdot |\mathbf{R}|^{K/2} \cdot \prod_{i=1}^{M} \Gamma\left(\frac{K+1-i}{2}\right), \quad K \geq M, \quad (20c)$$

and $\Gamma(x)$ is the gamma function, which for an integer $x = n \geq 1$ is equal to $(n-1)!$.

Here, the distribution of a random matrix is specified via a joint distribution of random elements that compose such a matrix [3, 9]. Thus, (20) presents an "economical" definition of the pdf $p(\mathbf{A}_r) = p(a_{i\ell})$, $i \in \overline{1, M}$, $\ell \in \overline{i, M}$, as a function of $M \cdot (M+1)/2$ scalar variables, which are completely specified by the real-valued diagonal and above-diagonal elements of the symmetric matrix $\mathbf{A}$ defined by (19).

If CM $\mathbf{R}$ is persymmetric, then under the condition (17), its ML estimate may be written as[1]

$$\hat{\mathbf{R}}_p = \frac{1}{K} \cdot \mathbf{A}_{rp}, \quad \mathbf{A}_{rp} = \frac{1}{2} \cdot \left(\mathbf{Y} \cdot \mathbf{Y}^T + \mathbf{\Pi}_M \cdot \mathbf{Y} \cdot \mathbf{Y}^T \cdot \mathbf{\Pi}_M\right). \quad (21)$$

The problem at hand is to derive the closed-form expression for the pdf of that matrix $\mathbf{A}_{rp}$.

B. The matrix defined by (21) is a sum of two symmetric matrices each being a result of a permutation of another one with respect to its secondary diagonal; thus, it is also symmetric and persymmetric at the same time that follows directly from definition (2). For even $M = 2 \cdot L$ (at this stage, we restrict ourselves by that assumption for the sake of simplicity), matrix (21) is defined by $L \cdot (L+1)$ random parameters—its elements $a_{i\ell}$, $i \in \overline{1, L}$; $\ell \in \overline{i, M+1-i}$.

A comparison of (21) with (19) reveals that the first term of matrix $\mathbf{A}_{rp}$ has Wishart distribution (20) with the parameter matrix $\mathbf{R}/2$, and the second term has the same Wishart distribution under the conditions (2). Vectors $\mathbf{\Pi}_M \cdot \mathbf{y}_i$, $i \in \overline{1, K}$ of the "inverted" sample $\mathbf{\Pi}_M \cdot \mathbf{Y}$ in (21), possess the same properties (17) as the initial vectors $\mathbf{y}_i$. If these terms are mutually independent, then their sum has the Wishart distribution analogous to (20) with $2 \cdot K - M$ degrees of freedom and the parameter matrix $\mathbf{R}/2$ [3–5]. However, for the terms of matrix $\mathbf{A}_{rp}$ defined by (21), this condition is not valid; therefore, its distribution should be different [34].

C. In order to find the desired pdf, we next partition the initial $2 \cdot L \times K$ matrix sample $\mathbf{Y} = [\mathbf{y}_i]_{i=1}^K$, $\mathbf{y}_i = \left[y_\ell^{(i)}\right]_{\ell=1}^{2L}$ into the $L \times K$ "upper" $\mathbf{Y}_\mathrm{U}$ and "lower" $\mathbf{Y}_\mathrm{L}$ blocks, so that

$$\mathbf{Y} = \begin{bmatrix} \mathbf{Y}_\mathrm{U} \\ \mathbf{Y}_\mathrm{L} \end{bmatrix}, \quad \begin{matrix} \mathbf{Y}_\mathrm{U} = [\mathbf{y}_{\mathrm{U}i}]_{i=1}^K, & \mathbf{y}_{\mathrm{U}i} = \left[y_\ell^{(i)}\right]_{\ell=1}^{L}, \\ \mathbf{Y}_\mathrm{L} = [\mathbf{y}_{\mathrm{L}i}]_{i=1}^K, & \mathbf{y}_{\mathrm{L}i} = \left[y_\ell^{(i)}\right]_{\ell=L+1}^{2L}. \end{matrix} \quad (22)$$

Let us introduce a linear transform of (22) performed with matrix $\mathbf{S}_M$ defined by (5), i.e.,

$$\mathbf{V} = [\mathbf{v}_i]_{i=1}^K = \mathbf{S}_M \cdot \mathbf{Y} = \begin{bmatrix} \mathbf{V}_\Sigma \\ \mathbf{V}_\Delta \end{bmatrix},$$
$$\mathbf{V}_\Sigma = \left[\mathbf{v}_{\Sigma i}\right]_{i=1}^K = \frac{1}{\sqrt{2}} \cdot (\mathbf{Y}_\mathrm{U} + \mathbf{\Pi}_L \cdot \mathbf{Y}_\mathrm{L}), \quad \mathbf{V}_\Delta = [\mathbf{v}_{\Delta i}]_{i=1}^K = \frac{1}{\sqrt{2}} \cdot (\mathbf{Y}_\mathrm{L} - \mathbf{\Pi}_L \cdot \mathbf{Y}_\mathrm{U}), \quad (23)$$

which allows rewrite (21), taking into account (6), as follows

$$\mathbf{A}_{rp} = \frac{1}{2} \cdot \left(\mathbf{S}_M^T \cdot \mathbf{V} \cdot \mathbf{V}^T \cdot \mathbf{S}_M + \mathbf{\Pi}_M \cdot \mathbf{S}_M^T \cdot \mathbf{V} \cdot \mathbf{V}^T \cdot \mathbf{S}_M \cdot \mathbf{\Pi}_M\right)$$
$$= \frac{1}{2} \cdot \mathbf{S}_M^T \cdot \left(\mathbf{V} \cdot \mathbf{V}^T + \mathbf{J}_M \cdot \mathbf{V} \cdot \mathbf{V}^T \cdot \mathbf{J}_M\right) \cdot \mathbf{S}_M.$$

It is easy to deduce that taking into account the properties (5) of matrix $\mathbf{J}_M$, the addends embraced in the above formula have identical $L \times L$ diagonal blocks and opposite in signs $L \times L$ off-diagonal blocks. Therefore, one can rewrite

$$\mathbf{A}_{rp} = \mathbf{S}_M^T \cdot \mathbf{B}_\mathrm{V} \cdot \mathbf{S}_M,$$
$$\mathbf{B}_\mathrm{V} = [b_{i\ell}]_{i,\ell=1}^{2L} = \begin{bmatrix} \mathbf{B}_\Sigma & \mathbf{0} \\ \mathbf{0} & \mathbf{B}_\Delta \end{bmatrix} = \mathbf{S}_M \cdot \mathbf{A}_{rp} \cdot \mathbf{S}_M^T, \quad (24a)$$

$$|\mathbf{B}_\mathrm{V}| = |\mathbf{B}_\Sigma| \cdot |\mathbf{B}_\Delta| = |\mathbf{A}_{rp}|, \quad (24b)$$

where the $L \times L$ diagonal blocks $\mathbf{B}_\Sigma$ and $\mathbf{B}_\Delta$ are expressed as follows:

$$\mathbf{B}_\Sigma = \left[b_{i\ell}^{(\Sigma)}\right]_{i,\ell=1}^{L} = \mathbf{V}_\Sigma \cdot \mathbf{V}_\Sigma T, \quad \mathbf{B}_\Delta = \left[b_{i\ell}^{(\Delta)}\right]_{i,\ell=1}^{L} = \mathbf{V}_\Delta \cdot \mathbf{V}_\Delta^T. \quad (25)$$

Taking into account the interrelations (24), the problem at hand is transformed now into the problem of derivation of the pdf of the auxiliary matrix $\mathbf{B}_\mathrm{V}$ (24).

D. First, note that due to orthogonality of matrix $\mathbf{S}_M$, the Jacobian of the transform, $\mathbf{Y} = \mathbf{S}_M^T \cdot \mathbf{V}$, is equal to unity; hence, the pdf $p(\mathbf{V})$ of the transformed sample $\mathbf{V}$ (23) under conditions (18) becomes

$$p(\mathbf{V}) = (2\pi)^{-K\cdot L}\cdot|\mathbf{R}|^{-K/2}\cdot exp\left\{-\frac{1}{2}tr\left(\mathbf{R}^{-1}\cdot\mathbf{S}_M^T\cdot\mathbf{V}\cdot\mathbf{V}^T\cdot\mathbf{S}_M\right)\right\}.$$

Using the property of the matrix product trace, $tr(\mathbf{A}\cdot\mathbf{B}) = tr(\mathbf{B}\cdot\mathbf{A})$, and taking into account (7)–(9), the latter formula can be rewritten as follows:

$$p(\mathbf{V}) = (2\pi)^{-K\cdot L}\cdot|\mathbf{R}_\Sigma|^{-K/2}\cdot|\mathbf{\Pi}_L\cdot\mathbf{R}_\Delta\cdot\mathbf{\Pi}_L|^{-K/2} \times\exp\left\{-\frac{1}{2}\cdot tr\left(\mathbf{R}_M^{-1}\cdot\mathbf{V}\cdot\mathbf{V}^T\right)\right\}.$$

Next, taking into account the explained above properties (7) and (23)–(25), we obtain

$$\begin{aligned} tr\left(\mathbf{R}_M^{-1}\cdot\mathbf{V}\cdot\mathbf{V}^T\right) &= tr\left(\mathbf{R}_\Sigma^{-1}\cdot\mathbf{V}_\Sigma\cdot\mathbf{V}_\Sigma^T\right) \\ &+ tr\left(\mathbf{\Pi}_L\cdot\mathbf{R}_\Delta^{-1}\cdot\mathbf{\Pi}_L\cdot\mathbf{V}_\Delta\cdot\mathbf{V}_\Delta^T\right) \\ &= tr\left(\mathbf{R}_M^{-1}\cdot\mathbf{B}_V\right), \end{aligned} \tag{26a}$$

that yield

$$p(\mathbf{V}) = p(\mathbf{V}_\Sigma)\cdot p(\mathbf{V}_\Delta) \tag{26b}$$

where

$$p(\mathbf{V}_\Sigma) = (2\pi)^{-K\cdot L/2}\cdot|\mathbf{R}_\Sigma|^{-K/2}\cdot\exp\left\{-\frac{1}{2}tr\left(\mathbf{R}_\Sigma^{-1}\cdot\mathbf{V}_\Sigma\cdot\mathbf{V}_\Sigma^T\right)\right\}, \tag{27a}$$

$$p(\mathbf{V}_\Delta) = (2\pi)^{-K\cdot L/2}|\mathbf{\Pi}_L\cdot\mathbf{R}_\Delta\cdot\mathbf{\Pi}_L|^{-K/2}\cdot\exp\left\{-\frac{1}{2}tr(\mathbf{\Pi}_L\cdot\mathbf{R}_\Delta^{-1}\cdot\mathbf{\Pi}_L\cdot\mathbf{V}_\Delta\cdot\mathbf{V}_\Delta^T)\right\}. \tag{27b}$$

The properties (17) and (4) of the CM blocks admit the following representations

$$\overline{\mathbf{y}_{Ui}\cdot\mathbf{y}_{Ui}^T} = \mathbf{R}_{11},\quad \overline{\mathbf{y}_{Li}\cdot\mathbf{y}_{Ui}^T} = \mathbf{\Pi}_L\cdot\mathbf{R}_{12}\cdot\mathbf{\Pi}_L,$$
$$\overline{\mathbf{y}_{Ui}\cdot\mathbf{y}_{Li}^T} = \mathbf{R}_{12},\quad \overline{\mathbf{y}_{Li}\cdot\mathbf{y}_{Li}^T} = \mathbf{\Pi}_L\cdot\mathbf{R}_{11}\cdot\mathbf{\Pi}_L,\quad i\in\overline{1,K},$$

and using the definitions (23), (22), and (7), it is easy to deduce that matrices $\mathbf{R}_\Sigma$ and $\mathbf{\Pi}_L\cdot\mathbf{R}_\Delta\cdot\mathbf{\Pi}_L$, which specify the entries in the corresponding expressions (27), can be expressed as follows,

$$\mathbf{R}_\Sigma = \overline{\mathbf{v}_{\Sigma i}\cdot\mathbf{v}_{\Sigma i}^T},\quad \mathbf{\Pi}_L\cdot\mathbf{R}_\Delta\cdot\mathbf{\Pi}_L = \overline{\mathbf{v}_{\Delta i}\cdot\mathbf{v}_{\Delta i}^T},\quad i\in\overline{1,K}. \tag{28}$$

In doing so, it is easy to observe that K– variate "summ", $\mathbf{V}_\Sigma$ and "difference", $\mathbf{V}_\Delta$; samples (23) of the random $L = M/2$ – variate vectors $\mathbf{v}_{\Sigma i}$ and $\mathbf{v}_{\Delta i}$ $(i\in\overline{1,K})$ have normal distributions (27), and matrices $\mathbf{B}_\Sigma$ and $\mathbf{B}_\Delta$ formed via (25) have Wishart distributions with $K - M$ degrees of freedom and the parameter matrices $\mathbf{R}_\Sigma$ and $\mathbf{\Pi}_L\cdot\mathbf{R}_\Delta\cdot\mathbf{\Pi}_L$, respectively, i.e.,

$$p(\mathbf{B}_\Sigma) = W_L^{(\mathbf{R})}(\mathbf{B}_\Sigma, K, \mathbf{R}_\Sigma), \tag{29a}$$

$$p(\mathbf{B}_\Delta) = W_L^{(\mathbf{R})}(\mathbf{B}_\Delta, K, \mathbf{\Pi}_L\cdot\mathbf{R}_\Delta\cdot\mathbf{\Pi}_L). \tag{29b}$$

On the other hand, due to the mutual independence of samples $\mathbf{V}_\Sigma$ and $\mathbf{V}_\Delta$ that follow from (26), matrices $\mathbf{B}_\Sigma$ and $\mathbf{B}_\Delta$ defined by (25) are also mutually independent, and their joint density is, therefore, $p(\mathbf{B}_\Sigma, \mathbf{B}_\Delta) = p(\mathbf{B}_\Sigma)\cdot p(\mathbf{B}_\Delta)$. Multiplying these densities (29a) and (29b) and taking into account (26), (24), and (8), we obtain the density $p(\mathbf{B}_V)$ of matrix $\mathbf{B}_V$ defined by (24),

$$p(\mathbf{B}_V) = \frac{|\mathbf{B}_V|^{(K-L-1)/2}\cdot\exp\left\{-\frac{1}{2}tr\left(\mathbf{R}_M^{-1}\cdot\mathbf{B}_v\right)\right\}}{2^{K\cdot L}\cdot\pi^{L\cdot(L-1)/2}\cdot|\mathbf{R}_M|^{K/2}\cdot\prod_{i-1}^{L}\Gamma^2\left(\frac{K+1-i}{2}\right)}. \tag{30}$$

Each of two symmetric $L\times L$ matrices $\mathbf{B}_\Sigma$ and $\mathbf{B}_\Delta$ in the arguments of $p(\mathbf{B}_\Sigma, \mathbf{B}_\Delta)$ are defined by $L\cdot(L+1)/2$ parameters, so the number of such parameters in matrix $\mathbf{B}_V$ (24) is equal to $L\cdot(L+1)$ that exactly coincides with the number of parameters that determine matrix $\mathbf{A}_{rp}$ (21). Therefore, to obtain the desired pdf $p(\mathbf{A}_{rp})$ using (30), it is enough to define the Jacobian of the transform (24) that relates $\mathbf{B}_V$ and $\mathbf{A}_{rp}$.

Using (5) and (24), it is easy to deduce that

$$b_{i\ell} = a_{i\ell} + a_{i,2\cdot i+1-\ell},\quad b_{2\cdot L+1-\ell,\,2\cdot L+1-i} = a_{i\ell} - a_{i,2\cdot L+1-\ell},$$
$$i\in\overline{1,\,L};\quad \ell\in\overline{i,L}.$$

Then, the Jacobian matrix of the transform (24) can be written as $\mathbf{I}_{L\cdot(L+1)/2}\otimes\begin{bmatrix}1 & -1\\ 1 & 1\end{bmatrix}$ where $\otimes$ defines the Kroneker product, and hence, that Jacobian is equal to $2^{L\cdot(L+1)/2}$.

Replacing in (30) matrix $\mathbf{B}_V$ by its representation (24a) and taking into account (24b), (9), and (8), we obtain

$$p(\mathbf{A}_{rp}) = \frac{|\mathbf{A}_{rp}|^{(K-L-1)/2}\cdot\exp\left\{-\frac{1}{2}tr\left(\mathbf{R}^{-1}\cdot\mathbf{A}_{rp}\right)\right\}}{2^{(2\cdot K-L-1)\cdot L/2}\cdot\pi^{L\cdot(L-1)/2}\cdot|\mathbf{R}|^{K/2}\cdot\prod_{i-1}^{L}\Gamma^2\left(\frac{K+1-i}{2}\right)}. \tag{31}$$

The latter formula describes the desired pdf of the real symmetric and persymmetric random matrix $\mathbf{A}_{rp}$ of the ML estimate $\hat{\mathbf{R}}_p$ (21) of the real and also persymmetric CM $\mathbf{R}$ of an even order $M = 2\cdot L$ defined above in (2) and (17). This formula has the same form as the Wishart distribution (20) of the matrix $\mathbf{A}_r$ (19) from the ML estimate $\hat{\mathbf{R}} = K^{-1}\cdot\mathbf{A}_r$ of GCM. However, for formula (31), the reduced number of parameters that determine PCM has resulted in increased on $L = M/2$ number of degrees of freedom. That is why this formula could be considered as modified Wishart distribution of the ML estimate $\hat{\mathbf{R}}_p$ (21) of the real PCM $\mathbf{R}$ of an even order $M = 2\cdot L$.

4 Distribution density of ML estimate of complex persymmetric CM

A. Let the random complex normal $M-$ variate vectors $\mathbf{y}_i = \left[y_\ell^{(i)}\right]_{\ell=1}^{M} = \mathbf{y}_i' + j\cdot\mathbf{y}_i''$ of the $K-$ variate sample $\mathbf{Y} = [\mathbf{y}_i]_{i=1}^{K}$ be mutually independent and have zero means and identical non-negative definite complex Hermitian $M \times M$ CMs, $\mathbf{C} = [c_{i\ell}]_{i,\ell=1}^{M} = \mathbf{C}' + j\cdot\mathbf{C}''$, i.e.,

$$\mathbf{Y} = \mathbf{Y}' + j\cdot\mathbf{Y}'' = [\mathbf{y}_i]_{i=1}^{K},\ \mathbf{y}_i \sim CN(0,\mathbf{C}),\ \overline{\mathbf{y}_i} = 0,$$
$$\overline{\mathbf{y}_i\cdot\mathbf{y}_\ell^*} = \mathbf{C}\cdot\delta(i-\ell),\ \ i,\ell\in 1,K. \tag{32a}$$

The latter means [8, 12] that real $\mathbf{y}_i'$ and imaginary $\mathbf{y}_i''$ parts of vectors $\mathbf{y}_i$ $(i\in 1,K)$ are zero means jointly normal real-valued vectors. Then, the $2\cdot M-$ variate vectors

$$\mathbf{g}_i^T = \left[\mathbf{y}_i'^T,\ \ \mathbf{y}_i''^T\right] \sim N(0,\mathbf{Q}),\ \ \overline{\mathbf{g}i} = 0,$$
$$\overline{\mathbf{g}_i\cdot\mathbf{g}_\ell^T} = \mathbf{Q}\cdot\delta(i-\ell),\ \ i,\ell\in 1,K \tag{32b}$$

are also mutually independent with zero means and identical $2\cdot M \times 2\cdot M$ CMs

$$\mathbf{Q} = \overline{\mathbf{g}_i\cdot\mathbf{g}_i^T} = \begin{bmatrix} \overline{\mathbf{y}_i'\cdot\mathbf{y}_i'^T} & \overline{\mathbf{y}_i'\cdot\mathbf{y}_i''T} \\ \overline{\mathbf{y}_i''\cdot\mathbf{y}_i'^T} & \overline{\mathbf{y}_i''\cdot\mathbf{y}_i''T} \end{bmatrix} = \frac{1}{2}\cdot\begin{bmatrix} \mathbf{C}' & -\mathbf{C}'' \\ \mathbf{C}'' & \mathbf{C}' \end{bmatrix},\ \ i\in 1,K. \tag{32c}$$

The joint distribution of the sample $\mathbf{Y}$ in that case is given by [8, 12]

$$p(\mathbf{Y}) = \pi^{-K\cdot M}\cdot|\mathbf{C}|^{-K}\cdot\exp\left\{-tr\left(\mathbf{C}^{-1}\cdot\mathbf{A}_c\right)\right\}, \tag{33}$$

where

$$\mathbf{A}_c = [a_{i\ell}]_{i,\ell=1}^{M} = \sum_{i=1}^{K}\mathbf{y}_i\cdot\mathbf{y}_i^* = \mathbf{Y}\cdot\mathbf{Y}^* = \mathbf{A}_c^* = K\cdot\hat{\mathbf{C}}. \tag{34}$$

is the $M \times M$ sample complex CM. Under conditions (32), the matrix $\hat{\mathbf{C}} = K^{-1}\cdot\mathbf{A}_c$ in (34) specifies an ML estimate of the general type complex CM $\mathbf{C}$ [6–12], whereas matrix $\mathbf{A}_c$ is characterized by the complex Wishart distribution, $W_M^{(\mathbf{C})}(\mathbf{A}_c, K, \mathbf{C})$, with $K-M+1$ degrees of freedom and the parameter matrix $\mathbf{C}$ [6, 8, 9], i.e.,

$$p(\mathbf{A}_c) = W_M^{(\mathbf{C})}(\mathbf{A}_c, K, \mathbf{C}) = \frac{\mathbf{F}_M^{(\mathbf{C})}(\mathbf{A}_c, K, \mathbf{C})}{\mathbf{f}_M^{(\mathbf{C})}(K, \mathbf{C})}, \tag{35a}$$

$$\mathbf{F}_M^{(\mathbf{C})}(\mathbf{A}_c, K, \mathbf{C}) = |\mathbf{A}_c|^{K-M}\cdot\exp\left\{-tr\left(\mathbf{C}^{-1}\cdot\mathbf{A}_c\right)\right\}, \tag{35b}$$

$$\mathbf{f}_M^{(\mathbf{C})}(K, \mathbf{C}) = \pi^{M\cdot(M-1)/2}\cdot|\mathbf{C}|^{K}\cdot\prod_{i-1}^{M}\Gamma(K+1-i),\ \ K\geq M. \tag{35c}$$

Here, the pdf of the complex matrix $\mathbf{C}$ is treated as the joint distribution of its random real and imaginary parts [6–10]. Thus, (35a) specifies a non-negative function of M^2 parameters

$$p(\mathbf{A}_c) = p\left(a_{11}, a_{22}, \ldots, a_{MM}, a_{i\ell}', a_{i\ell}''\right),\ \ i\in 1, M-1,$$
$$\ell\in i+1, M.$$

Such parameters are completely defied by the real diagonal elements a_{ii} $(i\in 1, M)$ of the random Hermitian complex matrix $\mathbf{A}_c$ (34) and $M\cdot(M-1)$ real $(a_{i\ell}')$ and imaginary $(a_{i\ell}'')$ parts of its above-diagonal elements $a_{i\ell} = a_{i\ell}' + j\cdot a_{i\ell}''$, $(i\in 1,\ M-1;\ \ell\in i+1,\ M)$.

If CM $\mathbf{C}$ is persymmetric, then under the conditions (32), its ML estimate admits the following representation [28–31, 27–37]:

$$\hat{\mathbf{C}}_p = \frac{1}{K}\cdot\mathbf{A}_{cp},$$
$$\mathbf{A}_{cp} = \frac{1}{2}\left(\mathbf{Y}\cdot\mathbf{Y}^* + \mathbf{\Pi}_M\cdot\mathbf{Y}^{\sim}\cdot\mathbf{Y}^T\cdot\mathbf{\Pi}_M\right) = \mathbf{A}_{cp}^*$$
$$= \mathbf{\Pi}_M\cdot\tilde{\mathbf{A}}_{cp}\cdot\mathbf{\Pi}_M. \tag{36}$$

Thus, the problem at hand now is to find the distribution density of the matrix $\mathbf{A}_{cp}$ in (36).

B. By construction, this matrix $\mathbf{A}_{cp}$ is Hermitian and persymmetric as a sum of two Hermitian matrices each being a result of permutation of another one with respect to the secondary diagonal. Therefore, such $\mathbf{A}_{cp}$ is completely specified by $M\cdot(M+1)/2$ real-valued scalar parameters, among which there are

$$z = \varepsilon\left[\frac{M}{2}\right]\cdot\varepsilon\left[\frac{M+1}{2}\right] = \begin{cases} (L-1)\cdot L, & M = 2\cdot L-1, \\ L^2, & M = 2\cdot L, \end{cases} \tag{37}$$

the matrix imaginary parts $(a_{i\ell}'')$, and the rest $M\cdot(M+1)/2 - z$ real parts $(a_{i\ell}')$ of the elements $a_{i\ell}$, $i\in 1, L$; $\ell\in i, M+1-i$ that explicitly specify the whole matrix $\mathbf{A}_{cp}$. In (37), $\varepsilon[x]$ represents the integer part of the embraced variable x.

From a comparison of (36) with (34), it follows that the first addend in matrix $\mathbf{A}_{cp}$ is characterized by the distribution, $W_M^{(\mathbf{C})}(\mathbf{A}_c, K, \mathbf{C}/2)$. The second addend has the same distribution as well, since under the condition (11), vectors $\mathbf{\Pi}_M\cdot\tilde{\mathbf{y}}_i$ $(i\in 1,K)$ of the "reverse" and complex conjugate sample $\mathbf{\Pi}_M\cdot\mathbf{Y}^{\sim}$ possess the same properties as the initial vectors, $\mathbf{y}_i$. The samples $\mathbf{Y}$ and $\mathbf{\Pi}_M\cdot\mathbf{Y}^{\sim}$

are mutually uncorrelated, i.e., $\overline{\mathbf{Y}\cdot\left(\mathbf{\Pi}_M\cdot\mathbf{Y}^{\sim}\right)^*}=0$ [8, 12]; however, they are not jointly normal [34]. Absence of mutual correlation does not mean mutual independence that does not allow to represent the joint pdf $p\,(\mathbf{Y},\mathbf{\Pi}_M\cdot\mathbf{Y}^{\sim})$ via the product $p\,(\mathbf{Y})\cdot p\,(\mathbf{\Pi}_M\cdot\mathbf{Y}^{\sim})$. In addition, the distribution $W_M^{(\mathbf{C})}\,(\mathbf{A}_c,2K,\mathbf{C}/2)$ specifies the density of the sum in (36) only under the conditions of mutual independence of the addends.

C. Let us consider the transform of the sample matrix $\mathbf{Y}$ performed by the unitary matrix $\mathbf{T}$ defined in (12), i.e.,

$$\mathbf{V}=\{\mathbf{v}_i\}_{i=1}^{K}=\mathbf{T}\cdot\mathbf{Y}=\mathbf{V}_\Sigma+j\cdot\mathbf{V}_\Delta, \tag{38a}$$

$$\mathbf{V}_\Sigma=\left\{\mathbf{v}_{\Sigma i}\right\}_{i=1}^{K}=\frac{1}{\sqrt{2}}\left(\mathbf{Y}'+\mathbf{\Pi}_M\cdot\mathbf{Y}''\right),\quad \mathbf{V}_\Delta=\{\mathbf{v}_{\Delta i}\}_{i=1}^{K}=\frac{1}{\sqrt{2}}\left(\mathbf{Y}''-\mathbf{\Pi}_M\cdot\mathbf{Y}'\right), \tag{38b}$$

Using (13) and (38), matrix $\mathbf{A}_{cp}$ defined by (36) admits the following representation

$$\mathbf{A}_{cp}=\frac{1}{2}\cdot\mathbf{T}^*\cdot\left(\mathbf{V}\cdot\mathbf{V}^*+\mathbf{V}^{\sim}\cdot\mathbf{V}^T\right)\cdot\mathbf{T}.$$

Obviously, the addends in braces in this equality are complex conjugate, thus

$$\mathbf{A}_{cp}=\mathbf{T}^*\cdot\mathbf{B}_\mathbf{V}\cdot\mathbf{T} \tag{39}$$

where

$$\mathbf{B}_\mathbf{V}=[b_{i\ell}]_{i,\ell=1}^{M}=\mathrm{Re}\,(\mathbf{V}\cdot\mathbf{V}^*)=\mathbf{B}_\Sigma+\mathbf{B}_\Delta=\mathbf{B}_\mathbf{V}^T, \tag{40a}$$

$$\mathbf{B}_\Sigma=\left[b_{i\ell}^{(\Sigma)}\right]_{i,\ell=1}^{M}=\mathbf{V}_\Sigma\cdot\mathbf{V}_\Sigma^T,\quad \mathbf{B}_\Delta=\left[b_{i\ell}^{(\Delta)}\right]_{i,\ell=1}^{M}=\mathbf{V}_\Delta\cdot\mathbf{V}_\Delta^T. \tag{40b}$$

The representation (39) yields the following equalities

$$\mathbf{B}_\mathbf{V}=\mathbf{T}\cdot\mathbf{A}_{cp}\cdot\mathbf{T}^*,\quad |\mathbf{B}_\mathbf{V}|=|\mathbf{A}_{cp}|, \tag{41}$$

that reduce the problem at hand to deriving the pdf of the real symmetric matrix $\mathbf{B}_\mathbf{V}$.

D. Note that due to (32a) and (32c), CMs of the "summary" $\mathbf{v}_{\Sigma i}$ and the "difference" $\mathbf{v}_{\Delta i}$ $(i\in 1,K)$ vectors in samples $\mathbf{V}_\Sigma$ and $\mathbf{V}_\Delta$ (38b) are identical and equal to

$$\overline{\mathbf{v}_{\Sigma i}\cdot\mathbf{v}_{\Sigma\ell}^T}=\overline{\mathbf{v}_{\Delta i}\cdot\mathbf{v}_{\Delta\ell}^T}=\mathbf{C}_\Sigma\cdot\delta\,(i-\ell),\quad \mathbf{C}_\Sigma=\mathbf{C}_r/2,\quad i,\ell\in 1,K, \tag{42}$$

whereas (as a consequence of unitary $\mathbf{T}$, and the properties specified by (9) and (33)) the density $p(\mathbf{V})$ of the transformed sample $\mathbf{V}$ (38a) becomes

$$p\,(\mathbf{V})=(2\cdot\pi)^{-K\cdot M}\left|\mathbf{C}_\Sigma\right|^{-K}\exp\left\{-\frac{1}{2}\cdot tr\left(\mathbf{C}_\Sigma^{-1}\cdot\mathbf{V}\cdot\mathbf{V}^*\right)\right\} \tag{43}$$

where matrix $\mathbf{C}_r$ has been defined in (14).

Taking into account a symmetry of matrices $\mathbf{C}_r$ and $\mathbf{C}_\Sigma$, and the expressions (40), it is easy to verify the following equalities

$$\begin{aligned} tr\,(\mathbf{C}_\Sigma^{-1}\cdot\mathbf{V}\cdot\mathbf{V}^*)&=tr\left\{\mathbf{C}_\Sigma^{-1}\cdot\mathrm{Re}\,(\mathbf{V}\cdot\mathbf{V}^*)\right\}\\ &=tr\left(\mathbf{C}_\Sigma^{-1}\cdot\mathbf{V}_\Sigma\cdot\mathbf{V}_\Sigma^T\right)\\ &\quad+tr\left(\mathbf{C}_\Sigma^{-1}\cdot\mathbf{V}_\Delta\cdot\mathbf{V}_\Delta^T\right). \end{aligned} \tag{44}$$

Those (43) can be also re-expressed as

$$p(\mathbf{V})=p(\mathbf{V}_\Sigma,\mathbf{V}_\Delta)=p(\mathbf{V}_\Sigma)\cdot p(\mathbf{V}_\Delta) \tag{45}$$

where

$$p(\mathbf{V}_\Sigma)=(2\cdot\pi)^{-K\cdot M/2}\,|\mathbf{C}_\Sigma|^{-K/2}\cdot\exp\left\{-\frac{1}{2}\cdot tr\left(\mathbf{C}_\Sigma^{-1}\cdot\mathbf{V}_\Sigma\cdot\mathbf{V}_\Sigma^T\right)\right\}, \tag{46a}$$

$$p(\mathbf{V}_\Delta)=(2\cdot\pi)^{-K\cdot M/2}\cdot\left|\mathbf{C}_\Sigma\right|^{-K/2}\cdot\exp\left\{-\frac{1}{2}\cdot tr\left(\mathbf{C}_\Sigma^{-1}\cdot\mathbf{V}_\Delta\cdot\mathbf{V}_\Delta^T\right)\right\}. \tag{46b}$$

From (18), (20), and (40), it follows now that the pdf(s) of the matrices $\mathbf{B}_\Sigma$ and $\mathbf{B}_\Delta$ in (40) can be expressed as

$$p\left(\mathbf{B}_\Sigma\right)=W_M^{(\mathbf{R})}\left(\mathbf{B}_\Sigma,K,\mathbf{C}_\Sigma\right),\quad p(\mathbf{B}_\Delta)=W_M^{(\mathbf{R})}\left(\mathbf{B}_\Delta,K,\mathbf{C}_\Sigma\right). \tag{47a}$$

and because of (45), these matrices $\mathbf{B}_\Sigma$ and $\mathbf{B}_\Delta$ are mutually independent.

The pdf of the sum (40) is therefore given by

$$p(\mathbf{B}_\mathbf{V})=W_M^{(\mathbf{R})}\left(\mathbf{B}_\mathbf{V},2K,\mathbf{C}_\Sigma\right)=\frac{|\mathbf{B}_\mathbf{V}|^{(2K-M-1)/2}\cdot\exp\left\{-\frac{1}{2}tr\left(\mathbf{C}_\Sigma^{-1}\cdot\mathbf{B}_\mathbf{V}\right)\right\}}{2^{M\cdot K}\cdot\pi^{M\cdot(M-1)/4}\cdot\left|\mathbf{C}_\Sigma\right|^{K}\cdot\prod_{i-1}^{M}\Gamma\left(\frac{2K+1-i}{2}\right)}. \tag{47b}$$

This formula has been already derived in somewhat different way in [35, 38]. In these works, it has been used in accordance with methodology [7, 9, 10] in order to attain the objectives been set, which, however, did not include a derivation of the pdf of the complex Hermitian persymmetric $M\times M$ matrix $\mathbf{A}_{cp}$ (36). At the same time, it is quite simple to proceed to this pdf form the pdf

(47b) by determination of a Jacobian of the transform (41) which connects the matrices $\mathbf{B_V}$ and $\mathbf{A}_{cp}$.

The symmetric $M \times M$ matrix $\mathbf{B_V}$ is defined by $M \cdot (M+1)/2$ parameters, whose number exactly coincides with the number of parameters that specify the Hermitian persymmetric matrix $\mathbf{A}_{cp}$. For elements $a_{i\ell} = a'_{i\ell} + j \cdot a''_{i\ell}$ of that matrix, the following equalities

$$\alpha_{i\ell} = \alpha_{M_\ell M_i} = \tilde{\alpha}_{M_\ell M_i} = \tilde{\alpha_{i\ell}}, \quad M_k = M + 1 - k,$$
$$\alpha'_{i\ell} = \alpha'_{M_\ell M_i} = \alpha'_{M_i M_\ell} = \alpha''_{\ell i}, \alpha''_{i\ell} = \alpha''_{M_\ell M_i} = -\alpha''_{M_i M_\ell}$$
$$= -\alpha''_{\ell i}, i, \ell \in 1, M$$

hold.

Next, taking into account (12), we can express the elements of matrix $\mathbf{B_V}$ (41) as follows:

$$b_{i\ell} = \alpha'_{i\ell} - \alpha''_{i, M_\ell}, \quad b_{M_\ell M_i} = \alpha'_{i\ell} + \alpha''_{i, M_\ell},$$

$$b_{i, M_i} = \alpha'_{i, M_i}, i \in 1, M, \ell \in i, M,$$

that allow to compute the Jacobian of the transform (41)

$$\det \left[\begin{array}{c:c} \mathbf{I}_z \otimes \begin{bmatrix} 1 & -1 \\ 1 & 1 \end{bmatrix} & \mathbf{0} \\ \hline \mathbf{0} & \mathbf{I}_L \end{array} \right] = \det \left[\mathbf{I}_z \otimes \begin{bmatrix} 1 & -1 \\ 1 & 1 \end{bmatrix} \right] = 2^z, \quad z = \varepsilon \left[\frac{M}{2} \right] \cdot \varepsilon \left[\frac{M+1}{2} \right]. \tag{48}$$

Replacing in (47b) matrix $\mathbf{B_V}$ by its representation (41) and taking into account (48), (42), (16), and (15) yields

$$p(\mathbf{A}_{cp}) = \frac{|\mathbf{A}_{cp}|^{(2K-M-1)/2} \exp\{-tr(\mathbf{C}^{-1} \cdot \mathbf{A}_{cp})\}}{2^z \cdot \pi^{M \cdot (M-1)/4} \cdot |\mathbf{C}|^K \cdot \prod_{i-1}^{M} \Gamma\left(\frac{2K+1-i}{2}\right)}, K \geq L = \varepsilon \left[\frac{M+1}{2} \right]. \tag{49}$$

The latter formula completely defines the desired pdf of the complex Hermitian persymmetric $M \times M$ matrix $\mathbf{A}_{cp}$ present in the ML estimate $\hat{\mathbf{C}}_p$ (36) of the Hermitian PCM $\mathbf{C}$ specified in (11) and (32). This formula has the same form as the Wishart's–Goodman's pdf (35) of the matrix $\mathbf{A}_c$ (34) from the ML estimate $\hat{\mathbf{C}} = K^{-1} \cdot \mathbf{A}_c$ of GCM. However, for formula (49), the reduced number of parameters that determine PCM has resulted in increased on $(M-1)/2$ number of degrees of freedom. That is why this formula could be considered as modified Wishart's–Goodman's distribution of the ML estimate $\hat{\mathbf{C}}_p$ (36) of complex PCM $\mathbf{C}$ of an order M.

Note that in a particular case of $M = 1$, when $L = 1$, $z = 0$, $|\mathbf{C}| = c_{11} = \overline{\left|\mathbf{y}_1^{(i)}\right|^2} = \sigma^2$ and $\mathbf{A}_{cp} = a_{11} = \sum_{i=1}^{K} \left|\mathbf{y}_1^{(i)}\right|^2 = \mathbf{A}_c$, formula (49) is transformed into

$$p(\mathbf{A}_{cp}) = p(\mathbf{A}_c) = p(a_{11})$$
$$= \frac{1}{\sigma^2 \cdot (K-1)!} \cdot \left(\frac{a_{11}}{\sigma^2}\right)^{K-1} \cdot \exp\left(-\frac{a_{11}}{\sigma^2}\right), \tag{50}$$

i.e., the pdf (49) turns into the Erlang distribution (50) with the shape and scale parameters, K and σ^2, respectively. Such pdf (50) characterizes, in an explicit statistical sense, the pdf of a sum of K squared magnitudes of independent complex normal random variables with zero means and equal variances σ^2 [39].

5 Exemplifying practical usage of the derived distributions

Distributions (31) and (49) of a persymmetric estimation CM (21) and (36) resemble the pdf(s) (20) and (35) of a general type CM estimates (19) and (34) but with an increased number of the degrees of freedom. In connection with this, the well-known properties of real [1–5] and complex [6–10] Wishart distributions (with relevant modifications) are transferred into the derived here distributions. Here beneath, we feature an importance of those distributions referring to some characteristic SP examples.

A. A non-degenerate transformation

$$\mathbf{B}_{rp} = \mathbf{U} \cdot \mathbf{A}_{rp} \cdot \mathbf{U} \tag{51}$$

of a $2L \times 2L$ real persymmetric matrix $\mathbf{A}_{rp}$ (21) distributed via (31) with the non-random symmetric and persymmetric $2 \cdot L \times 2 \cdot L$ matrix $\mathbf{U} = \mathbf{U}^T = \mathbf{\Pi}_M \cdot \mathbf{U} \cdot \mathbf{\Pi}_M$ gives rise to the random symmetric and persymmetric matrix $\mathbf{B}_{rp}$ (51) with the same distribution but the transformed parametric matrix[2]

$$\mathbf{G} = \mathbf{U} \cdot \mathbf{R} \cdot \mathbf{U}. \tag{52}$$

Indeed, under the conditions (21), such matrix $\mathbf{B}_{rp}$ (51) can be expressed as

$$\mathbf{B}_{rp} = \frac{1}{2}\left(\mathbf{U} \cdot \mathbf{Y} \cdot \mathbf{Y}^T \cdot \mathbf{U} + \mathbf{U} \cdot \mathbf{\Pi}_{2L} \cdot \mathbf{Y} \cdot \mathbf{Y}^T \cdot \mathbf{\Pi}_{2L} \cdot \mathbf{U}\right)$$
$$= \frac{1}{2}\left(\mathbf{V} \cdot \mathbf{V}^T + \mathbf{\Pi}_{2L} \cdot \mathbf{V} \cdot \mathbf{V}^T \cdot \mathbf{\Pi}_{2L}\right), \tag{53}$$

where $\mathbf{V} = \mathbf{U} \cdot \mathbf{Y} = \{\mathbf{v}_i\}_{\ell=1}^{K}$ is the K- variate sample composed of $2 \cdot L$ - variate random vectors

$$\mathbf{v}_i = N(0, \mathbf{G}), \quad \overline{\mathbf{v}_i} = 0, \quad \overline{\mathbf{v}_i \cdot \mathbf{v}_\ell^T} = \mathbf{G} \cdot \delta(i - \ell), \quad i, \ell \in 1, K. \tag{54}$$

The pdf of matrix $\mathbf{B}_p$ (51) (for a fixed given $K \geq L$) can therefore be expressed as

$$p(\mathbf{B}_{rp}) = \frac{|\mathbf{B}_{rp}|^{(K-L-1)/2} \cdot \exp\{-\frac{1}{2}tr(\mathbf{G}^{-1}\cdot\mathbf{B}_{rp})\}}{2^{(K-\frac{L+1}{2})\cdot L} \cdot \pi^{\frac{L\cdot(L-1)}{2}} \cdot |\mathbf{G}|^{\frac{K}{2}} \cdot \prod_{i-1}^{L} \Gamma^2\left(\frac{K+1-i}{2}\right)}. \quad (55)$$

This formula permits ease computing of the Jacobian $\left|\frac{\partial(\mathbf{B}_{rp})}{\partial(\mathbf{A}_{rp})}\right| = \frac{p(\mathbf{A}_{rp})}{p(\mathbf{B}_{rp})}$ of the transform (51). Using (31) and taking into account (52), we obtain $\left|\frac{\partial(\mathbf{B}_{rp})}{\partial(\mathbf{A}_{rp})}\right| = |\mathbf{U}|^{L+1}$.

Similarly, the use of the complex matrix (36) (characterized by distribution (49)) in the transform $\mathbf{B}_{cp} = \mathbf{U}\cdot\mathbf{A}_{cp}\cdot\mathbf{U}$ (for a Hermitian and persymmetric $\mathbf{U}$) yields the same distribution $p(\mathbf{B}_{cp})$ (49) for $\mathbf{B}_{cp}$ but with the properly transformed parametric matrix $\mathbf{G}_c = \mathbf{U}\cdot\mathbf{C}\cdot\mathbf{U}$. The Jacobian of the transform is given by $\left|\frac{\partial(\mathbf{B}_{cp})}{\partial(\mathbf{A}_{cp})}\right| = |\mathbf{U}|^{M+1}$.

Note that the computations of the corresponding Jacobians become intractable without knowledge of the analytically closed expressions (31) and (49) for the corresponding pdf(s).

B. In the example, let us compare mean values of relative bias

$$\Delta(\alpha) = \frac{\overline{s(\alpha)-\hat{s}(\alpha)}}{s(\alpha)} = 1-\overline{\hat{v}(\alpha)}, \quad \hat{v}(\alpha) = \frac{\hat{s}(\alpha)}{s(\alpha)} \quad (56)$$

between random (estimate) spectral function (SF)

$$\hat{s}(\alpha) = \left(\mathbf{x}^*(\alpha)\cdot\hat{\mathbf{C}}^{-1}\cdot\mathbf{x}(\alpha)\right)^{-1} \quad (57a)$$

of Capon method [7, 18, 19] and true value of this SF

$$s(\alpha) = \left(\mathbf{x}^*(\alpha)\cdot\mathbf{C}_p^{-1}\cdot\mathbf{x}(\alpha)\right)^{-1}. \quad (57b)$$

The latter is inversely proportional to a quadratic form of complex steering vector $\mathbf{x}(\alpha) = \mathbf{x}'(\alpha) + j\cdot\mathbf{x}''(\alpha)$ with matrix $\mathbf{C}_p^{-1}$ being inverse to Hermitian PCM $\mathbf{C}_p$.

As an estimate of this matrix, we will use in (57a) following matrices

$$\hat{\mathbf{C}} = \begin{cases} K^{-1}\cdot\mathbf{A}_c & (a) \\ K^{-1}\cdot\mathbf{A}_{cp} & (b) \end{cases} \quad (58)$$

with defining matrices $\mathbf{A}_c$ (34) and $\mathbf{A}_{cp}$ (36) which obey pdfs (35) and (49), respectively. In the latter case, we will also assume that the steering vector $\mathbf{x}(\alpha)$ obeys a condition

$$\mathbf{x}(\alpha) = \mathbf{x}_p(\alpha) = c\cdot\mathbf{\Pi}_M\cdot\tilde{\mathbf{x}}_p(\alpha), \quad |c|^2 = 1, \quad (59)$$

which is completely natural for CS receive channels.

As is shown in [7, 10], in the case (a)

$$\hat{v}(\alpha) = K^{-1}\cdot d, \quad (60)$$

where d is a random variable with the independent on α Erlang's pdf

$$p_d(x) = ((\delta-1)!)^{-1}\cdot x^{\delta-1}\cdot\exp\{-x\}, \quad \delta = \delta_g = K-M+1$$

with the shape parameter δ_g and the scale parameter equal to unity [39]. Its mean is $\bar{d} = \delta_g$. Therefore, by virtue of (60), $\overline{\hat{v}(\alpha)} = K^{-1}\cdot\bar{d} = 1-(M-1)/K$, so that

$$\Delta(\alpha) = \Delta_g = (M-1)/K. \quad (61)$$

In the case (b), let us use the representation (39) for the matrix $\mathbf{A}_{cp}$. Then, taking into account the properties (13) of the matrix $\mathbf{T}$ (12), we will obtain for the SF $\hat{s}(\alpha)$ (57a) the following

$$\hat{s}(\alpha) = K^{-1}\cdot\left(\mathbf{z}^*(\alpha)\cdot\mathbf{B}_{\mathrm{V}}^{-1}\cdot\mathbf{z}(\alpha)\right)^{-1}, \quad \mathbf{z}(\alpha) = \mathbf{T}\cdot\mathbf{x}(\alpha),$$

where $\mathbf{B}_{\mathrm{V}}$ is the matrix (40) with the pdf (47). Under conditions (59), the vector

$$\mathbf{z}(\alpha) = (1-j)\cdot\mathbf{x}_\Delta(\alpha)/\sqrt{2}, \quad \mathbf{x}_\Delta(\alpha) = \mathbf{x}'(\alpha)-\mathbf{x}''(\alpha),$$

and the latter SF is transformed to the formula

$$\hat{s}(\alpha) = K^{-1}\cdot\left(\mathbf{x}_\Delta^*(\alpha)\cdot\mathbf{B}_{\mathrm{V}}^{-1}\cdot\mathbf{x}_\Delta(\alpha)\right)^{-1},$$

which has a quadratic form of real-valued vector $\mathbf{x}_\Delta(\alpha)$ with real-valued symmetric matrix $\mathbf{B}_{\mathrm{V}}$, with pdf (47), in denominator.

Next, using the methodology [7, 9, 10], it is possible to demonstrate that, under considered conditions, quantity $\hat{v}(\alpha)$ (56) obeys following equality similar to (60)

$$\hat{v}(\alpha) = K^{-1}\cdot d_1, \quad (62)$$

where d_1 is a random variable with the independent on α pdf

$$p_{d_1}(x) = \Gamma(\delta_p)^{-1}\cdot x^{\delta_p-1}\cdot\exp\{-x\}. \quad \delta_p = K-(M-1)/2.$$

For odd M, this distribution become the Erlang's one [39] with the shape parameter δ_p and the scale parameter equal to unity. That is why mean value $\bar{d}_1 = \delta_p$, and, by virtue of (60) and (56),

$$\overline{\hat{v}(\alpha)} = K^{-1}\cdot\overline{d_1} = 1-(M-1)/(2\cdot K),$$
$$\Delta(\alpha) = \Delta_p = (M-1)/(2\cdot K) = \Delta_g/2.$$

Thereby, under considered conditions, for the same training sample size K, the estimate (58b) reduces as great as twice the bias (56) of SF estimate (57) in contrast to the estimate (58a). This is equivalent to the statement that equal values of bias (56) are provided by the estimate (58b) at the twice smaller training sample size K.

C. Note, that, under conditions (59), the quadratic form in (57a) could be computed in more simple way by using the estimate (58b) instead of (58a). This is easy to follow by rewriting it as

$$\mathbf{x}^*(\alpha)\cdot\hat{\mathbf{C}}^{-1}\cdot\mathbf{x}(\alpha) = \begin{cases} K\cdot q_g(\alpha), & q_g(\alpha)=\mathbf{x}^*(\alpha)\cdot\mathbf{w}_g(\alpha), \quad \mathbf{w}_g(\alpha)=\mathbf{A}_c^{-1}\cdot\mathbf{x}(\alpha), \quad \text{(a)} \\ K\cdot q_p(\alpha), & q_p(\alpha)=\mathbf{x}_p^*(\alpha)\cdot\mathbf{w}_p(\alpha), \quad \mathbf{w}_p(\alpha)=\mathbf{A}_{cp}^{-1}\cdot\mathbf{x}_p(\alpha). \quad \text{(b)} \end{cases} \tag{63}$$

Matrix $\mathbf{A}_{cp}^{-1}$, being inverse to Hermitian persymmetric matrix, is also Hermitian persymmetric one, i.e., $\mathbf{A}_{cp}^{-1}=\mathbf{\Pi}_M\cdot\left(\widetilde{\mathbf{A}_{cp}}\right)^{-1}\cdot\mathbf{\Pi}_M$. That is why, under conditions (59), vector $\mathbf{w}_p(\alpha)=c\cdot\mathbf{\Pi}_M\cdot\widetilde{\mathbf{w}_p}(\alpha)$ and thus it is completely determined by the half ($M/2$) of its components which could be computed at the expense of $\approx M^2/2$ multiplications. Approximately $M/2$ multiplications are enough in order to compute the scalar product $q_p(\alpha)$. Thus, an amount of computations necessary to calculate the quadratic form in (57a) based on (58b) could be twice less than based on (58a).

D. Similar gains in the amount of computations and efficiency (including an efficiency in terms of criteria different from (56)) could be achieved in the systems with CS receive channels also by using other kinds of PCM ML estimates (considered, particularly, in [30–32, 35, 36, 37, 38–19]).

6 Conclusions

The main result of this work is the derivation of the pdfs (37) and (49) of random $M\times M$ real-valued and complex-valued ML estimates (21) and (36) of persymmetric CMs (2) and (11) of multivariate Gaussian processes and fields. Such CMs arise in numerous practical applications, particularly, in the tasks of space-time adaptive signal processing in systems with central symmetry of receive channels [20–32, 27–37, 38, 16, 17]. The derived pdfs have the same form as the classical Wishart's pdf and Wishart's–Goodman's pdf (20) and (35) for GCM ML estimates, but with the number of degrees of freedom being increased approximately on $M/2$. This is due to the approximately half less number of determining parameters (elements) of the PCM. That is why, in the systems with the CS receive channels, the derived distributions appeal to such importance as that of the classical Wishart and Wishart's–Goodman's pdfs in systems with arbitrary receive channels.

Reduced dimensionality of parameters vector for PCM in CS systems increases an efficiency of adaptive signal processing based on ML estimates (21) and (36) as compared with ML estimates (19) and (34). The gain depends on the efficiency criterion and additional conditions which take into account the task specificity. Nevertheless, in the above-considered example as well as in numerous other practically important cases, the adaptive processing based on estimates (21) and (36) under central symmetry of space-time receive channels could provide for some conditions at the expense of K_p training samples, the efficiency (in terms of different criteria) being close to that provided by the estimates (19) and (34) at the expense of $K\approx 2\cdot K_p$ training samples [34, 35, 36, 37].

It is essential that, taking into account the structure specificity of utilized matrices and vectors, it is possible to make signal processing in CS systems based on ML estimates (21) and (36) as well as their variants [30–32, 36, 37] less computationally consuming.

General considerations allow to assume a possibility to obtain similar gain not only in case of Gaussian stochastic processes but also in case of other stochastic processes. The latter, in particular, could be subject to exponential distribution or Weibull one. However, a rigorous proof of this hypothesis is unavailable to the author, since for such non-Gaussian processes, there are currently unknown neither their correlation matrices' ML estimates analogous to (19) and (34) nor these estimates' pdfs analogous to Wishart's (20) pdf and Wishart's–Goodman's (35) one.

Finally, note that statistical characteristics of different functions of ML estimates of Gaussian processes' PCM could be obtained without explicit use of their pdfs (31) and (49) what was illustrated, in particular, in [35, 36, 37, 38, 16, 17]. Nevertheless, the pdfs (31) and (49) are also useful in such case because they allow to perform only one step of transformations similar to (9) and (39) and then to use the methodology [7, 9, 10] in order to find statistical characteristics of functions of GCM ML estimates. Such approach seems to be the easiest one and methodologically reasonable. Namely, this approach is used by the author for comparative analysis of a number of "superresolving" spectral estimation methods in systems with CS receive channels. The results of this analysis are planned to be discussed in a special paper.

In closing, the author would like to thank all five reviewers for the time and effort with this paper.

7 Endnotes

[1]For place saving, we omit the derivation of formula (21), as it can be easily obtained according to the procedure employed in [28] when deriving the ML estimate of the Hermitian persymmetric CM.

[2]In application to distribution (35), this property is known as the Goodman theorem [8–10].

Abbreviations

AA: antenna array; CM: correlation matrix; CS: centrally symmetric; GCM: general type correlation matrix; ML: maximum likelihood; PCM: persymmetric correlation matrices; pdf: probability density function; SAR: synthetic aperture radar; SF: spectral function; SINR: signal-to-(interference + noise) ratio; SP: signal processing.

Competing interests

The author declares that he has no competing interests.

Acknowledgements

The author is very grateful to Yu. I. Abramovich and V. M. Koshevyy for the helpful discussions and insightful comments that helped to improve the paper.

References

1. J Wishart, The generalised product moment distribution in samples from a normal multivariate population. Biometrika **20A**(1–2), 32–52 (1928). doi:10.1093/biomet/20A.1-2.32
2. M Hazewinkel (ed.), *Encyclopaedia of Mathematics, Vol. 9 (Sto–Zyg)* (Kluwer, Dordrecht, 1993)
3. TW Anderson, *An introduction to multivariate statistical analysis*, 3rd edn. (John Wiley & Sons, Hoboken NJ, 2003)
4. H Cramér, *Mathematical methods of statistics* (Princeton University Press, Princeton, N.J., 1946)
5. MH DeGroot, *Optimal statistical decisions* (McGraw-Hill, New York, 1969)
6. NR Goodman, Statistical analysis based on a certain multivariate complex Gaussian distribution (an introduction). The Annals of Mathematical Statistics **34**(1), 152–177 (1963). doi:10.1214/aoms/1177704250
7. J Capon, NR Goodman, Probability distributions for estimators of the frequency-wavenumber spectrum. IEEE Proceedings **58**(10), 1785–1786 (1970). doi:10.1109/PROC.1970.8014
8. DR Brillinger, *Time series: data analysis and theory* (Holden Day, Inc., San Francisco, 1981)
9. IS Reed, JD Mallett, LE Brennan, Rapid convergence rate in adaptive arrays. IEEE Trans. Aerosp. Electron. Syst. **AES-10**(6), 853–863 (1974). doi:10.1109/TAES.1974.307893
10. LE Brennan, IS Reed, An adaptive array signal processing algorithm for communications. IEEE Trans. Aerosp. Electron. Syst. **AES-18**(1), 124–130 (1982). doi:10.1109/TAES.1982.309212
11. YD Shirman, VN Manzhos, *Theory and techniques of radar information processing in a background of interference* (Radio i Sviaz, Moscow, 1981) (in Russian)
12. RA Monzingo, TW Miller, *Introduction to adaptive arrays* (John Wiley & Sons, New York, 1980)
13. VG Repin, GP Tartakovskiy, *Statistical synthesis under prior uncertainty and adaptation of information systems* (Soviet Radio, Moscow, 1977) (in Russian)
14. H Wang, L Cai, On adaptive multiband signal detection with the SMI algorithm. IEEE Trans. Aerosp. Electron. Syst. **26**(5), 768–773 (1990). doi:10.1109/7.102712
15. H Wang, L Cai, On adaptive multiband signal detection with the GLR algorithm. IEEE Trans. Aerosp. Electron. Syst. **27**(2), 225–233 (1991). doi:10.1109/7.78296
16. C Hao, S Gazor, G Foglia, B Liu, C Hou, Persymmetric adaptive detection and range estimation of a small target. IEEE Trans. Aerosp. Electron. Syst. **51**(4), 2590–2604 (2015). doi:10.1109/TAES.2015.140517
17. J Liu, G Cui, H Li, B Himed, On the performance of a persymmetric adaptive matched filter. IEEE Trans. Aerosp. Electron. Syst. **51**(4), 2605–2614 (2015). doi:10.1109/TAES.2015.140633
18. DI Lekhovytskiy, PM Flekser, *Statistical analysis of quasi-harmonic spectral estimation resolution with Capon's method, Proceedings of International Scientific and Technical Conference "Modern Radiolocation", Kyiv, Ukraine, vol. 1*, 1994, pp. 66–71. in Russian
19. DI Lekhovytskiy, YS Shifrin, Statistical analysis of "superresolving" methods for direction-of-arrival estimation of noise radiation sources under finite size of training sample. Signal Process. **93**(12), 3382–3399 (2013). doi:10.1016/j.sigpro.2013.03.008
20. YV Shkvarko, Unifying regularization and Bayesian estimation methods for enhanced imaging with remotely sensed data—part I: theory. IEEE Trans. Geosci. Remote Sens. **42**(5), 923–931 (2004). doi:10.1109/TGRS.2003.823281
21. YV Shkvarko, Unifying regularization and Bayesian estimation methods for enhanced imaging with remotely sensed data—part II: implementation and performance issues. IEEE Trans. Geosci. Remote Sens. **42**(5), 932–940 (2004). doi:10.1109/TGRS.2003.823279
22. YV Shkvarko, Unifying experiment design and convex regularization techniques for enhanced imaging with uncertain remote sensing data—part I: theory. IEEE Trans. Geosci. Remote Sens. **48**(1), 82–95 (2010). doi:10.1109/TGRS.2009.2027695
23. YV Shkvarko, Unifying experiment design and convex regularization techniques for enhanced imaging with uncertain remote sensing data—part II: adaptive implementation and performance issues. IEEE Trans. Geosci. Remote Sens. **48**(1), 96–111 (2010). doi:10.1109/TGRS.2009.2027696
24. YV Shkvarko, J Tuxpan, SR Santos, ℓ2–ℓ1 structured descriptive experiment design regularization based enhancement of fractional SAR imagery. Signal Process. **93**(12), 3553–3566 (2013). doi:10.1016/j.sigpro.2013.03.024
25. YV Shkvarko, J Tuxpan, SR Santos, Dynamic experiment design regularization approach to adaptive imaging with array radar/SAR systems. Sensors **11**(5), 4483–4511 (2011). doi:10.3390/s110504483
26. RL Stratonovich, *Principles of adaptive reception* (Soviet Radio, Moscow, 1973) (in Russian)
27. A De Maio, D Orlando, An invariant approach to adaptive radar detection under covariance persymmetry. IEEE Trans. Signal Process. **63**(5), 1297–1309 (2015). doi:10.1109/TSP.2014.2388441
28. R Nitzberg, Application of maximum likelihood estimation of persymmetric covariance matrices to adaptive processing. IEEE Trans. Aerosp. Electron. Syst. **AES-16**(1), 124–127 (1980). doi:10.1109/TAES.1980.308887
29. EI Lifanov, VA Likharev, Estimate of the covariation matrix of stationary interference. Telecommunications and Radio Engineering **37–38**(5), 103–105 (1983)
30. VI Zarytskyi, VN Kokin, DI Lekhovytskiy, VV Salamatin, Recurrent adaptive processing algorithms under condition of central symmetry of space-time reception channels. Radiophysics and Quantum Electronics **28**(7), 592–598 (1985). doi:10.1007/BF01034102
31. VA Averochkin, PE Baranov, VS Tokolov, Effectiveness of adaptive filters with real weight coefficients. Radioelectron. Commun. Syst. **30**(4), 80–82 (1987)
32. VM Koshevyy, VV Radionov, Evaluation of limiting rate of convergence of algorithms for signal adaptive processing for a class of structures of noise correlation matrices. Telecommunications and Radio Engineering **45**(6), 36–41 (1991)
33. MB Sverdlik, VE Shpatakovskiy, Estimation of the potential convergence rate of the adaptive signal processing in equispace receive channels. Radiotekhnika i Elektronika **34**(4), 760–766 (1989) (in Russian)
34. YI Abramovich, AY Gorokhov, On an estimation of the convergence rate of adaptive interference compensation filters with a persymmetrical correlation matrix. J. Commun. Technol. Electron. **38**(7), 9–21 (1993)
35. VM Koshevyy, VV Radionov, Effectiveness of adaptive filters with central symmetry of receiving channels. Radiotekhnika i Elektronika **39**(11), 1779–1788 (1994) (in Russian)
36. SA Vorobyov, *Reduced complexity blind unitary prewhitening with application to blind source separation. Paper presented at the 2005 1st IEEE International Workshop on Computational Advances in Multi-Sensor Adaptive Processing, Puerto Vallarta, Mexico, 13–15 December*, 2005. doi:10.1109/CAMAP.2005.1574214
37. DI Lekhovytskiy, DV Atamanskiy, IG Kirillov, VI Zarytskyi, Comparison of adaptive processing efficiencies for arbitrary and centrosymmetrical arrays. Antennas **44**(1), 99–103 (2000) (in Russian)
38. L Cai, H Wang, A persymmetric multiband GLR algorithm. IEEE Trans. Aerosp. Electron. Syst. **28**(3), 806–816 (1992). doi:10.1109/7.256301
39. NAJ Hastings, JB Peacock, *Statistical distributions: a handbook for students and practitioners* (Butterworths, London, 1975)
40. VL Girko, *Multivariate statistical analysis* (Vyshcha Shkola, Kyiv, 1988) (in Russian)

8

Multi-target simultaneous ISAR imaging based on compressed sensing

Gang Li*, Qingkai Hou, Shiyou Xu and Zengping Chen

Abstract

Conventional range-Doppler (RD) inverse synthetic aperture radar (ISAR) imaging method utilizes coherent integration of consecutive pulses to achieve high cross-range resolution. It requires the radar to keep track of the target during coherent processing intervals (CPI). This restricts the radar's multi-target imaging ability, especially when the targets appear simultaneously in different observing scenes. To solve this problem, this paper proposes a multi-target ISAR imaging method for phased-array radar (PAR) based on compressed sensing (CS). This method explores and exploits the agility of PAR without changing its structure. Firstly, the transmitted pulses are allocated randomly to different targets, and the ISAR image of each target can be then reconstructed from limited echoes using CS algorithm. A pulse allocation scheme is proposed based on the analysis of the target's size and rotation velocity, which can guarantee that every target gets enough pulses for effective CS imaging. Self-adaptive mechanism is utilized to improve the robustness of the pulse allocation method. Simulation results are presented to demonstrate the validity and feasibility of the proposed approach.

1 Introduction

Inverse synthetic aperture radar (ISAR) can generate images of targets with high resolution in two dimensions. It usually transmits wideband waveform to obtain high-range resolution and utilizes coherent integration of multi-pulse to achieve high cross-range resolution [1]. This is the basic idea of range-Doppler (RD) imaging. It requires both appropriate rotation angle (usually 3°–5° for RD imaging) and consecutive pulses during coherent processing intervals (CPI) [2].

To the best of our knowledge, most ISARs in practice can only generate images one target at a time. Since the RD imaging method requires consecutive echoes, the radar must track the target for a long period. The observing scene of radar is always a limited region defined by the radar's receiving range gate and the beam width. Therefore, the observing scene of ISAR must be focused on the target during the CPI. In some applications, the radar needs to observe several targets appearing in different observing scenes simultaneously, as shown in Fig. 1. Such scenes are quite common for military air defense radars or space surveillance radars. Modern PAR with active electronically scanning phased-array antenna can change the frequency and beam direction of signal between pulses readily [3]. Therefore, PARs are widely applied in multi-target radars, such as long-range air defense radars and missile-tracking radars.

Although PAR can achieve multi-target detection and tracking comfortably by allocating the pulses to each target, there are still some challenges in imaging them simultaneously. As is well known, the maximum pulse repetition frequency (PRF) of radar is limited by the observing distance to prevent range ambiguity. Meanwhile, the radar still needs to assign some pulses for target detection, tracking, and other functions [4]. Hence, the PAR's pulses may be inadequate for the coherent integration of each target. This paper aims to exploit the flexibility of PAR and to achieve better performance in multi-target imaging.

Recently, CS has drawn great attention in data acquisition and signal processing. It suggests that the signal can be sampled at sub-Nyquist rate and be reconstructed correctly if the signal is sparse or compressive in some basis or transform domain [5–9]. ISAR imaging based on CS is also an active research area since the targets often show sparse reflections and occupy only limited pixels in the imaging results [10, 11]. It has been proposed in [12] that ISAR image can be reconstructed

* Correspondence: lg19860521@163.com
College of Electronic Science and Engineering, National University of Defense Technology, Changsha, Hunan 410073, China

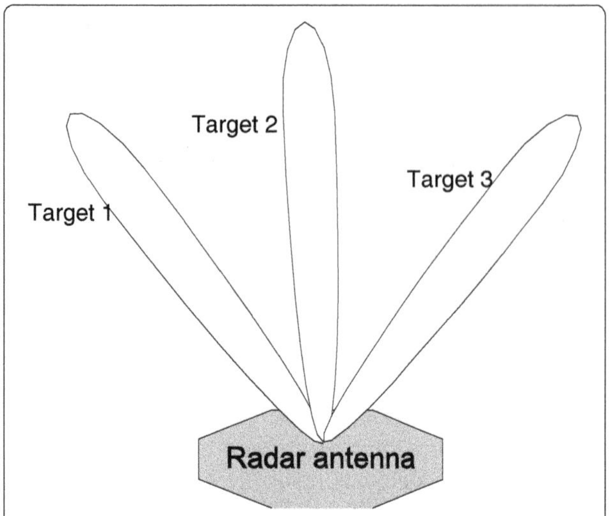

Fig. 1 Scenario of multi-target for PAR ISAR radar

using much fewer pulses than RD algorithm with random pulse repetition interval (PRI). At present, most of the research on CS imaging is aimed at a single target and has achieved some research results [7–10, 12]. Considering the requirement of radar multi-target observation and imaging, this paper tries to use the CS imaging method to improve the ability of simultaneous multi-target radar imaging.

Inspired by CS and the flexibility of PAR, we allocate the pulses randomly to multiple targets appearing in different observing scenes. The radar illuminates one target at one pulse and changes target from pulse to pulse. The observing sequence is arranged randomly to realize non-uniform sampling in the cross-range dimensions of each target. Such random sampling can insure that the measurement matrix satisfies the restricted isometry property (RIP), which is the sufficient criterion for effective reconstruction in CS [13, 14]. Another major contribution of this paper is that we propose a pulse allocating strategy based on detailed analysis of CS ISAR imaging. Besides random sampling, the sizes and rotation velocities of targets are also determining factors for pulse allocation. This allocation of pulse guarantees that every target obtains enough measurements for effective CS reconstruction. The key innovation of this method is fully utilizing the limited resource of radar pulses to implement multi-target imaging, based on the image sparsity and CS algorithms. After random observation, the measurement matrices for the targets are different from each other; thus, the images are reconstructed separately using CS algorithms. Experiment results are provided to demonstrate the validity of this observing strategy and imaging method.

This paper is organized as follows. In Section 2, the mathematic model of ISAR imaging is built and the CS imaging method is presented. In Section 3, the multi-target observing scheme and reconstructing method of ISAR image are presented based on CS. The experiment results and analysis are provided in Section 4, and conclusions are given in Section 5.

2 CS ISAR imaging using limited pulses

2.1 Model of range-Doppler ISAR imaging

Assume that the translational motion of the target has been compensated using conventional methods [15–17]. The target can be treated as a platform which rotates around the center *O*, as shown in Fig. 2. Suppose the transmitted linear frequency modulation (LFM) signal is

$$S_T(t) = \mathrm{rect}\left(\frac{t}{T_\mathrm{P}}\right)\exp\left(j2\pi\left(f_c t + \frac{1}{2}\gamma t^2\right)\right) \quad (1)$$

where $\mathrm{rect}(u) = \begin{cases} 1, & |u|\le 1/2 \\ 0, & |u| > 1/2 \end{cases}$, f_c represents the center frequency, T_p is the pulse width, γ is he frequency modulation rate, and t is the fast time. The echo reflected by the scattering point locating at $P(x, y)$ after matched filtering pulse compression can be written as

$$s_\mathrm{R}(t, t_\mathrm{s}) = \beta\mathrm{sinc}\left(T_\mathrm{p}\gamma\left(t - \frac{2R(t_\mathrm{s})}{c}\right)\right)\exp\left(-j4\pi\frac{R(t_\mathrm{s})}{\lambda}\right) \quad (2)$$

where β is the backward scattering intensity of $P(x,y)$, λ is the wavelength of signal, t is the fast time, and t_s is the slow time. $R(t_\mathrm{s})$ is the instantaneous distance from $P(x, y)$ to radar and at t_s

$$R(t_\mathrm{s}) = R_0 + y\cos\theta(t_\mathrm{s}) + x\sin\theta(t_\mathrm{s}) \quad (3)$$

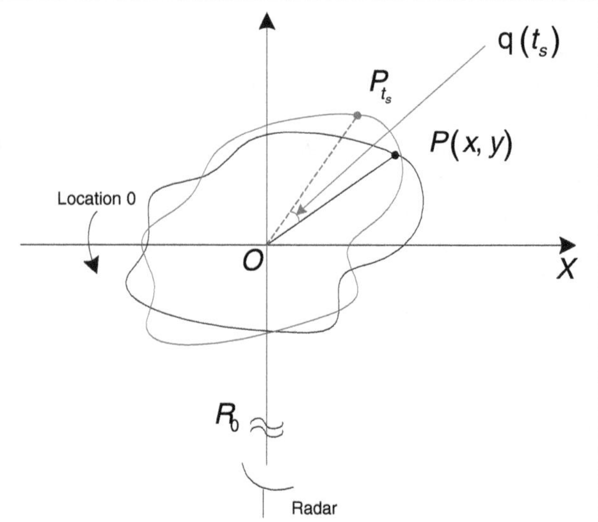

Fig. 2 Geometry of the scattering point *p*

where $\theta(t_s)$ is the instantaneous rotation angle of the mth pulse. Since the rotation angle is usually very small in ISAR, the $R(t_s)$ can be approximated as

$$R(t_s) \approx R_0 + y + x\theta(t_s) \quad (4)$$

In Eq. (4), $\theta(t_s)$ can be approximated by Taylor expansion as

$$\theta(t_s) \approx \omega t_s + 0.5\alpha t_s^2 + \sigma(t_s^2) \quad (5)$$

where ω and α are rotation velocity and acceleration, respectively. Therefore, the echo can be approximated as

$$s_R(t, t_s) \approx \beta \operatorname{sinc}\left(T_P\gamma\left(t - \frac{2(R_0 + y)}{c}\right)\right) \exp\left(-j4\pi\left(\frac{R_0 + y + x(\omega t_s + 0.5\alpha t_s^2)}{\lambda}\right)\right) \quad (6)$$

Suppose the total number of range cells is M and there are K scatters in the mth range cell. The rotational motion is assumed to be stationary. After neglecting the constant term and high-order term, the signal of the mth range cell can be denoted as

$$\begin{aligned} s_m(t_s) &\approx \sum_{k=1}^{K} \beta \operatorname{sinc}\left(T_P\gamma\left(t - \frac{2(R_0 + y)}{c}\right)\right) \exp\left(-j4\pi\left(\frac{R_0 + y + 0.5\alpha t_s^2}{\lambda}\right)\right) \exp\left(-j2\pi\left(\frac{2x_k\omega}{\lambda}\right)t_s\right) \\ &\approx \sum_{k=1}^{K} \beta \operatorname{sinc}\left(T_P\gamma\left(t - \frac{2(R_0 + y)}{c}\right)\right) \exp\left(-j4\pi\left(\frac{R_0 + y}{\lambda}\right)\right) \exp\left(-j2\pi\left(\frac{2x_k\omega}{\lambda}\right)t_s\right) \\ &= \sum_{k=1}^{K} \beta_k \exp\left(-j2\pi\left(\frac{2x_k\omega}{\lambda}\right)t_s\right) \end{aligned} \quad (7)$$

where $\beta_k = \beta sinc\left(T_P\gamma\left(t - \frac{2(R_0+y)}{c}\right)\right) \exp\left(-j4\pi\left(\frac{R_0+y}{\lambda}\right)\right)$, which denotes the kth scattering point's intensity. In RD imaging, the cross-range compression is achieved by applying a Fourier transform in the cross-range dimension. Let $f_k = \frac{2x_k\omega}{\lambda}$ denote the Doppler frequency of the kth scatter, and we can achieve the compression result of the mth range cell as

$$s_m(f_d) = \sum_{k=1}^{K} \beta_k \delta(f_d - f_k) \quad (8)$$

Considering the sampling window in the cross-range domain, the $\delta(\bullet)$ function will be substituted by $\sin c(\bullet)$.

If we build a dictionary Ψ and the ith column of Ψ is $\psi_i = \exp[-j2\pi f_d(i)t_s]$, Eq. (7) can be rewritten in the matrix form as

$$s_m = \Psi\beta_m + n \quad (9)$$

where s_m is the vector form of $s_m(t_s)$, β_m is the vector which denotes the scatters distribution in the mth range cell, and n is the measuring noise. The whole image of the target is obtained after cross-range compression of all M range cells.

2.2 CS ISAR imaging using random pulses

In most ISAR cases, there are only a few strong scattering points in one range cell, and the number of scattering centers is much smaller than the number of pulses. Therefore, the vector β is sparse, and the echoes of target are compressive in the cross-range dimension. CS ISAR imaging method has been proposed in [12] to reconstruct the image using much fewer pulses than RD algorithm with random PRI. In this paper, further study about CS ISAR imaging is carried on and some conditions are given for effective CS imaging.

First, to achieve effective reconstruction in CS, the number of measurements must exceed the theoretical minimal number [6].

$$M > O(K \cdot \log N) \quad (10)$$

where K is the sparse level and N is the length of the measured sparse signal. In the context of CS ISAR imaging, the sparse level K is the number of cross-range bins which are occupied by target in image, and Eq. (10) determines the minimal number of transmitted pulses for the target.

Second, the cross-range resolution in conventional RD imaging is defined by the wavelength of transmitted signal λ and the target's rotational angle Θ during the CPI, which is denoted as

$$\Delta_c = \frac{\lambda}{2\Theta} \quad (11)$$

The rotation angle Θ is usually 3°–5° because the smaller angle is inadequate for high resolution and the migration through resolution cell (MTRC) will occur if Θ is larger [18]. Moreover, the sampling rate in the cross-range dimension, e.g., the PRF of radar, must be at least twice the Doppler bandwidth of the target, which is proportional to the target's rotation velocity. Hence, targets with different rotation velocities need different PRFs for equivalent cross-range resolution. Faster rotation means that the CPI for one image is shorter and a higher PRF is required. The reference [19] suggests that the expected resolution of CS reconstructed image is restricted by the incoherency of the sensing matrix. In CS ISAR imaging, since the random pulses are the subset of Nyquist-sampled pulses in RD imaging, Eq. (11) still determines the cross-range resolution, and enough rotation angle is also required for high resolution.

According to the above analysis, we give the following two conditions that the random measurements must satisfy to achieve effective CS ISAR imaging.

2.2.0.1 Condition 1. The number of random pulses M is more than the minimal measurements needed by CS, as (10).

2.2.0.2 Condition 2. The rotation angle of the target during CPI is approximately 3°-5°, which is the same as RD method. This guarantees the reconstructed image own the same cross-range resolution as RD imaging result.

3 CS multi-target simultaneous imaging

3.1 Basic idea of multi-target observation

Based on the CS ISAR imaging, a multi-target imaging method is proposed for PAR in this section. As introduced in Section 1, there may be multiple targets in different observing scenes, but the radar can only observe one target at one pulse. Instead of illuminating one target during the whole CPI, the pulses can be allocated to all the targets and the observing sequence is arranged randomly. Therefore, the PRI for each target is non-uniform and the measurements of every target are random sampling, which coincides with the CS imaging method condition for single target in [12].

Suppose there are four different targets, and Fig. 3 shows the sequence of transmitted pulses, which are allocated randomly. As a simple example, the pulses are allocated to four targets with equal proportion in Fig. 3, e.g., the probability of being illuminated for each target is equal. However, such an equal proportion is apparently too simple for the practical applications. The emphasis of this section is to determine the allocating proportions of pulses for different targets.

In the train of transmitted pulses, the illuminated target of each pulse can be treated as an independent and identically distributed (I.I.D.) random variable A. $A \in \{0, 1, 2 \cdots L\}$, where L is the number of targets. $A_m = i(0 < i \leq L)$ means the mth pulse illuminates the ith target, while $A_m = 0$ means no target is observed, e.g., this pulse is not used in any target's imaging. The probability distribution of A determines the allocation proportions of pulses for different targets.

To obtain effective CS measurements for each target, random allocation of pulses must ensure that the measurements of every target satisfy the two conditions presented in Section 2. Based on this, we propose an algorithm to determine the probability distribution of A.

For condition 1, the key problem is to determine the sparse level of target, namely the size of target in cross-range dimension. For coarse estimation, the target's size can be estimated from the radar cross-section (RCS) [20] and high-resolution range profiles (HRRPs) of the targets. Although these methods cannot provide accurate estimation of the cross-range size of target, they can help to determine the sparse level of target roughly. Together with the expected resolution of ISAR image Δ_c, the sparse level of target k_i can be estimated by

$$K_i = D_i / \Delta_c \tag{12}$$

where D_i is the estimated size of target. Therefore, the number of pulses M_i needed for each target can be calculated in Eq. (10).

As for condition 2, the CPI of a target depends on its rotation velocity ω with respect to the radar line of sight. For space objects, the rotation velocity ω can be estimated from the orbit information. While for other non-cooperate targets, the ω can be estimated from Doppler analysis of target's echoes. Reference [21] suggests that the received signal of range bin can be approximated as cubic phase signals, and the ratio of the third-order phase coefficient to the first-order phase coefficient is just the square of the rotation velocity. We use this algorithm to estimate the rotation velocity ω_i of each target, and the CPI τ_i of target can be obtained by

$$\tau_i = \frac{\bar{\Theta}}{\omega_i} \tag{13}$$

where $\bar{\Theta}$ is the typical rotation angle for ISAR imaging and is set to be $\bar{\Theta} = 4°$.

Based on those estimations, the least number of pulses and CPIs of each target are determined. We use $\bar{\rho}_i$ to denote the equivalent average PRF for the ith target, and $\bar{\rho}_i$ is given as

$$\bar{\rho}_i = \frac{M_i}{\tau_i} \tag{14}$$

It proposes that the allocating probability for different target is proportional to the equivalent average PRF $\bar{\rho}_i$ of each target. The probability distribution of A_m follows

$$P(A_m = i) = \frac{\bar{\rho}_i}{f_{\text{PRF}}} \tag{15}$$

where f_{PRF} is the actual PRF with Nyquist sampling rate in the conventional RD imaging. Besides, the maximum number of targets that the radar can observe simultaneously can be derived as

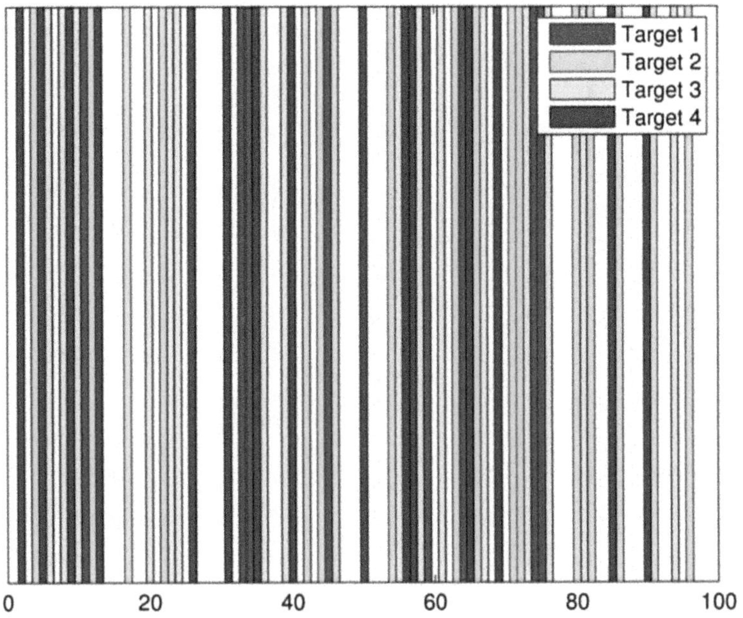

Fig. 3 An example of random pulse allocation for four targets

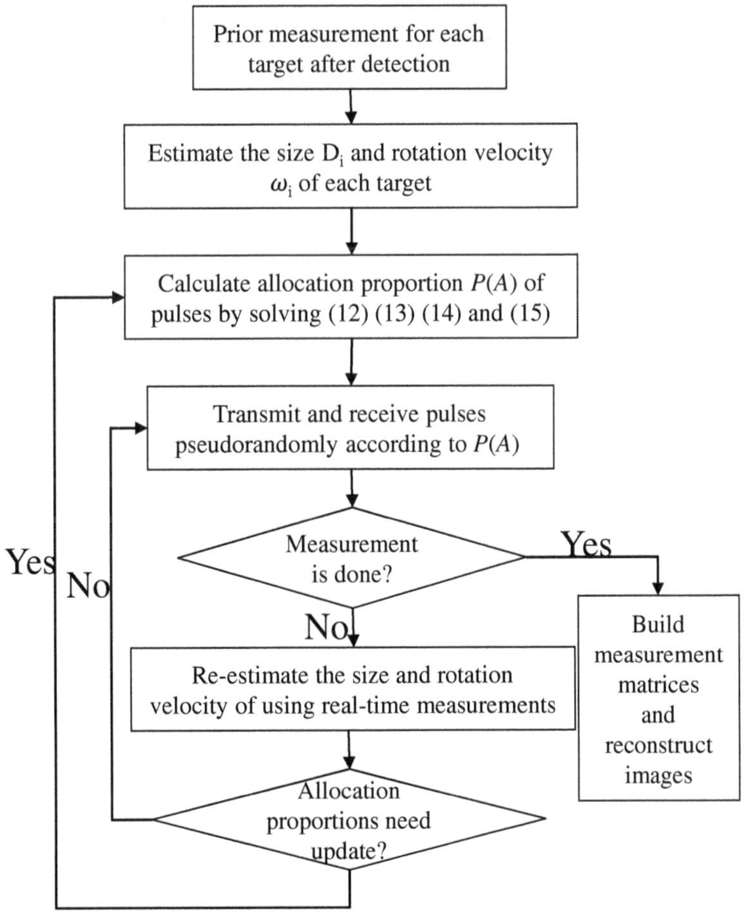

Fig. 4 Flow chart of compressive measurement for multiple targets

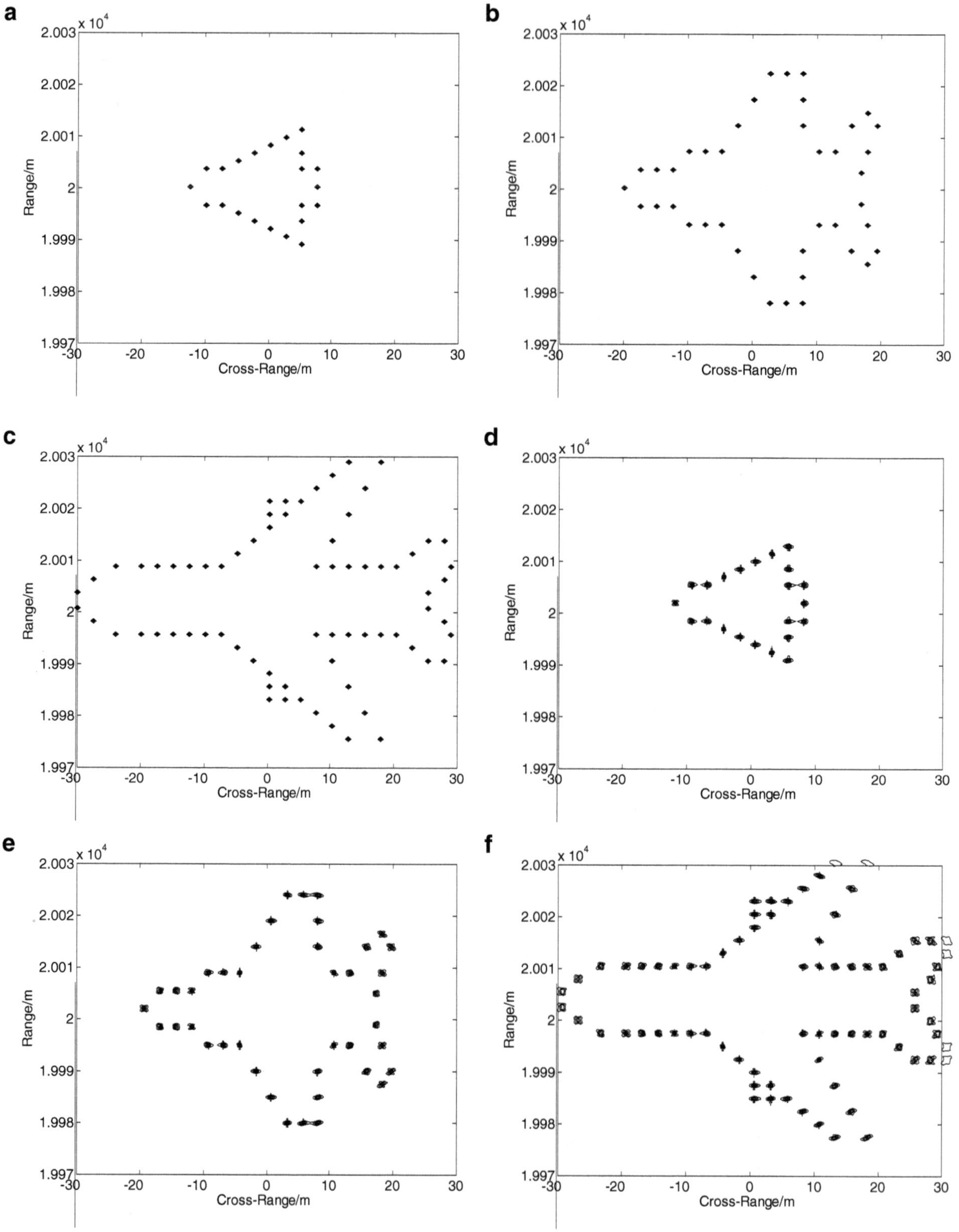

Fig. 5 Reflectivity distribution and conventional RD imaging results of three simulated targets. (**a**)-(**c**) are the point scattering models of the three targets; (**d**)-(**f**) are the conventional RD imaging results of three simulated targets

$$\sum_{i=1}^{L} \bar{\rho}_i \leq f_{\text{PRF}} \tag{16}$$

If targets number L exceeds this limitation, the pulse allocation cannot guarantee that enough measurements are acquired for each target.

For the convenience of radar management, the estimation of sparse level and rotation velocity can be obtained as prior information for multi-target CS imaging. Specifically, this can be done after the radar detection and tracking process; then, the wideband pulses for imaging are transmitted pseudo-randomly according to the estimated probability density $P(A_m)$.

3.2 Adaptive pulse allocating method

The estimations of rotation velocity and target size are very important for the multi-target CS imaging method. However, the estimation results in practice are usually inaccurate due to the influence of noise and clutters. Besides, the prior measurements before imaging may be insufficient or incorrect to determine the appropriate pulse allocating proportions. Considering this, an improved adaptive observing strategy for multiple targets is introduced in this section. With the development of digital processing, the modern radar systems can own more powerful real-time processing ability. During CS imaging, some real-time analysis can be carried out to estimate the velocities and sizes of the targets. This allows us to update the allocating proportions of pulses during observation.

In three situations, we need to re-calculate the allocating proportions for different targets. (1) Some targets disappear from the radar's view and do not need imaging anymore; then, it is eliminated from the targets list. (2) A new target is detected and is added into the imaged targets list. (3) The estimations of targets' velocities and sizes are considerably different from the current ones.

The self-adapting allocation proportions can improve the robustness of the multi-target observing method. For convenience of understanding, a flow chart is presented to interpret the work mode of radar in the adaptive CS imaging method, as shown in Fig. 4.

The sequence of pulses must be memorized in the radar system because it is essential to build the measurement matrices of each target, which will be discussed in Section 3.3.

Limited by the real-time capability of the radar system and the complexity of CS reconstructing algorithms, it is difficult to realize real-time image reconstruction using limited pulses. Once it is solved with faster algorithms, the iterative method can be employed in the flow of multi-target observation. Instead of estimating the sizes and velocities of targets based on the RCS and HRRPs, the quality of real-time imaging results can be employed to evaluate whether the pulse allocation proportion is effective. In the following observation, more pulses will be allocated to those targets with blurred images. The most reasonable proportions will be established after several iterations. This is the unsolved issue that we are investigating in the future work.

3.3 Reconstruction images of multiple targets

In ISAR imaging, the non-cooperative motion of target must be compensated to make the echoes consistent with the model of rotated platform in Fig. 2. References [22] and [23] suggest the method that minimizes entropy of average range profile, and the eigenvector method can be utilized to solve the range alignment and phase correction of random pulses. Reference [24] proposed a method to solve the problem of motion compensation when pulses are inconsecutive. Combining Eq. (9), the echoes after compensation can be denoted as

$$y_m = \Phi \Psi \beta_m + n \tag{17}$$

where matrix Φ is the random measurement matrix, and vectors y_m and n are the measurements of mth range cell and the measured noise, respectively. The cross-range image β_m of mth range cell can be reconstructed by solving

$$\min \left\| \hat{\beta}_m \right\|_1 \quad \text{s.t.} \quad \| y_m - \Phi \Psi \beta \|_2 \leq \varepsilon \tag{18}$$

where $\hat{\beta}_m$ is the reconstruction of vector β and ε is the noise level. It is the typical optimization problem in CS and there are some algorithms to solve it, such as basis pursuit (BP), orthogonal matching pursuit (OMP), Bayesian algorithms [25], and smoothed ℓ_0 algorithm (SL0). The SL0 [26] has a good tradeoff between accuracy and complexity [27]. Different from most greedy algorithms and BP algorithms, the sparsity level of an original signal is not necessary for SL0 method. Therefore, it is quite suitable for CS radar imaging, since the number of scattering centers is unknown until the image is obtained.

The first step of reconstructing multi-target images is to build the measurement matrices for each target. In conventional Nyquist sampling, the measurement matrix is the identity matrix I_i, and the size N_i of matrix I_i is

Table 1 Parameter setting of three targets in simulation

Target	Range (km)	Rotation velocity 1 (°/s)	Rotation velocity 2 (°/s)
Target 1	100	2.0	1.0
Target 2	120	2.0	2.5
Target 3	90	2.0	5.0

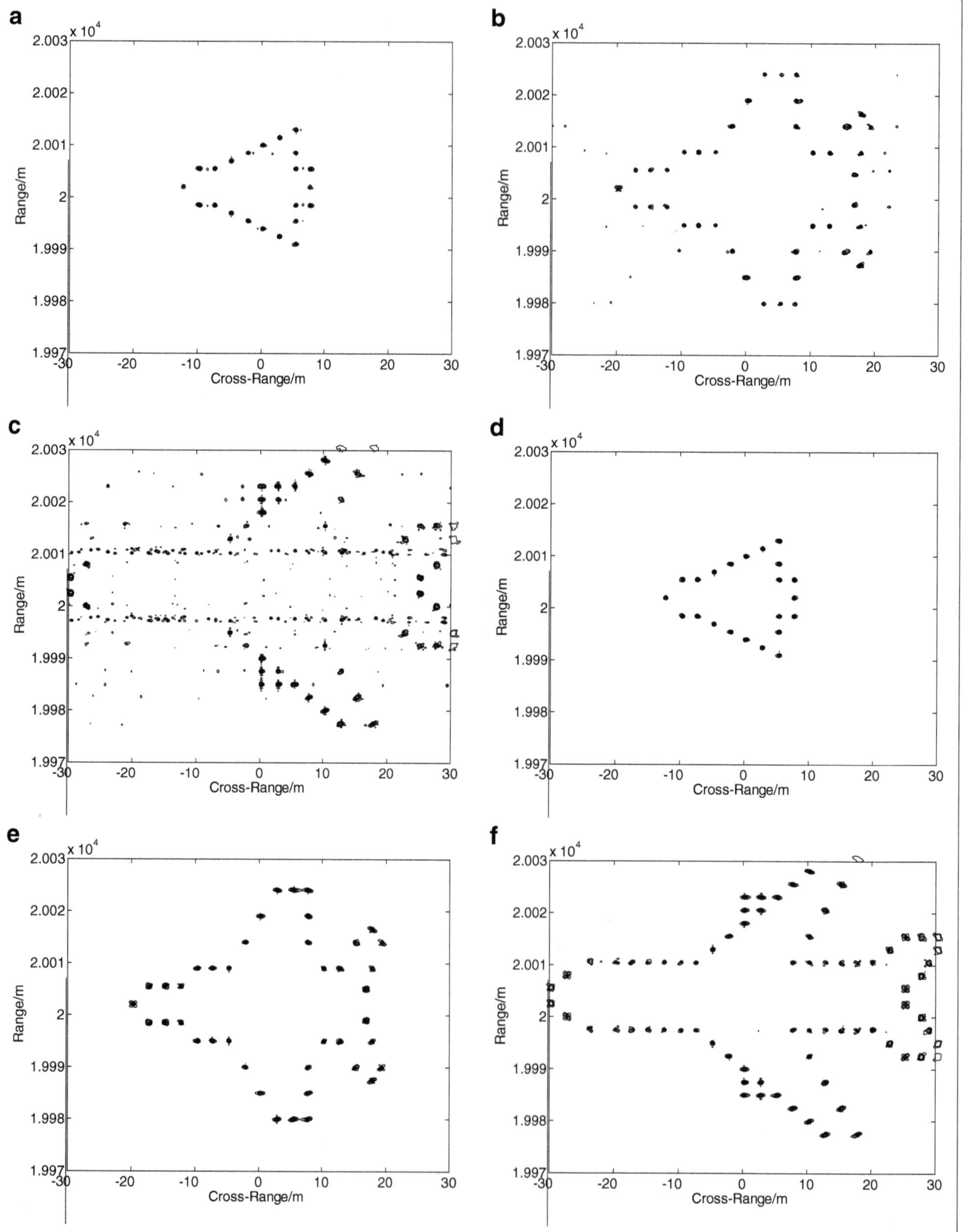

Fig. 6 The pulse allocating proportion affected by the size of target. **a**–**c** Reconstructed images when pulses are allocated randomly to three targets with the same probability. **d**–**f** Reconstructed images when the allocating proportions are decided by the size of targets

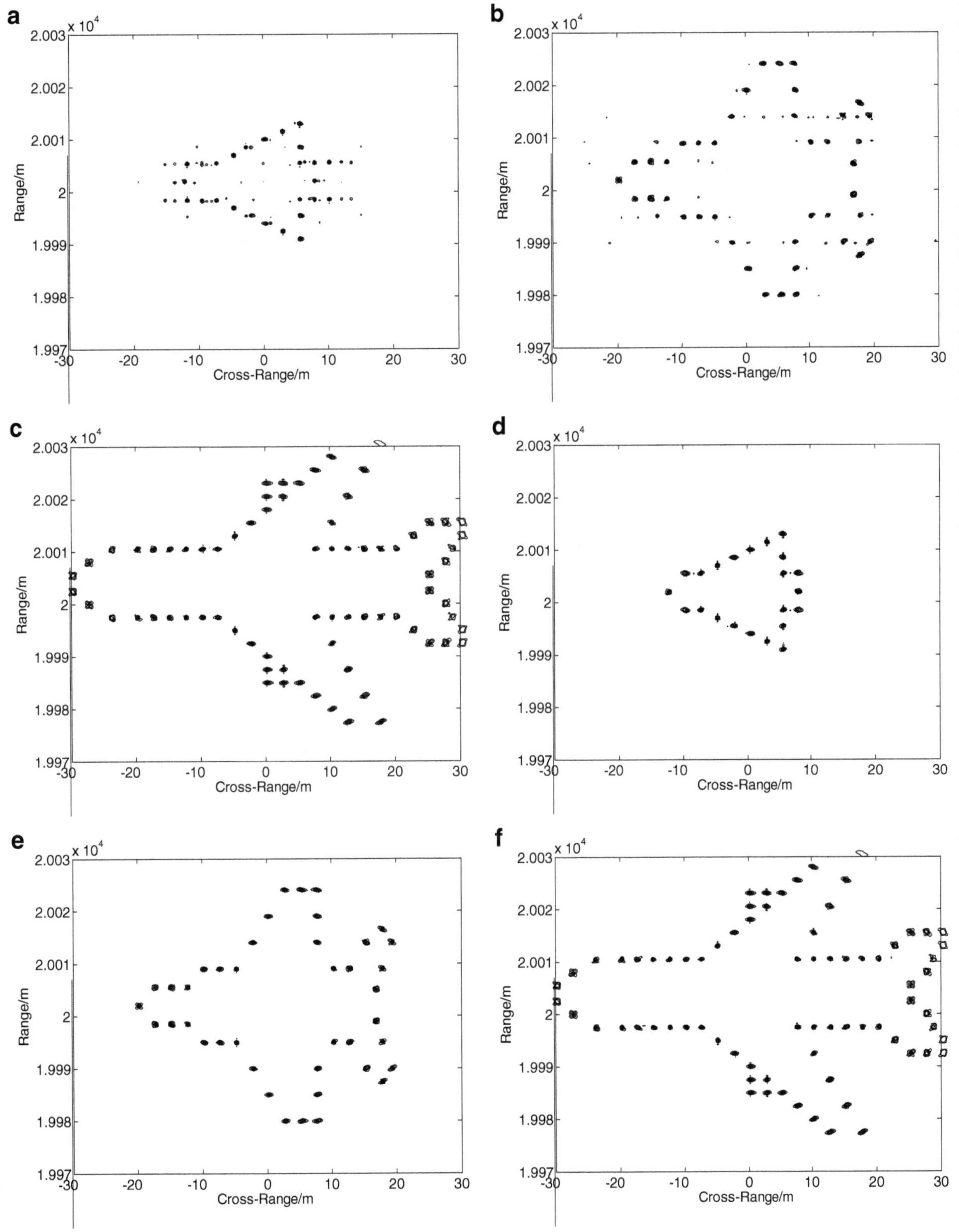

Fig. 7 The pulse allocating proportion affected by the rotation velocity of target. **a**–**c** Reconstructed images when the pulses are allocated without consideration of the different rotation velocities of targets. **d**–**f** CS reconstructed images when the pulses allocation proportion is calculated according to both the sizes and the different rotation velocities of targets

the number of pulses transmitted during corresponding CPI τ_i, and

$$N_i = f_{\mathrm{PRF}} \times \tau_i \tag{19}$$

In CS multi-target imaging, the pulses are randomly allocated in CPI for each target. Hence, the measurement matrix Φ_i of the ith target's echo in Eq. (17) can be obtained by selecting corresponding rows from I_i according to the random sequence of pulses. The selected indices of rows are determined by the indices of the pulses that illuminate the ith target.

Then, the images can be reconstructed by solving Eq. (18) for each target separately. The reconstructing performance and analysis will be given in Section 4.

4 Simulation results

To verify the validity of the proposed observing strategy and imaging method, some simulations are performed in this section. Suppose the parameters of the transmitted LFM signal are as follows. The bandwidth is $B = 300$ MHz, the carrier frequency is $f_c = 10$ GHz, the pulse width is $\tau_c = 50$ μs, and the PRF of radar is $f_{\mathrm{PRF}} = 1000$ Hz.

In the simulation, three aeroplanes with different sizes are selected as the targets, which locate in different observing scenes. The point scattering models of the three targets are given in Fig. 5. The parameters of the three targets are presented in Table 1. As shown in Fig. 5, the sizes of three targets are different, and the sparse level K_i of target is determined by the number of scattering points in the cross-range dimension. The simulations are carried out in two steps.

In the first experiment, the simulation is carried out to testify the effectiveness of target sizes on the allocation proportions of pulses. The rotation velocities of three targets are set to be the same, as shown in the third column of Table 1. If we allocate the radar pulses equally, without considering the difference of target sizes, the reconstructed images of three targets are shown in Fig. 6a–c. As we can see, target 3 has the biggest size, and the corresponding reconstructed image is blurred seriously. However, the images of the other two targets are well focused. Then, we use Eq. (15) to calculate the allocating proportions for three targets, and the proportion is about 2:3:4. As shown in Fig. 6d–f, all targets are allocated with enough pulses, and thus, the images are all well focused.

In the second experiment, the difference of rotation velocities is considered and the rotation velocities of the three targets are set as the fourth column of Table 1. The CPIs of three targets can be calculated to be about $\tau_1 = 5.0$ s, $\tau_2 = 2$ s, and $\tau_3 = 1$ s, respectively. First, the allocating probability is calculated by Eq. (15) without considering the difference of rotation velocities. As shown in Fig. 7a–c, the reconstructed images of targets 1 and 2 are blurred. The reason is that the two targets rotate much faster than target 3 and the allocated pulses are inadequate in their CPIs. Fig. 7d–f shows the reconstructed images when the allocating proportions of pulses are calculated according to both sizes and rotation velocities of three targets. Images with better quality are obtained for all targets.

The results of the simulations and comparison are consistent with the theoretical analysis in this paper. Hence, the proposed multi-target imaging method is proved to be reasonable and effective.

5 Conclusions

In order to implement multi-target simultaneous ISAR imaging, an observing strategy and CS imaging method is proposed in this paper. The CS theory is introduced into multi-target imaging, and a random pulse allocating method is proposed based on the flexibility of PAR. Multi-target simultaneous imaging is realized by controlling the beam directions of radar pulses, without changing the architecture and working mode of PARs. The method can take full advantage of radar resources and obtain images for multiple targets using much less pulses than conventional RD method. Although every target gets very limited pulses, the sparsity of ISAR images and the theory of CS guarantee effective reconstruction of images. The allocation proportion is calculated based on the sizes and rotation velocities of targets. A self-adapting observing flow is designed for practical radar applications, which improves the robustness of the proposed method. SL0 algorithm is employed to reconstruct images of targets from random pulses. The simulation results testify the conclusion in this paper and prove the feasibility of the proposed method.

Competing interests

The authors declare that they have no competing interests.

Acknowledgements

This work was supported by the National Natural Science Foundation of China (Grant Nos. 61471373).

References

1. C Ozdemir, *Inverse Synthetic Aperture Radar Imaging With MATLAB Algorithms* (John Wileyand Sons, INC, Hoboken, New Jersey, 2012)
2. F Zhou, X Bai, M Xing, Z Bao, Analysis of wide-angle radar imaging. IET Radar, Sonar and Navigation **5**(4), 449–457 (2011)
3. Pirkl M. and Holpp W., *From research to application: how phased array radars conquered the real world*, 14th International Radar Symposium, pp.17-22, 2013
4. M Zatman., in Proceedings of IEEE Radar Conference. Radar resource management for UESA(IEEE Radar Conference, Long Beach, California, 2002)
5. DL Donoho, Compressed sensing. IEEE Trans Inf Theory **52**(4), 1289–1306 (2006)
6. EJ Cand`es, J Romberg, T Tao, Robust uncertainty principles: exact signal reconstruction from highly incomplete frequency information. IEEE Trans Inf Theory **52**, 489–509 (2006)

7. MA Herman, T Strohmer, High-resolution radar via compressed sensing. IEEE Trans Signal Process **57**, 2275–2284 (2009)
8. JHG Ender, On compressive sensing applied to radar. Signal Process **90**, 1402–1414 (2010)
9. X Bai, F Zhou, M Xing, Z Bao, High-resolution radar imaging of air-targets from sparse azimuth data. IEEE Trans on Aerospace and Electronic Systems **48**(2), 1643–1655 (2012)
10. MG Amin, F Ahmad, Compressive sensing for through-the-wall radar imaging. J Electronic Imaging **22**, 030901 (2013)
11. D Li, X Li, Y Cheng, Y Qin, H Wang, Radar coincidence imaging in the presence of target-motion-induced error. J Electronic Imaging **23**, 023014 (2014)
12. L Zhang, M Xing, C-W Qiu, J Li, Z Bao, Achieving higher resolution ISAR imaging with limited pulses via compressed sampling. IEEE Geosci Remote Sens Lett **6**, 567–571 (2009)
13. JA Tropp, AC Gilbert, Signal recovery from random measurements via orthogonal matching pursuit. IEEE Trans Inf Theory **53**, 4655–4666 (2007)
14. EJ Candes, The restricted isometry property and its implications for compressed sensing. C R Acad Sci Paris, Ser I **346**, 589–592 (2008)
15. J Wang, D Kasilingam, Global range alignment for ISAR. IEEE Trans Aerosp Electron Syst **39**, 351–357 (2003)
16. Y Wang, H Ling, V Chen, ISAR motion compensation via adaptive joint time-frequency technique. IEEE Trans Aerosp Electron Syst **34**, 670–677 (1998)
17. RP Perry, RC Dipietro, R Fante, in Proceedings of IEEE National Radar Conference. Coherent Integration With Range Migration Using Keystone Formatting(IEEE National Radar Conference, Boston, MA,2007)
18. M Xing, R Wu, J Lan, Z Bao, Migration through resolution cell compensation in ISAR imaging. IEEE Geosci Remote Sens Lett **1**, 141–144 (2004)
19. J Ender, in Proceedings of 14th International IEEE Radar Symposium. A brief review of compressive sensing applied to radar. (IRS 2013, Dresden, Germany, 2013)
20. R Lambour, N Rajan, T Morgan, I Kupiec, E Stansbery, Assessment of orbital debris size estimation from radar cross-section measurements. Adv Space Res **34**(No. 5), 1013–1020 (2004). Space Debris
21. Y Wang, Y Jiang, A novel algorithm for estimating the rotation angle in isar imaging. IEEE Geosci Remote Sens Lett **5**, 608–609 (2008)
22. D Zhu, X Yu, Z Zhu, in Proceedings of 2011 IEEE CIE International Conference on Radar. Algorithms for compressed ISAR autofocusing. (2011 IEEE CIE International Conference on Radar,Chengdu,China, 2011)
23. D Zhu, L Wang, Y Yu, Q Tao, Z Zhu, Robust isar range alignment via minimizing the entropy of the average range profile. IEEE Geosci Remote Sens Lett **6**, 204–208 (2009)
24. Q Hou, L Fan, S Su, Z Chen, Compensation of phase errors for compressed sensing based ISAR imagery using inadequate pulses. Progress In Electromagnetics Research M **41**, 125–138 (2015)
25. S Ji, Y Xue, L Carin, Bayesian compressive sensing. IEEE Transctions on Signal Processing **56**, 2346–2356 (2008)
26. GH Mohimani, M Babaie-Zadeh, C Jutten, A fast approach for overcomplete sparse decomposition based on smoothed l0 norm. IEEE Trans Signal Process **57**, 289–301 (2007)
27. J Liu, S Xu, X Gao, X Li, Compressive radar imaging methods based on fast smoothed l0 algorithm. 2012 International Workshop on Information and Electronics Engineering **29**, 2209–2213 (2012). Elsevier Ltd

9

Instruction scheduling heuristic for an efficient FFT in VLIW processors with balanced resource usage

Mounir Bahtat[1*], Said Belkouch[1], Philippe Elleaume[2] and Philippe Le Gall[2]

Abstract

The fast Fourier transform (FFT) is perhaps today's most ubiquitous algorithm used with digital data; hence, it is still being studied extensively. Besides the benefit of reducing the arithmetic count in the FFT algorithm, memory references and scheme's projection on processor's architecture are critical for a fast and efficient implementation. One of the main bottlenecks is in the long latency memory accesses to butterflies' legs and in the redundant references to twiddle factors. In this paper, we describe a new FFT implementation on high-end very long instruction word (VLIW) digital signal processors (DSP), which presents improved performance in terms of clock cycles due to the resulting low-level resource balance and to the reduced memory accesses of twiddle factors. The method introduces a tradeoff parameter between accuracy and speed. Additionally, we suggest a cache-efficient implementation methodology for the FFT, dependently on the provided VLIW hardware resources and cache structure. Experimental results on a TI VLIW DSP show that our method reduces the number of clock cycles by an average of 51 % (2 times acceleration) when compared to the most assembly-optimized and vendor-tuned FFT libraries. The FFT was generated using an instruction-level scheduling heuristic. It is a modulo-based register-sensitive scheduling algorithm, which is able to compute an aggressively efficient sequence of VLIW instructions for the FFT, maximizing the parallelism rate and minimizing clock cycles and register usage.

Keywords: FFT, VLIW, Scheduling heuristic, Twiddle factors, Modulo scheduling, Software pipelining

1 Introduction

The discrete Fourier transform (DFT) is a used transform for spectral analysis of finite-domain discrete-time signals. It is widely employed in signal processing systems. For decades, studies have been done to improve the algorithmic efficiency of this technique and this is still an active research field. The frequency response of a discrete signal $x[n]$ can be computed using the DFT formula over N samples as in (1).

$$X[k] = \sum_{n=0}^{N-1} x[n] W_N^{nk} \qquad (1)$$

For $k \in \{0,\ldots,N-1\}$ where $W_N^{nk} = e^{-j(2\pi/N)nk}$

* Correspondence: mnr.bahtat@gmail.com
[1]LGECOS Lab, ENSA-Marrakech of the Cadi Ayyad University, Marrakech, Morocco
Full list of author information is available at the end of the article

The DFT algorithmic complexity is $O(N^2)$. In order to reduce this arithmetic count and therefore enhancing its implementation efficiency, a set of methods were proposed. These methods are commonly known as fast Fourier transforms (FFTs), and they present a valuable enhancement in complexity of $O(N\log(N))$. FFT was first discovered by Gauss in the eighteenth century and re-proposed by Cooley and Tukey in 1965 [1]. The idea is based on the fundamental principle of dividing the computation of a DFT into smaller successive DFTs and recursively repeating this process. The fixed-radix category of FFT algorithms mainly includes radix-2 (dividing the DFT into 2 parts), radix-4 (into 4 parts), radix-2^2, and radix-8 [2]. Mixed-radix FFTs combine several fixed-radix algorithms for better convenience [3]. Split-radix FFTs offer lower arithmetic count than the fixed or mixed-radix, using a special irregular decomposition [4, 5]. Also, a recursive FFT can be implemented as in [6], and a combination between the decimation-in-frequency (DIF) and the decimation-in-time (DIT) FFT is proposed in [7].

The FFT algorithm has been implemented for either hardware or software, on different platforms. Hardware IP implementations on ASIC or FPGA can provide real-time high-speed solutions but lack flexibility [8]. Equivalent implementations on general purpose processors (GPP) offer flexibility, but it is generally slower and cannot meet high real-time constraints. Multi-core digital signal processors (DSPs) are interesting hardware platforms achieving the tradeoff between flexibility and performance. These are sharing with FPGAs a well-earned reputation of being difficult for developing parallel applications. As a result, several languages (such as OpenCL) seeking to exploit the power of multi-cores while remaining platform independent has been recently explored [9, 10]. OpenCL for instance is an industry's attempt to unify embedded multi-core programming, allowing data parallelism, SIMD instructions, and data locality as well [11].

Modern low-power multi-core DSP architectures attracted many real-time applications with power restrictions. One of the primary examples in this field is the C6678 multi-core DSP from Texas Instruments, which can provide up to 16 GFLOPS/watt. In [12], a real-time low-power motion estimation algorithm based of the McGM gradient model has been implemented in the TI C6678 DSP, exploiting DSP features and loop-level very long instruction word (VLIW) parallelism. The implementation provided significant power efficiency gains toward high-end current architectures (multi-core CPUs, many-core GPUs). In [13], a low-level optimization of the 4-, 8-, and 16-point FFTs in the C6678 DSP is presented.

The most recent high-end DSP architectures are VLIW, which mainly support an instruction-level parallelism (ILP) feature, offering the possibility to execute simultaneously multiple instructions and a data-level parallelism allowing the access to multiple data during each cycle. Therefore, these kinds of processors are known to have greater performance compared to RISC or CISC, even having simpler and more explicit internal design. However, unlike superscalar processors where parallelism opportunities are discovered by hardware at the run time, VLIW DSPs leave this task to the software compiler. It has been shown that constructing an optimal compiler performing instruction mapping and scheduling in VLIW architectures is an NP-Complete problem [14]. Toward this increasingly difficult task, compilers have been unable to capitalize on these existing features and often cannot produce efficient code [15].

Several compilation techniques tackled this problem. A classical method is called the list scheduling [16] and it schedules instructions within a single block, by building a directed acyclic dependency graph (DAG) (as in Fig. 1). Trace scheduling was introduced afterwards by Fisher [17], which selects and acts on acyclic paths having the highest probability of execution (called traces). The trace scheduling was unable to properly optimize loops; then, a more effective solution to this specific problem was proposed by software pipelining [18]. The most successful technique of software pipelining is known as the modulo scheduling [19]. We have proposed an efficient enumeration-based heuristic for modulo scheduling in [20].

One of the bottlenecks toward an efficient FFT implementation on these VLIW DSP platforms is memory latencies. Indeed, in addition to the memory access of

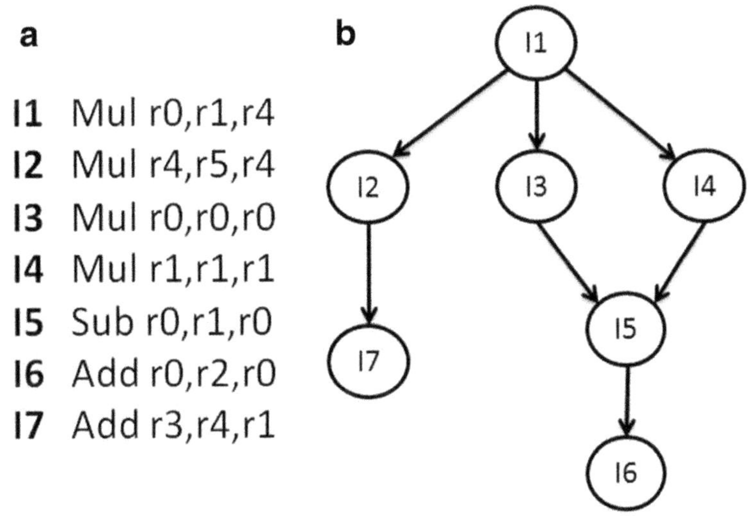

Fig. 1 Dependency graph (**b**) of an instruction block (**a**)

butterflies' inputs and outputs over several stages ($\log_2(N)$ stages for a radix-2 FFT, shown in Fig. 2), conventional algorithms excessively and redundantly load twiddle factors (W_N^k). These latter are classically stored as a N-sized complex vector, requiring $O(N\log(N))$ accesses. In [21], a novel memory reference reduction method is introduced by grouping butterflies using the same twiddle factors together; therefore decreasing the number of memory references due to twiddle factors in DSPs by 76 %. Another FFT scheme is presented in [22], reducing the memory access frequency and multiplication operations. Also, other results in [23] decrease the number of twiddle accesses by an asymptotic factor of $\log(N)$, based on G and G^T transforms. On the other hand, the FFT performance is tightly dependent to the processor's architecture and its memory and cache structure. Kelefouras et al. [24] propose a methodology to speed up the FFT algorithm depending on the memory hierarchy of processor's architecture. State-of-the-art FFT libraries such as FFTW [25–27] and UHFFT [28] maximize the performance by adapting to the hardware at run time, usually using a planner, searching over a large space of parameters in order to pick the best implementation. The FFTS in [29] claims an efficient cache-oblivious FFT scheme that is not requiring any machine-specific calibration.

In the present paper, we propose an efficient modulo-like FFT scheduling for VLIW processors. Our implemented methodology allows better core-level resource balance, exploiting the fact that the twiddle factors can be calculated recurrently using multipliers and entirely generated in masked time. The resulting scheme created a vital balance between the computation capability and the data bandwidth that are required by the FFT algorithm, taking into account the VLIW architecture. Moreover, an important amount of input buffers can be freed since twiddle factors are no longer stored, nor referenced from memory, avoiding significant memory stalls. Since the recurrent computation of twiddle factors using multipliers induces a processing error, a tradeoff parameter between accuracy and speed is introduced.

Besides, our proposed implementation methodology takes into account the memory hierarchy, the memory banks, the cache size, the cache associativity, and its line size, in order to well adapt the FFT algorithm to a broad range of embedded VLIW processors. The bit reversal was efficiently designed to take advantage of the cache structure, and a mixed scheme was proposed for FFT/iFFT sizes not fitting the cache size.

VLIW assembly code of the FFT/iFFT was generated using a scheduling heuristic. The proposed FFT-specific modulo instruction scheduling algorithm is resource-constrained and register-sensitive that uses controlled backtracking. This heuristic re-orders the scheduling array to accelerate the backtracking search for the best schedule within the NP-complete state space. Our algorithm applies a strict optimization on internally used registers, so that generating twiddle factors of the new

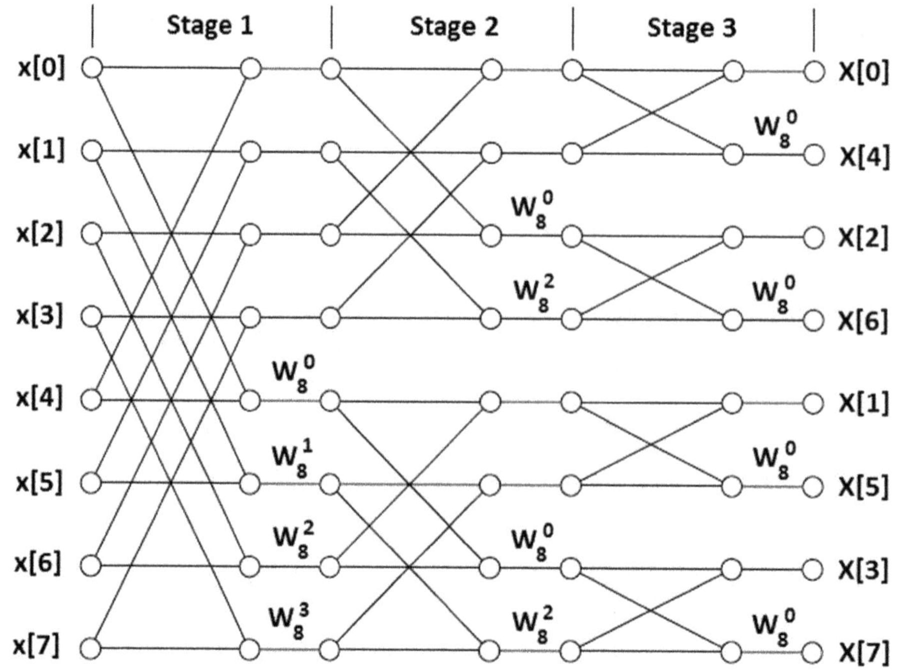

Fig. 2 8-point radix-2 DIF FFT

FFT scheme can be done effectively masked in parallel with other VLIW instructions.

The idea of recurrently generating twiddle factors during the FFT calculation is also discussed in our paper in [30]. In the present paper, we additionally propose a VLIW-generic recurrent FFT scheme and the related instruction scheduling generator.

In the following, a background on the FFT algorithm of interest is given in Section 2, we then present an overview on the VLIW DSP processors in Section 3, the new FFT strategy scheme is explained in Section 4, and the modulo-like scheduling of the suggested FFT is described in Section 5. Finally, experimental results are given in Section 6.

2 Background on the FFT algorithm of interest

Many factors other than the pure number of arithmetic operations must be considered for an efficient FFT implementation on a VLIW DSP, which can be derived from memory-induced stalls, regularity, and algorithm's projection on hardware VLIW architectures. Yet, one of the FFT algorithms that proved enough satisfaction on DSPs is the radix-4 FFT, mostly implemented by manufactures. This is mainly due to its relatively less access to memory (during $\log_4(N)$ stages vs. $\log_2(N)$ stages in a radix-2 scheme), additional to its regular, straightforward and less complex algorithm (compared for instance to split-radix FFTs, radix-8 and higher radix FFTs). The radix-4 FFT is usually used and mixed with a last radix-2 stage, enabling it to treat sizes that are power-of-2 and not only being limited to power-of-4 sizes.

We distinguish between two basic types of radix-4 algorithms: decimation-in-time (DIT) is the consequence of decomposing the input $x[n]$, and decimation-in-frequency (DIF) when decomposing the output $X[n]$. Both DIT and DIF present the same computational cost. In this paper, we will be only interested in DIF versions.

Building the radix-4 algorithm can be done starting from the DFT formula in (1) which can be rewritten in a decomposed form and consequently obtaining the DIF radix-4 butterfly description. An FFT computation is transformed into four smaller FFTs through a divide-and-conquer approach, making a radix-4 scheme with $\log_4(N)$ stages, each containing N/4 butterflies.

Through the given scheme, when the FFT input is in its natural order, the output will be arranged in the so-called digit-reversed order, which is defined depending on the used radix. Worthwhile to note that radix-2 FFT schemes present easier re-ordering process.

In 1996, He and Torkelson proposed in [31] a radix-4 variant, having the same computational complexity that they called a radix-2^2 FFT. Its main provided advantage is retaining the same butterfly structure as the radix-2 FFT and therefore preserving a bit-reversed order at the output. This is useful not only when re-ordering the output compared to 4-based digit-reversed re-ordering but also when mixing it with a last radix-2 stage, which in this case can be directly done, thanks to the instinct compatibility between radix-2 and radix-2^2 schemes. The new butterfly definition is given in Fig. 3 and the resulting algorithm's structure in Fig. 4.

The radix-2^2 FFT is adopted in this work and forms the basis of our new FFT scheme. Next, we describe the targeted VLIW family and the related state-of-art modulo scheduling.

3 VLIW DSP processors

3.1 Architecture overview

VLIW platforms allow several heterogeneous operations to be executed in parallel, due to multiple execution units in their architecture, achieving high computation capability (Fig. 5). In this case, the instruction size is increased depending on the number of units (usually 128 or 256 bits). Variable instruction sizes can be used as well to avoid additional NOP operations for code optimization. Although that each operation requires a number of cycles to execute, VLIW instructions can be fully pipelined; consequently, new operations can start in every cycle at every functional unit.

In VLIW processors, instructions are pipelined with an out-of-order execution, thus, iterations are initiated in parallel at a constant rate called the initiation interval (II) [19] (Fig. 6).

Among industrial VLIW platforms, we mention the Texas Instruments TMS320C6x, Texas Instruments 66AK2Hx, FreeScale StarCore MSC8x, ADI TigerSharc, and Infineon Carmel.

3.2 Background on the modulo scheduling

Modulo scheduling is a software pipelining technique, exploiting ILP to schedule multiple iterations of a loop in an overlapped form, initiating iterations at a constant rate called the initiation interval.

Modulo instruction scheduling schemes are mainly heuristic-based as finding an optimal solution is proven an NP-complete problem. Basic common operations of this technique include computing a lower bound of the initiation interval (denoted MII) which depends on provided resources and dependencies. Next, starting from this MII value, search for a valid schedule respecting hardware and graph dependency constraints. If no valid schedule could be found, increase the II value by 1 and search for a feasible schedule again. This last process is repeated until a solution is found. Higher performance is achieved for lower II; increasing II will reduce the

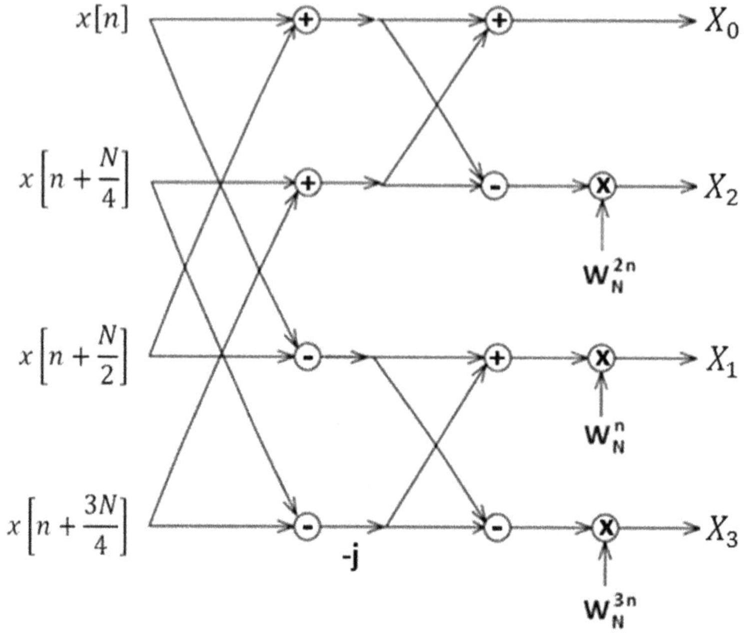

Fig. 3 Radix-2[2] butterfly

amount of used parallelism, however, this makes finding a valid schedule easier [32]. Main evoked techniques in the literature for modulo scheduling include iterative modulo scheduling (IMS) [19], which uses backtracking by scheduling and un-scheduling operations at different time slots searching for a better solution. Slack modulo scheduling [33] minimizes needed registers by reducing lifetimes of operands, using their scheduling freedom (or slack). Integrated register-sensitive iterative software pipelining (IRIS) [34] modifies the IMS technique to

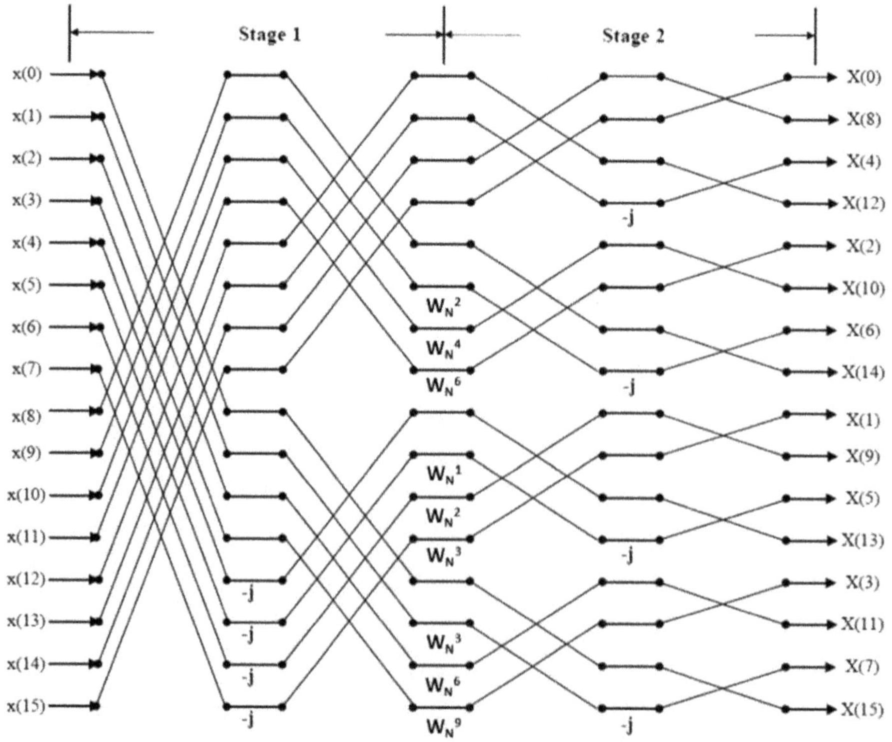

Fig. 4 16-point DIF radix-2[2] FFT

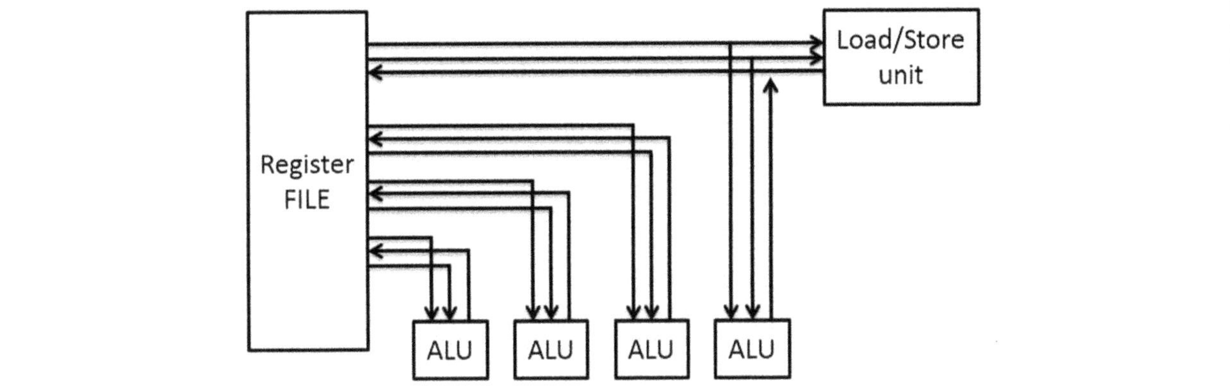

Fig. 5 Typical structure of a VLIW machine

minimize register requirements. Swing modulo scheduling (SMS) [35, 36] does not use backtracking but orders graph nodes guarantying effective schedules with low register pressure. The modulo scheduling with integrated register spilling (MIRS) in [37] suggests to integrate the possibility of storing data temporally out to memory (using spill code) when a schedule aims to exceed the number of available registers in the processor.

In general, the problem statement starts from a directed acyclic graph (DAG), with nodes representing operations of a loop, and edges for the intra- or inter-iteration dependencies between them. Those are valued at instructions' latencies. The wanted schedule must be functionally correct regarding data dependencies and hardware conflicts, minimizing both II and register usage, therefore reducing the execution time. Register pressure is a critical element to consider while searching for a schedule; a commonly used strategy is to minimize the lifetime of instruction's inputs/outputs.

Accordingly, modulo scheduling focuses on arranging instructions in a window of II slots called the kernel, when m iterations are overlapped within it, then m-1 iterations must be separately done before and after entering the kernel; those are called prolog and epilog, respectively. In order to reduce the code expansion issue that is naturally required by modulo scheduling (typically for the prolog/epilog parts), hardware facilities for software pipelining are implemented in VLIW.

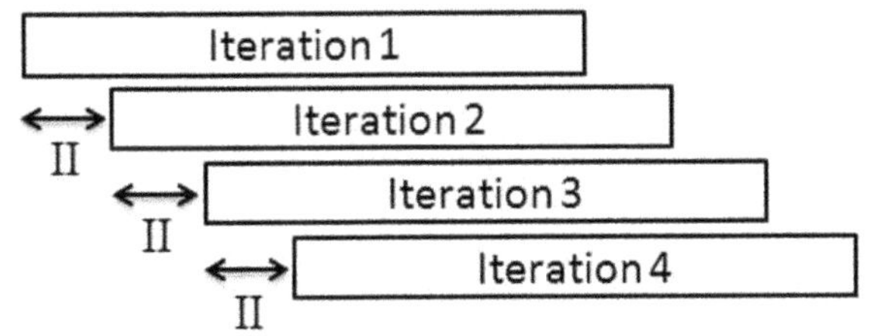

Fig. 6 Parallel initiation of iterations in VLIW cores

Next, our new FFT scheme is discussed for implementation possibilities on VLIW DSPs.

4 Our implementation methodology for the FFT on VLIW DSPs

4.1 A motivating example

The key idea behind the FFT scheme that we are proposing is to create a balance between the computation capability and the data bandwidth that are required by the FFT algorithm. In the following, we analyze the conventional FFT scheme regarding needed VLIW operations in a TI C66 device, in order to evaluate the default efficiency of resource usage.

The TI TMS320 C66 is a fixed and floating-point DSP. It contains eight cores, each working with a clock frequency of 1.0 to 1.25 GHz. A C66 CorePac core is able to execute up to eight separate instructions in parallel, thanks to the eight functional units in its VLIW structure as in Fig. 7. The maximum ability of one core is to execute 8 fixed/floating 32-bit multiplications per cycle using .M units, 8 fixed/floating 32-bit additions/subtractions per cycle using .L and .S units and loads/stores of 128-bit per cycle using .D units. The internal register files are composed of 64 32-bit registers [A31:A0 and B31:B0] [38].

As seen previously, the conventional radix-2^2 FFT algorithm needs $\log_4(N)$ stages (assuming N a power-of-4); and within each stage, a number of N/4 radix-2^2 butterflies are computed. Besides, there is a need of 8 loads/stores for each butterfly's legs, in addition to 3 load operations of twiddle factors as shown in Fig. 3; making a total of 11 loads/stores per butterfly. Moreover, eight complex additions/subtractions, three complex multiplications, and a special ($-j$) multiplication are required to complete the processing on a single butterfly.

Let us denote n_d the number of loaded/stored data in bytes during the whole FFT algorithm, n_m the total number of required real multiplications, n_a the total number of required real additions/subtractions, and n_j the total

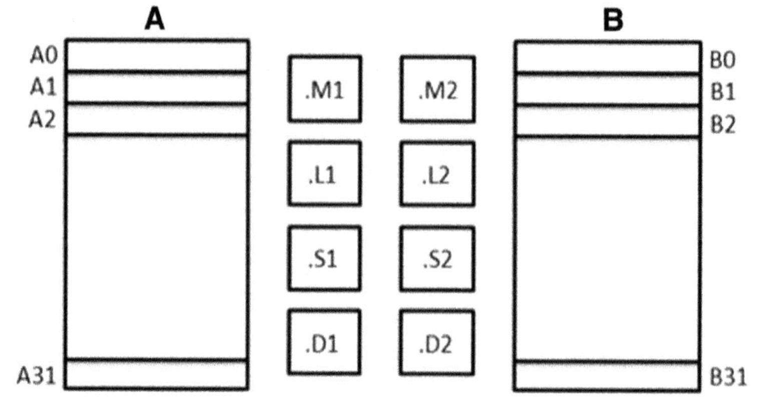

Fig. 7 The 8-way synoptic structure with 8 VLIW units (denoted as .M1/2, .L1/2, .S1/2 and .D1/2) and register files (A31:A0 and B31:B0) of a C66 core

number of (−*j*) multiplications. Then, the conventional algorithm needs the (n_d, n_m, n_a, n_j) expressed in (2) (always assuming N a power-of-4, denoting $B_N = N\log_4(N)/4$ as the total number of radix-4 butterflies). The n_d formula is scaled by a factor of 8 since the used samples are single-precision floating point, hence, coded in 8 bytes for both real and imaginary parts. The n_m formula takes into consideration that each complex multiplication is translated into 4 real multiplications, and the n_a formula sums the additions/subtractions that are needed in both complex additions/subtractions {16} and in complex multiplications {6}.

$$\begin{cases} n_d = 88\,B_N = 22\,Nlog_4N \\ n_m = 12\,B_N = 3\,Nlog_4N \\ n_a = 22\,B_N = \dfrac{11}{2}\,Nlog_4N \\ n_j = B_N = \dfrac{N}{4}log_4N \end{cases} \tag{2}$$

A VLIW core can especially issue loads/stores, multiplications, additions/subtractions, and (−*j*) multiplications in parallel. In the C66 core case, load/store capacity is 16 bytes per cycle using .D units (denoted next by p_d). Eight real floating-point single-precision multiplications can be done per cycle (p_m) using .*M* units and eight real floating-point single-precision additions/subtractions are achievable per cycle (p_a) using both .L and .S units. Finally, 2 multiplications by (−*j*) per cycle (p_j) using .L and .S units as well, those last are simplified into combinations of move and sign-change operations between real and imaginary parts.

According to these VLIW core capacities, the maximum peak performance in terms of clock cycles for the whole conventional FFT on device is equal to:

$$\text{MAX}\left(\frac{n_d}{p_d}, \frac{n_m}{p_m}, \frac{n_a}{p_a} + \frac{n_j}{p_j}\right) = \frac{11}{8} N\,log_4(N)$$

The minimal need for each set of operations on the given C66 VLIW core is shown in Fig. 8. The most optimized conventional way for implementing this algorithm at instruction level leads to the kernel form presented in Fig. 9. It shows butterfly's instructions mapping on the eight VLIW functional units (.D1, .L1, .S1 ...). Since each

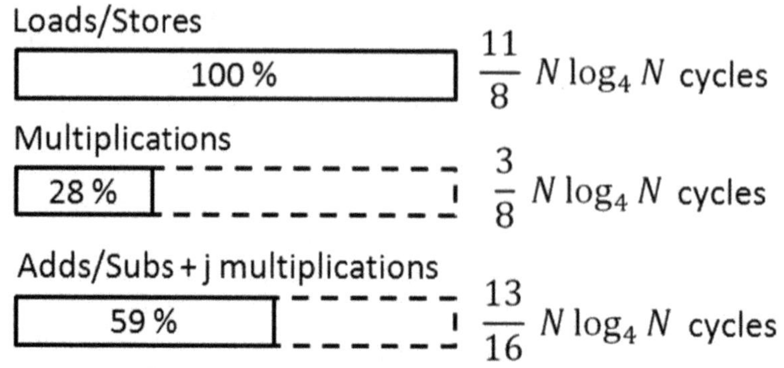

Fig. 8 Minimal need of the conventional FFT algorithm in terms of clock cycles on C66

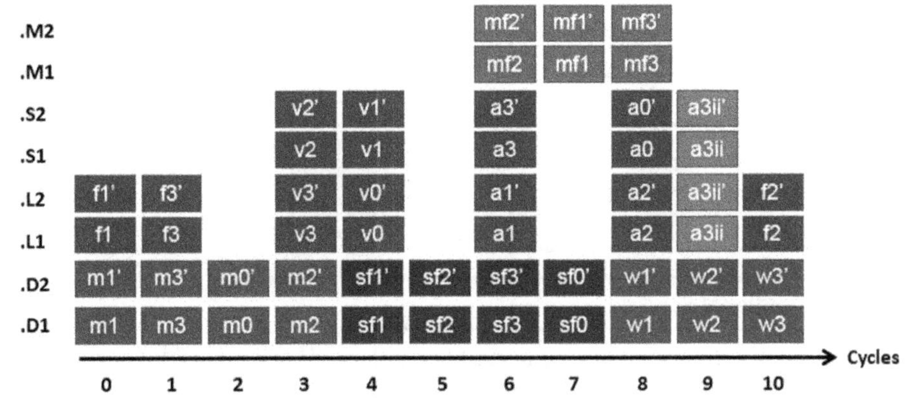

Fig. 9 The VLIW kernel form of the conventional FFT implementation on a C66 core (II = 11)

C66 core contains two side banks (*A* and *B*), we processed symmetrically one butterfly per side.

In Fig. 9, loads of the four butterfly's legs are marked by m0, m1, m2, and m3. Stores are represented by the entities sf0, sf1, sf2, and sf3. Additions and subtractions are referred as a0, a1, a2, a3, v0, v1, v2, and v3. A multiplication by $(-j)$ is translated into two operations on .L/.S units: a3ii (a3i1, a3i2). In addition, multiplications are marked by mf1, mf2, and mf3; and since we are processing complex data (with real and imaginary parts), extra additions are needed to complete the complex multiplication operation: f1, f2, f3. Finally, the symbols w1, w2, and w3 represent loads from memory of needed twiddle factors (W_N^k).

Hence, there is indeed an unbalance between the required computation capability and the load/store bandwidth for this VLIW case, making excessive loads/stores vs. lower use of computation units.

Our new method changes the structure of the algorithm to fit the VLIW hardware, creating a balance in resource usage, and therefore minimizing the overall clock cycles. In an attempt to reduce the load/store pressure, we suggest not to load twiddle factors but to generate them internally instead. This idea uses the fact that the twiddle factors in the n-indexed butterfly that are (W_N^{2n}, W_N^{n}, W_N^{3n}) can be deduced from the $(n-1)$-indexed butterfly according to these formulas: ($W_N^{2n} = W_N^{2(n-1)} W_N^2$, $W_N^n = W_N^{n-1} W_N$, $W_N^{3n} = W_N^{3(n-1)} W_N^3$). This trades loads/stores for multiplications/additions and makes an FFT scheme with butterflies that are dependent on each other; therefore, we cannot start the processing of the n-indexed butterfly if the $(n-1)$-indexed butterfly did not yet compute its twiddle factors.

We decide to process one butterfly per C66 core side bank as well, grouping two butterflies within a single larger iteration. Therefore, this makes an II large enough to wait for the generation of needed twiddle factors by subsequent pipeline stages (7 cycles are required on the TI C66 device in order to complete a floating-point complex multiplication).

This new scheme reduces the loads/stores in exchange with arithmetic operation increase (Fig. 10). Indeed, the number of needed cycles for loads/stores becomes $N \log_4(N)$ as twiddle factors are no more loaded, while the numbers of multiplications and additions/subtractions are increased to $3N\log_4(N)/4$ cycles and $N\log_4(N)$ cycles, respectively.

Our modulo scheduling heuristic that will be detailed in the next sections was able to generate the aggressively optimized schedule of Fig. 11 for the new FFT scheme. The obtained Initiation Interval (II) is 8 cycles instead of 11, fitting a limited core register set, despite adding extra arithmetic operations for twiddle factor generation. This enhances the raw needed time for the FFT by 27 % (excluding memory stall gains) over the conventional implementation with twiddle factors. Moreover, this scheme requires 0 % references to twiddle factors and 0 % space for their memory storage as well.

4.2 Proposed FFT implementation methodology

Our implemented methodology allows better core-level resource balance, exploiting the fact that the twiddle factors can be calculated recurrently using multipliers during the execution. The resulting scheme, regarding a VLIW architecture, created a vital balance between the computation capability and the data bandwidth that are required by the FFT algorithm. Besides, it takes into account the memory hierarchy, the memory banks, the cache size, the cache associativity, and its line size, in order to well adapt the FFT algorithm to a broad range of embedded VLIW processors. The bit reversal was efficiently designed to take advantage of the cache structure, and a mixed scheme was proposed for FFT/iFFT sizes not fitting the cache size.

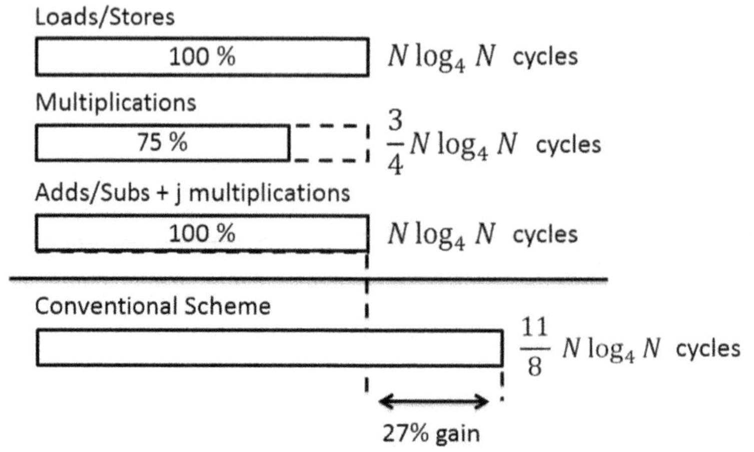

Fig. 10 Bandwidth and computation power's comparison for the new scheme on C66 cores

4.2.1 A recurrent FFT scheme without memory references of twiddle factors

The proposed FFT scheme generates twiddle factors using multipliers instead of loading them from a pre-computed array. Those are recurrently computed from previously handled butterflies. Therefore, the processing of the n-indexed butterfly is time-constrained by the (n – 1)-indexed butterfly.

Let us denote t_w the latency time in terms of cycles that is needed to compute a twiddle factor from a previously calculated one; consequently, if an iteration processes one butterfly, then the II must be greater than or equal to t_w, waiting the required time to generate twiddle factors for the next iteration.

For maximum FFT performance, the initiation interval must be minimized, expressed for our new FFT as MII = MAX(RCPB {required cycles per butterfly} for loads/stores, RCPB for multiplications, RCPB for adds/subs and j multiplications, t_w).

In order to mask the effect of t_w on II, we unroll a number of U successive iterations into a single large one, reducing dependencies to between groups of merged iterations. The new MII expression becomes MII = MAX(U × RCPB for loads/stores, U × RCPB for multiplications, U × RCPB for adds/subs and j multiplications, t_w).

In the earlier equation, $3U$ twiddle factors per group are deduced from $3U$ previously calculated ones, which reduces dependencies toward the constant delay t_w. The minimum value of U minimizing MII (having MII > t_w) will be denoted U_m next. During each n-indexed group of U_m butterflies, there is a need of $3U_m$ twiddle factors which are computed from those in the (n – 1)-indexed group as in (3) (denoting twiddle factors by $\gamma_{n,k}$). On the

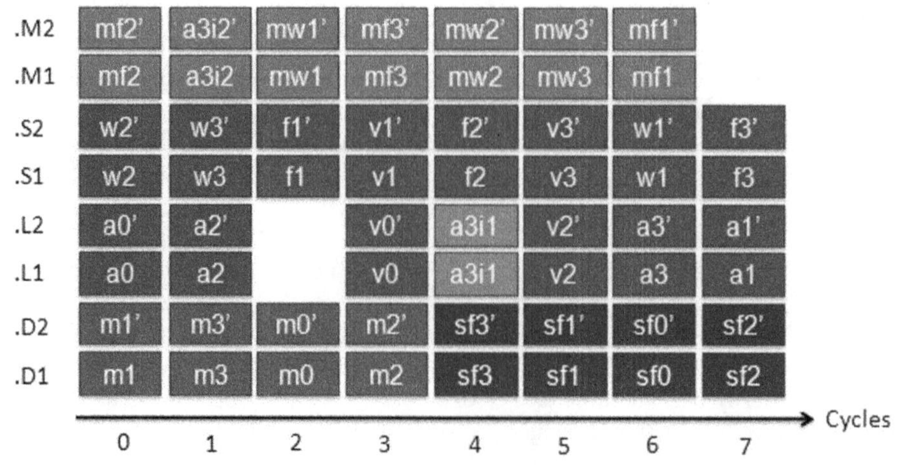

Fig. 11 The best FFT schedule on C66 returned by the heuristic (a kernel of II = 8)

other hand, treating many butterflies simultaneously per iteration requires the usage of more VLIW core registers.

$$\begin{cases} y_{n,k}^2 = y_{n-1,k}^2 W_N^{2U_m} \\ y_{n,k} = y_{n-1,k} W_N^{U_m} \\ y_{n,k}^3 = y_{n-1,k}^3 W_N^{3U_m} \end{cases} \quad (3)$$

For $0 \le k < U_m$ and $1 \le n < \frac{N}{4U_m}$ Denoting $y_{n,k} = W_N^{nU_m+k}$

The resulting structure of a group of U_m butterflies composing a single larger iteration is shown in Fig. 12. The minimum II will be then expressed as follows:

$$\text{MII} = \text{MAX}\Big(U_m n'_d/(p_d B_N), U_m n'_m/(p_m B_N), U_m\left(n'_a/p_a + n'_j/p_j\right)/B_N\Big)$$

with (n'_d, n'_m, n'_a, n'_j) are the new needs in terms of arithmetic and load/store operations expressed as in (4).

$$\begin{cases} n'_d = 64\,B_N = 16\,Nlog_4N \\ n'_m = 24\,B_N = 6\,Nlog_4N \\ n'_a = 28\,B_N = 7\,Nlog_4N \\ n'_j = B_N = \dfrac{N}{4}log_4N \end{cases} \quad (4)$$

Consequently, this new scheme reduces memory accesses by 27 %, making an implementation advantage on a broad range of architectures as most FFT algorithms use memory extensively. In addition to that, it gives an opportunity to use the non-exploited VLIW units for a possibly masked generation of twiddle factors. Besides, since it is not an obvious task to generate an efficient pipelined schedule (having II = MII) with respect to hardware constraints and available core registers, we suggest in later sections an aggressive FFT-specific scheduling heuristic.

This scheme requires 0 % references to twiddle factors and 0 % space for their memory storage as well, making significant gains on related memory latencies.

The key parameters of our scheme are the VLIW core features (p_d, p_m, p_a, p_j, t_w). By computing the MII_1 when using an FFT scheme with loaded twiddle factors (using n_d, n_m, n_a, and n_j, expressed in Eq. (2)), and MII_2 when using an FFT scheme with recurrent computation of twiddle factors (using n'_d, n'_m, n'_a, and n'_j, expressed in Eq. (4)), then if $\text{MII}_1 < \text{MII}_2$, the provided VLIW core would not be applicable for the proposed scheme; otherwise, the minimal gain is expressed as $100(\text{MII}_1 - \text{MII}_2)/\text{MII}_1$.

4.2.2 Setup code integration within the pipelined flow

The previous section described low-level instruction mapping of the most inner loop of the new FFT scheme. In order to complete the FFT/iFFT implementation, intermediate setup iterations (representing outer loops) must be injected into the pipelined flow of iterations. The straightforward way is to completely drain the last iterations of the inner loop, executing the setup code (constants reset, pointers updates ...), and then resuming the pipelined execution; this turns to be time-consuming due to the time needed for the prolog/epilog parts. Indeed, if the dynamic length (DL) denotes the number of cycles that are needed by an inner loop iteration for its processing, then the whole FFT will at least require $B_N\text{MII}/Um$ + (DL-II)(N/48 – 1/3) cycles (assuming N a power-of-4). The integer expression (N/48 – 1/3) counts the number of interrupts that must be done to the inner loop kernel, assuming that the last two FFT stages can be especially treated and done without setup code merging. For $N = 4k$ on the C66 for example, we can see that the setup code interruptions represent 7 % of the main processing.

VLIW architectures can support the merging of setup codes into the pipelined iterations (the case of C66), making it possible to add a customized iteration in concurrence with others without draining the process. Therefore, we can insert an additional II cycle iteration, setting up changes required by outer loops to begin the next sequence of inner loop iterations; needing only $B_N\text{MII}/Um$ + II(N/48 – 1/3) cycles on the whole FFT/iFFT routine. This enhances the efficiency, representing only 2.7 % of the main processing when $N = 4k$ on C66 cores.

4.2.3 Cache-efficient bit reversal computation

The FFT naturally returns an N-sized output with a bit-reversed order, post re-ordering data is necessary. Bit reversing an element at a 0-based index k consists of replacing it into the position index m, such that m is obtained by reversing $\log_2(N)$ bits of the binary form of k. Processors usually implement hardware bit reversal of a 32-bit integer, hence, the wanted function can be obtained by left-shifting an index 32-$\log_2(N)$ times and bit-reversing the whole word afterwards.

In order to increase computation efficiency, one can integrate the re-ordering step into the last stage of the FFT/iFFT, rather than creating a separate routine. One encountered difficulty in bit reversal is accessing scattered positions of memory, causing many memory stalls. Indeed, commonly used architectures of L1D cache are to divide it into several banks, such that simultaneous accesses to distinct banks are possible, while many concurrent accesses to the same bank induce latencies. In processors' architectures that allow multiple data to be accessed in a cycle, the L1D cache level is divided into banks that are defined by lower bits of an address (AMD's processors, TI C6x DSPs, ...). In the C66 CorePac architecture for example, there is 8 L1D banks such that the address range [$4b + 32k$; $4(b + 1) + 32k$

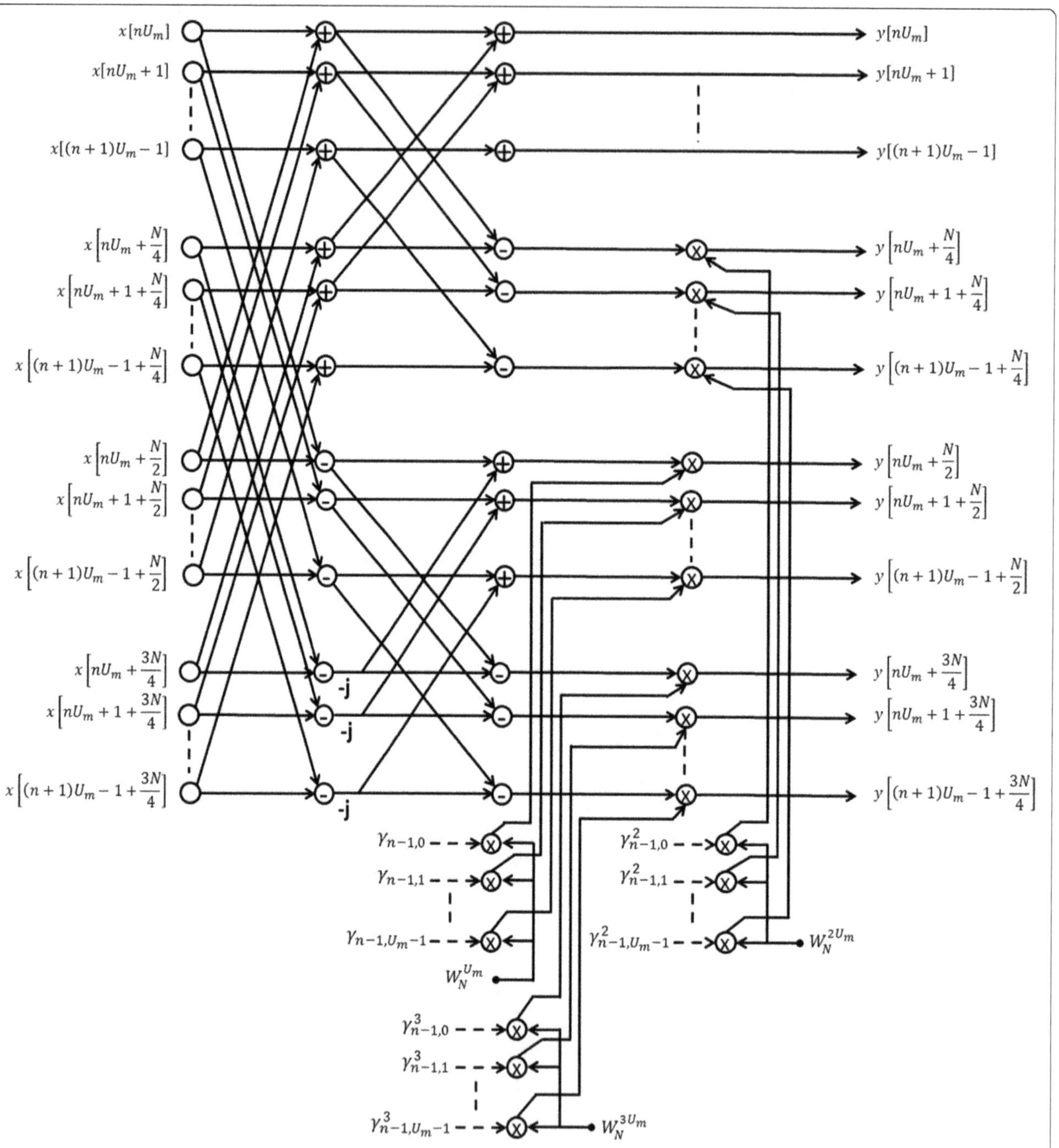

Fig. 12 The n-indexed group of U_m butterflies in the proposed FFT structure

[(where k and b are integers) is linked with the bank number b ($b \in [0,7]$).

It turns out that store indexes related to first butterflies (0, $N/2$, $N/4$, ...) all usually belong to the same memory bank (as long as N gets high values); consequently, 2 parallel stores in a constructed kernel will likely target different addresses from the same bank, inducing stalls. Besides, it is recommended to access consecutive addresses, to be possibly merged into larger accesses by subsequent data paths.

The straightforward implementation provides no successive stores, neither avoiding bank conflicts. A possible enhancement could be achieved by trying to bit-reverse input indexes on the last FFT stage instead of output ones. Resulting structure of this FFT/iFFT stage is described below (processing four butterflies per iteration):

```
i = 0;
loop N/16 times
br = bit_reverse(i);
load_legs(br, br + 1, br + 2, br + 3);
load_legs(N/2 + br, N/2 + br + 1, N/2 + br + 2, N/2 + br + 3);
load_legs(N/4 + br, N/4 + br + 1, N/4 + br + 2, N/4 + br + 3);
load_legs(3 N/4 + br, 3 N/4 + br + 1, 3 N/4 + br + 2, 3 N/4 + br + 3);
process_butterflies();
store_legs(i, i + N/2, i + N/4, i + 3 N/4);
store_legs(i + 1, i + N/2 + 1, i + N/4 + 1, i + 3 N/4 + 1);
store_legs(i + 2, i + N/2 + 2, i + N/4 + 2, i + 3 N/4 + 2);
store_legs(i + 3, i + N/2 + 3, i + N/4 + 3, i + 3 4 + 3);
i = i + 4;
end loop
```

Doing so, we can always issue parallel stores targeting different memory banks and then avoiding bank conflicts (for example, data (i) at a specific bank in parallel with data $(i+1)$ at another bank). Furthermore, 4 consecutive store accesses are now possible. In this case, butterflies are processed in an order that provides the maximum of consecutive stores.

During the FFT, in-place computation on an input buffer is performed until the last stage, where stored data are put into the output buffer. Processing 2, 4, or more butterflies per iteration increases register pressure; we have applied the same scheduling heuristic that will be described later to find a feasible implementation with advanced constraints on data accesses. Found schedule has II = MII with all constraints verified ensuring consecutive stores and avoiding bank conflicts. Obtained performance of the FFT routine with bit reversal was similar to an FFT without bit reversal.

For FFT sizes that are power-of-2 and not power-of-4, an additional radix-2 stage is added; that is where the bit reversal is merged in the same manner.

4.2.4 Adapting the FFT to the cache associativity

When the FFT size is greater than the allocated cache size, the considered radix-2^2 scheme may present some inefficiency toward the L1D cache. The L1D cache is composed of a number of cache lines (usually of 64 bytes), used to store external data prior to their use by the CPU. A cache miss occurs when the requested data is not yet available into the cache; in this case, the CPU is stalled waiting for a cache line to be updated. Many cache structures were used in CPU architectures: direct-mapped cache associates each address of the external memory with a unique position into the cache (therefore with one cache line); as a result, two addresses that are separated by a multiple of the cache size could not survive into the cache at the same time. An advanced mechanism is called the set-associative cache, where the cache memory is divided into a number of p ways, such that when a cache miss occurs, data is transferred to the way whose cache line is the least recently used (LRU); consequently, there are p unique locations into the cache for every address. The main advantage for increasing the associativity is to let non-contiguous data survive into cache lines without overwriting each other (without cache thrashes).

A radix-2^2 butterfly loads their legs from the indexes: 0, $N/4$, $N/2$, and $3N/4$. All this data should exist in the cache at the same time. If the L1D cache is 2-way set-associative and denoting L1D_S the allocated cache size in bytes, no cache thrash would happen if N is less than or equal to L1D_S/8. Otherwise, cache lines for indexes (0 and $N/2$) or ($N/4$ and $3\,0/4$) will overwrite each other continuously, decreasing then the cache efficiency. A solution to this consists of applying radix-2 FFTs for larger sizes, until the size (L1D_S/8) where radix-2^2 can be used without cache thrashes. Indeed, while radix-2 FFTs only access elements at indexes like (0 and $N/2$), no cache thrash would occur no matter how large N is; as long as the cache is 2-way set-associative.

A radix-2 FFT without references of twiddle factors was similarly built and generated using our scheduling heuristic leading to a schedule of II = MII (merging 4 radix-2 butterflies in a single iteration).

Denoting the cache associativity parameter by CACHE_A, the pseudo-code of our adapted FFT scheme regarding cache is written below:

```
function fft_cache()
begin
step = N;
while (step > L1D_S/8 and CACHE_A < 4) loop
for (k = 0;k < N/step)
fft_radix2_stage(input + k*step, step);//radix-2 fft
step = step/2;
end loop
for (k = 0;k < N/step)
fft(input + k*step, step);//radix-2^2 fft
bit_reversal(input, output);
end
```

A bit reversal routine was designed separately in this case and cache-optimized; the II(MII) was extended in order to optimally (fully) treat 4 cache lines in each iteration.

Using a radix-2 FFT for first stages is making a slight drop on the overall efficiency. In fact, a full-radix-2 scheme requires more time than a full-radix-2^2 scheme (on C66 cores, it needs $N\log_2(N)$ cycles at peak performance instead of $N\log_4(\mathrm{N})$). Even so, its gain is far dominant for large FFTs avoiding cache thrashes. For example, the 16*k*-FFT performance on C66 cores using a full-radix-2^2 scheme is 367,890 cycles; it decreased to 245,206 cycles (33 % gain) using the scheme-avoiding cache thrashing.

The inverse FFT is the same as a FFT, except the fact that it uses conjugated twiddle factors and $(1/N)$ extra multiplications added to the last stage. These modifications can be performed without decreasing performance, by exploiting the ILP feature of VLIW processors.

4.2.5 FFT scheme accuracy

A possible side effect of the proposed implementation is a slightly reduced precision. Indeed, internally computed twiddle factors in a recurrent fashion are less accurate than those loaded pre-computed using trigonometric functions. We introduce in Fig. 13 a tradeoff parameter (tradeoff_factor) between accuracy and speed. The tradeoff scheme injects more pre-computed twiddle factors within the FFT flow instead of using only one, which reduces error accumulation effects. However, since the pipeline is regularly stopped to process more pre-computed twiddle factors, the speed performance slightly drops.

The key idea of the algorithm in Fig. 13 is to use more than one pre-computed twiddle factor per FFT stage in order to limit the error propagation. Indeed, if the tradeoff_factor is 0 then only 1 twiddle factor will be used to feed the whole FFT process. Otherwise, 2^(tradeoff_factor)/2 pre-computed twiddle factors will be used per each FFT stage. We will denote next the tradeoff_factor by T.

The calculation error of twiddle factors using the repeated multiplication algorithm grows as $O(N)$ as shown in [39]. Therefore, using our tradeoff method, the twiddle factors accuracy would be expressed as follows:

$$|\omega_N^k - \widehat{\omega}_N^k| \leq \left(4\frac{\sqrt{3}}{3} + \frac{\sqrt{2}}{2}\right)\left(\frac{N}{2^{T+1}\,U_m}\right)u, k < N$$

where $\widehat{\omega}^{Nk}$ is the approximated twiddle factor value and u is the unit roundoff. For IEEE-754 single-precision floating point, the unit roundoff is equal to $u = 5.96 \times 10^{-8}$.

For increasing values of T, the method's accuracy increases, but also the FFT time increases according to the following formula:

```
function fft_tradeoff (tradeoff_factor)
begin
  if (tradeoff_factor==0)
  begin
    fft(input, output, N, w[1]);
    return;
  end
  ss=N/ (2^(tradeoff_factor-1));
  step=N;  j_s=1;
  while (step>4) loop
    ss_cnt=step/ss;
    for (k=0;k<N/step)
    begin
      j=j_s;
      if (ss_cnt>1)
      begin
        for (s=0;s<ss_cnt)
          fft_radix2p2_stage(input+k*step+s*ss, ss, w[j++]);
      else
        fft_no_last_stage(input+k*step, step, w[j:log4(step)]);
        step=16;
      end
    end
    step=step/4;  j_s=j;
  end loop
  last_fft_stage(input, output, step);
end
```

Fig. 13 Pseudo-code for an FFT scheme with an accuracy-tradeoff parameter

$$\frac{B_N MII}{U_m} + II\left(\frac{N}{48}-\frac{1}{3}\right) + 2^{T-1}(DL-II)log_4(N)$$

Where DL denotes the dynamic length of an inner loop iteration. The T parameter creates then a tradeoff factor between accuracy and speed.

5 Instruction scheduling heuristic for FFT/iFFT implementations on VLIW

5.1 Introduction

According to the proposed FFT scheme, a group of U_m butterflies must be processed during a single iteration. Furthermore, extra operations are added to compute the needed twiddle factors in the masked time; these make an iteration with largely increased operations to be scheduled during II = MII within a limited core register set. The data dependence graph of this inner loop FFT iteration is shown in Fig. 14; each node of the graph (among $30U_m$ nodes) can be executed in 1 functional unit of the VLIW core.

In a TI C66 device for instance, and as we aspire the schedule to be done for II = MII = 8, the kernel can be able then to execute up to 64 nodes (due to the 8-way VLIW architecture). It leads to a functional unit pressure of 60 per 64 possible slots (94 % of unit pressure); this shows the difficulty class of the actual scheduling problem, in the presence of a limited register set.

The new FFT scheme merges U_m totally independent butterflies in a single iteration, making it possible to symmetrically divide the computation on processors with symmetric core-bank structure (ADI TigerShark, TI C66 [Fig. 7], ...). This will have the effect to reduce the problem size by half (on $U_m/2$ butterflies), and avoid core-bank communication which is therefore usually limited with many other constraints.

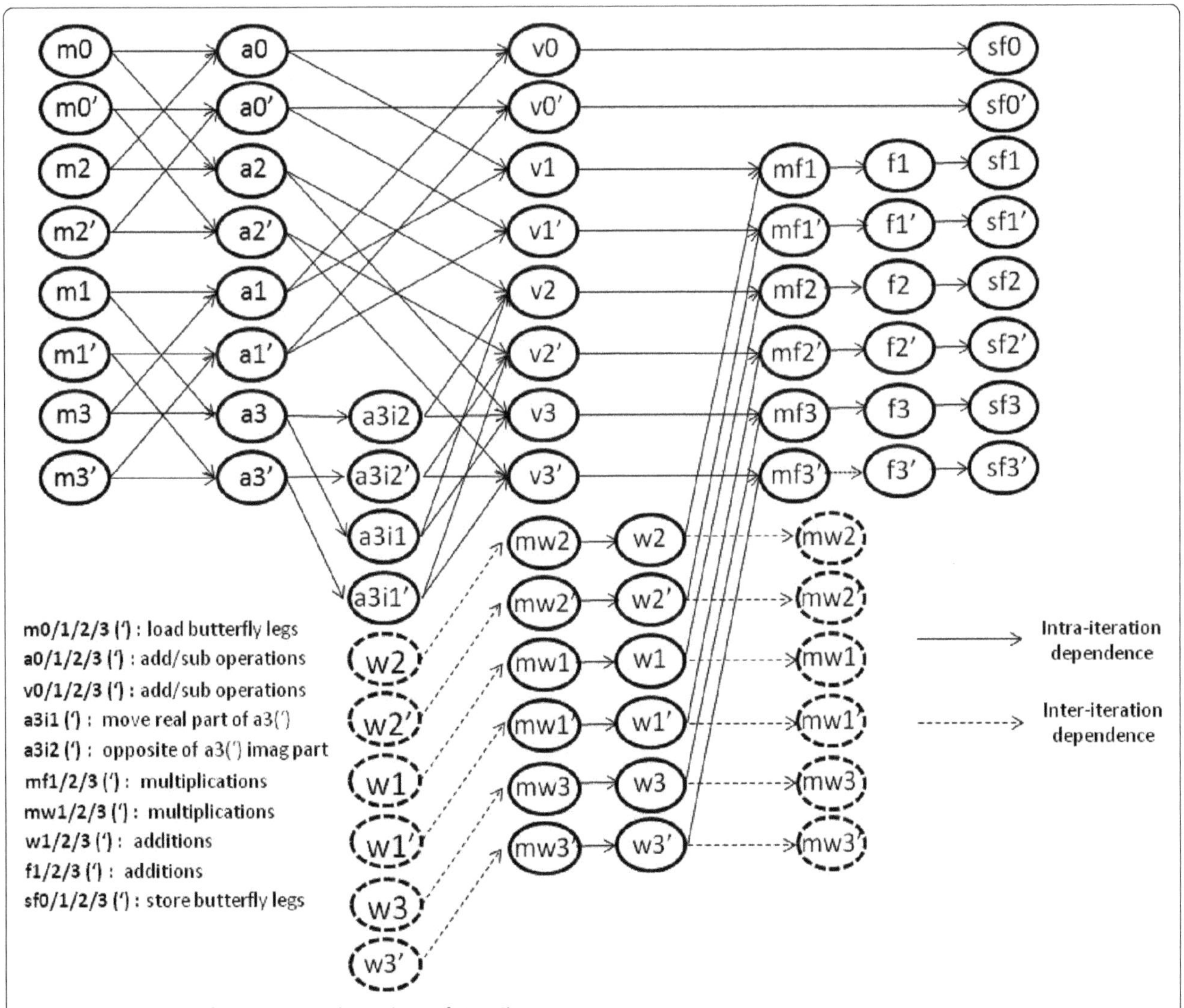

Fig. 14 Iteration DAG of the new FFT scheme (case of $U_m = 2$)

Each node of the graph is associated with a specific assembly instruction, requiring input/output operands with precise sizes, and a list of possible functional units for execution (an example of some TI C66 instructions in Table 1).

At the core-register level, the FFT algorithm will need to allocate a number of registers exclusively to store data pointers, constants, counters, and twiddle factors. First, 1 register is needed to store a counter on the iteration loop; 4 registers per butterfly to contain pointers on input and output butterfly legs; 1 register for the FFT stride; 3 registers per butterfly for jump offsets; 1 register for a pointer on the final output buffer; 1 register as a stack pointer (where some core-registers are spilled). Besides, 3 register pairs are exclusively needed for $(W_N^{U_m}, W_N^{2U_m}, W_N^{3U_m})$, and $3Um$ twiddle factors per butterfly must be allocated as well. Left registers must be used for operand allocation of the entire FFT/iFFT DAG. Our scheduling algorithm must take into account this limiting register constraint.

One of the most efficient scheduling heuristic is SMS as evaluated in [32, 35, 36]. Applying SMS on our FFT problem in the TI C66 core, it produced a schedule of II = MII with a minimum register usage of 20 per core side (40 needed registers), which is greater than the available registers for the DAG allocation, meaning that this is not an implementable schedule. Our scheduling technique aims to find a valid schedule with II = MII and a minimum register requirement in a reasonable time.

5.2 A proposed modulo scheduling algorithm

The new scheduling algorithm starts with ordering the graph nodes for a one core side into a 1-dimensional array, such that if a node is j-indexed into this array, all of its predecessors must be indexed less than j. This is the case as the scheduling algorithm that will be presented next uses this generated array-order to schedule/un-schedule graph nodes in a backtracking fashion and computes the best starting time of each node (regarding register lifetime) based on all of its already scheduled predecessors. The scheduling order is critical and our algorithm uses a special ordering of graph nodes, which will be presented later.

For each node on the ordered list, we define two parameters that are node possible start time (NPST) and node end time (NET), which describe the freedom or possible slots in the actual schedule; they are defined according to (5). We define as well the node start time (NST) as the effective start time, varying between NPST and NET, and pred_i being the ith predecessor of a node. Special freedom ranges were attributed for root nodes not having any predecessor and those with inter-iteration dependences.

$$\begin{aligned} \text{NPST(node)} &= \max_i(\text{NST}(\text{pred}_i) + \text{DS}(\text{pred}_i) + 1) \\ \text{NET(node)} &= \text{II}-1 + \min_i(\text{NST}(\text{pred}_i) + \text{DS}(\text{pred}_i) + 1) \end{aligned} \tag{5}$$

Based on slot freedom of each node on the formed ordered list, we schedule them in a 2-dimensional kernel starting from their NPST. When it is not feasible to schedule an operation due to a unit or write conflict, other possible units are tried or another cycle in [NPST + 1; NET] is used in a backtracking mode. The algorithm is lifetime-sensitive, integrating an accumulative measure of how much time the returned operands remain in core registers before being used. This criterion at a graph node is defined as the total lifetimes since results are being returned by all its predecessors before being consumed by this node; it is expressed in (6) (NRS ["node result size"] is the size in terms of core-registers for a node's results). Notice that this provided lifetime is weighted by the amount of registers that are presented and pended for use. The scheduling algorithm should minimize the overall accumulative lifetime which takes into consideration every node of the graph; in this case, register usage is in general also minimized.

$$\begin{aligned} &\text{lifetime(node)} \\ &\quad = \sum_i \text{NRS}(\text{pred}_i)\Big(\text{NST(node)}-\text{NST}(\text{pred}_i) \\ &\quad -\text{DS}(\text{pred}_i)\Big) \end{aligned} \tag{6}$$

The total length of the accumulative lifetime divided by II gives a lower bound on register pressure, denoted AvgLive. Despite the fact that a minimized AvgLive gives smaller register usage, it does not necessarily provide the lowest. For example, a found schedule with a total lifetime of 110 requires a minimum of 17 registers, while another schedule with a lifetime of 118 required only a minimum of 16 registers. A better register lower bound is computed considering overlapped lifetimes over II cycles, getting

Table 1 Instructions' features of some TI C66 operations

Instruction	Operand size (op1, op2, dst) [in number of core registers]	Delay slot latency (DS)	Possible execution units
DADDSP	(2, 2, 2)	2	L, S
DSUBSP	(2, 2, 2)	2	L, S
CMPYSP	(2, 2, 4)	3	M
STDW	(2, 0, 1)	0	D
LDDW	(1, 0, 2)	4	D
ADD	(1, 1, 1)	0	L, S, D

an array (called LiveVector) of II elements as described in [33]. The maximum among the LiveVector values was named the MaxLive, which is a precise lower bound measure of the number of needed registers. It was shown in [33] that a schedule requires at most MaxLive + 1 registers.

Our algorithm merges the calculation of the MaxLive in the search process, informing of register pressure at any partial schedule. This serves us to efficiently cut off useless branches in the state space, reducing significantly the scheduling time. The pseudo-code of our scheduling algorithm is given in Fig. 15.

As the state space cannot be scanned entirely due to its NP-Complete nature despite MaxLive cut-offs, we propose to make smaller successive searches with different starting points on the search space. This is having the advantage to make finding a better schedule faster. Indeed, if we are not able to find a better solution within a specified amount of backtracking tries (100*M* nodes as an example), then it is more likely because first placed operations constrain the efficiency and therefore must be changed. The algorithm starts then with an initial ordering in the scheduling array, subsequently, if the backtracking amount limit is reached, the scheduling array is re-ordered according to specific rules and the search process starts again using a new initial state; this sequence is repeated until a solution fitting available registers is found.

The re-ordering part tries to guarantee different initial schedules and a fast convergence rate. The main used criteria while sorting is that when an operation *v* is unscheduled, next operations to be rescheduled must be those who maximize their effect on this operation *v*. In order to illustrate this criteria; let's take an example and assume that the scheduling array is arranged as follows: {mw1, mw2, mw3, m0, m1, m2, m3, a0, a1, a2, a3, a3i1, a3i2, v0, v1, v2, v3, f1, f2, f3, sf0, sf1, sf2, sf3, w1, w2, w3}.

Next, we assume that operations until "sf3" were placed successfully into the kernel and found a valid slot. If the operation "w1" cannot be placed into the schedule (either because it presents higher MaxLive pressure, or no free place could be found within its slots freedom range), then the algorithm will reschedule the previous operation in the scheduling array which is "sf3" and checking if this enhanced scheduling opportunities for "w1". It will not have an effect, because "sf3" is not sharing the same resource unit as "w1" nor among its direct predecessors. Hence, rescheduling "sf3", "sf2", "sf1", or "sf0" merely leads to useless states; only "mw1" (its direct predecessor) or operations using the same unit resource could have a chance to make a valid placement for "w1". In order to avoid scanning useless states first, a better order should have been done (making "mw1" close to "w1" in the scheduling array for example).

Accordingly, re-ordering the scheduling array will take those considerations:

If an operation is *j*-indexed into this array, all its predecessors must be indexed less than *j* {1}

Each operation must be close as possible to its direct predecessors {2}

Each operation must be close as possible to operations using the same unit resource {3}

Operations with larger input/output sizes are more critical to re-ordering considerations {4}

We next define for each graph node on the ordered list, a measure on its rescheduling easiness, denoted RF. It expresses how much a graph node meets the previously mentioned criteria regarding its indexing order into the scheduling array. Equation (7) defines the considered RF for a graph node operation op:

$$\mathrm{RF(op)} = \left(2\mathrm{op.id} - \frac{1}{\mathrm{op.pn}} \sum_{i=1}^{\mathrm{op.pn}} \mathrm{op.pred}[i]\mathrm{.id} - \frac{1}{\mathrm{op.cn}} \sum_{i=1}^{\mathrm{op.cn}} \mathrm{op.conc}[i]\mathrm{.id} \right) \mathrm{op.bs} \quad (7)$$

The ".id" field in (7) represents the ordering position of a node within the array. The *pn* and *cn* fields denotes respectively the number of predecessors of *op* and the number of concurrent operations using the same unit resource as *op* and which are indexed less than its index. The formula is scaled by the number of registers (buffers size ".bs") that are required by *op*.

The sum of all RF for every operation in the array reflects the ordering penalty (referred next by OrdP). A better ordering should have a minimized sum. The re-ordering routine generates a number of ordering possibilities; the one having the minimal penalty is picked and used next. This routine is as follows (assuming the array is presented with condition {1} verified):

```
function change_order(Sch_Array)
begin
loop
choose op: an operation from the Sch_Array;
min_i = index(op);
max_i = min(index(successors(op)));
//if no successor, set max_i to upper bound
choose a position s in the range [min_i, max_i-1];
move in array operation from position min_i to s;
compute the OrdP;
compare it to the best penalty found so far;
end loop
return the order having the lowest OrdP;
end
```

```
registers_pressure_goal=12; // setting the stop condition
best_registers_pressure=+∞; // best registers usage found so far
while (best_registers_pressure>registers_pressure_goal) {
        inits(); // re-assign startup conditions on the kernel
        change_order(sch_array); // re-order the scheduling array
        search(0); // start the search process, placing the 0-indexed operation
}
/* the search function definition */
cut_count=100M; // stop searching if 100M nodes are discovered
LiveVector={0};
void search(int op_index) {
        if (cut_count==0) return;
        else cut_count--;
        MaxLive=max(LiveVector);
        if (MaxLive >= best_registers_pressure) return; // if worst then a previously found solution, cut-off
        if (op_index >= op_number) { // all operations were placed, a valid schedule is found
                best_registers_pressure=MaxLive;
                report solution;
                return;
        }
        op=sch_array[op_index];
        updateNPSTandNET(op); // update NPST and NET values for each node
        for (i ∈ [op.NPST , op.NET] ) { // through possible scheduling slots
                x=i mod II;
                for (y ∈ op.possible_units) { // through possible units
                        if (fit_constraints(op,x,y)) { // check if resource/write constrainsts are valid
                                kernel[x][y]=op ; // schedule an operation
                                updateLiveVector(op); // modify the LiveVector
                                search(op_index+1); // try to schedule the next operation (recursive call)
                                kernel[x][y]=NULL; // un-schedule this operation
                                resetLiveVector(op); // modify-back the LiveVector
                        }
                }
        }
}
```

Fig. 15 Pseudo-code of our scheduling algorithm

The presented heuristic in this section was tested on a TI C66 VLIW core and generated an efficient schedule with II = MII and MaxLive = 12 during few minutes. Figure 16 shows the ordering penalty effect on the convergence speed. The resulting kernel form for the FFT/iFFT on C66 is shown in Fig. 11.

Our proposed scheduling algorithm aggressively minimized register usage, enhancing the MaxLive by a factor of 1.7 in the TI C66 core, toward the SMS scheduling method (which returned a MaxLive of 20), making an FFT completely without memory references of twiddle factors implementable.

The key parameters of our scheduling method are mainly the computed MII and U_m in Section 4.2.1, the number of symmetric clusters (denoted SymC) in the VLIW core (The method would schedule U_m/SymC butterflies per cluster, reducing the algorithmic problem size by a factor of SymC). The scheduling is also dependent on the VLIW instruction's delay slots, operand sizes, and their possible execution units and on the number of available core registers per cluster.

6 Implementation and experimental results

Subsequent implementation strategy for the FFT/iFFT was implemented in the high-end TMS320 C6678 VLIW DSP and in the 66AK2H12 DSP, using the Standard C66 Assembly. Data samples were single-precision complex floating point, with imaginary parts in odd indexes and real parts in even ones. During benchmarks, L1D/L1P was fully used as cache. Input/output buffers are stored into the memory L2 (512 Kbytes in C6678, 1 Mbytes in 66AK2H12). Moreover, the program code is mapped to

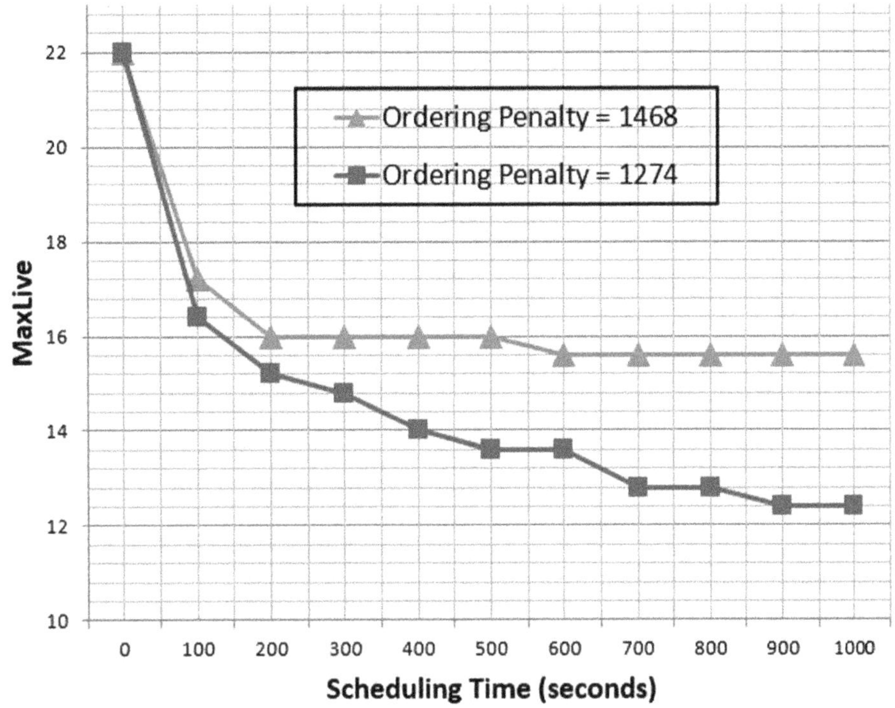

Fig. 16 The effect of the ordering penalty on the convergence speed

the local memory L2. Experimented FFT sizes are in the range [256, 64*k*], which correspond to most signal processing applications. The comparison is made with the most vendor-tuned linear assembly-optimized FFT of TI (found in the DSPLib version 3.1.1.1), with the TI compiler's optimizations all active (-o3, version 7.3.2).

A common efficiency measure for the FFT algorithm will be used, which is the number of cycles per pseudo-radix-2 butterfly (that we will denote as CPPR2B), defined by the FFT cycle count divided by $N\log_2(N)/2$. A perfect FFT implementation on the CorePac C66 would have a CPPR2B of 1; otherwise, it will be greater than 1. Performance comparison between our new FFT/iFFT (bit reversal included) and the optimized TI routines is presented in Fig. 17 and Table 2 (results are for 1 core of C6678, running at the frequency of 1 GHz).

Our presented FFT implementation shows great improvements over TI; the peak performance was reached for $N = 4k$, as the limited cache associativity made our special optimization to take place for $N = 8k$ and larger, inducing relatively less efficiency for integrating radix-2 stages. Small FFTs usually suffer from non-negligible overhead toward main processing. We are then able to reach an average gain of 50.56 % (2 times acceleration) over TI's routines, with a maximum performance of 1.119 CPPR2B (89.36 % of absolute efficiency). This obtained gain is explained by the proved 27 % gain in Section 4, the suppressed latencies of twiddle factors and by the other described optimizations.

Besides the speed performance, our FFT saves 50 % of input buffers toward conventional (TI) FFT routines (Table 3). Indeed, our scheme does not require twiddle factors to be stored nor to be referenced from external memory.

The bit reversal computation did not affect the performance for FFT sizes less than 8*k* (0 % increase due to our cache-efficient bit reversal optimization), while it increased the cycles count by an average of 18.4 % starting from 8*k* sizes; the loss represents the price of the time needed to process bit reversal separately for large FFTs. Besides, the proposed FFT/iFFT adaptation to the cache associativity is having at least a gain of 69 % in terms of efficiency. The inverse FFT was optimally reformed such that its performance overlapped with the FFT routine, despite the fact it included extra arithmetic operations.

Figure 18 shows the relative RMS error comparison between the new FFT and TI's one. The proposed FFT using 1 twiddle factor (tradeoff factor of 0) achieves for instance an RMS error of about 1E-05 (FFT size of 4*k*), against 5E-07 for TIs. Our FFT variant with a tradeoff factor of 1 (using $\log(N)$ pre-computed twiddle factors) achieved about a 10 times enhancement in terms of precision, preserving exactly the same presented speed performance. For most signal processing applications, this FFT accuracy is enough, and we can see for instance that the signal on FFT-noise ratio (SNR) we achieve in Fig. 18 for a 4*k*-FFT is about 107 dB, compared to

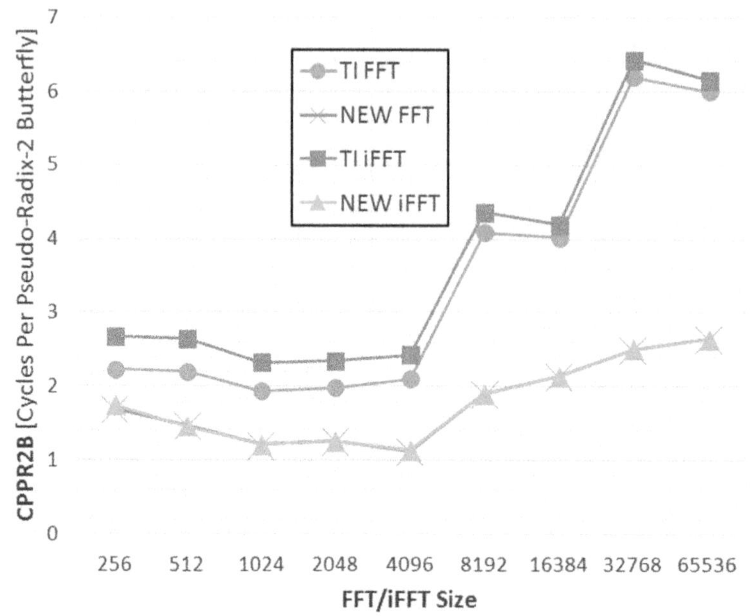

Fig. 17 Performance comparison between the new FFT and TIs in C66 cores

127 dB for the TI FFT and to 138 dB for the maximum achievable SNR of an IEEE-754 single-precision floating point. Worth to note that a 16-bit ADC converter has an SQNR of about 84 dB [40] (which is even less than the SNR due to FFT's computation accuracy); the SQNR is usually raised by coherent signal processing gains (e.g., a 4*k*-FFT processing can increase the SQNR by 33 dB or by 10 $\log_{10}(N/2)$ dB).

On the other hand, our scheduling heuristic generates the kernel codes of the FFT/iFFT and aggressively optimizes the number of cycles and registers' usage. It is able to compute the best schedule respecting tight pressure constraints with a fast convergence rate, overcoming results given by SMS by a factor of 1.7 (40 % gain) on the found MaxLive. The best generated schedule of instructions with a MaxLive = 12 was computed within 2- to 15-min range.

Furthermore, a 4*k*-sample floating-point FFT was performed in-chip during 2.6 μs within a 10-W power consumption in a TI 66AK2H12 DSP device, making a remarkable FFT implementation efficiency of 9.5 GFLOPS/watt. This makes it possible for use in several compute-intensive applications, such as radar processing [41]. Our work has been used within the official FFT library of Texas Instruments [42].

In contrast to previous works, on-the-fly generation of twiddle factors as in [43–45] used the CORDIC algorithm or related generation designs to compute the needed twiddle factors instead of performing ROM accesses. These techniques target hardware FFT designs in FPGAs or ASICs and are not applicable for CPU or DSP platforms. Indeed, the idea of generating twiddle factors using multipliers (or equivalent operations) in software for CPU/DSP is usually avoided, as it requires in most cases more latency than FFT schemes with pre-computed twiddle

Table 2 Performance comparison between the new FFT/iFFT and TIs

Implementation	FFT size	CPPR2B	Cycles	Relative gain over TI (%)
New FFT	1*k*	1.206	6175	37.62
TI FFT	1*k*	1.933	9899	-
New FFT	4*k*	1.119	27502	46.65
TI FFT	4*k*	2.097	51547	-
New FFT	8*k*	1.896	100979	53.63
TI FFT	8*k*	4.090	217782	-
New iFFT	1*k*	1.211	6198	47.89
TI iFFT	1*k*	2.323	11894	-
New iFFT	4*k*	1.130	27779	53.50
TI iFFT	4*k*	2.431	59745	-
New iFFT	8*k*	1.896	100977	56.59
TI iFFT	8*k*	4.368	232613	-

Table 3 Twiddle factor (TF) storage/reference comparison

Implementation	FFT size	Number of stored TF	Number of memory references due to TF
New FFT	512	1	1
TI FFT	512	512	511
FFT of [21] in C64x	512	254	127
New FFT	1*k*	1	1
TI FFT	1*k*	1024	1023
FFT of [21] in C64x	1*k*	510	255

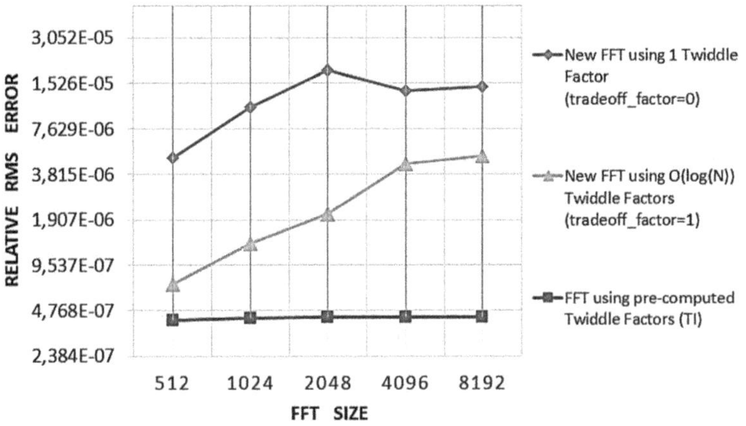

Fig. 18 RMS error comparison between the new FFT and TIs in C66 cores

factors. To the best of our knowledge, no published work proposed a software-efficient solution to do an FFT with in-generation of twiddle factors. The idea becomes possible with recent high-end VLIW processors, where we have to issue parallel instructions computing the twiddle factors in the masked time; however, it requires proper scheduling and low-level control on the execution pattern to be done successfully.

7 Conclusions

In the present paper, a new radix-2^2-based FFT/iFFT scheme is proposed to fit VLIW processors. This structure made a balance between the VLIW computation capabilities and the data bandwidth pressure, optimally exploiting parallelism opportunities and reducing memory references to twiddle factors, leading to an average gain of 51 % on efficiency toward the most assembly-optimized and vendor-tuned FFT on a high-end VLIW DSP. Our implementation methodology took into account the VLIW hardware resources and the cache structure, adapting the FFT algorithm to a broad range of embedded VLIW processors. On the other hand, a resource-constrained and register-sensitive modulo scheduling heuristic was designed to find the best low-level schedule to our FFT scheme, minimizing clock cycles and register usage using controlled backtracking, generating efficient assembly-optimized FFT with balanced resource usage.

Competing interests

The authors declare that they have no competing interests.

Acknowledgements

This research is sponsored in part by a Research and Development Contract from Thales Air Systems.

Author details

[1]LGECOS Lab, ENSA-Marrakech of the Cadi Ayyad University, Marrakech, Morocco. [2]Thales Air Systems, Paris, France.

Received: 23 October 2015 Accepted: 14 March 2016
Published online: 31 March 2016

References

1. JW Cooley, JW Tukey, An algorithm for the machine calculation of complex Fourier series. Math. Comput. **19**, 297–301 (1965)
2. GD Bergland, A radix-eight fast-Fourier transform subroutine for real-valued series. IEEE Trans. On Electroacoust. **17**(2), 138–144 (1969)
3. RC Singleton, An algorithm for computing the mixed radix fast Fourier transform. IEEE Trans. Audio Electroacoust. **1**(2), 93–103 (1969)
4. P Duhamel, H Hollmann, Split radix FFT algorithm. Electronics Letters **20**, 14–16 (1984)
5. D Takahashi, An extended split-radix FFT algorithm. IEEE Signal Processing Letters **8**(5), 145–147 (2001)
6. AR Varkonyi-Koczy, A recursive fast Fourier transform algorithm. IEEE Trans. on Circuits and Systems, II **42**, 614–616 (1995)
7. A Saidi, Decimation-in-time-frequency FFT algorithm. Proc. ICAPSS **3**, 453–456 (1994)
8. BM Baas, A low-power, high-performance, 1024-point FFT processor. IEEE J. Solid-State Circuits **34**(3), 380–387 (1999)
9. R Weber et al., Comparing hardware accelerators in scientific applications: a case study. IEEE Trans. Parallel Distrib. Syst. **22**(1), 58–68 (2011). doi:10.1109/TPDS.2010.125
10. T Fryza, J Svobodova, F Adamec, R Marsalek, J Prokopec, Overview of parallel platforms for common high performance computing. Radioengineering **21**(1), 436–444 (2012)
11. Jia-Jhe Li, Chi-Bang Kuan, Tung-Yu Wu, and Jenq Kuen Lee. Enabling an OpenCL compiler for embedded multicore DSP systems. In Proceedings of the 2012 41st International Conference on Parallel Processing Workshops (ICPPW '12). (IEEE Computer Society, Washington, DC, USA, 2012), p. 545-552
12. Francisco D. Igual, Guillermo Botella, Carlos García, Manuel Prieto, Francisco Tirado, Robust motion estimation on a low-power multi-core DSP. EURASIP Journal on Advances in Signal Processing. **99**, 1-15 (2013)
13. T. Fryza and R. Mego, Low level source code optimizing for single/multi/core digital signal processors, Radioelektronika (RADIOELEKTRONIKA), 2013 23rd International Conference, Pardubice, 2013, pp. 288-291. doi:10.1109/RadioElek.2013.6530933
14. JA Fisher, P Faraboschi, C Young, Embedded computing: A VLIW approach to architecture, compilers, and tools. (Morgan Kaufmann Publishers Inc., San Francisco, CA, USA, 2005), ISBN: 9780080477541.
15. V Z˘Zivojnovi'c, Compilers for digital signal processors. DSP & Multimedia Technology Magazine **4**(5), 27–45 (1995)
16. J. P. Grossman, Compiler and architectural techniques for improving the effectiveness of VLIW compilation. [Online]. Available:http://www.ai.mit.edu/projects/aries/Documents/vliw.pdf [24-Mars-2016]
17. JA Fisher, Trace scheduling: a technique for global microcode compaction. IEEE Trans. Comput. **30**(7), 478–490 (1981)
18. L Monica, *Software pipelining: an effective scheduling technique for VLIW machines* (Proc. SIGPLAN '88 Conference on Programming Language Design and Implementation, Atlanta, 1988), pp. 318–328

19. B Ramakrishna Rau, *Iterative modulo scheduling: an algorithm for software pipelining loops*. Proc. 27th Annual International Symposium on Microarchitecture, 1994, pp. 63–74
20. M. Bahtat, S. Belkouch, P. Elleaume, P. Le Gall, Fast enumeration-based modulo scheduling heuristic for VLIW architectures, in 26th International Conference on Microelectronics (ICM), 2014, pp. 116-119, 2014. doi: 10.1109/ICM.2014.7071820
21. Y Wang, Y Tang, Y Jiang, JG Chung, SS Song, MS Lim, Novel memory reference reduction methods for FFT implementation on DSP processors. IEEE Trans. Signal Process **55**, 2338–2349 (2007). doi:10.1109/TSP.2007.892722
22. Y Jiang, T Zhou, Y Tang, Y Wang, Twiddle-factor-based FFT algorithm with reduced memory access, in *Proc. 16th Int. Symp. Parallel Distrib. Process* (IEEE Computer Soc, Washington, 2002), p. 70
23. K.J. Bowers, D.E. Shaw Res, New York, NY, USA; R.A. Lippert, R.O. Dror, D.E. Shaw, Improved twiddle access for fast Fourier transforms. IEEE Trans. Signal Process. **58**(3), 1122–1130 (2010)
24. VI Kelefouras, G Athanasiou, N Alachiotis, HE Michail, A Kritikakou, CE Goutis, A methodology for speeding up fast Fourier transform focusing on memory architecture utilization. IEEE Trans. Signal Process **59**(12), 6217–6226 (2011)
25. M Frigo, SG Johnson, The fastest Fourier transform in the west, in *Proc. Int. Conf. Acoust., Speech, Signal Process. (ICASSP)*, 1998
26. M Frigo, A fast Fourier transform compiler. SIGLAN Not. **39**, 642–655 (2004)
27. S Johnson, M Frigo, A modified split-radix FFT with fewer arithmetic operations. IEEE Trans. Signal Process **55**(1), 111–119 (2006)
28. D Mirkovic, L Johnsson, Automatic performance tuning in the UHFFT library, in *Computational Science—ICCS 2001* (Springer, New York, 2001), pp. 71–80
29. AM Blake, IH Witten, MJ Cree, The fastest Fourier transform in the south. IEEE Trans. Signal Process **61**(19), 4707–4716 (2013)
30. M. Bahtat, S. Belkouch, P. Elleaume, P. Le Gall, Efficient implementation of a complete multi-beam radar coherent-processing on a telecom SoC, in 2014 International Radar Conference (Radar), pp. 1-6, 2014. doi: 10.1109/RADAR.2014.7060412
31. S He, M Torkelson, A new approach to pipeline FFT processor, in *Proc. IEEE Parallel Processing Symp*, 1996, pp. 766–770
32. J.M. Codina, J. Llosa, A. González, A comparative study of modulo scheduling techniques, Proceedings of the 16th international conference on Supercomputing ICS 02(2002), **13**(1), 97. ACM Press
33. RA Huff, Lifetime-sensitive modulo scheduling, In Proc. of the ACM SIGPLAN '93 Conf. on Programming Language Design and Implementation. 258-267(1993)
34. AK Dani, VJ Ramanan, R Govindarajan, Register-sensitive software pipelining. Parallel Processing Symposium, 1998. (IPPS/SPDP, Orlando, FL, 1998), p. 194-198
35. J. Llosa, A. González, E. Ayguadé, M. Valero, Swing modulo scheduling: a lifetime-sensitive approach, PACT '96 Proceedings of the 1996 Conference on Parallel Architectures and Compilation Techniques. (Boston, MA, 1996), p. 80-86
36. J Llosa, E Ayguade, A Gonzalez, M Valero, J Eckhardt, Lifetime-sensitive modulo scheduling in a production environment. IEEE Trans. Comput. **50**(3), 234–249 (2002)
37. J Zalamea, J Llosa, E Ayguade, M Valero, Register constrained modulo scheduling. IEEE Trans. Parallel Distrib. Syst. **15**(5), 417–430 (2004)
38. TMS320C6678, Multicore fixed and floating-point digital signal processor, Data Manual, Texas Instruments. SPRS691E. March 2014. [Online]. Available: www.ti.com/lit/gpn/tms320c6678 [25-Mars-2016]
39. M Tasche, H Zeuner, Improved roundoff error analysis for precomputed twiddle factors. J. Comput. Anal. Appl. **4**(1), 1–18 (2012)
40. JJ Alter, JO Coleman, Radar digital signal processing, Chapter 25 in Merrill I. Skolnik, Radar Handbook, Third Edition, (McGraw-Hill, 2008)
41. A Klilou, S Belkouch, P Elleaume, P Le Gall, F Bourzeix, MM Hassani, Real-time parallel implementation of pulse-Doppler radar signal processing chain on a massively parallel machine based on multi-core DSP and serial RapidIO interconnect. EURASIP Journal on Advances in Signal Processing **2014**, 161 (2014)
42. Texas Instruments. FFT library for C66X floating point devices, C66X FFTLIB, version 2.0. [Online]. Available: http://www.ti.com/tool/FFTLIB [25-Mars-2016]
43. Sang Yoon Park; Nam Ik Cho; Sang Uk Lee; Kichul Kim; Jisung Oh, Design of 2K/4K/8K-point FFT processor based on CORDIC algorithm in OFDM receiver, Communications, Computers and signal Processing, 2001. PACRIM. 2001 IEEE Pacific Rim Conference on, vol. 2, no., pp. 457,460 vol. 2, 2001. doi:10.1109/PACRIM.2001.953668
44. T Pitkänen, T Partanen, J Takala, Low-power twiddle factor unit for FFT computation. Embedded Computer Systems: Architectures, Modeling, and Simulation Lecture Notes in Computer Science **4599**(2007), 65–74 (2007)
45. JC Chi, SG Chen, *An efficient FFT twiddle factor generator* (Proc. European Signal Process. Conf, Vienna, 2004)

10

Robust and adaptive diffusion-based classification in distributed networks

Patricia Binder*, Michael Muma and Abdelhak M. Zoubir

Abstract

Distributed adaptive signal processing and communication networking are rapidly advancing research areas which enable new and powerful signal processing tasks, e.g., distributed speech enhancement in adverse environments. An emerging new paradigm is that of multiple devices cooperating in multiple tasks (MDMT). This is different from the classical wireless sensor network (WSN) setup, in which multiple devices perform one single joint task. A crucial first step in order to achieve a benefit, e.g., a better node-specific audio signal enhancement, is the common unique labeling of all relevant sources that are observed by the network. This challenging research question can be addressed by designing adaptive data clustering and classification rules based on a set of noisy unlabeled sensor observations. In this paper, two robust and adaptive distributed hybrid classification algorithms are introduced. They consist of a local clustering phase that uses a small part of the data with a subsequent, fully distributed on-line classification phase. The classification is performed by means of distance-based similarity measures. In order to deal with the presence of outliers, the distances are estimated robustly. An extensive simulation-based performance analysis is provided for the proposed algorithms. The distributed hybrid classification approaches are compared to a benchmark algorithm where the error rates are evaluated in dependence of different WSN parameters. Communication cost and computation time are compared for all algorithms under test. Since both proposed approaches use robust estimators, they are, to a certain degree, insensitive to outliers. Furthermore, they are designed in a way that they are applicable to on-line classification problems.

Keywords: Adaptive distributed classification, Clustering, Labeling, Robust, Outlier, Multi device multi task (MDMT)

1 Introduction

Recent advances in distributed adaptive signal processing and communication networking are currently enabling novel paradigms for signal and parameter estimation. Based on the principles of adaptive filtering theory [1], a network of devices with node-specific interests adaptively optimizes its behavior, e.g., to jointly solve a decentralized least mean squares problem [2–6]. Under this new paradigm, multiple devices cooperate in multiple tasks (MDMT). This is different from the classical wireless sensor network setup, in which multiple devices perform one single joint task [2].

The MDMT paradigm can be beneficial, e.g., for speech enhancement in adverse environments [7]. Consider, for example, distributed audio signal enhancement in a public area, such as an airport, a train-station, etc. By cooperating with each other, various devices (e.g., smart-phones, hearing aids, tablets) benefit in enhancing their node-specific audio source of interest, given a received mixture of interfering sound sources [2, 8], e.g., by suppressing noise and interfering sound sources that are not of interest to the user.

Note that in such scenarios, the devices must operate under stringent power and communication constraints and the transmission of observations to a fusion center (FC) is, in many cases, infeasible or undesired. A crucial first step in order to achieve a benefit, e.g., a better node-specific audio signal enhancement, is the common *unique labeling* of all relevant speech sources that are observed by the network [8]. Also in other MDMT signal-enhancement tasks, such as image enhancement, it is of practical importance to answer the question: who observes what? [9].

*Correspondence: binder@spg.tu-darmstadt.de
Signal Processing Group, Technische Universität Darmstadt, 64283 Darmstadt, Germany

This challenging research question can be tackled by designing adaptive data clustering and classification rules where each sensor collects a set of unlabeled observations that are drawn from a known number of classes. In particular, object or speaker labeling can be solved by in-network adaptive classification algorithms where a minimum amount of information is exchanged among single-hop neighbors. Various methods have been proposed that deal with distributed data clustering and classification, e.g., [8–24]. In the last few years, several distributed adaptive strategies, such as incremental, consensus, and diffusion least mean squares algorithms have been developed [25]. In [17], a distributed K-Means (DKM) algorithm that uses the consensus strategy was proposed.

In this paper, we provide an adaptive and robust hybrid diffusion-based approach which extends our previously published algorithm [21] by a robust distance measure that improves the classification/labeling performance, especially if the covariances of the clusters differ significantly. Robust methods become necessary whenever the distribution of the extracted features is heavy tailed or contains outliers [26, 27] due to errors in the feature estimation step. A scenario containing a high amount of outliers, as depicted in Fig. 1, complicates the classification considerably. In such a scenario, we propose to base the classification/labeling on robust adaptive centroid estimation and data clustering.

Contributions: Two robust in-network distributed classification algorithms, i.e., the RDiff K-Med and the CE RDiff K-Med, are proposed. It is shown that the performance of the first algorithm can be approached by the second algorithm with a considerably lower between-sensor communication cost. Unlike the DKM, which serves as a benchmark, the proposed algorithms are adaptive, instead of working with a batch of data. They are thus applicable to real-time classification problems. Furthermore, they are robust against outliers in the feature vectors and can handle non-stationary features. An extensive simulation-based performance analysis is provided that investigates the error rates in dependence of different WSN parameters, and also considers communication cost and computation time.

Organization: Section 2 provides the problem formulation, Section 3 provides a brief introduction to the topic of robust estimation of class centroid and covariance. Section 4 is dedicated to the proposal and description of two robust diffusion-based classification algorithms, while Section 5 provides an extensive Monte-Carlo simulation study. Section 6 concludes the paper and provides future research directions.

2 Problem formulation and data model

Consider a network with J nodes distributed over some geographic region (see Fig. 2). Two nodes are connected if they are able to communicate directly with each other. The set of nodes connected to node $j \in 1, \ldots, J =: \mathcal{J}$ is called the neighborhood of node j and is denoted by $\mathcal{B}_j \subseteq \mathcal{J}$. The communication links between the nodes are symmetric and a node is always connected to itself. The number of nodes connected to node j is called the degree of node j and is denoted by $|\mathcal{B}_j|$.

This paper is concerned with adaptive data clustering and classification/labeling when each sensor collects

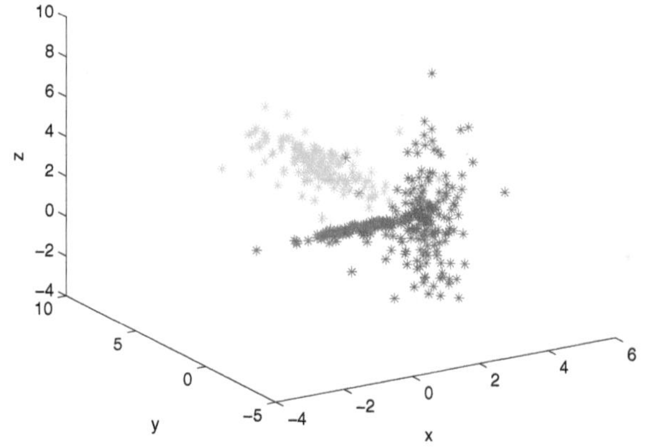

Fig. 1 Three data clusters containing outlying feature vectors

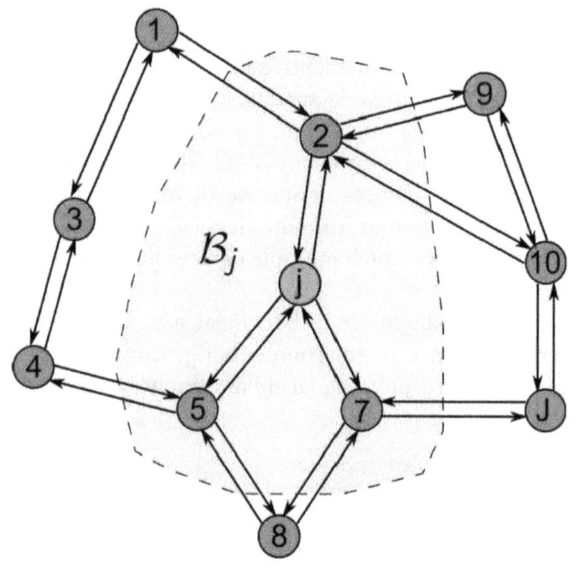

Fig. 2 Sensor network showing the neighborhood of node j, denoted by $\mathcal{B}_j$

a set of unlabeled observations that are drawn from a known number of classes. This task should be accomplished in a decentralized manner by communicating only within directly connected neighborhoods $\mathcal{B}_j$, instead of transmitting all observations to a master node or FC. Each observation is assumed to belong to a certain class $\mathcal{C}_k$ with $k \in 1, \ldots, K$ with k denoting the label of the given class. The total number of classes K is assumed to be known, or estimated a priori. Each class is described by a number of application dependent descriptive statistics (features). The feature estimation process is an application-specific research area of its own (see, e.g., [8, 9]) and is not considered in this article, where we seek for generic adaptive robust clustering and classification methods. In the following, it is assumed that the feature extraction has already been performed, so that the uncertainty of the feature estimation within each class can be modeled by a probability distribution, e.g., the Gaussian. Further, we account for estimation errors in the feature extraction process that we consider as outliers, thus arriving at the following observation model for feature vectors at time instant $n, n = 1, \ldots, N$:

$$\boldsymbol{d}_{jkn} = \boldsymbol{w}_k + \boldsymbol{e}_{jkn} + \boldsymbol{o}_{jn}. \tag{1}$$

Here, $\boldsymbol{w}_k$ denotes the class centroid, $\boldsymbol{e}_{jkn}$ represents the class-specific uncertainty term with covariance matrix $\boldsymbol{\Sigma}_{jk}$, $\boldsymbol{o}_{jn}$ denotes the outlier term which models disturbances of an unspecified density and $\boldsymbol{d}_{jkn}, \boldsymbol{w}_k, \boldsymbol{e}_{jkn} \in \mathbb{R}^q$. $\boldsymbol{e}_{jkn}$ is assumed to be temporally and spatially independent, i.e.,

$$\mathbb{E}\{\boldsymbol{e}_{jn}^* \boldsymbol{e}_{lm}\} = \sigma_{e,j}^2 \cdot \delta_{jl} \cdot \delta_{nm} \tag{2}$$

with $j, l = 1, \ldots, J$, $n, m = 1, \ldots, N$ and δ denoting the Kronecker delta function. $\boldsymbol{e}_{jkn}$ is assumed to be zero mean. For reasons of clarity, we drop the index k in the observation vectors and refer to them as $\boldsymbol{d}_{jn}$.

The aim of this paper is thus to enable every node j to assign each observation to a cluster k based on an estimated feature $\mathbf{d}_{jn}$. The classification/labeling should be real-time capable so that a new observation can be assigned on-line without the necessity of all recorded observations being available. Furthermore, outliers in Eq. (1) should not have a huge effect on the labeling performance. This will be achieved by using robust techniques to estimate the class centroids and covariances, as well as robust distance measures, as described in the next section.

3 Robust estimation of class centroid and covariance

The presence of even a small amount of outliers in a data set can have a high impact on classical estimators like the sample mean vector and sample covariance matrix. Though these estimators are optimal under the Gaussian noise assumption, they are extremely sensitive to uncharacteristic observations in the data [26]. For this purpose, robust estimators have been developed which are, to a certain degree, resistant towards outliers in the data.

In the following, a short overview of the concept of M-estimation for the multivariate case is presented, as required by our methods. For a more detailed treatment of the fundamental concepts, see, e.g., [26, 28].

The hybrid classification approach developed in this paper involves estimating the mean and covariance for vector-valued data $\mathbf{d}_{jn} = (d_{1jn}, d_{2jn}, \ldots, d_{qjn})^T$ with $\mathbf{d}_{jn} \in \mathbb{R}^q$, where q is the dimension of the feature space.

In the univariate case, it is possible to define the robust estimates of location and dispersion separately. In the multivariate case, In order to obtain equivariant estimates, it is of advantage to estimate location and dispersion simultaneously [28].

The multivariate Gaussian density is

$$f_{\mathbf{D}}(\mathbf{d}; \mathbf{w}, \boldsymbol{\Sigma}) = \frac{1}{\sqrt{|\boldsymbol{\Sigma}|}} h_{\mathbf{D}}(g_{\mathbf{D}}(\mathbf{d}; \mathbf{w}, \boldsymbol{\Sigma})) \tag{3}$$

where $|\boldsymbol{\Sigma}|$ denotes the determinant of $\boldsymbol{\Sigma}$, $h_X(x) = c\exp(-x/2)$ with $c = (2\pi)^{-q/2}$ and $g_{\mathbf{D}}(\mathbf{d}; \mathbf{w}, \boldsymbol{\Sigma}) = (\mathbf{d} - \mathbf{w})^T \boldsymbol{\Sigma}^{-1} (\mathbf{d} - \mathbf{w})$.

Let $\mathbf{d}_{j1}, \ldots, \mathbf{d}_{jN}$ be an i.i.d. sample from a density of the form (3). M-estimates of the cluster centroids and covariance matrices are defined as solutions of the general system equations

$$\sum_{n=1}^{N} \phi_1(g_{\mathbf{D}}(n))(\mathbf{d}_{jn} - \hat{\mathbf{w}}_k) = \mathbf{0}_q \tag{4}$$

$$\frac{1}{N-1} \sum_{n=1}^{N} \phi_2(g_{\mathbf{D}}(n))(\mathbf{d}_{jn} - \hat{\mathbf{w}}_k)(\mathbf{d}_{jn} - \hat{\mathbf{w}}_k)^T = \hat{\boldsymbol{\Sigma}}_k, \tag{5}$$

where the functions ϕ_1 and ϕ_2 may be chosen differently. Uniqueness of solutions of (4) and (5) requires that $g_{\mathbf{D}}\phi_2(g_{\mathbf{D}})$ is a nondecreasing function of $g_{\mathbf{D}}$ [28].

A common choice are *Huber's functions* [29] with

$$\rho(\mathbf{d}) = \begin{cases} \mathbf{d}_{jn}^2 & , \text{if } |\mathbf{d}_{jn}| \leq \mathbf{c}_{\text{hub}} \\ 2\mathbf{c}_{\text{hub}} |\mathbf{d}_{jn}| - \mathbf{c}_{\text{hub}}^2 & , \text{if } |\mathbf{d}_{jn}| > \mathbf{c}_{\text{hub}} \end{cases} \tag{6}$$

and

$$\phi_{1,2}(\mathbf{d}) = \frac{\partial \rho(\mathbf{d})}{\partial \mathbf{d}} \quad (7)$$

with $\mathbf{c}_{\text{hub}}$ denoting the Huber's tuning constant. The function $\rho(\mathbf{d})$ from Eq. (6) shows quadratic behavior in the central region while increasing linearly to infinity. Outliers are therefore assigned less weight than data close to the model. Note that all maximum likelihood estimators are also M-estimators.

4 Proposed methods

In this section, two new robust in-network distributed classification algorithms are presented that extend our previously published algorithm [21] by a robust distance measure that improves the classification/labeling performance, especially if the covariances of the clusters differ significantly.

Since we have no training data available for the classification process, the general idea of the methods is to split the classification/labeling procedure into two main steps: in a *local clustering phase* each node calculates a preliminary estimate of the cluster characteristics (i.e., centroids and covariances) of each cluster using a small number of feature vectors. These preliminary estimates serve as an initialization for the subsequent *global classification phase*. Here, based on these estimates, a new feature is classified using a robust distance measure. The aim is to improve the local classification result by a combination of local processing and communication between the agents.

An advantage of this procedure is that this hybrid approach turns into a mere classification algorithm when the cluster characteristics are known beforehand. In this case, the local clustering phase is not needed.

The methods are based on the diffusion LMS strategy that was introduced in [30]. In this way, the classification is adaptive and can handle streaming data coming from a distributed sensor network. Since the communication cost between the nodes should be kept as low as possible, the second approach is designed with reduced in-network communication. A robust design makes sure that the proposed algorithms are, to a certain degree, resistant towards outliers in the feature vectors. In the following, the two proposed approaches are described in detail.

4.1 Robust distance-based K-medians clustering/classification over adaptive diffusion networks (RDiff K-Med)

The first proposed hybrid classification methodology is the "Robust Distance-Based Clustering/Classification Algorithm over Adaptive Diffusion Networks" (RDiff K-Med). It begins with a local initialization phase where each node j collects a number of N_t observations and performs K-medians clustering on these observations. In this way, each node locally partitions its first N_t observations $\mathbf{D}_{jn} = \{\mathbf{d}_{jn}, n = 1, \ldots, N_t\}$ into k sets $\mathcal{C}_k$ so that the ℓ_1-distance within each cluster is minimized:

$$\arg\min_{\mathbf{w}_k} \sum_{k=1}^{K} \sum_{n=1}^{N_t} \|\mathbf{d}_{jn} - \mathbf{w}_k\|_1 \quad (8)$$

Each center is the component-wise median of the points of each cluster. The features assigned to each class $\mathcal{C}_k$ are stored in an initial feature matrix $\boldsymbol{S}^0_{jk}$. Based on all elements in $\boldsymbol{S}^0_{jk}$, local intermediate estimates of the cluster centroid $\boldsymbol{\psi}^0_{jk}$ and covariance matrix $\boldsymbol{\Sigma}^0_{jk}$ are determined. In the following, the calculation steps are presented in detail.

First, as robust local initial estimate of the cluster center, compute the column-wise median of $\boldsymbol{S}^0_{jk}$

$$\hat{\boldsymbol{\psi}}^0_{jk} = \text{median}\left(\boldsymbol{S}^0_{jk}\right). \quad (9)$$

$\hat{\boldsymbol{\psi}}^0_{jk}$ is thus obtained by computing the median separately for each spatial direction of all elements in $\boldsymbol{S}^0_{jk}$.

Next, proceed by computing a robust local initial estimate of the cluster covariances. In this paper, we compare three estimators, i.e. the sample covariance, Huber's M-estimator and a computationally simple robust covariance estimator based on the median absolute deviation (MAD).

The sample covariance matrix estimate is given by

$$\hat{\boldsymbol{\Sigma}}^0_{jk} = \frac{1}{N_t - 1} \sum_{n=1}^{N_t} \left(\mathbf{d}_{jn} - \hat{\boldsymbol{\psi}}^0_{jk}\right) \left(\mathbf{d}_{jn} - \hat{\boldsymbol{\psi}}^0_{jk}\right)^H. \quad (10)$$

Huber's M-estimator, as defined in Eq. (6), is computed via an iteratively reweighted least-squares algorithm, as detailed in [28] with the previously computed $\hat{\boldsymbol{\psi}}^0_{jk}$ as location estimate.

In case of the MAD based covariance estimate, for each feature $\boldsymbol{d}_{jn}$ in $\boldsymbol{S}^0_{jk}$ the difference vector

$$\boldsymbol{d}_{\text{diff},jk} = |\boldsymbol{d}_{jn} - \text{median}\left(\boldsymbol{S}^0_{jk}\right)| \quad (11)$$

is calculated and stored in the matrix $\boldsymbol{S}^0_{\text{diff},jk}$. Based on the elements in $\boldsymbol{S}^0_{\text{diff},jk}$, the MAD is given by

$$\hat{\boldsymbol{\sigma}}^0_{jk} = 1.483 \cdot \text{median}\left(\boldsymbol{S}^0_{\text{diff},jk}\right) \quad (12)$$

and the corresponding covariance matrix is

$$\hat{\boldsymbol{\Sigma}}^0_{jk}(r,s) = \begin{cases} \left(\hat{\boldsymbol{\sigma}}^0_{jks}\right)^2, & \forall r = s = 1, \ldots, q \\ 0, & \forall r \neq s \end{cases} \tag{13}$$

with $\hat{\boldsymbol{\sigma}}^0_{jks}$ denoting the standard deviation estimate in each spatial direction of the feature space. Note that the covariance matrix calculated in Eq. (13) is a diagonal matrix. This computationally simple robust estimator is only applicable when the entries of the feature vectors are assumed to be independent of each other. The estimates of the sample covariance matrix and the M-estimator do not require this assumption and are, in general, not diagonal matrices.

Since the order in which the cluster centroids are stored by K-Medians is random, it may differ between two nodes. Thus, it has to be assured that the data which is exchanged by the nodes refers to the same classes. This is achieved by a unique initial ordering of the class centroids and covariance matrices among all nodes in the network: starting with the class centroids and covariance matrices stored for the first class of a preset reference node, all other nodes calculate the Euclidean distance of the respective entries corresponding to all stored classes and those of the first class of the reference node. The data with the smallest Euclidean distance to the reference entries are re-stored at the position corresponding to the first class. This procedure is repeated for all classes stored by the nodes in the network.

Having obtained a consistent data structure, each node j exchanges its own feature vectors $\boldsymbol{S}^0_{jk}$ for each class $\mathcal{C}_k$ with its neighbors $i \in \mathcal{B}_j$. All nodes store their own as well as the features received from their neighbors in an initial matrix $\boldsymbol{V}^0_{jk}$. In the following clustering/classification procedure, $\boldsymbol{S}^0_{jk}$ and $\boldsymbol{V}^0_{jk}$ are extended to $\boldsymbol{S}_{jkn}$ and $\boldsymbol{V}_{jkn}$ in every time step n by adding columns containing the new feature vectors received at time step n.

This completes the initialization phase, which is followed by the exchange phase, where each new observation $\mathbf{d}_{jn}$, $n = N_t + 1, \ldots, N$, is classified according to the following diffusion-procedure:

*1. **Exchange Step:*** If there are new, unshared feature vectors, each node j adds them to $\boldsymbol{V}_{jkn}$ and broadcasts them to its neighbors $i \in \mathcal{B}_j$.
*2. **Adaptation Step:*** Each node j determines preliminary local estimates $\hat{\boldsymbol{\psi}}_{jkn}$ and $\hat{\boldsymbol{\Sigma}}^*_{jkn}$ at time n based on the feature vectors stored in $\boldsymbol{V}_{jkn}$ analogously to –(13) with $\boldsymbol{V}_{jkn}$ replacing $\boldsymbol{S}_{jkn}$. In order to be capable of dealing with non-stationary time-varying signals, a window length l_w is introduced which limits the size of $\boldsymbol{V}_{jkn}$ by only retaining the latest l_w elements which were added to $\boldsymbol{V}_{jkn}$.
*3. **Exchange Step:*** Each node exchanges its intermediate estimates $\hat{\boldsymbol{\psi}}_{jkn}$ and $\hat{\boldsymbol{\Sigma}}^*_{jkn}$ with its neighbors.
*4. **Combination Step:*** Each node j adapts its estimates according to

$$\hat{\mathbf{w}}_{jkn} = \alpha \cdot \hat{\boldsymbol{\psi}}_{jkn} + (1-\alpha) \cdot \sum_{b \in \mathcal{B}_j/\{j\}} a_{bkn} \cdot \hat{\boldsymbol{\psi}}_{bkn} \tag{14}$$

and

$$\hat{\boldsymbol{\Sigma}}_{jkn} = \alpha \cdot \hat{\boldsymbol{\Sigma}}^*_{jkn} + (1-\alpha) \cdot \sum_{b \in \mathcal{B}_j/\{j\}} a_{bkn} \cdot \hat{\boldsymbol{\Sigma}}^*_{bkn} \tag{15}$$

with α denoting an adaptation factor which determines the weight which is given to the own estimate and the

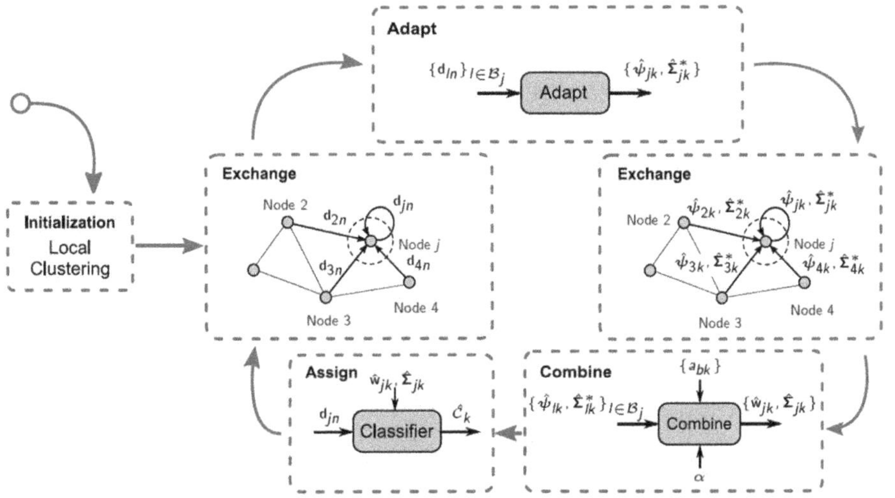

Fig. 3 Overview of the Robust Distance-Based K-Medians Clustering/Classification over Adaptive Diffusion Networks (RDiff K-Med) algorithm

neighborhood estimates, respectively, and a_{bkn} being a weighting factor chosen as

$$a_{bkn} = 1 / \left[\| \hat{\boldsymbol{\psi}}_{bk} - \mathrm{median}(\mathbf{V}_{jkn}) \|^2 \right] \tag{16}$$

with subsequent normalization such that $\sum_{b \in \mathcal{B}_j / \{j\}} a_{bkn} = 1$.

5. Classification Step: In the next step, feature vector $\boldsymbol{d}_{jn}$ is classified by evaluating its distance to each of the estimated class centroids $\hat{\boldsymbol{w}}_{jk}$. The considered distance measures are the Euclidean distance and the Mahalanobis distance given by

$$d_{\mathrm{Eucl}}(\boldsymbol{d}_{jn}, \hat{\boldsymbol{w}}_{jk}) = \sqrt{(\boldsymbol{d}_{jn} - \hat{\boldsymbol{w}}_{jk})^T (\boldsymbol{d}_{jn} - \hat{\boldsymbol{w}}_{jk})} \tag{17}$$

and

$$d_{\mathrm{Mahal}}(\boldsymbol{d}_{jn}, \hat{\boldsymbol{w}}_{jk}) = \sqrt{(\boldsymbol{d}_{jn} - \hat{\boldsymbol{w}}_{jk})^T \hat{\boldsymbol{\Sigma}}_{jk}^{-1} (\boldsymbol{d}_{jn} - \hat{\boldsymbol{w}}_{jk})}. \tag{18}$$

$\boldsymbol{d}_{jn}$ is assigned to the class $\mathcal{C}_k$ for which the respective distance is minimized.

With *Step 1*, the processing chain then starts at the beginning where the previously classified feature vectors are broadcasted to the neighborhood.

An overview of the *RDiff K-Med* algorithm is depicted in Fig. 3, a summary is provided in Table 1.

4.2 Communicationally Efficient Robust Distance-Based K-Medians Clustering/Classification over Adaptive Diffusion Networks (CE RDiff K-Med)

Since the *RDiff K-Med* may be demanding in terms of communication between sensors, which is a major contributor to the energy consumption of the devices [31], an algorithm is proposed which yields similar performance with reduced in-network communication: the "Communicationally Efficient Robust Distance-Based K-Medians Clustering/Classification over Adaptive Diffusion Networks" (CE RDiff K-Med).

The general procedure is similar to the RDiff K-Med except that there is no exchange of feature vectors between the nodes. The steps of the *CE RDiff K-Med* are the following:

1. Adaptation Step: Based on the feature vectors $\boldsymbol{d}_{jn}$ stored in $\boldsymbol{S}_{jkn}$, each node calculates its intermediate estimates $\hat{\boldsymbol{\psi}}_{jkn}$ and $\hat{\boldsymbol{\Sigma}}_{jkn}^*$ according to (9)–(13).

2. Exchange Step: Instead of broadcasting the entire feature vectors, the nodes share only their estimates of the cluster centers $\hat{\boldsymbol{\psi}}_{jkn}$ and the respective covariance matrices $\hat{\boldsymbol{\Sigma}}_{jkn}^*$ with their neighbors.

Table 1 Summary of the RDiff K-Med algorithm

	Algorithm: RDiff K-Med
	Local Clustering Phase
1.	**for the first** N_t **feature vectors do**
2.	**for all** $j = 1, \ldots, J$ **do**
3.	perform K-medians according to (8)
4.	calculate $\hat{\boldsymbol{w}}_{jk}^0$ and $\hat{\boldsymbol{\Sigma}}_{jk}^0$ via (9)-(13)
5.	store classified data in $\boldsymbol{S}_{jk}^0$
6.	**end for**
7.	**for all** $j = 1, \ldots, J$ **do**
8.	perform synchronization of cluster estimates
9.	**end for**
10.	**for all** $j = 1, \ldots, J$ **do**
11.	exchange $\boldsymbol{S}_{jk}^0$ with all neighbors $i \in \mathcal{B}_j$
12.	store received data in $\boldsymbol{V}_{jk}^0$
13.	**end for**
14.	**end for**
	Distributed Classification Phase
15.	**for** $n = N_t, N_t + 1, .., N$ **do**
16.	**for all** $j = 1, \ldots, J$ **do**
17.	broadcast an update for $\boldsymbol{V}_{jkn}$ to all neighbors $i \in \mathcal{B}_j$
18.	**end for**
19.	**for all** $j = 1, \ldots, J$ **do**
20.	determine $\hat{\boldsymbol{\psi}}_{jkn}$ and $\hat{\boldsymbol{\Sigma}}_{jkn}^*$ via (9)-(13)
21.	**end for**
22.	**for all** $j = 1, \ldots, J$ **do**
23.	broadcast $\hat{\boldsymbol{\psi}}_{jkn}$ and $\hat{\boldsymbol{\Sigma}}_{jkn}^*$ to all neighbors $i \in \mathcal{B}_j$
24.	**end for**
25.	**for all** $j = 1, \ldots, J$ **do**
26.	determine $\hat{\boldsymbol{w}}_{jk}(n)$ and $\hat{\boldsymbol{\Sigma}}_{jkn}$ via (14) & (15)
27.	calculate distances from feature vector $\boldsymbol{d}_{jn}$ to all $\hat{\boldsymbol{w}}_{jkn}$ by evaluating (17) or (18)
28.	assign $\boldsymbol{d}_{jn}$ to class $\mathcal{C}_k$ which minimizes (17) or (18)
29.	**end for**
30.	**end for**

3. Combine Step: Each sensor j combines its neighbor's estimates analogously to (14) and (15) in order to obtain improved estimates $\hat{\boldsymbol{w}}_{jkn}$ and $\hat{\boldsymbol{\Sigma}}_{jkn}$.

4. Classification Step: Based on the estimates determined in the previous step, the distance measure of the feature vector to the estimates of the class centroids is evaluated and $\boldsymbol{d}_{jn}$ is classified analogously to the RDiff K-Med. Subsequently, $\boldsymbol{d}_{jn}$ is added to $\boldsymbol{S}_{jkn}$.

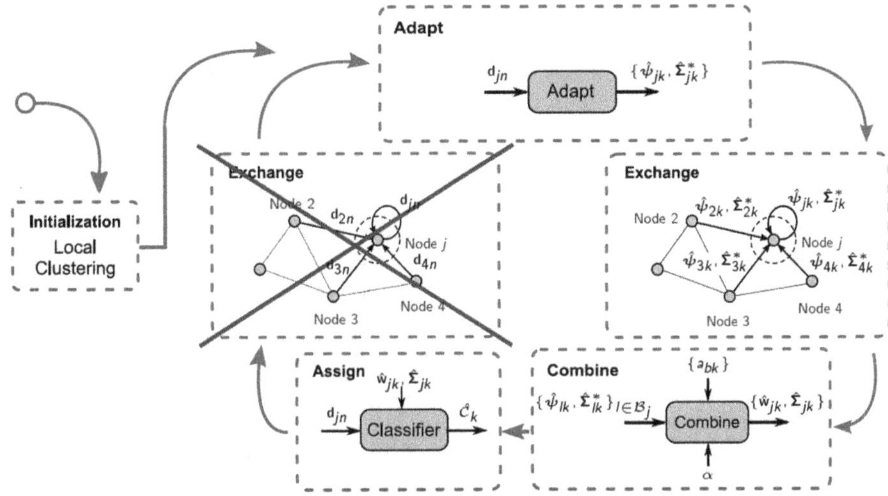

Fig. 4 Overview of the Communicationally Efficient Robust Distance-Based K-Medians Clustering/Classification over Adaptive Diffusion Networks (CE RDiff K-Med) algorithm

An overview of the *CE RDiff K-Med* algorithm is provided in Fig. 4, a summary is given in Table 2.

5 Numerical experiments

This section evaluates the performance of the proposed algorithm numerically in terms of the error rate in a broad range of conditions, i.e., different distributions of the outliers, different percentages of outliers in the feature vectors, different dimensions of the input data, different numbers of clusters and in terms of the adaptation speed in case of non-stationary data. Furthermore, the communication cost for different neighborhood sizes and the computation time as a function of the data dimension is considered. When reasonable, we compare our proposed method to the DKM [17].

5.1 Benchmark: distributed K-means (DKM)

As a benchmark, this paper considers the *Distributed K-Means* (DKM) algorithm by Forero et al., for details, see [17]. The basic idea of the DKM is to cluster the observations into a given number of groups, such that the sum of squared-errors is minimized, that is

$$\arg\min_{\mathbf{w}_k,\mu^p_{jnk}} \frac{1}{2}\sum_{j=1}^{J}\sum_{k=1}^{K}\sum_{n=1}^{N_j}\mu^p_{jnk}\|\mathbf{d}_{jn}-\mathbf{w}_k\|^2, \tag{19}$$

where $\mathbf{w}_k$ is the cluster center for class k, $\mu_{jnk} \in [0,1]$ is the membership coefficient of $\mathbf{d}_{jn}$ to class k, and $p \in [1,+\infty]$ is a tuning parameter. The DKM iteratively solves the surrogate augmented Lagrangian of a distributed clustering problem based on (19) while exchanging the resulting parameters among neighboring nodes.

Although the DKM achieves very good performance in many scenarios, a major drawback is that the clustering is

Table 2 Summary of the CE RDiff K-Med

Algorithm: CE RDiff K-Med
Local Clustering Phase
for the first N_t **feature vectors do**
for all $j = 1,\ldots,J$ **do**
perform K-medians according to (8)
calculate w^0_{jk} and $\hat{\boldsymbol{\Sigma}}^0_{jk}$ via (9)-(13)
store classified data in $\boldsymbol{S}^0_{jk}$
end for
for all $j = 1,\ldots,J$ **do**
perform synchronization of cluster estimates
end for
end for
Distributed Classification Phase
for $n = N_t, N_t+1, .., N$ **do**
for all $j = 1,\ldots,J$ **do**
calculate intermediate estimates $\hat{\boldsymbol{\psi}}_{jkn}$ and $\hat{\boldsymbol{\Sigma}}^*_{jkn}$ according to (9)-(13)
broadcast $\hat{\boldsymbol{\psi}}_{jkn}$ and $\hat{\boldsymbol{\Sigma}}^*_{jkn}$ to all neighbors $i \in \mathcal{B}_j$
end for
for all $j = 1,\ldots,J$ **do**
determine $\hat{\boldsymbol{w}}_{jkn}$ and $\hat{\boldsymbol{\Sigma}}_{jkn}$ via (14)
calculate distances from feature vector $\boldsymbol{d}_{jn}$ to all $\hat{\boldsymbol{w}}_{jkn}$ by evaluating (17) or (18)
assign $\boldsymbol{d}_{jn}$ to class $\boldsymbol{C}_k$ which minimizes (17) or (18)
end for
end for

performed based on all available data and that it may need a high number of iterations until it converges to its final solution. This property makes the DKM difficult to use in real-time applications where an observation needs to be classified based on streaming data, such as for example in speaker labeling for MDMT speech enhancement [2] or object labeling in MDMT video enhancement for camera networks [9]. In addition to that, the performance of the DKM is limited in scenarios where feature vectors contain outliers.

5.2 Simulation setup

The simulations are based on a scenario with $J = 10$ nodes which are randomly distributed in space. Each node is connected to the four neighboring nodes which have the smallest Euclidean distance. Unless mentioned otherwise, classification is performed on $K = 3$ classes with centers $\mathbf{w}_1 = (1,1,1)^T$, $\mathbf{w}_2 = (1,4,3)^T$, $\mathbf{w}_3 = (3,1,1)^T$. Each sample $\mathbf{d}_{jn}$ is drawn at random from class k from the density $\mathcal{N}(\mathbf{d}_{jn}; \mathbf{w}_k, \Sigma_k)$ with covariance matrices $\mathbf{\Sigma}_1 = (1, 0.01, 0.01)^T \mathbf{I}_3$, $\mathbf{\Sigma}_2 = (0.16, 4, 0.16)^T \mathbf{I}_3$ and $\mathbf{\Sigma}_3 = (0.25, 0.01, 4)^T \mathbf{I}_3$. Each node has $N_J = 80$ samples available, 20 for the initialization and 60 for real-time classification. K-Medians is run three times, and the result which minimizes (8) is used for the classification. The parameters for the benchmark algorithm DKM are set $p = \nu = 2$, where $p = 2$ enables soft clustering and $\nu = 2$ is the tuning parameter which yields the best results in the performance tests in [17]. The result is obtained having all $N_J = 80$ samples per node available. Since the performance of the DKM depends on the number of iterations, we provide simulation results for multiple choices of the amount of iterations.

The generation of outliers considers a certain percentage of samples to be replaced by a new sample which is drawn from a contaminating distribution (Gaussian or chi-square). The error rate is calculated based on the classified samples excluding any outliers. The displayed results represent the averages that are based on 100 Monte-Carlo runs.

5.3 Simulation results

In Fig. 5, the impact of the dimension of the feature vectors on the performance is depicted. The data is generated by concatenating the mean values and covariance matrices until they have the according dimension. For example, $\mathbf{w}_3 = (3,1,1)^T$ is changed to $\mathbf{w}_3 = (3,1,1,3,1,1)^T$ and $\mathbf{\Sigma}_3 = (0.25, 0.01, 4)^T \mathbf{I}_3$ becomes $\mathbf{\Sigma}_3 = (0.25, 0.01, 4, 0.25, 0.01, 4)^T \mathbf{I}_6$ in order to obtain data of dimension $q = 6$ and so on. For increasing data dimension, the error rates for all considered algorithms decreases continuously.

Figure 6 depicts the error rate of the algorithms under test as a function of the percentage of outliers in the data, where 0 % corresponds to the outlier free case. Here, the outliers are drawn at random from a Gaussian distribution with the density $\mathcal{N}((10, 10, 10)^T, \mathbf{I}_3)$. The simulation is run with the different estimators of covariance introduced in Section 3, the location is estimated using the median. The robust distance measures result in smaller error rates than the Euclidean distance.

Since in real-world scenarios, the outliers usually do not follow any specific distribution, the question arises how the algorithms deal with other types of outliers, e.g., from a skewed heavy tailed distribution. For the evaluation of this scenario, the outliers are now generated by a chi-square distribution with different degrees of freedom ν for each class: to a certain percentage of the feature vectors a vector is added which is drawn at random from a chi-square distribution where for each class, different values

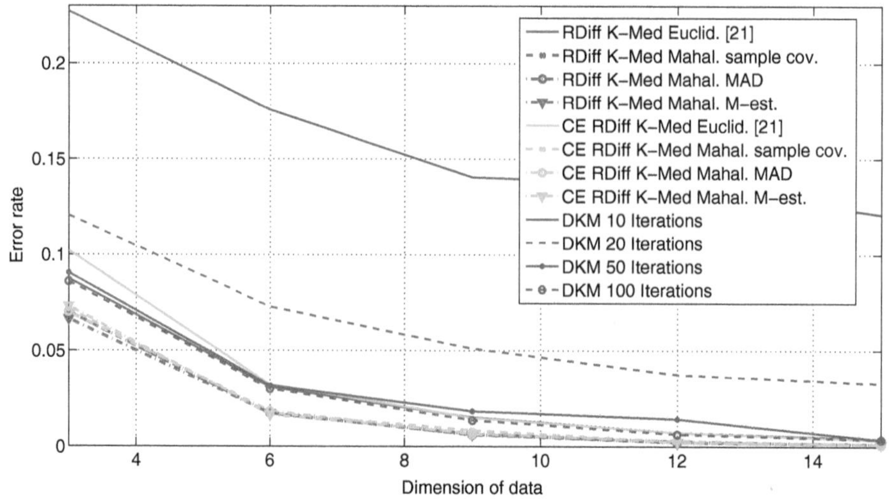

Fig. 5 Error rate as a function of the data dimension

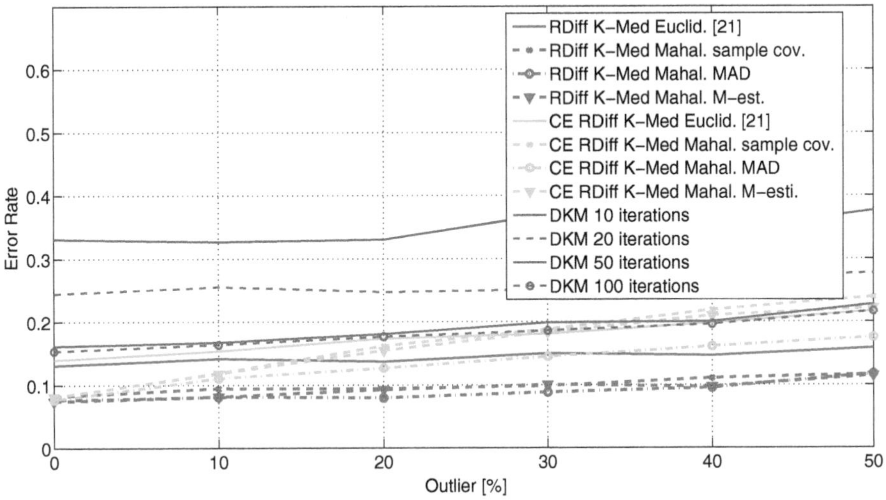

Fig. 6 Average error rate for different estimators of covariance as a function of the amount of outliers from a Gaussian distribution with the density $\mathcal{N}((10, 10, 10)^T, \mathbf{I}_3)$

for ν are chosen. This is done in order to create a non-symmetric outlier distribution instead of a constant shift of the mean of the outlier distribution for all classes. In this manner, for the first class $\mathcal{C}_1$, a randomly drawn vector of dimension q with $\nu_1 = 3$ is added to a certain number of data vectors, a vector with $\nu_2 = 5$ is subtracted from corresponding feature vectors of class $\mathcal{C}_2$ and for $\mathcal{C}_3$ a different random number is drawn for each direction in space: generated with $\nu_{3,1} = 4$, $\nu_{3,2} = 1$ and $\nu_{3,3} = 7$ for x, y and z direction, respectively, whereby $\nu_{3,2} = 1$ is subtracted from the y-component. For this simulation, a scenario is chosen with more distinct clusters with centroids $\mathbf{w}_1 = (1, 1, 1)^T$, $\mathbf{w}_2 = (0, 5, 3)^T$, $\mathbf{w}_3 = (3, 3, 7)^T$. The result is given in Fig. 7.

Figure 8 shows the error performance as a function of the number of feature vectors which are available per node. Both the DKM for $i = 10$ and $i = 20$ and the RDiff K-Med and CE RDiff K-Med with robust estimation methods show a slightly decreasing error rate with a growing number of feature vectors.

For the next experiment, we evaluate a more complex scenario consisting of eight clusters of different shapes and sizes distributed in space (see Fig. 9). The centroids are chosen as $\mathbf{w}_1 = (1, 0, 3)^T$, $\mathbf{w}_2 = (1, 4, 3)^T$,

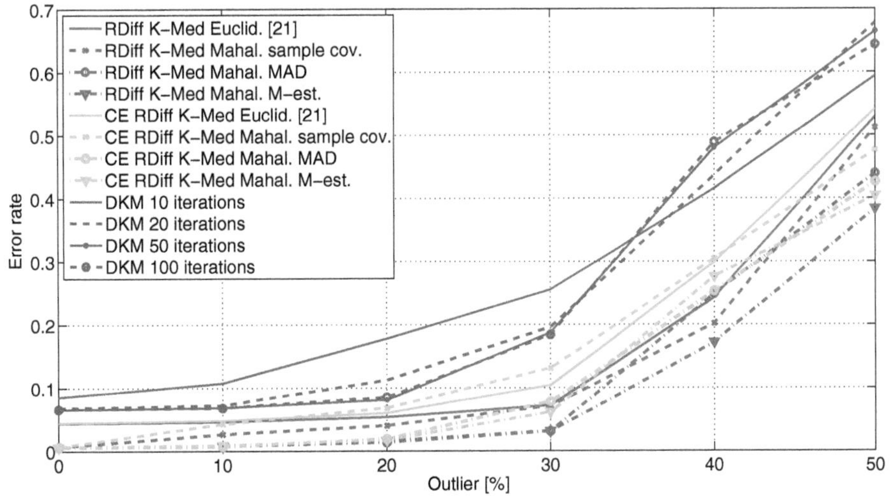

Fig. 7 Average error rate for different estimators of covariance as a function of the amount of outliers in the data, where the outliers follow a chi-square distribution

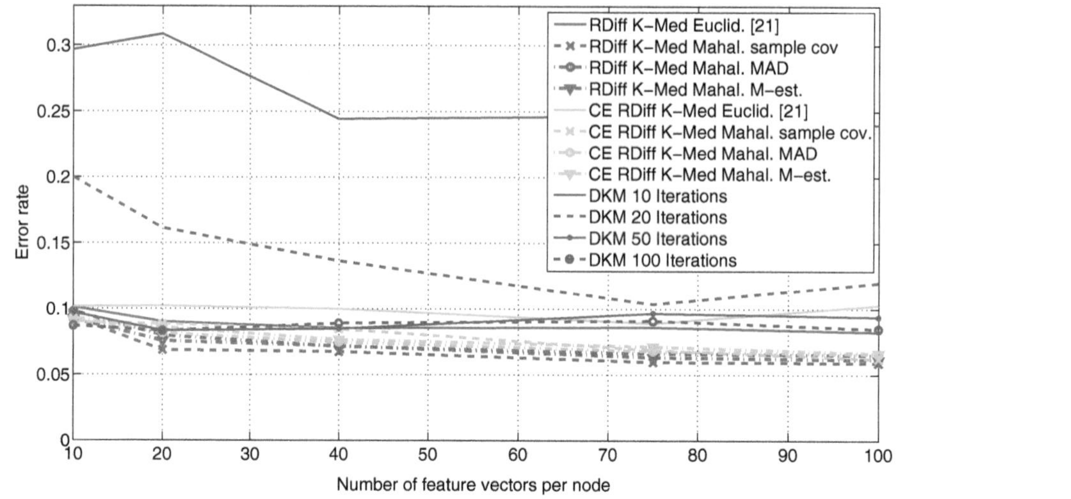

Fig. 8 Error rate as a function of the available number of feature vectors per node

$\mathbf{w}_3 = (1,0,6)^T$, $\mathbf{w}_4 = (-1,3,3)^T$, $\mathbf{w}_5 = (4,4,4)^T$, $\mathbf{w}_6 = (6,3,7)^T$, $\mathbf{w}_7 = (4.5,7,6)^T$ and $\mathbf{w}_8 = (2,4,7)^T$ with corresponding covariance matrices $\mathbf{\Sigma}_1 = (0.1,0.1,1)^T\mathbf{I}_3$, $\mathbf{\Sigma}_2 = (0.1,0.4,1)^T\mathbf{I}_3$, $\mathbf{\Sigma}_3 = (2,0.1,0.5)^T\mathbf{I}_3$, $\mathbf{\Sigma}_4 = (0.4,1.6,0.4)^T\mathbf{I}_3$, $\mathbf{\Sigma}_5 = (0.2,1.2,0.1)^T\mathbf{I}_3$, $\mathbf{\Sigma}_6 = (0.25,0.3,1.5)^T\mathbf{I}_3$, $\mathbf{\Sigma}_7 = (0.8,0.5,0.2)^T\mathbf{I}_3$ and $\mathbf{\Sigma}_8 = (0.5,0.5,0.3)^T\mathbf{I}_3$. The outliers are drawn randomly from a Gaussian distribution with the density $\mathcal{N}((10,10,10)^T,\mathbf{I}_3)$. The results are provided in Fig. 10.

The former performance studies were based on the assumption that the data is stationary. Next, it is examined how the proposed algorithms perform for non-stationary feature vectors. For this purpose the value of a single considered cluster centroid is instantly changed during the classification process. The adaptation speed of the RDiff K-Med and the CE RDiff K-Med is examined for different window sizes l_w and different values for α (see Eqs. (14) and (15)) by calculating the error which is given by the

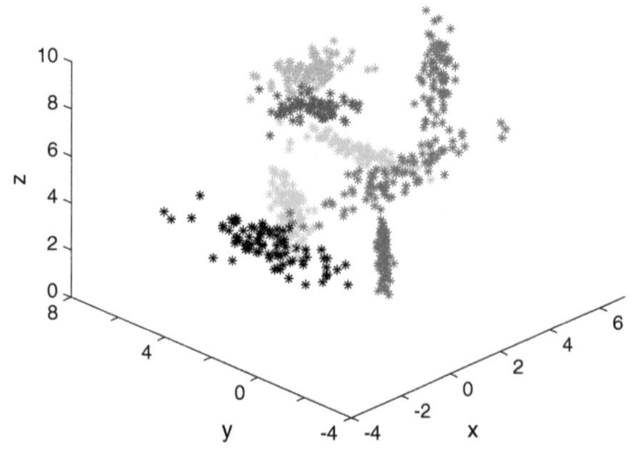

Fig. 9 Scenario with eight clusters of different shapes and sizes

norm of the difference between the true value and the estimate of the cluster centroid. Unlike the CE RDiff K-Med the RDiff K-Med stores not only its own feature vectors, but also the feature vectors from its neighborhood, it has ($|\ \mathcal{B}_j\ | + 1$) data vectors per time step available instead of only one. In order to make the window sizes for both algorithms comparable, l_w is chosen such that it contains the feature vectors of l_w time steps. As a consequence, the compared window length of the RDiff K-Med corresponds to ($|\ \mathcal{B}_j\ | + 1$) times the window length of the CE RDiff K-Med. The result is shown in Fig. 11. As depicted in the upper plot, a large window size results in a slower adaptation speed. The RDiff K-Med adapts faster to the true cluster centroid than the CE RDiff K-Med since its estimation is based on more available samples. However, the CE RDiff K-Med yields a smaller error compared to the RDiff K-Med when both have adapted to the true value. The choice of the factor α (see lower plot) has no significant impact on the RDiff K-Med. For the CE RDiff K-Med a smaller value for α (and therefore a higher weighting of the estimates of the neighboring nodes) leads to a higher adaptation speed. Since it has only a small amount of feature vectors available, this method is dependent on the data exchange with its neighbors.

5.4 Communication cost and computation time

Apart from the error rate, further performance measures of great importance are the communication cost as well as computation time. Since the communication costs contribute stronger to the energy consumption in the wireless devices than the computational costs [31], the former should be kept as low as possible. Figure 12 depicts the communication costs for the standard scenario in dependence of various neighborhood cardinalities of

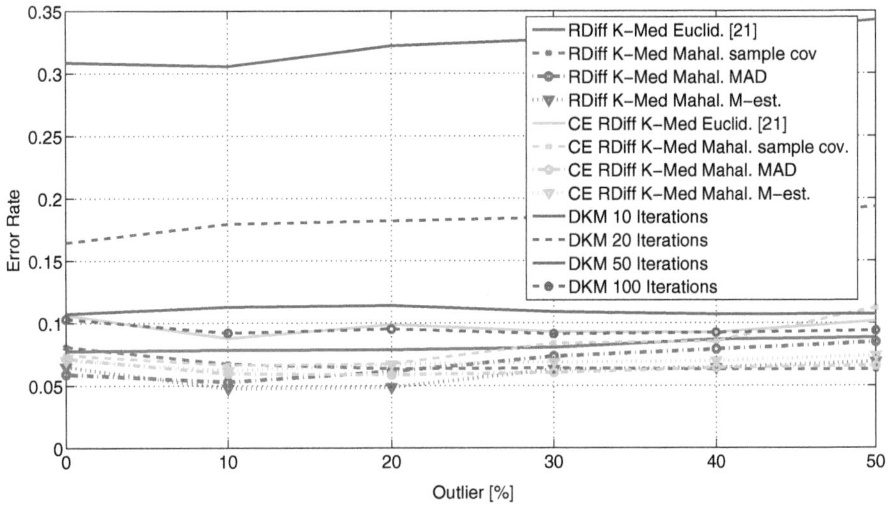

Fig. 10 Average error rate for different estimators of covariance as a function of the amount of outliers from a Gaussian distribution with the density $\mathcal{N}((10, 10, 10)^T, \mathbf{I}_3)$

each node. The communication cost displayed in Fig. 12 is specified in data units, where one matrix entry forms one unit. It becomes clear that the choice of the neighborhood size has a high impact on the communication costs. For the DKM the number of iterations is crucial. While for a small amount of clusters few iterations may be sufficient, the number of iterations that is necessary for a good performance increases for higher cluster numbers (see [17] for more detailed information) which results in strongly increasing communication costs.

The computation time as a function of the dimension of the data is provided by Fig. 13 and given in seconds (using an Intel Core i7 5820K). Whereas the DKM has a constant computation time independent of the data dimension, it increases with the data dimension for the proposed algorithms. The resulting computation time for using the M-estimator is notably higher than for the other approaches which makes it hardly real-time capable. The other estimation methods take equally long for each algorithm while the CE RDiff K-Med has a much shorter

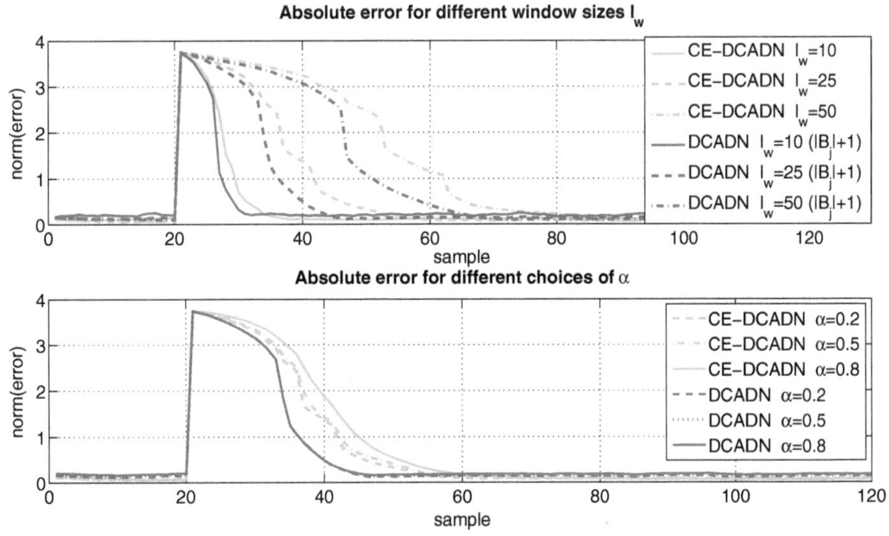

Fig. 11 Behavior of the norm of the difference vector of true and estimated cluster centroid for a non-stationary feature vector which changes abruptly at sample 21. In the upper figure, the norm of the error is depicted for $\alpha = 0.2$, the lower figure is obtained with $l_w = 25$ and $l_w = 25(|\mathcal{B}_j| + 1)$, respectively

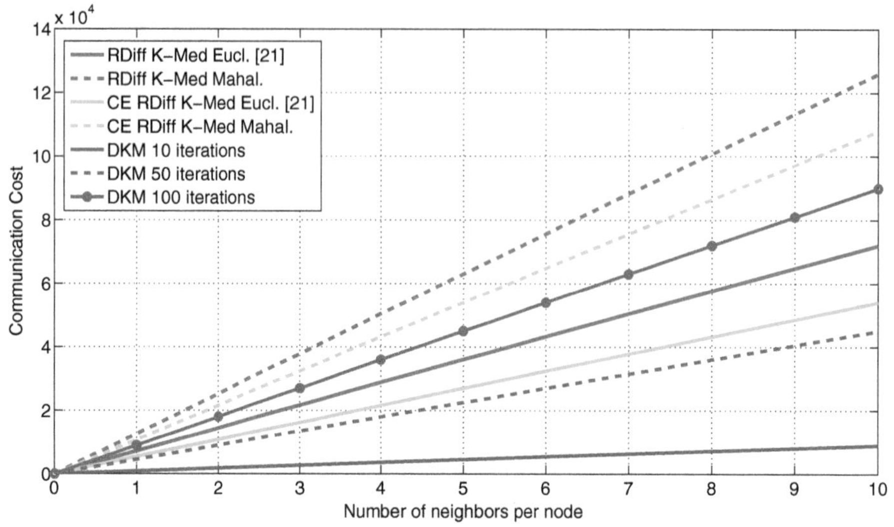

Fig. 12 Communication cost for different neighborhood sizes

computation time due to the smaller data sets it has to work with.

6 Conclusions

Two generic robust diffusion-based distributed hybrid classification algorithms were proposed, which can be adapted to various object/source labeling applications in a decentralized MDMT network. A performance comparison to the DKM was provided and the proposed methods showed promising results. Even in direct comparison with the DKM which permanently has access to all available samples, since it is operating in batch mode, our proposed online methods provide comparable error rates to the DKM using 50 iterations and more. Unlike the DKM, both the RDiff K-Med and CE RDiff K-Med are potentially real-time capable.

The choice of the distance metric has a considerable impact on the performance of the proposed classification algorithms. Using the Mahalanobis distance yields significantly smaller error rates compared to the Euclidean distance while resulting in higher communication costs and computation time.

Future work will include the application of this algorithm to real-world speech source labeling, object labeling in camera networks as well as labeling of semantic information based on occupancy grid maps for autonomous mapping and navigation with multiple rescue robots [32].

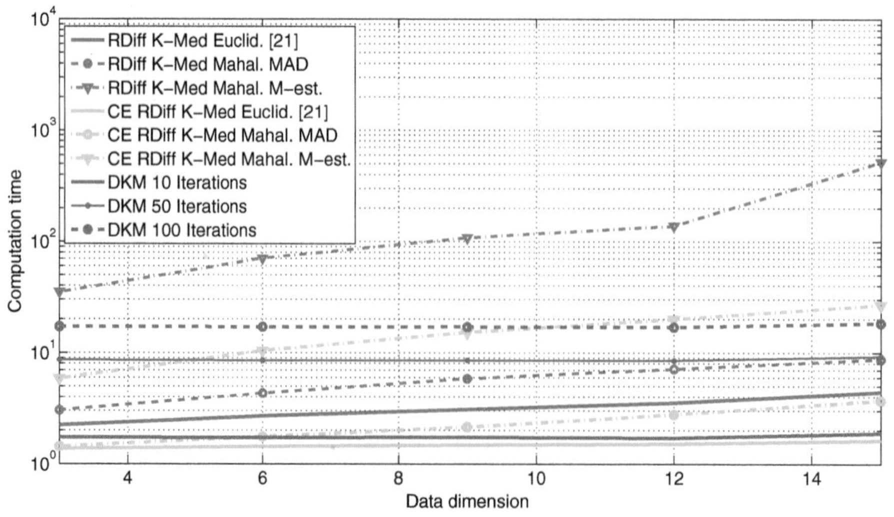

Fig. 13 Computation time in dependency on the dimension of the feature vectors

Competing interests
The authors declare that they have no competing interests.

Acknowledgements
This work of P. Binder was supported by the LOEWE initiative (Hessen, Germany) within the NICER project and by the German Research Foundation (DFG). The work of M. Muma was supported by the Future and Emerging Technologies (FET) programme within the Seventh Framework Programme for Research of the European Commission (HANDiCAMS), under FET-Open grant number: 323944.

References

1. E Hänsler, *Statistische Signale: Grundlagen und Anwendungen*. (Springer, Berlin, 2013)
2. A Bertrand, M Moonen, Distributed signal estimation in sensor networks where nodes have different interests. Signal Process. **92**(7), 1679–1690 (2012)
3. N Bogdanovic, J Plata-Chaves, K Berberidis, Distributed incremental-based LMS for node-specific adaptive parameter estimation. IEEE Trans. Signal Process. **62**(20), 5382–5397 (2014)
4. J Plata-Chaves, A Bertrand, M Moonen, in *Acoustics, Speech and Signal Processing (ICASSP), 2015 IEEE Int. Conf. on*. Distributed signal estimation in a wireless sensor network with partially overlapping node-specific interests or source observability, (2015), pp. 5808-5812
5. J Chen, C Richard, AH Sayed, Diffusion LMS over multitask networks. IEEE Trans. Signal Process. **63**(11), 2733–2748 (2015)
6. J Chen, C Richard, AH Sayed, Multitask diffusion adaptation over networks. IEEE Trans. Signal Process. **62**(16), 4129–4144 (2014)
7. E Hänsler, G Schmidt, *Speech and Audio Processing in Adverse Environments*. (Springer, Berlin, 2008)
8. S Chouvardas, M Muma, K Hamaidi, S Theodoridis, AM Zoubir, in *Proc. 40th IEEE Int. Conf. Acoustics, Speech and Signal Processing (ICASSP)*. Distributed robust labeling of audio sources in heterogeneous wireless sensor networks, (2015), pp. 5783–5787
9. FK Teklehaymanot, M Muma, B Béjar-Haro, P Binder, AM Zoubir, M Vetterli, in *Proc. 12th IEEE AFRICON (accepted)*. Robust diffusion-based unsupervised object labelling in distributed camera networks, (2015)
10. A D'Costa, A Sayeed, in *IEEE Military Communications Conference (MILCOM)*. Data versus decision fusion for distributed classification in sensor networks, vol. 1, (2003), pp. 585–5901
11. D Li, KD Wong, YH Hu, AM Sayeed, Detection, classification and tracking of targets in distributed sensor networks. Technical report, Department of Electrical and Computer Engineering, University of Wisconsin-Madison, USA
12. F Fagnani, S Fosson, C Ravazzi, A distributed classification/estimation algorithm for sensor networks. SIAM J Control Optim. **52**(1), 189–218 (2014)
13. M Hai, S Zhang, L Zhu, Y Wang, in *Ind. Control and Electron. Eng. (ICICEE), 2012 Int. Conf. On*. A survey of distributed clustering algorithms, (2012), pp. 1142–1145
14. E Kokiopoulou, P Frossard, Distributed classification of multiple observation sets by consensus. IEEE Trans. Signal Process. **59**(1), 104–114 (2011)
15. B Malhotra, I Nikolaidis, J Harms, Distributed classification of acoustic targets in wireless audio-sensor networks. Comput. Netw. **52**(13), 2582–2593 (2008)
16. RD Nowak, Distributed em algorithms for density estimation and clustering in sensor networks. IEEE Trans. Signal Process. **51**(8), 2245–2253 (2003)
17. P Forero, A Cano, GB Giannakis, et al., Distributed clustering using wireless sensor networks. IEEE J. Sel. Topics Signal Process. **5**(4), 707–724 (2011)
18. S-Y Tu, AH Sayed, Distributed decision-making over adaptive networks. IEEE Trans. Signal Process. **62**(5), 1054–1069 (2014)
19. D Wang, J Li, Y Zhou, in *IEEE/SP 15th Workshop on Stat. Signal Process. (SSP)*. Support vector machine for distributed classification: a dynamic consensus approach, (2009), pp. 753–756
20. X Zhao, AH Sayed, Distributed clustering and learning over networks. IEEE Trans. Signal Process. **63**(13), 3285–3300 (2015)
21. P Binder, M Muma, AM Zoubir, in *Proc. 40th IEEE Int. Conf. Acoustics, Speech and Signal Processing (ICASSP)*. Robust and computationally efficient diffusion-based classification in distributed networks, (Brisbane, Australia, 2015), pp. 3432–3436
22. X Zhao, AH Sayed, in *Proc. International Workshop on Cognitive Information Processing (CIP)*. Clustering via diffusion adaptation over networks, (2012), pp. 1–6
23. AH Sayed, Adaptation, learning, and optimization over networks. Found. Trends Mach. Learn. **7**(4-5), 311–801 (2014)
24. S Khawatmi, AM Zoubir, AH Sayed, in *Proc. 23rd European Signal Processing Conf. (EUSIPCO). Nice, France*. Decentralized clustering over adaptive networks, (Nice, France, 2015), pp. 2745–2749
25. AH Sayed, Adaptive networks. Proc. IEEE. **102**(4), 460–497 (2014)
26. AM Zoubir, V Koivunen, Y Chakhchoukh, M Muma, Robust estimation in signal processing: a tutorial-style treatment of fundamental concepts. Signal Process. Mag. IEEE. **29**(4), 61–80 (2012)
27. PA Forero, V Kekatos, GB Giannakis, Robust clustering using outlier-sparsity regularization. IEEE Trans. Signal Process. **60**(8), 4163–4177 (2012)
28. R Maronna, D Martin, V Yohai, *Robust Statistics*. (John Wiley & Sons, Chichester, 2006)
29. PJ Huber, et al., Robust estimation of a location parameter. Ann. Math. Stat. **35**(1), 73–101 (1964)
30. FS Cattivelli, AH Sayed, Diffusion LMS strategies for distributed estimation. IEEE Trans. Signal Process. **58**(3), 1035–1048 (2010)
31. D Estrin, L Girod, G Pottie, M Srivastava, in *IEEE Int. Conf. Acoustics, Speech and Signal Processing (ICASSP)*. Instrumenting the world with wireless sensor networks, vol. 4, (2001), pp. 2033–2036
32. S Kohlbrecher, J Meyer, T Graber, K Petersen, U Klingauf, O von Stryk, in *RoboCup 2013: Robot World Cup XVII*. Hector open source modules for autonomous mapping and navigation with rescue robots (Springer, Berlin, 2014), pp. 624–631

11

Cognitive radar ambiguity function optimization for unimodular sequence

Jindong Zhang, Xiaoyan Qiu*, Changli Shi and Yue Wu

Abstract

An important characteristic of a cognitive radar is the capability to adjust its transmitted waveform to adapt to the radar environment. The adaptation of the transmit waveform requires an effective framework to synthesize waveforms sharing a desired ambiguity function (AF). With the volume-invariant property of AF, the integrated sidelobe level (ISL) can only be minimized in a certain area on the time delay and Doppler frequency shift plane. In this paper, we propose a new algorithm for unimodular sequence to minimize the ISL of an AF in a certain area based on the phase-only conjugate gradient and phase-only Newton's method. For improving detection performance of a moving target detecting (MTD) radar system, slow-time ambiguity function (STAF) is defined, and the proposed algorithm is presented to optimize the range-Doppler response. We also devise a cognitive approach for a MTD radar by adaptively altering its sidelobe distribution of STAF. At the simulation stage, the performance of the proposed algorithm is assessed to show their capability to properly shape the AF and STAF of the transmitted waveform.

Keywords: Cognitive radar, Unimodular sequence synthesis, Optimization algorithm, Ambiguity function, Slow-time ambiguity function

1 Introduction

Cognitive radar (CR) is established by the notion of a cognitive cycle, in which the two key aspects are perception of the environment and control exercised on the environment by virtue of feedback of the information that was learnt through perception. Figure 1 summarizes the essence of cognitive radar in its most basic forms. In cognitive radar system, how the transmitted waveform adapts in response to information about the radar environment is a key enabling step [1]. Many of the research efforts have been devoted to radar waveform optimization methods, which have been developed based on different performance objectives. For detecting a particular target in the presence of additive signal-dependent noise, waveform optimization method, developed by Guerci [2, 3], is evaluated in terms of the signal-to-interference-plus-noise ratio (SINR) under a particular model of the system, interference, clutter, and targets. For estimating the parameters of a target from a given ensemble, the radar waveform should be designed to maximize the mutual information (MI) between the received signal and the target ensemble [4]. Besides, exploiting a variety of knowledge sources, the radar can locate the range-Doppler bins where strong unwanted returns are predicted and synthesize a waveform whose ambiguity function (AF) exhibits low values in those interfering bins. In the previous work in [5], the idea of designing the slow-time ambiguity function (STAF) of the transmit waveform in a CR system has been discussed.

In radar systems, unimodular (i.e., constant modulus) sequences are usually exploited and optimized for transmission. The integrated sidelobe level (ISL) of the autocorrelation function (ACF) is often used to express the goodness of the correlation properties of a given sequence. A transmitted sequence with low ISL value reduces the risk that the echo signal of the weak target of interest is drawn in the sidelobes of the strong one or clutter interference [6]. Additionally, the unimodular sequence has low peak-to-average power ratio (PAR) which is especially desired for the transmitter [7]. A lot of literature has been focused on the topic of unimodular sequence synthesis with good properties (in particular, the ACF with low ISL values) and the many references included. These unimodular synthesis methods can be summarized into two types. The first

*Correspondence: qxynuaa@126.com
College of Electronic and Information Engineering, Nanjing University of Aeronautics and Astronautics, Nanjing 210016, China

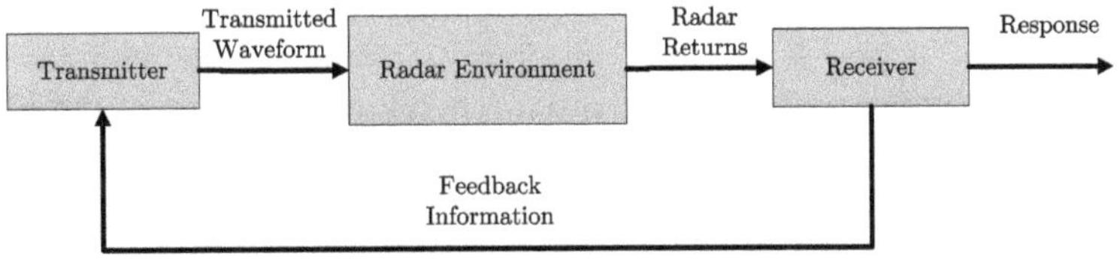

Fig. 1 Cognitive radar in its most basic form

is to use some famous sequences, such as the Golomb sequence [8], Frank sequence [9], and a pseudo random sequence, which have been proved with low sidelobes and applied in the radar systems successfully. The second is to synthesize the sequence with minimized ISL metric by the optimization algorithms [10–12]. Because the problem of reducing the ISL metric may have multiple local minima, the exhaustive search algorithm has been proposed in [12]. The computational burden of this kind of algorithm increases significantly as the sequence length increases. Some optimization algorithms have been designed as the local minimization algorithms to overcome this default [13–17]. Most of these algorithms can obtain fast convergence in descent gradient and provide quick solutions. It is worthwhile to mention that the cyclic algorithms proposed in [13] can design unimodular sequences that have virtually zero autocorrelation sidelobes in a specified lag interval and long sequences.

In this paper, we mainly consider the ambiguity function synthesis problem for unimodular sequences. According to Woodward's definition, AF is a two-dimensional function defined on the time delay and Doppler frequency shift plane. The AF is defined as follows:

$$\chi(\tau,f_d)=\int_{-\infty}^{\infty}s(t)s^*(t+\tau)e^{j2\pi f_d t}dt, \tag{1}$$

where τ and f_d denote the time delay and Doppler frequency shift, respectively, and $s(t)$ is the radar waveform. It describes the matched filter response to the target signature. The shape of AF indicates the range and Doppler resolutions of the radar system. It also demonstrates the matched filter output with respect to the interference produced by unwanted returns. It should come with no surprise that extensive research on AF synthesis exists in the literature [18–23]. Despite so much effort on this problem, few methods can synthesize the desired AF successfully. In [22], the cross ambiguity function was considered instead of AF. A pair of the waveform and receiving filter was developed simultaneously. Aubry et al. [23] deal with the design of phase-coded pulse train, which approximately maximizes the detection performance. A similarity constraint between the ambiguity functions of the devised waveform and the pulse train encoded with the prefixed sequence is required. De Maio et al. [5] also discuss the design problem of phase-coded pulse train. The average value of the STAF of the transmitted signal over some range-Doppler bins is minimized with prior information.

Note that the volume of a AF, which is defined as

$$V=\int_{-\infty}^{\infty}\int_{-\infty}^{\infty}|\chi(\tau,f_d)|^2d\tau df_d \tag{2}$$

is equal to the energy of $s(t)$. The volume-invariant property of AF prevents the synthesis of an ideal AF that has a high narrow peak in the origin and zero sidelobes everywhere else. In this paper, we mainly focus on the synthesis of an AF that has a clear area close to the origin or minimized ISL in a certain area on the time delay and Doppler frequency shift plane.

Additionally, it is known that a moving target detecting (MTD) radar system is designed to observe the target in range-Doppler bins [6]. Its detection performance is considerably affected by the range-Doppler response of the waveform used to illuminate the operation environment. Considering that a MTD radar transmits a burst of pulses in slow time, the STAF is defined to evaluate the range-Doppler response.

The main contribution of this paper is as follows:

(1) For optimizing the shape of an AF, the optimization algorithm is proposed based on the phase-only conjugate gradient (POCG) and phase-only Newton's method (PONM), which have been successfully applied in optimizing the phased array radar beam pattern.
(2) We extend the PCA and present an algorithm for optimizing the shape of STAF.
(3) A cognitive approach for a MTD radar system is also provided in this work. The radar system can adaptively alternate its sidelobe distribution of STAF according to the interested area and clutter distribution on the time delay and Doppler frequency shift plane. This scheme is especially attractive for detecting a target with a small radar cross section (RCS) in a heavy clutter scenario.

The rest of this work is organized as follows. Section 2 discusses the formulation of the ambiguity function synthesis problem of unimodular sequence, and the optimization method based on POCG and PONM are proposed. Section 3 defines the STAF and extends the optimization algorithm for optimizing the shape of STAF of a MTD radar system. A cognitive workflow is also given. Several numerical examples are presented in Section 4. Finally, concluding remarks and directions for future research are presented in Section 5.

2 Ambiguity function synthesis

2.1 Problem formulation

We consider a monostatic radar that transmits a burst of pulses. The transmit signal can be written as

$$s(t) = \sum_{k=1}^{N} s_k p_k(t), \tag{3}$$

where N denotes the number of subpulses, s_k is the sequence code of the kth subpulse, and $p_k(t)$ is the pulse-shaping function. The typical form of $p_k(t)$ is the rectangular pulse and can be expressed as

$$p_k(t) = \frac{1}{\sqrt{t_p}}\text{rect}\left(\frac{t-(k-1)t_p}{t_p}\right), \tag{4}$$

where t_p is the time duration of subpulses and

$$\text{rect}(t) = \begin{cases} 1, \ 0 \le t \le 1; \\ 0, \ \text{elsewhere}. \end{cases} \tag{5}$$

Under the above assumptions, the AF of the transmit signal $s(t)$ can be given by

$$\begin{aligned} \chi_s(\tau,f_d) &= \int_{-\infty}^{\infty} s(t)s^*(t+\tau)e^{j2\pi f_d t}dt \\ &= \sum_{k=1}^{N}\sum_{l=1}^{N} s_k s_l^* \chi_p^{(k,l)}(\tau,f_d), \end{aligned} \tag{6}$$

where

$$\begin{aligned} \chi_p^{(k,l)}(\tau,f_d) &= \int p_k(t)p_l^*(t+\tau)e^{j2\pi f_d t}dt \\ &= e^{j\pi f_d(2k-1)t_p} \cdot \frac{t_p - |\tau-(k-l)t_p|}{t_p} \\ &\times \frac{\sin\pi f_d\left(t_p - |\tau-(k-l)t_p|\right)}{\pi f_d\left(t_p - |\tau-(k-l)t_p|\right)}, \\ &(k-l-1)t_p \le \tau \le (k-l+1)t_p \end{aligned} \tag{7}$$

denotes the cross ambiguity function (CAF) of the pulse-shaping functions $p_k(t)$ and $p_l(t)$.

The AF $\chi_s(\tau,f_d)$ can be rewritten as

$$\chi_s(\tau,f_d) = \mathbf{s}^H\mathbf{R}(\tau,f_d)\mathbf{s}, \tag{8}$$

where $\mathbf{s} = [s_1, s_2, \ldots, s_N]^T \in \mathbb{C}^N$, $\mathbb{C}^N$ denotes the complex N-space, $(\cdot)^T$ and $(\cdot)^H$ indicate transpose and conjugate transpose of a vector or matrix, respectively, and

$$\mathbf{R}(\tau,f_d) = \begin{pmatrix} \chi_p^{(1,1)}(\tau,f_d) & \cdots & \chi_p^{(1,N)}(\tau,f_d) \\ \vdots & & \vdots \\ \chi_p^{(N,1)}(\tau,f_d) & \cdots & \chi_p^{(N,N)}(\tau,f_d) \end{pmatrix} \tag{9}$$

is the subpulse CAF matrix, which is fixed once the pulse-shaping function and the number of subpulses N are given. Therefore, the shape of the AF $\chi_s(\tau,f_d)$ is directly determined by the sequence codes $\{s_k\}_{k=1}^N$ or the phase variables $\{\phi_k\}_{k=1}^N$ of $\{s_k\}_{k=1}^N$.

For the convenience of simplification, the time delay and Doppler frequency shift plane, i.e., $\tau - f_d$ plane, is discretized into grids with sufficient precision. The spacing of the grids is t_p in the time-delay axis and $1/(Mt_p)$ in the Doppler frequency shift axis. By substituing $\tau = nt_p$ and $f_d = m/(Mt_p)$ in Eq. (7), we have

$$\chi_p^{(k,l)}(n,m) = \begin{cases} e^{j\pi(2k-1)m/M}, & k = l+n; \\ 0, & \text{elsewhere} \end{cases} \tag{10}$$

and obtain the discretized AF (DAF), which can be expressed as

$$\chi_s(n,m) = \mathbf{s}^H\mathbf{U}_{n,m}\mathbf{s}, \tag{11}$$

where $\mathbf{U}_{n,m} = \mathbf{R}\left(nt_p, m/(Mt_p)\right)$.

In this work, we aim at synthesizing the AF with a clear area close to the origin or minimized ISL in a certain area on $\tau - f_d$ plane. Considering that the shape of AF can be controlled by the shape of DAF, we exploit the ISL metric of DAF, which is described as

$$\text{ISL} = \sum_{(n,m)\subset I_\Omega} |\chi_s(n,m)|^2, \tag{12}$$

where I_Ω is the subset of the range and Doppler bins $(nt_p, m/Mt_p)$ on $\tau - f_d$ plane. Additionally, the synthesized sequence should have constant modulus, i.e.,

$$s_k = e^{j\phi_k}, k = 1, \ldots, N \tag{13}$$

where ϕ_k is the phase of the kth sequence code s_k. Therefore, we can think of synthesizing the unimodular sequence $\mathbf{s}$ as minimizing the ISL metric in Eq. (12) over the unimodular sequence set.

The ambiguity function synthesis problem in this paper can be formulated as

$$\begin{aligned} \min & \sum_{(n,m)\subset I_\Omega} |\mathbf{s}^H\mathbf{U}_{n,m}\mathbf{s}|^2 \\ \text{s.t.} & \quad |s_k| = 1, \quad k = 1, 2, \ldots, N \end{aligned} \tag{14}$$

The objective function in Eq. (14) is a quartic form, which is relatively difficult to tackle. With the conclusions in [24], the objective function is also a non-convex function. Moreover, the constraint set is a non-convex set. Hence, this problem is a non-convex optimization problem. The paper [25] has suggested that maximum block improvement (MBI) algorithms are capable of providing some good-quality solutions to this kind of problem in polynomial time. A simplified and more practical method relies on the exploitation of a simpler criterion (in particular, a quadratic function) to replace the quartic function [26].

In general, constrained optimization problems such as this one can be difficult to deal with because we must simultaneously perform the optimization and satisfy the constraint. It is worthwhile to point out that unconstrained gradient-based algorithms can be generalized to the constant modular constraint case. Therefore, the constrained optimization problem can be transformed to be unconstrained. With the derivatives of the objective function with respect to the phases, a local optimum can be obtained by gradient-based algorithms, such as the conjugate-gradient method and Newton's method. However, a local minima can also be found in the gradient equation by successive iterations if the Hessian matrix is (semi) positive definite. Furthermore, the application of the iterative algorithm is computational efficient and easy to realize.

Based on the above considerations, accounting for the complicated form of the objective function, we can obtain the local optimum in the first-order and second-order derivatives instead. Although the Hessian matrix is not (semi) positive definite, we can exploit the diagonal loading technique to make it so.

2.2 Optimization analysis

As already highlighted, a highly multi-modal optimization objective inevitably appears in Eq. (14). It is hard for us to obtain the global optimum by the analytical expression or the optimization method. In this section, we expect to find the local optimum for the problem in Eq. (14) and propose a computationally efficient approach.

The first-order and second-order derivatives of the objective function in Eq. (14) can be respectively given by

$$\frac{\partial \text{ISL}}{\partial \phi} = \sum_{(n,m)\subset I_\Omega} \text{Re}\left[\left(\mathbf{s}^H \mathbf{U}_{n,m}\mathbf{s}\right)^* \text{Im}\left(\mathbf{s}^* \odot \mathbf{U}_{n,m}\mathbf{s}\right)\right] \tag{15}$$

$$\begin{aligned}\frac{\partial^2 \text{ISL}}{\partial \phi \partial \phi^T} = &\sum_{(n,m)\subset I_\Omega} \text{Re}\left[\left(\mathbf{s}^H \mathbf{U}_{n,m}\mathbf{s}\right)^* \mathbf{U}_{n,m} \odot \mathbf{s}\mathbf{s}^H\right] \\ &+ \text{Im}\left(\mathbf{s}^* \odot \mathbf{U}_{n,m}\mathbf{s}\right) \text{Im}\left(\mathbf{s}^* \odot \mathbf{U}_{n,m}\mathbf{s}\right)^H,\end{aligned} \tag{16}$$

where $\phi = [\phi_1, \phi_2, \ldots, \phi_N]^T \in \mathbb{R}^N$, $\mathbb{R}^N$ denotes real N-space and $\text{Re}(\cdot)$ and $\text{Im}(\cdot)$ represent the real and imaginary part of a complex number, respectively (see the derivation in Appendix B).

The set of the local minimum (including its global optima) is simply a subset of the stable points $\{\widetilde{\mathbf{s}}\}$, which can be characterized by

$$\left.\frac{\partial \text{ISL}}{\partial \phi}\right|_{\mathbf{s}=\widetilde{\mathbf{s}}} = 0. \tag{17}$$

Moreover, $\widetilde{\mathbf{s}}$ is also a local minimum if and only if

$$\left.\frac{\partial^2 \text{ISL}}{\partial \phi \partial \phi^T}\right|_{\mathbf{s}=\widetilde{\mathbf{s}}} \geq 0. \tag{18}$$

Namely, the Hessian matrix of the ISL metric is required to be (semi) positive definite. With the positive definiteness of $\frac{\partial^2 \text{ISL}}{\partial \phi \partial \phi^T}$, the stable points $\{\widetilde{\mathbf{s}}\}$ form the set of the local minimum.

In the following discussion, we express the Hessian matrix in Eq. (18) as $\mathbf{U}^{\ddagger}$. Note that this matrix can be (semi) positive definite using the diagonal loading technique, which implies

$$\mathbf{U}^{\ddagger} + \lambda N^2 \mathbf{I} \geq 0, \tag{19}$$

where $\mathbf{I}$ is an identity matrix, λ is a constant coefficient, which should satisfy $\lambda + \delta_{min}(\mathbf{U}^{\ddagger})/N^2 \geq 0$, and $\delta_{min}(\mathbf{U}^{\ddagger})$ denotes the smallest singular value of the Hessian matrix $\mathbf{U}^{\ddagger}$.

We also note that (see the proof in Appendix C)

$$\mathbf{s}^H \mathbf{U}_{0,0}\mathbf{s} = N^2 \mathbf{I}, \tag{20}$$

and

$$\begin{aligned}&\text{Re}[\,(\mathbf{s}^H \mathbf{U}_{0,0}\mathbf{s})^* \mathbf{U}_{0,0} \odot \mathbf{s}\mathbf{s}^H] \\ &+ \text{Im}(\mathbf{s}^* \odot \mathbf{U}_{0,0}\mathbf{s})\text{Im}(\mathbf{s}^* \odot \mathbf{U}_{0,0}\mathbf{s})^H = N^2 \mathbf{I},\end{aligned} \tag{21}$$

where $\odot$ denotes Hadamard (element-wise) product of matrices, and $\mathbf{U}_{0,0} = \mathbf{I}$. Hence, the corresponding optimization problem in (14) can be transformed to

$$\begin{aligned}\min \sum_{(n,m)\subset I_\Omega} \rho &= \left|\mathbf{s}^H \mathbf{U}_{n,m}\mathbf{s}\right|^2 + \lambda \left|\mathbf{s}^H \mathbf{U}_{0,0}\mathbf{s}\right|^2 \\ \text{s.t.} \quad |s_k| &= 1, \quad k = 1, 2, \ldots, N.\end{aligned} \tag{22}$$

The first-order and second-order derivatives of the objective function in Eq. (14) can be respectively given by

$$\frac{\partial \rho}{\partial \phi} = \sum_{(n,m)\subset I_\Omega} \text{Re}\left[\left(\mathbf{s}^H \mathbf{U}_{n,m}\mathbf{s}\right)^* \text{Im}\left(\mathbf{s}^* \odot \mathbf{U}_{n,m}\mathbf{s}\right)\right] \tag{23}$$

$$\begin{aligned}\frac{\partial^2 \rho}{\partial \phi \partial \phi^T} = &\sum_{(n,m)\subset I_\Omega} \text{Re}\left[\left(\mathbf{s}^H \mathbf{U}_{n,m}\mathbf{s}\right)^* \mathbf{U}_{n,m} \odot \mathbf{s}\mathbf{s}^H\right] \\ &+ \text{Im}\left(\mathbf{s}^* \odot \mathbf{U}_{n,m}\mathbf{s}\right) \text{Im}\left(\mathbf{s}^* \odot \mathbf{U}_{n,m}\mathbf{s}\right)^H + \lambda N^2 \mathbf{I}.\end{aligned} \tag{24}$$

Due to the fact that such a diagonal loading does not change the solution of the equality function in Eq. (15), the local minimum $\bar{\mathbf{s}}$ can now be obtained by

$$\sum_{(n,m)\subset I_\Omega} \text{Re}\left[\left(\bar{\mathbf{s}}^H \mathbf{U}_{n,m}\bar{\mathbf{s}}\right)^* \text{Im}\left(\bar{\mathbf{s}}^* \odot \mathbf{U}_{n,m}\bar{\mathbf{s}}\right)\right] = 0 \tag{25}$$

over the constant modulus set. This equation is also equivalent to the following expression as (see the proof in Appendix D).

$$\sum_{(n,m)\subset I_\Omega} \mathrm{Re}\left[j\left(\bar{\mathbf{s}}^H \mathbf{U}_{n,m}\bar{\mathbf{s}}\right)^* \left(\bar{\mathbf{s}}^* \odot \mathbf{U}_{n,m}\bar{\mathbf{s}}\right)\right] = 0. \quad (26)$$

Consequently, a local minimum $\bar{\mathbf{s}}$ can be characterized by

$$\sum_{(n,m)\subset I_\Omega} \left(\bar{\mathbf{s}}^H \mathbf{U}_{n,m}\bar{\mathbf{s}}\right)^* \mathbf{U}_{n,m}\bar{\mathbf{s}} = \nu\bar{\mathbf{s}} \quad (27)$$

or

$$\sum_{(n,m)\subset I_\Omega} \left(\bar{\mathbf{s}}^H \mathbf{U}_{n,m}\bar{\mathbf{s}}\right)^* \mathbf{U}_{n,m} = \nu\mathbf{I}, \quad (28)$$

where ν is a real number.

2.3 Optimization method

The conjugate gradient method is used to compute the optimizing value of a function defined on a vector space, using only first derivation information. The only difference between the standard conjugate gradient method and the phase-only conjugate gradient method is that lines in Euclidean space must be replaced by lines on the N-torus, i.e., for a phase-only vector $\mathbf{s}$, direction $\mathbf{h}_c = \partial\rho/\partial\phi$, and step size t

$$e^{jt\mathrm{Diag}(\mathbf{h}_c)}\mathbf{s} \quad \rightarrow \quad \mathbf{s} + t\mathbf{h}_c. \quad (29)$$

Newton's method can provide quadratic convergence to an optimum solution. However, the Hessian matrix must be computed at every step, and there is the possibility of converging to a nonoptimum critical point. The experience of applying such algorithms is to first use the conjugate gradient method to get a close solution and then use Newton's method to achieve the solution within machine accuracy. Newton's iteration is obtained by moving in the direction

$$\mathbf{h}_n = -\left(\frac{\partial^2\rho}{\partial\phi\partial\phi^T}\right)^{-1}\frac{\partial\rho}{\partial\phi} = -\mathbf{U}^{\ddagger(-1)}\mathbf{h}_c. \quad (30)$$

Let $\mathbf{s}_i$ and $\mathbf{s}_{i+1}$ be the sequence at the ith and $(i+1)$th iteration. The detailed steps incorporating the phase-only conjugate gradient method and the phase-only Newton's method are given as follows:

1. Select $\phi_0 \in \mathbb{R}_N$, compute $\mathbf{g}_0 = \mathbf{h}_0 = \partial\rho\left(\mathbf{s}_0\right)/\partial\phi$, and set $i = 0$.
2. For $i = 0, 1, \ldots, N_c$, compute t_i such that
$$\rho\left(e^{jt_i\mathrm{Diag}(\mathbf{h}_i)}\mathbf{s}_i\right) > \rho\left(e^{jt\mathrm{Diag}(\mathbf{h}_i)}\mathbf{s}_i\right)$$
for all $t > 0$ (line optimization).
3. Set $\mathbf{s}_{i+1} = e^{jt_i\mathrm{Diag}(\mathbf{h}_i)}\mathbf{s}_i$.
4. Set
$$\mathbf{g}_{i+1} = \frac{\partial\rho\left(\mathbf{s}_{i+1}\right)}{\partial\phi}$$
$$\mathbf{h}_{i+1} = \mathbf{g}_{i+1} + \gamma_i\mathbf{h}_i$$
$$\gamma_i = \frac{\left(\mathbf{g}_{i+1} - \mathbf{g}_i\right)^T \mathbf{g}_{i+1}}{\|\mathbf{g}_i\|^2}.$$
5. Set $i = i + 1$; if $i < N_c$, go to Step 2; or else, go to Step 6.
6. Compute
$$\mathbf{U}^\ddagger(\mathbf{s}_i) = \frac{\partial^2\rho(\mathbf{s}_i)}{\partial\phi\partial\phi^T}$$
$$\mathbf{h}_i = -\mathbf{U}^{\ddagger(-1)}(\mathbf{s}_i)\mathbf{g}_i.$$
7. Set $i = i+1$; go to Step 6 until $\|\rho(\mathbf{s}_{i+1}) - \rho(\mathbf{s}_i)\|_2^2 < \varepsilon$, where ε is a predefined parameter.

The algorithm of POCG requires on the order of $8\ell N^2 + \ell N$ real floating point operations (flops) to form the gradient vector , where ℓ is the number of samples available. Per iteration, it requires $8\ell N^2 + \ell N$ flops to compute the gradient, and $2N$ flops to compute the updated search direction.

The algorithm of PONM requires on the order of $8\ell N^2 + N^2$ flops to form the Hessian matrix, $2N^3/3 + N^2/4 + 2N$ flops to perform matrix inversion, and $4N(N-1)$ to perform the production of a matrix and a vector.

2.4 Selection of parameter λ

In optimization algorithms of POCG and PONM, the local/gobal optimum is obtained by successive iterations. It should be pointed out that the Hessian matrix $\mathbf{U}^\ddagger$ varies with the synthesized sequence at the optimization process, and the parameter λ_i should change with the smallest singular value of $\mathbf{U}^\ddagger(\mathbf{s}_i)$ to guarantee the positive definiteness of the Hessian matrix.

Two methods can be used to make the Hessian matrix positive definite. The first is to use a large-enough value for λ, and this will make λ a constant value. The second is to calculate the eigenvalues and eigenvector of $\mathbf{U}^\ddagger(\mathbf{s}_i)$ at every iteration. Note that the matrix inversion of $\mathbf{U}^\ddagger(\mathbf{s}_i)$ is also required at every iteration, and $\mathbf{U}^\ddagger(\mathbf{s}_i) = \sum_{l=1}^{w_i}\delta_l\mathbf{v}_i^l\mathbf{v}_i^{lH}$, where $w_i = \mathrm{rank}(\mathbf{U}^\ddagger(\mathbf{s}_i))$. The matrix inversion of $\mathbf{U}^\ddagger(\mathbf{s}_i)$ after diagonal loading by λ_i can be given by

$$\mathbf{U}^{\ddagger(-1)}(\mathbf{s}_i) = \sum_{l=1}^{w_i}\frac{1}{\delta_l + \lambda_i}\mathbf{v}_i^l\mathbf{v}_i^{lH}, \quad (31)$$

where $\lambda_i + \delta_{\min}(\mathbf{U}^\ddagger(\mathbf{s}_i)) > 0$.

3 Slow-time ambiguity function synthesis in cognitive MTD radar

Motivated by higher performance requirements, the radar system now can exploit different environmental information, such as geographic information database, meteorological data, previous scans and some electromagnetic reflectivity, and spectral clutter models [27]. In this paper, we consider a cognitive MTD radar system which can observe the range and Doppler bins where clutter or interference is foreseen. This radar can then transmit a burst of waveforms whose STAF generates low sidelobe values in those bins.

3.1 STAF optimization

Now, we consider a monostatic MTD radar system which transmits a coherent burst of P slow-time pulses. The transmitted pulses can be written as

$$x(t) = \sum_{i=0}^{P-1} s(t - iT_r), \tag{32}$$

where T_r is the pulse repetition interval, and $T_r \gg Nt_p$.

From the viewpoint of matched filtering and MTD processing, we define the slow-time ambiguity function $\vartheta(\tau, f_d)$ as

$$\begin{aligned}\vartheta(\tau, f_d) &= \int_{-\infty}^{\infty} x(t)x^*(t-\tau)e^{j2\pi f_d t}dt \\ &= \sum_{i=0}^{P-1} e^{-j2\pi i f_d T_r} \int_{-\infty}^{\infty} s(t)s^*(t-\tau)e^{j2\pi f_d t}dt \\ &= \sum_{i=0}^{P-1} e^{-j2\pi i f_d T_r} \chi_s(\tau, f_d), \\ & -(T_r - Nt_p) \le \tau \le (T_r - Nt_p).\end{aligned} \tag{33}$$

Note that

$$\sum_{i=0}^{P-1} e^{-j2\pi i f_d T_r} = e^{-j2\pi(P-1)f_d T_r} \frac{\sin(\pi P f_d T_r)}{\sin(\pi f_d T_r)}. \tag{34}$$

$\vartheta(\tau, f_d)$ can also be written as

$$\vartheta(\tau, f_d) = e^{-j2\pi(P-1)f_d T_r} \frac{\sin(\pi P f_d T_r)}{\sin(\pi f_d T_r)} \chi_s(\tau, f_d). \tag{35}$$

Hence, the STAF $\vartheta(\tau, f_d)$ can be regarded as the product of the Doppler weighted function and the AF $\chi_s(\tau, f_d)$.

By substituting $\tau = nt_p$ and $f_d = m/(Mt_p)$, the discretized form of $\vartheta(\tau, f_d)$ is given by

$$\begin{aligned}\vartheta(n, m) &= \sum_{i=0}^{P-1} e^{-j2\pi i f_d T_r} \chi_s(n, m) \\ &= e^{-j2\pi m(P-1)T_r/Mt_p} \frac{\sin(\pi m P T_r/Mt_p)}{\sin(\pi m T_r/Mt_p)} \chi_s(n, m).\end{aligned} \tag{36}$$

In this section, we intend to synthesize the STAF $\vartheta(n, m)$ with minimized ISL in the range-Doppler bins where the clutter exists. The ISL metric for STAF can be expressed as

$$\mathrm{ISL} = \sum_{(n,m)\subset I_C} |\vartheta(n, m)|^2, \tag{37}$$

where I_C is the subset of the range and Doppler bins, whose sidelobes are desired to be suppressed as much as possible at the output of the MTD processor.

Interested and clutter areas are depicted on the discretized time delay and Doppler frequency shift plane, respectively, in Fig. 2. Without loss of generality, the center of the interested area can be assumed to be the origin of the range-Doppler plane. This means that the matched filter and MTD processing response of clutter returns depend on the difference of its time delay and Doppler frequency shift with respect to those of the center of the interested area.

Taking into account that the synthesized waveform should have constant module, the STAF optimization problem for a MTD radar system can be summarized as

$$\begin{aligned}&\min \sum_{(n,m)\subset I_C} |\vartheta(n, m)|^2 \\ &\text{s.t.} |s_k| = 1, k = 1, 2, \ldots, N.\end{aligned} \tag{38}$$

(35) is equivalent to

$$\begin{aligned}&\min \sum_{(n,m)\subset I_C} |\rho_m \chi(n, m)|^2 \\ &\text{s.t.} |s_k| = 1, k = 1, 2, \ldots, N,\end{aligned} \tag{39}$$

where

$$\rho_m = \frac{\sin(\pi m P T_r/Mt_p)}{\sin(\pi m T_r/Mt_p)}. \tag{40}$$

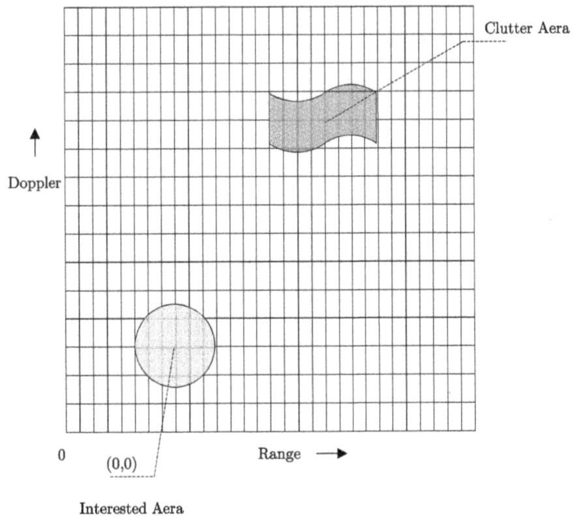

Fig. 2 Interested area and clutter area on the time delay and Doppler frequency shift plane

With the derivation in the previous section, the formulation can also be given by

$$\min \sum_{(n,m)\subset I_C} \left|\rho_m \mathbf{s}^{(t)H}\mathbf{U}_{n,m}\mathbf{s}^{(t)}\right|^2 + \lambda \left|\mathbf{s}^{(t)H}\mathbf{U}_{0,0}\mathbf{s}^{(t)}\right|^2$$
$$\text{s.t.} |s_k| = 1, k = 1, 2, \ldots, N. \tag{41}$$

The proposed optimization algorithm in Section 2.3 can also be used to solve this problem.

3.2 Workflow of a cognitive MTD radar

In Fig. 3, the workflow of a cognitive MTD radar is given. When the MTD radar begins to work, it utilizes some unimodular sequences with good AF or ACF properties for transmission. Then, range-Doppler processing is carried out for information extraction. With the extracted information associated with the target and clutter, the radar system begins to synthesize the unimodular sequence by our proposed algorithm. In the next coherent processing interval (CPI), the MTD radar will transmit a new designed sequence. The above process is repeated and the MTD radar system can operate in a dynamic environment with cognitive capability. This framework is especially attractive for the confirmation process. Once a target has been found by a standard radar waveform, detection can be confirmed reliably by transmitting the optimized waveform, which is matched to the operation scenario of the radar system.

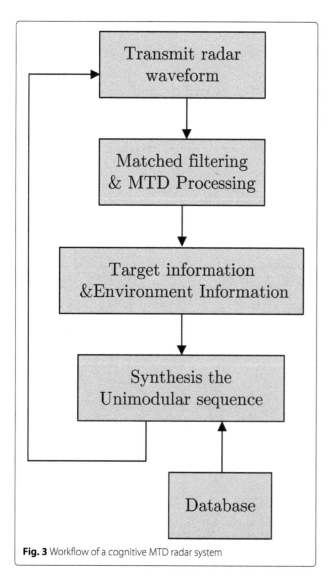

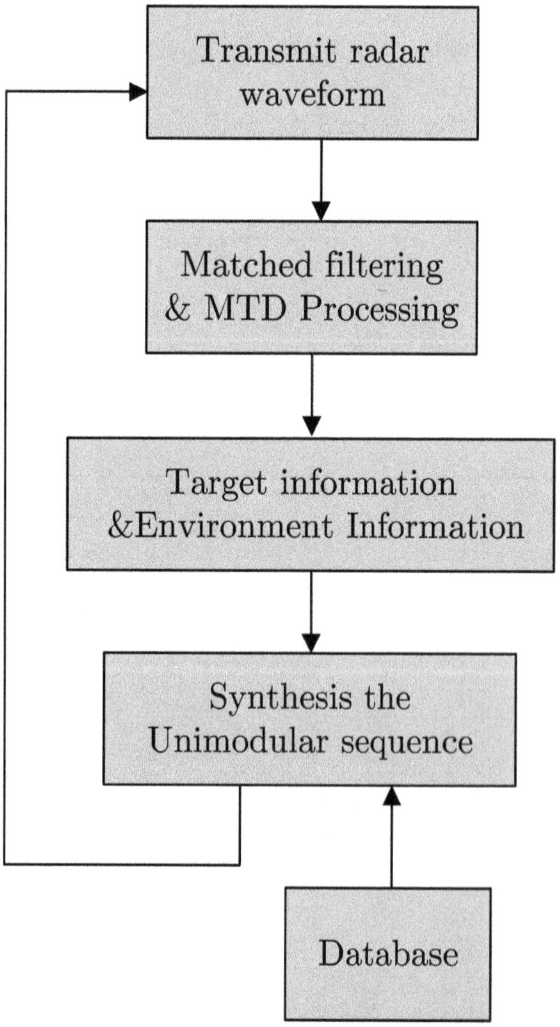

Fig. 3 Workflow of a cognitive MTD radar system

4 Numerical examples

In order to verify the effectiveness of the proposed algorithms, we will present several numerical examples, including the AF synthesis, STAF synthesis, and detection performance of a cognitive MTD radar. In the following examples, we all assume that the unimodular sequence has $N = 100$ subpulses with rectangular pulse-shaping. The time duration of each subpulse is t_p and that of the total waveform is $T = 100t_p$. The pulse repetition interval is $T_r = 10T$, and the number of pulses in a CPI is $P = 64$. In AF and STAF, the time delay axis τ is normalized by T and the Doppler frequency axis f is normalized by $1/T$. The convergence of the proposed algorithm will be tested by using randomly generated sequences in the initialization. In the iteration process, the parameter ϵ is set to be 10^{-3}.

4.1 AF synthesis

Suppose that $\Omega = \{(\tau,f_d)||\tau| < 0.2, |f_d| < 0.01, \tau f_d \neq 0\}$ is the interested area, which is near the origin but excludes the origin on $\tau - f_d$ plane. With randomly generated sequence in the initialization, PCA is applied to minimize the ISL metric of the AF of the synthesized sequence.

The AFs of the initialization sequence and synthesized sequence are shown in Fig. 4a,b. The AF in Fig. 4a presents high sidelobe values on the whole $\tau - f_d$ plane. The desired low sidelobes in the interested area of AF is obviously obtained in Fig. 4b. Therefore, the synthesized sequence has a good capability of separating and detecting closely spaced targets.

Figure 4c,d gives the zero-Doppler range profile cut and zero-delay Doppler profile cut of the AF in Fig. 4b. The sidelobes in the interested area is suppressed to about −40 dB in the time delay axis with $|\tau| < 0.2$. Due to the fact that the synthesized sequence has constant modulus, the zero-delay Doppler profile cut is a sinc function.

4.2 STAF synthesis

STAF can also be optimized by the algorithm, which has been suggested in Section 4. Two types of STAFs are both examined in this example. The first type has a clear area close to the origin on the time delay and Doppler frequency shift plane and is especially attractive for detecting

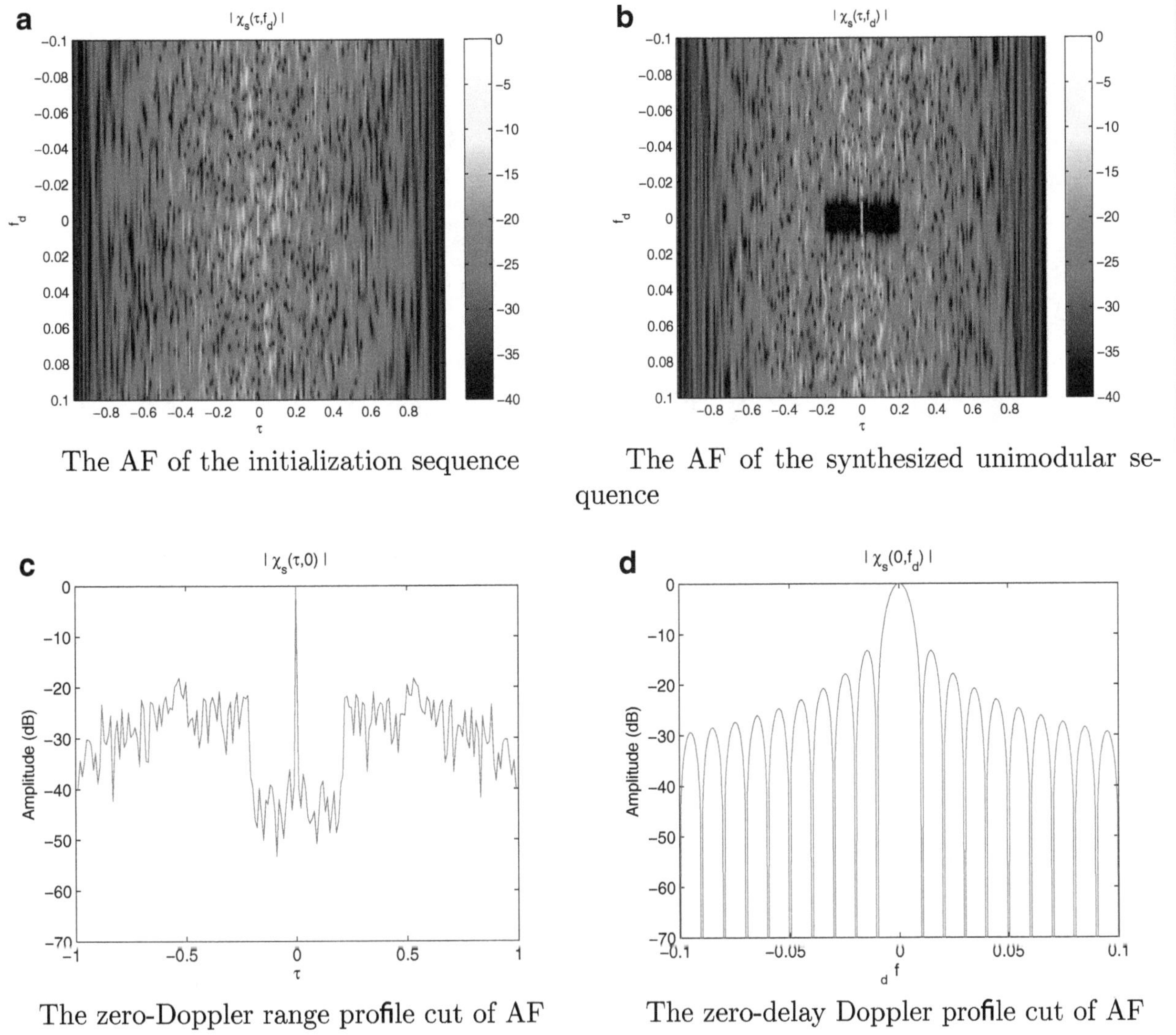

Fig. 4 AF synthesis for unimodular sequence. **a** The AF of the initialization sequence. **b** The AF of the synthesized unimodular sequence. **c** The zero-Doppler range profile cut of AF. **d** The zero-delay Doppler profile cut of AF

closely spaced targets. The specified area can be described as

$$\Omega_1 = \left\{(\tau, f_d) \, \| \tau \,| < 0.1, |f_d| < 5 \times 10^{-4}\right\}. \tag{42}$$

Figure 5a,b shows the desired and synthesized STAFs of the first type in log scale. The ISL of STAF in Ω_1 is minimized and the averaged sidelobe of the obtained sequence is suppressed to about −50 dB in Fig. 4b.

The seconde type has minimized ISL in a certain area, which is given by

$$\Omega_2 = \left\{(\tau, f_d) \,|0.3 < |\tau| < 0.5, \\ 4 \times 10^{-4} < |f_d| < 6 \times 10^{-4}\right\}. \tag{43}$$

The desired and synthesized STAFs of the seconde type are plotted in Fig. 5c,d. The ISL of STAF in Ω_2 is reduced and the averaged sidelobe of the obtained sequence is suppressed to about −70 dB in Fig. 5d.

4.3 STAF synthesis in a cognitive MTD radar system

In this example, a MTD radar system is designed as a CR system. The target and clutter distributions within the radar scene should be dynamically deciphered from the received backscattered signal, and these deciphered distributions over the STAF could then be used for the proposed synthesis approach. In Fig. 6a, the clutter distribution on the $\tau - f_d$ plane is plotted and a strong clutter block lies in

$$\Omega_C = \{(\tau, f_d)|0.3 < |\tau| < 0.5, \\ 4 \times 10^{-4} < |f_d| < 6 \times 10^{-4}\}. \tag{44}$$

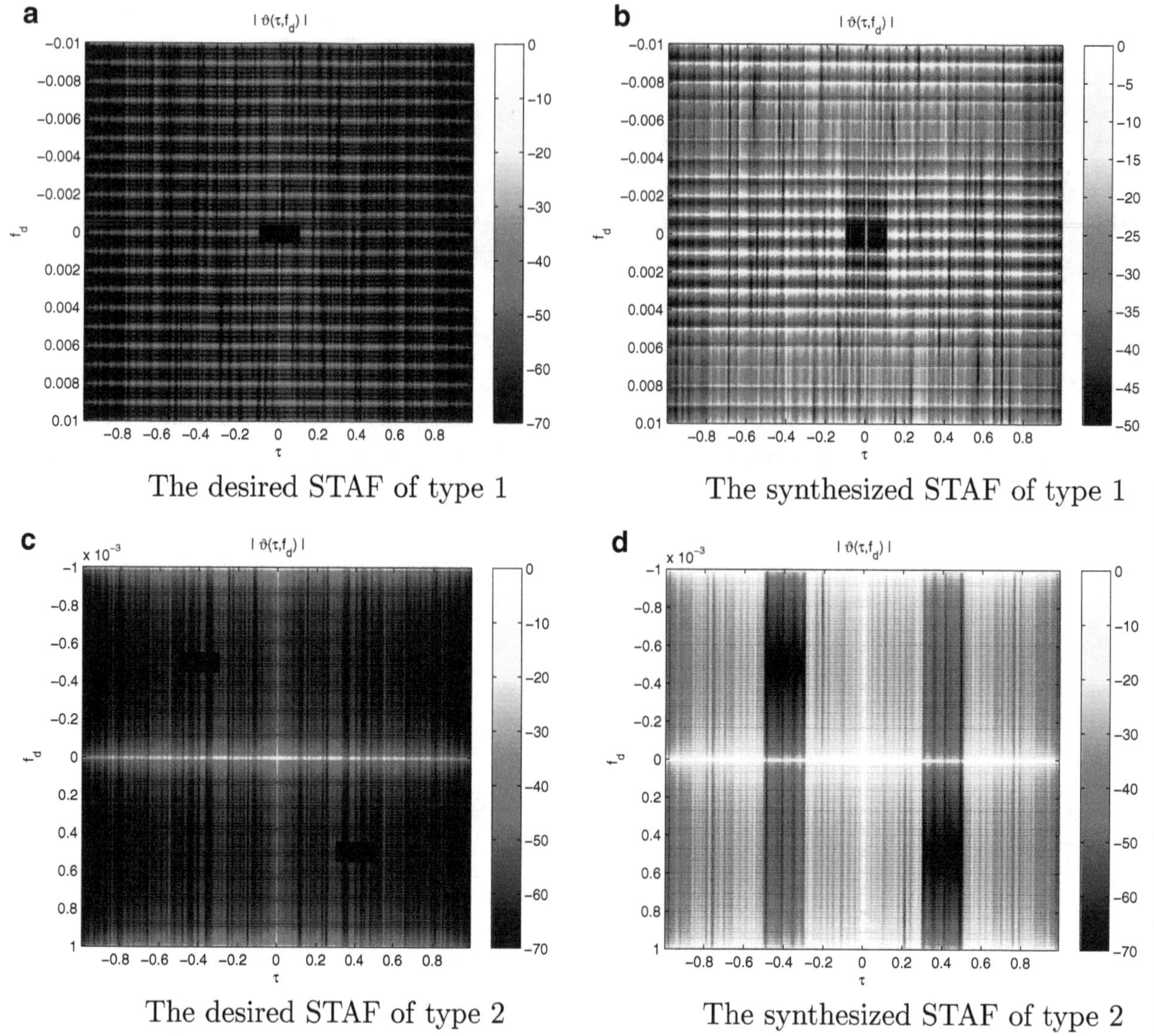

Fig. 5 STAF synthesis for unimodular sequence

For ease of simulation, the clutter in every range-Doppler bin can be treated as a stationary scattering point. Hence, the whole clutter return is the superposition of all the returns from every range-Doppler scattering point.

We also assume that the target distribution can be described as

$$\Omega_T = \{(\tau, f_d) | |\tau| < 0.1, |f_d| < 5 \times 10^{-4}\} \tag{45}$$

and consider the underlying scintillation on RCS based on different Swerling models for the moving target. The optimized shape of STAF is plotted in Fig. 6b, in which a low sidelobe is presented in the target and heavy clutter area.

According to the Swerling models, the RCS of a reflecting target can be described by the chi-square probability density function with specific degrees of freedom. In this example, Swerling I and III models are used in order to evaluate the detection performance of a cognitive MTD radar system. Swerling I and III models indicate a target whose magnitude of the backscattered signal is relatively constant during the dwell time. The RCS is constant from pulse to pulse but varies independently from scan to scan. For Swerling I model, its RCS varies according to a chi-square probability density function with two degrees of freedom. The density of probability of the RCS is given by the Rayleigh-Function

$$P(\sigma) = \frac{1}{\sigma_{\text{average}}} \cdot \exp\left\{\frac{-\sigma}{\sigma_{\text{average}}}\right\}. \tag{46}$$

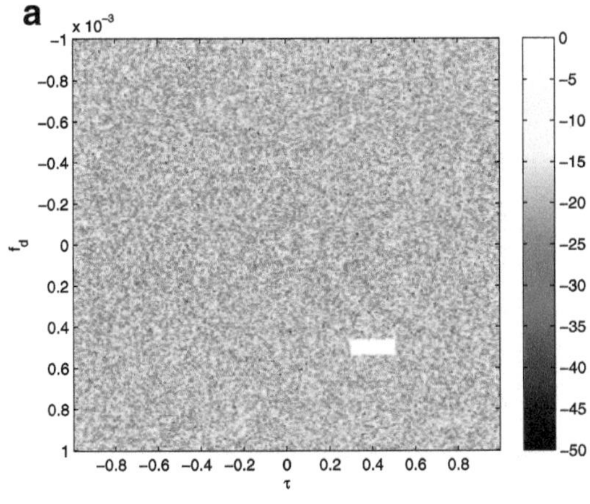

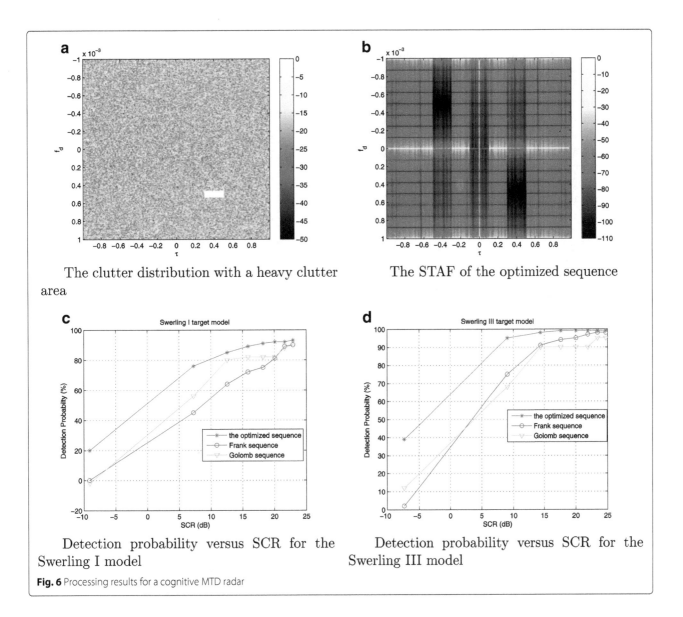

The clutter distribution with a heavy clutter area

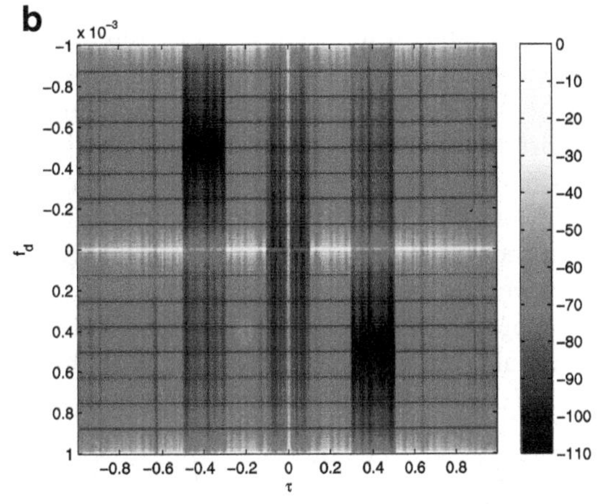

The STAF of the optimized sequence

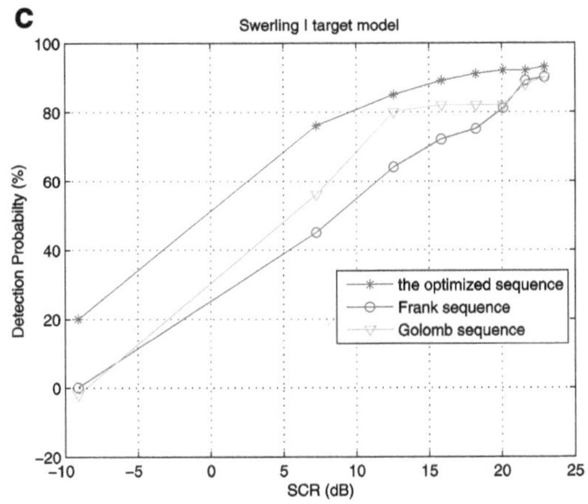

Detection probability versus SCR for the Swerling I model

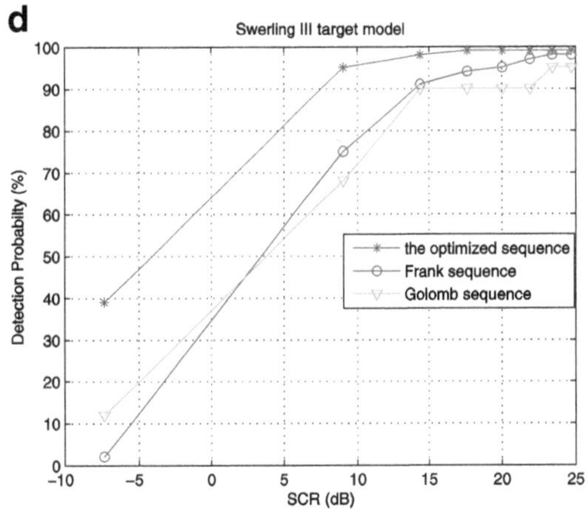

Detection probability versus SCR for the Swerling III model

Fig. 6 Processing results for a cognitive MTD radar

The Swerling III model is described like Swerling I but with four degrees of freedom. The scan-to-scan fluctuation follows a density of probability

$$P(\sigma) = \frac{4\sigma}{\left(\sigma_{\text{average}}\right)^2} \cdot \exp\left\{\frac{-2\sigma}{\sigma_{\text{average}}}\right\}. \tag{47}$$

In Eqs. (46) and (47), σ is the value of RCS, and σ_{average} is the mean value of RCS.

In order to evaluate the detection performance, signal-to-clutter ratio (SCR) is defined as

$$\text{SCR} = \frac{PT_r\sigma^2_{\text{average}}}{Mt_p \int\int C(\tau,f_d)d\tau df_d}, \tag{48}$$

where $C(\tau,f_d)$ is the clutter distribution. In this definition, the average scattering power of the Swerling target model is compared with the average power of all the clutter scattering points.

In Fig. 6c,d, considering the radar scene in Fig. 6a, the detection probability versus SCR is given for the Swerling I and III target models, and the detection probability of the optimized Frank and Golomb sequences are compared. As expected, the optimized sequence outperforms Frank and Golomb sequences, showing the performance of higher detection probability and suppressing the interference of the clutter returns from the output of MTD processing. Furthermore, as SCR increases, the detection probability is raised accordingly for both the Swerling I and III models. These two figures highlight the capability of the proposed algorithm to suitably shape the STAF of the transmitted waveform.

5 Conclusions

An algorithm was proposed to synthesize a unimodular sequence by minimizing the sidelobe values of AF in certain areas on the time delay and Doppler frequency shift plane. This algorithm can be convergent theoretically and practically and has been shown to be useful for ISL minimization of AF and STAF. The algorithm for synthesizing the unimodular sequence with the desired AF and STAF was built in this work.

A cognitive approach to devise waveforms for a MTD radar system was also put forward in this work. With this approach, the MTD radar system can adaptively optimize the STAF of its transmit waveform by minimizing the ISL metric of the interested area and clutter area on the time delay and Doppler frequency shift plane. The numerical example shows that better detection performance can be achieved by our proposed approach.

We note further that computational efficiency of Newton's method was limited by matrix inversion. This algorithm is better for the sequence with a length no longer than 10^4. Therefore, in the future work, we will try to find a better approach and a computation-saving method.

Appendix

Subpulse cross ambiguity function

In order to verify the subpulse CAF in Eq. (7), we rewrite the kth and lth subpulse CAF expressions as follows:

$$\chi_p^{(k,l)}(\tau,f_d) = \int_{-\infty}^{\infty} p_k(t)p_l^*(t+\tau)e^{j2\pi f_d t}dt,$$

where

$$p_k(t) = \text{rect}\left(\frac{t-(k-1)t_p}{t_p}\right), \quad (k-1)t_p \le t \le kt_p$$

$$p_l(t+\tau) = \text{rect}\left(\frac{t+\tau-(l-1)t_p}{t_p}\right),$$

$$(l-1)t_p \le (t+\tau) \le lt_p.$$

Note that the two subsets of t overlap with each other only when $\tau = (k-l)t_p + \tau'$, with $|\tau'| \le t_p$. The integral in Eq. (7) can be calculated in two cases.

Case 1. $-t_p \le \tau' < 0$

$$\chi_p^{(k,l)}(\tau,f_d) = \frac{1}{t_p}\int_{(k-1)t_p}^{kt_p+\tau'} e^{j2\pi f_d t}dt$$

$$= \frac{1}{t_p}\cdot\frac{e^{j2\pi f_d t}}{j2\pi f_d}\Big|_{(k-1)t_p}^{kt_p+\tau'}$$

$$= e^{j\pi f_d(2k-1)t_p}e^{j\pi f_d \tau'}\frac{\sin\pi f_d(t_p+\tau')}{\pi f_d(t_p+\tau')}\frac{t_p+\tau'}{t_p}.$$

With $f_d\tau' \ll 1$, the above equation can be simplified to

$$\chi_p^{(k,l)}(\tau,f_d) = e^{j\pi f_d(2k-1)t_p}\frac{\sin\pi f_d(t_p+\tau')}{\pi f_d(t_p+\tau')}\frac{t_p+\tau'}{t_p}.$$

Case 2. $0 \le \tau' \le t_p$

$$\chi_p^{(k,l)}(\tau,f_d) = e^{j\pi f_d(2k-1)t_p}\frac{\sin\pi f_d(t_p-\tau')}{\pi f_d(t_p-\tau')}\frac{t_p-\tau'}{t_p}.$$

Therefore, the subpulse CAF can be summarized with the following expression as

$$\chi_p^{(k,l)}(\tau,f_d) = e^{j\pi f_d(2k-1)t_p} \cdot \frac{\sin\pi f_d\left(t_p - |\tau-(k-l)t_p|\right)}{\pi f_d\left(t_p - |\tau-(k-l)t_p|\right)} \cdot \frac{t_p - |\tau-(k-l)t_p|}{t_p},$$

$$(k-l-1)t_p \le \tau \le (k-l+1)t_p.$$

Derivatives of ISL

It is assumed that $\mathbf{s} = \left(e^{j\phi_1}, e^{j\phi_2}, \ldots, e^{j\phi_N}\right)^T$ and noted that

$$\text{ISL} = \sum_{(n,m)\subset I_\Omega}\left|\mathbf{s}^H\mathbf{U}_{n,m}\mathbf{s}\right|^2 = \sum_{(n,m)\subset I_\Omega}\sum_{k,l}\left|\mathbf{U}_{n,m}(k,l)e^{j(\phi_l-\phi_k)}\right|^2.$$

Let $\gamma_{n,m}(\mathbf{s}) = \mathbf{s}^H\mathbf{U}_{n,m}\mathbf{s}$ and $1 \le k_0 \le N$, we have

$$\frac{\partial\text{ISL}}{\partial\phi_{k0}} = \sum_{(n,m)\subset I_\Omega}\left\{\frac{\partial\gamma_{n,m}(\mathbf{s})}{\partial\phi_{k0}}\gamma_{n,m}^*(\mathbf{s}) + \frac{\partial\gamma_{n,m}^*(\mathbf{s})}{\partial\phi_{k0}}\gamma_{n,m}(\mathbf{s})\right\} = \sum_{(n,m)\subset I_\Omega} 2\text{Re}\left\{\frac{\partial\gamma_{n,m}(\mathbf{s})}{\partial\phi_{k0}}\gamma_{n,m}^*(\mathbf{s})\right\},$$

where

$$\frac{\partial\gamma_{n,m}(\mathbf{s})}{\partial\phi_{k0}} = \text{Im}\left(e^{-j\phi_{k0}}\sum_l \mathbf{U}_{n,m}(k0,l)e^{j\phi_l}\right).$$

The first order derivative of ISL with respect to ϕ can be given by

$$\frac{\partial\text{ISL}}{\partial\phi} = 2\sum_{(n,m)\subset I_\Omega}\text{Re}\left\{\left(\mathbf{s}^H\mathbf{U}_{n,m}\mathbf{s}\right)^*\text{Im}\left(\mathbf{s}^*\odot\mathbf{U}_{n,m}\mathbf{s}\right)\right\}.$$

Similarly, the second order derivative can also be obtained by

$$\frac{\partial^2\text{ISL}}{\partial\phi\partial\phi^T} = \sum_{(n,m)\subset I_\Omega}\left\{\frac{\partial^2\gamma_{n,m}(\mathbf{s})}{\partial\phi\partial\phi^T}\gamma_{n,m}^*(\mathbf{s}) + \frac{\partial^2\gamma_{n,m}^*(\mathbf{s})}{\partial\phi\partial\phi^T}\gamma_{n,m}(\mathbf{s}) + \frac{\partial\gamma_{n,m}(\mathbf{s})}{\partial\phi}\frac{\partial\gamma_{n,m}^*(\mathbf{s})}{\partial\phi^T} + \frac{\partial\gamma_{n,m}^*(\mathbf{s})}{\partial\phi}\frac{\partial\gamma_{n,m}(\mathbf{s})}{\partial\phi^T}\right\},$$

where

$$\frac{\partial^2\gamma_{n,m}(\mathbf{s})}{\partial\phi\partial\phi^T} = \mathbf{U}_{n,m}\odot\mathbf{s}\mathbf{s}^H.$$

It can be simplified to

$$\frac{\partial^2 \text{ISL}}{\partial\phi\partial\phi^T} = 2 \sum_{(n,m)\subset I_\Omega} \text{Re}\left[\left(\mathbf{s}^H\mathbf{U}_{n,m}\mathbf{s}\right)^*\mathbf{U}_{n,m}\odot\mathbf{s}\mathbf{s}^H\right] + \text{Im}\left(\mathbf{s}^*\odot\mathbf{U}_{n,m}\mathbf{s}\right)\text{Im}\left(\mathbf{s}^*\odot\mathbf{U}_{n,m}\mathbf{s}\right)^H.$$

Proof of Eq. (20)

With the definition of the matrix $\mathbf{U}_{n,m}$, we have

$$\mathbf{U}_{0,0} = \mathbf{I}$$

and

$$\mathbf{s}^H\mathbf{U}_{0,0}\mathbf{s} = N^2.$$

Hence, the first item in Eq. (20) can be simplified and rewritten as

$$\text{Re}\left[\left(\mathbf{s}^H\mathbf{U}_{0,0}\mathbf{s}\right)^*\mathbf{U}_{0,0}\odot\mathbf{s}\mathbf{s}^H\right] = N^2\mathbf{I}.$$

We also note that

$$\mathbf{s}^*\odot\mathbf{U}_{0,0}\mathbf{s} = \mathbf{1},$$

where $\mathbf{1} = [1,1,\ldots,1]^T$. The second item in Eq. (20) can also be expressed as

$$\text{Im}\left(\mathbf{s}^*\odot\mathbf{U}_{0,0}\mathbf{s}\right)\text{Im}\left(\mathbf{s}^*\odot\mathbf{U}_{0,0}\mathbf{s}\right)^H = \mathbf{0}.$$

With the above two equations, we can obtain the equality in Eq. (20), which is expressed as

$$\text{Re}\left[\left(\mathbf{s}^H\mathbf{U}_{0,0}\mathbf{s}\right)^*\mathbf{U}_{0,0}\odot\mathbf{s}\mathbf{s}^H\right] + \text{Im}\left(\mathbf{s}^*\odot\mathbf{U}_{0,0}\mathbf{s}\right)\text{Im}\left(\mathbf{s}^*\odot\mathbf{U}_{0,0}\mathbf{s}\right)^H = N^2\mathbf{I}.$$

Equality proof

As indicated in Section "Derivatives of ISL", we have

$$\frac{\partial\gamma_{n,m}(\mathbf{s})}{\partial\phi} = -j\left(\mathbf{s}^*\odot\mathbf{U}_{n,m}\mathbf{s}\right) + j\left(\mathbf{s}^*\odot\mathbf{U}_{n,m}\mathbf{s}\right)^* = \text{Im}\left(\mathbf{s}^*\odot\mathbf{U}_{n,m}\mathbf{s}\right).$$

Eq. (26) can be rewritten as

$$\sum_{(n,m)\subset I_\Omega}\text{Re}\left[\left(\bar{\mathbf{s}}^H\mathbf{U}_{n,m}\bar{\mathbf{s}}\right)^*\text{Im}\left(\bar{\mathbf{s}}^*\odot\mathbf{U}_{n,m}\bar{\mathbf{s}}\right)\right] = \sum_{(n,m)\subset I_\Omega}\left\{-\text{Re}\left[j\left(\bar{\mathbf{s}}^H\mathbf{U}_{n,m}\bar{\mathbf{s}}\right)^*\left(\mathbf{s}^*\odot\mathbf{U}_{n,m}\mathbf{s}\right)\right] + \text{Re}\left[j\left(\bar{\mathbf{s}}^H\mathbf{U}_{n,m}\bar{\mathbf{s}}\right)^*\left(\mathbf{s}^*\odot\mathbf{U}_{n,m}\mathbf{s}\right)^*\right]\right\} = 0.$$

An equality can be obtained the above equation , and expressed as

$$\sum_{(n,m)\subset I_\Omega}\sum_{(n,m)\subset I_\Omega}\text{Re}\left[j\left(\bar{\mathbf{s}}^H\mathbf{U}_{n,m}\bar{\mathbf{s}}\right)^*\left(\mathbf{s}^*\odot\mathbf{U}_{n,m}\mathbf{s}\right)\right] = \sum_{(n,m)\subset I_\Omega}\text{Re}\left[j\left(\bar{\mathbf{s}}^H\mathbf{U}_{n,m}\bar{\mathbf{s}}\right)^*\left(\mathbf{s}^*\odot\mathbf{U}_{n,m}\mathbf{s}\right)^*\right].$$

This expression can be expanded by the real and imaginary part of $\bar{\mathbf{s}}^H\mathbf{U}_{n,m}\bar{\mathbf{s}}$ and $\mathbf{s}^*\odot\mathbf{U}_{n,m}\mathbf{s}$, and given by

$$\sum_{(n,m)\subset I_\Omega} -\text{Im}\left[\bar{\mathbf{s}}^H\mathbf{U}_{n,m}\bar{\mathbf{s}}\right]\text{Re}\left[\mathbf{s}^*\odot\mathbf{U}_{n,m}\mathbf{s}\right] + \text{Re}\left[\bar{\mathbf{s}}^H\mathbf{U}_{n,m}\bar{\mathbf{s}}\right]\text{Im}\left[\mathbf{s}^*\odot\mathbf{U}_{n,m}\mathbf{s}\right] = \sum_{(n,m)\subset I_\Omega}\text{Im}\left[\bar{\mathbf{s}}^H\mathbf{U}_{n,m}\bar{\mathbf{s}}\right]\text{Re}\left[\mathbf{s}^*\odot\mathbf{U}_{n,m}\mathbf{s}\right] + \text{Re}\left[\bar{\mathbf{s}}^H\mathbf{U}_{n,m}\bar{\mathbf{s}}\right]\text{Im}\left[\mathbf{s}^*\odot\mathbf{U}_{n,m}\mathbf{s}\right]$$

which implies

$$\sum_{(n,m)\subset I_\Omega}\text{Im}\left[\bar{\mathbf{s}}^H\mathbf{U}_{n,m}\bar{\mathbf{s}}\right]\text{Re}\left[\mathbf{s}^*\odot\mathbf{U}_{n,m}\mathbf{s}\right] = 0.$$

Note that from

$$\sum_{(n,m)\subset I_\Omega}\text{Re}\left[\left(\bar{\mathbf{s}}^H\mathbf{U}_{n,m}\bar{\mathbf{s}}\right)^*\text{Im}\left(\bar{\mathbf{s}}^*\odot\mathbf{U}_{n,m}\bar{\mathbf{s}}\right)\right] = \sum_{(n,m)\subset I_\Omega}\text{Re}\left[\left(\bar{\mathbf{s}}^H\mathbf{U}_{n,m}\bar{\mathbf{s}}\right)^*\right]\text{Im}\left[\left(\bar{\mathbf{s}}^*\odot\mathbf{U}_{n,m}\bar{\mathbf{s}}\right)\right] = 0,$$

we can obtain

$$\sum_{(n,m)\subset I_\Omega}\left\{\text{Im}\left[\bar{\mathbf{s}}^H\mathbf{U}_{n,m}\bar{\mathbf{s}}\right]\text{Re}\left[\mathbf{s}^*\odot\mathbf{U}_{n,m}\mathbf{s}\right] + \text{Re}\left[\left(\bar{\mathbf{s}}^H\mathbf{U}_{n,m}\bar{\mathbf{s}}\right)^*\right]\text{Im}\left[\left(\bar{\mathbf{s}}^*\odot\mathbf{U}_{n,m}\bar{\mathbf{s}}\right)\right]\right\} = \sum_{(n,m)\subset I_\Omega}\text{Re}\left[j\left(\bar{\mathbf{s}}^H\mathbf{U}_{n,m}\bar{\mathbf{s}}\right)^*\left(\bar{\mathbf{s}}^*\odot\mathbf{U}_{n,m}\bar{\mathbf{s}}\right)\right].$$

Competing interests

The authors declare that they have no competing interests.

Acknowledgements

This work was supported by the National Natural Science Foundation of China under grant 61201367, the Natural Science Foundation of Jiangsu Province under grant BK2012382, the Aeronautical Science Foundation of China under grant 20142052019, the Fundamental Research Funds for Central Universities under grant NS2016042, and the Cooperative Innovation Foundation Project in Jiangsu Province under grant BY2014003-5.

References

1. S Haykin, Cognitive radar: a way of the future. IEEE Signal Process. Mag. **23**(1), 30–40 (2006)
2. PG Grieve, JR Guerci, Optimum matched illumination reception radar. U.S. Patent S517552 (1992)
3. SU Pillai, HS OH, DC Youla, JR Guerci, Optimum transmit-receiver design in the presence of signal-dependent interference and channel noise. IEEE Trans. Inf. Theory. **46**(2), 577–584 (2000)
4. MR Bell, Information theory and radar waveform. IEEE Trans. Inf. Theory. **39**(5), 1578–1597 (1993)
5. S A De Maio, Y De Nicola, ZQ Huang, S Luo, Zhang, Design of phase codes for radar performance optimization with a similarity constraint. IEEE Trans. Signal Process. **57**(2), 30–40 (2009)
6. M Skolnik, *Radar Handbook*, 3rd ed. (McGraw Hill, New York, 2008)
7. N Levanon, E Mozeson, *Radar Signals*. (NY, Wiley, 2004)
8. N Zhang, SW Golomb, Polyphase sequence with low autocorrelations. IEEE Trans. Inf. Theory. **39**(3), 1085–1089 (1993)
9. R Frank, Polyphase codes with good nonperiodic correlation properties. IEEE Trans. Inf. Theory. **9**(1), 43–45 (1963)

10. CD Groot, D Wurtz, KH Hoffmann. Low autocorrelation binary sequences: exact enumeration and optimization by evolutionary strategies.Optimization. **23**(4), 369–384 (1992)
11. HD Schotten, HD Luke, On the search for low correlated binary sequences. Int. J. Electron. Commun. **59**(2), 67–78 (2005)
12. S Mertens, Exhaustive search for low-autocorrelation binary sequences. J. Phys. A. **29**, 473–481 (1996)
13. P Stocia, H He, J Li, New algorithms for designing unimodular sequences with good correlation properties. IEEE Trans. Signal Process. **57**(4), 1415–1425 (2009)
14. J Li, P Stoica, X Zheng, Signal synthesis and receiver design for MIMO radar imaging. IEEE Trans. Signal Process. **56**(8), 3959–3968 (2008)
15. M Soltanalian, P Stoica, Computational design of sequences with good correlation properties. IEEE Trans. Signal Process. **60**(5), 2180–2193 (2012)
16. P Stoica, H He, J Li, On designing sequences with impulse-like periodic correlation. IEEE Trans. Signal Process. Lett. **16**(8), 703–706 (2009)
17. M Soltanalian, P Stoica, Designing unimodular codes via quadratic optimization is not always hard. IEEE Trans. Signal Process. **57**(6), 1221–1234 (2009)
18. S Sussman, Least-square synthesis of radar ambiguity functions. IEEE Trans. Inf. Theory. **8**(3), 246–254 (1962)
19. JD Wolf, GM Lee, CE Suyo, Radar waveform synthesis by mean-square optimization techniques. IEEE Trans. on Aero. Elec. Sys. **5**(4), 611–619 (1968)
20. I Gladkova, D Chebanov, in *International Conference on Radar Systems, Toulouse*. On the synthesis problem for a waveform having a nearly ideal ambiguity functions, (France, 2004), pp. 1–5
21. YI Abramovich, BG Danilov, AN Meleshkevich, Application of integer programming to problems of ambiguity function optimization. Radio Eng. Elect. Phys. **22**(5), 48–52 (1977)
22. H He, P Stocia, in *Acoustics, Speech and Signal Processing (ICASSP) 2011 IEEE International Conference on*. On synthesizing cross ambiguity functions, (Prague, 2011), pp. 3536–3539
23. A Aubry, A De Maio, B Jiang, S Zhang, Ambiguity function shaping for cognitive radar via complex quartic optimization. IEEE Trans. Signal Process. **61**(22), 5603–5619 (2013)
24. S Boyd, L Vandenberghe, *Convex Optimization*. (Cambridge Univ. Press, Cambridge, 2004)
25. B Chen, S He, Z Li, S Zhang, Maximum block improvement and polynomial optimization. SIAM J. Optimiz. **22**(11), 87–107 (2012)
26. M Soltanalian, P Stoica, Designing unimodular codes via quadratic optimization. IEEE Trans. Signal Process. **62**(5), 1221–1234 (2014)
27. JR Guerci, *Cognitive Radar, The Knowledge-Aided Fully Adaptive Approach*. (Artech House, Norwood, MA, 2010)

12

Interval type 2 fuzzy localization for wireless sensor networks

Noura Baccar[1*] and Ridha Bouallegue[2]

Abstract

Indoor localization in wireless sensor networks (WSN) is a challenging process. This paper proposes a new approach to solve the localization problematic. A fuzzy linguistic localization scheme is proposed. Based on interval type 2 fuzzy logic (IT2FL), a signal processing of the radio signal strength indicator (RSSI) minimizes the uncertainty in RSSI measurements from anchors caused by the indoor obstacles. The fuzzy system subdivides the map on fuzzy sets described by a new fuzzy location indicator (FLI). Fluctuations on RSS fingerprints are then reduced thanks to the IT2FL in the input side and the FLI in the output side. Experimentations were done in the Cynapsys indoor environment on a WSN test bed. The experimental results prove higher success rate in position estimations thanks to the FLI concept and the superiority of interval type 2 fuzzy logic to handle signal fluctuations.

Keywords: Interval type 2 fuzzy logic, Signal processing, Wireless sensor network, Localization

1 Introduction

Do we really need *x*, *y*, and *z* coordination for indoor localization? When we are subjected to human localization process, we refer generally to linguistic localization (near to the desk, next to the window in front of the TV...). Thus, a fuzzification of this problematic will change our angle of view and enlarge our perception of localization methods from Euclidean geometrical equations and signal propagation models to more opened intelligent and pervasive computing.

The availability and diversity of wireless communication (wireless area networks (WAN), wireless sensor networks (WSN)...) give researchers a huge amount of creative areas. Those available transmitted data and indicators may be exploited in applications to facilitate human being life. Smart buildings, smart homes, and ubiquitous cities are the trends of leading projects in pioneer companies. Hence, the progress in WSN deployment for "smart" purposes, besides the implication of those huge technological companies in this field, give a big motivation to innovate in various communication techniques. Mobility and localization are indeed two constraining factors relative to WSN design problematic. Many emerging context-aware applications are stand on location-based services (LBS).

Since that, geo-localization in WSN has been the subject of many researches. For outdoor as well as indoor environment, the use of computational intelligence in localization techniques is not a new invented methodology. However, the specific nature of the indoor environment (shadowing, reflection, path loss...) originates depth investigation using different optimization techniques. Type 1 fuzzy logic (T1FL) is one of those techniques for geometrical localization and as a clustering-based methodology. Nevertheless, there has not been any attempt to investigate the usage of interval type 2 fuzzy logic (IT2FL) in indoor geo-localization. But, it was proved that the use of IT2FL in complex real-word applications presenting a high level of uncertainty in measurements performs better [1–3]. In control theory, some industrial application results were presented in [4], and the type 2 fuzzy logic controller (FLC) was applied to three domains: industrial control, mobile robot control, and ambient intelligent environment control. The author proved that type 2 FLC for each application provides smooth responses outperforming always the type 1 counterparts. This is due to the powerful paradigm of type 2 FLC to handle the high level of uncertainties present in real-world environments.

In [5], a data-driven IT2 fuzzy logic modeling framework is presented and very good computational efficiency was demonstrated through real industrial case study posing particular challenges in terms of data uncertainty comparing

* Correspondence: baccar_noura@hotmail.com
[1]Innov'COM/ENIT/Cynapsys, University Tunis El Manar, Tunis, Tunisia
Full list of author information is available at the end of the article

to type 1 fuzzy logic. The superiority of IT2FL to type 1 in handling measurement uncertainties in real-world applications was also proved in [6] and [7].

Since the localization problematic that we discuss here is based on radio signal strength indicator which is submitted to a high level of fluctuations and uncertainty in indoor environments and Interval Type 2 Fuzzy Localization System (IT2FLS) was proved to give better results dealing with data uncertainty, the use of IT2FLS may give similar results on the radio frequency (RF)-based localization.

In this paper, a new approach on fuzzy geo-localization is proposed. Based on a linguistic concept, the expert builds an adaptive fuzzy model to the target environment. In a first learning stage, he defines the distribution of anchor nodes in a manner to cover all target space. Then, he ranges the radio signal strength indicator (RSSI) using linguistic fuzzy descriptors {low, medium, or high}. Because of the instability in the indoor RSSI measurements, an IT2FL processing is programmed. On the other hand, the expert clustered the target map on fuzzy sets using a new fuzzy location indicator (FLI). Thus, for each FLI, the expert takes the RSS fingerprints and proceeds to rule base building. Through semantic relations, the geometrical map dispositions are fuzzified to an "if-then" linguistic description. In the online stage, signals are submitted to IT2 fuzzification and then aggregated using the inference engine of the fuzzy localization system (FLS). The FLI is defuzzified to a crisp value describing the location zone in the map. Experiments in the Cynapsys indoor environment have proved the effectiveness of this approach.

This paper is organized as follows. Section 2 will present the background of localization algorithm based on fuzzy logic. Section 3 will detail the proposed approach concepts. In Section 4, the experimentation process and the results are discussed. Finally, the paper is summarized by a conclusion and perspectives.

2 Background

Two main technological choices are basic for the design of localization systems: the localization technology and the positioning technique. Firstly, location-based systems are generally RF-based technologies. Thanks to the speedy progress of nanotechnology [8] (the ease to reach receivers and sensors) that heavily involves short-range communications notably WiFi, Bluetooth, and ZigBee, localization applications become available and some are based on hybrid systems, from robotic guiding [9] to location-based services. In their survey [10], Liu et al. present existent indoor applications in the market and their different performance criteria. They concluded that fingerprinting schemes are better on indoor open areas.

Secondly, the localization techniques can be classified in three categories. The first one consists of deterministic techniques, classified as geometrical methods. They are range-based and estimate the target coordination through multi-lateration, triangulation, angulation, angle of arrival (AoA), and time of arrival (TOA) needing most of the time specific hardware. In their work, Yan et al. [11] presented a fuzzy-based geometrical probabilistic method to deal with non-light-of-sight (NLOS) conditions. Although it presents good results, their algorithm needs complex calculations and depends on the known and precision of anchor coordination.

On the other side, a big number of research works consider the probabilistic approaches [10] like Bayesian algorithms [12] and a third localization process is based on machine learning approaches [13–15], using SVM [16] and neural network-based algorithms [17]. In this category, K-nearest neighbor (KNN) classification was deeply investigated in fingerprinting algorithms [14, 18, 19]. It shows promoting results in terms of offering adequate estimation accuracy; however, a big number of anchors are required to reach this accuracy.

Fuzzy logic was exploited in two manners: geometric fuzzification concept [20] and rule-based fuzzification concept. Wang et al. [20] demonstrate that the fuzzy geometric approach outperforms the traditional least squares approach. However, this approach is costly while it requires velocity and azimuth angle measurements. Besides, the system is only adaptable to linear trajectories and not for the various kinds of fuzzy observer trajectories. Fan et al. [21] suggest the use of fuzzy logic in a recursive least squares filter. Although it proposes a different methodology to process noise unlike statistical models, it uses the classical coordinate-based localization technique in a way raising the filtering processes leading to the increase of computational complexity.

Garcia-Valverde et al. in [22] and [23] have worked on a mobile application based on fuzzy logic. They build an adaptive rule-based model to the system. Through a T1 fuzzification in RSS classification, the used technique is able to automatically learn offline and online to adapt in order to deal with the environmental changes. It reaches 82.22 % of success accuracy. But to handle RSS fluctuations, they used two alternatives: a heuristic preprocessing algorithm and a responsive universal based on trim-like operation to remove peaks and drops and on a modified standard deviation-based technique applied to the last received RSSI values for every access point. On the other side, paper [24] investigates the RSS-based range-free fuzzy ring method. This approach proves good performance face to radio propagation irregularity. However, it is computational intensive and difficult in experimental deployments while it depends on the propagation model parameter estimation.

In [25], the author uses T1FL for RSS clustering and the FLS creates linear equations to estimate the location zone. This system provides 95 % accuracy in positioning, whereas it has big granularity in localization (zones and not rooms) which are relatively away from each other and without providing results in case of adjacent rooms.

Furthermore, IT2FL was not used for localization. It is used generally in WSN for clustering sensed data. Although Liang and Wang in [26] presented a methodology to simulate uncertainty on RSSi and to cluster measurements, it was not exploited on localization. In literature, no real experiments on indoor mobile application based on type 2 fuzzy logic were found and this is the main contribution of this paper.

Our anchor-based proposed approach provides high granularity in location definition. It uses no preprocessing algorithm but the IT2 in the fuzzification phase which will handle RSS fluctuations. The following section will give all details of the proposed approach.

3 Proposed approach

Generally, when working on geo-localization, geometric positioning is used to calculate the coordinates of mobile nodes. Little work referred to "linguistic" geo-localization. In our proposed linguistic approach, calculation of the mobile's node position is based on hierarchical fuzzy clustering process. As presented in Fig. 1, in the first learning phase, the target space is subdivided in zones characterized by a FLI. The FLI is incremented in order to respect continuity in the geometric space and translation between rooms. This continuity in FLI will guarantee the continuity in fuzzy space where each room is considered as a fuzzy set (FS). Thus, each room is described by a fuzzy vector of FLIn.

In each FLI, RSS measurements are collected from anchor nodes in the data base (DB). Those measurements are processed using interval type 2 fuzzy logic algorithm to minimize instability of this indicator through its footprint of uncertainty (FOU) property. Based on the created DB, the expert extracts the linguistic rules to form the rule base of the fuzzy process.

On the online phase, RSSi measurements are first fuzzified using IT2 process as described in Fig. 2 and transmitted to the inference engine which will proceed to implication and aggregation methods referring to the rule base. The aggregated type 2 output will be then type-reduced to a fuzzy type 1 FLI. Finally, the defuzzification module will conclude the location estimation process by calculating the crisp corresponding FLI.

3.1 Fuzzy interval type 2 input processing

An intelligent localization algorithm is proposed based on "interval type 2 fuzzy logic" for input processing. Type 2 FLS is generally used when the circumstances are too unknown to determine exact membership grade like when the training data is affected by noise. In a big number of control and clustering applications, higher accuracy has been proved using the IT2 fuzzy logic [27]. Satvir et al.

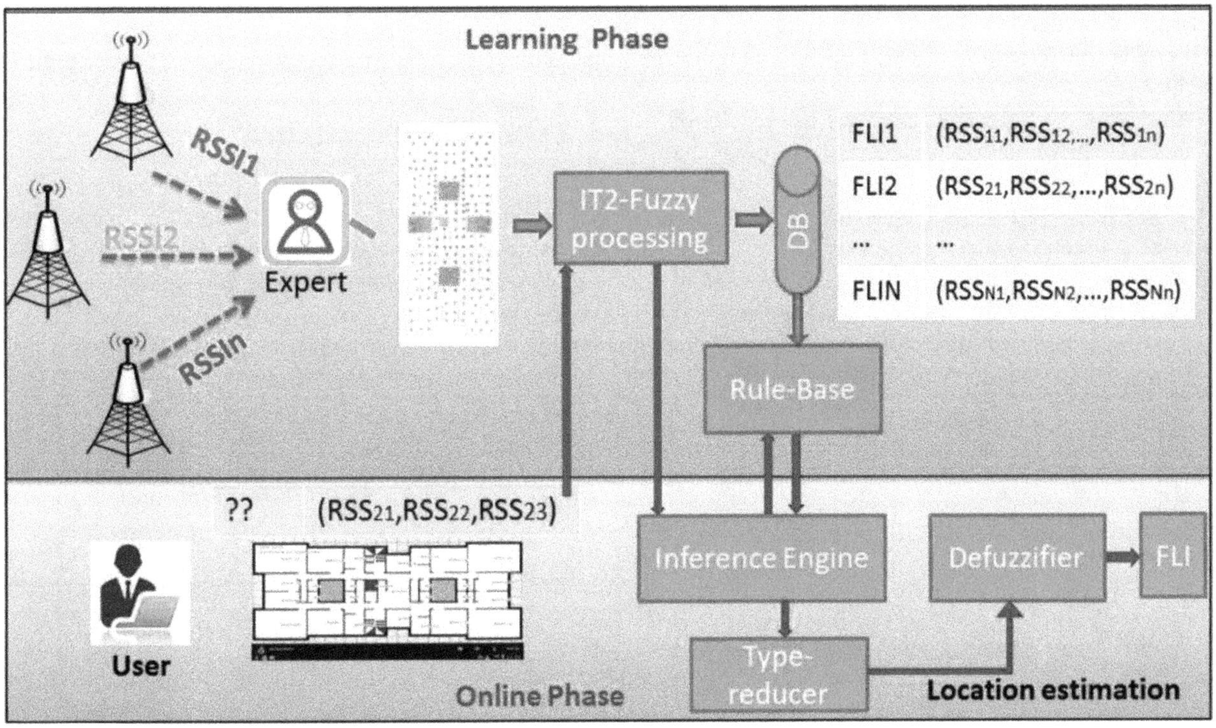

Fig. 1 General fuzzy localization approach diagram

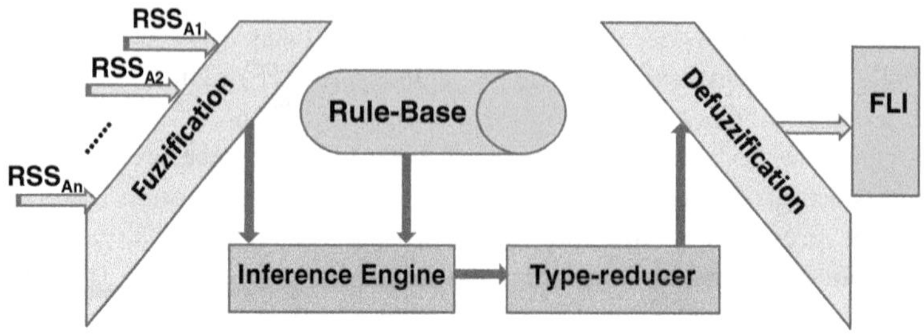

Fig. 2 Interval type 2 fuzzy process

[27] proved the viability of interval type 2 over type 1 FLSs through implemented systems in real environment. IT2 handled the presented noise by its uncertainty modeling property.

In their work [28], Aladi et al. demonstrated the relationship between the FOU size and the amount of uncertainty and noise in a given environmental setting. Thus, considering the target space as fuzzy sets will incorporate fluctuations in RSS measurements. An RSS vector in a zone will not be as specific as it was saved in the learning phase. The fuzzification process will limit this specificity and takes into consideration the instability of signal propagation in the indoor environment.

Two approaches exist to design an IT2FLS: the first approach is partially dependent and based on a type 1 FLS design and then a translation to the IT2FLS. Thus, a faster comparative study between T1 and the IT2 could be easily done. The second approach relies on a direct design of predefined IT2FLS parameters and thus avoids the effect of translation from T1 which may not give the best results.

As in this work, we intend to compare the results of the T1 and IT2 in localization error, and to prove the superiority of IT2 upon T1, the first approach is used. Thus, we will preserve the basic structure (the number of membership functions and the rule base).

Zadeh defines "Fuzzy Logic is determined as a set of mathematical principles for knowledge representation based on degrees of membership rather than on crisp membership of classical binary logic." RSS is T1 FS representing RSSi(t) in the fuzzy domain. Based on the Zadeh theory, it can be defined as

$$\mathrm{RSS} = \int_{D_{RSS}} \mu_{RSS}(x)/x \tag{1}$$

where D_{RSS} is the universe of discourse: $D_{\mathrm{RSS}} = [-100,-70]$; μ_{RSS} is the membership function (MF): $\mu_{\mathrm{RSS}}: D_{\mathrm{RSS}} \rightarrow [0, 1]$; and "∫"denotes the collection of all points $x \in D_{\mathrm{RSS}}$ with associated membership grade $\mu_{\mathrm{RSS}}(x)$

Consider an IT2FS $\widetilde{\mathrm{RSS}}$ described based on the definition in [29]:

$$\begin{aligned}\widetilde{\mathrm{RSS}} &= \int_{x\in D_{\widetilde{\mathrm{RSS}}}} \int_{u\in J_{x\subseteq[0,1]}} \mu_{\widetilde{\mathrm{RSS}}(x,u)}/(x,u)\\ &= \int_{x\in D_{\widetilde{\mathrm{RSS}}}} \left[\int_{u\in J_{x\subseteq[0,1]}} 1/u\right]/x\end{aligned} \tag{2}$$

where x is the primary variable in $D_{\widetilde{\mathrm{RSS}}} = [-100,-70]$; $u \in [0, 1]$ the secondary variable in the domain $J_{x\subseteq[0,1]}$ at each $x \in \mathrm{D}_{\widetilde{\mathrm{RSS}}}$; and the amplitude of $\mu_{\widetilde{\mathrm{RSS}}(x,u)}$ is the secondary grade of $\widetilde{\mathrm{RSS}}$, equals 1 for $\forall x \in \mathrm{D}_{\widetilde{\mathrm{RSS}}}$ and $\forall u \in J_x \subseteq [0, 1]$.

$\widetilde{\mathrm{RSS}}$ is described by its FOU, shown in the right part of Fig. 3 using the upper and the lower membership functions $\mu_{\overline{\mathrm{RSS}}}$ and $\mu_{\underline{\mathrm{RSS}}}$ [29] as

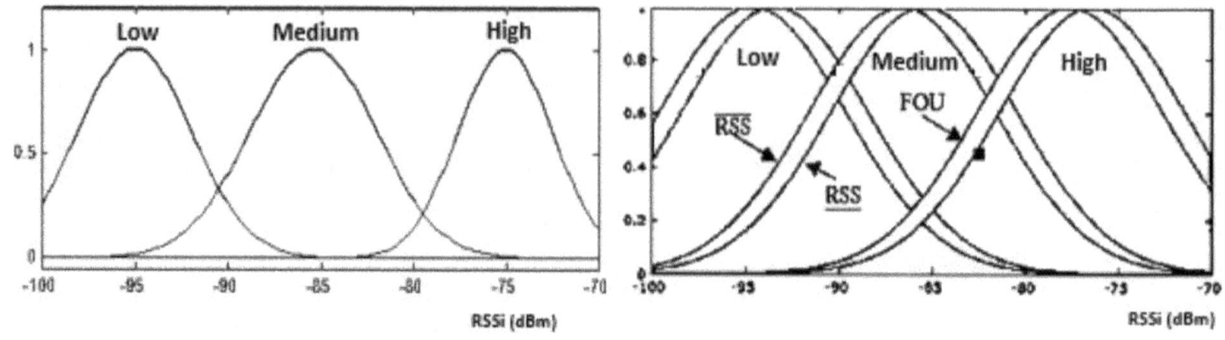

Fig. 3 Type 1 (*left*) and interval type 2 (*right*) RSS fuzzy sets (dBm)

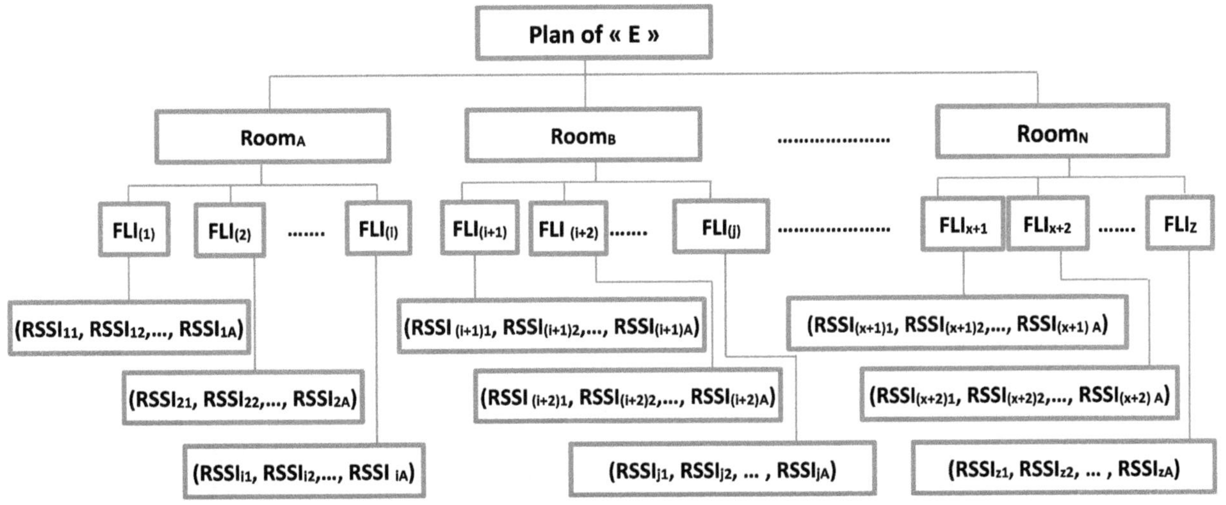

Fig. 4 Fuzzy location indicator (FLI) diagram

$$\mathrm{FOU}\left(\widetilde{\mathrm{RSS}}\right) = \cup_{\forall\, x\in J_x}\left(\mu_{\overline{\mathrm{RSS}}}\,, \mu_{\underline{\mathrm{RSS}}}\right) \tag{3}$$

The FOU is not uniform in the FS's region. With an assumption that the noise/uncertainty is uniform, a FOU construction method gave rise to an equal amount of uncertainty in the memberships.

In order to ensure a uniform FOU, based on the work of Aladi et al. [28] considering the FOU size, it is expressed using the parameter $c \in [0,1]$. For $c = 0$, MFs are of type 1 FS, and for $c = 1$, they are an IT2 set with a very wide FOU. Thus, the upper and lower MFs are expressed as follows:

$$\mu_{\overline{\mathrm{RSS}}} = \min\left[\mu_{RSS}(x) + \frac{c}{2}, 1\right] \tag{4}$$

$$\mu_{\underline{\mathrm{RSS}}} = \min\left[\max\left[\mu_{RSS}(x) - \frac{c}{2}, 0\right], 1-c\right] \tag{5}$$

Gaussian membership functions are considered in both T1 and IT2FLS.

3.2 Output processing: the FLI

Through a linearization process of the 2D plan, the tagged environment "E" will be hierarchized in N fuzzy sets, Z fuzzy subsets (FLI).

To be localized, a mobile node sends a message to the nearest anchor in its coverage. The anchor stands by and replies by a beacon message to the sender. This message indicates the RSSI measurement and will be classified in a FLI classified in the set {Room_A, Room_B,...,Room_N} (Fig. 4).

Thus, the fuzzy set "Room_A" is defined by Room_A = {FLI1, FLI2,..., FLIn}. Hence, Room_B will be Room_B = {FLIn + 1, FLIn + 2,..., FLIn + m} and so on for each room (Fig. 5). Those FSs are represented by type 1 triangular membership functions (Fig. 6).

The FLI specification will be equivalent to the FSs of Rssi vector in each room.

The variation in each FLI will specify the interval of each membership function. For FLI = 1, an interval of the lowest measured Rssi for FLI = 1 and the higher measured one for the same FLI will be determined.

A subset Room$_A$ of the set FLI is induced by its membership function $\mu_{\mathrm{Room\_A}}$ mapping the indicators of the FLI with the elements of the unity interval [0, 1], $\mu_{\mathrm{Room\_A}}$: FLI → [0, 1] (Fig. 6).

3.3 FLS

Considering the correlation between input fuzzy RSS sets and the output FLI, a Mamdani model is used, with the following characteristics:

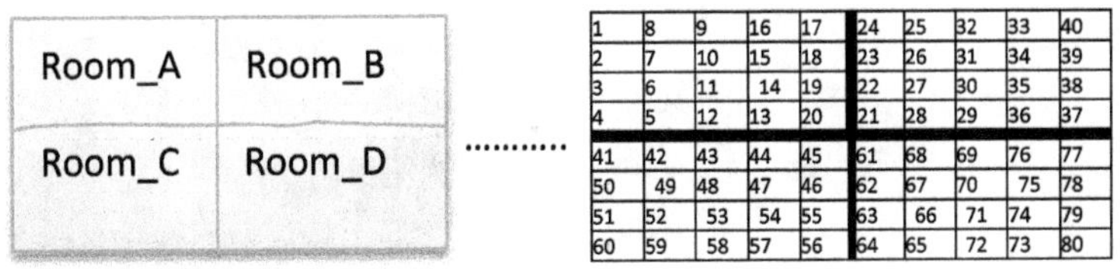

Fig. 5 Fuzzy location indicator (FLI) definition for room identification

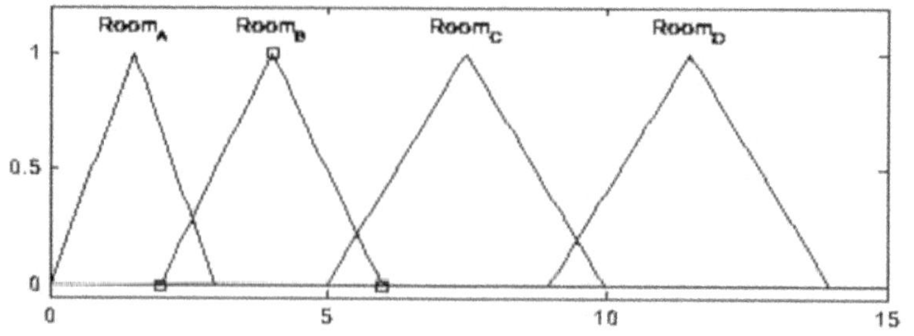

Fig. 6 Membership functions of the FLI

"Fuzzification = 'Interval Type 2'"
"Approach = 'Principal MF + FOU'"
"TNorm = 'Product'"
"SNorm = 'Probor'"
"Implication Method = 'Product'"
"Aggregation Method = 'Probor'"
"Type Reduction Method = 'LoM'"
"Defuzzification Method = 'Minimum'"
Details of those methods may be found in [28] and [30].

4 Experimental results and discussion

4.1 Experimental test bed

For the experimental setup, we considered the implementation of a localization platform in the indoor environment of the Cynapsys Company (Fig. 7). The experimental bench is realized by the deployment of a WSN platform. The choice of the communication protocol and kit was restricted by the used sensors in Cynapsys for their smart home project. This platform is based on an STM32W108C kit set of four application boards to build a mesh network (two standard boards (MB851) and two with power amplifiers (MB954)). STM32W108 is a ZigBee RF4CE and IEEE 802.15.4 certified platform. The boards integrate a 2.4-GHz, IEEE802.15.4 compliant transceiver and a 32-bit ARM®-CortexTM M3 microprocessor. Thus, it allows evaluating IEEE 802.15.4 capabilities and developing a testing localization application.

Let us consider the plan of Cynapsys as our test bed. Three STM32W108 boards are deployed as anchors. Figure 9 shows there dispositions in a way their range covers all the target zones.

The mobile node MB954 is attached to an i5 Pc through a USB cable. The expert takes five fingerprints in each indicated zone along the target space: {Open_Space, Pythagore_meeting_room, Pythagore_corridor, Reception, Descartes_meeting_room, Descartes_corridor, RD_room}.

The localization process is composed of two main phases. The first one is the "learning phase." In this stage, the expert saves the fingerprints relative to each room. In the second stage, the system proceeds to a fuzzy localization process.

4.2 Software developments

4.2.1 Network creation

The implementation of the localization platform was started by connecting the STM32W108 boards and building the network. In the first place, the choice of network topology was made based on the application needs. It is necessary to keep in obvious fact that the mobile board must be able to communicate directly with anchors so that we obtain the value of the RSSI between these two nodes and not with regard to another node which has broadcast the message. Based on the optimized MAC library IEEE 802.15.4, three possible topologies for the network are possible. The first one is star topology. In this type of network, all nodes are directly connected to the coordinator. Thus, there is no direct communication if we place more than one mobile. The second topology is in a tree where nodes which are

Fig. 7 Experimental setup of the localization test bed

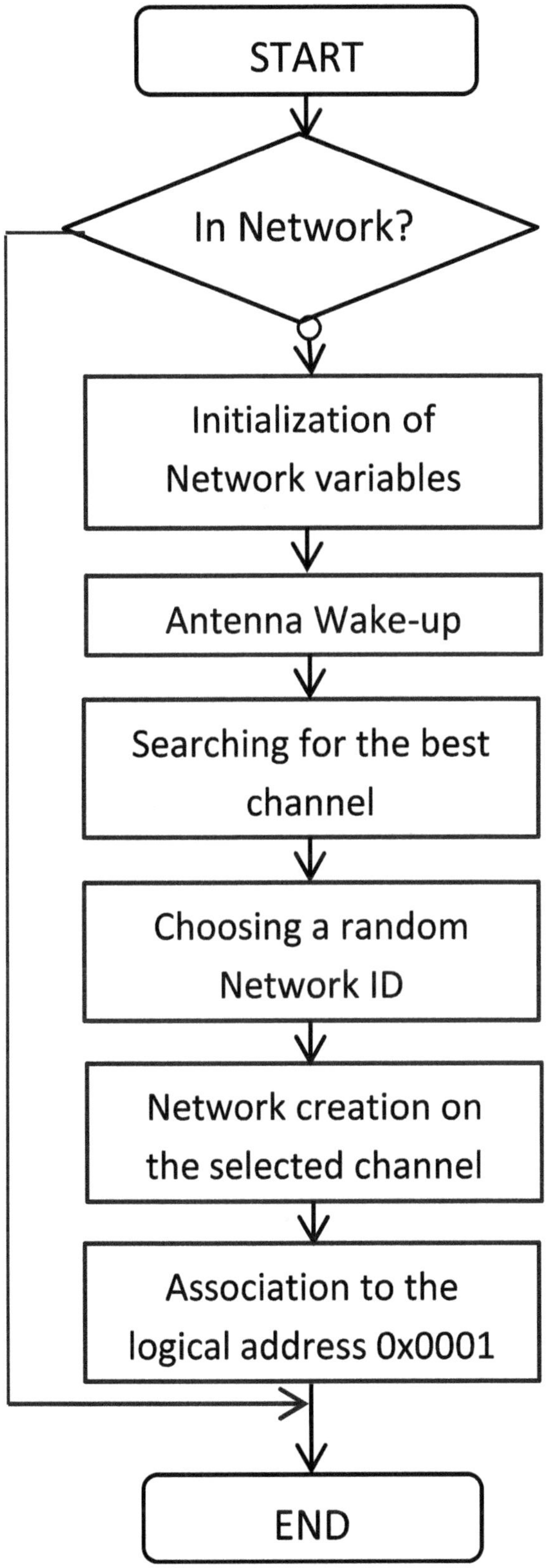

Fig. 8 Wireless sensor network creation diagram

in various connections of the tree are not in direct contact what does not suit our application. The final proposed topology is meshed where nodes are in direct contact. This topology suits our case.

Hence, the embedded program is charged of RSSI collection and sending. The functions realized by the embedded system are the following ones: firstly, to establish a wireless network, then connecting cards on the same network; secondly, to assure a stable communication between them. In addition to making requests to collect RSSI from various anchors, it sends the RSSI vector collected and realizes commands reading via USB to manage card behavior.

The "Simple MAC" library is used for the program. One of its functions is the callback function named "ST_RadioReceiveIsrCallback" which is going to serve us to get back the value of the RSSI. The callback function types are generally functions of interruption which runs automatically in case of an event. In our case, the "ST_RadioReceiveIsrCallback" function runs in the reception of a message. It allows getting back the package in question, the time of arrival, if it contains errors, and the RSSI. Thanks to this function, the recovery of the RSSI of every message is possible; thus, it is enough to send any message to be able to know the RSSI with the transmitter.

To realize the communication between boards, it is necessary first of all to create a private network. The creation of the network is only realized by the coordinator which plays the role of a server. As indicated in Fig. 8, all at first begin by making out a choice, if the boards are already in a network or not. If not, the coordinator proceeds to the initialization of the network intern variables, and then, it wakes up the radio. Next, it looks for the best channel (energetic side) and it chooses randomly one ID for the network, and then, the latter is created in the chosen channel. Finally, it attributes the logical address 1 in the table of address. The protocol was developed in IAR Embedded Workbench for ARM 6.50 and loaded on the STM32W108 boards using a programmer and debugger J-Link of flash memory JTAG.

4.2.2 Input fuzzification

As we considered in the localisation test bed of three anchors, three fuzzy inputs are defined: ZRSS1, ZRSS2, and ZRSS3. Their properties are as defined in Table 1 defined the same way for ZRSS2 and ZRSS3 on the Generalized Fuzzy System toolbox on Matlab R2014. The universe of discourse (UOD) was defined based on the experimental measurements, and FOU was defined as 2.

4.2.3 Output FLI definition

The testing environment for localization on Cynapsys was divided into 20 zones. Each zone is defined by its

Table 1 Fuzzy interval type 2 ZRSS1 properties

ZRSS1	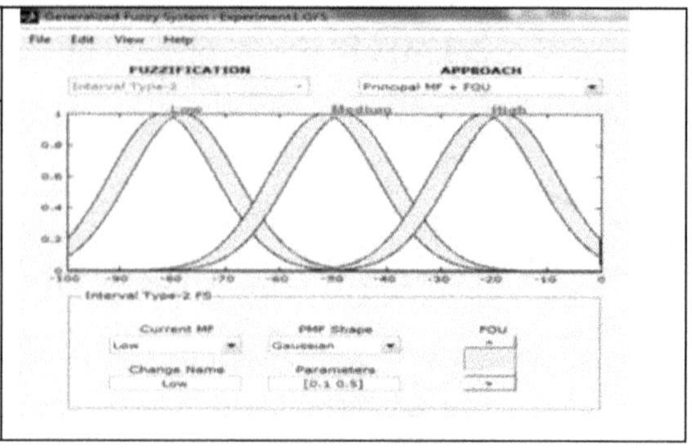
UOD = [-100 0] NumMFUNs = 3 MF1 = 'Low':'Gaussian', [10 -80],FOU = 2 MF2 = 'Medium':'Gaussian',[10 -50],FOU = 2 MF3 = 'High':'Gaussian',[10 -20],FOU = 2	

FLI, and every room is considered as a type 1 triangular fuzzy set presented in Fig. 9 from the left to the right and with the following parameters:

"MF1 = 'Open_Space':'Triangular',[0 1.5 3]"
"MF2 = 'Pythagore_room':'Triangular',[2.5 3.5 5]"
"MF3 = 'Pythagore_corridor':'Triangular',[4.5 6 8]"
"MF4 = 'Reception':'Triangular',[7 9 11]"
"MF5 = 'Descartes_room':'Triangular',[10 12 14]"
"MF6 = 'Descartes_corridor':'Triangular',[13 15 17]"
"MF7 = 'RD_room':'Triangular',[16 18 20]"

4.2.4 Rule base creation

Twenty-one rules were defined based on the expert linguistic evaluations. Some rules were technically impossible and were not considered, for example, IF (ZRSS1 IS Medium) (ZRSS2 IS High) (ZRSS3 IS High) is impossible, the mobile node cannot be near anchor 2 and anchor 3 in the same time.

1. IF (ZRSS1 IS Low) (ZRSS2 IS Low) (ZRSS3 IS Low)THEN (FLI IS Open_Space)(1)
2. IF (ZRSS1 IS Low) (ZRSS2 IS Low) (ZRSS3 IS Medium)THEN (FLI IS Open_Space)(1)
3. IF (ZRSS1 IS Low) (ZRSS2 IS Low) (ZRSS3 IS High)THEN (FLI IS Open_Space)(1)
4. IF (ZRSS1 IS Low) (ZRSS2 IS Medium) (ZRSS3 IS Low)THEN (FLI IS Open_Space)(1)
5. IF (ZRSS1 IS Low) (ZRSS2 IS High) (ZRSS3 IS Medium)THEN (FLI IS Open_Space)(1)
6. IF (ZRSS1 IS Medium) (ZRSS2 IS Low) (ZRSS3 IS Low)THEN (FLI IS Open_Space)(1)
7. IF (ZRSS1 IS Medium) (ZRSS2 IS Low) (ZRSS3 IS Medium)THEN (FLI IS Open_Space)(1)
8. IF (ZRSS1 IS Medium) (ZRSS2 IS Low) (ZRSS3 IS High)THEN (FLI IS Open_Space)(1)
9. IF (ZRSS1 IS Medium) (ZRSS2 IS Medium) (ZRSS3 IS Low)THEN (FLI IS Open_Space)(1)
10. IF (ZRSS1 IS Medium) (ZRSS2 IS Medium) (ZRSS3 IS Medium)THEN (FLI IS Open_Space)(1)
11. IF (ZRSS1 IS Low) (ZRSS2 IS Medium) (ZRSS3 IS Medium)THEN (FLI IS Open_Space)(1)
12. IF (ZRSS1 IS Low) (ZRSS2 IS Medium) (ZRSS3 IS High)THEN (FLI IS Open_Space)(1)
13. IF (ZRSS1 IS Low) (ZRSS2 IS High) (ZRSS3 IS Medium)THEN (FLI IS Open_Space)(1)
14. IF (ZRSS1 IS Medium) (ZRSS2 IS High) (ZRSS3 IS Low)THEN (FLI IS Open_Space)(1)
15. IF (ZRSS1 IS Medium) (ZRSS2 IS High) (ZRSS3 IS Medium)THEN (FLI IS Open_Space)(1)
16. IF (ZRSS1 IS High) (ZRSS2 IS Low) (ZRSS3 IS Low)THEN (FLI IS Open_Space)(1)

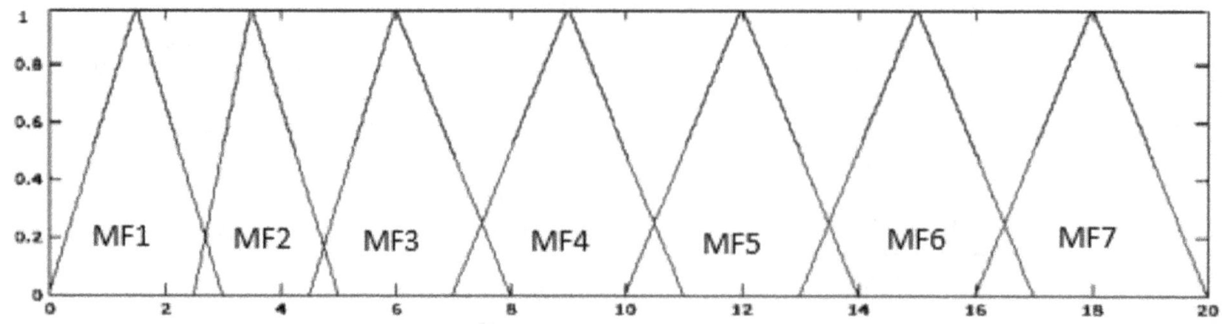

Fig. 9 FLI membership functions (MFs)

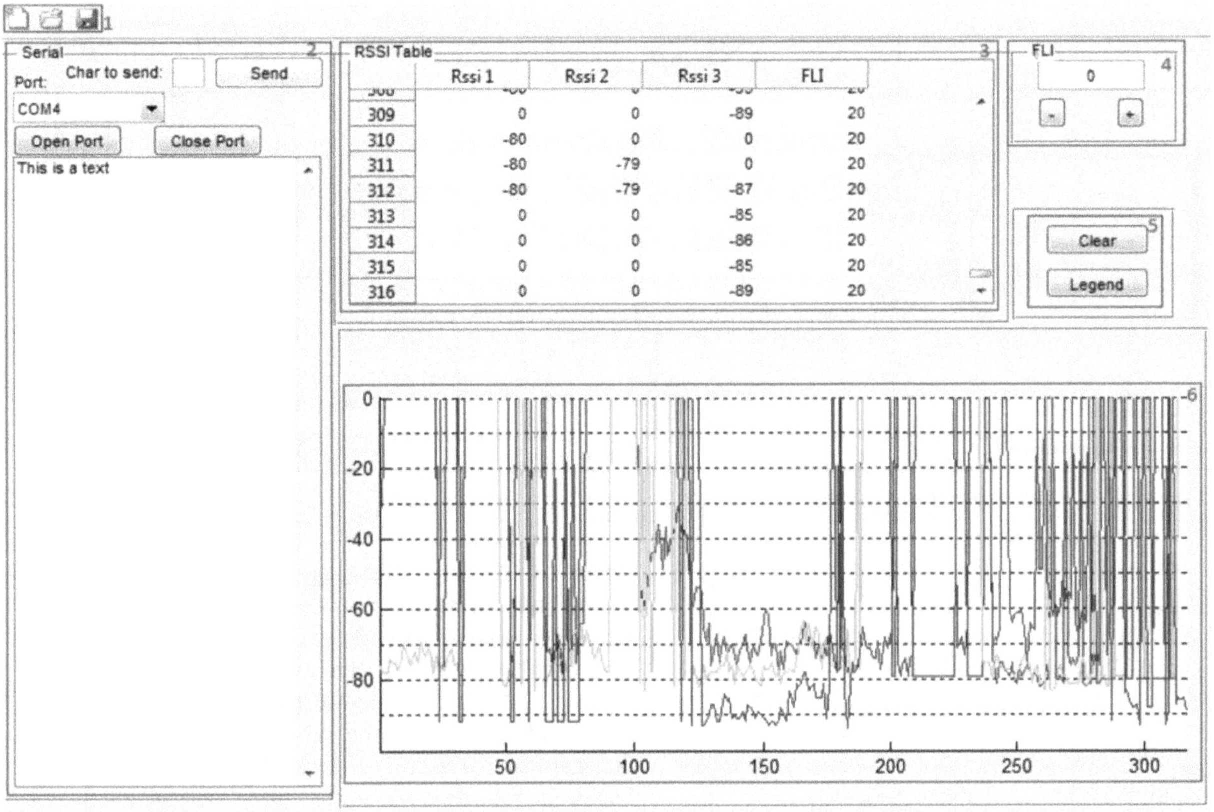

Fig. 10 Fingerprinting GUI

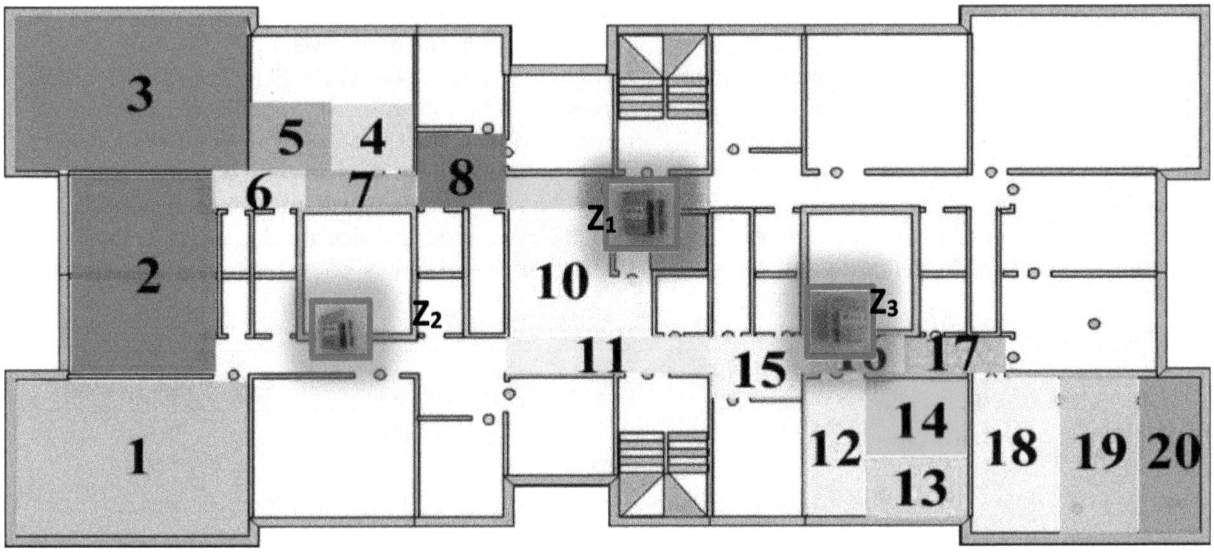

Fig. 11 Experimental setup of the localization bench

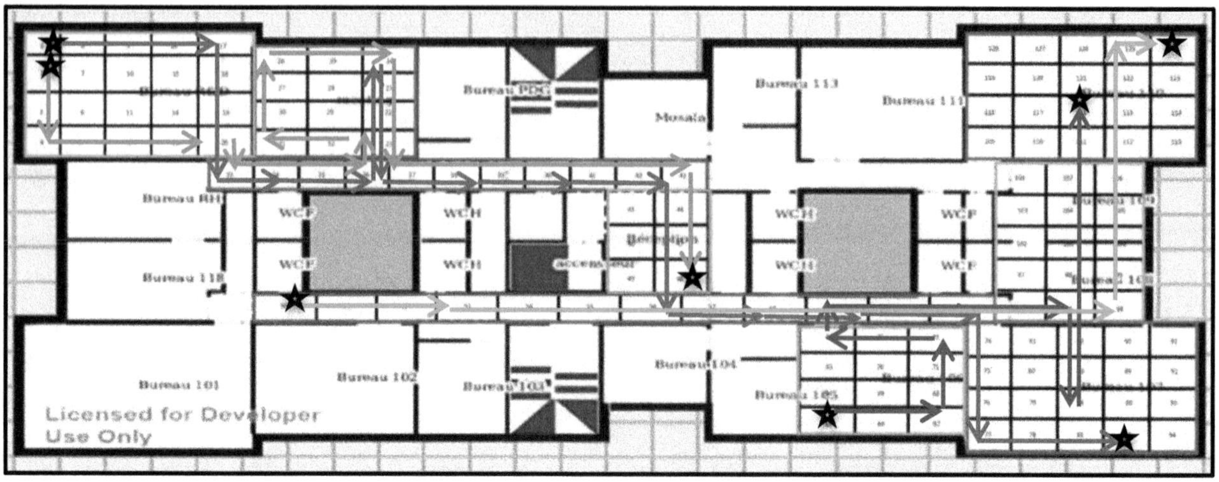

Fig. 12 Experimental scenarios on the Cynapsys map

17.IF (ZRSS1 IS High) (ZRSS2 IS Low) (ZRSS3 IS Medium)THEN (FLI IS Open_Space)(1)
18.IF (ZRSS1 IS High) (ZRSS2 IS Low) (ZRSS3 IS High)THEN (FLI IS Open_Space)(1)
19.IF (ZRSS1 IS High) (ZRSS2 IS Medium) (ZRSS3 IS Low)THEN (FLI IS Open_Space)(1)
20.IF (ZRSS1 IS High) (ZRSS2 IS Medium) (ZRSS3 IS Medium)THEN (FLI IS Open_Space)(1)
21.IF (ZRSS1 IS High) (ZRSS2 IS Medium) (ZRSS3 IS High)THEN (FLI IS Open_Space)(1)

4.2.5 Experimental platform

Using Matlab R2014, a fuzzy localization platform was developed. The graphical user interface (GUI) presents two windows. The first one, shown in Fig. 10, is dedicated to fingerprinting. In the second red rectangle of Fig. 10, the communicating interface between the anchor nodes and the mobile node linked to the PC through the "COM4" port.

The second interface processes those measurements and displays the calculated FLI on the map as presented in Fig. 11.

4.3 Experimental scenarios

Two test cases were defined. In the first test case, the target environment where divided into 20 zones as shown in Fig. 11. The average zone's area is 20 m^2. In the second test case, we divided the target environment into 130 zones with an average area of 2.25 m^2. For each test case, five scenarios were evaluated through five trajectories and four of them are shown in Fig. 12: blue, orange, and purple and the other trajectory repeats the fingerprinting trajectory; hence, it tested all the zones. For each trajectory, we started from the star point in a defined zone.

Then, relying on the RSSI measurements from the ZigBee anchors Z_1, Z_2, and Z_3, the system calculates the FLI, and using the algorithm below, the localization process is evaluated.

4.4 Results and discussion

While this work is based on a linguistic localization, the performance of the design is evaluated through the success and failure rate of the estimated position in the zone level and in the room level.

For the first test case where FLI = 20, Table 2 details success rates in both zone and room levels. The true estimated position was mentioned by the user as correct during evaluation for two characteristics: is it the correct zone? And is it the correct room? Saved answers in the data base are used to calculate the success rate. From the fifth trajectories, less success rate was recorded for

Table 2 Experimental results for FLI = 20

Scenarios	Total positions	True estimated position	True estimated room	Success rate in the zone level (%)	Success rate in the room level (%)
Fingerprinting trajectory	120	105	107	87.5	89.16
Red trajectory	65	57	57	87.69	87.69
Orange trajectory	18	16	16	88.88	88.88
Purple trajectory	30	24	25	80	83.33
Blue trajectory	30	25	25	83.33	83.33

Table 3 Experimental results for FLI = 130

Scenarios	Total positions	True estimated position	True estimated room	Success rate in the zone level (%)	Success rate in the room level (%)
Fingerprinting trajectory	120	98	110	81.66	91.66
Red trajectory	65	55	59	84.61	90.76
Orange trajectory	18	16	16	88.88	88.88
Purple trajectory	30	24	28	80	93.33
Blue trajectory	30	22	25	73.33	83.33

the longer trajectory where all zones are crossed. Errors in the zone level are not necessarily errors in the room level. In the purple trajectory, for example, six errors were noticed. One error was a wrong zone but in the correct room, and the others are wrong zones and wrong room estimation. Higher success rate was recorded on the orange trajectory positions. This is due to the fact that this trajectory presents a simple path where less neighboring rooms and zones cause similarity. Hence, the average success rate in the zone level is 85.48 %, and the average success rate for the room level is 86.47 % which is an excellent positioning rate.

For the second test case where FLI = 130, harder work was done to collect five fingerprints in a 2.25 m^2 zone. Their experimental results presented in Table 3 shows an average success rate in the zone level as 81.69 % and an average success rate in the room level as 89.59 %. In comparison to the first case, the success rate in the zone level was decreased but the success in the room level was increased. This is because the number of zones in a room rises, for example for RD room, it was only 3 zones and became 20 zones. Hence, the positioning errors in the zones become more frequent. Besides, errors when taking fingerprintings have higher probability to occur while zones are small (2.25 m^2) and fingerprints in the same room are nearly similar.

On the other side, the localization system was tested using a T1 RSS signal processing. For FLI = 20, the average success rate has remarkably decreased in the zone level to 75.59 % and the average success rate for the room level to 77.4 %. For FLI = 130, it decreases to 72.39 % in the zone level and to 78.88 % in the room level. Hence, the use of IT2 fuzzy logic has enhanced the performance of the system by 10 % as presented in Fig. 13, despite that the FLI approach has proved good localization precision regards to fuzzy systems.

Further experiments were conducted on the R&D room (8 m × 5.5 m) to calculate the average localization error (The localization error is measured as the Euclidean distance between the actual and the estimated locations). For three anchor boards (STM32W108), 200 fingerprints were taken through 40 FLI in the target zone. Thirty-five locations were considered for evaluation. For the sake of consistency and completeness, we use our gathered data to evaluate our proposed IT2FL algorithm and two non-fuzzy algorithms: the KNN-based localization method and the lateration algorithm.

The KNN method is based on comparative searches of the profiled fingerprints to choose the K closest profiled samples in terms of minimizing the RSS discordance between the query RSS sample and the profiled ones.

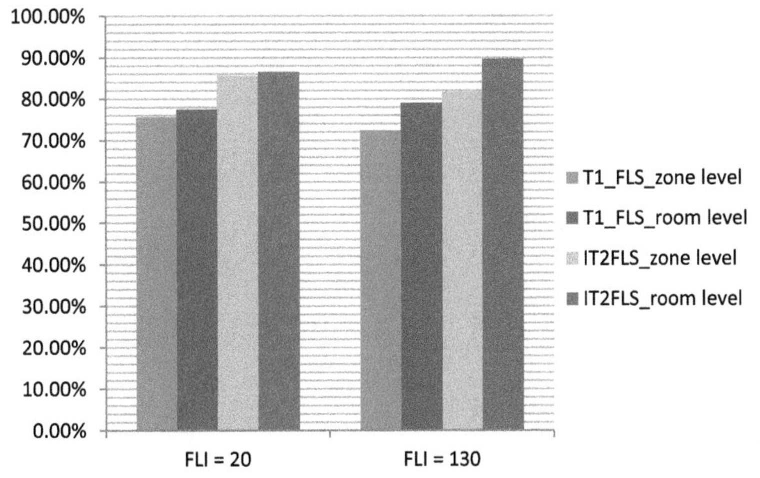

Fig. 13 Success rate in T1 and IT2FLS for FLI = 20 and 130

Table 4 Comparative experimental results of the average localization error between fuzzy and non-fuzzy algorithms

Localization algorithm	Average localization error (m)
IT2FLS	0.8
K-nearest neighbor (KNN)	1.1
Lateration	1.9

The weighted coordinates of these K samples generate the estimated location.

For the lateration-based localization algorithm, a log-normal shadowing propagation model is configured as follows:

$$\mathrm{RSS}(i) = \mathrm{RSS0}{-}10 * \mathrm{np} * \log(d(i)/d0) + \sigma \tag{6}$$

where RSS0 parameter refers to the initial signal strength in $d0$ (for our experimental bed RSS0 = −63 dBm, for $d0$ = 1 m), np is the path loss parameter np = 2.25 (considering an indoor office environment), and σ is the standard deviation of valid RSSI values per link. We use the profiled fingerprints to estimate $\sigma = 4.9$ dB. Then, the system of equation system is solved using a standard least squares approach [31] deducing the average error distance.

Table 4 exhibits the average localization error of the testing fingerprinting sets. The experimental results of our proposed approach outperform the two non-fuzzy localization-based algorithms followed by the KNN-based and then by the lateration method. The integration of interval type 2 fuzzification has limited the effect of RSSi fluctuations. Hence, the proposed localization system performs better regarding the obstacle's presence in indoor environments. It integrates a linguistic classification approach, simplifying the KNN-based classifications and reducing the heavy calculations found in the lateration method.

5 Conclusions

This paper proposed a linguistic fuzzy modeling focused on interpretability for localization of mobile nodes in wireless sensor networks. The uncertainty in the linguistic localization system was processed in two ways: in the first place, an interval type 2 fuzzification was proposed to handle RSSI fluctuations. Secondly, a fuzzy location indicator (FLI) was considered to handle geometric repartitions of fuzzy fingerprints. Experimentations have proved a high success rate either for the zone level or the room level. Besides, the superiority of IT2FL to T1FL to minimize RSSI uncertainties has been proved.

In the future work, we intend to work on the automatic generation of the rule base through a neuro-fuzzy algorithm (GARIC), in addition to automating the FLI recording through a preprogrammed drone.

Competing interests

The authors declare that they have no competing interests.

Acknowledgements

These works of research and innovation are made within a MOBIDOC thesis, financed by the European Union (EU) within the framework of the PASRI program, and partially supported by Cynapsys IT Enterprise. We give our thanks to Mootez Jridi and Meher Houidi for their assistances.

Author details

[1]Innov'COM/ENIT/Cynapsys, University Tunis El Manar, Tunis, Tunisia.
[2]Innov'COM, University Carthage, Tunis, Tunisia.

References

1. R Martinez, O Castillo, LT Aguilar, Optimization of interval type-2 fuzzy logic controllers for a perturbed autonomous wheeled mobile robot using genetic algorithms. Inf Sci **179**(13), 2158–2174 (2009)
2. C-H Hsu, C-F Juang, Evolutionary robot wall-following control using type-2 fuzzy controller with species-DE-activated continuous ACO. IEEE Trans. Fuzzy Syst. **21**(1), 100–112 (2013)
3. R John, P Innocent, M Barnes, Type 2 fuzzy sets and neuro-fuzzy clustering of radiographic tibia images. Proceedings of the Sixth IEEE International Conference in Fuzzy Systems **3**, 1375–1380 (1997)
4. H Hagras, Type-2 FLCs: a new generation of fuzzy controllers. IEEE Comput. Intell. Mag. **2**(1), 30–43 (2007)
5. A Rubio Solis, G Panoutsos, Interval type-2 radial basis function neural network: a modelling framework. IEEE Trans. Fuzzy. Syst. **23**(2), 457–473 (2015)
6. R Sepúlveda, O Castillo, P Melin, A Diaz, O Montiel, *Handling Uncertainty in Controllers Using Type-2 Fuzzy Logic*. Proceeding of the 2005 IEEE International Conference on Fuzzy Systems,USA, 2005, pp. 248–253
7. J Mendel, Type-2 fuzzy sets and systems: an overview. IEEE Comput. Intell. Mag. **2**(2), 20–29 (2007)
8. ABI . Research, "Indoor location technologies," US, AN-1331 https://www.abiresearch.com/market-research/product/1016891-indoor-location-technology-oems/. (2014)
9. P Steinhaus, M Strand, R Dillmann, Autonomous robot navigation in human-centered environments based on 3D data fusion. EURASIP J. Adv. Signal Process. **2007**(86831), 1–10 (2006)
10. H Liu, H Darabi, P Banerjee, J Liu, Survey of wireless indoor positioning techniques and systems. IEEE T. Syst. Man CY. C. **37**(6), 1067–1080 (2007)
11. J Yan, K Yu, L Wu, Fuzzy modeling, maximum likelihood estimation, and Kalman filtering for target tracking in NLOS scenarios. EURASIP J. Adv. Signal Process. **2014**, pp. 1-16 (2014)
12. M.R. Morelande, B. Moran, M. Brazil, "Bayesian node localisation in wireless sensor networks," in *Acoustics, Speech and Signal Processing. ICASSP 2008. IEEE International Conference on*, Las Vegas pp. 2545-2548 , (2008)
13. H. Ahmadi and R. Bouallegue, "Comparative study of learning-based localization algorithms for Wireless Sensor Networks: Support Vector regression, Neural Network and Naïve Bayes," *Wireless Communications and Mobile Computing Conference (IWCMC) proceedings, Dubrovnik*, pp. 1554–1558, 2015.
14. IT Haque, C Assi, Profiling-based indoor localization schemes. IEEE Syst. J. **9**(1), 76–85 (2015)
15. MA Alsheikh, S Lin, D Niyato, H-P Tan, Machine learning in wireless sensor networks: algorithms, strategies, and applications. IEEE Commun. Surv. Tutorials **16**(4), 1996–2018 (2014)
16. A Ukil, *Support Vector Machine, Chapter 4, Intelligent Systems and Signal Processing in Power Engineering* (Springer-Verlag, Berlin, 2007)
17. L Gogolak, S Pletl, D Kukolj, Neural network-based indoor localization in WSN environments. Acta. Polytechnica. Hungarica. **10**(6), 221–235 (2013)
18. P. Bahl and V. N. Padmanabhan, "RADAR: an in-building RF-based user location and tracking system," in *INFOCOM 2000. Nineteenth Annual Joint Conference of the IEEE Computer and Communications Societies. Proceedings. IEEE pp 775–784 vol.2*, Tel Aviv (2000). http://ieeexplore.ieee.org/xpl/articleDetails.jsp?arnumber=832252&newsearch=true&queryText=RADAR:%20an%20in-building%20RFbased%20user%20location%20and%20tracking%20system

19. T. Oktem, D. Slock, "Pairwise error probability analysis for power delay profile fingerprinting based localization, pp. 1–5.," in *Vehicular Technology Conference (VTC Spring), 2011 IEEE 73rd*, Yokohama (2011). http://ieeexplore.ieee.org/xpl/articleDetails.jsp?reload=true&arnumber=5956780
20. R. Wang, W. Cao, W. Wan, Location discovery based on fuzzy geometry in passive sensor networks. *Int Journal of Digital Multimedia Broadcasting. , vol. 2011, Article ID 851951, 6 pages. doi:10.1155/2011/851951 Hindawi Pub. Co,* (2011)
21. E Fan, W-x Xie, Z-x Liu, Maneuvering target tracking using fuzzy logic-based recursive least squares filter. EURASIP J. Adv. Signal Process. **53**(53), 1–16 (2014)
22. T Garcia-Valverde, A Garcia-Sola, A Gomez-Skarmeta, J Botia, H Hagras, J Dooley, V Callaghan, "An adaptive learning fuzzy logic system for indoor localisation using Wi-Fi in ambient intelligent environments". Proc. FUZZ-IEEE **1**(8), Brisbane, pp 10–15 (2012)
23. T Garcia-Valverde, A Garcia-Sola, H Hagras, J Dooley, V Callaghan, J Botia, A fuzzy logic-based system for indoor localization using WiFi in ambient intelligent environments. IEEE Trans. Fuzzy Systems **21**(4), 702–718 (2013)
24. A Velimirovic, G Lj, M Djordjevic, M Velimirovic, M Jovanovic, A fuzzy set based approach to range-free localization in wireless sensor networks. Ser.:Elec.Energ. **23**(2), 227–244 (2010)
25. A. Salazar, A. L and G. Licea, "Estimating indoor zone-level location using Wi-Fi RSSI fingerprinting based on fuzzy inference system," *ICMEAE, Conf proceedings, Morelos* pp. 19–22, 2013.
26. Q. Liang and L. Wang, "Sensed Signal Strength Forecasting for Wireless Sensors Using Interval Type-2 Fuzzy Logic System," in The 14th IEEE International Conference on Fuzzy Systems (FUZZ '05) pp. 25-30., 2005.
27. S. Satvir, S. G. Inderjeet, S. Sarabjeet and D. Gaurav, "Application of type-2 fuzzy logic—a review," *International Conference on Communication, Computing & Systems(ICCCS) proceedings, Punjab* pp. 259–263, 2014.
28. J. Aladi, C. Wagner, J. Garibaldi, "Type-1 or interval type-2 fuzzy logic systems—on the relationship of the amount of uncertainty and FOU size," *Fuzzy Systems (FUZZ-IEEE), 2014 IEEE International Conference on, Beijing* pp. 2360–2367, 2014.
29. A. Sadeghian, J. Mendel, H. Tahayori, "Advances in type-2 fuzzy sets: theory and applications", Springer. Vol 30 (2013)
30. JM Mendel, *Uncertain Rule-Based Fuzzy Logic Systems Introduction and New Directions* (Prentice Hall, Indiana , 2001). http://www.informit.com/store/uncertain-rule-based-fuzzy-logic-systems-introduction-9780130409690.
31. K Langendoen, N Reijers, Distributed localization in wireless sensor networks: a quantitative comparison. J. Comput. Netw. **43**(3), 499–518 (2003). http://dx.doi.org/10.1016/S1389-1286(03)00356-6

13

Multiple access interference in MIMO-CDMA systems under Rayleigh fading: statistical characterization and applications

Khalid Mahmood[1], Syed Muhammad Asad[1], Muhammad Moinuddin[2], Azzedine Zerguine[3*] and Lahouari Cheded[4]

Abstract

A major limiting factor in the performance of multiple-input-multiple-output (MIMO) code division multiple access (CDMA) systems is multiple access interference (MAI) which can reduce the system's capacity and increase its bit error rate (BER). Thus, a statistical characterization of the MAI is vital in analyzing the performance of such systems. Since the statistical analysis of MAI in MIMO-CDMA systems is quite involved, especially when these systems are fading, existing works in the literature, such as successive interference cancellation (SIC) or parallel interference cancellation (PIC), employ suboptimal approaches to detect the subscriber without involving the need for MAI statistics. The knowledge of both MAI and noise statistics plays a vital role in various applications such as the design of an optimum receiver based on maximum likelihood (ML) detection, evaluation of the probability of bit error, calculation of the system's capacity, evaluation of the outage probability, estimation of the channel's impulse response using methods including the minimum mean-square-error (MMSE), the maximum likelihood(ML), and the maximum a posteriori probability (MAP) criterion. To the best of our knowledge, there is no existing work that explicitly evaluates the statistics of the MAI-plus-noise in MIMO fading channels. This constitutes the prime objective of our proposed study here. In this work, we derive the expressions for the probability density function (PDF) of MAI and MAI-plus-noise in MIMO-CDMA systems in the presence of both Rayleigh fading channels and additive white Gaussian noise. Moreover, we evaluate the probability of the bit error rate in the presence of optimum reception using a ML receiver. Our theoretical findings can provide a reliable basis for both system design and various performance analyses of such systems. Our simulation results show that the theoretical findings are very well substantiated.

1 Introduction

In spite of their numerous advantages, MIMO-CDMA systems suffer from a major drawback in MAI which can reduce their capacity and increase their BER, thus resulting in a degraded system performance. Hence, a statistical analysis of MAI becomes a very important factor in the performance analysis of these systems.

In CDMA systems, each user is assigned a unique spreading code. These orthogonal codes should ideally provide perfect isolation from other subscribers so as to maintain error-free communication among all users. However, in reality, the orthogonality between these codes is difficult to preserve due to asynchronism and channel delay spread at the receiving end. While both asynchronism and channel delay spread exist on the uplink, only channel delay spread can be seen on the downlink of the channel. A correlation receiver, which in a multipath channel turns into a Rake receiver, cannot perfectly separate the signals in the case of multiple users. This lack of separation leads to MAI causing a system performance degradation, which may lead to unacceptable error performances for moderate user loads.

Most of the reported research work is done on characterization of single-input single-output (SISO) CDMA systems and is based only on approximations, such as the standard Gaussian approximation (SGA) [1], improved Gaussian approximation (IGA) [2] and simplified IGA (SIGA) [3]. The central limit theorem is applied in SGA

*Correspondence: azzedine@kfupm.edu.sa
[3]Department of Electrical Engineering, King Fahd University of Petroleum and Minerals, Dhahran 31261, Kingdom of Saudi Arabia
Full list of author information is available at the end of the article

to get an approximate sum of additive white Gaussian noise processes (AWGNP). These approximations are widely used because of their ease of application but can exhibit major drawbacks. For example, the SGA overestimates the system's performance, thus making the use of approximations an even more severe problem when the number of users is small [2]. The Standard Hermite polynomial error correction method was employed in [4] to improve the accuracy of SGA. In [5], the improved Gaussian approximation (IGA) method was used based on both the derivation of the conditional characteristic function of MAI and on bounds on its error probability for binary direct-sequence spread-spectrum multiple access (DS-SSMA) systems. In the case where the number of users is low, IGA has outperformed the SGA [2] but at the cost of an increased in computational complexity which makes it a major limitation for this method. The IGA was later simplified and renamed as the simplified IGA (SIGA) in [6].

Another approach adopted by researchers to find the BER of the DS/SSMA scheme is to ignore MAI completely. Most of these techniques are basically an extension of previously studied inter-symbol interference (ISI) techniques. Some of these techniques are moment space method, characteristic function method, moments method, and the approximate Fourier series method. It has been reported in the literature that these techniques are superior to the central limit theorem-based techniques in approximating the BER but involve higher computational costs. A study of the signal-to-noise ratio (SNR) of Rician fading channels at the correlator receiver's output was done by [7]. The BER performance of the DS-CDMA system in frequency non-selective Rayleigh fading channels for deterministic sequences using the SGA approach was evaluated in [8]. The characteristic function (CF) technique was utilized to assess the performance of the spread spectrum multiple access (SSMA) scheme in an AWGN environment in [9]. The CF method used to evaluate the performance of the DS-SSMA scheme in multipath fading channels with multipath intersymbol interference was applied in [10] without taking into account the MAI effect. An approximate Fourier series technique was utilized in [11, 12] to evaluate the BER performance in selective and non-selective Rayleigh fading environments. System degradation caused by an imperfect chip and phase synchronization were also assessed in this technique.

For a given SNR, the BER dependency on the number of users is analyzed in [13], where a closed-form expression for the CF of MAI for asynchronous operation in a Rayleigh fading environment was obtained. An expression for a single integral for overall BER is derived therein.

The conditional CF of MAI together with bounds on the probability error rate for the DS-SSMA scheme are obtained here, whereas [14] derived only the average probability of error at the correlation receiver's output for binary as well as quaternary synchronous and asynchronous DS-SSMA schemes which use a random signature sequence.

The probability density function (PDF) of MAI for a synchronous downlink CDMA in an AWGN case was derived in [15]. This result is then used to derive the conditional probability density function of the MAI, ISI, and noise in multi-carrier code division multiple access scheme (MC-CDMA) provided that the fading environment is known. The PDF of both the MAI and the inter carrier interference is also derived while assuming that the channel-fading effect in CDMA system is known.

A new unified approach to MAI analysis in fading environments was presented in [16], assuming that the channel phase is either known or has been perfectly estimated. Random behavior of the channel fading is also included in [16] to get realistic results for the PDF of MAI and noise. Also, the analysis does not make any simplifying assumptions on the MAI and provides a complete statistical characterization of MAI.

Accurate statistical analysis of MAI in MIMO-CDMA systems has not received much attention from researchers, as indicated by the few published studies available in the literature, mainly because the computational complexities it involves. So, to alleviate these complexities, researchers in the past either used some strong assumptions, for example Gaussian assumption for interference in MIMO system [17], or suboptimal approaches to detect the subscriber without involving the need for MAI statistics such as in SIC [18] and PIC [19]. In [20, 21], other types of spreading codes are used. These codes, known as chaotic codes, are nonlinear with good correlation properties. In [20], the MAI is analyzed using the Gaussian distribution approximation and in [21] the performance was analyzed under a fading channel scenario in the MIMO case, where in contrast to existing works, an exact characterization of the MAI in a Rayleigh fading environment is developed for MIMO-CDMA systems. Consequently, explicit closed-form expressions for both the PDFs of MAI and MAI plus noise were derived for a Rayleigh fading channel. Recently in [22], the approach of [16] was used to analyze the MAI in MIMO-CDMA systems which was later used in [23] to design minimum mean-square-error (MMSE) estimate of fading channels in the presence of MIMO systems. Although, the work in [22] has provided the derivation for the MAI statistics and the work in [23] has provided MMSE estimator design based on this statistics, but there can be many other interesting applications of the derived MAI statistics in practical scenarios which these work failed to provide. In this present work, we aimed to provide more comprehensive treatment of the MAI statistics in MIMO-CDMA systems. More importantly, we have provided many interesting applications in Section 5 such as the design of optimum receiver, derivation of probability of bit error rate and the derivation for the probability of outage in MIMO-CDMA systems in the presence of Rayleigh flat fading in addition to the design of MMSE estimator. Moreover, we have also highlighted some future research directions/challenges that can be dealt via utilizing the proposed framework of MAI statistics analysis.

1.1 Main contributions

In this work, the main contributions are outlined next.

1. Expressions for the PDF of MAI and MAI and noise in MIMO-CDMA systems in the presence of both Rayleigh fading channel and additive Gaussian noise are derived.
2. Three important applications that utilize the newly-derived statistics of MAI are provided and analyzed.
    (a) In the first application, an optimum receiver based on ML detection criterion is developed. For this, a new expression for the probability of BER, which is of prime importance in the study of any communication system, is also derived.
    (b) In the second application, a new expression for the minimum mean-square-error (MMSE) channel estimation of Rayleigh fading using our derived MAI statistics, is derived.
    (c) In the final application, we derive the expression for the probability of outage for MIMO-CDMA systems
3. Although our analysis deals with only a Rayleigh fading channel, our methodology is nevertheless generalized and can be applied to other fading channels.
4. In the last section, we also highlighted some future applications for MIMO-CDMA systems that can employ the proposed framework of designing MAI statistics.

1.2 Paper organization

The paper is organized as follows. Section 2 describes the system model used for the analysis. Section 3, where the analysis of the PDF of MAI is carried out is followed by Section 4 which describes the analysis of the PDF of MAI-plus-noise. Two important and pertinent applications that utilize the analyses, namely the optimum receiver design using the ML criterion and the MMSE channel estimation, are presented in Section 5. Section 6 presents simulation and numerical results to corroborate the theoretical findings of this work. Finally, Section 7 concludes the paper.

2 System model

In this paper, a synchronous DS–CDMA transmitter model for the downlink of a mobile radio network with N transmit and M receive antennas is considered as shown in Fig. 1. Consider a flat-fading channel whose complex impulse response between the nth transmitter and m^{th} receiver for the lth symbol is given by

$$H_{mn}^{l}(t) = h_{mn}^{l} e^{j\phi_l} \delta(t) \quad (1)$$

where h_{mn}^{l} is the lth channel tap between the nth transmitter and the mth receiver whose value becomes unity for the AWGN channel, and ϕ_l is the phase of the complex channel for the lth symbol. Thus, for a Rayleigh fading channel, the PDF of h_{mn}^{l} will be:

$$f_{h_{mn}^{l}}(x) = \frac{x}{\sigma_{h_{mn}}^{2}} \exp\left(-\frac{x^2}{2\sigma_{h_{mn}}^{2}}\right), \quad \text{for } x > 0, \quad (2)$$

where $\sigma_{h_{mn}}^{2}$ represents the variance of the real and imaginary Gaussian component in the Rayleigh fading. Assuming that the receiver is able to perfectly track the phase of the channel, the detector in the mth receiver then observes the following signal:

$$r_m(t) = \sum_{n=1}^{N} \sum_{l=-\infty}^{\infty} \sum_{k=1}^{K} A^k b_n^{l,k} s_n^{l,k}(t) h_{mn}^{l} + \eta_m(t), \quad m = 1, 2, \ldots, M \quad (3)$$

where K represents the number of users, $s_n^{l,k}(t)$ is the rectangular signature waveform with random PN signature sequence of the kth user defined in the $(l-1)\,T_b \leq t \leq lT_b$, T_b and T_c are the bit period and the chip interval, respectively, related by $N_c = T_b/T_c$, $\{b_n^{l,k}\}$ is the input bit stream of the kth user, A^k is the transmitted amplitude of the kth user, and ν_m is the additive white Gaussian noise with zero mean and variance σ_ν^2 at the mth receiver. The cross-correlation between the signature sequences of users j and k for the lth symbol is given by

$$\rho_l^{k,j} = \int_{(l-1)T_b}^{lT_b} s_n^k(t) s_n^j(t) dt = \sum_{i=1}^{N_c} c_{l,i}^k c_{l,i}^j, \quad (4)$$

where $\left\{c_{l,i}^k\right\}$ is the normalized spreading sequence (so as to make the autocorrelations of the signature sequences unity) of user k for the lth symbol. The receiver consists of a matched filter at the front end, which is matched to the signature waveform of the desired user. In our analysis, the desired user will be user 1. Thus, the matched filter's

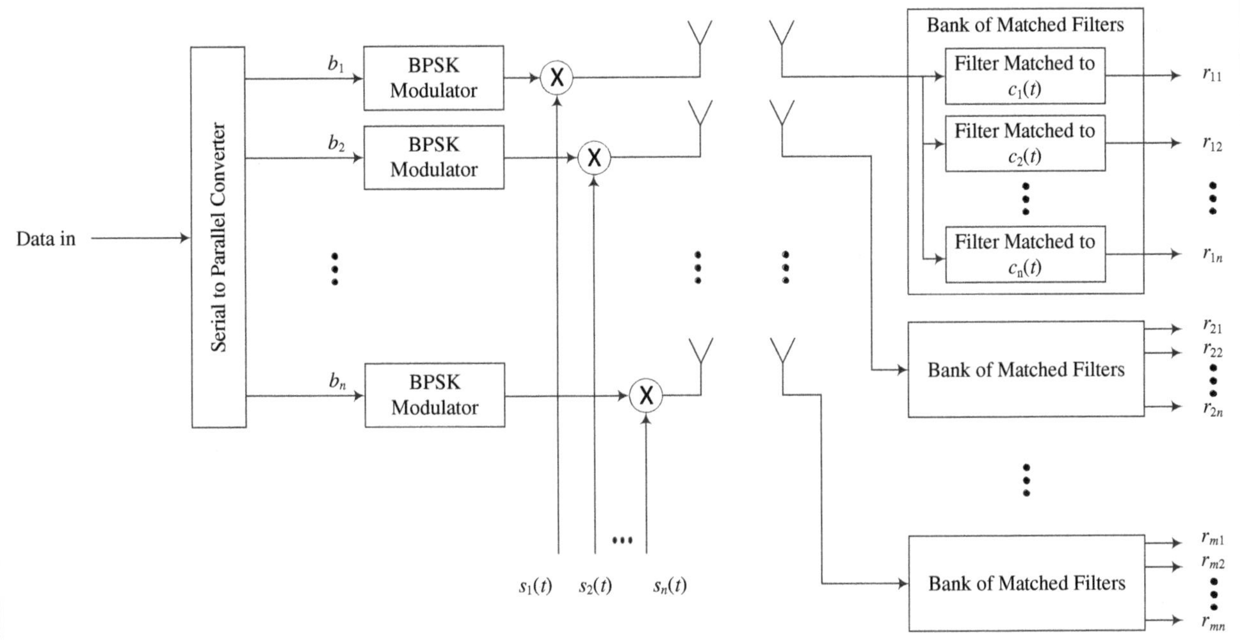

Fig. 1 A block diagram of MIMO-CDMA transmitter and receiver system

output for the lth symbol at the mth receiver can be written as follows:

$$y_m^l = \int_{(l-1)T_b}^{lT_b} r_m(t) s_m^{l,1}(t) dt = \sum_{n=1}^{N} A^1 b_n^{l,1} h_{mn}^l + z_m^l + \eta_m, \quad m = 1, 2, \ldots M, \tag{5}$$

where z_m^l is the MAI at the mth receiver for the lth symbol in the presence of the fading channel h_{mn}^l and is given by

$$z_m^l = \sum_{n=1}^{N} \sum_{k=2}^{K} A^k b_n^{l,k} \rho_n^{k,1} h_{mn}^l, \quad m = 1, 2, \ldots M \tag{6}$$

which can also be expressed as follows

$$z_m^l = \sum_{n=1}^{N} I_{mn}^l h_{mn}^l, \quad m = 1, 2, \ldots, M \tag{7}$$

where the random variable $I_{mn}^l = \sum_{k=2}^{K} A^k b_n^{l,k} \rho_n^{k,1}$, which is nothing but MAI in AWGN environment, is shown to follow Gaussian behavior in [16], that is, $I_{mn}^l \sim \mathcal{N}\left(0, \sigma_I^2\right)$ where $\sigma_I^2 = \frac{A^2(K-1)}{N_c}$. For the sake of tractability of the analysis, we have assumed the same behavior for random variable I_{mn}^l in the MIMO system.

3 PDF of MAI in MIMO-CDMA systems

In order to find the PDF of the random variable $U_n^l = I_{mn}^l h_{mn}^l$, we use the assumption of statistical independence of $I^{l,k}$ and h_{mn}^l as follows

$$f_U(u) = \int_{-\infty}^{\infty} \frac{1}{|x|} f_I\left(\frac{u}{x}\right) f_{h_{mn}^l}(x) dx, \quad x > 0$$
$$= \int_0^{\infty} \frac{1}{x} \frac{1}{\sqrt{2\pi\sigma_I^2}} \exp\left(-\frac{u^2}{2x^2\sigma_I^2}\right) \frac{x}{\sigma_{h_{mn}}^2} \times \exp\left(-\frac{x^2}{2\sigma_{h_{mn}}^2}\right) dx,$$

which is found to be

$$f_U(u) = \frac{1}{2\sigma_I \sigma_{h_{mn}}} \exp\left(-\frac{|u|}{\sigma_{h_{mn}} \sigma_I}\right) \tag{8}$$

The characteristic function of the random variable U_n^l can be then be evaluated as

$$\Phi_{U_n}(\omega) = E\left[e^{iwU}\right] = \frac{1}{2\sigma_I \sigma_{h_{mn}}} \int_{-\infty}^{\infty} \exp(i\omega u) \exp\left(-\frac{|u|}{\sigma_{h_{mn}} \sigma_I}\right) du$$

$$\Phi_{U_n}(\omega) = \frac{1}{\omega^2 \sigma_{U_n}^2 + 1} \tag{9}$$

where[1] $\sigma_{U_n}^2 = \sigma_I^2 \sigma_{h_{mn}}^2$. Since the interferers are assumed to be independent of, but not identical to, each other, it can therefore be observed from (7) that the characteristic function of z_m^l will be the product of N characteristic functions of the independent random variables U_n^l, that is,

$$\Phi_Z(\omega) = \prod_{n=1}^{N} \Phi_{U_n}(\omega) = \prod_{n=1}^{N} \frac{1}{\omega^2 \sigma_{U_n}^2 + 1} \tag{10}$$

Inverse-Fourier transforming the above characteristic function will yield:

$$\begin{aligned} f_Z(z) &= \mathcal{F}^{-1}\left[\Phi_Z(\omega)\right] \\ &= \frac{1}{2\pi}\int_{-\infty}^{\infty}\exp\left(-i\omega z\right)\prod_{n=1}^{N}\frac{1}{\omega^2\sigma_{U_n}^2+1}d\omega \end{aligned} \tag{11}$$

The above integral is evaluated in Appendix A for two different scenarios: (1) $\sigma_{U_n}^2$ have distinct values for each n and (2) $\sigma_{U_n}^2$ are equal for all n. As a result, expression for the PDF of z can be shown to

$$f_Z(z) = \begin{cases} \sqrt{\frac{2|z|}{\pi\sigma_U}}\frac{1}{(2\sigma_U)^N}\frac{(|z|)^{N-1}}{\Gamma(N)}K_{N-\frac{1}{2}}\left(\frac{|z|}{\pi\sigma_U}\right) & \text{for identical } \sigma_{U_n}^2, \\ \frac{1}{2}\sum_{n=1}^{N}\frac{C_n e^{-\frac{|z|}{\sigma_{U_n}}}}{\sigma_{U_n}} & \text{for distinct } \sigma_{U_n}^2. \end{cases} \tag{12}$$

where C_n is defined in (59) (see Appendix A) and $K_\mu(z)$ is the Bessel function for imaginary arguments [24] and it is defined in (67). The PDF of MAI in (12) for the distinct scenario shows that the MAI experienced at any receiving antenna is a sum of Laplacian distributed random variables. It can be easily seen that by setting $N = 1$ in the above, the PDF of MAI will reduce to a single Laplacian random variable, which is consistent with the result obtained in [16].

3.1 Variance of MAI

The MAI term is already defined in (7). Since it is assumed that the interferers are independent and zero mean (zero mean is due to the fact that $E\left[I_{mn}^l\right] = 0$), the variance of total MAI in MIMO-CDMA system (denoted by σ_z^2) can be evaluated as follows:

$$\sigma_z^2 = \sum_{n=1}^{N}E\left[\left(I_{mn}^l\right)^2\right]E\left[\left(h_{mn}^l\right)^2\right] = \sum_{n=1}^{N}2\sigma_I^2\sigma_{h_{mn}}^2, \tag{13}$$

In the special case when $\sigma_{h_{mn}}^2 = \sigma_h^2$ for all m and n, we get

$$\sigma_z^2 = 2N\sigma_I^2\sigma_h^2, \tag{14}$$

4 PDF of MAI-plus-noise

In order to find the PDF of the MAI-plus-noise, we consider κ_m^l to be a random variable resulting in MAI-plus-noise, that is,

$$\kappa_m^l = z_m^l + \eta_m^l \qquad m = 1, 2, \ldots, M \tag{15}$$

where η_m^l is the AWGN part. Thus, the PDF of the random variable κ_m^l can be evaluated by the convolution of the PDFs of z_m^l and η_m^l as follows:

$$\begin{aligned} f_{\kappa_m^l}(\kappa) &= f_Z(z) * f_\eta(\eta) \\ &= \int_{-\infty}^{\infty} f_Z(t) f_\eta(\kappa - t)\, dt \\ &= \sum_{j=1}^{N}\frac{C_n}{2\sigma_{U_n}}\beta_n \end{aligned} \tag{16}$$

where β_n is the integral defined as

$$\beta_n = \frac{1}{\sqrt{2\pi}\sigma_\eta}\int_{-\infty}^{\infty}\exp\left(-\frac{|t|}{\sigma_{U_n}} - \frac{(\kappa - t)^2}{2\sigma_\eta^2}\right)dt \tag{17}$$

and can be evaluated using the technique of "completing the square" and by employing the definition of the error complement function erfc(x) [24]. This yields

$$\begin{aligned} \beta_n = &\frac{e^{\frac{\sigma_\eta^2}{2\sigma_{U_j}^2}}}{2}e^{\frac{-\kappa}{\sigma_{U_n}}}\operatorname{erfc}\left(\frac{\sigma_\eta}{\sqrt{2}\sigma_{U_n}} - \frac{\kappa}{\sqrt{2}\sigma_\eta}\right) \\ &+ e^{\frac{\kappa}{\sigma_{U_n}}}\operatorname{erfc}\left(\frac{\sigma_\eta}{\sqrt{2}\sigma_{U_n}} + \frac{\kappa}{\sqrt{2}\sigma_\eta}\right) \end{aligned} \tag{18}$$

Now, using the fact that

$$\begin{aligned} \Gamma\left(\frac{1}{2}, x; b\right) = &\frac{\sqrt{\pi}}{2}\exp\left(-2\sqrt{b}\right)\operatorname{erfc}\left(\sqrt{x} - \sqrt{b/x}\right) \\ &+ \exp\left(2\sqrt{b}\right)\operatorname{erfc}\left(\sqrt{x} + \sqrt{b/x}\right) \end{aligned} \tag{19}$$

where

$$\Gamma\left(a, x; b\right) := \int_x^{\infty} t^{a-1}\exp\left(-t - b/t\right)dt.$$

is the *generalized incomplete gamma function* [25].

We can express the PDF $f_{\kappa_m^l}(\kappa)$ as

$$f_{\kappa_m^l}(\kappa) = \frac{1}{2\sqrt{\pi}}\sum_{n=1}^{N}\mathcal{A}_n\Gamma\left(\frac{1}{2}, \mathcal{B}_n; \frac{\kappa^2}{\mathcal{C}_n}\right) \tag{20}$$

where, for compactness purposes, the symbols $\mathcal{A}_n = \frac{C_n}{\sigma_{U_n}}\exp\left(\mathcal{B}_n\right)$, $\mathcal{B}_n = \frac{\sigma_\eta^2}{2\sigma_{U_n}^2}$ and $\mathcal{C}_n = 4\sigma_{U_n}^2$ have been introduced.

5 Important applications involving the utilization of the exact MAI statistics

As stated earlier, MAI introduces an overhead on CDMA systems, which acts as a limiting factor in system performance. It is evident from previous work that the performance analysis of CDMA systems has not really utilized the exact statistics of MAI. Therefore, system designs based on approximated MAI statistics have lead to poor system performance. In this work, in order that the knowledge of the exact MAI statistics does indeed remarkably improve system performance, we present here two important applications to emphasize this point. These applications are listed below and discussed in the ensuing subsections:

- design of an optimum MIMO-CDMA receiver using the ML criterion.
- design of MMSE channel estimator for Rayleigh fading in MIMO-CDMA systems.
- derivation of probability of outage for Rayleigh fading in MIMO-CDMA systems.

5.1 Design of an optimum MIMO-CDMA receiver using the ML criterion

Both the design and characteristics of optimum receivers in the presence of AWGN for different modulation methods have been extensively covered in the literature [26]. It is reported in the literature that the optimum detector for a AWGN channel is comprised of a correlation demodulator or a matched filter followed by an optimum decision rule, and is based on the maximum a posteriori probability (MAP) criterion when the a priori probabilities of the transmitted signal are unequal, and the ML criterion when these a priori probabilities are equal. Decisions based on any of the criteria used depend on the conditional PDF of the received vector at the output of either the matched filter or the correlator, whichever is used. In our analysis, the ML criterion is utilized, since we are using the case where the a priori probabilities of the transmitted signal are equal.

BER is defined as the number of bits received in error with respect to the total number of bits received at a particular receiver. BER performance is considered to be a very important criterion for CDMA systems as it determines the quality of transmission as well as the amount of data that can be transmitted per unit of bandwidth. Since all users contribute to the interference levels at the receiving side, the BER of each user increases when several users try to access the same channel simultaneously. Subsequently, the maximum number allowable of users is determined by the amount of interference which can be tolerated [27]. This section deals with the design of an optimum receiver in the presence of MAI-plus-noise for a Rayleigh fading environment. The probability of error is derived here for the maximum likelihood receiver and the simulation results obtained here support our analytical finding.

At the front end of the optimum receiver, a matched filter is placed, and is matched to the desired subscriber, which in our case, is user 1. The output of the matched filter that is matched to the signature waveform of the desired user for the lth symbol can be written as

$$y^l_m = w^l_{m,i} + \kappa^l_m \qquad i = 1,2 \qquad \text{(for BPSK signals)} \tag{21}$$

where $w^l_{m,i}$ is the desired symbol in a MIMO system. If E_b represents the energy-per-bit, then $w^l_{m,i}$ is given by either $+N\alpha_i\sqrt{E_b}$ or $-N\alpha_i\sqrt{E_b}$ for BPSK signals. From the output of the matched filter given in (5), the desired signal is given by $\sum_{n=1}^{N} A^1 b^{l,1}_n h^l_{mn}$, where the channel taps α_i are no longer individual Rayleigh fading contributions but are rather a sum of all Rayleigh fading contributions. This can be seen as

$$\sum_{n=1}^{N} A^1 b^{l,1}_n h^l_{mn} = A^1 b^{l,1} \sum_{n=1}^{N} h^l_{mn} \tag{22}$$

where we are assuming that the same data is being transmitted from each antenna for a given user (i.e., $b^{l,1}_n = b^{l,1}\ \forall\ n$). Thus, $\alpha^l = \sum_{n=1}^{N} h^l_{mn}$ represents the sum of N independent Rayleigh random variables whose PDF can be obtained from ([28] Eq. 4a–b) as

$$f_\alpha(\alpha) = \frac{\alpha^{2N-1} e^{-\frac{\alpha^2}{2\psi}}}{2^{N-1}\psi^N (N-1)!}, \tag{23}$$

where $\psi = \frac{\sigma^2}{N}\left[(2N-1)!!\right]^{1/N}$, $(2N-1)!! = (2N-1)(2N-3)\cdots 3.1$, $\alpha = x/\sqrt{N}$, x is the normalized Rayleigh random variable and N is the number of transmitters.

For BPSK signaling, the conditional PDF $p\left(y^l_m|w^l_{m,1}\right)$ can be obtained by using (20) as

$$p\left(y^l_m|w^l_{m,1}\right) = \frac{1}{2\sqrt{\pi}} \sum_{n=1}^{N} A_n \Gamma\left(\frac{1}{2}, \mathcal{B}_n; \frac{\left(y^l_m - N\alpha_i\sqrt{E_b}\right)^2}{\mathcal{C}_n}\right) \tag{24}$$

For the case when $w^l_{m,1}$ and $w^l_{m,2}$ have equal a priori probabilities, then according to the ML criterion, the optimum test statistic is the likelihood ratio $\left(\Lambda = p\left(y^l_m|w^l_{m,1}\right)/p\left(y^l_m|w^l_{m,2}\right)\right)$. Now assuming that the channel attenuation (α^l) is deterministic, therefore any transmission error that has occurred is only due to the MAI-plus-noise contribution term $(Z^l_{m,i})$. It is shown in [16] that this MAI-plus noise term has a zero mean and a zero skewness, which shows its symmetric behavior about its mean. Consequently, the conditional PDF $p\left(y^l_m|w^l_{m,1}\right)$ with deterministic channel attenuation will also be symmetric, thus resulting in the threshold for the ML optimum receiver being its mean value of zero. Finally, the probability of error, given that $w^l_{m,1}$ is transmitted, is found to be:

$$P\left(e|w_{i,1}\right) = \int_{-\infty}^{0} p\left(y_m^l|w_{m,1}^l\right) dy_m^l$$
$$= \frac{1}{2\sqrt{\pi}} \sum_{n=1}^{N} \int_{-\infty}^{0} \mathcal{A}_n \Gamma\left(\frac{1}{2}, \mathcal{B}_n; \frac{\left(y_m^l - N\alpha_i\sqrt{E_b}\right)^2}{\mathcal{C}_n}\right) dy_m^l \tag{25}$$
$$= \frac{1}{2} \sum_{n=1}^{N} C_n \exp\left(\frac{\sigma_\eta^2}{2\sigma_I^2\sigma_\alpha^2}\right) \int_{\sigma_\eta^2/2\sigma_I^2\sigma_\alpha^2}^{\infty} e^{-t} \text{erfc}\left(\sqrt{\frac{\alpha^2 N^2 E_b}{4\sigma_I^2\sigma_\alpha^2 t}}\right) dt \tag{26}$$

where we have replaced the constants $\mathcal{A}_n$, $\mathcal{B}_n$, and $\mathcal{C}_n$ in (25) by their respective expressions mentioned right after (20). In the derivation of BER, we require the PDF of α^2 for which we need the PDF of α. In order to get the PDF of α^2, we need to apply a transformation to the random variable α to get the PDF of the squared one. This carried out as follows: We define a new random variable

$$\gamma_\kappa = \frac{\alpha^2 N^2 E_b}{4\sigma_I^2\sigma_\alpha^2 t} \tag{27}$$

The mean of γ_κ, i.e., $\overline{\gamma_\kappa} = E[\gamma_\kappa]$ can be found as

$$\overline{\gamma_\kappa} = E[\gamma_\kappa] = \frac{E\left[\alpha^2\right] N^2 E_b}{4\sigma_I^2\sigma_\alpha^2 t} = \frac{2\psi N N^2 E_b}{4\sigma_I^2\sigma_\alpha^2 t} = \frac{\psi N^3 E_b}{2\sigma_I^2\sigma_\alpha^2 t} \tag{28}$$

From (27) we have

$$\alpha = \frac{2}{N}\sqrt{\frac{\gamma_\kappa \sigma_I^2\sigma_\alpha^2 t}{E_b}} \tag{29}$$

So the PDF of γ_κ can be found by the transformation method as

$$f_{\gamma_\kappa}(\gamma_\kappa) = \left.\frac{f_\alpha(\alpha)}{|d\gamma_\kappa/d\alpha|}\right|_{\alpha=\frac{2}{N}\sqrt{\frac{\gamma_\kappa\sigma_I^2\sigma_\alpha^2 t}{E_b}}} \tag{30}$$

where $\frac{d\gamma}{d\alpha}$ can be found by differentiating (27) to get

$$\frac{d\gamma}{d\alpha} = \frac{\alpha N^2 E_b}{2\sigma_I^2\sigma_\alpha^2 t} = \frac{2}{N}\sqrt{\frac{\gamma_\kappa\sigma_I^2\sigma_\alpha^2 t}{E_b}} \times \frac{N^2 E_b}{2\sigma_I^2\sigma_\alpha^2 t} \tag{31}$$

The expression for the BER is evaluated in Appendix A and can be setup as

$$P(e) = \frac{1}{2}\sum_{j=1}^{N} C_j 2^{1-N} \exp\left(\frac{\sigma_\eta^2}{2\sigma_I^2\sigma_\alpha^2}\right)\left(\frac{\sigma_I^2\sigma_\alpha^2}{\psi N^2 E_b}\right)^N \frac{\Gamma(2N)}{\Gamma(N+1)} \times I_j \tag{32}$$

where

$$I_j = \int_{\sigma_\eta^2/2\sigma_I^2\sigma_\alpha^2}^{\infty} e^{-t} t^N {}_2F_1\left(N, N+\frac{1}{2}; N+1, -\frac{2\sigma_I^2\sigma_\alpha^2 t}{\psi N^2 E_b}\right) dt \tag{33}$$

There is no closed-form expression for the above integral and so it was evaluated numerically.

5.2 Design of MMSE channel estimator for Rayleigh fading in MIMO-CDMA systems

In order to ascertain the impact of the above analysis from an application perspective, a pilot-aided MIMO channel estimation scheme is devised which extends the original work done in [29]. The estimation is based on the MMSE criterion. Taking the sum of Rayleigh fading in the MIMO system for the lth symbol to be $\alpha^l = \sum_{n=1}^{N} h_{mn}^l$, we define the signal of the desired user as

$$x \triangleq b^1\alpha \tag{34}$$

where we have dropped the time index for simplicity. Denoting the estimate of x by $\hat{x}$, the mean-square-error cost function for the MMSE estimate is

$$J = E\left[(x-\hat{x})^2\right] \tag{35}$$

The solution of the cost function in Eq. (35) is well known and is given by [30]

$$\hat{x}(y) = E\left[x \mid y\right] = \int_{-\infty}^{\infty} x f_{x|y}(x \mid y)\, dx \tag{36}$$

The estimate of $\hat{x}$ will lead us to the estimate of $\hat{\alpha}$ from (34)

$$\hat{\alpha} = \frac{\hat{x}}{b^1} \tag{37}$$

In order to evaluate $\hat{x}$, we require the conditional PDF $f_{x|y}(x \mid y)$, which can be obtained, using Bayes theorem as [30]

$$f_{x|y}(x \mid y) = \frac{f_{y|x}(y \mid x) f_x(x)}{f(y)} \tag{38}$$

To use (38), we need to evaluate first $f_x(x)$. Since the random variable x is the product of two random variables b^1 and α, its PDF can be evaluated using the procedure of the random variable transformation as follows:

$$f_x(x) = \int_0^{\infty} \frac{1}{\lambda} f_\alpha(\lambda) f_b\left(\frac{x}{\lambda}\right) d\lambda \tag{39}$$

where $f_b(b) = 0.5\left[\delta(b+1) + \delta(b-1)\right]$and $f_\alpha(\alpha)$ is the PDF of the sum of Rayleigh fading random variables given in (23). Inserting both PDFs in (39), the integral results in

$$f_x(x) = \frac{\mathcal{G}}{\psi^N} x^{2N-1} \exp\left(-\frac{x^2}{2N\psi}\right) \tag{40}$$

where $\mathcal{G} = \left(\frac{1}{\sqrt{N}}\right)^{2N}\left(\frac{1}{2}\right)^{N}\frac{1}{(N-1)!}x^{2N-1}$. The conditional PDF of $f_{y|x}(y \mid x)$, which can be found by (20), is given by

$$f_{y|x}(y \mid x) = \frac{1}{2\sqrt{\pi}}\sum_{n=1}^{N}\mathcal{A}_n\Gamma\left(\frac{1}{2},\mathcal{B}_n;\frac{(y-x)^2}{\mathcal{C}_n}\right) \quad (41)$$

Using the fact that $\forall\, y$

$$f(y) = \int_{-\infty}^{\infty} f_{y|x}(y \mid x) f_x(x)dx \quad (42)$$

Plugging both (40) and (41) in (42) yields

$$f(y) = \frac{1}{2\sqrt{\pi}}\frac{\mathcal{G}}{\psi^N}\sum_{n=1}^{N}\mathcal{A}_n I_{n(1)} \quad (43)$$

where $I_{n(1)}$ is given by

$$I_{n(1)} = \int_{-\infty}^{\infty}\Gamma\left(\frac{1}{2},\mathcal{B}_n;\frac{(y-x)^2}{\mathcal{C}_n}\right)\exp\left(-\frac{x^2}{2N\psi}\right)dx \quad (44)$$

Substituting the PDFs of $f(y)$ and $f_{y|x}(y \mid x)$ in (38) and using (36) through some mathematical simplification, we get

$$\hat{x} = \sum_{n=1}^{N}\frac{I_{n(2)}}{I_{n(1)}} \quad (45)$$

where $I_{n(2)}$ is given by

$$I_{n(2)} = \int_{-\infty}^{\infty} x^{2N}\Gamma\left(\frac{1}{2},\mathcal{B};\frac{(y-x)^2}{\mathcal{C}}\right)\exp\left(-\frac{x^2}{2Nb}\right)dx \quad (46)$$

Although the integrals in (44) and (46) cannot be evaluated analytically, there are various numerical integration techniques to evaluate these numerically [31]. Hence, the estimate in (45) can be used in (37) to get the MMSE estimate of the Rayleigh fading channel for MIMO-CDMA system.

6 Outage probability

It is well known that outage probability is used as a performance measure for a communication link when signal to interference-plus-noise ratio (SINR) is a random quantity. This happens when we deal with random channel as in the case fading.

The outage probability is the probability that the received SINR is below certain threshold (corresponding to a minimum required rate) in a given duration. Thus, the outage probability (denoted by P_{out}) can be expressed as

$$P_{out} = Pr[SINR \leq \zeta] \quad (47)$$

where ζ is a certain threshold to meet the required minimum rate. In our case, the instantaneous SINR can be expressed as

$$SINR = \frac{S}{\sigma_z^2 + \sigma_\eta^2} \quad (48)$$

where $S = \left(\sum_{n=1}^{N} A^1 b_n^{l,1} h_{mn}^l\right)^2$ represents the instantaneous desired signal power which make the SINR a random quantity. Here, $\sigma_z^2 = E\left[\left(z_m^l\right)^2\right]$ and $\sigma_\eta^2 = E\left[\left(\eta_m^l\right)^2\right]$ represent the MAI power and the noise power, respectively. In order to evaluate the MAI power, we make use of the probability of MAI expression derived in (12). Thus, we can evaluate σ_z^2 as

$$\sigma_z^2 = \int_{-\infty}^{\infty} z^2 f_Z(z)dz = \int_{-\infty}^{\infty} z^2\frac{1}{2}\sum_{n=1}^{N}\frac{C_n e^{-\frac{|z|}{\sigma_{U_n}}}}{\sigma_{U_n}}dz \quad (49)$$

Since, the PDF of MAI is even symmetric due to the term $|z|$, we can simplify the above as

$$\sigma_z^2 = \sum_{n=1}^{N}\frac{C_n}{\sigma_{U_n}}\int_0^{\infty} z^2\sum_{n=1}^{N} e^{-\frac{z}{\sigma_{U_n}}}dz \quad (50)$$

Now, by employing a change of variable with $t = -\frac{z}{\sigma_{U_n}}$, we can set up the above as

$$\sigma_z^2 = \sum_{n=1}^{N}\sigma_{U_n}^2 C_n\int_0^{\infty} t^2 e^{-t}dt \quad (51)$$

Next, by using the definition of gamma function $\Gamma(\alpha) = \int_0^{\infty} t^{\alpha-1} e^{-t}dt$ and knowing the fact that $\Gamma(1) = 1$, we conclude that

$$\sigma_z^2 = \sum_{n=1}^{N}\sigma_{U_n}^2 C_n \quad (52)$$

Now, we turn our attention to characterize the instantaneous desired signal power (S). To do so, we first utilize the formulation given in (22) which allows us to write S as

$$S = \left(A^1 b^{l,1}\right)^2\left(\sum_{n=1}^{N} h_{mn}^l\right)^2 \quad (53)$$

Since we are focusing on BPSK modulation, we have $\left(A^1 b^{l,1}\right)^2 = 1$. As a result, the random variable S can be formulated as $S = \alpha^2$ where α is the sum of N independent Rayleigh random variables whose PDF is given in (23). Eventually, this provides the following PDF of random variable S

$$f_S(s) = \frac{s^{N-1}e^{-\frac{s}{2\psi}}}{2^N\psi^N(N-1)!}, \quad (54)$$

Outage probability is given by

$$P_{out} = \int_0^{\zeta\left(\sigma_z^2+\sigma_\eta^2\right)} f_S(s)ds$$
$$= \int_0^{\zeta\left(\sigma_z^2+\sigma_\eta^2\right)} \frac{s^{N-1}e^{-\frac{s}{2\psi}}}{2^N\psi^N(N-1)!}ds \quad (55)$$

By using the change of variable $t = \frac{s}{2\psi}$, we get

$$P_{out} = \frac{1}{(N-1)!}\int_0^{\frac{\zeta\left(\sigma_z^2+\sigma_\eta^2\right)}{2\psi}} t^{N-1}e^{-t}dt \quad (56)$$

Finally, by utilizing the definition of incomplete gamma function (i.e., $\gamma(\alpha, x) \triangleq \int_0^x t^{\alpha-1}e^{-t}dt$), we obtain

$$P_{out} = \frac{1}{(N-1)!}\gamma\left(N, \frac{\zeta\left(\sigma_z^2+\sigma_\eta^2\right)}{2\psi}\right) \quad (57)$$

7 Simulation results

In this section, we present some simulation results to validate our theoretical findings. The simulation setup consists of two different scenarios of 2×2 and 4×4 MIMO systems. The CDMA system used here relies on the use of random signature sequences of length 31. The waveform chosen for the PN signatures are rectangular chip waveforms. The channel noise is taken to be an additive white Gaussian noise with an SNR of 20 dB. The Rayleigh channel is chosen to be flat and slow-fading. The simulation results are discussed according to the various tasks in the ensuing subsections.

7.1 Investigation on MAI statistics

In this section, we aim to investigate the effect of different parameters on the PDF of the MAI and MAI-plus-noise, namely the effect of the number of transmitting and receiving antennas, length of the pseudo-random-noise (PN) sequence used, and the number of users in the system. Moreover, we validate the theoretically derived results for the PDF of MAI and MAI-plus-noise by comparing them with various simulation experiments.

Figure 2 shows the effect of system's diversity order on the PDF of MAI. As can be seen, the variance of MAI increases with an increase in diversity. This is consistent with our theoretical predictions in that the severity of the interference would increase in the presence of such diversity because the cumulative effect of all the interferences emerging from the various transmitting channels. The effect of the length of the signature sequence on the PDF of MAI can be seen in Fig. 3 where the MIMO system used is a 4 × 4 one. This is also consistent with the results reported in [16]. The variance of MAI decreases with an increase in the length of the PN sequence.

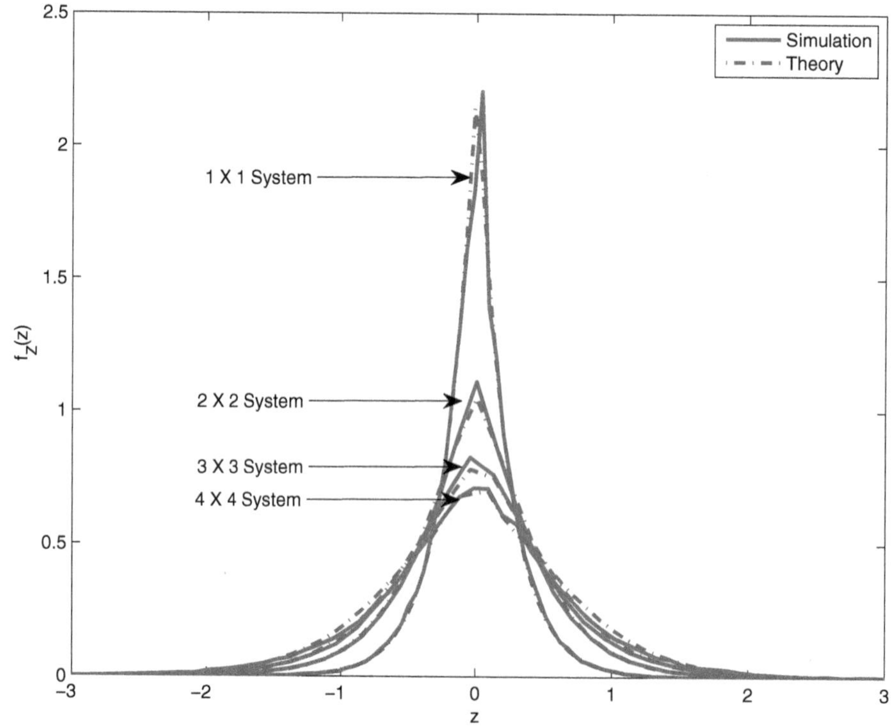

Fig. 2 PDF of MAI for different scenarios of transmit and receive antennas

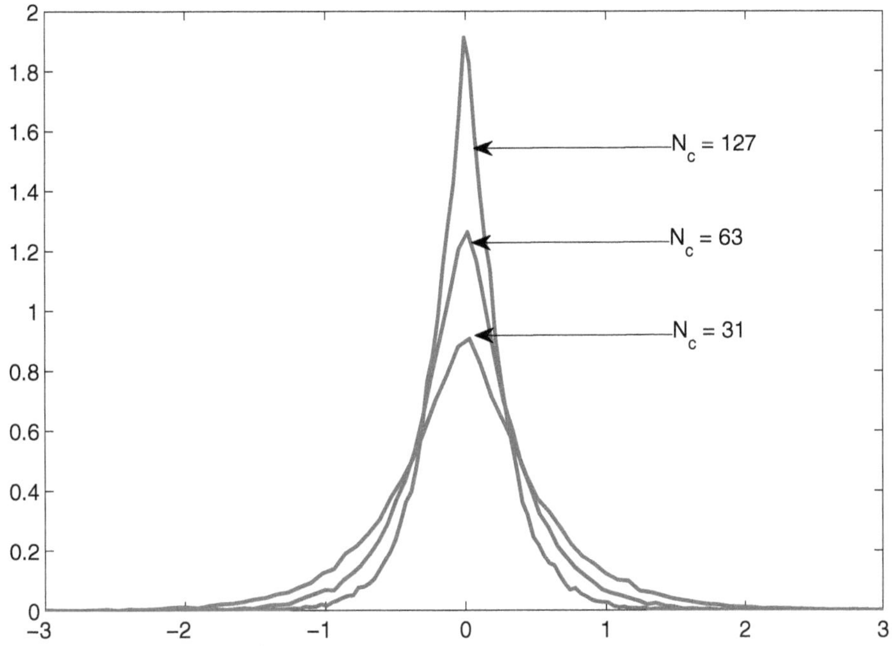

Fig. 3 PDF of MAI for 4 × 4 MIMO system under various lengths of PN sequences

Table 1 shows the comparison between the analytical and experimental variances in each case, which corroborates our theoretical analysis. As shown in our analysis, the MIMO-MAI is a sum of Laplacian-distributed random variables. Thus, to ascertain this fact, it is necessary to test the kurtosis of the MIMO-MAI. Table 1 lists the kurtosis of the MAI which is gradually increasing as the signature length increases. The decrease in the signature sequence's length would result in MAI in AWGN becoming Gaussian while affecting the MAI under the fading environment at the same time. Although from simulation, it cannot be predicted whether the MIMO-MAI would exhibit any Gaussian behavior. However, it can be safely assumed that for a short-enough signature length, the MIMO-MAI would assume a Gaussian behavior. This fact is also observed in Fig. 3.

Figure 4 shows the effects of interference on both the PDF of MAI-plus-noise and on the system's performance. It is intuitive to predict that the system will be severely degraded by an increase in the number of users. As the number of users increases, the power of the MAI experienced by the desired user will also increase as depicted in Fig. 4. Table 2 lists the experimental kurtosis of MAI-plus-noise under different capacity and diversity scenarios to test the Gaussianity assumption. In all the cases studied, the kurtosis increases with an increase in the system's user capacity. Particularly for the 2 × 2 MIMO case, the MAI-plus-noise behaves more like a Gaussian signal as its kurtosis gets closer to that of a Gaussian distribution which is 3. Moreover, it can be seen that the kurtosis decreases with an increase in number of users. For example, in case of 2 × 2 MIMO with 20 users, it reduces to 3.14 which is very close to Gaussian behavior. This is due to the fact that larger number of users makes the MAI approaching to the Gaussian behavior by virtue of the central limit theorem.

Figure 5 shows the effect of diversity on the PDF of the MAI-plus-noise. Even though a MIMO-CDMA system will provide higher data rates with an increase in reliability, the system will be severely degraded by such limiting factors as capacity and diversity. The results shown here motivate the fact that any receiver design for such a system will have to take such factors into account.

Table 1 Kurtosis and variance of MAI in a 4 × 4 MIMO system with $K = 10$

	$N_c = 31$	$N_c = 63$	$N_c = 127$	$N_c = 255$
Experimental kurtosis of MAI	4.02	4.11	4.16	4.21
Experimental variance	1.1689	0.5736	0.2823	0.1411
Analytical variance	1.1613	0.5714	0.2835	0.1412

7.2 Comparing proposed MAI statistics with the SGA

In this section, we compare the proposed MAI statistics with the well-known existing approximation of SGA. For this purpose, we use 4 × 4 MIMO CDMA systems. Number of users selected are $K = 10$ and $K = 20$ for the two separate experiments. These results are reported in Figs. 6 and 7, respectively. For the theoretical result, we plotted

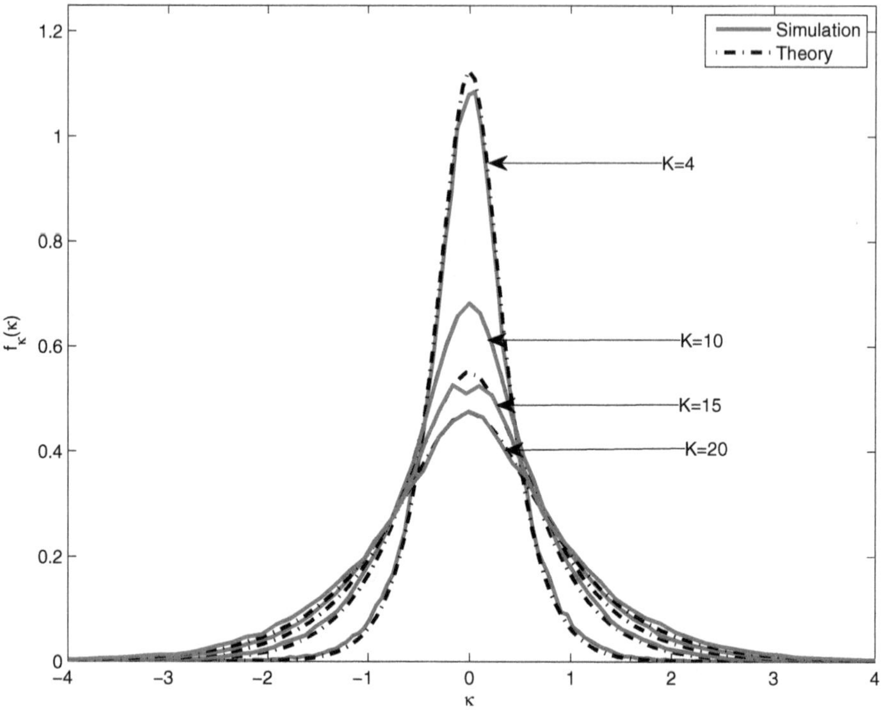

Fig. 4 PDF of MAI-plus-noise under different numbers of users in the system

the PDF of MAI derived in (12). It can be easily depicted from these results that the well-known SGA is failed to correctly model the statistics of the MAI in the MIMO-CDMA systems. On the other hand, the proposed analysis provides a good match with the simulation results in both scenarios which shows that the derived theoretical results for the PDF of MAI are valid for both smaller and larger number of users. This also justifies our claim that the MAI cannot be approximated as Gaussian distributed random variable in the MIMO-CDMA systems.

7.3 Probability of bit error rate

To validate the theoretical findings, simulations are carried out and results are discussed below. The simulation setup used random signature sequences of length 31 and rectangular chip waveforms. The measurement noise is taken to be additive white Gaussian with an SNR of 20 dB.

Table 2 Experimental kurtosis of MAI-plus-noise under different system's capacity with $N_c = 31$

MIMO system	2 × 2	3 × 3	4 × 4
$K = 4$	3.77	4.28	4.63
$K = 10$	3.30	3.90	4.02
$K = 15$	3.18	3.80	3.94
$K = 20$	3.14	3.71	3.83

Figure 8 shows the performance of CDMA systems in a flat Rayleigh fading environment for a 2 × 2 MIMO system and a 1 × 1 SISO system [16] where the number of system users is set to $K = 5$ and $K = 15$. It is evident from the result that the proposed analytical findings closely match the experimental ones. It is also evident that the MIMO system performs significantly better by achieving a lower BER as compared to the SISO system, especially for the lower number of users $K = 5$. However, an increase in the number of users severely degrades the BER performance due to the resulting increase in MAI. This intuitive fact is well-corroborated by our analysis. The theory-simulation mismatch in the low SNR is mainly due to the relatively high noise power. Moreover, the sum of Rayleigh fading used in the derivation of BER is only an approximation valid for small arguments only. This also contributes somewhat to this mismatch.

Figure 9 shows the BER performance of a MIMO-CDMA system versus the number of users in the system. Again, and as expected, we see a close match between the simulation and analytical results. When compared to the SISO system in [16], the MIMO-CDMA system achieves a significantly improved BER performance. It can be seen that the BER performance of the system degrades as the MAI experienced by each user increases.

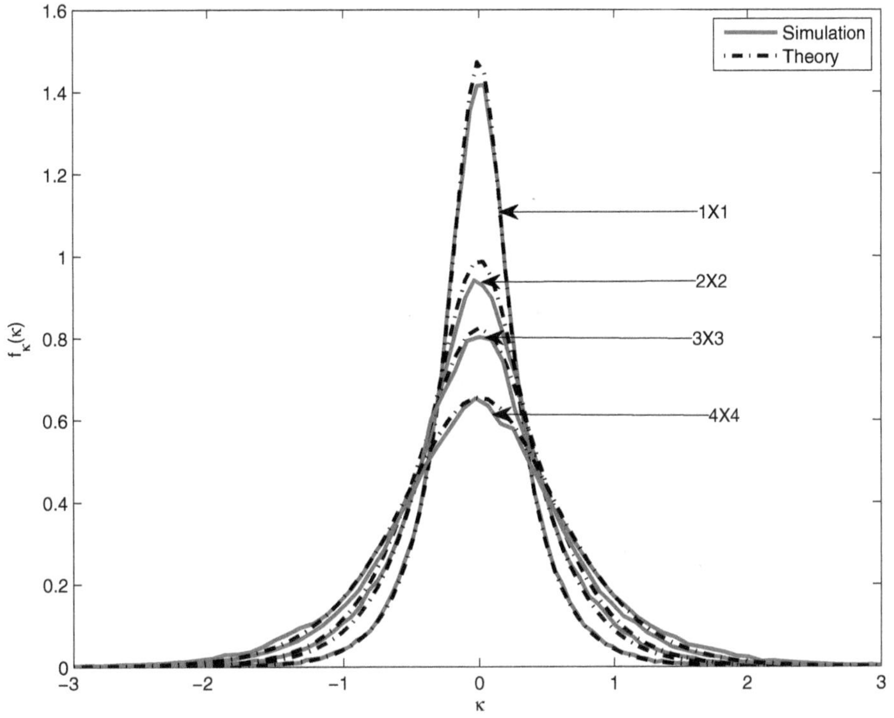

Fig. 5 PDF of MAI-plus-noise for different scenarios of transmit and receive antennas

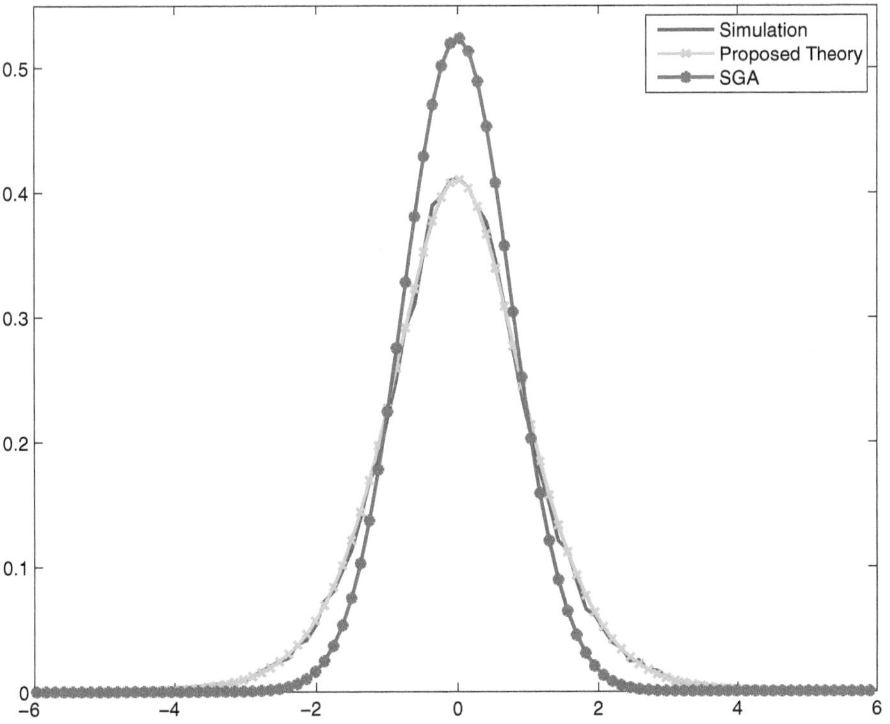

Fig. 6 Comparing the PDF of MAI with SGA in MIMO-CDMA systems for $K = 10$

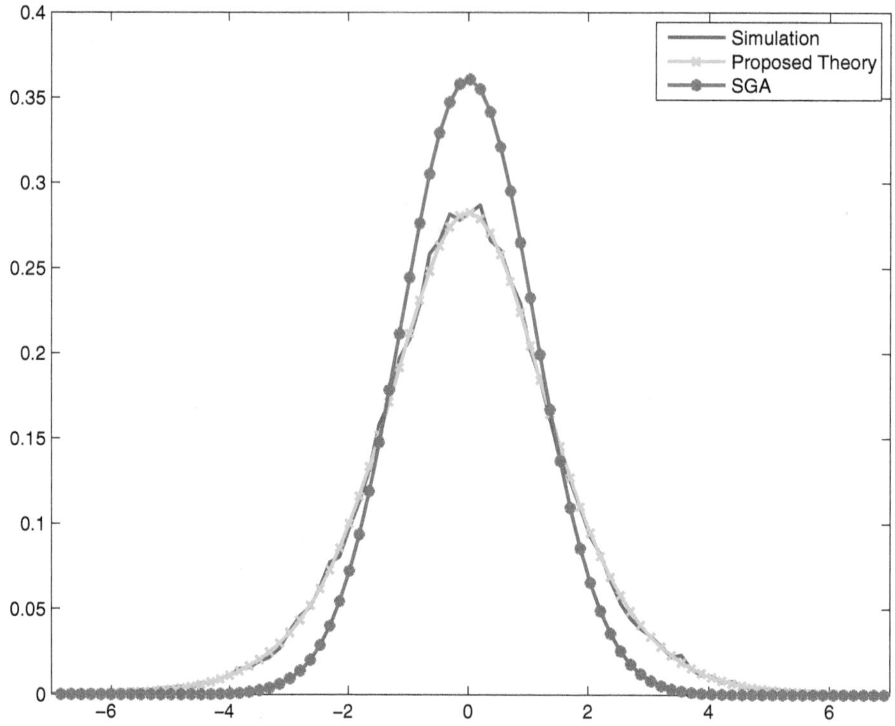

Fig. 7 Comparing the PDF of MAI with SGA in MIMO-CDMA systems for $K = 20$

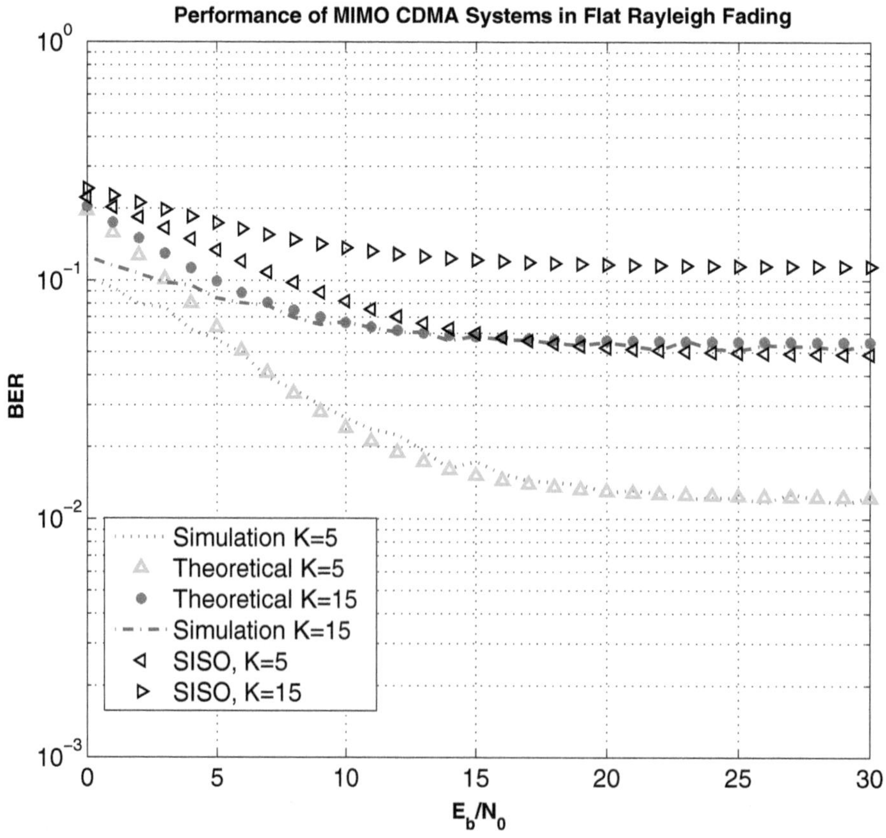

Fig. 8 BER performance of MIMO-CDMA system versus SNR

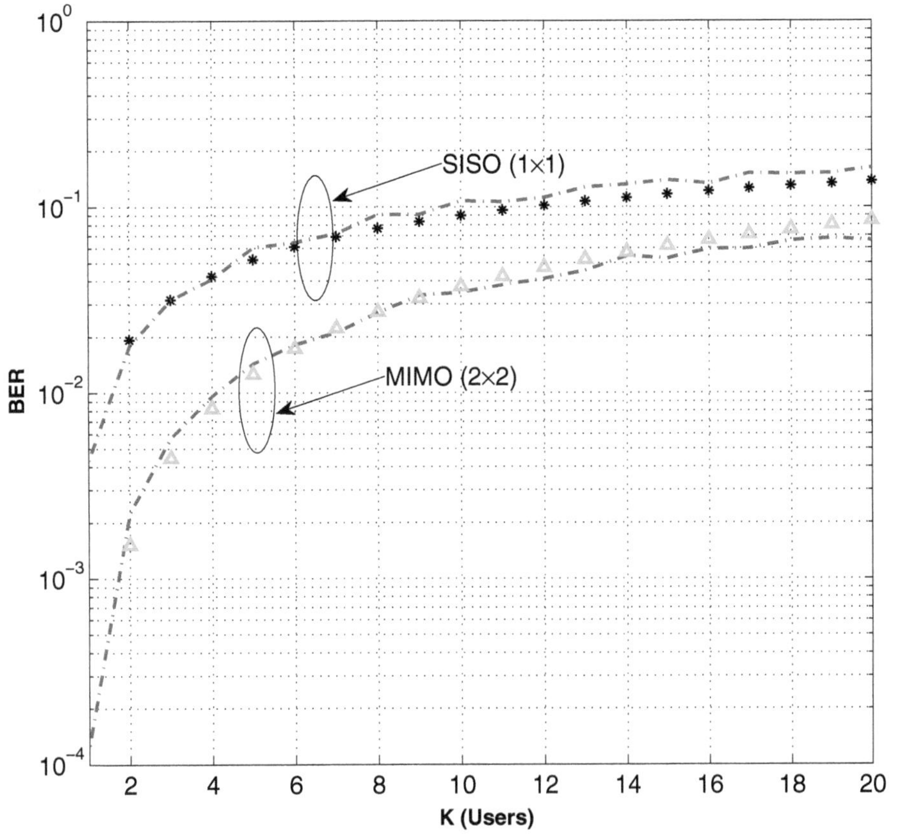

Fig. 9 BER Performance of MIMO-CDMA System versus number of users

7.4 Channel estimation

In this simulation, we have used a 2 × 2 MIMO system to estimate the channel taps for the flat Rayleigh fading channel based on (37) and (45). The estimator was tested for $K = 4$, $K = 6$, and $K = 10$ users. Figure 10 shows the mean-square-error performance of the estimator versus the SNR for a flat MIMO Rayleigh channel. As is evident from Fig. 10, the MMSE estimator based on our analysis is able to estimate the channel by minimizing the error for $K = 4$ users. As the MAI severely degrades the performance of the system, the estimator is unable to track channel variations for a higher number of users in the system, as is seen for the case of $K = 6$ and $K = 10$ in the Fig. 10. This is mainly due to the fact that any existing useful information on the channel is simple swamped by the accumulated effect of the contributions to the MAI by the large number of users.

7.5 Probability of outage

In this section, we compare the results for the probability of outage obtained via simulation and the proposed theoretical results given in (57). The results are compared for four users (i.e. $K = 4$). The other system parameters are the same as mentioned in previous experiments. The results are shown in Fig. 11. It can be observed that there is an excellent agreement between the simulation result and the one obtained via the proposed theoretical analysis.

8 Conclusions

In this work, a thorough statistical analysis of MAI and MAI-plus-noise in MIMO-CDMA systems has been performed in the presence of Rayleigh fading channel. the major contribution of this work is the statistical characterization of MAI without relying on any Gaussian assumption as is usually reported in the literature. Consequently, the analysis results in new closed-form expressions for the PDF of MAI and MAI-plus-noise. It is found that the derived PDF of MAI is in the form of summation of Laplacian distributed random variables while the PDF of MAI-plus-noise is found to be summation of generalized incomplete gamma functions. These PDFs are found to be a function of key factors such as the number of users, number of antennas, spreading code length, channel variance and noise variance. Moreover, the effect of these parameters on the PDF of MAI has been investigated through simulations whose results have shown a close agreement with the theoretical findings. As applications, we have demonstrated how the derived statistics can

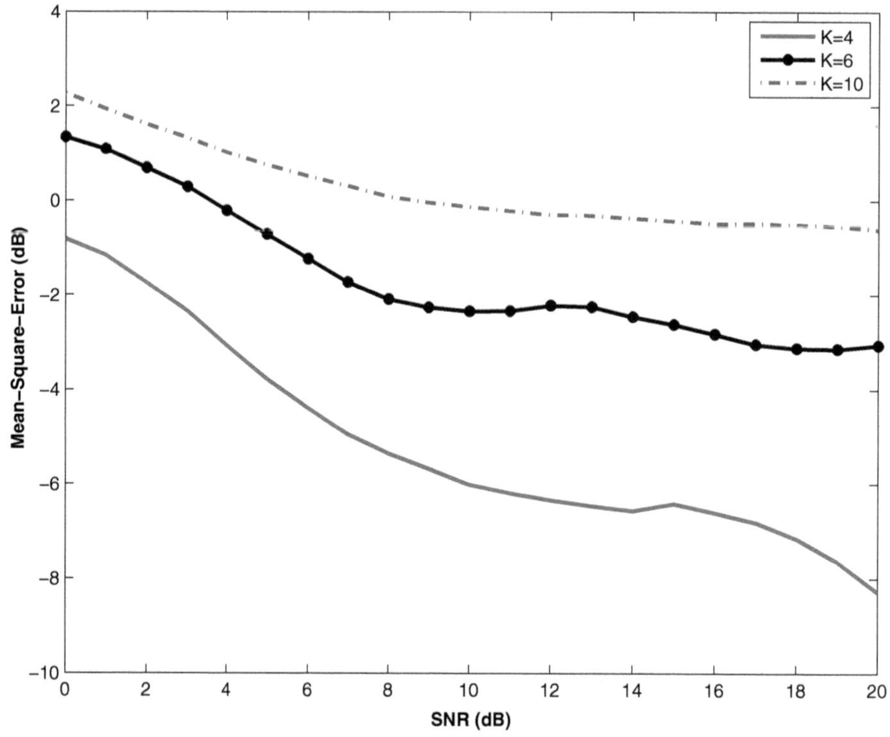

Fig. 10 Mean-square-error performance of the proposed channel estimator

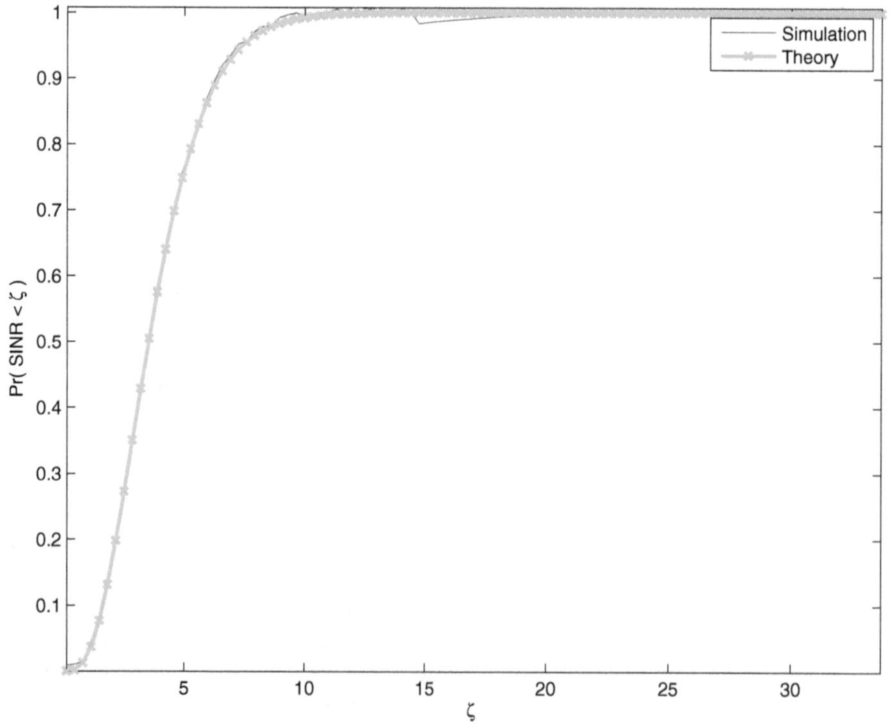

Fig. 11 Probability of outage for Rayleigh fading in MIMO-CDMA systems

be utilized for designing the optimum coherent receiver, derivation for the expression of probability of bit error rate, derivation of MMSE channel estimator for Rayleigh fading, and derivation for the probability of outage in fading environment. For future work, our analysis can provide a platform for many interesting applications in MIMO-CDMA systems. For example, one can utilize the expression for probability of outage to design a receiver that can optimization the system performance by minimizing the probability of outage. Another interesting application can be the design of optimum algorithm for MIMO antenna selection by joint minimization of receive probability of outage. In addition, our work can extended to frequency selective channels and asynchronous systems. Thus, we believe that our work will open new research directions to solve various challenging problems in MIMO communication systems.

Endnote

[1]Note that $\sigma^2_{U_n}$ is just an intermediate variable and it does not represent the true variance of the random variable U^l_n. The actual variance of the U^l_n is equal to $2\sigma^2_I\sigma^2_{h_{mn}}$ as $E\left[(h^l_{mn})^2\right] = 2\sigma^2_{h_{mn}}$.

Appendix A

Evaluation of $\frac{1}{2\pi}\int_{-\infty}^{\infty}\frac{\exp(-i\omega z)}{\prod_{n=1}^{N}\left(\omega^2\sigma^2_{U_n}+1\right)}d\omega$

To evaluate the integral in (11), we consider two different scenarios: (1) $\sigma^2_{U_n}$ have distinct values for each n and (2) $\sigma^2_{U_n}$ are equal for all n.

Scenario 1: For distinct $\sigma^2_{U_n}$

For the first scenario, we perform a partial fraction expansion of the product in (10) as follows:

$$\prod_{n=1}^{N}\frac{1}{\omega^2\sigma^2_{U_n}+1} = \sum_{n=1}^{N}\frac{C_n}{\omega^2\sigma^2_{U_n}+1} \tag{58}$$

where constant C_n in the numerator is given by

$$C_n = \frac{\left(\sigma^2_{U_n}\right)^{N-1}}{\prod_{j=1,j\neq n}^{N}\left(\sigma^2_{U_n}-\sigma^2_{U_j}\right)} \tag{59}$$

Thus, the inverse Fourier transform can be set up as

$$\begin{aligned} f_Z(z) &= \mathcal{F}^{-1}\left[\Phi_Z(\omega)\right] \\ &= \frac{1}{2\pi}\int_{-\infty}^{\infty}\exp(-i\omega z)\sum_{n=1}^{N}\frac{C_n}{\omega^2\sigma^2_{U_n}+1}d\omega \\ &= \sum_{n=1}^{N}\frac{C_n}{2\pi}\int_{-\infty}^{\infty}\frac{\exp(-i\omega z)}{\omega^2\sigma^2_{U_n}+1}d\omega \end{aligned} \tag{60}$$

which is a sum of N inverse Fourier transforms. The inner integral can be easily evaluated using the residue theory [24] as

$$\frac{1}{2\pi}\int_{-\infty}^{\infty}\frac{e^{-i\omega z}}{\omega^2\sigma^2_{U_n}+1}d\omega = \frac{e^{-\frac{z}{\sigma_{U_n}}}}{2\sigma_{U_n}}\left(e^{\frac{2z}{\sigma_{U_n}}\theta(-z)+\theta(z)}\right) \tag{61}$$

where $\theta(z)$ is the unit step function. The result in (61) can be simplified as

$$\frac{1}{2\pi}\int_{-\infty}^{\infty}\frac{e^{-i\omega z}}{\omega^2\sigma^2_{U_n}+1}d\omega = \frac{1}{2}\frac{e^{-\frac{|z|}{\sigma_{U_n}}}}{\sigma_{U_n}} \tag{62}$$

Finally, after substituting the result for the above integral in (60), the PDF of the MAI with distinct $\sigma^2_{U_n}$ is found to be given in (12).

Scenario 2: For identical $\sigma^2_{U_n}$

For the second scenario of identical $\sigma^2_{U_n}$ (say $\sigma^2_{U_n} = \sigma^2_U$ for all n), we can set up the integral in (11) as

$$\frac{1}{2\pi}\int_{-\infty}^{\infty}\frac{\exp(-i\omega z)}{\left(\omega^2\sigma^2_U+1\right)^N}d\omega \tag{63}$$

which can be solved using the residue theory [24] to obtain

$$\frac{1}{2\pi}\int_{-\infty}^{\infty}\frac{\exp(-i\omega z)}{\left(\omega^2\sigma^2_U+1\right)^N}d\omega = \frac{1}{(2\sigma_U)^N}\frac{(|z|)^{N-1}}{\Gamma(N)}W_{0,N-\frac{1}{2}}\left(\frac{2|z|}{\sigma_U}\right) \tag{64}$$

where $W_{\lambda,\mu}(z)$ is called *Whittaker function* and it is defined as [24]

$$W_{\lambda,\mu}(z) = \frac{z^{\mu+\frac{1}{2}}e^{-z/2}}{\Gamma\left(\mu-\lambda+\frac{1}{2}\right)}\int_0^{\infty}e^{-zt}t^{\mu-\lambda+\frac{1}{2}}(1+t)^{\mu+\lambda+\frac{1}{2}}dt \tag{65}$$

For the special case when $\lambda = 0$, the Whittaker function can be related to the *Bessel function for imaginary arguments* (denoted as $K_\mu(z)$) as follows [24]

$$W_{0,\mu}(z) = \sqrt{\frac{z}{\pi}}K_\mu\left(\frac{z}{2}\right) \tag{66}$$

where, the Bessel function for imaginary arguments is defined as [24]

$$K_\mu(z) = \frac{1}{2}\left(\frac{z}{2}\right)^\mu\int_0^{\infty}\frac{e^{-t-z^2/4t}}{t^{\mu+1}}dt, \quad |\arg(z)| < \frac{\pi}{2}, \quad Re\left(z^2\right) > 0 \tag{67}$$

Thus, by using the above relation, we can simplify the result of integral in (64) to

$$\frac{1}{2\pi}\int_{-\infty}^{\infty}\frac{\exp(-i\omega z)}{\left(\omega^2\sigma^2_U+1\right)^N}d\omega = \sqrt{\frac{2|z|}{\pi\sigma_U}}\frac{1}{(2\sigma_U)^N}\frac{(|z|)^{N-1}}{\Gamma(N)}K_{N-\frac{1}{2}}\left(\frac{|z|}{\pi\sigma_U}\right) \tag{68}$$

Finally, the PDF of the MAI with identical $\sigma_{U_n}^2$ is obtained after substituting the above solution and it is given in (12).

Derivation of Eq. (32)

Using (23) and (50) and after some mathematical manipulation, the PDF of γ_κ can be setup as

$$f_{\gamma_\kappa}(\gamma_\kappa) = \frac{\gamma_\kappa^{N-1}\left(\frac{N}{\overline{\gamma_\kappa}}\right)^N \exp\left(-\frac{N\gamma_\kappa}{\overline{\gamma_\kappa}}\right)}{(N-1)!} \tag{69}$$

For $N = 1$, the PDF of γ_κ reduces to

$$f_{\gamma_\kappa}(\gamma_\kappa) = \frac{1}{\overline{\gamma_\kappa}} e^{-\gamma_\kappa/\overline{\gamma_\kappa}} \tag{70}$$

which is consistent with [16]. As the channel attenuation is taken to be deterministic then γ_κ is also deterministic. If α_i is taken to be random then the above conditional PDF in (26) will have to be averaged over the PDF of γ_κ. So the average probability of error in BPSK symbols can be obtained as

$$\begin{aligned} P(e) &= \int_0^\infty P(e|w_{i,1})\, p(\gamma_\kappa)\, d\gamma_\kappa \\ &= \frac{1}{2}\sum_{j=1}^{N} C_j \exp\left(\frac{\sigma_\eta^2}{2\sigma_I^2\sigma_\alpha^2}\right)\int_0^\infty \left[\int_{\sigma_\eta^2/2\sigma_I^2\sigma_\alpha^2}^\infty e^{-t}\operatorname{erfc}\left(\sqrt{\gamma_\kappa}\right) dt\right] \\ &\times \frac{\gamma_\kappa^{N-1}\left(\frac{N}{\overline{\gamma_\kappa}}\right)^N \exp\left(-\frac{N\gamma_\kappa}{\overline{\gamma_\kappa}}\right)}{(N-1)!} d\gamma_\kappa \end{aligned} \tag{71}$$

Rearranging the above we get

$$\begin{aligned} P(e) &= \frac{1}{2}\sum_{j=1}^{N} C_j \exp\left(\frac{\sigma_\eta^2}{2\sigma_I^2\sigma_\alpha^2}\right)\int_{\sigma_\eta^2/2\sigma_I^2\sigma_\alpha^2}^\infty e^{-t}\left(\frac{N}{\overline{\gamma_\kappa}}\right)^N \\ &\times \left[\int_0^\infty \gamma_\kappa^{N-1}\exp\left(-\frac{N\gamma_\kappa}{\overline{\gamma_\kappa}}\right)\operatorname{erfc}\left(\sqrt{\gamma_\kappa}\right) d\gamma_\kappa\right] dt \end{aligned} \tag{72}$$

The inner integral can be evaluated as

$$I_{\gamma_\kappa} = \int_0^\infty \gamma_\kappa^{N-1}\exp\left(-\frac{N\gamma_\kappa}{\overline{\gamma_\kappa}}\right)\operatorname{erfc}\left(\sqrt{\gamma_\kappa}\right) d\gamma_\kappa$$

$$I_{\gamma_\kappa} = 2^{1-2N}\Gamma(2N)\, {}_2F_1\left(N, N+\frac{1}{2}; N+1, -\frac{N}{\overline{\gamma_\kappa}}\right)/\Gamma(N+1)$$

The above result is again consistent with [16] for $N = 1$ which yields $I_{\gamma_\kappa} = \overline{\gamma_\kappa}\left(1-\sqrt{\frac{\overline{\gamma_\kappa}}{1+\overline{\gamma_\kappa}}}\right)$. Replacing in the above integral in (72) and rearranging terms, we get

$$\begin{aligned} P(e) &= \frac{1}{2}\sum_{j=1}^{N} C_j 2^{1-N}\exp\left(\frac{\sigma_\eta^2}{2\sigma_I^2\sigma_\alpha^2}\right)\left(\frac{\sigma_I^2\sigma_\alpha^2}{\psi N^2 E_b}\right)^N \frac{\Gamma(2N)}{\Gamma(N+1)} \\ &\times \int_{\sigma_\eta^2/2\sigma_I^2\sigma_\alpha^2}^\infty e^{-t} t_2^N F_1\left(N, N+\frac{1}{2}; N+1, -\frac{2\sigma_I^2\sigma_\alpha^2 t}{\psi N^2 E_b}\right) dt \end{aligned} \tag{73}$$

Competing interests

The authors declare that they have no competing interests.

Acknowledgements

The authors acknowledge the support provided by the Deanship of Scientific Research at KFUPM under Research Grant SB111012.

Author details

[1]Electrical and Electronics Technology Department, Affiliated Colleges at Hafr Al Batin, King Fahd University of Petroleum and Minerals, P. O. Box 1803, Hafr Al Batin 31991, Saudi Arabia. [2]Electrical and Computer Engineering, King Abdulaziz University, Jeddah, Saudi Arabia. [3]Department of Electrical Engineering, King Fahd University of Petroleum and Minerals, Dhahran 31261, Kingdom of Saudi Arabia. [4]Department of Systems Engineering, King Fahd University of Petroleum and Minerals, Dhahran 31261, Kingdom of Saudi Arabia.

References

1. M Pursley, D Sarwate, Performance evaluation for phase-coded spread-spectrum multiple-access communication—part ii: code sequence analysis. Commun. IEEE Trans. **25**, 800–803 (1977)
2. RK Morrow Jr, JS Lehnert, Bit-to-bit error dependence in slotted ds/ssma packet systems with random signature sequences. Commun. IEEE Trans. **37**, 1052–1061 (1989)
3. JM Holtzman, in *Communications, 1991. ICC '91, Conference Record*. A simple, accurate method to calculate spread spectrum multiple access error probabilities, vol. 3 (IEEE International Conference on, Denver, CO, 1991), pp. 1633 -1636
4. B Long, J Hu, P Zhang, Method to improve gaussian approximation accuracy for calculation of spread-spectrum multiple-access error probabilities. Electron. Lett. **31**, 529 -531 (1995)
5. J Lehnert, M Pursley, Error probabilities for binary direct-sequence spread-spectrum communications with random signature sequences. Commun. IEEE Trans. **35**, 87–98 (1987)
6. JJM Holtzman, A simple, accurate method to calculate spread-spectrum multiple-access error probabilities. Commun. IEEE Trans. **COM-40**, 461–464 (1992)
7. D Borth, M Pursley, Analysis of direct-sequence spread-spectrum multiple-access communication over rician fading channels. Commun. IEEE Trans. **27**(10), 1566–1577 (1979)
8. C Gardner, J Orr, Fading effects on the performance of a spread spectrum multiple access communication system. Commun. IEEE Trans. **27**(1), 143–149 (1979)
9. E Geraniotis, M Pursley, Error probability for direct-sequence spread-spectrum multiple-access communications—part ii: approximations. Commun. IEEE Trans. **30**(5), 985–995 (1982)
10. E Geraniotis, Direct-sequence spread-spectrum multiple-access communications over nonselective and frequency-selective rician fading channels. Commun. IEEE Trans. **34**(8), 756–764 (1986)
11. MO Sunay, PJ McLane, in *Global Telecommunications Conference, 1996. GLOBECOM'96.'Communications: The Key to Global Prosperity*. Calculating error probabilities for DS-CDMA systems: when not to use the Gaussian approximation, vol. 3 (IEEE, London, 1996), pp. 1744–1749
12. MO Sunay, PJ McLane, Probability of error for diversity combining in DS CDMA systems with synchronization errors. Eur. Trans. Telecommun. **9**(5), 449–463 (1998)
13. J Cheng, NC Beaulieu, Accurate DS-CDMA bit-error probability calculation in Rayleigh fading. Wirel. Commun. IEEE Trans. **1**(1), 3–15 (2002)
14. J Lehnert, M Pursley, Error probabilities for binary direct-sequence spread-spectrum communications with random signature sequences. Commun. IEEE Trans. **35**, 87–98 (1987)
15. W Mee Jang, L Nguyen, P Bidarkar, MAI and ICI of synchronous downlink MC-CDMA with frequency offset. Wirel. Commun. IEEE Trans. **5**, 693–703 (2006)
16. M Moinuddin, AUH Sheikh, A Zerguine, M Deriche, A unified approach to ber analysis of synchronous downlink CDMA systems with random signature sequences in fading channels with known channel phase. EURASIP J. Adv. Signal Process. **2008**, 1–13 (2008)

17. JO Mark, MNM Saad, BB Samir, in *National Postgraduate Conference (NPC), 2011*. Average BER perfomance and spectral efficiency for MIMO orthogonal MC DS-CDMA system over Nakagami-m fading channels, (Kuala Lumpur, 2011), pp. 1–6
18. P Li, RC de Lamare, R Fa, Multiple feedback successive interference cancellation detection for multiuser mimo systems. Wirel. Commun. IEEE Trans. **10**(8), 2434–2439 (2011)
19. H Huang, H Viswanathan, GJ Foschini, in *Global Telecommunications Conference, 1999. GLOBECOM '99*. Achieving high data rates in CDMA systems using blast techniques, vol. 5, (1999), pp. 2316–2320
20. G Kaddoum, M Coulon, D Roviras, P Chargé, Theoretical performance for asynchronous multi-user chaos-based communication systems on fading channels. Signal Process. **90**(11), 2923–2933 (2010)
21. G Kaddoum, F Gagnon, Performance analysis of STBC-CSK communication system over slow fading channel. Signal Process. **93**(7), 2055–2060 (2013)
22. K Mahmood, SM Asad, M Moinuddin, A Zerguine, S Paul, in *Statistical Signal Processing (SSP), 2014*. Statistical analysis of multiple access interference in Rayleigh fading environment for MIMO CDMA systems (IEEE Workshop on, Gold Coast, VIC, 2014), pp. 412–415
23. K Mahmood, SM Asad, OB Saeed, M Moinuddin, A Zerguine, in *Communications, Signal Processing, and their Applications (ICCSPA), 2015*. Rayleigh fading channel estimation using MMSE estimator for MIMO-CDMA systems (International Conference on, Sharjah, 2015), pp. 1–4
24. IS Gradshteyn, IM Ryzhik, *Table of Integrals, Series, and Products*, 7th edn. (Academic Press, London, U.K., 2007)
25. MA Chaudhry, SM Zubair, *On A Class Of Incomplete Gamma Functions with Applications*. (Chapman & Hall CRC, 2002)
26. JG Proakis, *Digital communications*, 4th edn. (Mc Graw-Hill, United States, 2001)
27. C D'Amours, AO Dahmane, Bit error rate performance of a MIMO-CDMA system employing parity-bit-selected spreading in frequency nonselective Rayleigh fading. Int. J. Antennas Propagation. **2011**, 1–8 (2011)
28. J Hu, S Member, NC Beaulieu, accurate simple closed-form approximations to Rayleigh sum distributions and densities. **9**(2), 109–111 (2005)
29. MN Iqbal, M Moinuddin, in *Multitopic Conference (INMIC), 2011 IEEE 14th International*. Pilot-aided rayleigh fading channel estimation using MMSE estimator for DS-CDMA system, (Karachi, 2011), pp. 347–350
30. AJ Hayter, *Probability and statistics for engineers and scientists*, 4th edn. (Cengage Learning, Mason, OH, United States, 2012)
31. TV K'arm'an, M Biot, *Mathematical methods in engineering*, (McGraw-Hill, United States, 1940)

Filtered-X Least Mean Fourth (FXLMF) and Leaky FXLMF adaptive algorithms

Ali M. Al Omour, Abdelmalek Zidouri, Naveed Iqbal and Azzedine Zerguine*

Abstract

Adaptive filtering algorithms promise an improvement of the active noise control (ANC) problem encountered in many scenarios. Just to name a few, the Filtered-X Least Mean Square (FXLMS) algorithm, the Leaky FXLMS (LFXLMS) algorithm, and other modified LMS-based algorithms have been developed and utilized to combat the ANC problem. All of these algorithms enjoy great performance when the signal-to-noise ratio (SNR) is high. On the other hand, when the SNR is low, which is a known trend in ANC scenarios, the performance of these algorithms is not attractive. The performance of the Least Mean Fourth (LMF) algorithm has never been tested on any ANC scenario under low or high SNR. Therefore, in this work, reflecting the development in the LMS family on the LMF, we are proposing two new adaptive filtering algorithms, which are the Filtered-X Least Mean Fourth (FXLMF) algorithm and the Leakage-based variant (LFXLMF) of the FXLMF algorithm. The main target of this work is to derive the FXLMF and LFXLMF adaptive algorithms, study their convergence behaviors, examine their tracking and transient conduct, and analyze their performance for different noise environments. Moreover, a convex combination filter utilizing the proposed algorithm and algorithm robustness test is carried out. Finally, several simulation results are obtained to validate the theoretical findings and show the effectiveness of the proposed algorithms over other adaptive algorithms.

1 Introduction

Adaptive filtering algorithms are by now omnipresent in a variety of applications, such as plant modeling, adaptive equalization, and system identification, to name a few [1–8]. Add to that, noise control and noise cancelation are important issues whose effects adaptive filtering algorithms strive to mitigate. Active noise control (ANC) techniques use adaptive filtering algorithms to cancel the effect of acoustic noise, by playing anti-noise signal estimated from the noise source itself.

The Least Mean Square (LMS) algorithm suffers from problems, such as a degradation in the algorithm efficiency, due to the presence of a filter in the auxiliary or error path, as in the case of the ANC technique, as well as slow convergence, instability of the algorithm, increased residual noise power, and lower convergence rate. These constraints urged researchers to enhance the performance of the conventional LMS algorithm [9–11].

The Filtered-X LMS (FXLMS) algorithm is considered as the cornerstone for ANC applications [12–15]. In this algorithm, an identical copy of the secondary path, mainly used to solve the instability problem and to eliminate the noise from the primary signal, is used to filter the input before the adaptive algorithm uses it in order to adjust the coefficient vector of the adaptive filter, as depicted in Fig. 1 [9]. More details about the different parameters in Fig. 1 will be given in the next section.

In the last decade, intensive research was carried out for the purpose of enhancing the performance of the FXLMS algorithm. In [14], a new stochastic analysis for the FXLMS algorithm was introduced, using an analytical model not based on the independence theory [16], to derive the first moment of the adaptive weight filter. The main assumption of this work was to ignore the correlation between the data vector and the weights and compare the correlation between data vectors, preserving past and present data vector correlations. This model was validated for both white and colored primary input signals and shows stability even when using large step sizes.

The FXLMS algorithm is preferred because of its inherent stability and simplicity, but sometimes, the adaptive filter suffers from high noise levels caused by low-frequency resonances, which may cause nonlinear distortion due to overloading of the secondary source.

* Correspondence: azzedine@kfupm.edu.sa
Electrical Engineering Department, KFUPM, Dhahran, Saudi Arabia

This problem was solved by adding output power constraints to the cost function, as was proposed in the Leaky FXLMS (LFXLMS) algorithm [17]. Moreover, the LFXLMS reduces the numerical error in the finite precision implementation and limits the output power of the secondary source to avoid nonlinear distortion. The LFXLMS increases the algorithm's stability, especially when a large source strength is used.

Another modification of the FXLMS algorithm is the Modified FXLMS (MFXLMS) algorithm [15]. Since the FXLMS exhibits poor convergence performance, the MFXLMS proposes a better convergence and reduces the computational load.

The LMS may suffer from divergence due to the insufficient spectral excitation, like a sinusoid signal without noise, which consequently may cause overflow for the weight vector during the updating process. This divergence problem can be resolved by proposing a leak term during the update process of the weight vector. Of course, this will result in lesser performance; however, the leakage factor is controlled, which is necessary to balance for the lost performance. In addition, this will add complexity, but more robustness of the adaptive filter is achieved, as was done in the case of the Leaky LMS (LLMS) algorithm.

In [17], a stochastic analysis for the LFXLMS algorithms was proposed without resorting to the independence theory. Furthermore, to strengthen their work, the authors assumed an inexact estimation for the secondary path, which is the case in most practical implementations for the adaptive filter.

Due to very low input signal, the Leaky LMS algorithm proposed in [18] aims to reduce the stalling effect, where the gradient estimate is too small to adjust the coefficients of the algorithm. Moreover, the leakage term stabilized the LMS algorithm successfully. Also, the LLMS solved the problem of bursting in short-distance telephones when they added the adaptive echo canceller [19].

A very important extension of the LMS algorithm is the Least Mean Fourth (LMF) algorithm [20], where the cost function for LMF algorithm, defined in terms of the error signal ($e(n)$) is given by

$$J_{\mathrm{LMF}}(n) = E\left[e^4(n)\right]. \tag{1}$$

The LMF weights converge proportionally to the LMS weights. The performance of the LMF algorithm has never been tested on any ANC scenario under low or high signal-to-noise ratio (SNR). In this work, we propose two new algorithms, the Filtered-X LMF (FXLMF) and Leaky FXLMF (LFXLMF) algorithms. We analyze the convergence behaviors and examine the performance of both of them. This is carried out under different statistical input signals and noise for the mean and mean square error of the adaptive filter weights, depending on secondary path modeling error using an energy conservation relation framework. These two algorithms are expected to have a high effectiveness on the ANC issue at an extra computational complexity. Monte Carlo simulations used to assess the analytical assumptions, as well as the accuracy of the proposed model, are verified and assessed.

This paper is organized as follows: Section 1 provides an introduction and a literature review. In Section 2, analytical derivations for the FXLMF and LFXLMF algorithms are presented. Section 3 proposes the convex combination of the FXLMF algorithm with the FXLMS algorithm. Simulation results are presented in Section 4, and finally, the conclusions and future work are presented in Section 5.

2 Analysis

Figure 1 illustrates the block diagram of an ANC and illustrates the location of the secondary path $\boldsymbol{S}$ and its estimated secondary path $\hat{\boldsymbol{S}}$. The secondary path is a transfer function which can be represented by a group of a digital-to-analog (D/A) converter, a power amplifier, a

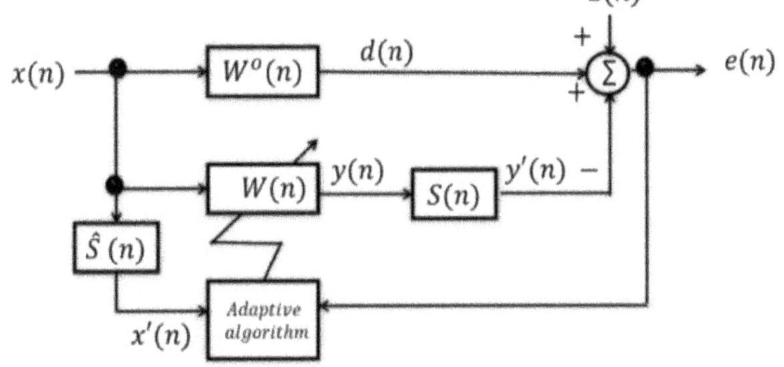

Fig. 1 Block diagram for ANC system

canceling loudspeaker, an error microphone, and an (A/D) converter.

The realization of the secondary path is usually obtained using a system identification technique. For this work, the assumption used considers an inexact estimation for the secondary path which may cause errors on the number of coefficients or on their values as was done in [21]. Consequently, the values of the secondary path will be as $\hat{\boldsymbol{S}} \neq \boldsymbol{S}$, and the filter coefficients' number $\hat{M} \neq M$. Table 1 describes the different parameters used in Fig. 1.

Referring to Fig. 1, the error signal is given by

$$e(n) = d(n) - y'(n) + z(n), \tag{2}$$

where $d(n)$ is the desired response and $y(n)$ is the output of the adaptive filter given by

$$y(n) = \boldsymbol{x}^T(n)\boldsymbol{w}(n) = \boldsymbol{w}^T(n)\boldsymbol{x}(n), \tag{3}$$

$y'(n)$ is the output of the secondary path

$$\begin{aligned} y'(n) &= \sum_{i=0}^{M-1} s_i y(n-i) \\ &= \sum_{i=0}^{M-1} s_i \boldsymbol{x}^T(n-i)\boldsymbol{w}(n-i), \end{aligned} \tag{4}$$

and $z(n)$ is the active noise. Finally, the filtered input signal is given as

$$x'(n) = \sum_{i=0}^{\hat{M}-1} \hat{s}_i \boldsymbol{x}(n-i). \tag{5}$$

For the case of an exact approximation for the secondary path, that is $\boldsymbol{S} = \hat{\boldsymbol{S}}$, the input signal, $\boldsymbol{x}(n)$, will be filtered by $\boldsymbol{S}$.

2.1 Development of FXLMF algorithm

Using the block diagram in Fig. 1, the cost function for the FXLMF algorithm is given by the following relation:

$$J_{\text{FXLMF}}(n) = E\left[e^4(n)\right], \tag{6}$$

Table 1 Parameters and their descriptions used in Fig. 1

Adaptive filter weights	$\boldsymbol{w}(n) = [w_0(n)\ w_1(n) \ldots w_{N-1}(n)]^T$
Stationary input signal	$\boldsymbol{x}(n) = [x(n)\ x(n-1) \ldots x(n-N+1)]^T$
Secondary path	$\boldsymbol{S} = [s_0\ s_1 \ldots s_{M-1}]^T$
Estimate of the secondary path	$\hat{\boldsymbol{S}} = [\hat{s}_0\ \hat{s}_1 \ldots \hat{s}_{M-1}]^T$
Primary (desired) signal	$d(n)$
Stationary noise process	$z(n)$
Number of tap weight coefficients	N
Number of the secondary path coefficients	M

where the error signal, $e(n)$, is given below as the difference between the output signal from the secondary path and the primary signal, that is,

$$e(n) = d(n) - \sum_{i=0}^{M-1} s_i \boldsymbol{x}^T(n-i)\boldsymbol{w}(n-i) + z(n). \tag{7}$$

During the course of derivations, we will resort to the same assumptions, used in the literature [17–23], to simplify our algorithms. These assumptions are as follows:

2.1.1 Assumption A1

$\boldsymbol{x}(n)$ is the input signal, a zero mean wide-stationary Gaussian process with variance σ_x^2, and $\boldsymbol{R}_{i,j} = E[\boldsymbol{x}(n-j)\boldsymbol{x}^T(n-i)] > 0$ is a positive definite autocorrelation matrix of the input signal.

2.1.2 Assumption A2

$z(n)$ is the measurement noise, an independent and identically distributed (i.i.d) random variable with zero mean and variance $\sigma_z^2 = E[z^2(n)]$, and there is no correlation between the input signal and the measurement noise. In other words, the sequence $z(n)$ is independent of $\boldsymbol{x}(n)$ and $\boldsymbol{w}(n)$. The measurement is assumed to have an even probability density function.

Assuming that the vector $\boldsymbol{w}$ is fixed, then the cost function looks like the following:

$$\begin{aligned} J_{\text{FXLMF}} = &\left\{\left(\sum_{i=0}^{M-1}\sum_{j=0}^{M-1}\sum_{k=0}^{M-1}\sum_{l=0}^{M-1} s_i s_j s_k s_l\, E[\boldsymbol{x}^T(n-l)\boldsymbol{x}(n-k)\,\boldsymbol{x}^T(n-j)\boldsymbol{x}(n-i)]\right)\right\}\|\boldsymbol{w}\|^4 \\ &-4\left\{\left(\sum_{i=0}^{M-1}\sum_{j=0}^{M-1}\sum_{k=0}^{M-1} s_i s_j s_k\, E[d(n)\boldsymbol{x}(n-k)\,\boldsymbol{x}^T(n-j)\boldsymbol{x}(n-i)]\right)\right\}\|\boldsymbol{w}\|^3 \\ &+6\left\{\left(\sum_{i=0}^{M-1}\sum_{j=0}^{M-1} s_i s_j\, E\left[d^2(n)\,\boldsymbol{x}(n-j)\,\boldsymbol{x}^T(n-i)\right]\right)\right. \\ &\left.+\sigma_z^2\left(\sum_{i=0}^{M-1}\sum_{j=0}^{M-1} s_i s_j\, E[\boldsymbol{x}(n-j)\,\boldsymbol{x}^T(n-i)]\right)\right\}\|\boldsymbol{w}\|^2 \\ &-4\left\{\left(\sum_{i=0}^{M-1} s_i\, E\left[d^3(n)\,\boldsymbol{x}^T(n-i)\right]\right)\right. \\ &\left.-\sigma_z^2\left(\sum_{i=0}^{M-1} s_i\, E[d(n)\boldsymbol{x}^T(n-i)]\right)\right\}\|\boldsymbol{w}\| \\ &+\left\{\left(E\left[d^4(n)\right] + \sigma_z^2 - 4\,E\left[z^3(n)\right]E\left[d(n)\right] + 6\,\sigma_d^2\sigma_z^2\right)\right\}. \end{aligned} \tag{8}$$

To obtain the optimal weight vector for the cost function, we take the derivative of Eq. (8) with respect to $\boldsymbol{w}$ and set it to zero. Discarding the noise, $z(n)$, the derivative of Eq. (8) will be

$$\frac{\partial J_{\mathrm{FXLMF}}(n)}{\partial \boldsymbol{w}(n)} = \|\boldsymbol{w}\|^3 - 3\left(\tilde{\boldsymbol{R}}_{s^4}^{-1}\tilde{\boldsymbol{P}}_{d,s^3}\right)\|\boldsymbol{w}\|^2 + 3\tilde{\boldsymbol{R}}_{s^4}^{-1}\left(\tilde{\boldsymbol{P}}_{d^2,s^2}\right) \times \|\boldsymbol{w}\| - \tilde{\boldsymbol{R}}_{s^4}^{-1}\left(\tilde{\boldsymbol{P}}_{d^3,s}\right), \tag{9}$$

where

$$\tilde{\boldsymbol{R}}_{s^2} = \sum_{i=0}^{M-1}\sum_{j=0}^{M-1} s_i s_j \, E\left[\boldsymbol{x}(n-j)\boldsymbol{x}^T(n-i)\right] = \sum_{i=0}^{M-1}\sum_{j=0}^{M-1} s_i s_j \, \boldsymbol{R}_{i,j},$$

$\boldsymbol{R}_{i,j} = E\ [\boldsymbol{x}(n-j)\boldsymbol{x}^T(n-i)]$ is the input autocorrelation matrix,

$$\tilde{\boldsymbol{P}}_{d,s} = \sum_{j=0}^{M-1} s_j \, E\left[d(n)\boldsymbol{x}(n-j)\right] = \sum_{j=0}^{M-1} s_j P_{d,j},$$

$\boldsymbol{P}_{d,j} = E\ [d(n)\boldsymbol{x}(n-j)]$ is the cross-correlation between the input and the primary signals,

$$\tilde{\boldsymbol{R}}_{s^4} = \sum_{i=0}^{M-1}\sum_{j=0}^{M-1}\sum_{k=0}^{M-1}\sum_{l=0}^{M-1} s_i s_j s_k s_l \, E[\boldsymbol{x}^T(n-l)\boldsymbol{x}(n-k)\,\boldsymbol{x}^T(n-j)\boldsymbol{x}(n-i)] = \sum_{i=0}^{M-1}\sum_{j=0}^{M-1}\sum_{k=0}^{M-1}\sum_{l=0}^{M-1} s_i s_j s_k s_l \, \boldsymbol{R}_{i,j,k,l}\,,$$

$$\tilde{\boldsymbol{P}}_{d,s^3} = \sum_{i=0}^{M-1}\sum_{j=0}^{M-1}\sum_{k=0}^{M-1} s_i s_j s_k \, E\left[d(n)\boldsymbol{x}(n-k)\,\boldsymbol{x}^T(n-j)\boldsymbol{x}(n-i)\right] = \sum_{i=0}^{M-1}\sum_{j=0}^{M-1}\sum_{k=0}^{M-1} s_i s_j s_k \, \boldsymbol{P}_{d,i,j,k},$$

$$\tilde{\boldsymbol{P}}_{d^2,s^2} = \sum_{i=0}^{M-1}\sum_{j=0}^{M-1} s_i s_j \, E\left[d^2(n)\,\boldsymbol{x}(n-j)\,\boldsymbol{x}^T(n-i)\right] = \sum_{i=0}^{M-1}\sum_{j=0}^{M-1} s_i s_j \boldsymbol{P}_{d^2,i,j},$$

and

$$\tilde{\boldsymbol{P}}_{d^3,s} = \sum_{i=0}^{M-1} s_i \, E\left[d^3(n)\,\boldsymbol{x}^T(n-i)\right] = \sum_{i=0}^{M-1} s_i \, \boldsymbol{P}_{d^3,i}.$$

Equation (9) has three solutions, and the optimal solution is given by

$$\boldsymbol{w_o} = \tilde{\boldsymbol{R}}_{s^2}^{-1}\tilde{\boldsymbol{P}}_{d,s}. \tag{10}$$

2.2 Mean behavior for the FXLMF algorithm

The FXLMF algorithm is governed by the following recursion:

$$\boldsymbol{w}(n+1) = \boldsymbol{w}(n) - \frac{\mu}{4}\,\frac{\partial J_{\mathrm{FXLMF}}(n)}{\partial \boldsymbol{w}(n)}, \tag{11}$$

where the instantaneous gradient can be approximated as

$$\frac{\partial \hat{j}_{\mathrm{FXLMF}}(n)}{\partial \boldsymbol{w}(n)} \approx -4\, e^3(n) \sum_{i=1}^{\hat{M}-1} \hat{s}_i \boldsymbol{x}^T(n-i) \tag{12}$$

due to the absence of the exact knowledge of the secondary path. Substituting Eqs. (2)–(5) and (11) in (10), the adaptive weight vector update is given by

$$\begin{aligned}
\boldsymbol{w}(n+1) = {} & \boldsymbol{w}(n) + \mu \sum_{i=0}^{\hat{M}-1} \hat{s}_i \, d^3(n)\boldsymbol{x}(n-i) \\
& -3\mu\left(\sum_{i=0}^{M-1}\sum_{j=0}^{\hat{M}-1} s_i \hat{s}_j \, d^2(n)\boldsymbol{x}(n-j)\boldsymbol{x}^T(n-i)\boldsymbol{w}(n-i)\right) \\
& +3\mu\left(\sum_{i=0}^{M-1}\sum_{j=0}^{M-1}\sum_{k=0}^{\hat{M}-1} s_i s_j \hat{s}_k \, d(n)\boldsymbol{x}(n-k)\boldsymbol{x}^T(n-j)\,\boldsymbol{x}(n-i)\boldsymbol{w}(n-j)\,\boldsymbol{w}^T(n-i)\right) \\
& -6\mu\left(\sum_{i=0}^{M-1}\sum_{j=0}^{\hat{M}-1} s_i \hat{s}_j \, z(n)\, d(n)\boldsymbol{x}(n-j)\boldsymbol{x}^T(n-i)\boldsymbol{w}(n-i)\right) \\
& -\mu\left(\sum_{i=0}^{M-1}\sum_{j=0}^{M-1}\sum_{k=0}^{M-1}\sum_{l=0}^{\hat{M}-1} s_i s_j s_k \hat{s}_l \, \boldsymbol{x}(n-l)\boldsymbol{x}^T(n-k)\,\boldsymbol{x}(n-j)\,\boldsymbol{x}^T(n-i)\boldsymbol{w}(n-k)\,\boldsymbol{w}^T(n-j)\boldsymbol{w}(n-i)\right) \\
& +3\mu\left(\sum_{i=0}^{M-1}\sum_{j=0}^{M-1}\sum_{k=0}^{\hat{M}-1} s_i s_j \hat{s}_k \, z(n)\boldsymbol{x}(n-k)\boldsymbol{x}^T(n-j)\,\boldsymbol{x}(n-i)\boldsymbol{w}(n-j)\,\boldsymbol{w}^T(n-i)\right) \\
& -3\mu\left(\sum_{i=0}^{M-1}\sum_{j=0}^{\hat{M}-1} s_i \hat{s}_j \, z^2(n)\boldsymbol{x}(n-j)\boldsymbol{x}^T(n-i)\boldsymbol{w}(n-i)\right) \\
& +\mu\left(\sum_{i=0}^{\hat{M}-1} \hat{s}_i \, z^3(n)\boldsymbol{x}(n-i)\right) + 3\mu\left(\sum_{i=0}^{\hat{M}-1} \hat{s}_i \, d(n)z^2(n)\boldsymbol{x}(n-i)\right) \\
& +3\mu\left(\sum_{i=0}^{\hat{M}-1} \hat{s}_i \, d^2(n)z(n)\boldsymbol{x}(n-i)\right).
\end{aligned} \tag{13}$$

To find the expectations for the terms on the right-hand side of Eq. (13), we resort to the following assumptions [1, 21]:

2.2.1 Assumption A3

Independence theory (IT) states that the taps of the input vector $x(n-i)$, $i = 0,1,2,\ldots$ are statistically dependent so that $E[\boldsymbol{x}(n-i)\boldsymbol{x}^T(n-j)] = E[\boldsymbol{x}(n-i)\boldsymbol{x}^T(n-j)\boldsymbol{x}(n-k)] = E[\boldsymbol{x}(n-l)\boldsymbol{x}^T(n-k)\boldsymbol{x}(n-j)\boldsymbol{x}^T(n-i)] = 0$, for any $i \neq j$, $i \neq j \neq k$, and $i \neq j \neq k \neq l$, respectively.

2.2.2 Assumption A4

Take into consideration the correlation between $\boldsymbol{x}(n-i)$, $\boldsymbol{x}(n-j)$, $\boldsymbol{x}(n-k)$, and $\boldsymbol{x}(n-l) \forall\, i, j, k, l$ and ignore the correlation between $\boldsymbol{w}(n-v)$ and $\boldsymbol{x}(n-i)$ or $\boldsymbol{x}(n-j)$ or $\boldsymbol{x}(n-k) \forall\, i, j, k$.

Using assumption *A3*, the mean weight update recursion for the FXLMF algorithm will look like the following:

$$
\begin{aligned}
E[\boldsymbol{w}(n+1)] = {} & E[\boldsymbol{w}(n)] + \mu \sum_{i=0}^{\hat{M}-1} \hat{s}_i \boldsymbol{P}_{d^3,i} - 3\mu \left(\sum_{i=0}^{M-1} \sum_{j=0}^{\hat{M}-1} s_i \hat{s}_j \boldsymbol{P}_{d^2,i,j} E[\boldsymbol{w}(n-i)] \right) \\
& + 3\mu \left(\sum_{i=0}^{M-1} \sum_{j=0}^{M-1} \sum_{k=0}^{\hat{M}-1} s_i s_j \hat{s}_k \boldsymbol{P}_{d,i,j,k} E[\boldsymbol{w}(n-j)\boldsymbol{w}^T(n-i)] \right) \\
& - \mu \left(\sum_{i=0}^{M-1} \sum_{j=0}^{M-1} \sum_{k=0}^{M-1} \sum_{l=0}^{\hat{M}-1} s_i s_j s_k \hat{s}_l \boldsymbol{R}_{i,j,k,l} E[\boldsymbol{w}(n-k)\boldsymbol{w}^T(n-j)\boldsymbol{w}(n-i)] \right) \\
& - 3\mu \sigma_z^2 \left(\sum_{i=0}^{M-1} \sum_{j=0}^{\hat{M}-1} s_i \hat{s}_j \boldsymbol{R}_{i,j} E[\boldsymbol{w}(n-i)] \right) + 3\mu \sigma_z^2 \left(\sum_{i=0}^{\hat{M}-1} \hat{s}_i \boldsymbol{P}_{d,i} \right).
\end{aligned}
\tag{14}
$$

Consequently, after taking into account the independence theory, Eq. (14) looks like the following:

$$
\begin{aligned}
E[\boldsymbol{w}(n+1)] = {} & E[\boldsymbol{w}(n)] + \mu \hat{s}_0 E\left[d^3(n)\boldsymbol{x}^T(n)\right] \\
& - 3\mu \left(\sum_{i=0}^{\min(\hat{M},M)-1} s_i \hat{s}_i \boldsymbol{P}_{d^2,i,j} E[\boldsymbol{w}(n-i)] \right) \\
& - 3\mu \sigma_z^2 \left(\sum_{i=0}^{\min(\hat{M},M)-1} s_i \hat{s}_i \boldsymbol{R}_{i,j} E[\boldsymbol{w}(n-i)] \right) \\
& + 3\mu \left(\sum_{i=0}^{\min(\hat{M},M)-1} s_i s_i \hat{s}_i \boldsymbol{P}_{d,i,j,k} E[\boldsymbol{w}(n-i)\boldsymbol{w}^T(n-i)] \right) \\
& + 3\mu \sigma_z^2 \hat{s}_0 E[d(n)\boldsymbol{x}(n)] \\
& - \mu \left(\sum_{i=0}^{\min(\hat{M},M)-1} s_i s_i s_i \hat{s}_i \boldsymbol{R}_{i,j,k,l} E[\boldsymbol{w}(n-i)\boldsymbol{w}^T(n-i)\boldsymbol{w}(n-i)] \right).
\end{aligned}
\tag{15}
$$

Since in a practical situation, an exact modeling for the secondary path cannot be achieved, which may lead to incorrect number of tap weights, such as $\hat{M} < M$ or may have the same number of taps but they do not have the same $\hat{S} \neq S$. Here, we consider the case of overestimation for the secondary path, as was the case for Eq. (12). Moreover, to study the steady-state condition, we assume that the optimal solution of tap weights is governed by $\lim_{n \to \infty} E[\boldsymbol{w}(n+1)] = \lim_{n \to \infty} E[\boldsymbol{w}(n)] = \boldsymbol{w}_\infty$; as a result,

$$
\boldsymbol{w}_\infty \approx \boldsymbol{w}_o = \tilde{\boldsymbol{R}}_{s^2}^{-1} \tilde{\boldsymbol{P}}_{d,s} \tag{16}
$$

2.3 Second moment analysis for FXLMF algorithm

Using Eq. (7), the mean square error (MSE) for the FXLMF algorithm is obtained:

$$
\begin{aligned}
\mathrm{MSE}_{\mathrm{FXLMF}}(n) &= E\left[e^2(n)\right] \\
&= E\left[d^2(n)\right] - 2\sum_{i=0}^{M-1} s_i E[d(n)\boldsymbol{x}(n-i)] E[\boldsymbol{w}(n-i)] \\
&\quad + \sum_{i=0}^{M-1} \sum_{j=0}^{M-1} s_i s_j E[\boldsymbol{x}(n-j)\boldsymbol{x}^T(n-i)] E[\boldsymbol{w}(n-i)\boldsymbol{w}^T(n-i)] \\
&\quad + E[z^2(n)] \quad = \sigma_d^2 - 2\sum_{i=0}^{M-1} s_i \boldsymbol{P}_{d,i} E[\boldsymbol{w}(n-i)] \\
&\quad + \sum_{i=0}^{M-1} \sum_{j=0}^{M-1} s_i s_j \boldsymbol{R}_{i,j} E[\boldsymbol{w}(n-i)\boldsymbol{w}^T(n-i)] + \sigma_z^2.
\end{aligned}
\tag{17}
$$

Next, to find the minimum mean square error (MMSE), we need to substitute the optimal solution of the FXLMF algorithm (16) in (17); moreover, the optimal error is given by

$$
e_o(n) = d(n) - \sum_{i=0}^{M-1} s_i \boldsymbol{x}^T(n-i) \boldsymbol{w}_o \tag{18}
$$

Relying on the orthogonality principle [1, 2], the input signal will be orthogonal to the error, and noting that $\sigma_d^2 = \tilde{\boldsymbol{P}}_{d,s}^{*} \tilde{\boldsymbol{R}}_{s^2}^{-1} \tilde{\boldsymbol{P}}_{d,s}$, where σ_d^2 is the power of the desired response and $\tilde{\boldsymbol{P}}_{d,s}$ and $\tilde{\boldsymbol{R}}_{s^2}$ have been already defined in Section 2.1, the $\mathrm{MMSE}_{\mathrm{FXLMF}}$ can be expressed as follows:

$$
\mathrm{MMSE}_{\mathrm{FXLMF}} = \sigma_z^2 \tag{19}
$$

2.4 FXLMF algorithm stability

Choosing the right value of step size ensures that the algorithm will converge. The FXLMF algorithm weight update equation is given by

$$
\boldsymbol{w}(n+1) = \boldsymbol{w}(n) + \mu\, e^3(n)\, x'(n). \tag{20}
$$

Then, the algorithm converges when $E[\boldsymbol{w}(n+1)] = E[\boldsymbol{w}(n)]$, that is, the expected value of the weight adjustment term will be zero:

$$
\mu E\left[e^3(n)\, x'(n)\right] = 0
$$

or

$$
\mu E\left[\left(d(n) - \sum_{i=0}^{M-1} s_i \boldsymbol{x}^T(n-i) \boldsymbol{w}(n-i) + z(n) \right)^3 \left(\sum_{i=0}^{M-1} s_i \boldsymbol{x}^T(n-i) \right) \right] = 0, \tag{21}
$$

since

$$
\begin{aligned}
e(n) &= d(n) - \sum_{i=0}^{M-1} s_i \boldsymbol{x}^T(n-i) \boldsymbol{w}(n-i) + z(n) \\
&= \sum_{i=0}^{M-1} s_i \boldsymbol{x}^T(n-i) \boldsymbol{w}_o - \sum_{i=0}^{M-1} s_i \boldsymbol{x}^T(n-i) \boldsymbol{w}(n-i) + z(n).
\end{aligned}
\tag{22}
$$

The weight error vector is defined as

$$\boldsymbol{v}(n) = \boldsymbol{w}(n) - \boldsymbol{w_o}. \quad (23)$$

Hence,

$$e(n) = z(n) - \sum_{i=0}^{M-1} s_i \boldsymbol{x}^T(n-i)\boldsymbol{v}(n). \quad (24)$$

Using Eqs. (23) and (24) in Eq. (19), then

$$\boldsymbol{v}(n+1) = \boldsymbol{v}(n) + \mu\left(z(n) - \sum_{i=0}^{M-1} s_i \boldsymbol{x}^T(n-i)\boldsymbol{v}(n)\right)^3 \left(\sum_{i=0}^{M-1} s_i \boldsymbol{x}^T(n-i)\right). \quad (25)$$

The value of $\boldsymbol{v}(n)$ approaches zero when the algorithm converges, and therefore, higher order terms of $\mathbf{v}(n)$ can be ignored, and as a result, the weight error update equation can look like

$$\begin{aligned}\boldsymbol{v}(n+1) &\cong \boldsymbol{v}(n) \\ &+ \mu\left(z^3(n) - 3\sum_{i=0}^{M-1} s_i z^2(n)\boldsymbol{x}^T(n-i)\boldsymbol{v}(n)\right) \\ &\times \left(\sum_{i=0}^{M-1} s_i \boldsymbol{x}^T(n-i)\right).\end{aligned} \quad (26)$$

Following assumptions *A1* and *A2* that the noise is independent of the input signal and independent of the weight error vector, the expected value of Eq. (26) results into

$$\begin{aligned}E[\boldsymbol{v}(n+1)] &= E[\boldsymbol{v}(n)] - \mu\left\{3\sigma_z{}^2 \sum_{i=0}^{M-1}\sum_{j=0}^{M-1} s_i E[\boldsymbol{x}(n-j)\boldsymbol{x}^T(n-i)]E[\boldsymbol{v}(n)]\right\} \\ &= \left[I - \mu\left(3\sigma_z{}^2 \tilde{\boldsymbol{R}}_{s^2}\right)\right]E[\boldsymbol{v}(n)].\end{aligned} \quad (27)$$

Since the autocorrelation matrix $\boldsymbol{R}_{i,j} > 0$, the range of the step size for the FXLMF algorithm can be shown to be given by

$$0 < \mu < \frac{2}{3\sigma_z{}^2 \lambda_{\max}\left(\tilde{\boldsymbol{R}}_{s^2}\right)}, \quad (28)$$

where $\lambda_{\max}\left(\tilde{\boldsymbol{R}}_{s^2}\right)$ represents the maximum eigenvalue of $\tilde{\boldsymbol{R}}_{s^2}$.

2.5 Development of Leaky FXLMF (LFXLMF) algorithm

In this section, the leaky version of the FXLMF algorithm is developed using assumptions *A1–A4*. Using the block diagram in Fig. 1, the cost function for the LFXLMF algorithm will be as follows:

$$J_{\text{LFXLMF}}(n) = E\left[e^4(n)\right] + \gamma\, \boldsymbol{w}^T(n)\boldsymbol{w}(n), \quad (29)$$

where γ is the leakage factor $\gamma \geq 0$. In the case where $\gamma = 0$, then the cost function will be for the FXLMF algorithm, and the error signal, $e(n)$, is given by

$$e(n) = d(n) - \sum_{i=0}^{M-1} s_i \boldsymbol{x}^T(n-i)\boldsymbol{w}(n-i) + z(n). \quad (30)$$

The derivative of the cost function with respect to $\boldsymbol{w}(n)$ will be as follows:

$$\begin{aligned}\frac{\partial J_{\text{LFXLMF}}(n)}{\partial \boldsymbol{w}(n)} &= \|\boldsymbol{w}\|^3 - 3\left(\tilde{\boldsymbol{R}}_{s^4}{}^{-1}\tilde{\boldsymbol{P}}_{d,s^3}\right)\|\boldsymbol{w}\|^2 \\ &+ 3\tilde{\boldsymbol{R}}_{s^4}{}^{-1}\left(\tilde{\boldsymbol{P}}_{d^2,s^2} + \frac{\gamma}{2}I\right)\|\boldsymbol{w}\| - \tilde{\boldsymbol{R}}_{s^4}{}^{-1}\tilde{\boldsymbol{P}}_{d^3,s}.\end{aligned} \quad (31)$$

2.6 Mean behavior of the adaptive weight vector for LFXLMF algorithm

Using the same block diagram used for the FXLMF algorithm in Fig. 1, the weight update equation for the LFXLMF algorithm is given by

$$\boldsymbol{w}(n+1) = \boldsymbol{w}(n) - \frac{\mu}{4}\frac{\partial J_{\text{LFXLMF}}(n)}{\partial \boldsymbol{w}(n)} = \left(1 - \mu\frac{\gamma}{2}\right)\boldsymbol{w}(n) + \mu\, e^3(n)\, x'(n), \quad (32)$$

where the instantaneous gradient can be approximated as follows:

$$\frac{\partial \hat{J}_{\text{LFXLMF}}(n)}{\partial \boldsymbol{w}(n)} \approx -4\, e^3(n) \sum_{i=1}^{\hat{M}-1} \hat{s}_i \boldsymbol{x}^T(n-i) + 2\gamma \boldsymbol{w}(n). \quad (33)$$

Since we do not have the exact knowledge of the secondary path, we can substitute Eqs. (2)–(4) and (32) in Eq. (31) to get the adaptive weight vector update expression as follows:

$$\begin{aligned}\boldsymbol{w}(n+1) &= \left(1 - \mu\frac{\gamma}{2}\right)\boldsymbol{w}(n) + \mu\left(\sum_{i=0}^{\hat{M}-1} \hat{s}_i\, z^3(n)\boldsymbol{x}(n-i)\right) \\ &+ \mu \sum_{i=0}^{\hat{M}-1} \hat{s}_i\, d^3(n)\boldsymbol{x}(n-i) - 3\mu\left(\sum_{i=0}^{M-1}\sum_{j=0}^{\hat{M}-1} s_i\hat{s}_j\, d^2(n)\boldsymbol{x}(n-j)\boldsymbol{x}^T(n-i)\boldsymbol{w}(n-i)\right) \\ &+ 3\mu\left(\sum_{i=0}^{M-1}\sum_{j=0}^{M-1}\sum_{k=0}^{\hat{M}-1} s_i s_j \hat{s}_k\, d(n)\boldsymbol{x}(n-k)\boldsymbol{x}^T(n-j)\,\boldsymbol{x}(n-i)\boldsymbol{w}(n-j)\,\boldsymbol{w}^T(n-i)\right) \\ &- 6\mu\left(\sum_{i=0}^{M-1}\sum_{j=0}^{\hat{M}-1} s_i\hat{s}_j\, z(n)d(n)\boldsymbol{x}(n-j)\boldsymbol{x}^T(n-i)\boldsymbol{w}(n-i)\right) \\ &+ 3\mu\left(\sum_{i=0}^{\hat{M}-1} \hat{s}_i\, d^2(n)z(n)\boldsymbol{x}(n-i)\right) \\ &- \mu\left(\sum_{i=0}^{M-1}\sum_{j=0}^{M-1}\sum_{k=0}^{M-1}\sum_{l=0}^{\hat{M}-1} s_i s_j s_k \hat{s}_l\, \boldsymbol{x}(n-l)\boldsymbol{x}^T(n-k)\,\boldsymbol{x}(n-j)\boldsymbol{x}^T(n-i)\, \boldsymbol{w}(n-k)\,\boldsymbol{w}^T(n-j)\boldsymbol{w}(n-i)\right) \\ &+ 3\mu\left(\sum_{i=0}^{M-1}\sum_{j=0}^{M-1}\sum_{k=0}^{\hat{M}-1} s_i s_j \hat{s}_k\, z(n)\boldsymbol{x}(n-k)\boldsymbol{x}^T(n-j)\,\boldsymbol{x}(n-i)\boldsymbol{w}(n-j)\,\boldsymbol{w}^T(n-i)\right) \\ &- 3\mu\left(\sum_{i=0}^{M-1}\sum_{j=0}^{\hat{M}-1} s_i\hat{s}_j\, z^2(n)\boldsymbol{x}(n-j)\boldsymbol{x}^T(n-i)\boldsymbol{w}(n-i)\right) \\ &+ 3\mu\left(\sum_{i=0}^{\hat{M}-1} \hat{s}_i\, d(n)z^2(n)\boldsymbol{x}(n-i)\right).\end{aligned} \quad (34)$$

Following assumptions $A1$–$A4$, the mean weight of the adaptive weight vector for LFXLMF algorithm is expressed as in the following:

$$\begin{aligned} E[\boldsymbol{w}(n+1)] = {} & \left(1-\mu\frac{\gamma}{2}\right)E\left[\boldsymbol{w}(n)\right] \\ & +\mu\sum_{i=0}^{\hat{M}-1}\hat{s}_i\,\boldsymbol{P}_{d^3,i}-3\,\mu\left(\sum_{i=0}^{M-1}\sum_{j=0}^{\hat{M}-1}s_i\hat{s}_j\;\boldsymbol{P}_{d^2,i,j}E[\boldsymbol{w}\,(n-i)]\right) \\ & +3\,\mu\left(\sum_{i=0}^{M-1}\sum_{j=0}^{M-1}\sum_{k=0}^{\hat{M}-1}s_is_j\hat{s}_k\,\boldsymbol{P}_{d,i,j,k}E[\boldsymbol{w}(n-j)\boldsymbol{w}^T(n-i)]\right) \\ & -\mu\left(\sum_{i=0}^{M-1}\sum_{j=0}^{M-1}\sum_{k=0}^{M-1}\sum_{l=0}^{\hat{M}-1}s_is_js_k\hat{s}_l\,\boldsymbol{R}_{i,j,k,l}E[\boldsymbol{w}(n-k)\boldsymbol{w}^T(n-j)\boldsymbol{w}(n-i)]\right) \\ & -3\,\mu\,\sigma_z^{\,2}\left(\sum_{i=0}^{M-1}\sum_{j=0}^{\hat{M}-1}s_i\hat{s}_j\,\boldsymbol{R}_{i,j}E[\boldsymbol{w}\,(n-i)]\right)+3\,\mu\,\sigma_z^{\,2}\left(\sum_{i=0}^{\hat{M}-1}\hat{s}_i\,\boldsymbol{P}_{d,i}\right). \end{aligned} \tag{35}$$

The mean weight of the adaptive weight vector for LFXLMF algorithm considering the independence theory looks like the following:

$$\begin{aligned} \mathrm{E}[\boldsymbol{w}(n+1)] = {} & \left(1-\mu\frac{\gamma}{2}\right)E[\boldsymbol{w}(n)]+\,\mu\,\hat{s}_0\,E\left[d^3(n)\boldsymbol{x}^T(n)\right] \\ & -3\,\mu\left(\sum_{i=0}^{\min(\hat{M},M)-1}s_i\hat{s}_i\,\boldsymbol{P}_{d^2,i,j}E[\boldsymbol{w}\,(n-i)]\right) \\ & +3\,\mu\left(\sum_{i=0}^{\min(\hat{M},M)-1}s_is_i\hat{s}_i\,\boldsymbol{P}_{d,i,j,k}E[\boldsymbol{w}(n-i)\boldsymbol{w}^T(n-i)]\right) \\ & -\,\mu\left(\sum_{i=0}^{\min(\hat{M},M)-1}s_is_is_i\hat{s}_i\boldsymbol{R}_{i,j,k,l}\,E[\boldsymbol{w}(n-i)\boldsymbol{w}^T(n-i)\boldsymbol{w}(n-i)]\right) \\ & -3\,\mu\sigma_z^{\,2}\left(\sum_{i=0}^{\min(\hat{M},M)-1}s_i\hat{s}_i\,\boldsymbol{R}_{i,j}E[\boldsymbol{w}\,(n-i)]\right) \\ & +3\,\mu\,\sigma_z^{\,2}(\hat{s}_0\,E[d(n)\boldsymbol{x}(n)]). \end{aligned} \tag{36}$$

2.7 Second moment analysis for LFXLMF

The performance analysis for the mean square error, $E[e^2(n)]$., of the LFXLMF algorithm is carried out, where the error is updated according to Eq. (7). Therefore, the MSE for the LFXLMF algorithm is obtained as follows:

$$\begin{aligned} \mathrm{MSE}_{\mathrm{LFXLMF}}(n) & = E\left[e^2(n)\right] \\ & = E\left[d^2(n)\right]-2\sum_{i=0}^{M-1}s_i\,E[d(n)\boldsymbol{x}(n-i)]E[\boldsymbol{w}(n-i)] \\ & +\sum_{i=0}^{M-1}\sum_{j=0}^{M-1}s_is_j\,E[\boldsymbol{x}(n-j)\boldsymbol{x}^T(n-i)]E[\boldsymbol{w}\,(n-i)\boldsymbol{w}^T\,(n-i)]+E[z^2(n)]. \\ & = \sigma_d^{\,2}-2\sum_{i=0}^{M-1}s_i\,\boldsymbol{P}_{d,i}\,E[\boldsymbol{w}(n-i)] \\ & +\sum_{i=0}^{M-1}\sum_{j=0}^{M-1}s_is_j\,\boldsymbol{R}_{i,j}\,E[\boldsymbol{w}\,(n-i)\boldsymbol{w}^T\,(n-i)]+\sigma_z^{\,2}. \end{aligned} \tag{37}$$

Following the steps used in deriving Eq. (19), here, we reach the same results for the MMSE of the LFXLMF as given by

$$\mathrm{MMSE}_{\mathrm{LFXLMF}} = \sigma_z^{\,2}. \tag{38}$$

2.8 LFXLMF algorithm stability

In the ensuing, the effect of the leakage factor γ on the stability of the LFXLMF algorithm is discussed. As was done in [21], the value of γ is determined by the filter designer using trial and error methodology. For this work, the range of the leakage factor can be found with respect to the step size μ. To do that, first, we start with the LFXLMF algorithm weight update:

$$\begin{aligned} \boldsymbol{w}(n+1) & = \left(1-\mu\frac{\gamma}{2}\right)\boldsymbol{w}(n)-\frac{\mu}{4}\,\frac{\partial \boldsymbol{J}_{\mathrm{LFXLMF}}(n)}{\partial \boldsymbol{w}(n)} \\ & = \left(1-\mu\frac{\gamma}{2}\right)\,\boldsymbol{w}(n)+\mu\,e^3(n)\,x'(n). \end{aligned} \tag{39}$$

The algorithm converges when $E[\boldsymbol{w}(n+1)] = E[\boldsymbol{w}(n)]$. In other words, the weight adjustment term will be zero, that is,

$$\begin{aligned} \mu\,E[\,e^3(n)\,x'(n)] = 0 \\ E\left[\left(d(n)-\sum_{i=0}^{M-1}s_i\boldsymbol{x}^T(n-i)\boldsymbol{w}+z(n)\right)^3\left(\sum_{i=0}^{M-1}s_i\boldsymbol{x}^T(n-i)\right)\right] = 0. \end{aligned} \tag{40}$$

But, since

$$\begin{aligned} e(n) & = d(n)-\sum_{i=0}^{M-1}s_i\boldsymbol{x}^T(n-i)\boldsymbol{w}+z(n) \\ & = \sum_{i=0}^{M-1}s_i\boldsymbol{x}^T(n-i)\boldsymbol{w_o}-\sum_{i=0}^{M-1}s_i\boldsymbol{x}^T(n-i)\boldsymbol{w}+z(n), \end{aligned} \tag{41}$$

and assuming fixed $\boldsymbol{w}$, then we can define the weight error vector

$$\boldsymbol{v}(n) = \boldsymbol{w}(n)-\boldsymbol{w_o}, \tag{42}$$

Hence, Eq. (41) looks like the following:

$$e(n) = z(n)-\sum_{i=0}^{M-1}s_i\boldsymbol{x}^T(n-i)\boldsymbol{v}(n). \tag{43}$$

Using Eqs. (42) and (43) in Eq. (39), one obtains

$$\begin{aligned} \boldsymbol{v}(n+1) = {} & \left(1-\mu\frac{\gamma}{2}\right)\boldsymbol{v}(n) \\ & +\mu\left(z(n)-\sum_{i=0}^{M-1}s_i\boldsymbol{x}^T(n-i)\boldsymbol{v}(n)\right)^3\left(\sum_{i=0}^{M-1}s_i\boldsymbol{x}^T(n-i)\right). \end{aligned} \tag{44}$$

The value of $\boldsymbol{v}(n)$ approaches zero when the algorithm converges so that we can ignore the high-order terms of $\boldsymbol{v}(n)$, and as a result, the weight error update equation can be written as

$$v(n+1) \cong \left(1-\mu\frac{\gamma}{2}\right)v(n) + \mu\left(z^3(n)-3\sum_{i=0}^{M-1} s_i z^2(n)\boldsymbol{x}^T(n-i)v(n)\right) \times \left(\sum_{i=0}^{M-1} s_i \boldsymbol{x}^T(n-i)\right). \quad (45)$$

To find the mean weight error, we need to take the expectation of Eq. (45), and relying on the assumptions *A1–A4*, the noise is independent of the input signal as well as the weight error vector. Consequently, the mean of the weight error vector is given by

$$E[v(n+1)] = \left(1-\mu\frac{\gamma}{2}\right)E[v(n)] -\mu\left\{3\sigma_z{}^2\sum_{i=0}^{M-1}\sum_{j=0}^{M-1} s_i E[\boldsymbol{x}(n-j)\boldsymbol{x}^T(n-i)]E[v(n)]\right\}$$

$$\mathrm{E}[v(n+1)] = \left(\left(1-\mu\frac{\gamma}{2}\right)I-\mu(3\sigma_z{}^2\boldsymbol{R}_{s^2})\right)E[v(n)]. \quad (46)$$

Assuming a positive definite autocorrelation matrix, $\boldsymbol{R}_{i,j} > 0$, the range of the leakage factor γ for LFXLMF algorithm is given by

$$\frac{3\sigma_z{}^2\lambda_{\max}(\tilde{\boldsymbol{R}}_{s^2})-1}{\frac{3}{2}\sigma_z{}^2\lambda_{\max}(\tilde{\boldsymbol{R}}_{s^2})} < \gamma < \frac{2}{\mu} \quad (47)$$

where $\lambda_{\max}(\tilde{\boldsymbol{R}}_{s^2})$ represents the maximal eigenvalue of $\tilde{\boldsymbol{R}}_{s^2}$. As can be seen from Eq. (48), the leakage factor has an effect on the step size.

3 Algorithms' convex combination

In this section, we examine the behavior of our algorithm through the convex combination approach, namely the convex combination with the FXLMF algorithm. The method of combining two algorithms is an interesting proposal. It aims to mix the output of each filter and highlights the best features of each individual algorithm. Then, it utilizes the features in the overall equivalent filter to improve the performance of the adaptive filter [24–29]. In this section, we will examine our proposed algorithms with members from the LMS and LMF families.

Figure 2 is the proposed block diagram for the convex combination of two filtered input signals, where the output of the overall combined filter can be given as in [25] by the following equation:

$$y(n) = \lambda(n)y'_1(n) + [1-\lambda(n)]y'_2(n) \quad (48)$$

where $y'_1(n)$ and $y'_2(n)$ are the output of the two filters and $\lambda(n)$ is the contribution or mixing parameter, where $0 \le \lambda(n) \le 1$. This parameter shows the percentage of involvement for each algorithm in the overall filter output. Therefore, the combined filter will extract the best features for each filter $\boldsymbol{w}_1(n)$ and $\boldsymbol{w}_2(n)$ individually. Assuming both filters $\boldsymbol{w}_1(n)$ and $\boldsymbol{w}_2(n)$ have the same size M, then the weight vector of the overall filter can be given as

$$\boldsymbol{w}(n) = \lambda(n)\boldsymbol{w}_1(n) + [1-\lambda(n)]\boldsymbol{w}_2(n). \quad (49)$$

Each filter is updated individually, depending on its own error $e_1(n)$ or $e_2(n)$, and the overall weight vector is updated according to the total error $e(n) = [d(n) - y(n) + z(n)]$ which adapts the mixing parameter $\lambda(n)$. Using the gradient descent method, we can minimize the fourth-order $e^4(n)$ and the second-order $e^2(n)$ errors for the overall filter. Based on that, we can use the convex combined filter over two scenarios.

In the first scenario, we will do the minimization for the quadratic error $e^2(n)$, where $\lambda(n)$ is the sigmoidal function given as

$$\lambda(n) = \frac{1}{1+e^{-a(n)}}, \quad (50)$$

and instead of doing the update equation with respect to $\lambda(n)$, we will define the update equation with respect to the changing value $a(n)$ as follows:

$$\begin{aligned} a(n+1) &= a(n)-\frac{\mu_{a^2}}{2}\frac{\partial e^2(n)}{\partial a(n)} \\ &= a(n)-\frac{\mu_{a^2}}{2}\frac{\partial e^2(n)}{\partial\lambda(n)}\frac{\partial\lambda(n)}{\partial a(n)} \\ &= a(n) + \mu_{a^2}e(n)[y'_1(n)-y'_2(n)]\lambda(n)[1-\lambda(n)]. \end{aligned} \quad (51)$$

The second scenario is to conduct the minimization for the fourth-order error of the overall filter; then, the updated equation with respect to $a(n)$ will be as the following:

$$\begin{aligned} a(n+1) &= a(n)-\frac{\mu_{a^4}}{4}\frac{\partial e^4(n)}{\partial a(n)} \\ &= a(n)-\frac{\mu_{a^4}}{4}\frac{\partial e^4(n)}{\partial\lambda(n)}\frac{\partial\lambda(n)}{\partial a(n)} \\ &= a(n) + \mu_{a^4}e^3(n)[y'_1(n)-y'_2(n)]\lambda(n)[1-\lambda(n)], \end{aligned} \quad (52)$$

where μ_{a^2} and μ_{a^4} are the step sizes for the overall filter, for the quadratic and fourth-order errors, respectively. In this work, we study the mean square performance for the convex-combined filter using the filtered input signal. Since the range of $\lambda(n)$ is between zero and one, we need to insure that the combined filter keeps adapting and does not stick with only one algorithm all the time. For this purpose, we have to reduce the interval of the mixing parameter by limiting the value of $a(n)$ inside $[1 - a^+, a^+]$; then, the range of the mixing parameter will be between $1 - \lambda^+ \le \lambda(n) \le \lambda^+$, as the following:

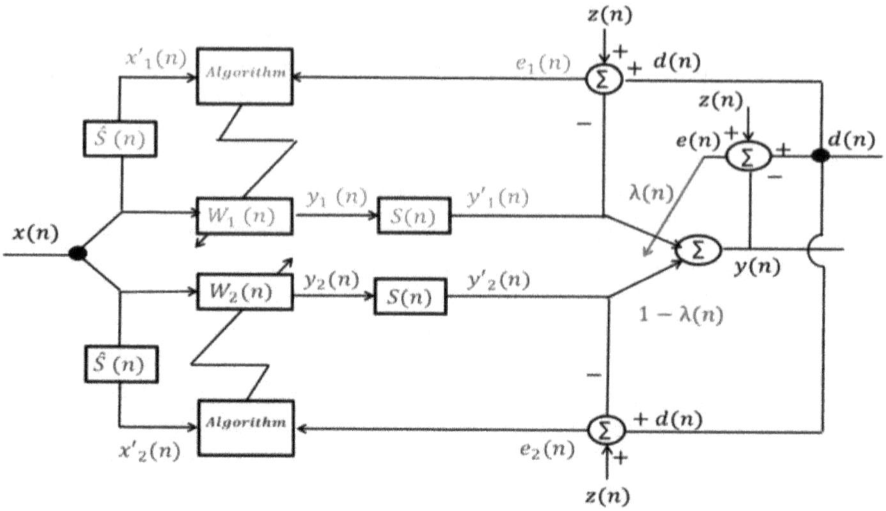

Fig. 2 Block diagram of adaptive convex combination for two filtered input signal algorithms

$$\lambda(n) = \begin{cases} 0.998, & a(n) > a^{+} \\ \lambda(n), & a^{+} \geq a(n) \geq -a^{+} \\ 0.002, & a(n) < -a^{+} \end{cases} \quad (53)$$

Simulations in Section 4 will investigate four cases, where the comparison will be done by using the FXLMF and FXLMS algorithms, as the two transversal filters are used in the convex combination, according to the second error order minimization.

4 Simulation results

Simulations in this section are divided into two parts. The first part examines the proposed algorithms in the mean square error and mean weight context. The simulation has been done for the FXLMF and LFXLMF algorithms under some conditions and environments. While in the second part, we test the concept of convex combinations over the FXLMF and FXLMS algorithms. Furthermore, comparisons with other algorithms are carried

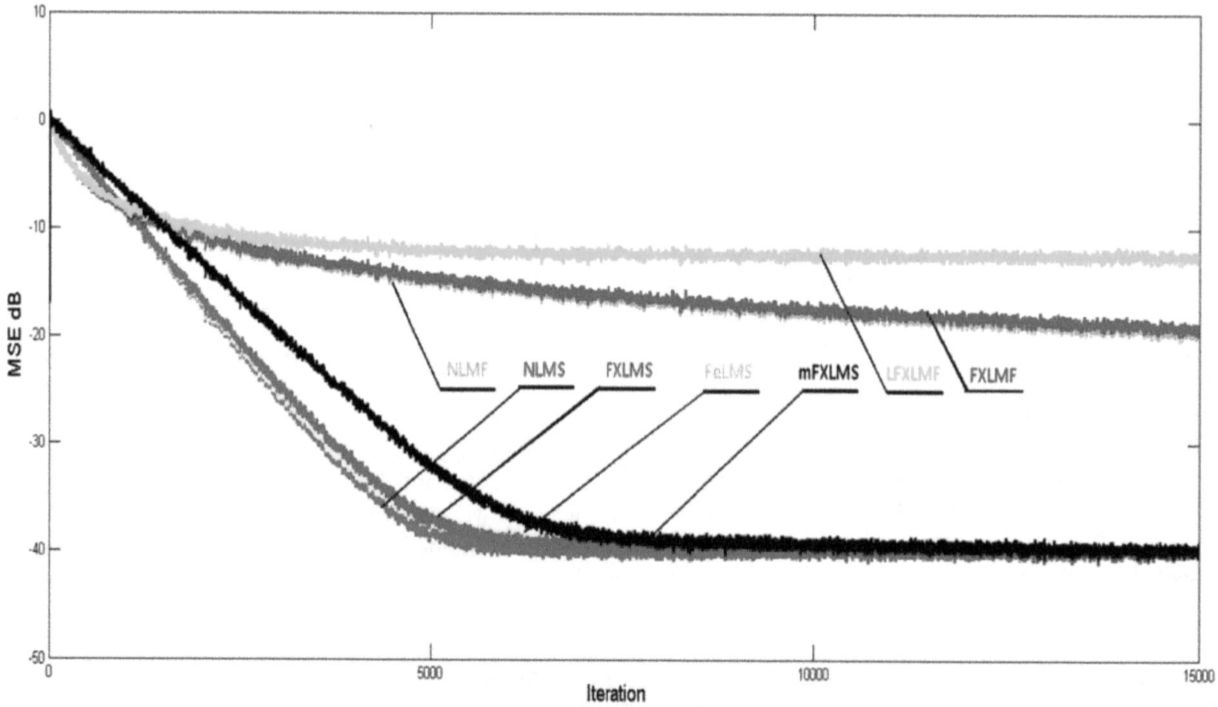

Fig. 3 Comparison over MSE for FXLMF and LFXLMF with other algorithms using fixed step size $\mu = 0.001$ and high SNR = 40 dB and Gaussian noise, leakage factor $\gamma = 0.05$

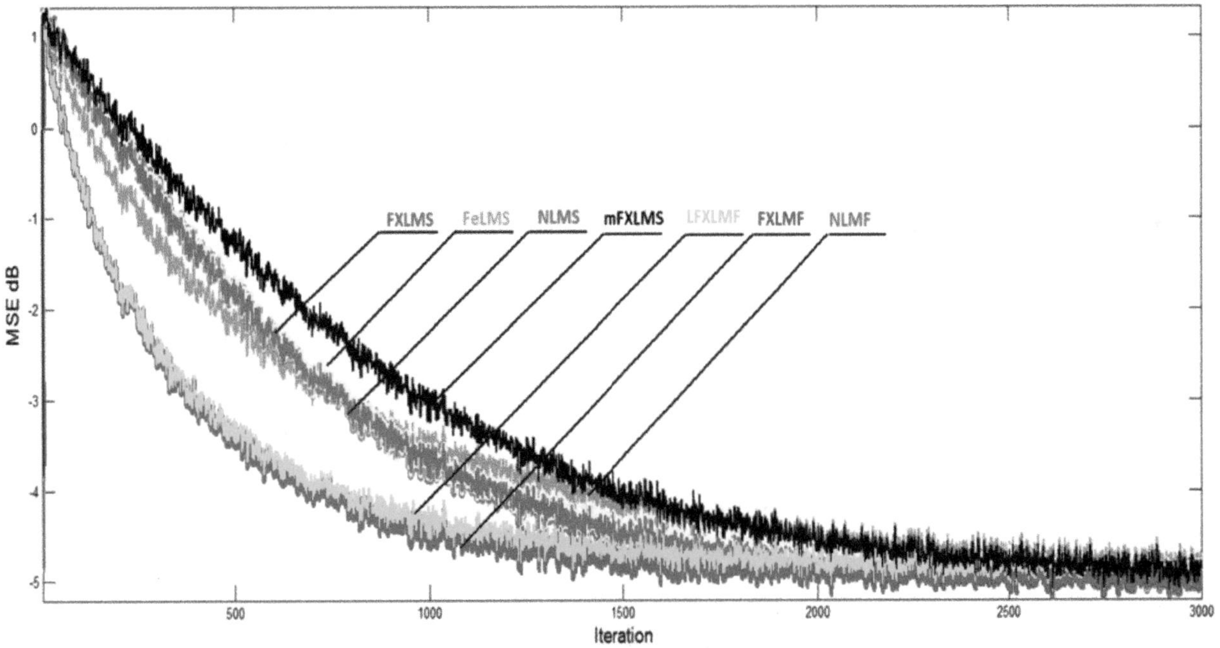

Fig. 4 Comparison over MSE for FXLMF and LFXLMF algorithms with other algorithms using fixed step size $\mu = 0.001$ and low SNR = 5 dB and Gaussian noise, leakage factor $\gamma = 0.05$

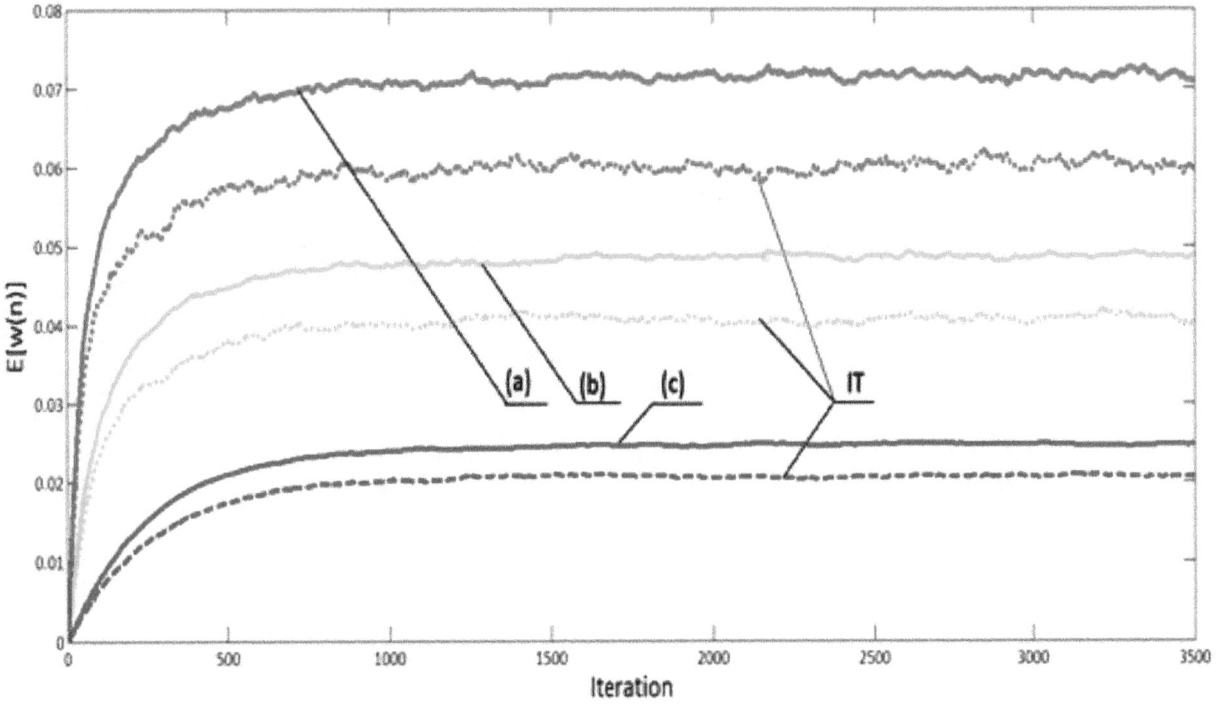

Fig. 5 Comparison over mean weight vector for FXLMF algorithms using different step sizes μ = [*red* = 0.001, *green* = 0.0005, *blue* = 0.0001] using Gaussian noise at low SNR = 5 dB. *Solid line*: proposed models (*a*), (*b*), and (*c*). *Dashed line*: IT model

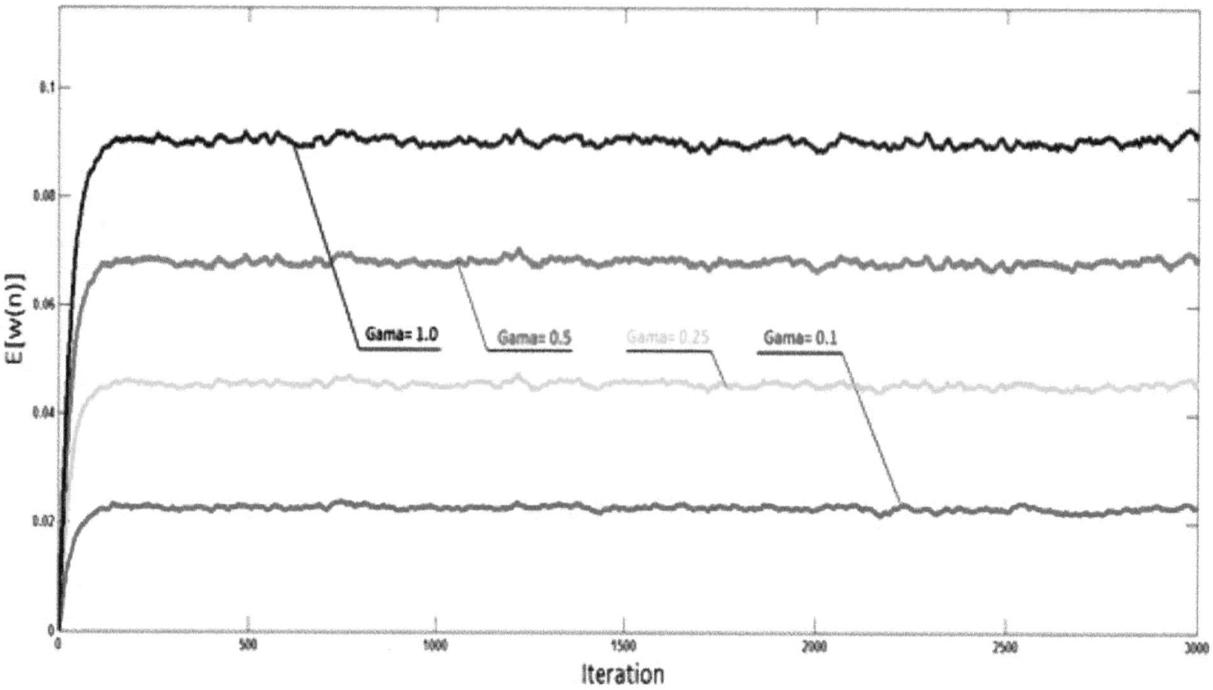

Fig. 6 Comparison over mean weight vector for LFXLMF algorithms using different leakage factors $\gamma = [0.1, 0.250, 0.50, 1]$ and fixed step size $\mu = 0.001$ using Gaussian noise at low SNR = 5 dB

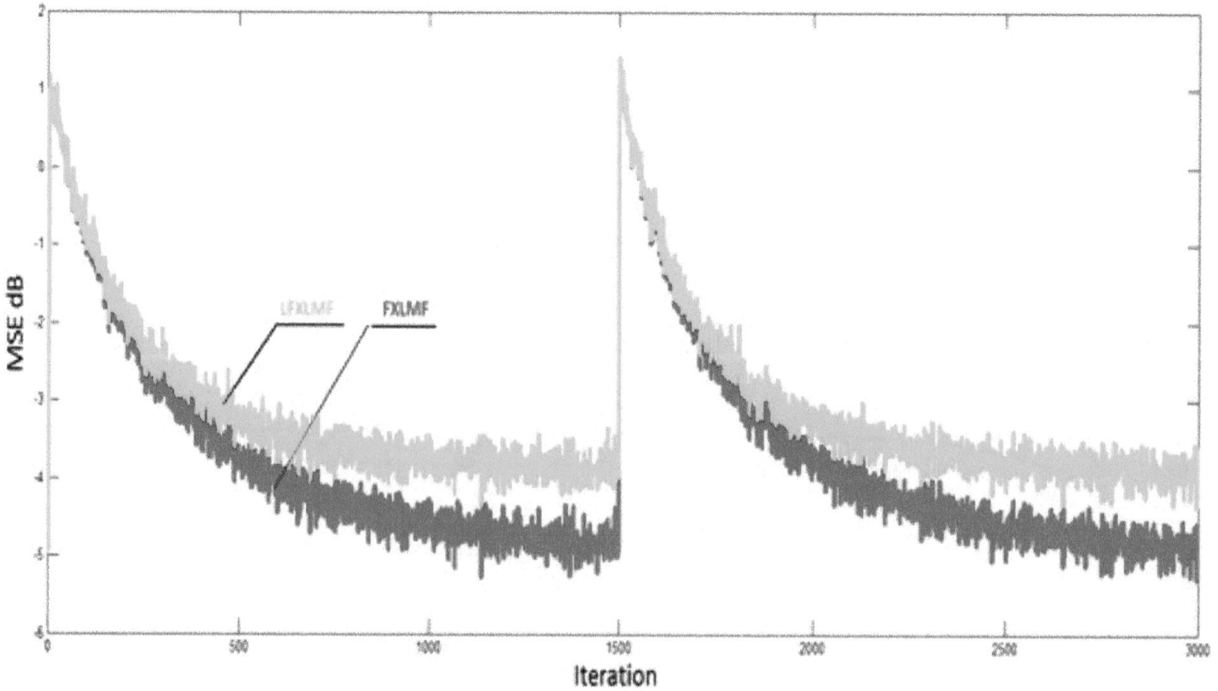

Fig. 7 MSE for the FXLMF and LFXLMF algorithm robustness using Gaussian noise at low SNR = 5 dB, fixed step size $\mu = 0.00125$, and leakage factor $\gamma = 0.50$

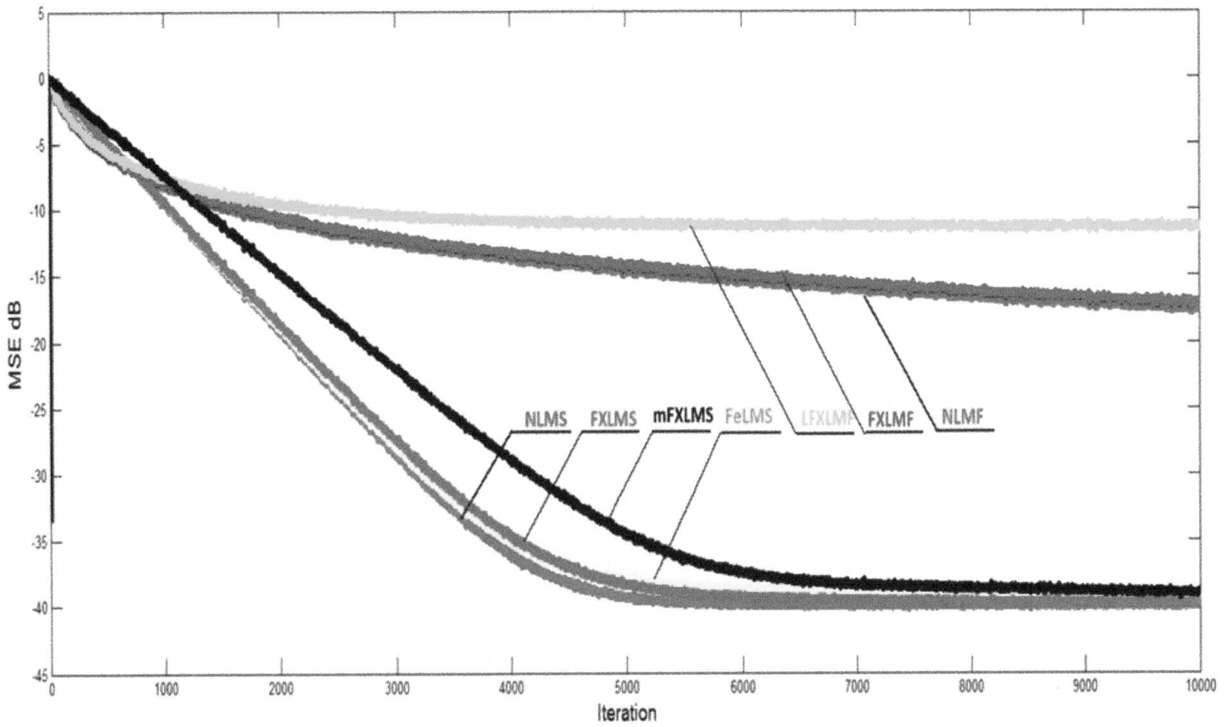

Fig. 8 Comparison over MSE for FXLMF and LFXLMF with other algorithms using a fixed step size $\mu = 0.001$ using uniform noise at high SNR = 40 dB and leakage factor $\gamma = 0.05$

out to show under which circumstances the new proposed algorithms outperform algorithms from the LMS family, in convergence. The plant vector used to filter the input signal is $\boldsymbol{wp}$ with nine taps where

$$wp = [\,0.0179 \quad 0.1005 \quad 0.2795 \quad 0.4896 \quad 0.5860 \quad 0.4896 \quad 0.2795 \quad 0.1005 \quad 0.0179\,].$$

In addition, for simplicity, we assume the secondary path and the estimated secondary path are equal $\boldsymbol{S} = \hat{\boldsymbol{S}} = [0.7756 \quad 0.5171 \quad -0.3620]$.

The result for all simulations are the average of 500 Monte Carlo simulations, the noise is white Gaussian for Figs. 3, 4, 5, 6, and 7 and uniform noise for Figs. 8, 9, 10, 11, and 12.

Next, Figs. 13, 14, 15, 16, 17, 18, and 19 are for the convex combination; we used both of the transversal filters to have the same adaptive algorithm but with different step sizes. Then, we did a comparison between the FXLMF and FXLMS algorithms at low and high SNR for white Gaussian noise. All previous simulations were done using the minimization for quadratic error equation.

Figure 3 shows a comparison of the mean square error MSE behavior for different algorithms from the LMS family (i.e., NLMS, FXLMS, FeLMS, MFXLMS), the NLMF, and our proposed ones. It can be shown that the FXLMF algorithm converges, and it will reach the white noise level after a large number of iterations. For the LFXLMF algorithm, it reaches the steady state level faster than the others and after almost 5000 iterations, but it converges to a higher white noise level at almost 12 dB. Using a larger step size μ may lead the algorithm to diverge.

Figure 4 shows a comparison of the mean square error MSE behavior for different algorithms with fixed step size but this time for low SNR with a value of 5 dB. We can clearly notice that the FXLMF and LFXLMF algorithms outperform other LMS family algorithms in speed of convergence, an advantage to our proposed algorithms with almost 500 iterations. FXLMF and LFXLMF almost have identical curves because we are using a small leakage factor γ.

Figure 5 shows the effect of changing the step size on the mean weight vector of the FXLMF algorithm; when we increase the values of the step size, the algorithm converges faster to the larger mean of the weight. Moreover, using assumption *A4* makes the algorithm converge to a higher mean weight level.

Figure 6 shows the effect of changing the leakage factor on the mean weight of the LFXLMF algorithm. We can see that increasing the value of the leakage factor will increase the mean weight of the LFXLMF algorithm and it does not affect the speed of convergence.

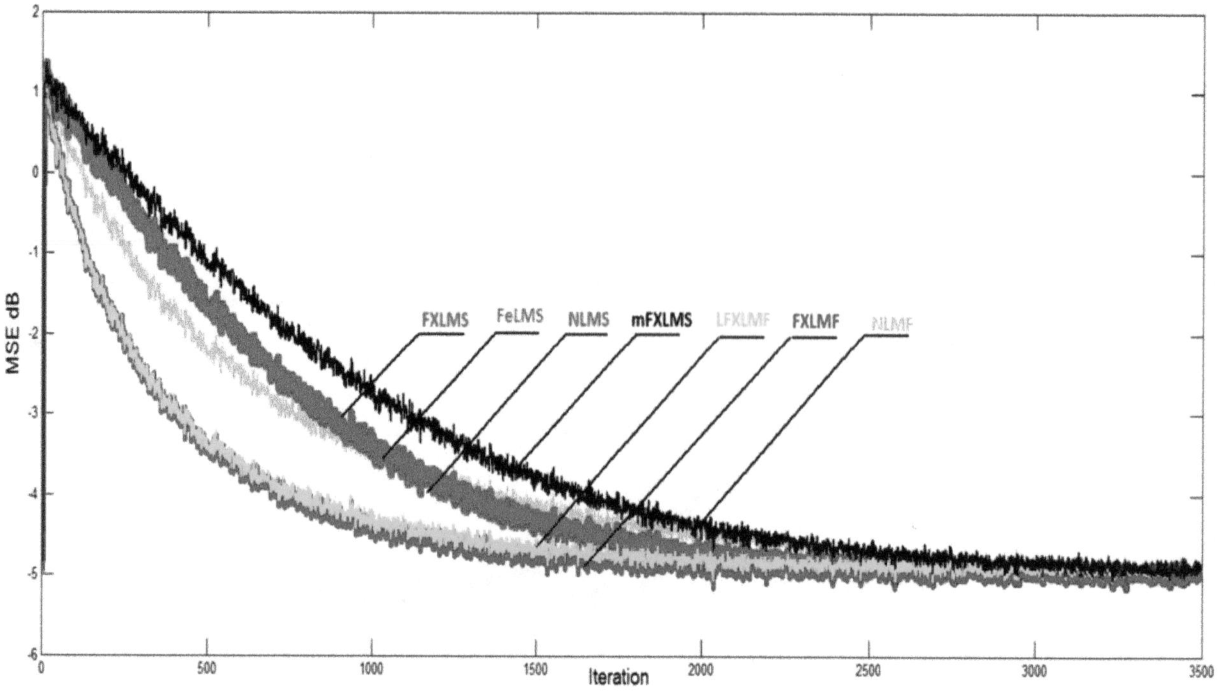

Fig. 9 Comparison over MSE for the FXLMF and LFXLMF algorithms with other algorithms using a fixed step size $\mu = 0.001$ and uniform noise at low SNR = 5 dB and leakage factor $\gamma = 0.05$

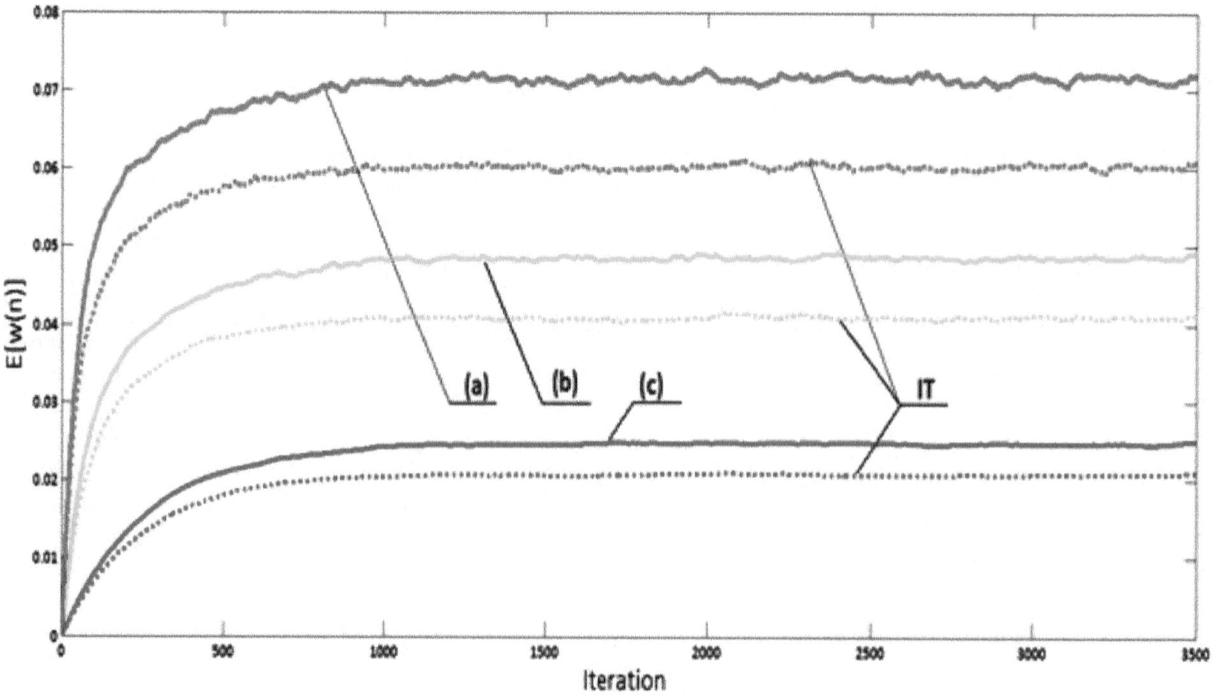

Fig. 10 Comparison over mean weight vector for FXLMF algorithms using different step sizes μ = [*red* = 0.001, *green* = 0.0005, *blue* = 0.0001] using uniform noise at low SNR = 5 dB. *Solid line*: proposed models (*a*), (*b*), and (*c*). *Dashed line*: IT model

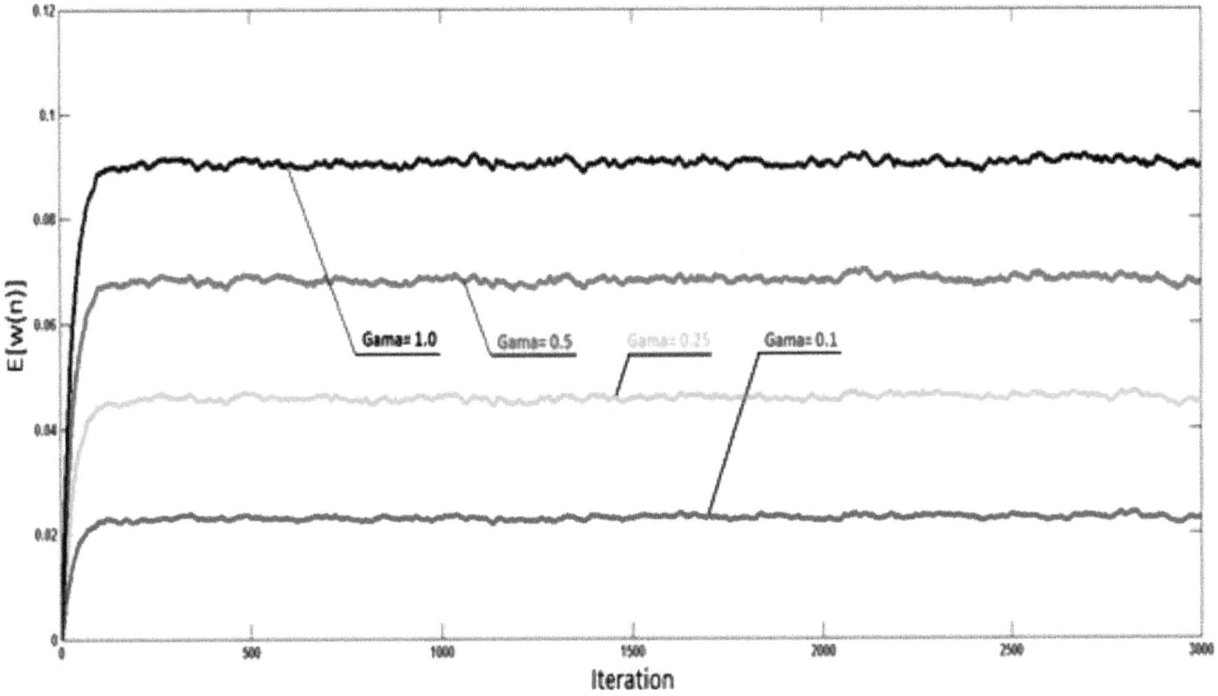

Fig. 11 Comparison over mean weight vector for LFXLMF algorithms using different leakage factors $\gamma = [0.1, 0.250, 0.50, 1]$ and fixed step size $\mu = 0.001$ using uniform noise at low SNR = 5 dB

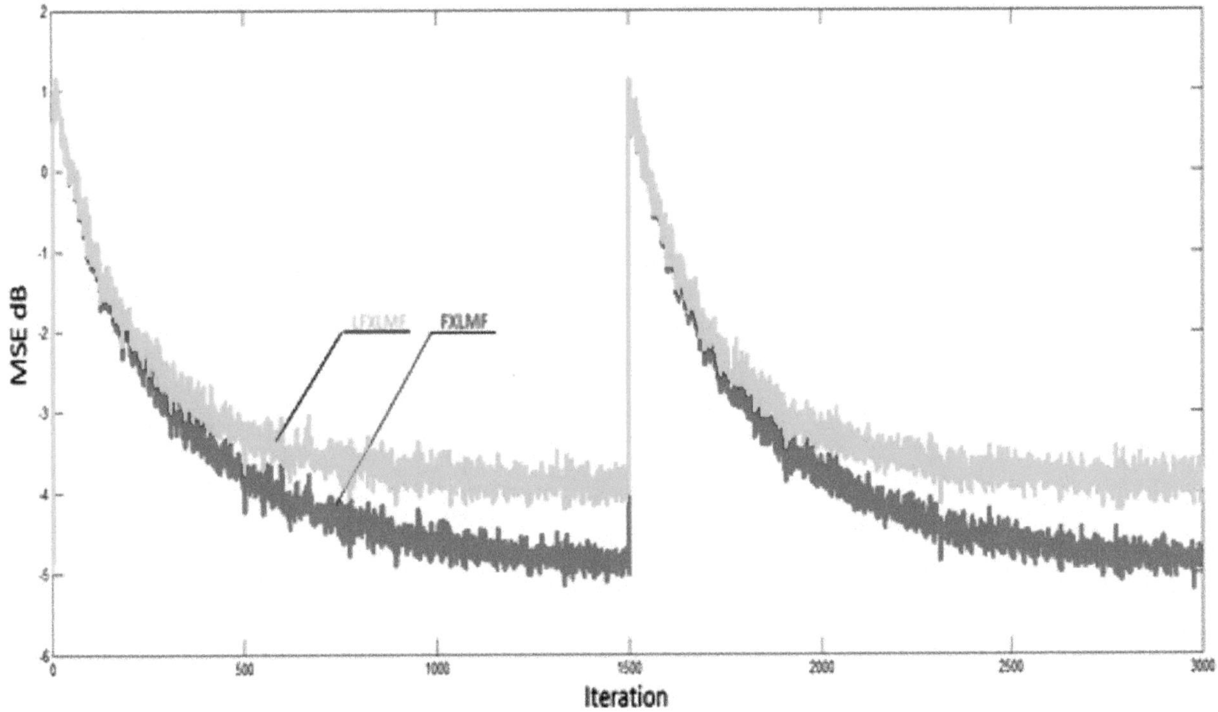

Fig. 12 MSE for the FXLMF and LFXLMF algorithm robustness using uniform noise at low SNR = 5 dB, fixed step size $\mu = 0.00125$, and leakage factor $\gamma = 0.50$

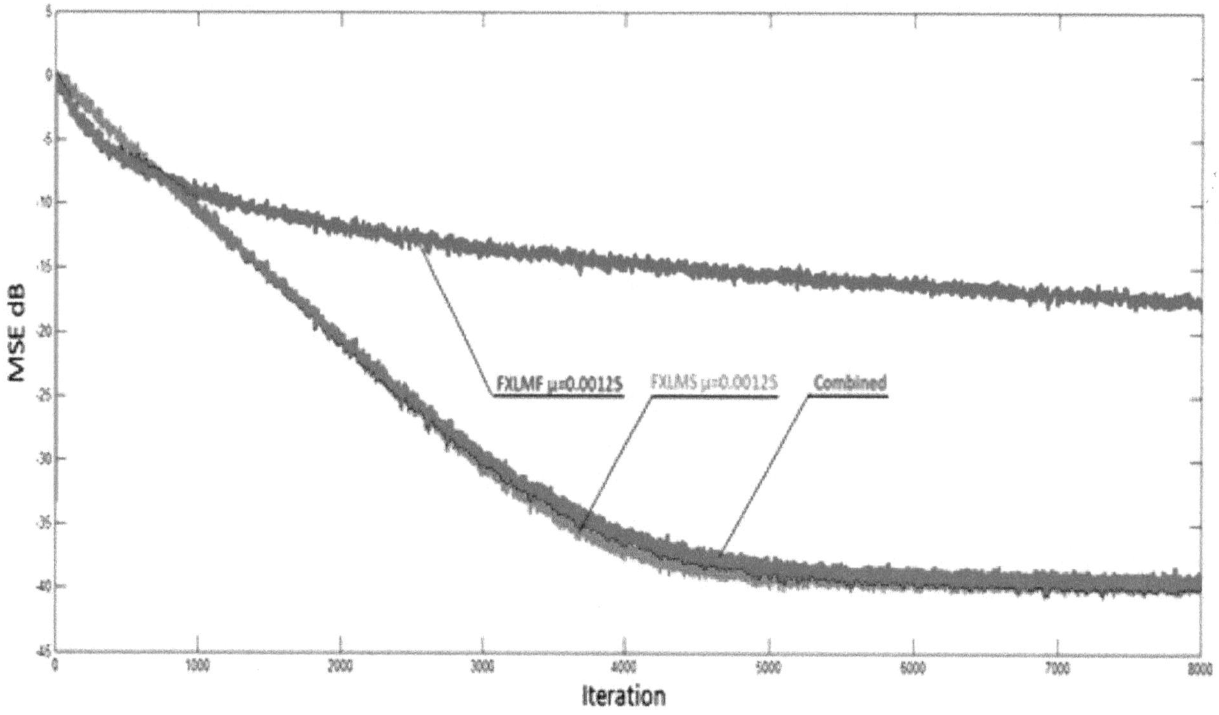

Fig. 13 MSE for combined FXLMF and FXLMS using Gaussian noise at high SNR = 40 dB and fixed step size $\mu = 0.00125$

Figure 7 shows the robustness of the proposed algorithms FXLMF and LFXLMF at low SNR and using Gaussian noise, when a sudden change occurred in the weight vector.

Figure 8 reports the performance of the algorithms when the uniform noise ids used instead of Gaussian, using the same conditions as we used before in Fig. 3. As we can see, we have almost the same result, since both the FXLMF and LFXLMF algorithms converge, where the first one keeps converging while the second one reaches the steady state faster.

Figure 9 is the same as Fig. 4 but using a fixed step size and uniform noise. In addition, the FXLMF and LFXLMF algorithms outperform the LMS family in convergence.

Figure 10 shows the effect of changing the step size on the mean weight vector of the FXLMF algorithm, and as

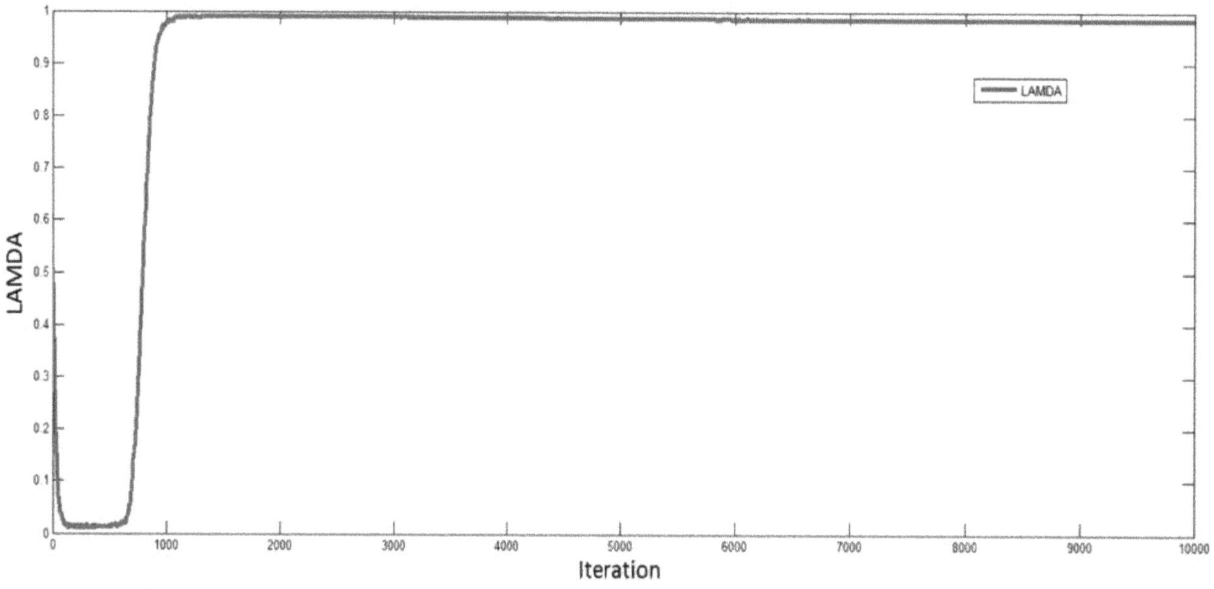

Fig. 14 Values of the mixing parameter $\lambda(n)$ for Fig. 13

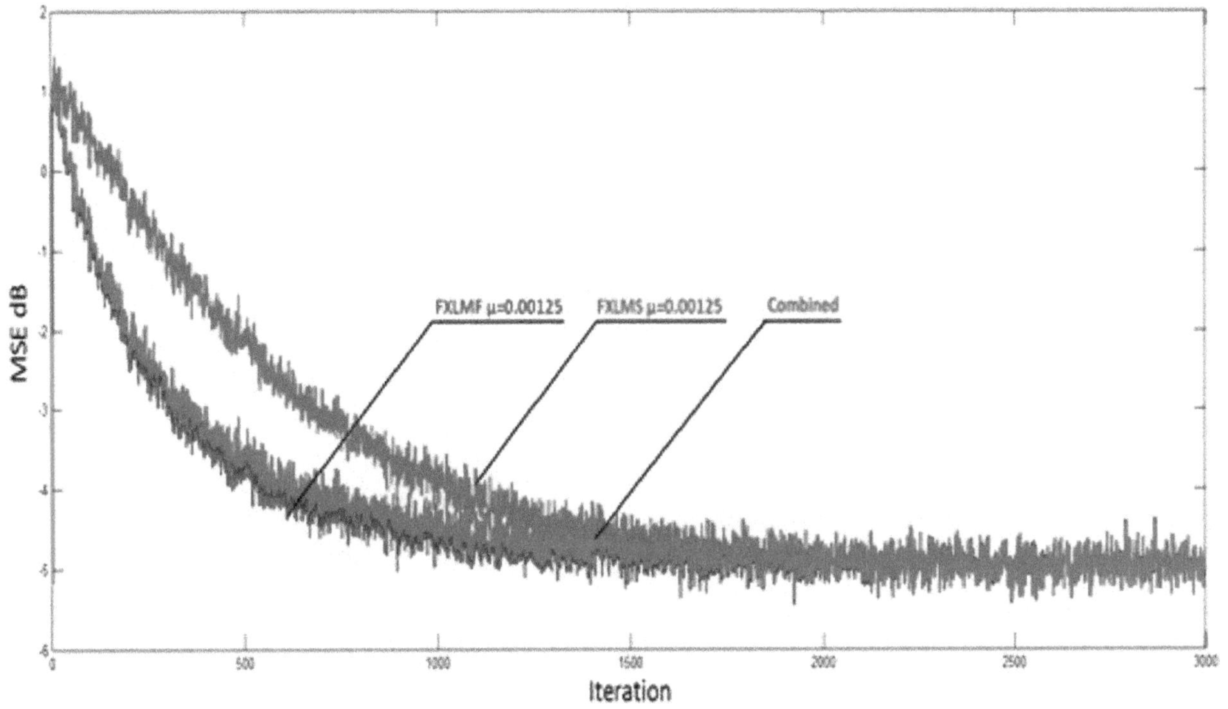

Fig. 15 MSE for combined FXLMF and FXLMS using Gaussian noise at low SNR = 5 dB and fixed step size $\mu = 0.00125$

depicted in Fig. 5, the algorithm converges faster as we increase the step size using uniform noise.

Figure 11 shows the effect of changing the leakage factor on the mean weight of the LFXLMF algorithm as shown in Fig. 6; increasing the value of the leakage factor will increase the mean weight of the LFXLMF algorithm.

Figure 12 shows the robustness of the proposed algorithms FXLMF and LFXLMF at low SNR and using uniform noise.

Figure 13 illustrates the behavior of the convex-combined filter of FXLMS and FXLMF algorithms; we can see at the beginning that the combined filter followed the FXLMF algorithm since it has a faster

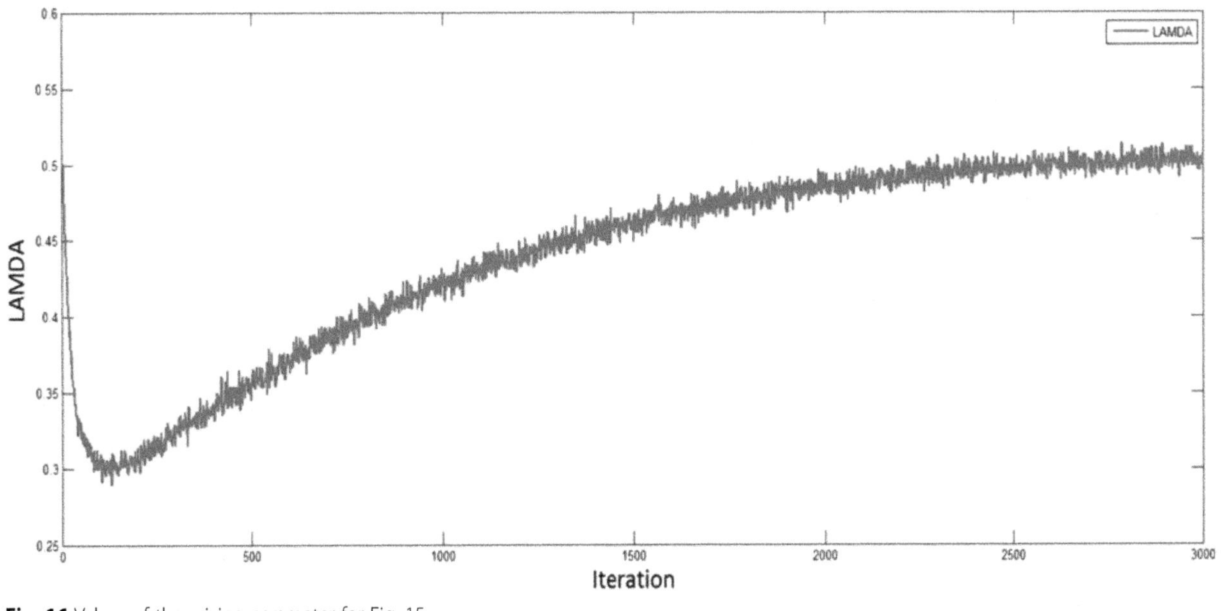

Fig. 16 Values of the mixing parameter for Fig. 15

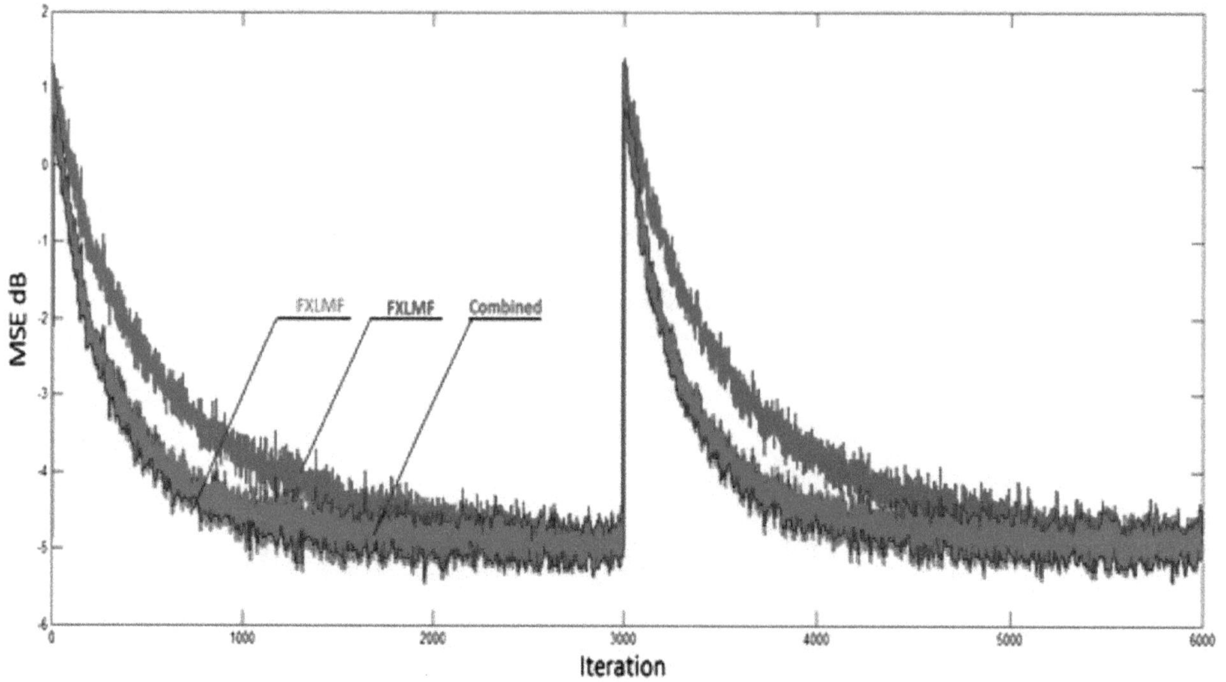

Fig. 17 MSE for combined FXLMF algorithm robustness using Gaussian noise at low SNR = 5 dB and fixed step sizes $\mu = 0.00125$ (*green*) and 0.000625 (*blue*)

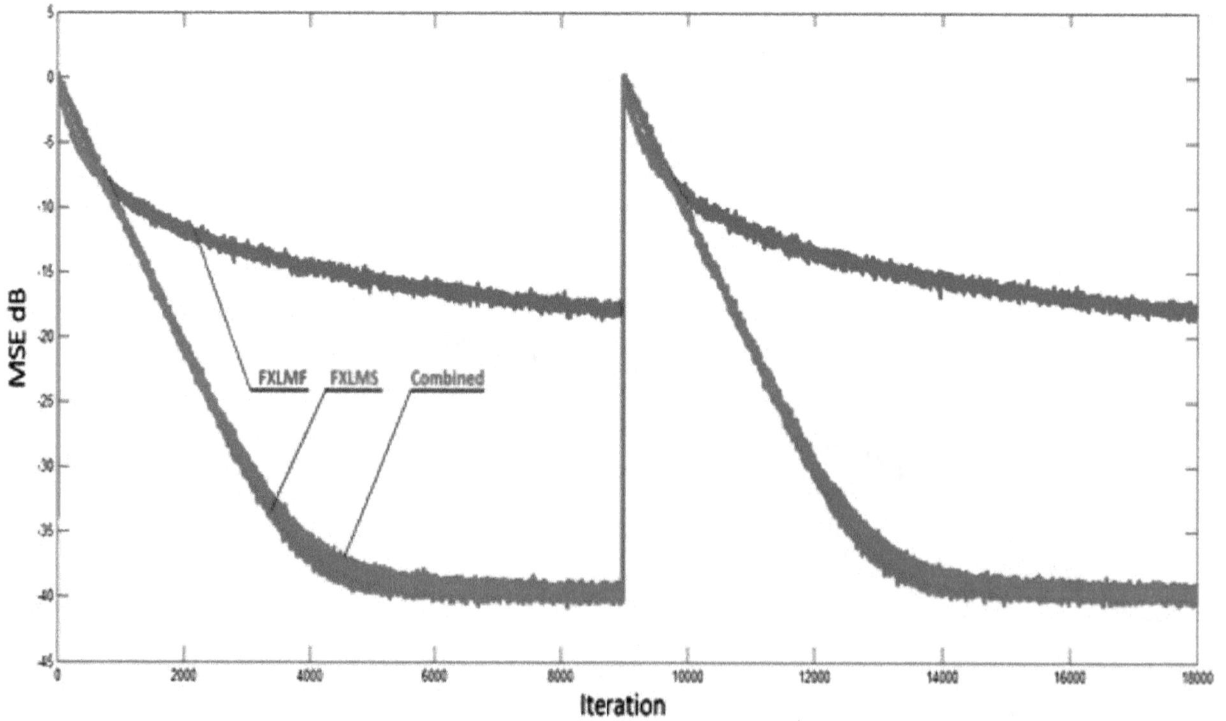

Fig. 18 MSE for the combined FXLMF and FXLMS algorithm robustness test using Gaussian noise at high SNR = 40 dB and fixed step size $\mu = 0.00125$

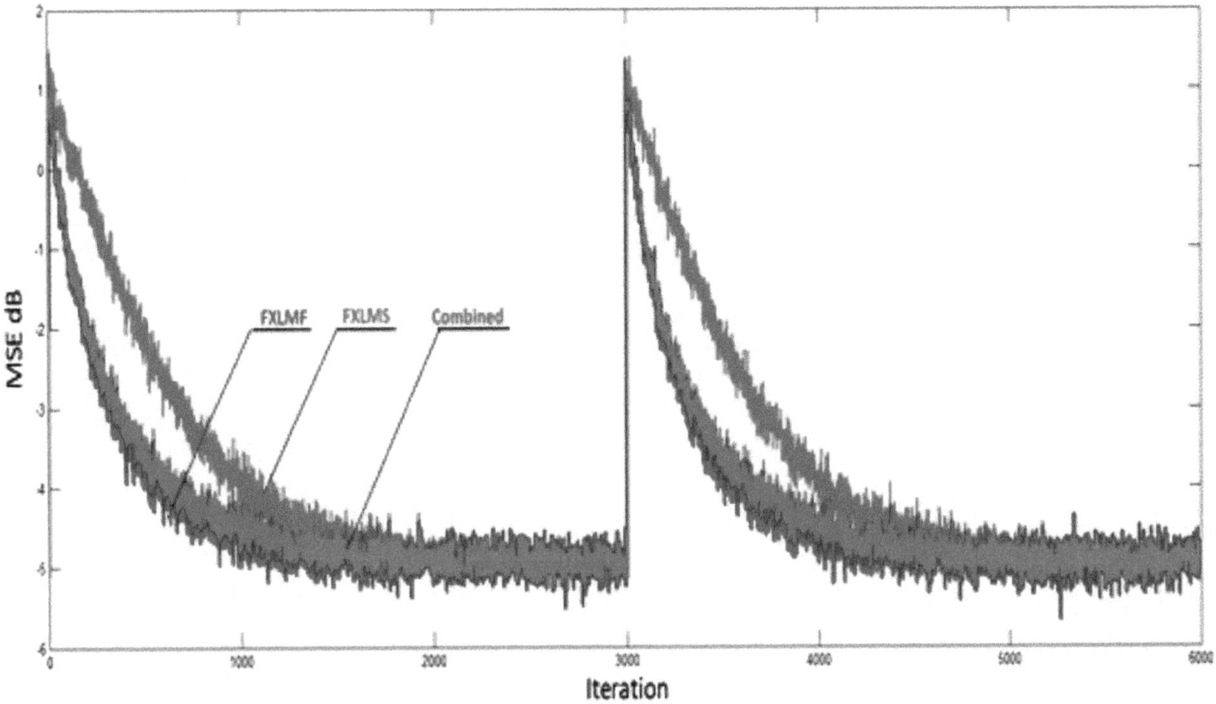

Fig. 19 MSE for combined FXLMF and FXLMS algorithm robustness test using Gaussian noise at low SNR = 5 dB and fixed step size $\mu = 0.00125$

speed of convergence. After that, the combined filter moved to the FXLMS algorithm, which showed better convergence at high SNR. Also, we can see from Fig. 14 the behavior of the mixing parameter $\lambda(n)$. We assume a 50 % mixing percentage as the initial case, then $\lambda(n)$ followed the FXLMF algorithm at the beginning where the FXLMF shows faster convergence, and after that, the mixing parameter switched to the other algorithm FXLMS where it has a better convergence. In Fig. 15, with the same environment as in Fig. 13 but with low SNR, the FXLMF algorithm outperforms the FXLMS algorithm and the combined filter followed the FXLMF algorithm at the beginning; then, when both algorithms have the same convergence, the

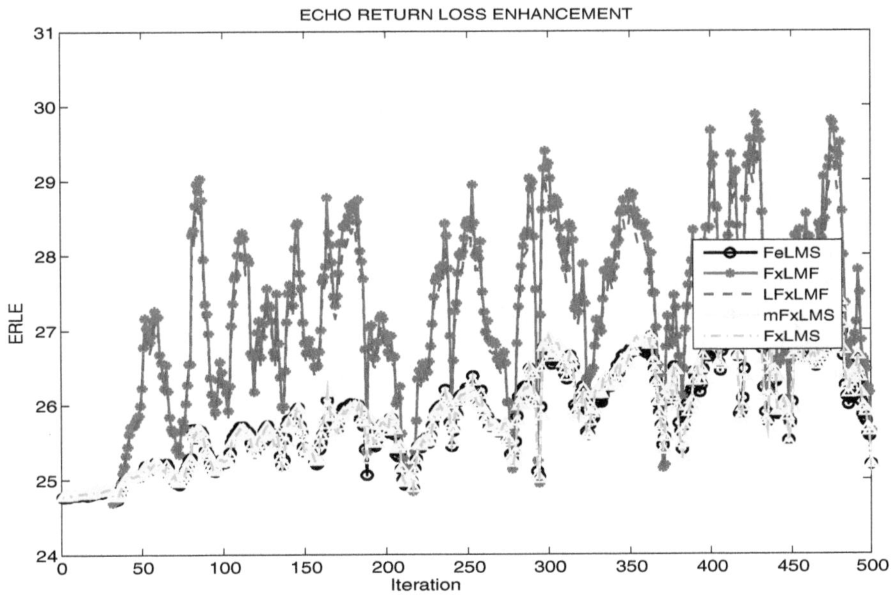

Fig. 20 ERLE performance of the FXLMF and LFXLMF algorithms

mixing parameter is $\lambda(n) = 50$ %. This is shown in Fig. 16.

Figure 17 shows the robustness of the convex-combined filter of FXLMF for two different step sizes at low SNR and using Gaussian noise. We can clearly see that the combined filter followed the one with a larger step size, which already shows better performance. Similarly, Fig. 18 shows the robustness of the convex-combined filter of the FXLMF and FXLMS algorithms at high SNR and using Gaussian noise. We can clearly see that the combined filter followed the FXLMF algorithm at the beginning and then switched to the FXLMS algorithm, which shows better performance at high SNR. Finally, Fig. 19 shows the robustness of the convex-combined filter of the FXLMF and FXLMS algorithms at low SNR and using Gaussian noise. We can clearly see that the combined filter followed the FXLMF algorithm all the time since it shows better performance than the FXLMS algorithm at low SNR.

Finally, the performance of the proposed algorithms is tested using the echo return loss enhancement (ERLE) metric. As can be depicted from Fig. 20, our proposed algorithms outperform the rest of the algorithms.

5 Conclusions

Two algorithms FXLMF and LFXLMF were proposed in this work; an analytical study and mathematical derivations for the mean weight adaptive vector and the mean square error for both algorithms have been obtained. Moreover, the step size and the leakage factor bound ranges were investigated.

From the literature, we received a good sense about proposing new algorithms to the LMF family, as was proposed before in the LMS. The FXLMF and LFXLMF algorithms successfully converge under a large range of SNR. Furthermore, we see the ability of both algorithms to converge under different environments of noise: Gaussian and uniform. However, the LMF family requires more computational complexity; our proposed algorithms were faster in convergence than members of the LMS family under some circumstances.

From the simulations, we saw that both algorithms converge well under relatively high SNR but they converge faster under low SNR. In addition, using a step size near the upper boundary will guarantee less time to converge; however, working close to the upper boundary of the step size ensures faster convergence, but we have to take the risk of algorithm divergence. Also, we see that a larger step size will increase the mean of the weight vector. Step size under the upper boundary is given in Eq. (28).

The leakage factor in the LFXLMF algorithm adds more stability to the algorithm, at the expense of reduced performance as was expected from the literature. The leakage factor boundaries were derived in Eq. (47).

The convex combination is an interesting proposal to get the best feature of two or more adaptive algorithms. We were able to successfully apply it using the FXLMF and FXLMS algorithms with different step sizes. In the other scenario, we applied the combination over the FXLMS and FXLMF algorithms and we noticed that the convex-combined filter, at every iteration, followed the best algorithm.

A robustness test was done for all the scenarios used, to ensure that the proposed algorithms are able to adapt in case of a sudden change in the tap weights of the filter, either in the transient or steady state stage.

Competing interests

The authors declare that they have no competing interests.

Acknowledgements

The authors would like to thank the anonymous reviewers for their feedback that had improved the quality of the paper. The authors acknowledge the support provided by the Deanship of Scientific Research at KFUPM.

References

1. S Haykin, *Adaptive filter theory*, 4th edn. (Prentice-Hall, Englewood Cliffs, NJ, 2002)
2. AH Sayed, *Adaptive filters* (Wiley, NJ, USA, 2008)
3. E Hänsler, G Schmidt, *Acoustic echo and noise control: a practical approach* (Wiley & Sons, New Jersey, 2004)
4. SM Kuo, DR Morgan, *Active noise control systems, algorithms and DSP implementation functions* (Wiley, New York, 1996)
5. B Widrow, D Shur, S Shaffer, On adaptive inverse control, in *Proc. 15th Asilomar Conf*, 1981, pp. 185–189
6. B. Widrow, S.D. Stearns, *Adaptive signal processing*, (Prentice-Hall, Upper-Saddle River, NJ, 1985)
7. WA Gardner, Learning characteristics of stochastic-gradient-descent algorithms: a general study, analysis and critique. Signal Processing **6**, 113–133 (1984)
8. B Widrow, ME Hoff, Adaptive switching circuits, in *Proc. Of WESCON Conv. Rec., part 4*, 1960, pp. 96–140
9. P Dreiseitel, E Hänsler, H Puder, Acoustic echo and noise control—a long lasting challenge, in *Proc EUSIPCO*, 1998, pp. 945–952
10. E Hänsler, GU Schmidt, Hands-free telephones—joint control of echo cancellation and postfiltering. Signal Processing **80**, 2295–2305 (2000)
11. C Breining, P Dreiscitel, E Hänsler, A Mader, B Nitsch, H Puder, T Schertler, G Schmidt, J Tilp, Acoustic echo control. An application of very-high-order adaptive filters. IEEE Signal Proc. Mag. **16**(4), 42–69 (1999)
12. E. Bjarnason, Analysis of the Filtered-X LMS algorithm. IEEE Trans. Speech Audio Process. **3**, 504–514 (1995)
13. OJ Tobias, JCM Bermudez, NJ Bershad, R Seara, Mean weight behavior of the Filtered-X LMS algorithm, in *Proc. IEEE Int. Conf. Acoust., Speech, Signal Process*, 1998, pp. 3545–3548
14. OJ Tobias, Stochastic analysis of the Filtered-X LMS algorithm, in *Ph.D dissertation* (Federal Univ, Santa Catarina, Brazil, 1999)
15. OJ Tobias, JCM Bermudez, NJ Bershad, Mean weight behavior of the Filtered-X LMS algorithm. IEEE Trans. Signal Process. **48**(4), 1061–1075 (2000)
16. JE Mazo, On the independence theory of equalizer convergence. Bell Syst. Tech. J. **58**, 963–993 (1979)
17. GJ Rey, RR Bitmead, CR Johnson, The dynamics of bursting in simple adaptive feedback systems with leakage. IEEE Trans. Circuits Syst. **38**, 475–488 (1991)
18. L Vicente, E Masgrau, Novel FxLMS convergence condition with deterministic reference. IEEE Trans. Signal Process. **54**, 3768–3774 (2006)

19. K Mayyas, T Aboulnasr, Leaky LMS algorithm: MSE analysis for Gaussian data. IEEE Trans. Signal Process. **45**(4), 927–934 (1997)
20. E. Walach, B. Widrow, The Least Mean Fourth (LMF) adaptive algorithm and its family. IEEE Trans. Inf. Theory. **IT-30**(2), (1984), pp. 275–283
21. O.J. Tobias, R. Seara, Leaky-FXLMS algorithm: stochastic analysis for Gaussian data and secondary path modeling Error. IEEE T. Speech Audi. P. **13**(6), 1217–1230 (2005)
22. RD Gitlin, HC Meadors Jr, SB Weinstein, The tap-leakage algorithm: an algorithm for the stable operation of a digitally implemented fractionally spaced equalizer. Bell Syst. Tech. J. **61**(8), 1817–1839 (1982)
23. O Khattak, A Zerguine, Leaky Least Mean Fourth adaptive algorithm. IET Signal Process. **7**(2), 134–145 (2013)
24. LA Azpicueta-Ruiz, M Zeller, AR Figueiras-Vidal, J Arenas-García, Least squares adaptation of affine combinations of multiple adaptive filters, in *Proc. of IEEE Intl. Symp. on Circuits and Systems, Paris, France*, 2010, pp. 2976–2979
25. JC Burgess, Active adaptive sound control in a duct: a computer simulation. J. Acoust. Soc. Am. **70**, 715–726 (1981)
26. SS Kozat, AC Singer, Multi-stage adaptive signal processing algorithms, in *Proc. 2000 IEEE Sensor Array Multichannel SignalWork- shop, Cambridge, MA*, 2000, pp. 380–384
27. AC Singer, M Feder, Universal linear prediction by model order weighting. IEEE Trans. Signal Process. **47**, 2685–2700 (1999)
28. M Niedz`wiecki, Multiple-model approach to finite memory adaptive filtering. IEEE Trans. Signal Process **40**, 470–473 (1992)
29. J. Arenas-Garcia, L.A. Azpicuet-Ruiz, M.T.M. Silva, V.H. Nascimento, A.H. Sayed, Combinations of adaptive filters: performance and convergence properties. IEEE Signal Proc. Mag. **33**, 120-140 (2016)

15

Robust adaptive filtering using recursive weighted least squares with combined scale and variable forgetting factors

Branko Kovačević[1], Zoran Banjac[2*] and Ivana Kostić Kovačević[3]

Abstract

In this paper, a new adaptive robustified filter algorithm of recursive weighted least squares with combined scale and variable forgetting factors for time-varying parameters estimation in non-stationary and impulsive noise environments has been proposed. To reduce the effect of impulsive noise, whether this situation is stationary or not, the proposed adaptive robustified approach extends the concept of approximate maximum likelihood robust estimation, the so-called M robust estimation, to the estimation of both filter parameters and noise variance simultaneously. The application of variable forgetting factor, calculated adaptively with respect to the robustified prediction error criterion, provides the estimation of time-varying filter parameters under a stochastic environment with possible impulsive noise. The feasibility of the proposed approach is analysed in a system identification scenario using finite impulse response (FIR) filter applications.

Keywords: Adaptive filtering, FIR filtering, M robust parameter estimation, Recursive weighted least squares, Variable forgetting factor, Recursive variance estimation, Non-stationary noise, Impulsive noise

1 Introduction

Adaptive filtering represents a common tool in signal processing and control applications [1–6]. An overview of methods for recursive parameter estimation in adaptive filtering is given in the literature [5–7]. There is, unfortunately, no recursive parameter estimation that is uniformly best. Recursive least squares (RLS) algorithm has been applied commonly in adaptive filtering and system identification, since it has good convergence and provides for small estimation error in stationary situations and under assumption that the underlying noise is normal [5–7]. In this context, however, two problems arise.

First, in the case of time varying parameters, forgetting factor (FF) can be used to generate only a finite memory, in order to track parameter changes [7, 8]. For a value of FF smaller than one, one can estimate the trend of non-stationarity very fast but with higher estimate variance, owing to smaller memory length. On the other hand, with a FF close to unity, the algorithm has wider memory length and needs rather a relatively long time to estimate the unknown coefficients. However, these coefficients are estimated accurately in stationary situations. Moreover, RLS with fixed value of FF (FFF) is not effective for tracking time-varying parameters with large variations. This makes it necessary to incorporate an adaptive mechanism in the estimator, resulting in the concept of variable FF (VFF). Several adaptation procedures have been discussed by changing the memory length of signal [7–13]. In particular, the methods referred as the parallel adaptation RLS algorithm (PA-RLS) and extended prediction error RLS-based algorithm (EPE-RLS) have a good adaptability in non-stationary situations [9–13]. In addition, both methods assume that the variance of interfering noise is known in advance.

The second problem arises in an application where the required filter output is contaminated by heavy tailed distributed disturbance, generating outliers [14–20]. Namely, the classical estimation algorithms optimise the sum of squared prediction errors (residuals) and, as a consequence, give the same weights to error signals, yielding a RLS type procedure. However, an adequate information about the statistics of additive noise is not

* Correspondence: zoran.banjac@viser.edu.rs
[2]School of Electrical and Computer Engineering, 283 Vojvode Stepe St., Belgrade, Serbia
Full list of author information is available at the end of the article

included in RLS computation. Possible approaches to robust system identification introduce a non-linear mapping of prediction errors. Although in the statistical literature, there are few approaches to robust parameter estimation, M robust approach (the symbol M means approximate maximum-likelihood) is emphasised, due to its simplicity for practical workers [15–23]. Robustified RLS algorithm, based on M robust principle, the so-called robustified recursive least square method (RRLS), uses the sum of weighted prediction errors as the performance index, where the weights are functions of prediction residuals [24–26]. However, M estimators provide for the solutions of the location parameters estimation problem [21–23]. As a consequence, in a situation of non-stationary noise signal with the time-varying variance, their efficiency should be bad [7, 24]. Therefore, a significant part of RRLS algorithm is the estimation of unknown noise variance or the so-called scale factor [15, 16, 24, 26]. A suitable practical robust solution is the median estimator based on absolute median deviations, named median of absolute median deviations (MAD) estimator [21–23]. However, RRLS algorithm of M robust type using MAD scale factor estimation is also found to be non-effective for tracking of time-varying parameters [7, 11, 24, 26]. For these reasons, neither of the stated algorithms alone can solve the both mentioned problems.

In this article, we design a new robust adaptive finite impulse response (FIR) system for dealing with these problems simultaneously. To alleviate the effects of non-stationary and impulsive noise, this algorithm extends the concept of M robust estimation to adaptive M robust algorithm with the estimation of both filter parameters and unknown noise variance simultaneously. The estimated noise variance, together with the robustified extended prediction error criterion, calculated on the sliding data frame of proper length, is used to define a suitable robust discrimination function, as a normalised measure of signal non-stationarity. In addition, the VFF is introduced by the linear mapping of robust discrimination function. This, in turn, enables the tacking of time-varying filter parameter under the impulsive noise. Simulation results demonstrate the effectiveness of the proposed algorithm, by the comparison with the conventional recursive least squares (RLS) using VFF based on the standard EPE criterion, and the adaptive M robust-based algorithm with only scale factor (RRLS).

2 Problem formulation

A commonly used adaptive FIR filtering scenario, expressed as a system identification problem, is presented in Fig. 1. Here, $x(k)$ is the random input signal, $d(k)$ is the required filter output, $n(k)$ is the noise or disturbance and $e(k)$ is the prediction error or residual. The

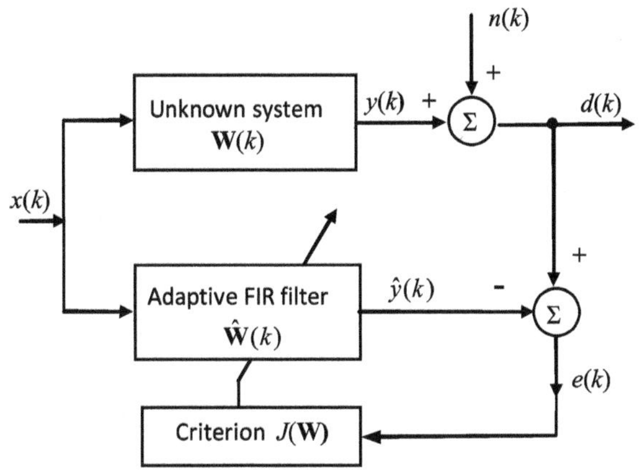

Fig. 1 System identification configuration

filter parameter vector, $\mathbf{W}(k)$, can be estimated recursively by optimising the prespecified criterion. The RLS algorithm with FF approaches the problem of estimation of non-stationary (time-varying) signal model parameters by minimising the sum of exponentially weighted squared residuals [5–7, 25, 26]. On the other hand, robust estimates are insensitive to outliers, but are inherently non-linear. Moreover, most robust regression procedures are minimization problems [15–26]. Specifically, M robust estimates are derived as minimization of the sum of weighted residuals, instead of the quadratic performance criterion in the classical RLS computation [21–23]. To combine these two approaches, let us define a new criterion as the sum of weighted residuals

$$J_k(\mathbf{W}, s) = \frac{1}{k}\sum_{i=1}^{k} \rho^{k-i}\phi\left(\frac{e(i,\mathbf{W})}{s}\right) \tag{1}$$

where the prediction error (residual) signal is given by

$$e(i,\mathbf{W}) = d(i) - \mathbf{X}^T(i)\mathbf{W} \tag{2}$$

with the regression vector, $\mathbf{X}(i)$, and the parameter vector, $\mathbf{W}$, being defined by

$$\mathbf{X}(k) = [x(k),\ x(k-1), \dots, x(k-n+1)]^T;\ \mathbf{W} = [w_1, w_2, \cdots, w_n]^T \tag{3}$$

Here, the quantities s and ρ represent the scale and forgetting factors, respectively. Moreover, $\mathbf{W}$ is the unknown filter parameter vector that has to be estimated. In addition, $\phi(\cdot)$ is a robust score, or loss, function, which has to suppress the influence of impulsive noise, generating outliers. Having in mind the importance of reducing the influence of outliers contaminating the Gaussian noise samples, $\phi(\cdot)$ should be similar to a quadratic function in the middle, but it has to increase more slowly in the tails than the quadratic one. In addition, its first derivative, $\psi(\cdot) = \phi'(\cdot)$, the so-called influence function in the statistical literatures, has to be bounded and continuous [21–23, 25, 26]. The first property provides that single outlier will not have a significant influence, while the second one provides that patchy or grouped outliers will not have a big impact. A possible choice, for example, is the Huber's robust loss function, with the corresponding influence function [21].

$$\psi(x) = \min\left\{\frac{|x|}{\sigma^2}, \frac{\Delta}{\sigma}\right\} \operatorname{sgn}(x) \quad (4)$$

Here, $\operatorname{sgn}(\cdot)$ is the signum function, σ is the noise standard deviation and Δ is a free parameter. This parameter can be adopted in such a way to provide for required efficiency robustness under the zero-mean white normal noise model [21–23]. The non-linear transformation of data based on (4) is known in the statistical literature as winsorization [21–23].

Taking the first partial derivate of (1) with respect to the elements of $\mathbf{W}$ in (3), say $\mathbf{W}_j, j = 1, 2, ..., n$, being equal to zero, we see that the minimization of (1) reduces to finding the solution of n non-linear algebraic relations:

$$\sum_{i=1}^{k} \rho^{k-i} \mathbf{X}_{ij} \psi\left(\frac{e(i,\mathbf{W})}{s}\right) = 0,\ j = 1, 2, ..., n \quad (5)$$

where $\mathbf{X}_{ij}$ is the element in the jth column of the row vector $\mathbf{X}^T(i)$ in (3), while $\psi(\cdot)$ is the first derivative of $\varphi(\cdot)$, $\psi(\cdot) = \varphi'(\cdot)$. Of course, for non-linear $\psi(\cdot)$, (5) must be solved by iterative numerical methods, and two suitable procedures are Newton-Raphson's and Ditter's algorithms, respectively, [27, 28]. Here, a slightly different approach is proposed using a weighted least-squares (WLS) approximation of (5). In this approach, the relation (5) is replaced by the following approximation

$$\sum_{i=1}^{k} \mathbf{X}_{ij} \beta(k,i) e(i,\mathbf{W}) \approx 0,\ j = 1, 2, ..., n \quad (6)$$

where the exponentially weighted robust term is given by

$$\beta(k,i) = \rho^{k-i} \omega(i, \mathbf{W}_0) \quad (7)$$

while its robust part is defined by

$$\omega(i,\mathbf{W}_0) = \begin{cases} \dfrac{\psi\left(\frac{e(i,\mathbf{W}_0)}{s}\right)}{\frac{e(i,\mathbf{W}_0)}{s}} & \text{if } d(i) \neq \mathbf{X}^T(i)\mathbf{W}_0 \text{ and } s \neq 0 \\ 1 & \text{if } d(i) = \mathbf{X}^T(i)\mathbf{W}_0 \text{ and/or } s = 0 \end{cases} \quad (8)$$

Here, $\mathbf{W}_0$ is an initial estimate of the parameter vector, $\mathbf{W}$, which can be obtained, for example, by using the conventional non-recursive LS estimator [5, 25, 26]. The solution of (6), say $\hat{\mathbf{W}}(k)$, represents a one-step non-recursive suboptimal M robust estimate of $\mathbf{W}$ in (3).

Application of the non-recursive M robust scheme (6)–(8) requires the non-linear residual transformation, $\psi(\cdot)$, and scaling factor, s, to be defined in advance. But, in general, the standard deviation, σ, in (4) is not known beforehand and has to be estimated somehow. A commonly used robust estimate of σ in the statistical literature is the median scheme, based on the absolute median deviations [21–23]

$$s = \frac{\text{median}|e_i - \text{median}(e_i)|}{0.6745},\quad i = 1, 2, ..., L \quad (9)$$

where L denotes the length of sliding data frame. The divisor 0.6745 in (8) is used because the MAD scale factor estimate, s, is approximately equal to the noise standard deviation, σ, if the sample size, L, is large and if samples actually arise from a normal distribution [21]. Moreover, because $s \approx \sigma$, Δ is usually taken to be 1.5 [21–23]. This choice will produce much better results, in comparison to the RLS method, when the corresponding noise probability density function (pdf) has heavier tails than the Gaussian one. Furthermore, it will remain good efficiency of RLS when the pdf is exactly normal [21–23].

The weighting term, ω, in (8) is not strictly related to the popular robust MAD estimation of the scale factor, s. This estimate guarantees that $s \neq 0$, but in the general case, a scale factor estimator may not guarantee that the estimate, s, should become equal to zero. This is the reason why the condition $s = 0$ is included in (8). Particularly, the application of a recursive robustified scale factor estimation requires the initial guess, $s(0)$, to be given beforehand. A common choice is $s(0) = 0$, but in the first few steps, the obtained estimate of scale factor can be equal to zero, so that the unit value of ω in (8) has to be chosen.

The proposed suboptimal M robust estimator (6)–(8) is numerically simpler than the ones oriented towards solving the non-linear optimization problem in (5), but it still remains complex computation. Namely, this method does not have an attractive recursive form and, therefore, is not computationally feasible as the RLS type estimators. Moreover, M robust approach is conservative and may degrade without further adaptation [15–20]. Starting from the proposed non-recursive M robust estimator (6)–(8), a simple and practically applicable recursive M robust parameter estimation procedure with both adaptive robustified scale and variable forgetting factors is derived in the next paragraph. Some alternative approaches for the scale factor adaptation can be found in the literature [15, 16, 24]. Moreover, the application of the EPE-based VFF for solving different practical problems is also discussed in the literature [12, 17–20, 29, 30]. However, similarly to sample mean and sample variance, the standard EPE approach is non-robust towards outliers [21–23]. Therefore, in the next chapter, an alternative M robust approach for generating VFF adaptively is proposed.

3 A new recursive robust parameter estimation algorithm with combined scale and forgetting factors

The solution of (6) can be also represented in the computationally more feasible recursive form, using the well-known algebraic manipulations (for more details, see Appendix 1), [25, 26]. This results in the parameter estimation algorithm

$$\hat{\mathbf{W}}(k) = \hat{\mathbf{W}}(k-1) + \mathbf{K}(k)e\left(k, \hat{\mathbf{W}}(k-1)\right) \quad (10)$$

$$e\left(k, \hat{\mathbf{W}}(k-1)\right) = d(k) - \mathbf{X}^T(k)\hat{\mathbf{W}}(k-1) \quad (11)$$

$$\mathbf{K}(k) = \frac{\mathbf{M}(k)\mathbf{X}(k)\omega(k)}{1+\mathbf{X}^T(k)\mathbf{M}(k)\mathbf{X}(k)\omega(k)}; \quad \mathbf{M}(k) = \frac{1}{\rho}\mathbf{P}(k-1) \quad (12)$$

$$\mathbf{P}(k) = \left(\mathbf{I} - \mathbf{K}(k)\mathbf{X}^T(k)\right)\mathbf{M}(k) \quad (13)$$

Here, the term $\omega(k)$ is defined by (8), when the initial estimate, $\mathbf{W}_0$, is replaced by the preceding estimate, $\hat{\mathbf{W}}(k-1)$, while the prediction error (residual) in (11) is given by (2), when the unknown parameter vector, $\mathbf{W}$, is substituted by $\hat{\mathbf{W}}(k-1)$.

Application of recursive M robust estimation algorithm (10)–(13) assumes the non-linear transformation, $\psi(\cdot)$ in (4), as well as the scale factor, s in (8), and the forgetting factor, ρ in (12), to be known. Since the scale factor, s, represents an estimate of the unknown noise standard deviation, σ, and the argument of non-linearity $\psi(\cdot)$ in (8) is the normalised residual, the non-linear transformation $\psi(\cdot)$ in (8) is defined by (4) with the unit variance, i.e. $\sigma = 1$. Particularly, if one choses the linear transformation in (8), $\psi(x) = x$, this results in the unit weight, $\omega(k) = 1$ in (8), and algorithm (10)–(13) reduce to the standard RLS algorithm with FF defined by (10) and (11), where the corresponding matrices, instead of (12) and (13), are given by [5, 25, 26]

$$\mathbf{K}(k) = \mathbf{P}(k-1)\mathbf{X}(k)\left[\rho + \mathbf{X}^T(k)\mathbf{P}(k-1)\mathbf{X}(k)\right]^{-1} \quad (14)$$

$$\mathbf{P}(k) = \frac{1}{\rho}\left(\mathbf{P}(k-1) - \frac{\mathbf{P}(k-1)\mathbf{X}(k)\mathbf{X}^T(k)\mathbf{P}(k-1)}{\rho + \mathbf{X}^T(k)\mathbf{P}(k-1)\mathbf{X}(k)}\right) \quad (15)$$

In addition, if one defines the Huber's non-linearity in (4) by using the non-normalised argument on the right-hand side of (4), yielding

$$\psi(x) = \min(|x|, \Delta\sigma)\text{sign}(x) \quad (16)$$

and approximate the first derivate, $\psi'(\cdot)$, by the weighted term $\omega(x) = \psi(x)/x$ in (8), together with the application of the winsorised residual, $\psi(e)$, instead of original one, e, in the parameter update equation (10), algorithm (10)–(13) can be rewritten as

$$\hat{\mathbf{W}}(k) = \hat{\mathbf{W}}(k-1) + \mathbf{P}(k)\mathbf{X}(k)\psi[e(k)] \quad (17)$$

$$\mathbf{P}(k) = \mathbf{P}(k-1) - \frac{\mathbf{P}(k-1)\mathbf{X}(k)\mathbf{X}^T(k)\mathbf{P}(k-1)\psi'[e(k)]}{1+\psi'[e(k)]\mathbf{X}^T(k)\mathbf{P}(k-1)\mathbf{X}(k-1)} \quad (18)$$

where the prediction error (residual), e,is given by (11).

The obtained algorithm in (3), (11), (16)–(18), represents the standard M robust RLS (RRLS), where the common approach is to estimate the unknown noise standard deviation, σ, by the MAD based scale factor in (9). This algorithm can be exactly derived by applying the Newton-Raphson iterative method for solving the non-linear optimization problem in (1), with the unit parameters s and ρ, respectively. Here, the non-linearity, ψ, in (16) represents the first derivative of the loss function, ϕ, in (1) [24–26]. It should be noted that the parameter update equation in (17) is non-linear, in contrast to the linear parameter update equation in (10). However, both procedures for generating the weighting matrix sequences, $P(k)$, in (12), (13), and (18), respectively, are non-linear. Later, it will be shown that the scheme for generating the weighting matrix is very important for achieving the practical robustness.

The proposed parameter estimation algorithm (10)–(13) are derived from the M robust concept that is conservative, so the quality of parameter estimates may degrade without further adaptations of s and ρ variables.

3.1 Adaptive robustified estimation of scale factor

As an adaptive robust alternative to the non-recursive robust MAD estimate in (9), the scale factor, s, can be estimated simultaneously with the filter parameter vector, $\mathbf{W}$. Namely, if $\bar{p}(n)$ is the pdf of zero-mean Gaussian white noise, $n(k)$, in Fig. 1, with the unit variance, then the pdf of noise with some variance, σ^2, is given by $p(n) = \bar{p}(n/\sigma)/\sigma$. Thus, one can define an auxiliary performance index, in the form of the conditional maximum-likelihood (ML) criterion, [25, 26].

$$J(\sigma/\mathbf{W}) = E\left\{F\left(\frac{e(k,\mathbf{W})}{\sigma}\right)/\mathbf{W}\right\}; \quad F(n) = -\ln(p(n)) \quad (19)$$

where $e(\cdot)$ is the prediction error signal in (11) and $E\{\cdot/\mathbf{W}\}$ represents the conditional mathematical expectation when the parameter vector, $\mathbf{W}$, is given. Furthermore, one can use the Newton's stochastic algorithm for recursive minimization of the performance index in (19) [25, 26].

$$s(k) = s(k-1) - \left[k\frac{\partial^2 J(s(k-1)/\hat{\mathbf{W}}(k-1))}{\partial\sigma^2}\right]^{-1}\left[k\frac{\partial J(s(k-1)/\hat{\mathbf{W}}(k-1))}{\partial\sigma}\right] \quad (20)$$

where $\hat{\mathbf{W}}(k)$ and $s(k)$ are the corresponding estimates, at time instant k, of $\mathbf{W}$ and σ, respectively. In addition, let us introduce the empirical approximation of the criterion (19) as

$$J_k(s/\hat{\mathbf{W}}) = \frac{1}{k}\sum_{i=1}^{k} F\left(\frac{e(i,\hat{\mathbf{W}})}{s}\right) \quad (21)$$

Under certain conditions, with k increasing, J_k in (21) approaches to J in (19). Moreover, since $p(n) = \bar{p}(n/\sigma)/\sigma$, one obtains from (19)

$$F(n) = \ln(\sigma) + f\left(\frac{n}{\sigma}\right);\ f\left(\frac{n}{\sigma}\right) = -\ln\left(\bar{p}\left(\frac{n}{\sigma}\right)\right) \quad (22)$$

In addition, with large k and by using the optimality conditions, yielding

$$\frac{\partial J(s/\hat{\mathbf{W}})}{\partial\sigma} \approx \frac{\partial J_k(s/\hat{\mathbf{W}})}{\partial s};\ \frac{\partial^2 J(s/\hat{\mathbf{W}})}{\partial\sigma^2} \approx \frac{\partial^2 J_k(s/\hat{\mathbf{W}})}{\partial s^2};\ J_{k-1}(s/\hat{\mathbf{W}}) \approx 0 \quad (23)$$

one obtains from (20)–(23) an approximate optimal solution in the recursive form

$$ks(k) = (k-1)s(k-1) + e(k,\hat{\mathbf{W}}(k-1))g(e(k,\hat{\mathbf{W}}(k-1))/s(k-1)) \quad (24)$$

or equivalently

$$ks^2(k) = (k-1)s^2(k-1) + e^2(k,\hat{\mathbf{W}}(k-1))\omega(k) \quad (25)$$

Here, the robust weighting term, $\omega(k)$, is defined by (8), when ψ function is changed by g function, while $\mathbf{W}_0$ is substituted by $\hat{\mathbf{W}}(k-1)$ and s by $s(k-1)$, respectively. As mentioned before, in M robust estimation, we wish to design estimators that are not only quite efficient in the situations when the underlying noise pdf is normal but also remain high efficiency in situations when this pdf possesses longer tails than the normal one, generating the outliers [21–27]. Thus, we can define M robust estimator not exactly as the ML estimator based on the standard normal pdf $\bar{p}(n)$, with zero-mean and unit variance, but ML estimator corresponding to a pdf $\bar{p}(n)$ that is similar to the standard Gaussian pdf in the middle, but has heavier tails than the normal one. This corresponds, for example, to the double exponential, or the Laplace pdf. Such choice corresponds further to the $f(\cdot)$ function in (22) being equal to the Huber's M robust score function, $\varphi(\cdot)$, in (1), with the first derivative, $\psi(\cdot) = \varphi'(\cdot)$, given by (4), [21–23]. Thus, in this case, $g(\cdot) = f'(\cdot)$ reduces to the ψ-function in (4), for which the noise standard deviation, σ, is equal to one. In addition, $\omega(k)$ in (25) is given by (8), with $\mathbf{W}_0$ and s being equal to $\hat{\mathbf{W}}(k-1)$ and $s(k-1)$, respectively. Furthermore, when the pdf, $\bar{p}(n)$, is the standard normal, the influence function $g(\cdot)$ is linear and the weighting term $\omega(k)$ in (25) becomes equal to one [13]. Finally, the application of the recursive algorithm (24) or (25) requires the initial guess $s(0)$ to be given beforehand, as it is done in Eq. (37).

The net effect is to decrease the consequence of large errors, named outliers. The estimator is then called robust. In algorithm (24) or (25), this goal is achieved through the weighting term in (8), where ψ is the saturation type non-linearity in (4). Thus, the function $\psi(\cdot)$ is linear for small and moderate arguments, but increases more slowly than the liner one for large arguments. Furthermore, in the normal case without outliers, one should want most of the arguments of the $\psi(\cdot)$ function to satisfy the inequality $|e(i,\mathbf{W}_0)| \le \Delta s$, because then $\psi(e(i,\mathbf{W}_0)/s) = e(i,\mathbf{W}_0)/s$ and ω in (8) is equal to unity. On the other hand, for large arguments satisfying $|e(i,\mathbf{W}_0)| > \Delta s$, the weighting term in (8) decreases monotonously with the argument absolute value and, as a consequence, reduces the influence of outliers.

For the scale estimation problem in question, the unknown noise variance is assumed to be constant. Therefore, after time increases, the derived recursive estimates (24) or (25) converge towards the constant value. Equations (24) and (25) represent the linear combination of the previous estimate and the robustly weighted current estimation error. The coefficients in the linear combination, $1 - 1/k$ and $1/k$, depend on the time step, k. Thus, as k increases, these coefficients converge towards unity and zero, respectively. As a consequence, after a sufficiently large time step, k, the correcting term in (24) and (25) that is multiplied by the coefficient $1/k$ is close to zero, so that the proposed algorithm eliminates the effect of possible outliers.

Moreover, in many practical problems, it is of interest to consider the situation in which the noise variance is time-varying. However, due to the described saturation effect, the proposed estimator cannot catch the changes. These situations can be covered by simple extension of Eqs. (24) and (25). A simple but efficient solution can be obtained by resetting. The forgetting or discounting factor, $1/k$, in (24) and (25) is then periodically reset to the unit value, for example each 100 steps, and the initial guess, $s(0)$, has to be set to the previous estimate.

3.2 Strategy for choosing adaptive robustifying variable forgetting factor

As mentioned before, the value of forgetting factor FF, ρ, belongs to the set of real numbers (0,1], as it has to give more heavily weights to the current samples, in order to provide for tracking of time-varying filter parameters. If a value of FF, ρ, is close to one, it needs rather long time to find the true coefficients. However, the parameter estimates should be with high quality in stationary situations. The speed of adaptation can be controlled by the asymptotic memory length, defined by [7, 25].

$$N = \frac{1}{1-\rho} \tag{26}$$

Thus, it follows from (26) that progressively smaller values of FF, ρ, provides an estimation procedure with smaller size of data window, what is useful in non-stationary applications.

If a signal is synthetised of sub-signals having different lengths of memory, changing between a minimum value, $N_{\min}$, and a maximum one, $N_{\max}$, the time-varying signal model coefficients can be estimated by using Eqs. (4), (8), (10–13), and (25), assigning to each sub-signal the corresponding FF, ρ, from (26), varying between $\rho_{\min}$ and $\rho_{\max}$. However, in practice, the memory length and the starting points of sub-signals are unknown in advance. Thus, one has to find the degree of signal non-stationarity, in order to generate the value of FF, ρ, in the next step. Although many adaptation procedures have been analysed by changing the memory length, the method using the extended prediction error (EPE) criterion is emphasised, since it involves rather easy computation, and has good adaptability in non-stationary situations, and a low variance in the stationary one [10, 12, 13]. Particularly, the extended prediction error criterion, as a local measure of signal non-stationarity, is defined by [10]:

$$E(k) = \frac{1}{L}\sum_{i=k-L+1}^{k} e^2\left(i, \hat{\mathbf{W}}(i-1)\right) \tag{27}$$

Here, $e(\cdot)$ is the prediction error, or residual, in (11), and the length of the sliding window L is a free parameter, which has to be set.

Thus, the quantity $E(k)$ in (27) represents a measure of the local variance of prediction residuals at the given sliding data frame of size L, and it contains the information about the degree of data non-stationarity. In addition, L should be a small number compared to the minimum asymptotic memory length, so that averaging does not obscure the non-stationarity of signal. Thus, the value of L represents the trade-off between the estimation accuracy and tracking ability of time varying parameters. Unfortunately, the EPE statistics in (27), like the sample mean and sample variance, lacks robustness towards outliers [21–23]. Therefore, we suggest to derive a robust alternative to the EPE criterion in (27) using the M robust approach. Thus, if the prediction errors $e(k)$ in (2) are assumed to be independent and identically distributed (i.i.d) random variables, a simple parameter estimation problem can be constructed. Define a random variable (r.v.), ζ, on the sample space Ω, from which the data $e(k)$, $k=1,2,\cdots,N$, are obtained. Based on empirical measurements, the mean, m_e, and variance, σ_e^2, of the unknown distribution of r.v., ζ, are to be estimated. As in (1), the robust M estimate $\hat{m}_e(N)$ of m_e is defined by

$$\sum_{k=1}^{N} \psi\left(\frac{e(k)-\hat{m}_e(N)}{s}\right) = 0 \tag{28}$$

where $\psi(\cdot)$ is the Huber's influence function in (4). Here, s is an estimate of the scale of the data $\{e(k)\}$. The estimating Eq. (28) is non-linear, and some form of WLS approximation, similar to (6), can be used for its solution. Moreover, a popular statistic s is the MAD estimation in (9). Although s in (9) is robust, it turns out to be less efficient than some other robust estimates of variance [21–23]. However, s is a nuisance parameter in the computation of m_e, and in this context, the efficient issue is not as crucial as in the estimation of the variance of the data, estimates of the latter being used in robustifying the EPE criterion (27) and setting the VFF. A more efficient estimator of the data variance should be based on the asymptotic variance formula for the location M estimate in (28). When $s=\sigma_e$, this formula is given by [21]

$$\mathrm{V} = \lim_{N\to\infty} E\{N[\hat{m}_e(N)-m_e]^2\} = \frac{\sigma_e^2 E\left\{\psi^2\left(\frac{e(k)-m_e}{\sigma_e}\right)\right\}}{E^2\left\{\psi'\left(\frac{e(k)-m_e}{\sigma_e}\right)\right\}} \tag{29}$$

A natural estimate of V in (29) is

$$\hat{\mathrm{V}}_N = s^2\frac{\frac{1}{N}\sum_{k=1}^{N}\psi^2\left(\frac{e(k)-\hat{m}_e(N)}{s}\right)}{\frac{1}{N}\sum_{k=1}^{N}\psi'\left(\frac{e(k)-\hat{m}_e(N)}{s}\right)} \tag{30}$$

where $\hat{\mathrm{V}}_N$ in (30) would appear to be a reasonable estimate of σ_e^2, with $\hat{m}_e(N)$ being the M estimate of m_e in (28). Therefore, given $m_e=0$, producing $\hat{m}_e(N)=0$ and the estimate s from the recursive M robust scale estimate, $s(k)$, in (25), a possible M robust alternative of the EPE criterion in (27) is given by

$$E_r(k) = s^2(k)\frac{\sum_{i=k-L+1}^{k}\psi^2\left(\frac{e\left(i,\hat{\mathbf{W}}(i-1)\right)}{s(i)}\right)}{\sum_{i=k-L+1}^{k}\psi'\left(\frac{e\left(i,\hat{\mathbf{W}}(i-1)\right)}{s(i)}\right)} \quad (31)$$

where $\psi(\cdot)$ is the Huber's influence function in (4), with $\sigma = 1$ and $\Delta = 1.5$. If $\psi(\cdot)$ is a linear function, $\psi(x) = x$, than the criterion (31) reduces to the standard EPE criterion in (27), under the assumption that the scale factor estimate, $s(i)$, $i = k - L + 1, \cdots, k$, on the sliding data frame of length L is close to the $s(k)$ value.

On the other hand, the total noise variance robust estimate in (25) is rather insensitive to the local non-stationary effects. Therefore, in order to make the estimation procedure invariant to the noise level, one can define the normalised robust measure of non-stationarity or the so-called robust discrimination function

$$Q(k) = \frac{E_r(k)}{s^2(k)} \quad (32)$$

A strategy for choosing the VFF at current time instant, k, may now be defined by using the relations (25), (26), (31) and (32), that is

$$\rho(k) = 1 - \frac{1}{N(k)}, \quad N(k) = \frac{N_{\max}}{Q(k)} \quad (33)$$

Thus, the maximum asymptotic length, $N_{\max}$, will determine the adaptation speed. Furthermore, for a stationary signal with possible outliers, the quantity $E_r(k)$ in (31) will converge to the noise variance, yielding $Q(k) \approx 1$ and $N(k) = N_{\max}$. Finally, since (33) does not guarantee that FF, ρ, does not become negative, a reasonable limit has to be placed on FF, ρ, yielding

$$\rho(k) = \max\left\{1 - \frac{1}{N(k)}, \rho_{\min}\right\} \quad (34)$$

where $N(k)$ is given by the relations (25) and (31)–(33).

A brief description of the proposed algorithm with both scale and forgetting factors is given in Table 1. Since the proposed algorithm combines the three adaptive procedures (recursive robust parameter estimation, recursive robustified noise variance estimation and adaptive robustified variable forgetting factor calculation), the theoretical performance analysis is very difficult with the coupled algorithms. Therefore, the figure of merit of the proposed approach will be given by simulations in the next section. The following algorithms are tested:

1. Recursive robust weighted least squares type method, defined by (4), (8) and (10)–(13) together with the both recursive robust scale estimation in (25) and adaptive robustified VFF calculation in (31)–(34), denoted as RRWLSV (see Table 1).
2. Recursive least squares algorithm with exponentially weighted residuals defined by (11), (14) and (15) and VFF given by (27) and (32)–(34), denoted as RLSVF.
3. Recursive robustified least squares algorithm defined by (16)–(18) and MAD-based scale factor estimation in (9), denoted as RRLSS.

4 Experimental analysis

To analyse the performances of previously discussed methods, a linear parameter estimation scenario in stationary and non-stationary contexts, related to the additive noise, is applied (see Fig. 1) [10]. The required

Table 1 Summary of adaptive robust parameter estimation algorithm (10)–(13) with scale factor (25) and EPE-based VFF (27)–(30)

Step 1	Let at stage k, $k \geq N$, the parameter vector estimate $\hat{\mathbf{W}}(k-1)$, the scale estimates $s(k-1), \ldots, s(k-L+1)$, the error signals $e(k-1), \ldots, e(k-L+1)$ and the matrix $\mathbf{P}(k-1)$ from the $(L-1)$ previous stages are known.
Step 2	Take the current input, $x(k)$, and form the regression vector in (3) $\mathbf{X}^T(k) = \{x(k), x(k-1), \ldots, x(k-N+1)\}$ of length N, assuming that the $(N-1)$ most recent inputs are given.
Step 3	Take the current output, $d(k)$, and calculate the current error signal, $e(k)$, from (11) using $\mathbf{X}(k)$ from step 2, and define the current data frame $E_L = \{e(k), e(k-1), \ldots, e(k-L+1)\}$ of length $L < N$, assuming that the $(L-1)$ most recent errors are previously stored.
Step 4	Calculate the normalised error $e(k)/s(k-1)$ and the winsorised error $\psi(e(k)/s(k-1))$ from (4) with $\sigma = 1$; then calculate the weight $\omega(k)$ in (25) by using (8) with $\mathbf{W}_0 = \hat{\mathbf{W}}(k-1)$ and $s = s(k-1)$; finally, calculate the scale factor $s(k)$ from (25).
Step 5	Define the current data frame of normalised residuals $E_{NL} = \{e(k)/s(k), e(k-1)/s(k-1), \ldots, e(k-L+1)/s(k-L+1)\}$ from steps 1, 3 and 4; then calculate the robust discrimination function, $Q(k)$, in (28), using the data set E_{NL}; finally, calculate the VFF, $\rho(k)$, from (29) and (30).
Step 6	Calculate the winsorised error, $\psi(e(k)/s(k))$, from (4), with $\sigma = 1$ and by using $e(k)$ from step 3 and $s(k)$ from step 4; then calculate the weight, $\omega(k)$, in (8) by using (4) with $\mathbf{W}_0 = \hat{\mathbf{W}}(k-1)$ and $s = s(k)$.
Step 7	Calculate the matrix, $\mathbf{M}(k)$, in (12) with $\rho = \rho(k)$ from step 5; then calculate the matrix, $\mathbf{K}(k)$, in (12) by using $\mathbf{X}(k)$ from step 2 and $\omega(k)$ from step 6.
Step 8	Calculate the parameter vector update, $\hat{\mathbf{W}}(k)$, in (10), by using $d(k)$ and $e(k)$ from step 3, as well as $\mathbf{K}(k)$ from step 7.
Step 9	Calculate the weighting matrix, $\mathbf{P}(k)$, in (13) by using $\mathbf{M}(k)$ and $\mathbf{K}(k)$ from step 7, together with $\mathbf{X}(k)$ from step 2.
Step 10	Tune the time counter, that is increase the time index, $k \leftarrow k+1$, and go back to step 2.

filter output, $d(k)$, is generated by passing the standard white Gaussian sequence, $x(k)$, of the zero-mean and unit variance, through the FIR system of the ninth order, with the true values of parameters

$$\mathbf{W} = [0.1, 0.2, 0.3, 0.4, 0.5, 0.4, 0.3, 0.2, 0.1]^T \quad (35)$$

In addition, a zero-mean white additive noise, $n(k)$, with corresponding variance is involved to its output. The value of variance is adopted so to give the desired signal-to-noise ratio (SNR) at the signal segment in question, before the impulsive noise component is introduced. Four situations regarding the additive noise are considered: stationary context with fixed variance and possible outliers and non-stationary context with changing variance and possible outliers. The variances are chosen so to give the different values of SNR equal to 15, 20 and 25 dB, respectively. The outliers, generated by the impulsive noise, are produced using the model $n(k) = \alpha(k)A(k)$, with $\alpha(k)$ being an i.i.d binary sequence defined by the corresponding probabilities $P(\alpha(k) = 0) = 0.99$ and $P(\alpha(k) = 1) = 0.01$, respectively, and $A(k)$ is the zero-mean normal random variable with the variance $\text{var}\{A(k)\} = 10^4/12$ that is independent of the random variable $\alpha(k)$. The random variable $n(k)$ has zero-mean and variance proportional to $\text{var}\{A(k)\}$ (see Appendix 3).

A priory information of the impulsive noise is used to choose the length, $L = 5$, of the sliding window that capture the non-stationarity. This means that no more than one outlier, in average, is in the sliding data frame of size $L = 5$ during the robustified EPE calculation in (31) and MAD calculation in (9), respectively, when the fraction of outliers is 1 %.

The following algorithms, described in previous section, are tested: (1) the proposed adaptive robust filtering algorithm with the both robust adaptive scale and VFF, denoted as RRWLSV; (2) the conventional RLS with EPE based VFF, denoted as RLSVF; and (3) the standard M robust RLS with MAD-based scale factor, denoted as RRLS.

The analysed algorithms have been tested on both the time-varying parameter tracking ability and the log normalised estimation error norm

$$\text{NEE}(k) = 10\log\frac{\|\frown\mathbf{W}(k) - \mathbf{W}\|^2}{\|\mathbf{W}\|^2} \quad (36)$$

where $\|\cdot\|$ is the Euclidian norm, averaged on 30 independent runs. In each experiment, the following values are used to the initial conditions of analysed algorithms:

$$\frown\mathbf{W}(0) = 0,\ P(0) = 100 \times \mathbf{I},\ s(0) = 1 \quad (37)$$

with $\mathbf{I}$ being the identity matrix of corresponding order.

4.1 Time-varying parameter tracking in a stationary zero-mean white normal noise with possible outliers

In this experiment, the first filter parameter w_1 in (3) is changed using the trajectory depicted in Fig. 2. The variance of noise, $n(k)$, is taken so that the SNR of 25 dB is achieved before the impulsive noise component is added. Figure 3 gives a realisation of the zero-mean white Gaussian sequence without (Fig. 3a) and with impulsive component (Fig. 3b), respectively. In Figs. 4, 5 and 6, the true and the estimated trajectories of changing parameter, under the pure zero-mean white Gaussian noise, are shown. Moreover, the estimated scale and variable forgetting factors are also depicted in these figures. Figures 7, 8 and 9 give the simulation results in the case of zero-mean and white and Gaussian noise with outliers. Figures 10 and 11 depicted the normalised estimation error in (36) obtained in the two discussed stationary noise environments, for the three analysed algorithms.

The obtained results have shown that the algorithms RRWLSV and RLSVF provide good and comparable results, due to the application of VFF in the weighted matrix update equation (see Eqs. 10, 12, 14 and 15), while the algorithm RRLSS gives bad parameter tracking performance, since it uses the fixed unit value of FF in

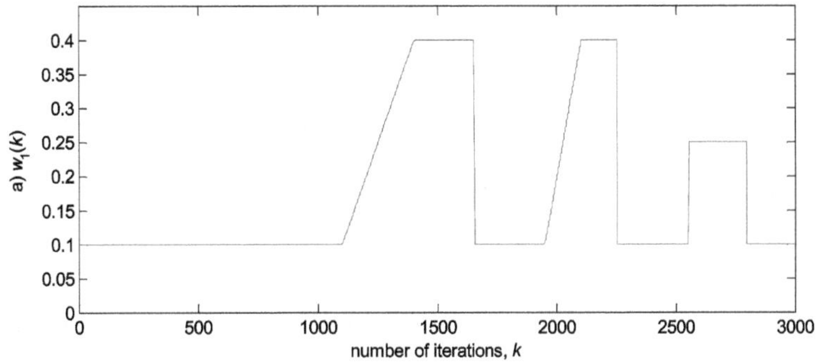

Fig. 2 Time varying parameter trajectory $w_1(k)$ in (3)

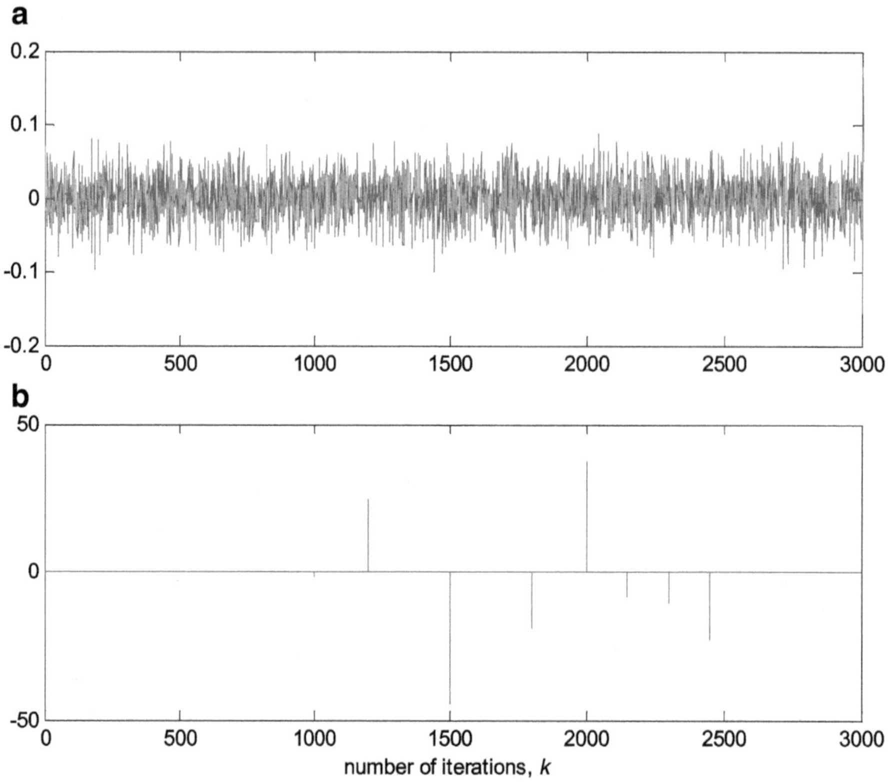

Fig. 3 Realisation of additive zero-mean white noise $n(k)$. **a** Pure zero-mean Gaussian samples (SNR = 25 dB). **b** Gaussian samples contaminated with outliers

(18), (see Figs. 4, 5, 6 and 10). Moreover, the results of simulations have indicated that the conventional RLS with VFF (RLSVF) is highly sensitive to outliers, since it does not use a robust influence function, ψ, in the parameter and weighted matrix update equations (see Eqs. 14 and 15). On the other hand, the RRLSS algorithm using scale factor estimation in (9), or combined the adaptive robustified scale and VFF factors (RRWLSV), are rather insensitive to outliers, due to the effect of robust influence function, ψ, in the parameter and weighted matrix update equations (Eqs. 17 and 18 or Eqs. 12 and 13). In addition, the algorithm RRWLSV has much better parameter tracking ability in the case of both time-varying parameters and impulsive noise environment than the algorithm RRLSS (see Figs. 7, 8, 9 and 11), due to the combined effects of scale factor and VFF (see Eqs. 12 and 13).

4.2 Time-invariant parameter tracking in a non-stationary zero-mean normal noise with possible outliers

In this experiment, the filter parameters are taken to be time invariant, but the noise variance is changed during the simulation, producing a non-stationary signal. The variance of additive noise, $n(k)$, is taken so that for the three sequential signal segments, the SNRs of 25, 15 and 20 dB, respectively, are produced, before the impulsive noise component is added. In order to obtain better capture of long-term non-stationarity, in the sense of achieving good estimates of noise level changes, the scale factor, s, is averaged on the data frame of 400 samples. On the other hand, this will not affect the ability of VFF algorithm to track the filter parameter changes. Figure 12 shows a realisation of noise, without (Fig. 12a) and with (Fig. 12b) impulsive noise component.

Figures 13 and 14 depict the obtained values of normalised estimation error (NEE) criterion in (36), without (Fig. 13) and with (Fig. 14) the presence of impulsive noise component.

In a pure zero-mean normal white noise environment (see, Fig. 12a), at the beginning of parameter estimation trajectory, all three discussed methods have similar behaviour (Fig. 13). Moreover, all three algorithms are rather insensitive to the changes of noise variance, due to the effects of scale factor estimations in (9) or (25), or VFF in (27)–(34) or (31)–(34), respectively, and give similar results at the whole parameter estimation trajectory, since there are no outliers (Fig. 13). The presented results in Fig. 14 indicated that the conventional RLS method with VFF (RLSVF) is highly sensitive to outliers, due to the lack of non-

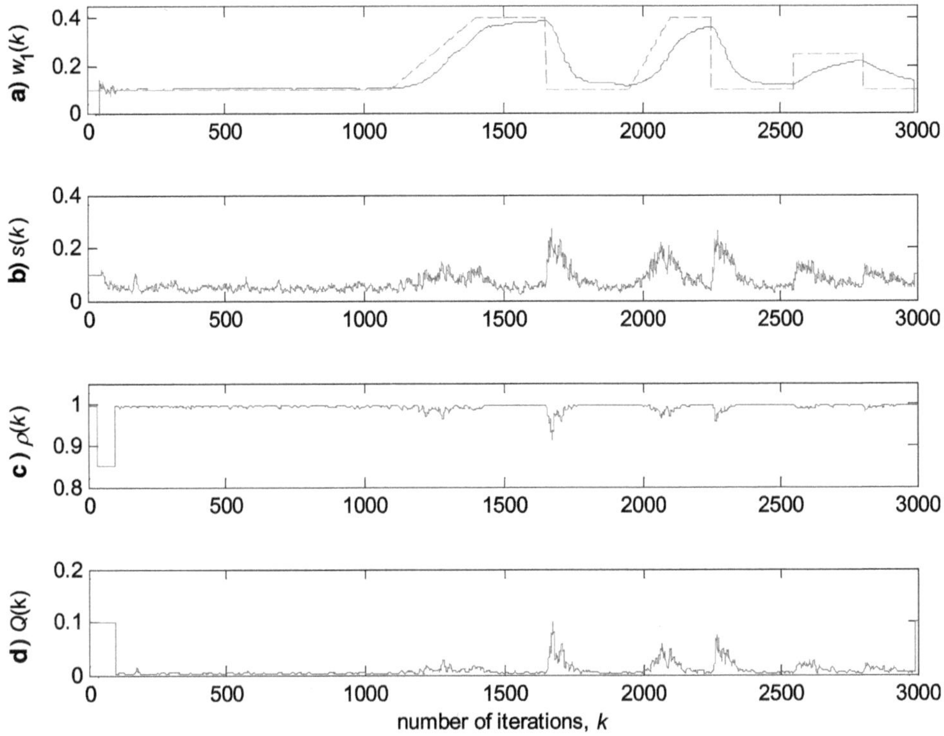

Fig. 4 Experimental results for RRWLSV algorithm in zero-mean white Gaussian noise (see Fig. 3a). **a** Estimated (*solid line*) and true parameter (*dashed line*) trajectories (see Fig. 2). **b** Scale factor estimation, $s(k)$. **c** VFF calculation, $\rho(k)$. **d** Discrimination function calculation, $Q(k)$

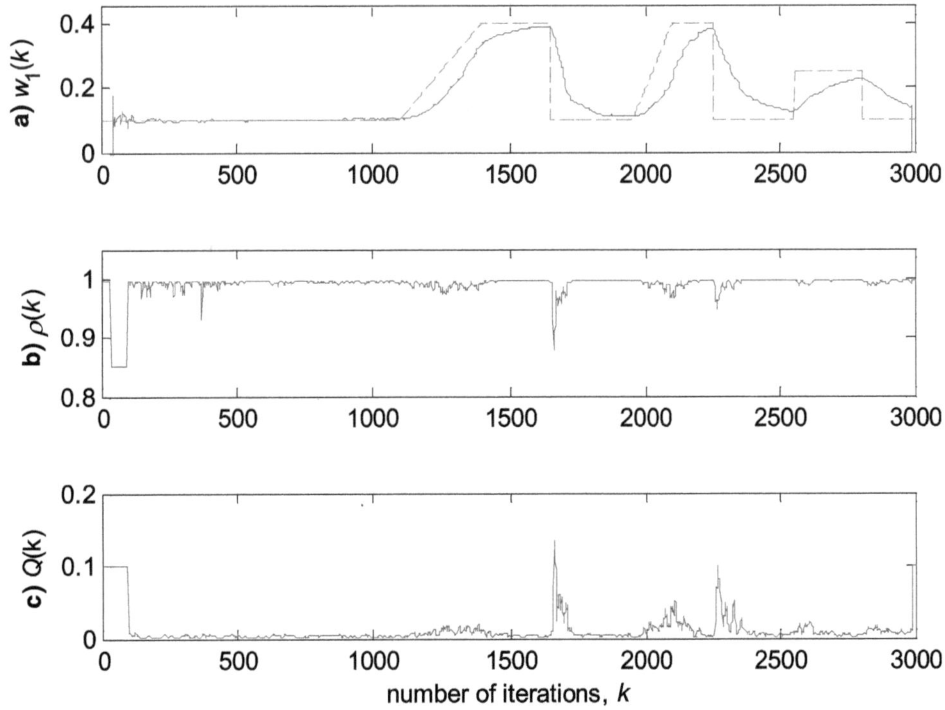

Fig. 5 Experimental results for RLSVF algorithm in zero-mean Gaussian noise (Fig. 3a). **a** Estimated (*solid line*) and true parameter (*dashed line*) trajectories (see Fig. 2). **b** VFF calculation, $\rho(k)$. **c** Discrimination function calculation, $Q(k)$

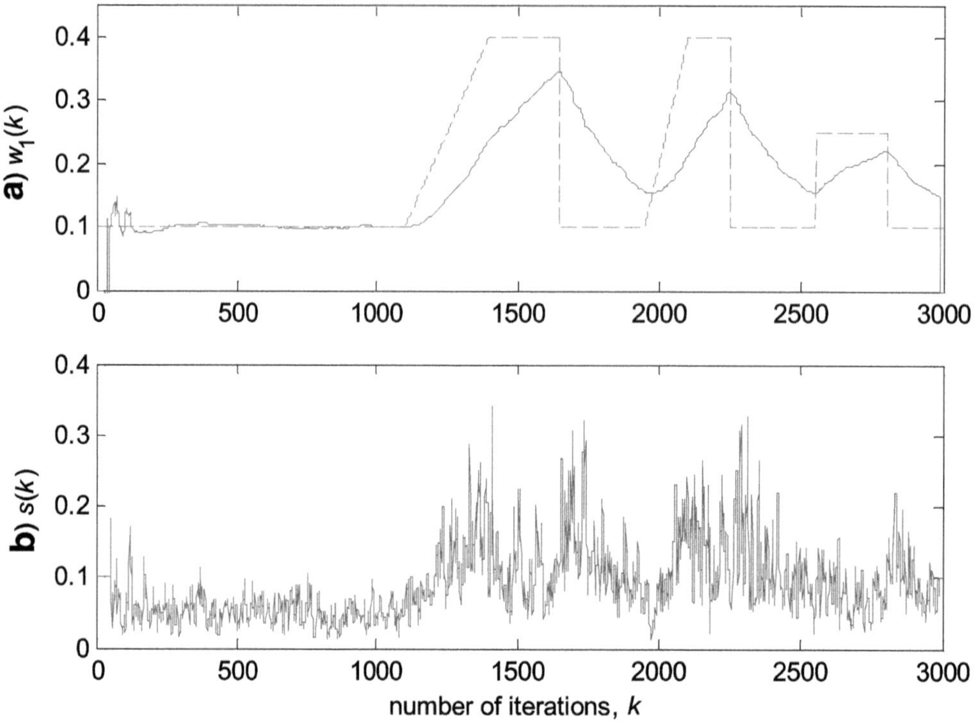

Fig. 6 Experimental results for RRLSS algorithm in zero-mean Gaussian noise (Fig. 3a). **a** Estimated (*solid line*) and true parameter (*dashed line*) trajectories (Fig. 2). **b** Scale factor estimation, $s(k)$

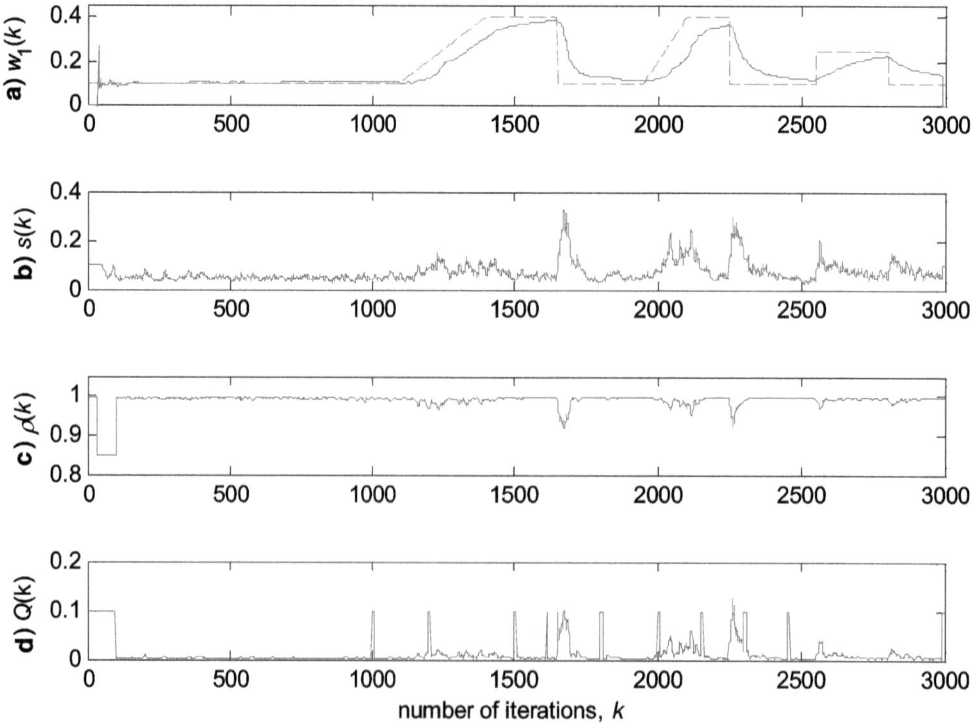

Fig. 7 Experimental results for RRWLSV algorithm in zero-mean Gaussian noise contaminated by outliers (Fig. 3b). **a** Estimated (*solid line*) and true parameter (*dashed line*) trajectories (Fig. 2). **b** Scale factor estimation, $s(k)$. **c** VFF calculation, $\rho(k)$. **d** Discrimination function calculation, $Q(k)$

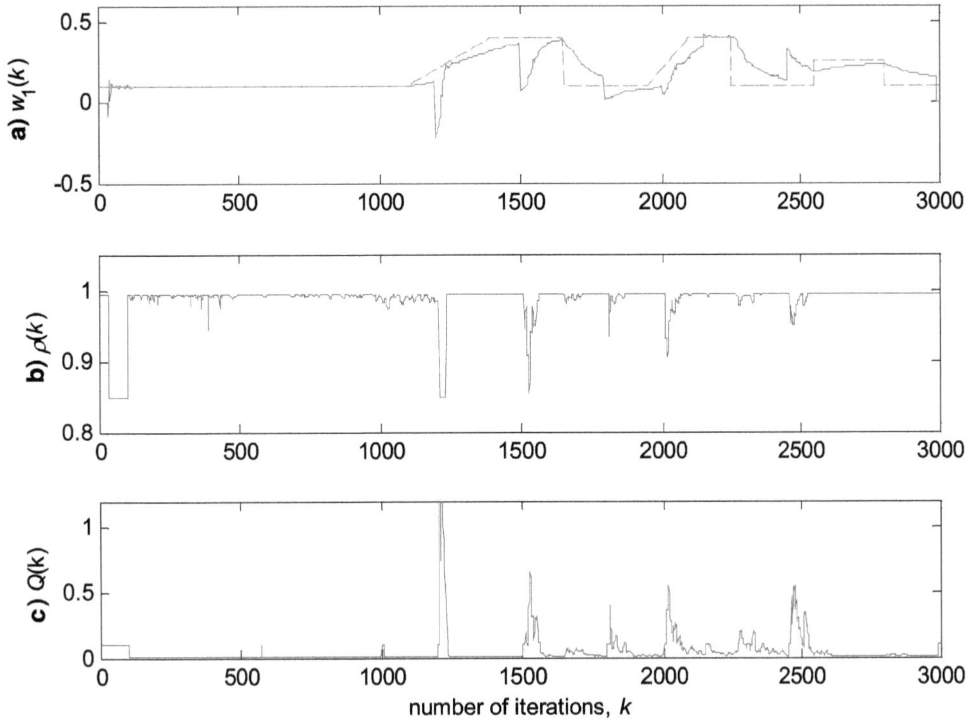

Fig. 8 Experimental results for RLSVF algorithm in zero-mean Gaussian noise contaminated by outliers (Fig. 3b). **a** Estimated (*solid line*) and true parameter (*dashed line*) trajectories (Fig. 2). **b** VFF calculation, $\rho(k)$. **c** Discrimination function calculation, $Q(k)$

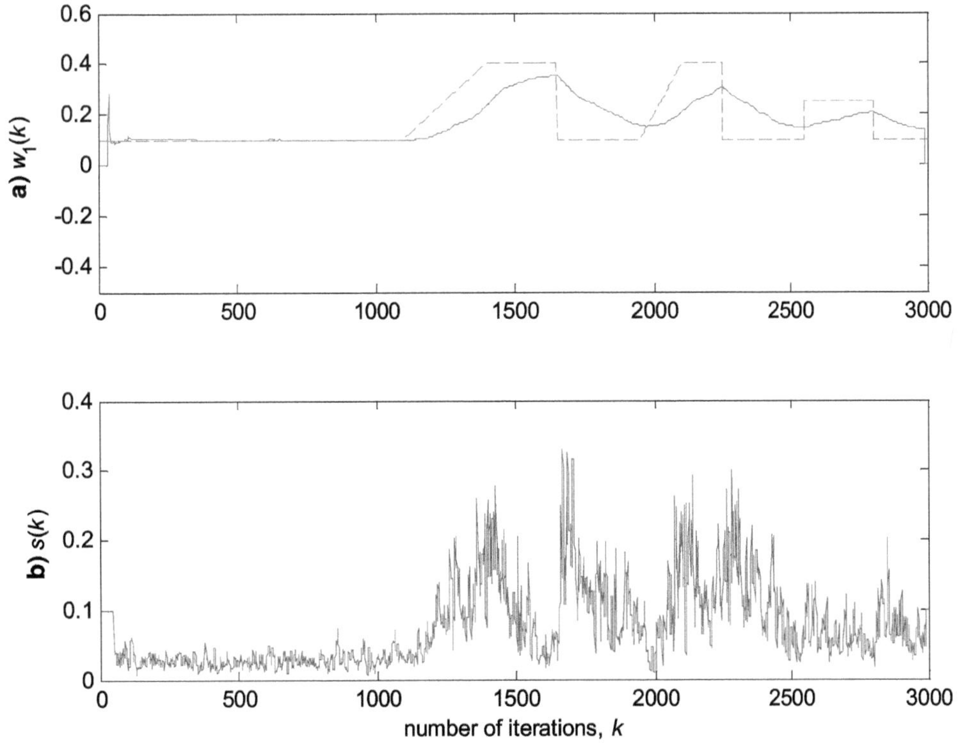

Fig. 9 Experimental results for RRLSS algorithm in zero-mean Gaussian noise contaminated by outliers (depicted in Fig. 3b). **a** Estimated (*solid line*) and true parameter (*dashed line*) trajectories (Fig. 2). **b** Scale factor calculation, $s(k)$

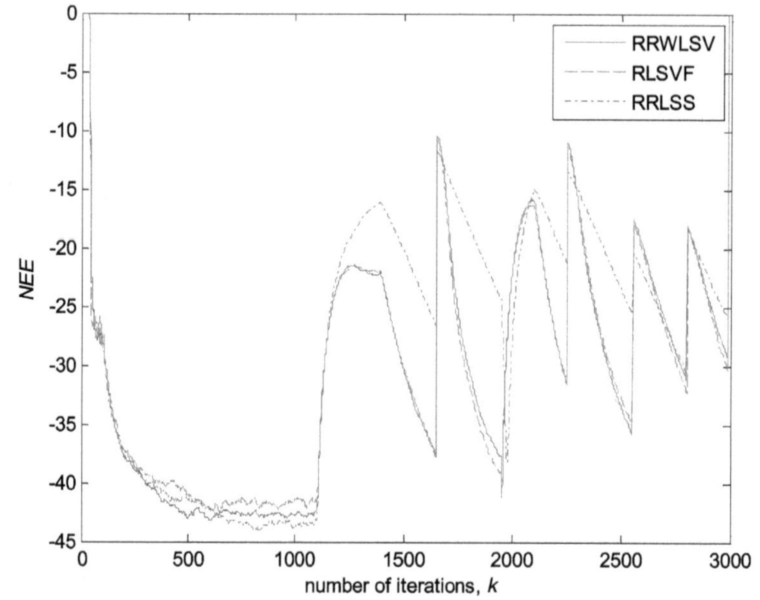

Fig. 10 Normalised estimation errors *NEE* in (36), for different algorithms, in stationary zero-mean white normal Gaussian noise (SNR = 25dB); Experimental conditions are given in Figs. 2 and Fig 3a

linear residual transformation, ψ (see Eqs. 14 and 15). On the other hand, the robust algorithms RRLSS and RRWLSV are rather insensitive to impulsive noise component, and give also comparable results, due to the effect of robust influence function, ψ, in the parameter and matrix update equations (see Eqs. 17 and 18 or Eqs. 12 and 13).

4.3 Time-varying parameter tracking in a non-stationary zero-mean normal noise with possible outliers

In this experiment, the simulation scenario is the combination of the previous two examples, with the exception that the first filter parameter, w_1, is adopted to be time-varying, using the parameters trajectory presented in Figs. 15, 16 and 17 depict the obtained *NEE* criterion

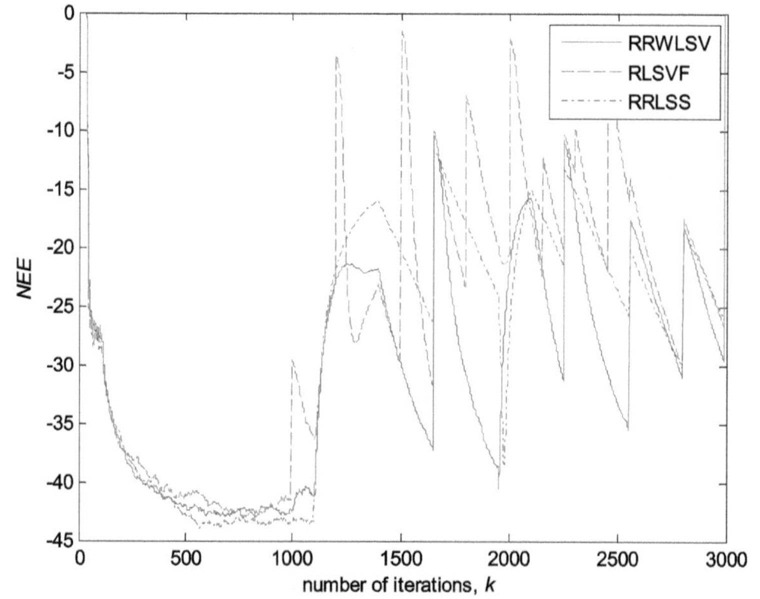

Fig. 11 Normalised estimation errors *NEE* in (36 for different algorithms in stationary zero-mean white normal noise (SNR = 25 dB) contaminated by outliers; experimental conditions are given in Figs. 2 and Fig 3b

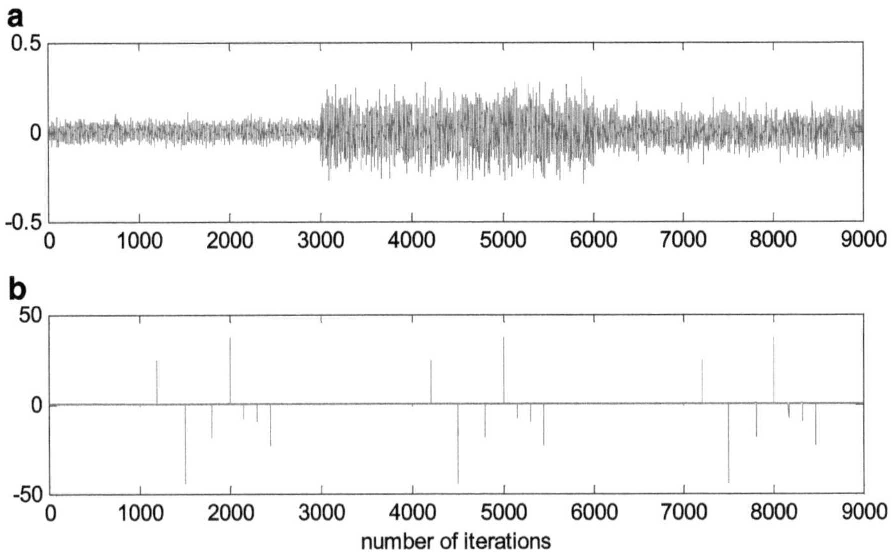

Fig. 12 Realisation of additive noise, $n(k)$. **a** Non-stationary zero-mean white normal noise samples with changing variances (SNR = 25, 15 and 20 dB). **b** Non-stationary zero-mean white normal noise samples, with changing variances, contaminated by outliers

(36), for different algorithms, without (Fig. 16) and with (Fig. 17) outliers, added to the non-stationary zero-mean normal noise with changing variance (see Fig. 12). The obtained results are in accordance to the conclusions derived from the previous two experiments.

In summary, the obtained results from the all three experiments have shown that, in order to properly estimate the time-varying parameters under the non-stationary and impulsive noise environment, both robustified VFF and adaptive M robust estimator with simultaneous estimation of parameters and scale factor (RRWLSV) are required. Moreover, an adequate non-linear residual transformation in the parameter update equation (Eq. 17 in RRLSS algorithm) is not sufficient for protecting well against the influence of outliers. Additionally, an important problem is also related to the way of recursive generation of the weighted matrix, **P**. It is found that the introduction of the Huber's saturation type non-linearity, ψ, coupled with the proper decrease of the weighted matrix, **P**, depending on the non-linearly transformed residuals and VFF (Eqs. 12

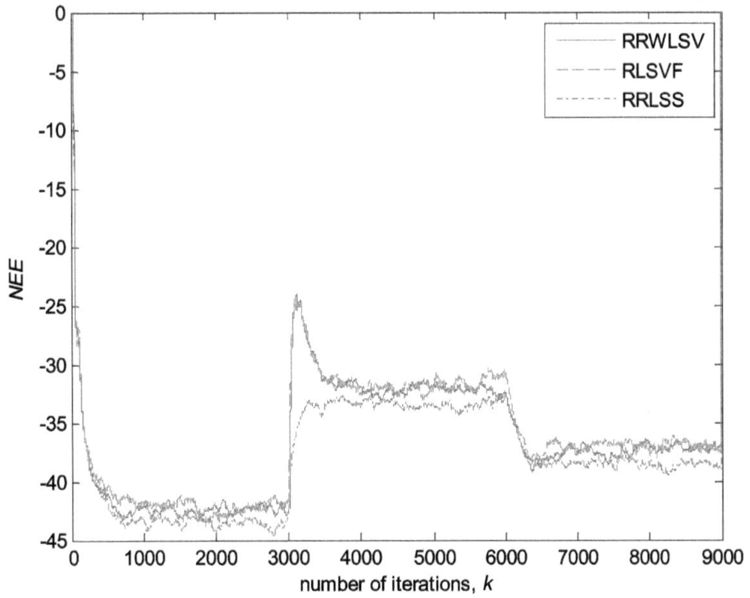

Fig. 13 Normalised estimation error norm (*NEE*), for different algorithms in non-stationary Gaussian noise environment (Fig. 12a), and fixed parameters in (35)

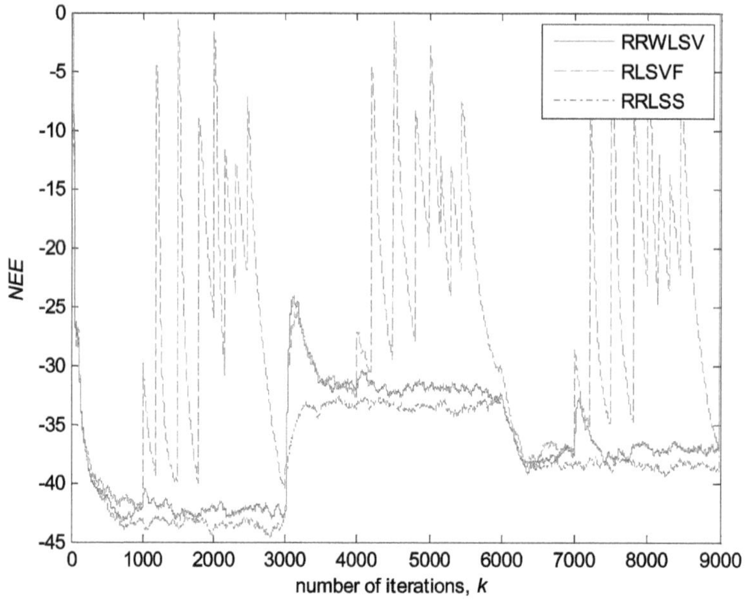

Fig. 14 Normalised estimation error norm *NEE*, for different algorithms in non-stationary and impulsive noise environment (Fig. 12b), and fixed parameters in (35)

and 13) provides low sensitivity to outliers and good parameter tracking performance (Figs. 4 and 7). The conventional M robust estimator (RRLSS) may converge very slowly, due to the introduction of the non-linearity first derivate, ψ', and the unit FF in the recursive generation of the weighted matrix (Eq. 18). Namely, large residual realisations, e, make the decrease of the weighted matrix, $\mathbf{P}$, very slow, since $\psi'(e) = 0$ in the saturation range (Eq. 18). This, in turn, results in an effect producing a slow convergence of parameter estimates (Figs. 6 and 9). The conventional RLS is also sensitive to outliers, but in a different way. In this algorithm, the weighted matrix, $\mathbf{P}$, is not influenced by the residuals (Eq. 15). As a consequence, the fast decrease of $\mathbf{P}$, independent of residuals, leads to the biased parameter estimates in the presence of outliers (see Fig. 8). In addition, the estimation of unknown noise variance (Eqs. 9 or 25) is essential to residual normalisation, in order to achieve a low sensitivity to the parameters defining the non-linear transformation of the prediction residuals in (4).

4.4 Influence of outlier statistics

A real outlier statistics is not exactly known in practice, so a low sensitivity to outliers is very important for achieving the practical robustness. The effect of desensitising the parameter estimates related to the influence of outliers is illustrated in Tables 2 and 3, depicting the evaluation of sample mean and sample variance of the NEE statistics (36), for different outlier probability and intensity. It can be observed that the proposed algorithm

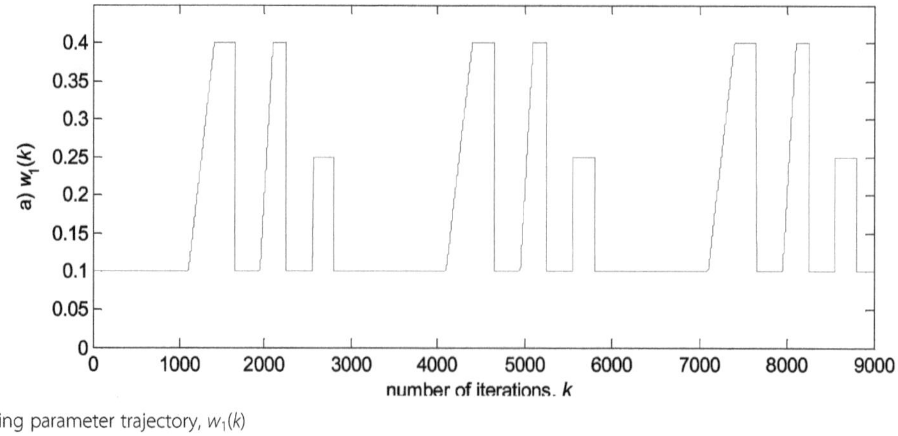

Fig. 15 Time varying parameter trajectory, $w_1(k)$

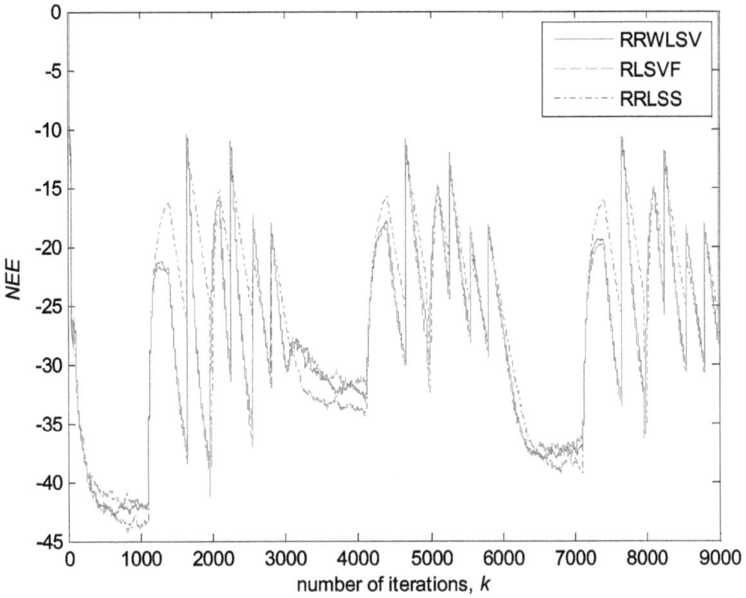

Fig. 16 Normalised estimation error norm (*NEE*), for different algorithms, in non-stationary zero-mean Gaussian noise environment (Fig. 12a) and the time-varying parameter trajectory (Fig. 15)

automatically damp out the effects of outliers, and it is rather insensitive to various fractions of outliers (see Table 2), up to 15 %, as well as to high level outliers (see Table 3). For higher percentage of outliers, more than 20 %, the normal noise model contaminated by outliers is not adequate. Furthermore, $s(k)$ is a nuisance parameter in the estimation of filter coefficients, as well as in the VFF computation. Its proper estimate is crucial for good performance of overall estimator, consisting of three coupled adaptive schemes. Since the complete algorithm performs quite well, this means that the estimation of scale factor also performs properly.

4.5 Influence of initial conditions

The proposed RRWLSV algorithm, exposed in Table 1, is non-linear and, consequently, may be highly influenced by the initial conditions, $\mathbf{W}(0)$ and $\mathbf{P}(0)$ in (33), respectively. However, from the practical point of view, a low sensitivity to the initial conditions represents the

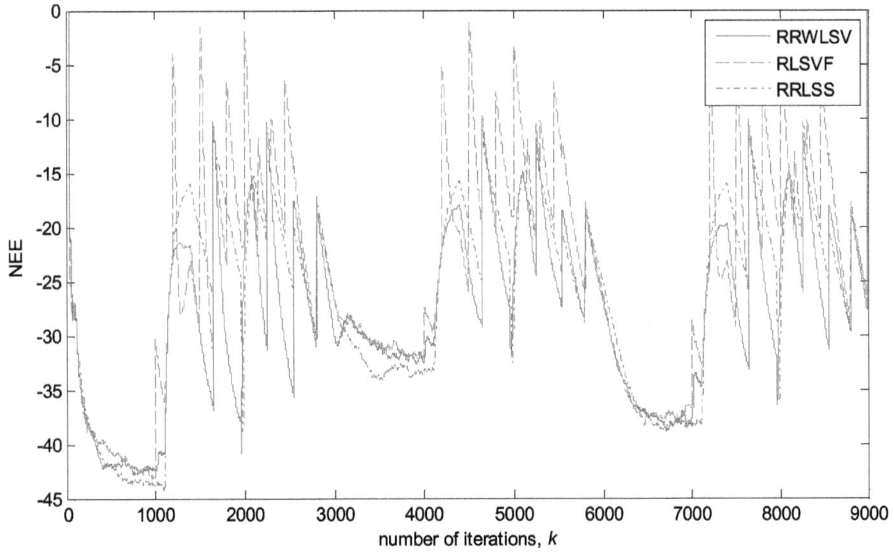

Fig. 17 Normalised estimation error norm (*NEE*), for different algorithms, in non-stationary noise contaminated by outliers (Fig. 12b), and the time-varying parameter trajectory (Fig. 15)

Table 2 The evaluation of the mean value and variance of *NEE*, for different outlier density, $\varepsilon = P(\alpha(k) = 1)$

ε	0.01	0.05	0.10	0.15	0.20	0.25	0.3
NEE							
Mean value	−30.2529	−30.6593	−30.1427	−30.3464	−24.4299	−18.6086	−14.2801
Variance	92.9838	95.1626	111.2679	112.4948	226.8080	322.398	410.0782

desirable performance measure. Table 4 illustrates the influence of the initial condition **P**(0) to the estimation error.

In general, large residual realisations in the initial steps, caused by large ‖**P**(0)‖, can make the decrease of ‖**P**(i)‖ very slow. This, in turn, may result in an undesirable effect producing a slow convergence of filter parameter estimates. However, the proposed RRWLSV algorithm is found to be relatively insensitive to the initial conditions, due to the proper way of generating of the weighting matrix, **P**(i), in (12) and (13), where the weighted term, $\omega(i)$ in (8), is used. This factor keeps the norm ‖**P**(i)‖ at values enough high for obtaining good convergence and, at the same time, enough small for preventing the described undesirable convergence effect. Similarly as in the experiment 4.1, it is observed that for higher values of ‖**P**(0)‖, the RRLSS algorithm converges very slowly. The reason lies in the introduction of the first derivative, ψ', instead of the weighted term ω in (8), in the weighted matrix update equation, **P**(i), in (18), which is equal to zero in the saturation range. Thus, large residuals in the initial steps, caused by large ‖**P**(0)‖, make the decrease of ‖**P**(i)‖ very slow. This, in turn, results in the described cumulative effect, producing a slow convergence of parameter estimates (see Table 4).

4.6 Influence of model order

The selection of model structure depends on the intended model application [31]. With the adopted FIR model structure, one has to select the order, n, of the parameter vector, **W** in (3). The model order should not be selected too low, since then, all system dynamics cannot be described properly. However, it should not be selected too high either, since the higher the model order, the most parameters need to be estimated and the higher the variance of the parameter estimates is. Thus, increasing the model order beyond the true order of the system will not add to the quality of the model. Hence, the model order is some sort of compromise between fitting the data and model complexity [32, 33]. Figure 18 illustrates the discussion through the obtained *NEE* criterion in (36), for the experimental conditions described in 4.1, in the cases of lower ($n = 7$), higher ($n = 12$) and exact ($n = 9$) model order of the FIR system.

4.7 Influence of additive noise correlations

The FIR model structure does not take into account the coloured additive noise. However, in general, additive noise, $n(k)$, may represent any kind of noise, with arbitrary colour. Such noise can be simulated by filtering a zero-mean white noise through a linear time-invariant (LTI) system [34, 35]. In this way, one can shape the fit of a time-invariant model under a stationary noise environment to the frequency domain. It can be shown that, in general case, the resulting estimate is a compromise between fitting the estimated constant model parameters to the true one and fitting the noise model spectrum to the prediction error spectrum [35]. In addition, the estimates can be improved by using prefilters. The analysis is based on the limit parameter value to which the parameter estimates converge asymptotically and corresponding limit criterion [35]. However, such an analysis is not possible on the short data sequences, whether the situation is stationary or not. Therefore, the answer to the question concerning the insensitivity to noise statistics, as well as the other questions related to the practical robustness, can be obtained only by simulations. Figure 19 depicts the obtained *NEE* criterion in (36), with the experimental conditions exposed in 4.1, but using the coloured noise with the given autocorrelation function in Fig. 20, [36]. The experimental results indicate that the proposed RRWLSV filtering algorithm copes satisfactorily with the coloured noise.

It should be noted that in a FIR model structure, the noise model is fixed and equal to the unit constant.

Table 3 The evaluation of the mean value and variance of *NEE*, for different outlier intensity, $\sigma_e^2 = \mathrm{var}A(k)$, where the nominal value is $\sigma_0^2 = 10^4/12$

σ_e^2	$10^{-2}\sigma_0^2$	$10^{-1}\sigma_0^2$	σ_0^2	$10\sigma_0^2$	$10^2\sigma_0^2$
NEE					
mean value	−30.8406	−30.3820	−30.4177	−30.4417	−30.3870
variance	94.2645	92.8128	94.9259	95.1020	94.6418

Table 4 The evaluation of the mean square error norm, ‖**P**(i)‖, for different initial conditions (experimental conditions are the same as in the experiment 4.1)

P(0)	10^2**I**	10**I**	**I**	0.1**I**
Iterations				
50	366.9852	36.6985	0.3670	0.3530
100	0.9492	0.4582	1.1870	1.3091
1000	0.0100	0.0092	0.0085	0.0119

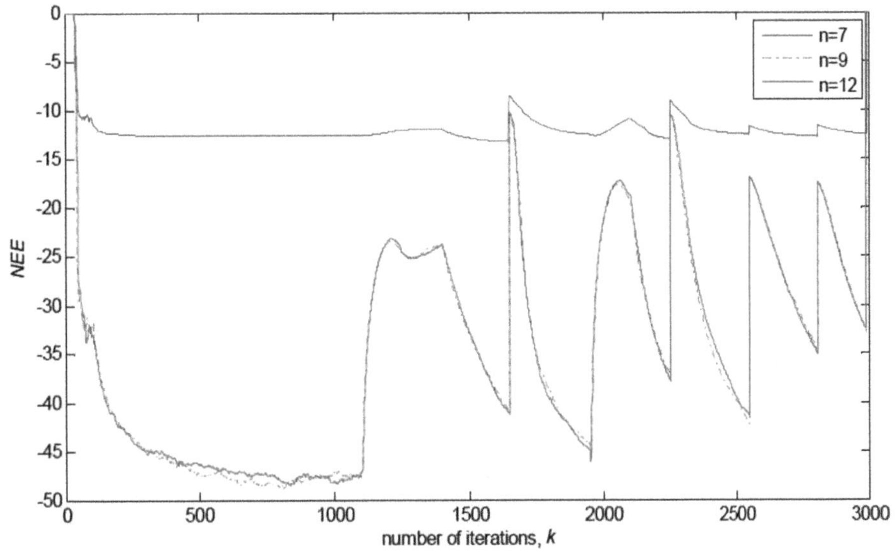

Fig. 18 Normalised estimation error norm (*NEE*) in (36), for the experimental conditions described in 4.1 (Figs. 2 and 3b) and the algorithm RRWLSV, in the cases of lower ($n = 7$), higher ($n = 12$) and exact ($n = 9$) model order

5 Conclusions

The estimation problem of time-varying adaptive FIR filter parameters in the situations characterised by non-stationary and impulsive noise environments has been discussed in the article. The posed problem is solved efficiently by application of a new adaptive robust algorithm, including a combination of the M robust concept, extended to the estimation of both filter parameters and unknown noise variance simultaneously, and adaptive robustified variable forgetting factor. The variable forgetting factor is determined by linear mapping of a suitably defined robust discrimination function, representing the ratio of robustified extended prediction error criterion, using M robust approach, and M robust type recursive estimate of noise variance. Since the robustified version of extended prediction error criterion is calculated on sliding data frame of proper length, it represents a robust measure of local data non-stationarity. On the other hand, the total noise variance robust recursive estimate is rather insensitive to the local non-stationarity effects, so that the adopted robust discrimination function represents a suitable normalised robust measure of the degree of signal non-stationarity. In addition, since the total noise variance, or the so-called scale factor, and variable forgetting factor are adaptively calculated with respect to the prediction errors, the proposed algorithm works properly in stationary and non-stationary situations with possible outliers. Simulation results have shown that the new method gives higher accuracies of parameter estimates, and ensures better parameter tracking ability, in

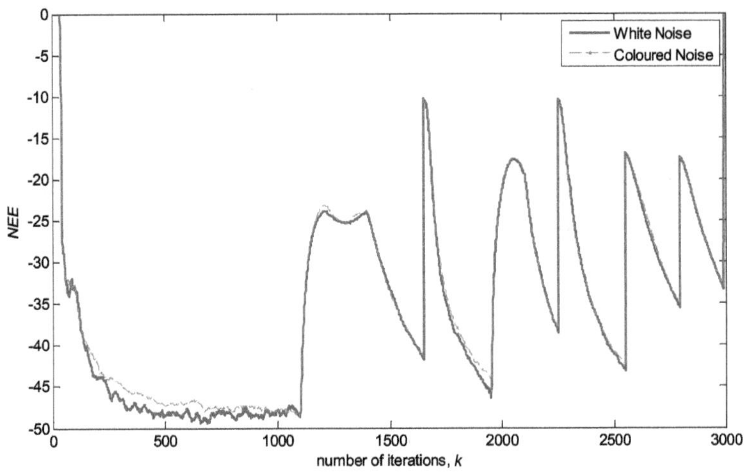

Fig. 19 Normalised estimation error norm (*NEE*) in (36), for the experimental conditions in the case of white and coloured noise (see Fig. 20)

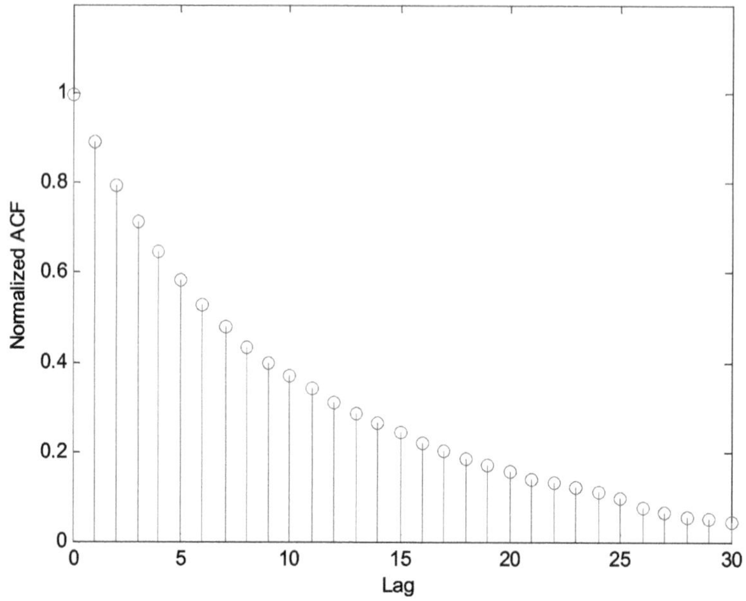

Fig. 20 Normalised autocorrelation function of coloured noise

comparison to the conventional least-squares algorithm with variable forgetting factor, and the standard M robust algorithm with scale factor estimation. Moreover, the standard least-squares algorithm with variable forgetting factor is very sensitive to outliers, while the new adaptive robust method with combined scale and variable forgetting factor, and the conventional M robust-based method, with scale factor, are rather insensitive to such a disturbance. However, the proposed adaptive M robust algorithm with combined scale and forgetting factors has much better parameter tracking performance than the conventional M robust algorithm with only scale factor. The experimental analysis has shown that the real practical robustness and good tracking performances are connected with both the non-linear transformation of prediction-residuals and an adequate recursive generation of the weighted matrix, depending on the non-linearity form and variable forgetting factor. Moreover, a recursive estimation of the unknown noise variance is essential for defining properly the non-linearity form. In summary, in order to properly estimate the time-varying parameters under the non-stationary and impulsive noise, both robustified variable forgetting factor and simultaneous adaptive M robust estimation of system parameters and unknown noise variance are required.

The proposed adaptive M robust estimators for generating scale factor and variable forgetting factor are general, while the adaptive M robust parameter estimation procedure depends on assumed signal, or system, model structure. Moreover, it can be easily applied to the other commonly used signal, or system models, including AR, ARX, ARMA and ARMAX models, respectively, or even non-linear models. Furthermore, the proposed adaptive robustified algorithm is the one that, with proper adaptation, can be used as a robust alternative to the conventional recursive least squares or Kalman filter, respectively. These applications arise in various fields, including speech processing, biomedical signal processing, image analysis, and failure detection in measurement and control.

6 Appendix 1

6.1 Derivation of relations (10)–(13).

The solution of (6) is given by

$$\hat{\mathbf{W}}(k) = \mathbf{R}^{-1}(k)\sum_{i=1}^{k}\beta(k,i)\mathbf{X}(i)d(i) \tag{38}$$

where

$$\beta(k,i) = \rho^{k-i}\omega(i) \tag{39}$$

with $\omega(i)$ being defined by (8) when $\mathbf{W}_0$ is replaced by $\hat{\mathbf{W}}(k-1)$. Moreover, $e(i, \mathbf{W})$ in (2) is defined by (11) with $\mathbf{W} = \hat{\mathbf{W}}(k-1)$, while the matrix $\mathbf{R}$ in (38) is given by

$$\begin{aligned}\mathbf{R}(k) &= \sum_{i=1}^{k}\beta(k,i)\mathbf{X}(i)\mathbf{X}^T(i)\\ &= \rho\sum_{i=1}^{k-1}\beta(k-1,i)\mathbf{X}(i)\mathbf{X}^T(i)\\ &\quad + \omega(k)\mathbf{X}(k)\mathbf{X}^T(k)\end{aligned} \tag{40}$$

from which it follows

$$\mathbf{R}(k) = \rho\mathbf{R}(k-1) + \omega(k)\mathbf{X}(k)\mathbf{X}^T(k) \quad (41)$$

Furthermore, one can also write

$$\sum_{i=1}^{k}\beta(k,i)\mathbf{X}(i)d(i) = \rho\sum_{i=1}^{k-1}\beta(k-1,i)\mathbf{X}(i)d(i) + \omega(k)\mathbf{X}(k)d(k) \quad (42)$$

Taking into account (38), one concludes from (42)

$$\sum_{i=1}^{k}\beta(k,i)\mathbf{X}(i)d(i) = \rho\mathbf{R}(k-1)\hat{\mathbf{W}}(k-1) + \omega(k)\mathbf{X}(k)d(k) \quad (43)$$

Furthermore, by calculating $\rho\mathbf{R}(k-1)$ from (41), and replacing it into (43), one obtains

$$\sum_{i=1}^{k}\beta(k,i)\mathbf{X}(i)d(i) = \left[\mathbf{R}(k)-\omega(k)\mathbf{X}(k)\mathbf{X}^T(k)\right]\hat{\mathbf{W}}(k-1) + \omega(k)\mathbf{X}(k)d(k) \quad (44)$$

Finally, by replacing (44) into (38), one obtains the relations (10) and (11) with the gain matrix

$$\mathbf{K}(k) = \mathbf{R}^{-1}(k)\omega(k)\mathbf{X}(k) \quad (45)$$

In addition, by introducing the weighting matrix $\mathbf{P}(k) = \mathbf{R}^{-1}(k)$, it follows from (41)

$$\mathbf{P}(k) = \left[\rho\mathbf{P}^{-1}(k-1) + \omega(k)\mathbf{X}(k)\mathbf{X}^T(k)\right]^{-1} \quad (46)$$

After applying the well-known matrix inversion lemma [25, 26]

$$(\mathbf{A}+\mathbf{BCD})^{-1} = \mathbf{A}^{-1}-\mathbf{A}^{-1}\mathbf{B}\left(\mathbf{C}^{-1}+\mathbf{D}\mathbf{A}^{-1}\mathbf{B}\right)^{-1}\mathbf{D}\mathbf{A}^{-1} \quad (47)$$

on (46) with $\mathbf{A} = \rho\mathbf{P}^{-1}(k-1)$, $\mathbf{B} = \mathbf{X}(k)$, $\mathbf{C} = \omega(k)$ and $\mathbf{D} = \mathbf{X}^T(k)$, one concludes from (47)

$$\mathbf{P}(k) = \frac{1}{\rho}\left\{\mathbf{P}(k-1)-\frac{\mathbf{P}(k-1)\mathbf{X}(k)\mathbf{X}^T(k)\mathbf{P}(k-1)}{\rho\omega^{-1}(k)\mathbf{X}^T(k)\mathbf{P}(k-1)\mathbf{X}(k)}\right\} \quad (48)$$

By substituting $\mathbf{R}^{-1}(k) = \mathbf{P}(k)$ from (48) into (45), one can write further

$$\mathbf{K}(k) = \frac{\mathbf{P}(k-1)\mathbf{X}(k)\omega(k)}{\rho+\mathbf{X}^T(k)\mathbf{P}(k-1)\mathbf{X}(k)\omega(k)} \quad (49)$$

Finally, by introducing $\mathbf{M}(k)$ from (12), and substituting (49) into (48), one obtains the relations (12) and (13), which completes the proof.

7 Appendix 2

7.1 Derivation of relations (24)–(25).

Starting from (21)–(23), one can write

$$kJ_k(s/\hat{\mathbf{W}}) = \ln(s) + (k-1)J_{k-1}(s/\hat{\mathbf{W}}) + f\left(\frac{e(k,\hat{\mathbf{W}})}{s}\right) \approx \ln(s) + f\left(\frac{e(k,\hat{\mathbf{W}})}{s}\right) \quad (50)$$

and

$$k\frac{\partial J_k(s/\hat{\mathbf{W}})}{\partial s} = \frac{1}{s} - \frac{e(k,\hat{\mathbf{W}})}{s^2}g\left(\frac{e(k,\hat{\mathbf{W}})}{s}\right) \quad (51)$$

where $g(\cdot) = f'(\cdot)$. Furthermore, one can also write from (19)

$$\frac{\partial J(\sigma/\hat{\mathbf{W}})}{\partial\sigma} = \frac{1}{\sigma} - E\left\{\frac{e(k,\hat{\mathbf{W}})}{\sigma^2}g\left(\frac{e(k,\hat{\mathbf{W}})}{\sigma}\right)\right\} \quad (52)$$

and

$$\frac{\partial^2 J(\sigma/\hat{\mathbf{W}})}{\partial\sigma^2} = -\frac{1}{\sigma^2} + E\left\{g'\left(\frac{e(k,\hat{\mathbf{W}})}{\sigma}\right)\frac{e^2(k,\hat{\mathbf{W}})}{\sigma^4}\right\} + \frac{2}{\sigma}E\left\{\frac{e(k,\hat{\mathbf{W}})}{\sigma^2}g\left(\frac{e(k,\hat{\mathbf{W}})}{\sigma}\right)\right\} \quad (53)$$

In the vicinity of the optimal solution, one concludes $\partial J(\sigma/\hat{\mathbf{W}})/\partial\sigma = 0$ in (52), from which it follows

$$E\left\{\frac{e(k,\hat{\mathbf{W}})}{\sigma^2}g\left(\frac{e(k,\hat{\mathbf{W}})}{\sigma}\right)\right\} = \frac{1}{\sigma} \quad (54)$$

Furthermore, by substituting (54) in (53), one obtains

$$\frac{\partial^2 J_k(s/\hat{\mathbf{W}})}{\partial s^2} \approx \frac{\partial^2 J(s/\hat{\mathbf{W}})}{\partial\sigma^2} = \frac{a}{s^2} \quad (55)$$

where the constant

$$a = 1 + E\left\{g'\left(\frac{e(k,\hat{\mathbf{W}})}{s}\right)\frac{e^2(k,\hat{\mathbf{W}})}{s^2}\right\} \approx 1 \quad (56)$$

Finally, if one substitutes (51), (55) and (56) into (20), one obtains an approximate optimal solution for the scale factor estimation in the recursive form (24). In addition, if we assume for the moment that $s(k-1)$ is close to $s(k)$, and take into account the relation (8), the expression (24) can be rewritten in the alternative form (25), which completes the proof.

8 Appendix 3

8.1 The derivation of mean value and variance of the random variable generating the outliers

The outliers $n(k)$ for each time step k are generated by the random variable (r.v.) $n = \alpha A$, representing the function of two variables, where α is the discrete binary r.v. taking the values $\alpha_1 = 0$ with the probability $p_1 = P\{\alpha = \alpha_1\}$, and $\alpha_2 = 1$ with the probability $p_2 = P\{\alpha = \alpha_2\}$, $p_1 + p_2 = 1$. Moreover, A is the continuous zero-mean r.v. with variance σ_A^2, and it is supposed that α and A are independent. The mean $E\{n\}$ can be determined directly in terms of the joint p.d.f. $f_{\alpha,A}(\alpha, A)$ without the need for evaluating p.d.f. of n, that is [35]

$$E\{n\} = E\{\alpha A\} = \int_{-\infty}^{\infty}\int_{-\infty}^{\infty} \alpha A f_{\alpha A}(\alpha, A) d\alpha dA = E\{\alpha\}E\{A\} = m_\alpha m_A \tag{57}$$

since α and A are independent, yielding $f_{\alpha A}(\alpha, A) = f_\alpha(\alpha)$-$f_A(A)$. However, due to the fact that $m_A = E\{A\} = 0$, one concludes $m_n = E\{n\} = 0$. The variance of r.v. n is given by

$$\sigma_n^2 = E\{n^2\} - E^2\{n\} = m_{2,n} - m_n^2 \tag{58}$$

where $m_{2,n}$ and m_n are non-centralized moments of the second and the first order, respectively. Similarly as before, the variance can be determined as

$$\sigma_n^2 = \sigma_{\alpha A}^2 = E\{(\alpha A)^2\} - E^2\{\alpha A\} \tag{59}$$

that is, since $E\{\alpha A\} = 0$

$$\sigma_{\alpha A}^2 = E\{\alpha^2 A^2\} = \int_{-\infty}^{\infty}\int_{-\infty}^{\infty} \alpha^2 A^2 f_{\alpha A}(\alpha, A) d\alpha dA = m_{2,\alpha} m_{2,A} \tag{60}$$

Here, $m_{2,\alpha} = \sigma_A^2$, since $m_A = 0$, while

$$m_{2,\alpha} = \alpha_1^2 p_1 + \alpha_2^2 p_2 = 0p_1 + 1p_2 = p_2 \tag{61}$$

from which it follows

$$\sigma_n^2 = p_2 \sigma_A^2;\ p_2 = P\{\alpha = 1\} = \varepsilon \tag{62}$$

where ε is the density or fraction of outliers.

Abbreviations

EPE: extended prediction error; FIR: finite impulse response; FF: forgetting factor; FFF: fixed value of forgetting factor; LS: least squares; M: approximate maximum-likelihood; MAD: median of absolute median deviations; ML: maximum-likelihood; *n*: parameter vecor order; *N*: memory length; NEE: normalised estimation error; PA: parallel adaptation; *Q*: discrimination function; RLS: recursive least squares; RLSVF: recursive least squares with variable forgetting factor; RRLS: robustified recursive least squares; RRLSS: robustified recursive least squares with scale factor; RRWLSV: robustified recursive weighted least squares with both scale and variable forgetting factors; SNR: signal-to-noise ratio; VFF: variable forgetting factor; WLS: weighted least-squares.

Competing interests

The authors declare that they have no competing interests.

Acknowledgments

This research was supported by Serbian Ministry of Education and Science (Project TR 32038 and III 42007)

Author details

[1]School of Electrical Engineering, University of Belgrade, Bulevar kralja Aleksandra 73, Belgrade, Serbia. [2]School of Electrical and Computer Engineering, 283 Vojvode Stepe St., Belgrade, Serbia. [3]Faculty of Informatics and Computing, Singidunum University, 32 Danijelova St., Belgrade, Serbia.

References

1. JV Candy, *Model-based signal processing* (John Wiley, New York, 2006)
2. SW Smith, *Digital signal processing: a practical guide for engineers and scientist* (Elsevier, Amsterdam, 2003)
3. SX Ding, *Model based fault diagnosis techniques, design schemes, algorithms, and tools* (Springer-Verlag, Berlin Heidelberg, 2008)
4. M Barkat, *Signal detection and estimation* (Artech House, Norwood, 2005)
5. M Verhaegen, V Verdult, *Filtering and system identification, a least squares approach* (Cambridge University Press, New York, 2012)
6. S Haykin, *Adaptive filter theory* (Prentice Hall, Pearson, 2013)
7. B Kovačević, Z Banjac, M Milosavljević, *Adaptive digital filters* (Springer-Verlag, Berlin, Heidelberg, 2013)
8. M Basseville, A Benveniste, *Detection of abrupt changes in signals and dynamical systems* (Springer-Verlag, Berlin, Heidelberg, 1986)
9. S Peters, DA Antoniou, A Parallel, Adaptation algorithm for recursive least squares adaptive filters in nonstationary environments. IEEE Trans Signal Process **43**(11), 2484–2494 (1995). doi:10.1109/78.482100
10. YS Cho, SB Kim, EJ Powers, Time-varying spectral estimation using AR models with variable forgetting factors. IEEE Trans Signal Process **39**(6), 1422–1426 (1991). doi:10.1109/78.136549
11. Z. Banjac, B. Kovačević, I. Kostić Kovačević, *Variable forgetting factor estimation in impulsive noise environment, Telecommunications Forum (TELFOR) 22nd, Belgrade, 25–27 November 2014, pp.* 449–452, doi:10.1109/TELFOR.2014.7034443
12. B. Kovačević, M. Milosavljević, M. Veinović, *Time-varying AR speech analysis using robust RLS algorithm with variable forgetting factor, Proceedings of the 12th IAPR International Conference on Pattern Recognition, (Jerusalem, 09–13 October 1994), vol* **3**, *pp.*211-213, doi:10.1109/ICPR.1994.577162
13. G Kvaščev, Ž Đurović, B Kovačević, I Kostić Kovačević, *Adaptive estimation of time-varying parameters in AR models with variable forgetting factor, Mediterranean Electrotechnical Conference MELECON, (Beirut, 13–16 April 2014), pp.* 68–73, doi:10.1109/MELCON.2014.6820509
14. J Chambers, A Alvonitis, A Robust, Mixed norm adaptive filter algorithm. IEEE Signal Process Lett **4**(2), 46–48 (1997)
15. Y Zou, SC Chan, TS Ng, Robust M-estimate adaptive filtering. IEE Proceedings Vis Image Signal Process **148**(4), 289–294 (2001)
16. Y Zou, SC Chan, TS Ng, A recursive least M-estimate (RLM) adaptive filter for robust filtering in impulse noise. Signal Process Lett IEEE **7**(11), 975–991 (2000)
17. HS Kim, JS Lim, SJ Baek, KM Sung, Robust Kalman filtering with variable forgetting factor against impulsive noise. IEICE Trans Fundam Electron Commun Comput Sci **E84-A**(1), 363–366 (2001)
18. T Yang, JH Lee, KY Lee, KM Sung, On robust Kalman filtering with forgetting factor for sequential speech analysis. Signal Process **63**(2), 151–156 (1997)
19. Y.Zhou, S. C. Chan, K. L. Ho, A new variable forgetting factor QR based recursive least M-estimate algorithm for robust adaptive filtering in impulsive noise environment, 14th European Signal Processing Conference, (Florence, 4–8 September 2006), pp. 1–5 IEEE http://ieeexplore.ieee.org/stamp/stamp.jsp?tp=&arnumber=7071126&isnumber=7065146 ISSN: 2219-5491
20. ZG Zhang, SC Chan, Recursive parametric frequency/spectrum estimation for nonstationary signals with impulsive components using variable forgetting factor. IEEE Trans Instrum Meas **62**(12), 3251–3264 (2013)
21. PJ Huber, EM Ronchetti, *Robust statistics* (John Wiley, New Jersey, 2009)
22. RR Wilcox, *Introduction to robust estimation and hypothesis testing* (Academic Press, Boston, 2012)

23. WN Venables, BD Ripley, *Modern applied statistics with S* (Springer, Berlin Heidelberg New York, 2002)
24. Z Banjac, B Kovačević, *Robust parameter and scale factor estimation in nonstationary and impulsive noise environments, in Proceedings of IEEE Conf. EUROCON, (Belgrade, 21–24. November, 2005), pp.* 1546–1549. doi:10.1109/EURCON.2005.1630261
25. L Ljung, T Soderstorm, *Theory and practice of recursive identification* (MIT Press, Cambridge, 1983)
26. YZ Tsypkin, *Foundations of informational theory of identification* (Nauka, Moscow, 1984)
27. M Veinović, B Kovačević, M Milosavljević, Robust nonrecursive AR speech analysis. Signal Process **37**(2), 189–201 (1994)
28. B Kovačević, M Veinović, M Milosavljević, M Marković, *Robust speech processing* (Springer Verlag, Berlin, Heidelberg, 2016). in press
29. AK Kohli, A Rai, Numeric variable forgetting factor RLS algorithm for second-order Volterra filtering. Circuits Syst Signal Process **32**(1), 223–232 (2013)
30. K Ak, A Rai, M Patel, Variable forgetting factor LS algorithm for polynomial channel model. ISRN Signal Process **2011**, Article ID 915259 (2011)
31. PPJ van den Bosch, AC van der Klauw, *Modeling, identification and simulation of dynamical systems* (CRC Press, Boca Raton, 1994)
32. R Stoica, R Eykhoff, R Janssen, T Soderstrorm, Model structure selection by cross validation. Internatt J Control **43**, 1841–1878 (1986)
33. H Akaike, Modern development of statistical methods, in *Trends and progress in system identification*, ed. by Eykhoff (Pergamon Press, New York, 1981), pp. 169–184
34. L Ljung, *System identification—theory for the user*, 2nd edn. (PTR Prentice Hall, Upper Saddle River, 1999)
35. B Kovačević, Ž Djurović, *Fundamentals of stochastic signals, systems and estimation theory: with worked examples* (Springer, Verlag, Berlin, 2008)
36. M Viswanathan, *Simulation of digital communication systems using Matlab*, 2013. http://www.gaussianwaves.com/simulation-of-digital-communication-systems-using-matlab-ebook. Accessed 01 march 2016

16

Co-channel interference suppression for multi-cell MIMO heterogeneous network

Yu Li[1] and Zufan Zhang[1,2*]

Abstract

The heterogeneous network, contains a macro cell and a grid of low power nodes with the same frequencies, can improve the system capacity and spectrum efficiency. Configuring low-power nodes that share the same spectrum with macro cell to form heterogeneous networks makes it more likely to improve the system capacity and spectrum efficiency, but inevitably, strong co-channel interference is the main barrier to further improvement for heterogeneous networks. This paper proposes an algorithm which combines the triangular decomposition and signal to leakage and noise ratio (SLNR) (TD-SLNR) to suppress strong co-channel interference in multi-cell multiple input and multiple output (MIMO) heterogeneous networks. Firstly, the proposed algorithm can reduce the number of inter-cell interferences in half. As a result of triangular decomposition, an equivalent interference channel model is extracted to eliminate the rest of interferences using SLNR and interference suppression matrix. Theoretical analysis shows that the proposed algorithm provides a potential solution to suppress the co-channel interference with low complexity and reduce the computation complexity without adding extra interference suppression matrices and computation complexity at receivers. Furthermore, the simulation results show that TD-SLNR algorithm can improve system capacity and energy efficiency comparing with the traditional SLNR algorithm.

Keywords: Multi-cell MIMO heterogeneous network, Co-channel interference, Signal leakage noise ratio, Triangular decomposition

1 Introduction

In the new generation of broadband mobile communication systems, multiple input and multiple output (MIMO) technique [1, 2] and heterogeneous networks [3–5] are key methods to enable the fast and reliable wireless communication access. On one hand, MIMO provides increased channel capacity and data rate using multiple antennas on both base stations and terminals. On the other hand, heterogeneous networks use hybrid networks with lower power nodes (pico, femto cells) and main nodes (macro cells) to achieve high-frequency efficiency and system capacity. The topology of a typical heterogeneous network consists of one macro cell and several pico/femto cells sharing the same frequency within the one area. Such networks bring co-channel interferences (CCI) which need to be eliminated in wireless communications [6–8]. For instance, users of the pico/femto cells are affected by the strong power signal from the macro cell, whereas high power terminals at the edge of macro and pico/femto cells produce strong interferences to the surrounding pico/femto cells. It is worthwhile to investigate methods to reduce or eliminate the CCI especially after MIMO be introduced to the heterogeneous networks.

At present, interference coordination is the key technology of interference suppression for heterogeneous network. The inter-cell interference in traditional networks can be significantly reduced by adjusting the spectrum allocation and transmission power among cells [9–11]. The inter-cell interference coordination requires a central control node to achieve parameter sending and so on. However, in heterogeneous network, a large of low power nodes are randomly allocated according to the demands of users; thus, the low power nodes cannot use the $X2$ interface [12], which will cause strong uplink and downlink interference to adjacent cells, such as the downlink dead zone and uplink blocking [8, 13]. Therefore, the novel interference coordination schemes

* Correspondence: zhangzf@cqupt.edu.cn
[1]School of Communications and Information Engineering, Chongqing University of Posts and Telecommunications, Chongqing 400065, China
[2]Chongqing Key Laboratory of Mobile Communication, Chongqing University of Posts and Telecommunication, Chongqing 400065, China

designed for heterogeneous network are proposed [14–16]. For example, in [10], a self-adaptive and flexible algorithm about spectrum utilization is proposed; this algorithm uses flexible spectrum utilization algorithm in cells formed by low power nodes while adopts fixed multiplexing schemes to manage interference in the macro cell. Meanwhile, there are many studies about interference suppression using various power control schemes for heterogeneous network [17, 18]. However, the interference coordination scheme based on the spectrum allocation cannot fully exploit the spectrum, and the interference coordination scheme based on the power control will result in higher computation complexity and a large number of signaling interactions. Furthermore, the application of interference coordination in actual deployment is usually restrained by many factors such as implementation complexity, central management, and distribution control; thus, we will focus on using the inter-cell interference elimination to suppress the interference in the heterogeneous network.

Currently, the interference elimination mainly includes two aspects, namely pre-coding design at transmitting end and the signal detection at receiving end, respectively. As for signal detection, it is usually limited by the achievement of channel state information, and it has high-complexity iterative detection process [19, 20]. As for the pre-coding design, CCI suppression can employ the block diagonalization pre-coding algorithm [21–24]. However, initially, this algorithm requires the number of transmitting antennas should be greater than the total number of all users' receiving antennas, which is difficult to satisfy. At present, some regularized versions of BD-type algorithms can deal with the limitation of the number of transmitting antennas [25, 26], but they are not referred to the application in multi-cell environment. Furthermore, BD algorithm will not take the problems of noise amplification into consideration; thus, it is unrealistic to put it into practice. Therefore, the signal to leakage and noise ratio (SLNR) algorithm proposed by Sadek is chosen to be the criterion of pre-coding design [27]. This algorithm maximizes the ratio of signal over the sum of leakage and noise, decomposes the multi-user MIMO system into multiple collateral and independent single-user MIMO systems, so that it is not restricted by the number of antennas, and gets the pre-coding matrices of each user independently, so the better interference suppression performance and extensive application scenarios can be obtained [28–31]. Moreover, in order to reduce the inter-cell co-channel interference, the interference alignment technology is adopted in multi-cell MIMO network [32, 33]. Generally, the interference alignment technology designs the interference suppression matrices at receivers and aligns the interference signal to the corresponding zero zones of interference suppression matrices to suppress the inter-cell co-channel interference. Though the interference alignment technology is helpful to suppress the inter-cell and intra-cell interference as well as enhance the system capacity, it will undoubtedly increase the number of interference suppression matrices at receivers and its corresponding computation complexity.

Summarized the previous works, this paper propose an interference suppression algorithm combining triangular decomposition and SLNR to solve the problems of the co-channel interference suppression for multi-cell MIMO heterogeneous network. The contributions and innovations of this paper are summarized as follows:

- This paper firstly discusses the interference situation of the network and then proposes an interference suppression algorithm combining triangular decomposition and SLNR under the considered network. This algorithm can reduce the number of inter-cell interferences in half through using triangular decomposition to the joint channel matrix, before interference suppression process at receiver.
- Based on the equivalent interference model, combining with the SLNR algorithm, this paper computes the pre-coding matrices of each user in each cell and the corresponding closed-form interference suppression matrices in detail according to the different interference situations of each cell.
- Considering the computation complexity, we compare the proposed algorithm with the traditional SLNR as well as the algorithm adopting interference alignment technology.
- We verify that comparing the proposed algorithm with traditional SLNR, a great improvement of system capacity and energy efficiency can be achieved. Furthermore, the impact of different number of data streams and antennas on the system performance is further analyzed.

The remainder of this paper is organized as follows. Section 2 mainly discusses the interference situations in multi-cell MIMO heterogeneous network. Section 3 makes a detailed introduction about the proposed algorithm which combines the triangular decomposition and SLNR. Furthermore, the computation complexity of the proposed algorithm with the traditional SLNR as well as the algorithm adopting interference alignment was compared. The simulation results will be discussed in Section 5. Finally, conclusions are presented in Section 6.

2 The interference situation discussion for multi-cell MIMO heterogeneous network

Multi-cell MIMO heterogeneous network consists of multiple macro cells and micro cells, and usually, the users are uniformly and randomly distributed in the cells. Figure 1 describes a universal downlink interference model in heterogeneous network, where the macro BS represents the macro base station in the network, the MUE represents the user belonging to macro BS, the pico BS indicates the base station in pico cell, and PUS represents the user belonging to pico BS. The circular region circled by dotted line is the coverage area of pico cell.

As shown in Fig. 1, there are two kinds of interferences in the model, including interference from macro BS to PUS and interference from pico BS to MUS. Due to the different path loss from pico BS to MUS, the received interference strength of different MUS is not the same. It is obvious that MUS1 may receive the strongest interference, MUS2 followed but also relatively strong, and MUS3 may receive the weakest interference strength. Furthermore, as the path loss from macro BS to MUS2 and MUS3 is much more than that to MUS1 and if we want to make the received signal to interference plus noise ratio (SINR) of each user the same, it is needed to increase the transmitting power of macro BS, which will result in strong interference from macro BS to PUS.

The uplink interference model in heterogeneous network is shown in Fig. 2. There are also two kinds of interference in the model, including interference from MUS to pico BS and interference from PUS to macro BS, respectively. According to the discussion of downlink, it may be considered that the interference from MUS1 and MUS2 to the uplink of pico BS is stronger enough: meanwhile, it is weaker to that of MUS3. However, the interference situations from MUS to the uplink of pico BS are quite different. If the macro BS requires the same receiving SINR from different MUS, but due to the different path loss of MUS1 and MUS2 to macro BS, the uplink transmission power of MUS2 should be much higher than that of MUS1, thus result in the interference from MUS2 to the uplink of pico BS is much stronger than the interference from MUS1 to the uplink of pico BS. Moreover, though MUS3 is far away from pico BS, the interference from MUS3 to the uplink of pico BS is the strongest. The path loss of MUS3 to macro BS is the

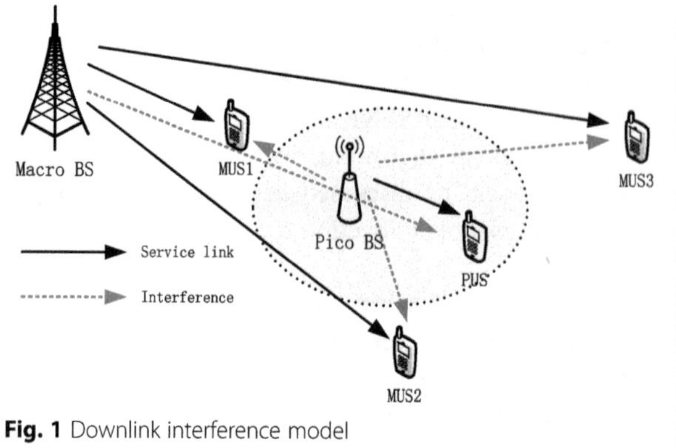

Fig. 1 Downlink interference model

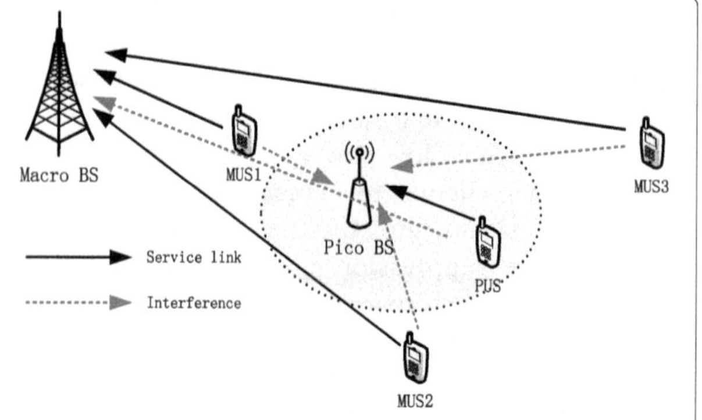

Fig. 2 Uplink interference model

largest one; so if macro BS requires the same receiving SINR from MUS3 and MUS1, the transmission power of MUS3 needs to be greatly enhanced; this results in the strongest interference from MUS3 to the uplink of pico BS. Similarly, the edge users of pico cell also need higher transmission power, which may result in interference to macro BS.

In conclusion, the interference situations in multi-cell MIMO heterogeneous network are absolutely different with that in traditional macro cell. According to the above discussion, we know that it is not suitable for the interference suppression of multi-cell MIMO heterogeneous network through judging the interference strength and designing the corresponding interference coordination scheme just according to the users' locations. Thus, this paper proposes an interference elimination algorithm for edge users, which can fully eliminate the interference according to the various interference situations on terminals.

For the convenience of analysis, the interference model has only one low-power cell. In the following, the system model of a multi-cell MIMO heterogeneous network is investigated, as shown in Fig. 3. Considering that there are K cells, including the low-power nodes such as macro cells and pico cells, they share the same spectrum. Thus, it is obvious that there are strong co-channel interferences exist in the system model, especially for the edge users. For the sake of convenience, it is supposed that there are only two edge users who not only receive the desired signals (the solid line represents in Fig. 3) from native cell but also receive the co-channel interference signals (the dotted line represents in Fig. 3) from other K-1 cells.

3 Co-channel interference suppression

Based on the system model considered above, supposing that the BS is equipped with N_t antennas, the user is equipped with N_r antennas, so constitutes a $(K, N_t) \times (2, N_r)$ MIMO interference channel model, as shown in Fig. 4. Due to the purpose of enabling the same signal space dimension that is provided by each transmitter, it can be assumed that each user has the same degrees of freedom d (Dof).

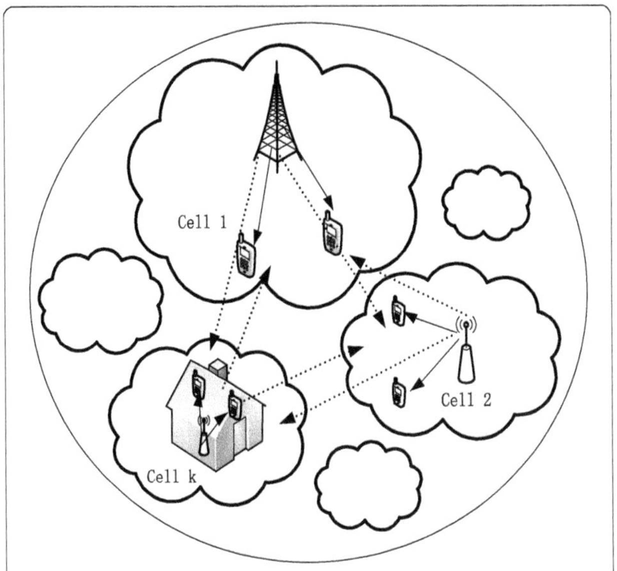

Fig. 3 System model

Thus, the received signal of ith user in kth cell can be expressed as

$$\mathbf{y}_{i,k}=\left(\mathbf{u}_{i,k}\right)^H\mathbf{H}_b^{i,k}\mathbf{w}_k\mathbf{x}_k+\left(\mathbf{u}_{i,k}\right)^H\sum_{b\neq k,b=1}^{K}\mathbf{H}_b^{i,k}\mathbf{w}_b\mathbf{x}_b+\left(\mathbf{u}_{i,k}\right)^H\mathbf{n}_{i,k} \tag{1}$$

where, $\mathbf{x}_k = [(\mathbf{x}_{1,k})^T, (\mathbf{x}_{2,k})^T]^T$ indicates the $2d \times 1$ data streams sent by the BS in kth cell; $\mathbf{x}_{1,k}$, $\mathbf{x}_{2,k}$ are the $d \times 1$ data streams sent by the BS in kth cell to users 1 and 2, respectively, satisfying the power constraint $E\left[\mathbf{x}_k^H\mathbf{x}_k\right] = P(k)$; $\mathbf{H}_b^{i,k}$ which represents the $N_r \times N_t$ channel matrix between the BS in the bth cell and the ith user in the kth cell; $\mathbf{u}_{i,k}$ is the intra-cell interference suppression matrix of the ith user in the kth cell, and $(\mathbf{u}_{i,k})^H\mathbf{u}_{i,k} = \mathbf{I}_d$; $\mathbf{w}_k = [\mathbf{w}_{1,k}, \mathbf{w}_{2,k}]$ is the $N_t \times 2d$ dimension pre-coding matrix; $\mathbf{w}_{1,k}$ and $\mathbf{w}_{2,k}$ are the $N_t \times d$ dimension pre-coding matrices of users 1 and 2 in the kth cell, respectively; $\mathbf{n}_{i,k}$ is the $N_r \times 1$ dimension additive white Gaussian noise with zero-mean, unit variance, and $E[\mathbf{n}_{i,k}(\mathbf{n}_{i,k})^H] = \mathbf{I}_{N_r}$.

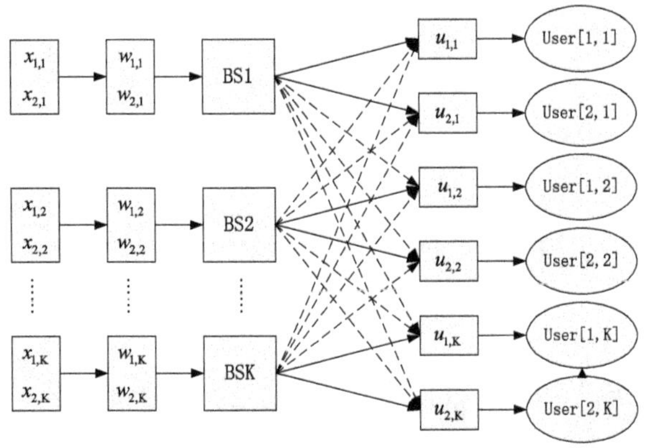

Fig. 4 Interference channel model

3.1 Triangular decomposition of the equivalent channel

From the point of joint channel matrix of all cells, this paper exploits triangular decomposition to the joint channel matrix. It can be seen from the discussion about the downlink interference in Section 2 that different base stations have different transmission power, which results in different degree of interference on users, and the base stations with higher transmission power have stronger co-channel interference to edge users of other cells. Thus, due to the different extent of interference on different users, it is needed to rank the receiving signal powers of users in different cells then obtain the suitable joint channel matrix by adjusting the row vectors of joint channel matrix.

Here, by computing the norms $\left\|\mathbf{H}_k^{i,k}\right\|_F^2$ of channel matrices between the base stations and the native users, the row vectors of joint channel matrix can be adjusted and ranked according to the values of norms. Besides, $\mathbf{H}_b^{i,k}$ can be further expressed as $T\mathbf{H}_b^{'i,k}R$,, where T and R are the power gains of transmitter and receiver, respectively. So the $\left\|\mathbf{H}_k^{i,k}\right\|_F^2$ norm of channel matrices between base stations and native users can be calculated [34].

$$\left\|\mathbf{H}_k^{i,k}\right\|_F^2=\sum_{j=1}^{N_t}\left\|h_j\right\|_2^2=\sum_{j=1}^{N_t}\lambda_j\left(\left(\mathbf{H}_k^{i,k}\right)^H\mathbf{H}_k^{i,k}\right) \tag{2}$$

where, λ_j is the jth eigenvalue of $\left(H_k^{i,k}\right)^H H_k^{i,k}$ matrix whose rank is N_t. It is observed that the $\left\|\mathbf{H}_k^{i,k}\right\|_F^2$ norm reflects the magnitude of the desired signal power of the ith user in the cell and the situation of transmission power of native base stations as well. Therefore, the row vectors of joint channel matrix can be adjusted and ranked according to $\left\|\mathbf{H}_k^{i,k}\right\|_F^2$. assuming that the $\left\|\mathbf{H}_k^{i,k}\right\|_F^2$ norms of the channel matrix of K cells are ranked as follows:

$$\left\|\mathbf{H}_a^{i,a}\right\|_F^2\geq\left\|\mathbf{H}_b^{i,b}\right\|_F^2\geq\cdots\geq\left\|\mathbf{H}_K^{i,K}\right\|_F^2 \tag{3}$$

According to the ranking result, corresponding cells are named as cell 1, cell 2,..., cell K.

In the following, the triangular decomposition of the equivalent channel will be discussed. The received signal of the ith user in the kth cell without interference suppression operation can be expressed as

$$\begin{aligned} \mathbf{y}_{i,k} &= \mathbf{H}_b^{i,k}\mathbf{w}_k\mathbf{x}_k + \sum_{b\neq k, b=1}^{K} \mathbf{H}_b^{i,k}\mathbf{w}_b\mathbf{x}_b + \mathbf{n}_{i,k} \\ &= \sum_{b=1}^{K} \mathbf{H}_b^{i,k}\mathbf{w}_b\mathbf{x}_b + \mathbf{n}_{i,k} \end{aligned} \tag{4}$$

According to the above comparison result of channel norms, the joint received signals Y of the whole system can be written as [35]

$$\mathbf{Y} = \begin{bmatrix} \mathbf{y}_1 \\ \mathbf{y}_2 \\ \vdots \\ \mathbf{y}_K \end{bmatrix} = \begin{bmatrix} \mathbf{y}_{1,1} \\ \mathbf{y}_{2,1} \\ \mathbf{y}_{1,2} \\ \mathbf{y}_{2,2} \\ \vdots \\ \mathbf{y}_{1,K} \\ \mathbf{y}_{2,K} \end{bmatrix} = \begin{bmatrix} \mathbf{H}_1^{1,1} & \mathbf{H}_2^{1,1} & \cdots & \mathbf{H}_K^{1,1} \\ \mathbf{H}_1^{2,1} & \mathbf{H}_2^{2,1} & \cdots & \mathbf{H}_K^{2,1} \\ \mathbf{H}_1^{1,2} & \mathbf{H}_2^{1,2} & \cdots & \mathbf{H}_K^{1,2} \\ \mathbf{H}_1^{2,2} & \mathbf{H}_2^{2,2} & \cdots & \mathbf{H}_K^{2,2} \\ \vdots & \vdots & \cdots & \vdots \\ \mathbf{H}_1^{1,K} & \mathbf{H}_2^{1,K} & \cdots & \mathbf{H}_K^{1,K} \\ \mathbf{H}_1^{2,K} & \mathbf{H}_2^{2,K} & \cdots & \mathbf{H}_K^{2,K} \end{bmatrix} \begin{bmatrix} \mathbf{w}_1\mathbf{x}_1 \\ \mathbf{w}_2\mathbf{x}_2 \\ \vdots \\ \mathbf{w}_K\mathbf{x}_K \end{bmatrix} + \begin{bmatrix} \mathbf{n}_{1,1} \\ \mathbf{n}_{2,1} \\ \mathbf{n}_{1,2} \\ \mathbf{n}_{2,2} \\ \vdots \\ \mathbf{n}_{1,K} \\ \mathbf{n}_{2,K} \end{bmatrix} = \mathbf{H}\mathbf{X} + \mathbf{n} \tag{5}$$

where,

$$\mathbf{X} = \begin{bmatrix} \mathbf{w}_1\mathbf{x}_1 \\ \mathbf{w}_2\mathbf{x}_2 \\ \vdots \\ \mathbf{w}_K\mathbf{x}_K \end{bmatrix}, \mathbf{y}_k = \begin{bmatrix} \mathbf{y}_{1,k} \\ \mathbf{y}_{2,k} \end{bmatrix}, \mathbf{n}_k = \begin{bmatrix} \mathbf{n}_{1,k} \\ \mathbf{n}_{2,k} \end{bmatrix}, k = 1, 2, ..., K.$$

Employing $\mathbf{H}_{bj} = \begin{bmatrix} \mathbf{H}_b^{1,j} \\ \mathbf{H}_b^{2,j} \end{bmatrix}$ to merge the channel matrices, $\mathbf{H}_{bj}$ is the joint channel matrix between two users in the jth cell and the base station in the bth cell; its dimension is $2N_r \times N_t$.. Thus, (5) can be rewritten as

$$\mathbf{Y} = \begin{bmatrix} \mathbf{y}_1 \\ \mathbf{y}_2 \\ \vdots \\ \mathbf{y}_K \end{bmatrix} = \begin{bmatrix} \mathbf{H}_{11} & \mathbf{H}_{21} & \cdots & \mathbf{H}_{K1} \\ \mathbf{H}_{12} & \mathbf{H}_{22} & \cdots & \mathbf{H}_{K2} \\ \vdots & \vdots & \cdots & \vdots \\ \mathbf{H}_{1K} & \mathbf{H}_{2K} & \cdots & \mathbf{H}_{KK} \end{bmatrix} \begin{bmatrix} \mathbf{w}_1\mathbf{x}_1 \\ \mathbf{w}_2\mathbf{x}_2 \\ \vdots \\ \mathbf{w}_K\mathbf{x}_K \end{bmatrix} + \begin{bmatrix} \mathbf{n}_1 \\ \mathbf{n}_2 \\ \vdots \\ \mathbf{n}_K \end{bmatrix} = \mathbf{H}\mathbf{X} + \mathbf{n} \tag{6}$$

where, $\mathbf{H} = \begin{bmatrix} \mathbf{H}_{11} & \mathbf{H}_{21} & \cdots & \mathbf{H}_{K1} \\ \mathbf{H}_{12} & \mathbf{H}_{22} & \cdots & \mathbf{H}_{K2} \\ \vdots & \vdots & \cdots & \vdots \\ \mathbf{H}_{1K} & \mathbf{H}_{2K} & \cdots & \mathbf{H}_{KK} \end{bmatrix}$ is the joint channel matrix of the whole system and its dimensions is $2KN_r \times KN_t$.

Then the joint channel matrix H is adjusted by the following triangular decomposition

$$\mathbf{H} = \begin{bmatrix} \mathbf{H}_{11} & \mathbf{H}_{21} & \cdots & \mathbf{H}_{K1} \\ \mathbf{H}_{12} & \mathbf{H}_{22} & \cdots & \mathbf{H}_{K2} \\ \vdots & \vdots & \cdots & \vdots \\ \mathbf{H}_{1K} & \mathbf{H}_{2K} & \cdots & \mathbf{H}_{KK} \end{bmatrix} = \begin{bmatrix} \mathbf{R}_{11} & & & \\ \mathbf{R}_{12} & \mathbf{R}_{22} & & \\ \vdots & \vdots & \ddots & \\ \mathbf{R}_{1K} & \mathbf{R}_{2K} & \cdots & \mathbf{R}_{KK} \end{bmatrix} \mathbf{U} = \mathbf{R}\mathbf{U} \tag{7}$$

where, $\mathbf{R}_{bj} = \begin{bmatrix} \mathbf{R}_b^{1,j} \\ \mathbf{R}_b^{2,j} \end{bmatrix}$ is the $2N_r \times N_t$ dimension matrix, and the dimension of $\mathbf{R}_b^{1,j}$ and $\mathbf{R}_b^{2,j}$ is $N_r \times N_t$, where $\boldsymbol{R}$ is the lower triangular matrix and its dimension is $2KN_r \times KN_t$,where $\boldsymbol{U}$ is unitary matrix and its dimension is $KN_t \times KN_t$. Thus, (6) can be equal to

$$\mathbf{Y} = \mathbf{H}\mathbf{X} + \mathbf{n} = \mathbf{R}\mathbf{U}\mathbf{X} + \mathbf{n} = \begin{bmatrix} \mathbf{R}_{11} & & & \\ \mathbf{R}_{12} & \mathbf{R}_{22} & & \\ \vdots & \vdots & \ddots & \\ \mathbf{R}_{1K} & \mathbf{R}_{2K} & \cdots & \mathbf{R}_{KK} \end{bmatrix} \mathbf{U} \begin{bmatrix} \mathbf{w}_1\mathbf{x}_1 \\ \mathbf{w}_2\mathbf{x}_2 \\ \vdots \\ \mathbf{w}_K\mathbf{x}_K \end{bmatrix} + \mathbf{n} \tag{8}$$

$$\text{Define} \begin{bmatrix} \mathbf{V}_1\mathbf{x}_1 \\ \mathbf{V}_2\mathbf{x}_2 \\ \vdots \\ \mathbf{V}_K\mathbf{x}_K \end{bmatrix} = \mathbf{U} \begin{bmatrix} \mathbf{w}_1\mathbf{x}_1 \\ \mathbf{w}_2\mathbf{x}_2 \\ \vdots \\ \mathbf{w}_K\mathbf{x}_K \end{bmatrix} \tag{9}$$

Thus, equation (8) can be rewritten as

$$\mathbf{Y} = \begin{bmatrix} \mathbf{y}_1 \\ \mathbf{y}_2 \\ \vdots \\ \mathbf{y}_K \end{bmatrix} = \begin{bmatrix} \mathbf{R}_{11} & & & \\ \mathbf{R}_{12} & \mathbf{R}_{22} & & \\ \vdots & \vdots & \ddots & \\ \mathbf{R}_{1K} & \mathbf{R}_{2K} & \cdots & \mathbf{R}_{KK} \end{bmatrix} \begin{bmatrix} \mathbf{V}_1\mathbf{x}_1 \\ \mathbf{V}_2\mathbf{x}_2 \\ \vdots \\ \mathbf{V}_K\mathbf{x}_K \end{bmatrix} + \begin{bmatrix} \mathbf{n}_1 \\ \mathbf{n}_2 \\ \vdots \\ \mathbf{n}_K \end{bmatrix} \tag{10}$$

As can be known from (10), the received signals without the complex interference suppression processing can be equivalent to

$$\mathbf{y}_1 = \begin{bmatrix} \mathbf{y}_{1,1} \\ \mathbf{y}_{2,1} \end{bmatrix} = \mathbf{R}_{11}\mathbf{V}_1\mathbf{x}_1 + \mathbf{n}_1 \tag{11}$$

$$\mathbf{y}_2 = \begin{bmatrix} \mathbf{y}_{1,2} \\ \mathbf{y}_{2,2} \end{bmatrix} = \mathbf{R}_{12}\mathbf{V}_1\mathbf{x}_1 + \mathbf{R}_{22}\mathbf{V}_2\mathbf{x}_2 + \mathbf{n}_2 \tag{12}$$

$$\mathbf{y}_k = \begin{bmatrix} \mathbf{y}_{1,k} \\ \mathbf{y}_{2,k} \end{bmatrix} = \mathbf{R}_{1k}\mathbf{V}_1\mathbf{x}_1 + \mathbf{R}_{2k}\mathbf{V}_2\mathbf{x}_2 + \cdots + \mathbf{R}_{kk}\mathbf{V}_k\mathbf{x}_k + \mathbf{n}_k \tag{13}$$

where, $\mathbf{R}_{bj}\mathbf{V}_b\mathbf{x}_b = \begin{bmatrix} \mathbf{R}_b^{1,j} \\ \mathbf{R}_b^{2,j} \end{bmatrix} \mathbf{V}_b\mathbf{x}_b = \begin{bmatrix} \mathbf{R}_b^{1,j}\mathbf{V}_b\mathbf{x}_b \\ \mathbf{R}_b^{2,j}\mathbf{V}_b\mathbf{x}_b \end{bmatrix}$, $b, j = 1, 2, ..., K$. When $b = j$, $\mathbf{R}_{bj}$ is the intra-cell equivalent channel matrix; When $b \neq j$, $\boldsymbol{R}_{bj}$ is the inter-cell equivalent channel matrix. $\mathbf{R}_b^{1,j}$ and $\mathbf{R}_b^{2,j}$, whose dimension is $N_r \times N_t$, represents the equivalent channel matrices between base stations of bth cell and user 1, user 2 in the jth cell, respectively. $\mathbf{V}_{1,k}$ and $\mathbf{V}_{2,k}$ represent the equivalent pre-coding matrices of user 1 and user 2 in the kth cell, and the dimension is $N_t \times d$, $\mathbf{V}_k = [\mathbf{V}_{1,k}, \mathbf{V}_{2,k}]$, is $N_t \times 2d$ dimension matrix, $k = 1,2,\ldots, K$.

Through the above analysis, the interference channel model described in Fig. 4 can be equivalent to that in Fig. 5.

As can be known from (11), after using the triangular decomposition for joint channel matrix, the users of cell 1 in equivalent model do not receive the interference from other cells (inter-cell interference) but only receive the intra-cell interference. As can be known from (12), the users of cell 2 only receive the interference from cell 1 and intra-cell interference. As can be known from (13), the users in the kth cell receive the interference from cells 1, 2,..., k-1 and the intra-cell interference. Therefore, the number of inter-cell interferences in half is reduced through using triangular decomposition for joint channel matrix, without other complex interference suppressing operation, which reduces the computation complexity at receiver.

In the following, considering to employ SLNR to design the pre-coding matrix $\mathbf{V}_{i,k}$ with the goal of eliminating the rest of inter-cell interference is to consider the meaning of the equivalent interference channel model in another way of thinking. Combined with (11), (12), and (13), it can be found that part of power that originally should be sent to native users in cell 1 was leaked to the users in cells 2, 3,..., K; thus, the SLNR is used to design pre-coding matrix $\mathbf{V}_{i,1}$ to eliminate the interferences in each of the cells caused by cell 1, then the interference suppression matrix $\mathbf{u}_{i,1}$ is used to eliminate the intra-cell interference of cell 1. Similarly, the base station in kth cell leaks part of power which originally should be sent to native users to the users of cell $k + 1$, $k + 2$,..., K; thus, the SLNR is used to design pre-coding matrix $\mathbf{V}_{i,k}$ to eliminate the interferences in each of the cells caused by cell k then also use interference suppression matrix $\mathbf{u}_{i,k}$ to eliminate intra-cell interference of cell k. Meanwhile, as shown in equivalent model, the base stations in cell K do not leak power to users in other cells: thus, the equivalent pre-coding matrix $\mathbf{V}_{i,K}$ can be used to suppress the intra-cell interference of cell K, so that the receiver in cell K does not need to increase intra-cell interference suppression matrix. It can be seen that the ultimate interference channel model can be simplified as Fig. 6 after using triangular decomposition and SLNR.

In conclusion, the algorithm reduce the number of inter-cell interferences in half using triangular decomposition, then the rest of interference is eliminated by using SLNR to design pre-coding matrix, so that the receiver does not need to design individual interference suppression matrix to eliminate inter-cell interference, which reduces the number of interference suppression matrices and simplifies the computation complexity at receiver. Besides, as can be known from (9) and matrix theory that dimension matching matrices satisfy $\text{span}(\mathbf{w}_k\mathbf{x}_k) = \text{span}(\mathbf{V}_k\mathbf{x}_k)$, that is to say, they can be spanned to the same space, which indicates that the triangular decomposition will not impact the degree of freedom, so the obtaining for equivalent model will not change the degree of freedom either. There is a need to explain that the proposed algorithm is implemented at base stations; meanwhile, it is assumed that all stations in this system can get channel matrix information through central control or circular polling mechanism, etc.

3.2 Interference suppressing algorithm combining triangular decomposition and SLNR

According to the above analysis, it can be found that the number of inter-cell interferences in half can be eliminated by employing triangular decomposition. In order to further

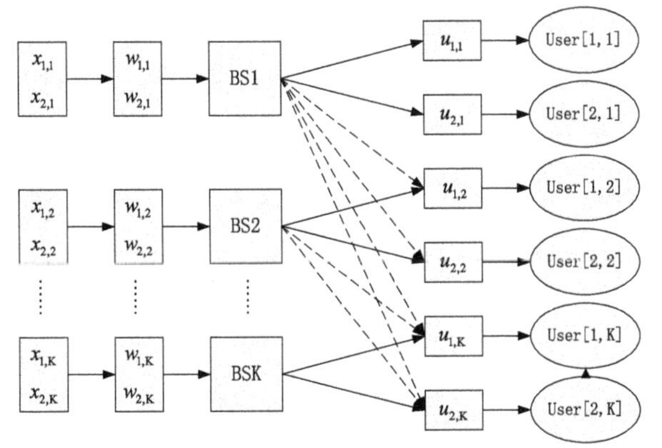

Fig. 5 Equivalent interference channel model

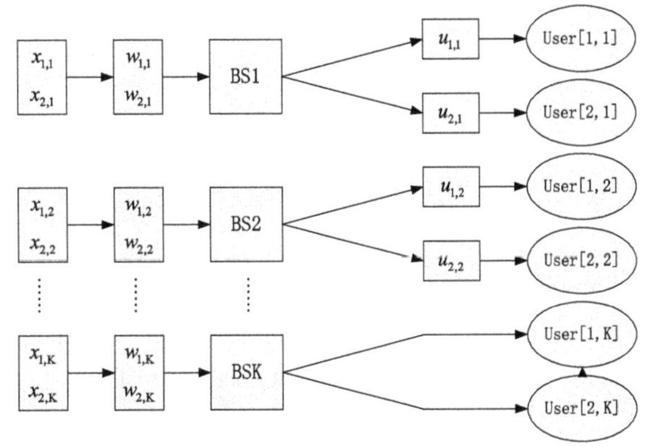

Fig. 6 Triangular decomposition SLNR interference channel model

decrease the number of the matrices at the receivers and the corresponding computation complexity, simplify the receivers processing; SLNR algorithm is employed to further suppress the inter-cell interferences. Next, for the convenience of analysis, we will take three cells as example to analyze the process of suppressing the interference for each cell in detail.

3.2.1 Interference suppression of cell 1

The users of cell 1 utilize the interference suppression matrix $\mathbf{u}_{i,1}$ to eliminate the intra-cell interference [35]. The received signal of the users in cell1 can be expressed as

$$\mathbf{r}_1 = \begin{bmatrix} \mathbf{r}_{1,1} \\ \mathbf{r}_{2,1} \end{bmatrix} = \begin{bmatrix} (\mathbf{u}_{1,1})^H \mathbf{y}_{1,1} \\ (\mathbf{u}_{2,1})^H \mathbf{y}_{2,1} \end{bmatrix} = \begin{bmatrix} (\mathbf{u}_{1,1})^H \mathbf{R}_1^{1,1} \mathbf{V}_1 \mathbf{x}_1 \\ (\mathbf{u}_{2,1})^H \mathbf{R}_1^{2,1} \mathbf{V}_1 \mathbf{x}_1 \end{bmatrix} + \begin{bmatrix} (\mathbf{u}_{1,1})^H \mathbf{n}_{1,1} \\ (\mathbf{u}_{2,1})^H \mathbf{n}_{2,1} \end{bmatrix} \tag{14}$$

Furthermore, the signal received by the ith user can be expressed as

$$\begin{aligned}\mathbf{r}_{i,1} &= (\mathbf{u}_{i,1})^H \mathbf{R}_1^{i,1} \mathbf{V}_1 \mathbf{x}_{i,1} + (\mathbf{u}_{i,1})^H \mathbf{n} \\ &= (\mathbf{u}_{i,1})^H \mathbf{R}_1^{i,1} \left(\mathbf{V}_{1,1} \mathbf{X}_{1,1} + \mathbf{V}_{2,1} \mathbf{X}_{2,1} \right) + (\mathbf{u}_{i,1})^H \mathbf{n}\end{aligned} \tag{15}$$

The user 1 needs to align the interference signal to the corresponding null space of the interference suppression matrix $\mathbf{u}_{1,1}$; thus, it should satisfy the following constraint:

$$\begin{cases} (\mathbf{u}_{1,1})^H \mathbf{R}_1^{1,1} \mathbf{V}_{2,1} = 0 \\ \text{rank}\left[(\mathbf{u}_{1,1})^H \mathbf{R}_1^{1,1} \mathbf{V}_{1,1} \right] = d \end{cases} \tag{16}$$

Therefore, $\mathbf{u}_{1,1}$ is the eigenvector corresponding to the minimum eigenvalue

$$\mathbf{u}_{1,1} = \nu_{\min}^{d} \left(\left(\mathbf{R}_1^{1,1} \mathbf{V}_{2,1} \right) \left(\mathbf{R}_1^{1,1} \mathbf{V}_{2,1} \right)^H \right) \tag{17}$$

Similarly, the interference suppression matrix of the user 2 in cell 1 should satisfy the following constraints:

$$\begin{cases} (\mathbf{u}_{2,1})^H \mathbf{R}_1^{2,1} \mathbf{V}_{1,1} = 0 \\ \text{rank}\left[(\mathbf{u}_{2,1})^H \mathbf{R}_1^{2,1} \mathbf{V}_{2,1} \right] = d \end{cases} \tag{18}$$

Therefore, the interference suppression matrix is

$$\mathbf{u}_{2,1} = \nu_{\min}^{d} \left(\left(\mathbf{R}_1^{2,1} \mathbf{V}_{1,1} \right) \left(\mathbf{R}_1^{2,1} \mathbf{V}_{1,1} \right)^H \right) \tag{19}$$

Considering formulas (11), (12), and (13), the users in cell 2 and cell 3 will receive the inter-cell interference from cell 1, combining the SLNR algorithm [36], that is to say, the user 1 in cell 1 not only leaks part of power to user 2 in cell 1 but also part of power to the users in cell 2 and cell 3. So the signal to leakage and noise ratio of use 1 in cell 1 is

$$\text{SLNR} = \frac{\left\| (\mathbf{u}_{1,1})^H \mathbf{R}_1^{1,1} \mathbf{V}_{1,1} \right\|_F^2}{\left\| (\mathbf{u}_{2,1})^H \mathbf{R}_1^{2,1} \mathbf{V}_{1,1} \right\|_F^2 + \sum_{i=1}^{2} \left\| (\mathbf{u}_{i,2})^H \mathbf{R}_1^{i,2} \mathbf{V}_{1,1} \right\|_F^2 + \sum_{i=1}^{2} \left\| \mathbf{R}_1^{i,3} \mathbf{V}_{1,1} \right\|_F^2 + N_r \sigma_{1,1}^2} \tag{20}$$

Since the power of transmitting data is normalized and $(\mathbf{u}_{i,k})^H \mathbf{u}_{i,k} = \mathbf{I}_k$, thus

$$SLNR = \frac{\left\| \mathbf{R}_1^{1,1} \mathbf{V}_{1,1} \right\|_F^2}{\left\| \mathbf{R}_1^{2,1} \mathbf{V}_{1,1} \right\|_F^2 + \sum_{i=1}^{2} \sum_{k=2}^{3} \left\| \mathbf{R}_1^{i,k} \mathbf{V}_{1,1} \right\|_F^2 + N_r \sigma_{1,1}^2} \tag{21}$$

Under the certain power constraint, the standard of SLNR algorithm that determines the pre-coding vector is to maximize the SLNR, which is to find the equivalent pre-coding matrix $\mathbf{V}_{1,1}$ satisfying the following two equations:

$$\begin{cases} \mathbf{V}_{1,1} = \arg\max \text{SLNR} \\ \left\| \mathbf{V}_{1,1} \right\|_F^2 = d \end{cases} \tag{22}$$

Rewritten the (21) as

$$\text{SLNR} = \frac{\left\| \mathbf{R}_1^{1,1} \mathbf{V}_{1,1} \right\|^2}{\left\| \tilde{\mathbf{R}}_1^{i,k} \mathbf{V}_{1,1} \right\|^2 + N_r \sigma_{1,1}^2} \tag{23}$$

According to the conclusions of generalized Rayleigh quotient, the pre-coding vectors are mutually orthogonal, the $\mathbf{V}_{1,1}$ is the eigenvectors corresponding to the d largest generalized eigenvalues of the matrix $\left\{ (\mathbf{R}_1^{1,1})^H \mathbf{R}_1^{1,1}, \left(\tilde{\mathbf{R}}_1^{i,k} \right)^H \tilde{\mathbf{R}}_1^{i,k} + N_r \sigma_{1,1}^2 I \right\}$, which enable maximize the SLNR, that is

$$\mathbf{V}_{1,1} \propto \max.\text{eigenvector}\left\{ (\mathbf{R}_1^{1,1})^H \mathbf{R}_1^{1,1}, \left(\tilde{\mathbf{R}}_1^{i,k} \right)^H \tilde{\mathbf{R}}_1^{i,k} + N_r \sigma_{1,1}^2 I \right\} \tag{24}$$

Similarly, the pre-coding matrix $\mathbf{V}_{2,1}$ of the user 2 in cell 1 should satisfy

$$\mathbf{V}_{2,1} \propto \max.\text{eigenvector}\left((\mathbf{R}_1^{2,1})^H \mathbf{R}_1^{2,1}, \left(\tilde{\mathbf{R}}_1^{i,k} \right)^H \tilde{\mathbf{R}}_1^{i,k} + N_r \sigma_{2,1}^2 \mathbf{I} \right) \tag{25}$$

3.2.2 Interference suppression of cell 2

The received signal of the users in cell 2 can be expressed as

$$\mathbf{r}_2 = \begin{bmatrix} \mathbf{r}_{1,2} \\ \mathbf{r}_{2,2} \end{bmatrix} = \begin{bmatrix} (\mathbf{u}_{1,2})^H \mathbf{y}_{1,2} \\ (\mathbf{u}_{2,2})^H \mathbf{y}_{2,2} \end{bmatrix} = \begin{bmatrix} (\mathbf{u}_{1,2})^H \mathbf{R}_1^{1,2}\mathbf{V}_1\mathbf{x}_1 \\ (\mathbf{u}_{2,2})^H \mathbf{R}_1^{2,2}\mathbf{V}_1\mathbf{x}_1 \end{bmatrix} + \begin{bmatrix} (\mathbf{u}_{1,2})^H \mathbf{R}_2^{1,2}\mathbf{V}_2\mathbf{x}_2 \\ (\mathbf{u}_{2,2})^H \mathbf{R}_2^{2,2}\mathbf{V}_2\mathbf{x}_2 \end{bmatrix} + \begin{bmatrix} (\mathbf{u}_{1,2})^H \mathbf{n}_{1,2} \\ (\mathbf{u}_{2,2})^H \mathbf{n}_{2,2} \end{bmatrix} \quad (26)$$

The acquisition of the intra-cell interference suppression matrix of the users in cell 2 is similar to that of users in cell 1; the constraints can be expressed as

$$\begin{cases} (\mathbf{u}_{1,2})^H \mathbf{R}_2^{1,2}\mathbf{V}_{2,2} = 0 \\ \text{rank}\left[(\mathbf{u}_{1,2})^H \mathbf{R}_2^{1,2}\mathbf{V}_{1,2}\right] = d \end{cases} \quad (27)$$

$$\begin{cases} (\mathbf{u}_{2,2})^H \mathbf{R}_2^{2,2}\mathbf{V}_{1,2} = 0 \\ \text{rank}\left[(\mathbf{u}_{2,2})^H \mathbf{R}_2^{2,2}\mathbf{V}_{2,2}\right] = d \end{cases} \quad (28)$$

Thus, interference suppression matrix can be expressed as

$$\mathbf{u}_{1,2} = v_{\min}^d\left(\left(\mathbf{R}_2^{1,2}\mathbf{V}_{2,2}\right)\left(\mathbf{R}_2^{1,2}\mathbf{V}_{2,2}\right)^H\right) \quad (29)$$

$$\mathbf{u}_{2,2} = v_{\min}^d\left(\left(\mathbf{R}_2^{2,2}\mathbf{V}_{1,2}\right)\left(\mathbf{R}_2^{2,2}\mathbf{V}_{1,2}\right)^H\right) \quad (30)$$

Similarly, it can be seen from formula (13) that the user 1 in cell 2 leaks the part of power to the user 2 in cell 2 as well as the users in cell 3. Combined with the SLNR algorithm, the signal to leakage and noise ratio can be expressed as

$$\text{SLNR} = \frac{\left\|(\mathbf{u}_{1,2})^H \mathbf{R}_2^{1,2}\mathbf{V}_{1,2}\right\|_F^2}{\left\|(\mathbf{u}_{2,2})^H \mathbf{R}_2^{2,2}\mathbf{V}_{1,2}\right\|_F^2 + \sum_{i=1}^{2}\left\|\mathbf{R}_2^{i,3}\mathbf{V}_{1,2}\right\|_F^2 + N_r\sigma_{1,2}^2} \quad (31)$$

Normalizing the power of transmitting data, and since $(\mathbf{u}_{i,k})^H\mathbf{u}_{i,k} = \mathbf{I}_k$, thus

$$\text{SLNR} = \frac{\left\|\mathbf{R}_2^{1,2}\mathbf{V}_{1,2}\right\|_F^2}{\left\|\mathbf{R}_2^{2,2}\mathbf{V}_{1,2}\right\|_F^2 + \sum_{i=1}^{2}\left\|\mathbf{R}_2^{i,3}\mathbf{V}_{1,2}\right\|_F^2 + N_r\sigma_{1,2}^2} \quad (32)$$

The confirmation for the equivalent pre-coding matrix $\mathbf{V}_{1,2}$ obtained from SLNR algorithm should satisfy the following two formulas

$$\begin{cases} \mathbf{V}_{1,2} = \arg\max \text{SLNR} \\ \left\|\mathbf{V}_{1,2}\right\|_F^2 = d \end{cases} \quad (33)$$

Rewritten the (32) as

$$\text{SLNR} = \frac{\left\|\mathbf{R}_2^{1,2}\mathbf{V}_{1,2}\right\|^2}{\left\|\tilde{\mathbf{R}}_2^{i,k}\mathbf{V}_{1,2}\right\|^2 + N_r\sigma_{1,2}^2} \quad (34)$$

$\mathbf{V}_{1,2}$is the eigenvectors corresponding to the d largest generalized eigenvalues of the matrix $\left\{\left(\mathbf{R}_2^{1,2}\right)^H\mathbf{R}_2^{1,2}, \left(\tilde{\mathbf{R}}_2^{i,k}\right)^H\tilde{\mathbf{R}}_2^{i,k} + N_r\sigma_{1,2}^2\mathbf{I}\right\}$, that will be able to maximize the SLNR, namely

$$\mathbf{V}_{1,2} \propto \max.\text{eigenvector}\left(\left(\mathbf{R}_2^{1,2}\right)^H\mathbf{R}_2^{1,2}, \left(\tilde{\mathbf{R}}_2^{i,k}\right)^H\tilde{\mathbf{R}}_2^{i,k} + N_r\sigma_{1,2}^2\mathbf{I}\right) \quad (35)$$

In a similar way, the pre-coding matrix $\mathbf{V}_{2,2}$ of the user 2 in cell 2 should satisfy

$$\mathbf{V}_{2,2} \propto \max.\text{eigenvector}\left(\left(\mathbf{R}_2^{2,2}\right)^H\mathbf{R}_2^{2,2}, \left(\tilde{\mathbf{R}}_2^{i,k}\right)^H\tilde{\mathbf{R}}_2^{i,k} + N_r\sigma_{2,2}^2\mathbf{I}\right) \quad (36)$$

3.2.3 Interference suppression of cell 3

The received signal of the users in cell 3 can be expressed as

$$\mathbf{r}_3 = \begin{bmatrix} \mathbf{r}_{1,3} \\ \mathbf{r}_{2,3} \end{bmatrix} = \begin{bmatrix} \mathbf{y}_{1,3} \\ \mathbf{y}_{2,3} \end{bmatrix} = \begin{bmatrix} \mathbf{R}_1^{1,3}\mathbf{V}_1\mathbf{x}_1 \\ \mathbf{R}_1^{2,3}\mathbf{V}_1\mathbf{x}_1 \end{bmatrix} + \begin{bmatrix} \mathbf{R}_2^{1,3}\mathbf{V}_2\mathbf{x}_2 \\ \mathbf{R}_2^{2,3}\mathbf{V}_2\mathbf{x}_2 \end{bmatrix} + \begin{bmatrix} \mathbf{R}_3^{1,3}\mathbf{V}_3\mathbf{x}_3 \\ \mathbf{R}_3^{2,3}\mathbf{V}_3\mathbf{x}_3 \end{bmatrix} + \begin{bmatrix} \mathbf{n}_{1,3} \\ \mathbf{n}_{2,3} \end{bmatrix} \quad (37)$$

As can be seen from formulas (11), (12), and (13), after triangular decomposition, the power that is sent by the BS in cell 3 does not leak to other cells, namely, result in no interferences to other cells. Therefore, the pre-coding matrices of each user in cell 3 are used to eliminate the intra-cell interferences, so the pre-coding matrix should satisfy the following constraints

$$\begin{cases} \mathbf{R}_3^{1,3}\mathbf{V}_{2,3} = 0 \\ \mathbf{R}_3^{2,3}\mathbf{V}_{1,3} = 0 \end{cases} \quad (38)$$

Moreover, the pre-coding matrix of the users 1, 2 in cell 3 can be expressed as

$$\begin{cases} \mathbf{V}_{1,3} = v_{\min}^d\left(\left(\mathbf{R}_3^{2,3}\right)^H\mathbf{R}_3^{2,3}\right) \\ \mathbf{V}_{2,3} = v_{\min}^d\left(\left(\mathbf{R}_3^{1,3}\right)^H\mathbf{R}_3^{1,3}\right) \end{cases} \quad (39)$$

Obviously, the receivers in cell 3 do not need intra-cell interference suppression matrix to eliminate the intra-cell interferences. Finally, the final pre-coding matrix $\mathbf{w}_{i,k}$ can be obtained through each equivalent pre-coding matrix $\mathbf{V}_{i,k}$.

4 Algorithm complexity analysis

4.1 Summarize the algorithm

The proposed algorithm that combines the triangular decomposition and SLNR can be implemented by three steps:

Step1. Employ the triangular decomposition for joint channel matrix $\boldsymbol{H}$ and then extract the equivalent interference channel model;

Step2. According to the equivalent interference channel model, exploit SLNR to compute the equivalent pre-coding matrices $V_{1,1}$, $V_{2,1}$, $V_{1,2}$, and $V_{2,2}$ to suppress the rest of inter-cell interference and then obtain $\mathbf{w}_{1,1}$, $\mathbf{w}_{2,1}$, $\mathbf{w}_{1,2}$ and $\mathbf{w}_{2,2}$;

Step3. Compute the intra-cell interference suppression matrices of users $\mathbf{u}_{1,1}$, $\mathbf{u}_{2,1}$, $\mathbf{u}_{1,2}$ and $\mathbf{u}_{2,2}$, respectively. Specially, the users in cell 3 use the equivalent pre-coding matrices $\mathbf{V}_{1,3}$ and $\mathbf{V}_{2,3}$ to eliminate the intra-cell interference, so the receiver does not need to add intra-cell interference suppression matrix any more.

4.2 Complexity analysis

Furthermore, the complexity of the triangular decomposition and SLNR algorithm is analyzed.

$\boldsymbol{A}$ and $\boldsymbol{B}$ are matrices whose dimensions are $m \times n, n \times k$, respectively; the complexity of operation $\mathbf{A} \times \mathbf{B}$ is $o(mnk)$. Thus, the complexity of operation $\left(\mathrm{H}_b^{i,k}\right)^H \mathrm{H}_b^{i,k}$ is $o(N_t^2 N_r)$, where, $\mathrm{H}_b^{i,k}$ is the channel matrix whose dimension is $N_r \times N_t$, and the complexity of eigenvalues operation for $N_t \times N_t$ dimension matrix $\boldsymbol{C}$ is $o(N_t^3)$. Therefore, the complexity of the algorithm that combines the triangular decomposition and SLNR can be concluded as follows:

Step1. Employ the triangular decomposition for $\boldsymbol{H}$, the according complexity is $o\left(2 \times 6^2 N_r^2 (3N_t - 6N_r/3)\right)$, namely, $o\left(3N_r^2 N_t - 2N_r^3\right)$;

Step2. Exploit SLNR algorithm to calculate the equivalent pre-coding matrices $V_{1,1}$, $V_{2,1}$, $V_{1,2}$, and $V_{2,2}$ to suppress the rest of inter-cell interference, the according complexity is $o\left(N_t^3\right) + o\left(N_t^2 N_r\right)$;

Step3. Compute the intra-cell interference suppression matrices of users $\mathbf{u}_{1,1}$, $\mathbf{u}_{2,1}$, $\mathbf{u}_{1,2}$ and $\mathbf{u}_{2,2}$, respectively. Specially, the users in cell 3 use the equivalent pre-coding matrices $\mathbf{V}_{1,3}$ and $\mathbf{V}_{2,3}$ to eliminate the intra-cell interference; the total complexity is $o\left(N_r^3\right) + o\left(N_t^3\right) + o\left(dN_r^2\right) + o\left(N_t^2 N_r\right) + o\left(dN_r N_t\right)$.

Therefore, according to above analysis, the total complexity of the proposed algorithm is $o\left(N_r^3\right) + o\left(N_t^3\right) + o\left(N_r^2 N_t\right) + o\left(N_t^2 N_r\right) + o\left(dN_r^2\right) + o\left(dN_r N_t\right)$.

However, exploit the interference alignment algorithm to suppress the rest of inter-cell interference, corresponding complexity is $o\left(N_r^2 N_t\right) + o\left(N_r^3\right) + o\left(d^3 N_r N_t^2\right) + o\left(d^3 N_t^3\right)$ [35]. Meanwhile, the complexity of the traditional SLNR without using triangular decomposition to the multi-cell MIMO interference system is $o\left(N_r^3\right) + o\left(N_t^3\right) + o\left(dN_r^2\right) + o\left(dN_r N_t\right) + o\left(N_t^2 N_r\right)$. It obviously seen that under the condition with certain configuration of antennas, the complexity of the proposed algorithm and the traditional SLNR are on the same order of magnitude, which means that the proposed algorithm without increasing complexity to the system compared with traditional SLNR algorithm. Furthermore, comparing with employing the interference alignment algorithm to compute the inter-cell interference suppression matrix at receiver [35], the proposed algorithm reduces the number of filters (matrices) at receiver, which is helpful to avoid more complex interference suppression process and have lower computation complexity as well as reduce costs of receiver.

5 Numerical results

In the downlink communication environment with co-channel interference of multi-cell MIMO heterogeneous network, the performance of the whole system will be affected by the antenna configurations both of transmitter and receiver; it will also be affected by the data streams sent by the transmitter. At present, the system capacity is usually used as one of the reference indexes to evaluate the system performance, and the energy consumption is a noteworthy problem as well. Thus, the system capacity and energy efficiency are chosen to be the indexes to evaluate the system performance. The system capacity is defined as $C = \log(1 + \mathrm{SINR}_k)$ (bps/Hz), and the energy efficiency is defined as the number of bits sent by in unit of energy and unit of bandwidth, namely, $\eta = \frac{\log(1+\mathrm{SINR}_k)}{P_k}$ (bit/Hz/J), SINR_k represents the signal to interference plus noise ratio of kth user and P_k represents the transmission power of kth user. Aiming at network environment is formed by three cells sharing the same frequency resource, in which each cell has two edge users. Assuming that all channels are flat Rayleigh fading channels with the elements that are independent identically distributed Gaussian random variables whose mean is 0, variance is 1.

Figure 7a, b shows the comparing results of system capacity and energy efficiency when the antenna configurations are 5×4, 10×8, and 15×12, respectively, and the numbers of received data streams (the degree of freedom) of each user are $d = 1, 2, 3$, the degree of system freedom are Dof = 6, 12, 18. As can be seen from Fig. 7, the system capacity and energy efficiency are obviously promoted with the increase of numbers of antenna as well as data streams. The reason for this phenomenon is the system obtains more diversity gains and the transmitter sends multiple collateral data streams simultaneously, which is very helpful to improve the system performance.

Figure 8a, b shows the comparing results of system capacity and energy efficiency in the same simulation

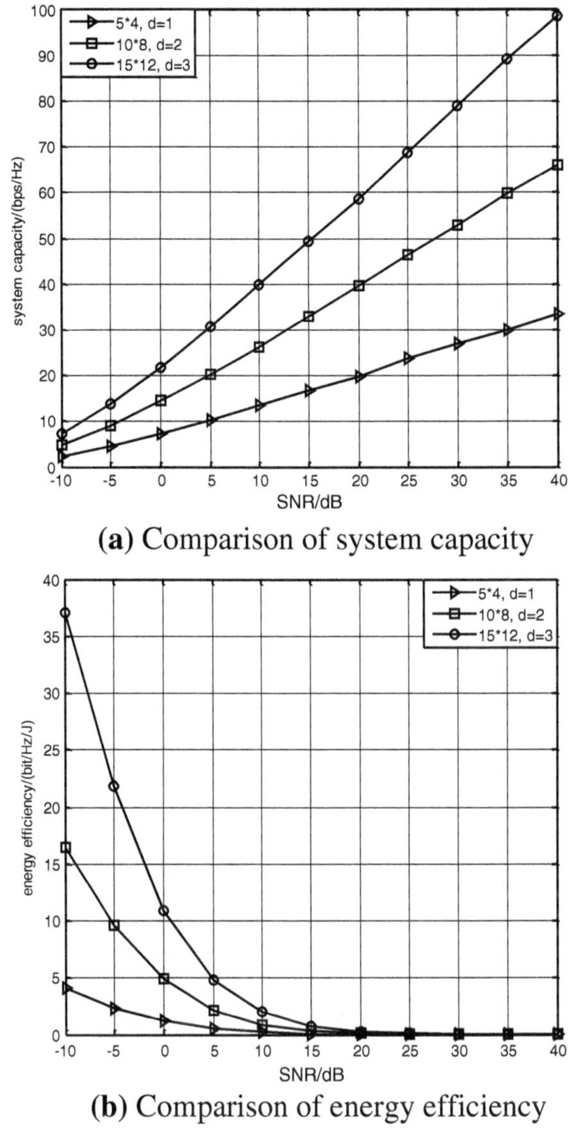

Fig. 7 System performance analysis. **a** Comparison of system capacity. **b** Comparison of energy efficiency

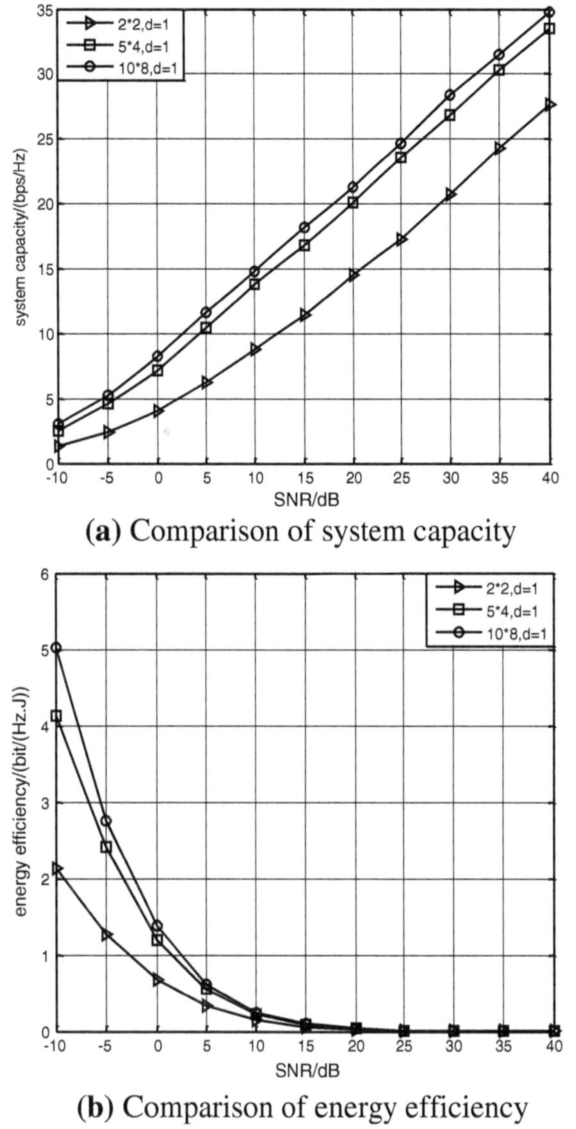

Fig. 8 Comparison of system performance with the same degree of freedom but different number of antennas. **a** Comparison of system capacity. **b** Comparison of energy efficiency

environment but $d = 1$, Dof = 6, and the antenna configurations are different. As can be known from Fig. 8, increasing the number of transmitting and receiving antenna can improve the system capacity and energy efficiency under the fixed Dof, especially the improvement of energy efficiency is more obvious. However, the further improvement of system performance is relatively slow with the increase of number of antenna. Thus, the antenna should be reasonably allocated according to the actual situation.

Figure 9a, b shows the comparing results of system capacity and energy efficiency with the same antenna configuration 10×8 and simulation environment, but different number of received data streams (the degree of freedom) $d = 1,2,3$, Dof = 6,12,18. As can be known from Fig. 9, the increasing of number of transmission data streams can improve the system capacity and energy efficiency obviously with fixed antenna configuration, and the improvement of energy efficiency is more obvious than system capacity as well. Therefore, it is needed to send multiple data simultaneously to improve system performance under the reasonable condition.

In the same simulation environment, Fig. 10a, b shows the results of system capacity and energy efficiency comparing the proposed triangular decomposition SLNR algorithm with traditional SLNR. As can be seen from Fig. 10, the proposed algorithm can greatly improve the system capacity comparing with the traditional SLNR under the same numbers of antennas and data streams.

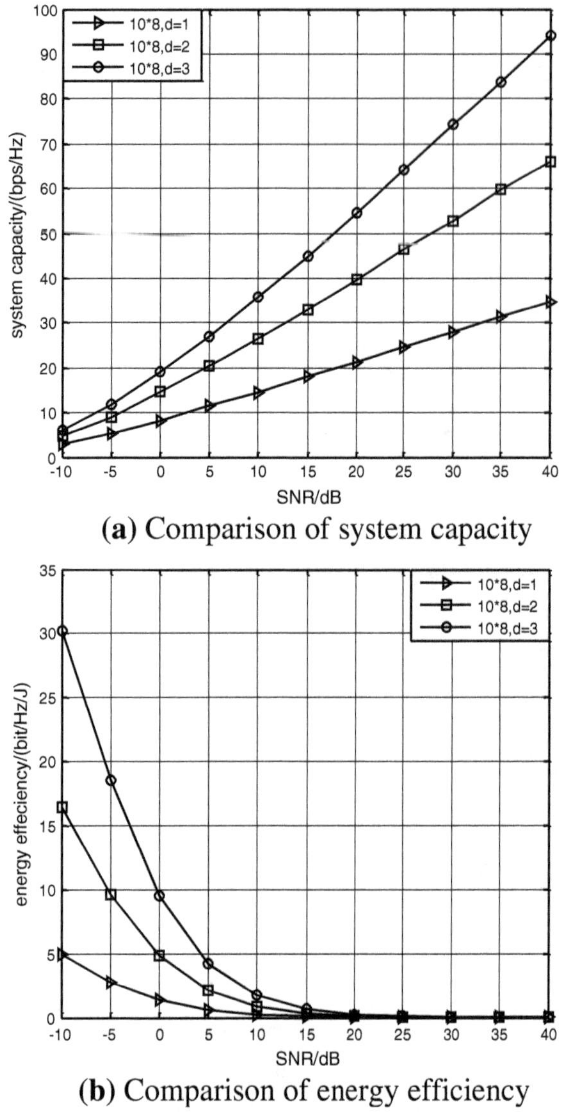

(a) Comparison of system capacity

(b) Comparison of energy efficiency

Fig. 9 Comparison of system performance with the same number of antennas but different number of degree of freedom. **a** Comparison of system capacity. **b** Comparison of energy efficiency

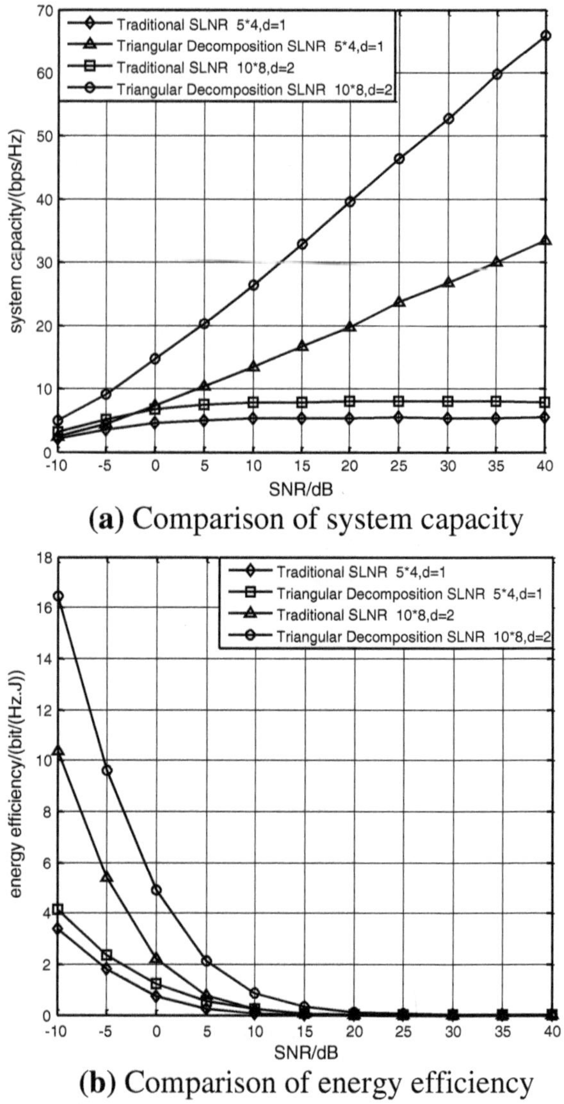

(a) Comparison of system capacity

(b) Comparison of energy efficiency

Fig. 10 Comparison of system performance with different algorithms. **a** Comparison of system capacity. **b** Comparison of energy efficiency

Meanwhile, it can be found from Fig. 10 that though the proposed algorithm does not have significant advantages in improving energy efficiency compared with the traditional SLNR, the proposed algorithm still has better performance than that of traditional SLNR in improving energy efficiency under the same condition.

It can be figured out that the traditional SLNR algorithm only reduce the inter-cell interference at receiver, the strong interference may weaken the interference suppression ability of SLNR, which causes the degradation of system performance. However, the proposed algorithm can reduce the number of inter-cell interferences in half before the interference suppression operation at receiver, so the interference environment at receiver is improved, and the application effect of the SLNR algorithm is enhanced; finally, the overall system performance is improved.

It should be noted that the analysis and studies of this paper are based on the ideal channel estimation and the actual method for obtaining channel state information is not further studied. Of course the acquisition of real-time channel state information under the actual channel condition can be studied in following. Furthermore, the performance of the proposed algorithm with real-time channel states information will be analyzed.

6 Conclusions

This paper firstly discusses the interference situations in multi-cell MIMO heterogeneous network. Aiming at the strong co-channel interference in multi-cell MIMO heterogeneous network, an algorithm that combines the triangular decomposition and SLNR has been proposed. The algorithm can reduce the number of inter-cell interferences in half through exploiting the triangular decomposition for equivalent channel matrix before the complex interference suppressing operation at receiver. Then based on the equivalent interference channel model extracted after triangular decomposition, the pre-coding matrices of each user in each cell and the corresponding closed-form interference suppression matrices are derived according to different interference situations in each cell. Furthermore, we compare the computation complexity of the proposed algorithm with traditional SLNR and interference alignment algorithm. Finally, the simulation results verify that the proposed algorithm can greatly improve the system capacity and energy efficiency compared with traditional SLNR algorithm. Meanwhile, the impact of different numbers of data streams and antennas on system performance is further analyzed.

Competing interests
The authors declare that they have no competing interests.

Acknowledgements
This work was supported in part by the National High Technology Research and Development Program of China (863 Program) under Grant No. 2014AA01A705, The National Natural Science Foundation of China under Grant No. 61440062, and the Program for Changjiang Scholars and Innovative Research Team in University under Grant No. IRT1299.

References
1. M Chiani, MZ Win, S Hyundong, MIMO networks: the effects of interference. IEEE Trans. Inf. Theory **56**(1), 336–349 (2010)
2. XR Jing, ZZ Zhou, Z Xu, A sequence detection method with adaptive channel tracking in time-varying multipath MIMO channels. J. Electron. Inf. Technol. **31**(8), 1930–1934 (2009)
3. A. Khandekar, N. Bhushan, T.F. Ji, V. Vanghi. LTE-advanced: heterogeneous networks. European Wireless Conference, 978-982 (2010).
4. A. Jabban, Y. Nasser, M. Helard, Performance analysis of heterogeneous networks based on SINR selection strategy. International Conference on Telecommunications, 1-5 (2013).
5. N. Himayat, S.P. Yeh, A.Y. Panah, Multi-radio heterogeneous networks: architectures and performance. International Conference on Computing, Networking and Communications, 252-258 (2014).
6. P. Palanisamy, S. Nirmala, Downlink interference management in femtocell networks—a comprehensive study and survey. International Conference on Information Communication and Embedded Systems, 747-754 (2013).
7. K.I. Pedersen, Y.Y. Wang, B. Soret, eICIC functionality and performance for LTE HetNet co-channel deployments. IEEE Vehicular Technology Conference, 1-5 (2012).
8. Y.J. Hong, L. Namyoon, B. Clerckx, System level performance evaluation of inter-cell interference coordination schemes for heterogeneous networks in LTE-A system. IEEE GLOBECOM Workshops, 690-694 (2010).
9. Z. Bakhti, S.S. Moghaddam, Inter-cell interference coordination with adaptive frequency-reuse for VoIP and data traffic in downlink of 3GPP-LTE. International Conference on Application of Information and Communication Technologies, 1-6 (2010).
10. C. He, F. Liu, H. Yang, Co-channel interference mitigation in MIMO-OFDM system. International Conference on Wireless Communications, Networking and Mobile Computing, 204-208 (2007).
11. A Bagayoko, I Fijalkow, P Tortelier, Power control of spectrum-sharing in fading environment with partial channel state information. IEEE Trans. Signal Process. **59**(5), 2244–2256 (2011)
12. 3GPP TR 36.814, Further advancements for E-UTRA physical layer aspects (Release 9), v. 2.0.0, Mar. 2010.
13. N Saquib, EE Hossain, LB Le, Interference management in OFDMA femtocell networks: issues and approaches. IEEE Wireless Commun. **19**(3), 86–95 (2012)
14. B. Li, An effective inter-cell interference coordination scheme for heterogeneous network. IEEE Vehicular Technology Conference, 1-5 (2011).
15. Y. Li, M.G. Peng, W. Hu, Adaptive heterogeneous interference coordination algorithm in uplink LTE-advanced systems. IEEE International Symposium on Personal Indoor and Mobile Radio Communications, 536-540 (2012).
16. J Mestre, N Pratas, *N R Prasad, Adaptive flexible spectrum usage algorithms in heterogeneous cell deployment IEEE International Symposium on Personal Indoor and Mobile Radio Communications, 253–257*, 2011
17. Q Li, RQ Hu, YR Xu, Y Qian, Optimal fractional frequency reuse and power control in the heterogeneous wireless networks. Wireless Communications. IEEE Trans. Wireless Commun. **12**(6), 2658–2668 (2013)
18. R.C. Xie, H. Ji, P.B. Si, Y. Li, Dynamic channel and power allocation in cognitive radio networks supporting heterogeneous services. IEEE Global Telecommunications Conference, 1-5 (2010).
19. P Marsch, G Fettweis, Uplink CoMP under a constrained backhaul and imperfect channel knowledge. IEEE Trans. Wireless Commun. **10**(6), 1730–1742 (2011)
20. P Li, RC de Lamare, Distributed iterative detection with reduced message passing for networked MIMO cellular systems. IEEE Trans. Vehicular Technol. **63**(6), 2947–2954 (2014)
21. Q.H. Spencer, M. Haardt, Capacity and downlink transmission algorithms for a multi-user MIMO channel. IEEE Conference on Signal, Systems and Computers, 1384-1388 (2002).
22. P Jungyong, L Byungju, S Byonghyo, A MMSE vector precoding with block diagonalization for multiuser MIMO downlink. IEEE Trans. Commun. **60**(2), 569–577 (2012)
23. Y Zeng, E Gunawan, YL Guan, Modified block diagonalization precoding in multicell cooperative networks. IEEE Trans. Vehicular Technol. **61**(8), 3819–3824 (2012)
24. J. An, Y.A. Liu, F. Liu, An efficient block diagonalization method for multiuser MIMO downlink. International Conference on Consumer Electronics, Communications and Networks, 145-148 (2012).
25. H Sung, S Lee, I Lee, Generalized channel inversion methods for multiuser MIMO systems. IEEE Trans Commun. **57**(11), 3489-3499 (2009)
26. K Zu, RC de Lamare, M Haardt, Generalized design of low-complexity block diagonalization type precoding algorithms for multiuser MIMO systems. IEEE Trans. Commun. **61**(10), 4232–4242 (2013)
27. M Sadek, A Tarighat, AH Sayed, A leakage based precoding scheme for downlink multi-user MIMO channels. IEEE Trans. Wireless Commun. **6**(5), 1711–1721 (2007)
28. X.Y. Zhang, C. He, L. Jiang, Successive SLNR based precoding for downlink multi-user MIMO systems. IEEE International Conference on Communications, 1-5 (2011).
29. P Piya, D Angela, A Simon, Equivalent expressions and performance analysis of SLNR precoding schemes: a generalisation to multi-antenna receivers. IEEE Commun. Lett. **17**(6), 1196–1199 (2013)
30. E. Saeid, V. Jeoti, B.B. Samir, Linear precoding for multi-cell processing multiuser MIMO systems. International Conference on Intelligent and Advanced Systems, 259-264 (2012).
31. K Wang, XD Zhang, On equivalence of SLNR-based precoding and RBD precoding. Electron. Lett. **48**(11), 662–663 (2012)
32. O Ayach, SW Peters, RW Heath, The practical challenges of interference alignment. IEEE Wireless Commun. **20**(1), 35–42 (2013)
33. G.C. Alexandropoulos, S. Papaharalabos, C.B. Papadias, On the performance of interference alignment under weak interference conditions. International Conference on Systems, Signals and Image Processing, 222-226 (2012).
34. XD Zhang, *Matrix analysis and applications* (Tsinghua University Press, Beijing, 2004)
35. XZ Xie, B Xu, WJ Lei, B Ma, Interference alignment algorithm based on orthogonal-triangular decomposition for edge users in 3-cell MIMO cellular networks. J Electron. Inf. Technol. **35**(5), 1031–1036 (2013)
36. XK Gao, Y Cui, YC Yu, An improved SLNR pre-coding with minimum BER sorting and iterative optimizing. J. Zhengzhou Univ. **33**(2), 19–23 (2012)

Permissions

All chapters in this book were first published in JASP, by Springer; hereby published with permission under the Creative Commons Attribution License or equivalent. Every chapter published in this book has been scrutinized by our experts. Their significance has been extensively debated. The topics covered herein carry significant findings which will fuel the growth of the discipline. They may even be implemented as practical applications or may be referred to as a beginning point for another development.

The contributors of this book come from diverse backgrounds, making this book a truly international effort. This book will bring forth new frontiers with its revolutionizing research information and detailed analysis of the nascent developments around the world.

We would like to thank all the contributing authors for lending their expertise to make the book truly unique. They have played a crucial role in the development of this book. Without their invaluable contributions this book wouldn't have been possible. They have made vital efforts to compile up to date information on the varied aspects of this subject to make this book a valuable addition to the collection of many professionals and students.

This book was conceptualized with the vision of imparting up-to-date information and advanced data in this field. To ensure the same, a matchless editorial board was set up. Every individual on the board went through rigorous rounds of assessment to prove their worth. After which they invested a large part of their time researching and compiling the most relevant data for our readers.

The editorial board has been involved in producing this book since its inception. They have spent rigorous hours researching and exploring the diverse topics which have resulted in the successful publishing of this book. They have passed on their knowledge of decades through this book. To expedite this challenging task, the publisher supported the team at every step. A small team of assistant editors was also appointed to further simplify the editing procedure and attain best results for the readers.

Apart from the editorial board, the designing team has also invested a significant amount of their time in understanding the subject and creating the most relevant covers. They scrutinized every image to scout for the most suitable representation of the subject and create an appropriate cover for the book.

The publishing team has been an ardent support to the editorial, designing and production team. Their endless efforts to recruit the best for this project, has resulted in the accomplishment of this book. They are a veteran in the field of academics and their pool of knowledge is as vast as their experience in printing. Their expertise and guidance has proved useful at every step. Their uncompromising quality standards have made this book an exceptional effort. Their encouragement from time to time has been an inspiration for everyone.

The publisher and the editorial board hope that this book will prove to be a valuable piece of knowledge for researchers, students, practitioners and scholars across the globe.

List of Contributors

S.-J. Fan, H.-T. Xiao and H.-Q. Fan
ATR, National University of Defense Technology, Changsha 410072, People's Republic of China

J.-P. Fan
College of Electronic Science and Engineering, National University of Defense Technology, Changsha 410072, People's Republic of China

Izaquiel L. Bessas, Flávio L. C. Pádua and Anisio Lacerda
Computer Science Department, Centro Federal de Educação Tecnológica de Minas Gerais, Av. Amazonas, 7675 Belo Horizonte, Brazil

Guilherme T. de Assis
Computer Science Department, Universidade Federal de Ouro Preto, Morro do Cruzeiro, Ouro Preto, Brazil

Rodrigo T. N. Cardoso
Departamento de Física e Matemática, Centro Federal de Educação Tecnológica de Minas Gerais, Av. Amazonas, 7675 Belo Horizonte, Brazil

M. Rizwan Tariq and Shuichi Ohno
Department of System Cybernetics, Hiroshima University, Saijo, Higashi-Hiroshima, Japan

Ondrej Slučiak and Markus Rupp
TU Wien, Institute of Telecommunications, Gusshausstrasse 25/E389, 1040 Vienna, Austria

Hana Straková and Wilfried Gansterer
University of Vienna, Faculty of Computer Science, Theory and Applications of Algorithms, Währingerstrasse 29, 1090 Vienna, Austria

Vasudev Kandade Rajan and Gerhard Schmidt
Digital Signal Processing and System Theory, University of Kiel, Kaiserstrasse 2, Kiel, Germany

Mohamed Krini and Klaus Rodemer
Division Acoustics, paragon AG, Schwalbenweg 29, Delbrueck, Germany

Jiufei Luo and Yi Zhang
School of Advanced Manufacture Engineering, Chongqing University of Posts and Telecommunications, Chongqing 400065, People's Republic of China

Shuaicheng Hou and Qi Ouyang
School of Automation, Chongqing University, Chongqing 400044, People's Republic of China

Xinyi Li
Department of Mechanical Engineering, Chongqing University, Chongqing 400044, People's Republic of China

David I. Lekhovytskiy
Kharkiv National University of Radio Electronics, 14 Lenin Avenue, 61166 Kharkiv, Ukraine

Gang Li, Qingkai Hou, Shiyou Xu and Zengping Chen
College of Electronic Science and Engineering, National University of Defense Technology, Changsha, Hunan 410073, China

Mounir Bahtat and Said Belkouch
LGECOS Lab, ENSA-Marrakech of the Cadi Ayyad University, Marrakech, Morocco

Philippe Elleaume and Philippe Le Gall
Thales Air Systems, Paris, France

Patricia Binder, Michael Muma and Abdelhak M. Zoubir
Signal Processing Group, Technische Universität Darmstadt, 64283 Darmstadt, Germany

Jindong Zhang, Xiaoyan Qiu, Changli Shi and Yue Wu
College of Electronic and Information Engineering, Nanjing University of Aeronautics and Astronautics, Nanjing 210016, China

Noura Baccar
Innov'COM/ENIT/Cynapsys, University Tunis El Manar, Tunis, Tunisia

Ridha Bouallegue
Innov'COM, University Carthage, Tunis, Tunisia

Khalid Mahmood and Syed Muhammad Asad
Electrical and Electronics Technology Department, Affiliated Colleges at Hafr Al Batin, King Fahd University of Petroleum and Minerals, P. O. Box 1803, Hafr Al Batin 31991, Saudi Arabia

Muhammad Moinuddin
Electrical and Computer Engineering, King Abdulaziz University, Jeddah, Saudi Arabia

Azzedine Zerguine
Department of Electrical Engineering, King Fahd University of Petroleum and Minerals, Dhahran 31261, Kingdom of Saudi Arabia

Lahouari Cheded
Department of Systems Engineering, King Fahd University of Petroleum and Minerals, Dhahran 31261, Kingdom of Saudi Arabia

Ali M. Al Omour, Abdelmalek Zidouri, Naveed Iqbal and Azzedine Zerguine
Electrical Engineering Department, KFUPM, Dhahran, Saudi Arabia

Branko Kovačević
School of Electrical Engineering, University of Belgrade, Bulevar kralja Aleksandra 73, Belgrade, Serbia

Zoran Banjac
School of Electrical and Computer Engineering, 283 Vojvode Stepe St., Belgrade, Serbia

Ivana Kostić Kovačević
Faculty of Informatics and Computing, Singidunum University, 32 Danijelova St., Belgrade, Serbia

Yu Li
School of Communications and Information Engineering, Chongqing University of Posts and Telecommunications, Chongqing 400065, China

Zufan Zhang
School of Communications and Information Engineering, Chongqing University of Posts and Telecommunications, Chongqing 400065, China
Chongqing Key Laboratory of Mobile Communication, Chongqing University of Posts and Telecommunication, Chongqing 400065, China

Index

O

P

Q

R

S

T

U

V

W

Printed in the USA
CPSIA information can be obtained
at www.ICGtesting.com
JSHW051430221024
72173JS00006B/1428